International
Warbirds

International Warbirds

*An Illustrated Guide to
World Military Aircraft,
1914–2000*

BY JOHN C. FREDRIKSEN
FOREWORD BY **WALTER BOYNE**

ABC-CLIO

Santa Barbara, California
Denver, Colorado
Oxford, England

Library of Congress Cataloging-in-Publication Data
Fredriksen, John C.
    International warbirds : an illustrated guide to world military aircraft,
1914–2000 / by John C. Fredriksen.
        p.   cm.
    Includes bibliographical references.
    ISBN 1-57607-364-5 (hardcover : alk. paper) — ISBN 1-57607-551-6
(e-book)
1. Airplanes, Military—Dictionaries.   I. Title.
UG1240.F74   2001
623.7'46—dc21

                                                                      2001002280

06   05   04   03   02   01   10 9 8 7 6 5 4 3 2 1

This book is also available on the World Wide Web as an e-book. Visit
abc-clio.com for details.

ABC-CLIO, Inc.
130 Cremona Drive, P.O. Box 1911
Santa Barbara, California 93116–1911

This book is printed on acid-free paper ∞.

Manufactured in the United States of America

CONTENTS

List of Aircraft by Era and Country of Manufacture   ix
Foreword, by Walter Boyne   xiii
Introduction   xv

Contents

Contents

LIST OF AIRCRAFT BY ERA AND COUNTRY OF MANUFACTURE

World War I, 1914–1919

Austria-Hungary
Aviatik C I
Aviatik D I
Etrich *Taube*
Hansa-Brandenburg C I
Hansa-Brandenburg D I
Lloyd C III
Lohner B VII
Phonix C I
Phonix D I
Ufag C I

France
Bleriot XI
Breguet 14
Caudron G III
Caudron G IV
Caudron R 11
Hanriot HD 1
Morane-Saulnier A 1
Morane-Saulnier L
Nieuport 11
Nieuport 17
Nieuport 28
Salmson 2A2
SPAD XIII

Germany
AEG C IV
AEG G IV
Albatros C XII

Albatros D V
DFW C V
Fokker D VII
Fokker D VIII
Fokker Dr I
Fokker E III
Friedrichshafen G III
Gotha G V
Halberstadt C V
Halberstadt CL IV
Halberstadt D II
Hannover CL III
Hansa-Brandenburg W 29
Junkers CL I
Junkers D I
Junkers J I
LFG Roland C II
LFG Roland D II
LVG C V
Pfalz D IIIa
Pfalz D XII
Rumpler C IV
Siemens-Schuckert D IV
Zeppelin Staaken R VI

Great Britain
Armstrong-Whitworth FK 8
Avro 504
Bristol F 2B
Bristol Scout D
de Havilland DH 2

de Havilland DH 4
de Havilland DH 9a
de Havilland DH 10 *Amiens*
Felixstowe F2A
Handley Page O/400
Martinsyde G 100 *Elephant*
Royal Aircraft Factory BE 2e
Royal Aircraft Factory FE 2
Royal Aircraft Factory RE 8
Royal Aircraft Factory SE 5a
Short 184
Sopwith 1½ *Strutter*
Sopwith *Camel*
Sopwith *Dolphin*
Sopwith *Pup*
Sopwith *Snipe*
Sopwith *Tabloid*
Sopwith Triplane
Vickers FB 5

Italy
Ansaldo SVA 5 *Primo*
Caproni Ca 310 Series
Macchi M 5

Russia
Anatra D
Sikorsky RBVZ *Ilya Muromets*
Sikorsky S 16

Golden Age, 1919–1939

Czechoslovakia
Avia B 534
Letov S 328

France
Amiot 143
Bleriot-SPAD S 510
Breguet 19
Dewoitine D 510
Farman F 222
LeO 20
Nieuport-Delage Ni-D 29

Germany
Arado Ar 68
Dornier Do 23
Heinkel He 51
Heinkel He 59
Heinkel He 70 *Blitz*
Henschel Hs 123
Junkers Ju 86

Great Britain
Armstrong-Whitworth *Siskin IIIA*
Blackburn *Shark*

Bristol *Bulldog*
de Havilland DH 82 *Tiger Moth*
Fairey *Flycatcher*
Fairey IIIF
Fairey *Swordfish*
Gloster *Gauntlet*
Gloster *Gladiator*
Handley Page *Heyford*
Hawker *Fury*
Hawker *Hart*
Supermarine *Stranraer*
Supermarine *Walrus*

Vickers *Vildebeest*
Vickers *Vimy*
Vickers *Wellesley*
Westland *Wapiti*

Italy
CANT Z 501 *Gabbiano*
Fiat CR 32 *Chirri*
Fiat CR 42 *Falco*

Savoia-Marchetti SM 81
   Pipistrello

Japan
Mitsubishi A5M
Mitsubishi G3M
Nakajima Ki 27

Netherlands
Fokker C V

Russia
Polikarpov I 15/I 153 *Chaika*
Polikarpov I 16
Polikarpov R5
Polikarpov U 2/Po 2
Tupolev SB 2
Tupolev TB 3

World War II, 1939–1945

Australia
Commonwealth CA 1 *Wirraway*
Commonwealth CA 12
   Boomerang

France
Bloch MB 152
Bloch MB 174
Breguet 691
Dewoitine D 520
LeO 451
Morane-Saulnier MS 406
Potez 63

Germany
Arado Ar 96
Arado Ar 196
Arado Ar 234 *Blitz*
Blohm und Voss Bv 138
Blohm und Voss Bv 222 *Wiking*
DFS 230
Dornier Do 18
Dornier Do 24
Dornier Do 217
Fieseler Fi 156 *Storch*
Flettner Fl 282 *Kolibri*
Focke-Wulf Fw 189 *Uhu*
Focke-Wulf Fw 190
Focke-Wulf Fw 200 *Condor*
Gotha Go 242
Heinkel He 111
Heinkel He 115
Heinkel He 177 *Greif*
Heinkel He 219 *Uhu*
Henschel Hs 129
Junkers Ju 52
Junkers Ju 87 *Stuka*
Junkers Ju 88
Junkers Ju 188
Junkers Ju 290
Messerschmitt Bf 109G
Messerschmitt Bf 110

Messerschmitt Me 163 *Komet*
Messerschmitt Me 262
Messerschmitt Me 321/323 *Gigant*
Messerschmitt Me 410 *Hornisse*

Great Britain
Airspeed *Horsa*
Airspeed *Oxford*
Armstrong-Whitworth *Whitley*
Avro *Anson*
Avro *Lancaster*
Blackburn *Skua* and *Roc*
Boulton-Paul *Defiant*
Bristol *Beaufighter*
Bristol *Beaufort*
Bristol *Blenheim*
de Havilland DH 98 *Mosquito*
Fairey *Barracuda*
Fairey *Battle*
Fairey *Firefly*
Fairey *Fulmar*
General Aircraft *Hamilcar*
Gloster *Meteor*
Handley Page *Halifax*
Handley Page *Hampden*
Hawker *Hurricane*
Hawker *Tempest V*
Hawker *Typhoon*
Miles *Master*
Short *Stirling*
Short *Sunderland*
Supermarine *Spitfire*
Vickers *Wellington*
Westland *Lysander*
Westland *Whirlwind*

Italy
CANT Z 506B *Airone*
CANT Z 1007 *Alcione*
Caproni Ca 310
Fiat Br 20 *Cignona*
Fiat G 50 *Freccia*

Macchi MC 200 *Saetta*
Macchi MC 202 *Folgore*
Piaggio P 108B
Reggiane Re 2000/2001 *Falco*
Savoia-Marchetti SM 79 *Sparviero*

Japan
Aichi D3A
Kawanishi H6K
Kawanishi H8K
Kawanishi N1K2 *Shiden Kai*
Kawasaki Ki 45 *Toryu*
Kawasaki Ki 48
Kawasaki Ki 61 *Hien*
Mitsubishi A6M *Reisen*
Mitsubishi G4M
Mitsubishi J2M *Raiden*
Mitsubishi Ki 21
Mitsubishi Ki 46
Mitsubishi Ki 67 *Hiryu*
Nakajima B5N
Nakajima B6N *Tenzan*
Nakajima J1N1 *Gekko*
Nakajima Ki 43 *Hayabusa*
Nakajima Ki 44 *Shoki*
Nakajima Ki 49 *Donryu*
Nakajima Ki 84 *Hayate*
Yokosuka D4Y *Suisei*
Yokosuka MXY 7 *Oka*
Yokosuka P1Y1 *Ginga*

Netherlands
Fokker D XXI
Fokker G I

Poland
PZL P 11 *Jedenastka*
PZL P 23 *Karas*
PZL P 37 *Los*

Russia
Beriev MBR 2

Ilyushin Il 2 *Shturmovik*
Ilyushin Il 4
Lavochkin La 5/7
Lavochkin LaGG 3

Mikoyan-Gurevich MiG 3
Petlyakov Pe 2
Petlyakov Pe 8
Tupolev Tu 2

Yakovlev Yak 3
Yakovlev Yak 9

Jet Age, 1946–2000

Argentina
FMA IA 58 *Pucara*

Brazil
Embraer EMB 312 *Tucano*

Canada
Avro Canada CF 100 *Canuck*
Canadair CL 28 *Argus*
Canadair CL 41 *Tutor*
de Havilland Canada DHC 1
    Chipmunk

China
Nanchang Q 5
Shenyang J 6/F 6

Consortia
Dassault/Dornier *Alphajet*
Panavia *Tornado*
SEPECAT *Jaguar*

Czechoslovakia
Aero L 29 *Delfin*
Aero L 39 *Albatros*

France
Aerospatiale AS 332 *Super*
    Puma/Cougar
Aerospatiale CM 170 *Magister*
Aerospatiale SA 321 *Super*
    Frelon
Aerospatiale SA 341/342 *Gazelle*
Aerospatiale SA 365 *Dauphin*/AS
    565 *Panther*
Dassault *Atlantique 2*
Dassault *Mirage 2000*
Dassault *Mirage F 1*
Dassault *Mirage III*
Dassault-Breguet *Super Etendard*

Germany
Dornier Do 27

MBB BO 105

Great Britain
Avro *Shackleton*
Avro *Vulcan*
Blackburn *Beverly*
Blackburn *Buccaneer*
British Aerospace *Harrier*
de Havilland DH 100 *Vampire*
de Havilland DH 110 *Sea Vixen*
de Havilland DH 112 *Venom/Sea*
    Venom
English Electric *Canberra*
English Electric *Lightning*
Folland *Gnat*
Gloster *Javelin*
Handley Page *Victor*
Hawker *Hunter*
Hawker *Sea Fury*
Hawker-Siddeley *Hawk*
Hawker-Siddeley *Nimrod*
Vickers *Valiant*
Westland *Lynx*
Westland *Scout/Wasp*

India
Hindustan HF 24 *Marut*

Israel
IAI *Kfir*

Italy
Aermacchi MB 339
Agusta A 109 *Hirundo*
Agusta A 129 *Mangusta*
Fiat G 91Y

Japan
Mitsubishi T 2/F 1
ShinMaywa US 1

Russia
Antonov An 2

Antonov An 12
Antonov An 22 *Antei*
Antonov An 124 *Ruslan*
Beriev Be 12 *Tchaika*
Ilyushin Il 28
Ilyushin Il 38
Ilyushin Il 76
Kamov Ka 27
Kamov Ka 50
Mikoyan-Gurevich MiG 15
Mikoyan-Gurevich MiG 21
Mikoyan-Gurevich MiG 23/27
Mikoyan-Gurevich MiG 25
Mikoyan-Gurevich MiG 29
Mikoyan-Gurevich MiG 31
Mil Mi 17
Mil Mi 24
Mil Mi 26
Myasishchev M 4 *Molot*
Sukhoi Su 17
Sukhoi Su 24
Sukhoi Su 25
Sukhoi Su 27
Tupolev Tu 16
Tupolev Tu 22
Tupolev Tu 22M
Tupolev Tu 95/142
Tupolev Tu 160
Yakovlev Yak 36

Spain
CASA C 101 *Aviojet*

Sweden
Saab J 29 *Tunnan*
Saab J 35 *Draken*
Saab JA 37 *Viggen*
Saab JAS 39 *Gripen*

Yugoslavia
SOKO G 4 *Super Galeb*
SOKO J 22 *Orao*

FOREWORD

John Fredriksen's book on international warbirds is a very welcome addition to the literature, for it goes beyond the conventional approach of most books on combat aircraft, which tend to emphasize only statistics, nomenclature, and operational history. John includes all of these, of course, but he adds a human dimension that enlivens each of his descriptions and lets us see behind the machine to the people involved.

As one reads through the book, three things become apparent. The first of these is the high quality of designers in all countries; the second is the critical nature of timing; and the third is the often overlooked importance of scale.

Fredriksen's apt capture of the essence of these airplanes is an impressive achievement. He makes you realize just how amazing is the ingenuity of aircraft designers and builders all over the world. It is really remarkable how designers in all countries, regardless of their size, were able to maintain a parity in the performance of their designs over the years, even when the resources of a particular country might not match the resources of another.

There are many illustrations of this phenomenon. If one examines the beautiful biplane fighters of the late 1920s and early 1930s, one finds such sterling examples as the American Curtiss P-6E, English Hawker *Fury*, Czech Avia B 534, Italian Fiat CR 32, Japanese Nakajima A2N, and Soviet Polikarpov I 15. Each aircraft was the product of its own design studio, and the designers had to accommodate the requirements of their armed service to the engines, equipment, and available materials. All were flown within roughly the same time frame, and all achieved roughly the same performance. A similar situation developed with the several generations of monoplane fighters, both those of the first generation (Boeing P-26, PZL 11, Polikarpov I 16) and of the second (Messerschmitt Bf 109G, Hawker *Hurricane*, Supermarine *Spitfire*).

Even well into World War II, when the immense industrial resources of the Allies began to take their toll, Axis designers were able to come up with competitive aircraft, for example, the Focke-Wulf Fw 190D, Macchi C 205, and Nakajima Ki 84. And when the chips were really down, the Germans managed to excel with the Messerschmitt Me 262. Similar resilience was shown by the Soviet designers, who managed to move a generation ahead in indigenous fighter design with such capable aircraft as the Yakovlev series of fighters, and do it under the pressure of relocating factories and workforces even as the fighting was going on. In all of these achievements, it is the Olympic spirit of the human desire to excel that stands out.

If one accepts the inherent ability of designers of all countries to come up with comparable aircraft, one next has to look into the matter of timing, which is almost always dictated by political, rather than practical, events. Poland, for example, had one of the most modern air forces in the world in the early 1930s—but was unable to modernize it in time for World War II. France was in the same boat; it had created one of the largest air forces in the world, only to see it go to rack and ruin as a succession of peacetime governments refused to spend the money to modernize it. When at last the funds did begin to flow, it was far too late, and France fought World War II with inadequate equipment and inadequate numbers.

A crucial example of timing may be found in the air forces of Great Britain and Germany. Germany had an advantage, as it could create an air force at the same time that it was creating a timetable for going to war—and could thus be sure that they would coincide. So when Hitler struck Poland on September 1, 1939, the Luftwaffe was filled with new and modern aircraft that were designed for the job they had to do.

Britain's situation was different. It had doddered along for years after World War I with open-cockpit biplanes fitted with fixed gear, two light machine guns, and a fixed-pitch propeller. Fortunately, two far-seeing companies, Hawker and Supermarine, were willing to speculate on the future with their *Hurricane* and *Spitfire* designs, building prototypes on spec and counting on the government to recognize their worth. (Coincidentally, at the same time, the Royal Air Force became convinced that fighters needed eight-gun armament and they were so equipped.) As it happened, the *Hurricane* and the *Spitfire* began to arrive in sufficient numbers just as the Battle of Britain commenced in 1940.

The case of the United States was different. Not only did it sit out the war for two years—until 1941—it had the advantage of the Anglo-French Purchasing Commission buying lots of aircraft and building up the U.S. industrial base. And this brings us to the third element: scale.

The aggressor nations—Germany, Japan, and, to a lesser extent, Italy—had a preconceived notion of how aerial warfare should take place. In each case they presumed that they would be the aggressor nation, that they would fight a sharp, swift war against a less well equipped opponent, and would then pause to regroup and reequip.

Their calculations indicated that a first-line air force of 3,000–4,000 aircraft would be adequate for the task. Great Britain and France thought along similar lines. Only in the Soviet Union and, to a far greater extent, in the United States did the planners envision operations on a grand scale. Incredibly enough, in the United States four men (Lieutenant Colonels Harold L. George and Haywood S. "Possum" Hansell Jr. and Majors Laurence S. Kuter and Kenneth W. Walker) would in nine days create Air War Plan Document–1, which would clearly and accurately outline the mammoth scale of American air operations.

Of the three elements under discussion—quality, timing, and quantity—the last ultimately proved to be of the greatest value. Germany and Japan were trapped by the early successes provided by the quality of their aircraft and the timing with which they were built. The successes merely confirmed their opinion that a small, highly trained air force was all that was necessary. When the tide of war changed, and massive numbers of enemy aircraft opposed them, they began frantically to build—but to no avail. Despite all their efforts (and Germany achieved an incredible 44,000 aircraft produced in 1944), it was far too little and far too late. The Allies' industrial output (mainly thanks to the United States and the Soviet Union and, to a lesser degree, Great Britain) had so far outstripped them in quantity that the war was already lost. And perhaps fittingly, the length of the war had switched the effect of timing, so that many new designs of the highest quality were now entering frontline Allied service.

It is to be hoped that John Fredriksen's fine book will be widely read by the decisionmakers in the United States, who might then see that having aircraft of high quality is often not enough; you must also have them in sufficient numbers to overcome a determined enemy.

Walter Boyne

INTRODUCTION

Airplanes are certainly fascinating machines. Since their invention in 1903, they continue capturing the world's imagination. Not surprisingly, aviation literature remains one of the most popular facets of the history genre. Year after year, an avalanche of picture books, directories, and histories—particularly about military aircraft—are published for the entertainment and enlightenment of interested readers, both professional and layperson alike. This sheer outpouring of literature can sometimes represent a problem for parties interested in testing the rather deep waters of this topic: How and where does one begin? This is an especially daunting proposition for students with little experience in historical research. Curiously, despite a highly developed body of literature available, aviation reference books have been less successful in bringing information quickly and easily to the attention of casual users. Most titles are, in fact, written by specialists with specialists in mind, or at least for readers steeped in the nuances of the technology. Neither is the coverage of world military aircraft afforded by these books necessarily uniform. Reference material on airplanes from World War I, World War II, and contemporary times are plentiful, but few address aeronautical developments of the so-called Golden Age (1919–1939). For students and laypersons interested in pursuing the aeronautical facts and feats of this essential period, this gap is an obstacle to effective research.

The present work is an attempt to address all the problems associated with aviation research books in general, reference books in particular. Drawing upon the success of my earlier volume (*Warbirds: An Illustrated Guide to U.S. Military Aircraft, 1915–2000*, published in 1999 by ABC-CLIO), *International Warbirds* is designed to address student inquiries about specific types of airplanes on a global scale. Simultaneously, it also contains sufficient breadth and depth to satiate most advanced researchers. However, unlike *Warbirds*, I drop all pretense toward comprehensiveness. That claim would require a book two or three times the size of this volume. Being restricted to only 336 entries, I was hard-pressed to assemble a list that was objective, far-reaching, and afforded good coverage of the most famous machines, not to mention a myriad of lesser-known ones. I believe I succeeded in compiling a useful, working survey. Naturally, any

thorough treatment of airplanes is going to be dominated by the big five: France, Germany, Great Britain, Japan, and Russia. All their famous aircraft, and a host of lesser types, are included. However, I went to great lengths to cover interesting machines from smaller countries, be they powerhouses like Israel and Canada, or developing nations like China, India, or Brazil. Wherever possible, I sought to accommodate as eclectic a collection of interesting or unusual airplanes from around the world as possible. I certainly wanted to avoid the usual Eurocentric approach to aviation history, for no one nation can claim a monopoly on military technology.

Given the constraints on space, my selection criteria were highly selective by necessity. I therefore chose aircraft that have been manufactured and actually deployed by military and naval units in some kind of squadron service. As in my previous venture, experimental prototypes—regardless of their celebrity or infamy—have been deliberately omitted. I believe my otherwise thorough coverage more than compensates for their absence.

To facilitate reader access, this book shares great commonality with its predecessor. Each entry consists of a photograph and a succinct account of each machine. Here I provide essential technical information such as dimensions, performance, power plant, armament, and service dates. Each narrative is carefully crafted to contextualize the airplanes in terms of development, deployment, and denouement. Special attention is paid to any record-breaking feats or unusual features that may have distinguished each in its time. Furthermore, everything has been rendered in direct, nontechnical prose for ease of comprehension. My goal throughout is to be exacting in scope without becoming burdensome in detail.

To facilitate additional inquiry, two detailed subject bibliographies are included in the rear matter of this book. This feature was added to counter a personal pique of mine with many so-called reference books about military aviation. On more than one occasion, I have become intrigued by entries discovered in the works of aeronautical mavens such as William Green, Bill Gunston, and Kenneth Munson, only to discover that no further references have been provided! Such material can, in fact, be uncovered eventually, but only after expending much time and effort. Therefore, I proffer two aviation bibliographies that are extensive and reflect some of the very latest literature available. The first (Aircraft Bibliography) painstakingly denotes printed materials available on an airplane-by-airplane basis. Wherever possible, material on the parent company is also provided for greater historical context. This assemblage has been carefully collected from *WorldCat* and other online sources to ensure that each book or magazine can be accessed through interlibrary loan. Furthermore, magazine articles, if not borrowed outright, can also be copied from many aviation museum libraries for a small charge, or ordered directly from the publisher. The second bibliography (General Bibliography) was culled from a vast number of titles pertaining to national aviation history. All are listed alphabetically by country, then in identical fashion by author. These materials represent the most recent titles on aviation literature anywhere. As previously noted, their availability was confirmed by *WorldCat*, and all should be easily obtained through loan or purchase.

I next sought to enhance this volume's utility through the addition of several appendixes. For the benefit of readers unacquainted with the history or applications of military aviation, Appendix 1: Aircraft by Mission identifies aircraft by the function they performed. Whenever an aircraft is employed in more than one mission, it is listed in each appropriate alphabetical category by name. Appendix 2: Museums is a listing of many of the biggest air museums from across the world. Appendix 3: Aircraft Journals and Magazines concludes the book by listing non-U.S. aviation magazines, many of which are in English or contain printed English-language translations.

The author would like to acknowledge and thank many people for their selfless contributions to this effort. Aviation author and scholar Walter Boyne needs no introduction, and his review of the manuscript and comments were extremely helpful. Walt was also generous enough to provide a Foreword that is both cogent and thought provoking. Also noted are John H. Bolthouse III and Miles Todd of the San Diego Aerospace Museum and Nilda Pergola-Jensen of the Defense Visual Information Center for their cheerful assistance in locating photographs. I am also deeply indebted to Joan McKenny and Dan Hagerdorn of the National Air and Space Museum, Smithsonian Institution. The same applies to Leo Opdyke of *World War I Aero*, Gerard Frawley of *Australian Aviation*, Avro Haav of Estonia, Jan Eric Keikke of the Netherlands, and Gordon G. Bartley of *British Aerospace*. Gratitude is also extended to that aviation research stalwart, Bill Hooper of the New England Air Museum Library, for both patience and permission to ransack—literally—his holdings. My editors, Alicia S. Merrit and Liz Kincaid, also warrant kudos for exemplary endurance in handling my many and impossible requests. Finally, I want to voice a personal note of thanks to aviation artist Charles Kourmphtes of Warwick, Rhode Island, Bob Gordon of Uncasville, Connecticut, for unfettered use of his private library, and Robert E. Schnare of the Henry E. Eccles Library, U.S. Naval War College, for access to his splendid facility. As with my previous endeavor, I could have neither begun nor finished this book without them.

John C. Fredriksen, Ph.D.

International Warbirds

Type: Reconnaissance; Light Bomber

Dimensions: wingspan, 44 feet, 1 inch; length, 23 feet, 5 inches; height, 12 feet
Weights: empty, 1,764 pounds; gross, 2,469 pounds
Power plant: 1 × 160–horsepower Mercedes liquid-cooled in-line engine
Performance: maximum speed, 98 miles per hour; ceiling, 16,400 feet; range, 400 miles
Armament: 2 × 7.92mm machine guns
Service dates: 1916–1918

The Allgemeine Elektrizitats Gesellschaft (AEG) C IV was an ungainly but functional two-seater used in World War I. Significantly, it pioneered the use of steel tubing in construction and was also deployed as an armored attack craft.

The firm AEG had aviation experience dating back to 1910. In 1914 it began developing a family of two-seat reconnaissance aircraft for the German army, commencing with the B I. During the next two years a series of similar aircraft was deployed with varying degrees of success until the most numerous model, the C IV, appeared in the summer of 1916. Like all AEG two-seaters, it possessed angular, rather unattractive lines and characteristic long wings. However, this model differed in the great extent that metal was used in construction. Unlike competing Aviatik, Albatros, and LVG aircraft, the C IV contained wing spars of welded steel tubing. The fuselage also consisted of steel tubing, being decked on the top with plywood and on the sides

with fabric. The C IV was powered by an excellent 160-horsepower Mercedes engine that sat partially exposed in the cowling, with a large "rhinoceros" exhaust stack protruding over the wing. For its class, it was also well-armed, with machine guns for both pilot and gunner. Around 400 C IVs were produced.

This AEG craft rendered excellent service in the field owing to its great physical strength and docile handling. Despite growing obsolescence, it lingered in frontline service until the Armistice of 1918. Previously, Germany's air force had introduced the concept of *infanterie flieger* (close support units) to assist the ground war. In 1917 a new version of the C IV, the J I, was introduced with a 200-horsepower engine, 860 pounds of armored plate, and two additional machine guns firing through the floorboards at a 45-degree angle. By 1918 further refinements culminated in the final J II model. A combined total of over 600 machines was delivered.

Type: Heavy Bomber

Dimensions: wingspan, 60 feet, 3 inches; length, 32 feet, 4 inches; height, 12 feet, 9 inches
Weights: empty, 4,410 pounds; gross, 8,003 pounds
Power plant: 2 × 260–horsepower Mercedes liquid-cooled in-line engines
Performance: maximum speed, 90 miles per hour; ceiling, 13,120 feet; range, 400 miles
Armament: 2 × 7.62mm machine guns; 772 pounds of bombs
Service dates: 1916–1918

The Allgemeine Elektrizitats Gesellschaft (AEG) G was a large but mediocre bomber that saw much service throughout World War I. Continually refined and improved, its performance never equaled that of Gotha and Friedrichshafen contemporaries.

In 1914 the AEG company began development of a large twin-engine aircraft in the *Grossflugzeug* (heavy bomber) category. It emerged in 1915 as the G I, a conventional snub-nosed biplane somewhat smaller than the Gotha and Friedrichshafen giants. It differed in having the engines mounted in a tractor, not pusher, configuration, with trademark "rhinoceros" exhaust stacks protruding up toward the wing. During the next year the G I was subjected to continual upgrades in design and power plants until the main production model, the G IV, appeared in 1916. Like all AEG products, it employed steel tubing in construction of the wing frames, fuselage, and tail assembly. This endowed the craft with great structural integrity, but at the cost of considerable weight. Thus the G IV never possessed the range or bomb load of other bombers in its class. Nevertheless, the German air service acquired an estimated 400 machines.

For such a nondescript aircraft, the G IV enjoyed an active and far-ranging combat career. Incapable of reaching England, they were employed in the Balkans and other secondary theaters where resistance was feeble. The lumbering giants bombed Bucharest and Salonika with impunity and also operated on the Italian front before being redeployed to France. There the quality of opposition was much higher and, with losses mounting, the G IVs were restricted to bombing enemy rear areas at night. Stripped of armament, they also flew long-range reconnaissance missions. In an attempt to improve the aircraft's performance, a final variant, the G V, was developed in 1917 with increased wingspan and greater bomb load. It emerged too late to affect the outcome of events, however, and by war's end only 40 AEG G-type aircraft remained in service.

Type: Trainer; Light Bomber

Dimensions: wingspan, 36 feet, 9 inches; length, 36 feet, 10 inches; height, 13 feet, 1 inch
Weights: empty, 7,297 pounds; gross, 13,999 pounds
Power plant: 1 × 4,400–pound thrust Rolls-Royce Viper turbojet engine
Performance: maximum speed, 560 miles per hour; ceiling, 48,00 feet; range, 311 miles
Armament: none, or up to 4,000 pounds of gunpods, bombs, or rockets
Service dates: 1979–

With all the looks and flair of an Italian sports car, the MB 339 is Macchi's latest attempt to capitalize on the success of its earlier MB 326. It combines good performance and great reliability at very modest cost.

In 1957 Macchi's Ermano Bazzochi broke company tradition by designing its first jet trainer, the MB 326. It was a stylish, low-wing craft that housed pupil and instructor under a long canopy. The craft exhibited sprightly performance and fine handling, and it was considerably less expense than other jet trainers in service. A single-seat light attack version, the MB 326K, was also developed and sold abroad to several countries. Needless to say, with a production run of 761 machines, Bazzochi's design was one of the most successful aircraft in Italian export history. By 1976 Macchi felt obliged to repeat its success with a newer, similar machine. That year the new MB 339 premiered, reflecting a logical progression of the older aircraft. The new design utilized 80 per-

cent of the MB 326's parts and even retained the tried-and-tested Rolls-Royce Viper engine. However, it sports a greatly revised nose section with staggered seating to allow instructors a better forward view. The tail has been enlarged and more advanced avionics fitted. The cockpit was also pressurized for ease of operation at high altitude. In 1977 the Italian Air Force purchased 101 copies as its primary jet trainer. The MB 339 has also been selected as the official mount of the *Frecce Tricolori* national acrobatic team.

Macchi also pursued development of a light strike version for ground attack. The MB 339C is an armed two-seater version that has been exported to New Zealand. The newer MB 339K *Veltro 2*, by comparison, seats one pilot only and is capable of carrying a variety of ordnance on several wing and fuselage hardpoints. An excellent aircraft, it remains to be seen if this racy little trainer can emulate the success of its celebrated ancestors.

Type: Trainer; Light Bomber

Dimensions: wingspan, 33 feet, 9 inches; length, 35 feet, 5 inches; height, 11 feet
Weights: empty, 5,212 pounds; gross, 7,231 pounds
Power plant: 1 × 1,962–pound thrust Motorlet M701c turbojet engine
Performance: maximum speed, 407 miles per hour; ceiling, 36,100 feet; range, 397 miles
Armament: none, or 440 pounds of bombs and 2 × 7.62mm gunpods
Service dates: 1963–

The *Delfin* (Dolphin) was the most important jet trainer of the now defunct Warsaw Pact. As it is phased out of service, small numbers of this docile craft are ending up in the hands of private collectors.

By 1958 the government of Czechoslovakia sought to replace its piston-powered trainers with a more modern jet equivalent. An Aero (a state industry) design bureau under Z. Rublic and K. Tomas responded with the L 29 prototype in April 1959. This was a midwing design with a high "T" tail unit and an elongated canopy seating a pupil and instructor in tandem. An advanced feature for the crew was synchronized ejection seats to avoid a midair collision while abandoning the airplane. The craft also possessed straight wings with air intakes at the roots, as well as robust landing gear. Although underpowered by Western standards, the L 29 exhibited good performance and easy handling. In 1960 a small preproduction batch was pitted against the PZL TS 11 and Yakovlev Yak 30 in a contest to be-

come the Warsaw Pact's standard military trainer. To the surprise of many, the little *Delfin* bested competing machines and entered full-scale production. By 1974 some 3,600 had been manufactured and adopted by air forces in the Soviet Union, Hungary, Romania, East Germany, and Bulgaria. This simple, robust machine was responsible for instructing huge numbers of Soviet bloc pilots who, in their day, constituted a formidable threat to the West.

Naturally, such a fine-handling, rugged jet had applications overseas in the hands of Soviet client states. The L 29 found ready customers in the employ of Afghanistan, Iraq, Nigeria, Egypt, Syria, and Uganda. The *Delfin* also made a decent ground-attack plane, and the Nigerian L 29s were readily employed as such during the 1968 civil war. Since the breakup of the Warsaw Pact, many L 29s continue training functions with Third World air forces. Others still find their way into private hands and are especially sought in the United States.

Type: Trainer; Light Bomber

Dimensions: wingspan, 31 feet; length, 39 feet; height, 15 feet
Weights: empty, 10,218 pounds; gross, 12,346 pounds
Power plant: 1 × 3,792–pound thrust Ivchenko AI-25 turbojet engine
Performance: maximum speed, 379 miles per hour; ceiling, 24,600 feet; range, 1,087 miles
Armament: none, or up to 2,205 pounds of bomb and rockets; 1 × 23mm cannon gunpod
Service dates: 1974–

Like its predecessor, the *Albatros* is a viceless trainer widely employed by members of the former Warsaw Pact. Fitted with sophisticated weapon pods, it also makes a capable light attack craft.

In 1966 the Aero design bureau was instructed to construct a successor to the numerous and successful L 29 *Delfins*. It was anticipated that this, too, would ultimately serve as the standard Warsaw Pact jet trainer. Considerable thought was given to the new machine, especially in terms of air intakes, and no less than four prototypes were built and flown before a final design was settled upon. The new L 39 *Albatros* flew in the fall of 1968 as an extremely attractive little jet. Although straight-winged like the L 29, it featured a lengthened, highly pointed nose with broader wing and tail surfaces. Moreover, being fitted with an Ivchenko AI 25 turbojet with twice the thrust of the older machine, it displayed marked improvements in performance. Another unique feature of the L 39 was its construction, which was modular.

The entire craft broke down into only three subassemblies (fuselage, wing, and tail unit) for ease of maintenance and repair. As predicted, the fine-flying *Albatros* was adopted as a standard trainer within Warsaw Pact air forces. More than 2,800 were constructed and deployed by the Soviet Union, East Germany, Bulgaria, Romania, and Albania. And because the L 39's lively performance allowed for the attachment of weapons pods, it also functioned as a flexible light attack aircraft.

After the collapse of the Soviet Union in 1991, the new Czech Republic continued developing and refining the basic *Albatros* design with a view toward greater export. The L 59 features a stronger turbofan engine, advanced avionics, and has been bought in quantity by Egypt. The new L 159 ALCA (*Advanced Light Combat Aircraft*) first flew in 1997 as a dedicated ground-attack weapon. Not surprisingly, the Czech view former Warsaw Pact members as their largest source of potential customers.

Aerospatiale AS 332 *Super Puma/Cougar* — France

Type: Transport; Reconnaissance; Antisubmarine

Dimensions: rotorspan, 51 feet, 2 inches; length, 61 feet, 4 inches; height, 15 feet, 1 inch
Weights: empty, 9,546 pounds; gross, 20,615 pounds
Power plant: 2 × 1,877–horsepower Turbomeca Makila turboshaft engines
Performance: maximum speed, 172 miles per hour; ceiling, 13,450 feet; range, 384 miles
Armament: none
Service dates: 1990–

The *Super Puma/Cougar* is the latest in a large, successful family of indigenously designed French helicopters. It was coproduced with Great Britain and serves in armies around the world.

In 1963 the French military requested procurement of a capable medium helicopter with troop-carrying capacity. The specification also mandated a capacity for all-weather operations, although it was understood that several years would lapse before such technology was developed. In 1965 Aerospatiale answered with the SA 330 *Puma*. Unlike the earlier *Super Frelon*, which was designed with Italian and U.S. help, the new machine was entirely French in origin. The *Puma* was a spacious helicopter featuring two overhead engines and retractable landing gear. Within two years the company reached an agreement to coproduce the craft with Westland of Great Britain, and it was built in large numbers for both nations. Many saw active service during the 1991 Gulf War with Iraq before being retired. A total of 697 were built before a new model, the SA 332 *Super Puma*, arrived in 1978. This was essentially a stretched version of the old machine with stronger engines, new undercarriage, and improved avionics. Another significant modification was employment of fiberglass rotors for enhanced performance. The *Super Puma* was originally intended for civilian use, and many were sold in France or exported abroad for such purposes. An SA 332 even serves as an official transportation vehicle for the French president. A variant is also employed by Romania (which fits them with antitank rockets) and Indonesia.

In 1990 continual refinement of the *Super Puma* induced the new owner, Eurocopter, to rename it the AS 532 *Cougar*. Subsequent modifications have also taken the basic design beyond its original role as a troop transport. *Cougars* are now capable of successfully conducting battlefield surveillance, antisubmarine, and antiship strike missions. Two important features are the ability to fly one hour without lubricants, and rotors that remain intact for at least 24 hours after being hit from ground fire. About 200 *Cougars* have been built for France, with a similar number on order.

Aerospatiale CM 170 *Magister* ———————————————————— France

Type: Trainer; Light Bomber

Dimensions: wingspan, 37 feet, 5 inches; length, 33 feet; height, 9 feet, 2 inches
Weights: empty, 4,740 pounds; gross, 7,055 pounds
Power plant: 2 × 882–pound thrust Turbomeca Marbore IIa turbojet engines
Performance: maximum speed, 444 miles per hour; ceiling, 36,090 feet; range, 575 miles
Armament: none
Service dates: 1956–

The gentle *Magister* was history's first jet trainer and one of the longest-employed. Built in large quantities, it continues today in both training and light strike functions.

After World War II, aviation engineer Pierre Maubossin made his reputation for pioneering the use of small jet engines on light aircraft and gliders. In 1950 the firm Fouga tapped his skill in responding to a French government specification for a new jet trainer—the world's first. Maubossin then originated a design that was practical, efficient, yet exuded a certain Gallic flair. The CM 170 was an all-metal, mid-wing design employing a unique vee, or "butterfly," tail. The straight wings were fitted with tiptanks. Powered by twin engines, the airducts were placed at the wing roots as pupil and instructor sat in tandem under a long plastic canopy. The Armee de l'Air was suitably impressed by the docile aircraft, which was both responsive and forgiving in all flight profiles. It entered production in 1956 as the *Magister* and was widely employed at aviation schools around

France. Not to be left behind, the Aeronavale followed suit and also purchased a navalized version, the CM 175 *Zephyr*, which featured structural strengthening and an arrester hook for carrier operations. At length Fouga passed into the hands of Potez, Sud-Aviation, and finally Aerospatiale, but production of the *Magister* continued unabated until 1970. A total of 622 were produced in France alone.

The low-price, high-performance CM 170 naturally attracted great interest from abroad, and several countries obtained manufacturing licenses to manufacture the *Magister* on their own. The biggest consumer was West Germany, which constructed 188 trainers, followed by Valmet of Finland with 62 and IAI in Israel with 36. This amounts to a total of 921 CM 170s worldwide. Israel found the craft potentially useful for light strike missions and actively employed it during several wars against Arab forces. These craft were fitted with a variety of gunpacks, bombs, and rockets. However, only a handful of French *Magisters* remain operational as trainers.

✪ Aerospatiale SA 321 *Super Frelon* ——————————— France

Type: Antisubmarine; Transport

Dimensions: rotorspan, 62 feet; length, 63 feet; height, 21 feet, 9 inches
Weights: empty, 15,130 pounds; gross, 28,660 pounds
Power plant: $3 \times 1,570$–horsepower Turbomeca IIIC turboshaft engines
Performance: maximum speed, 171 miles per hour; ceiling, 10,325 feet; range, 633 miles
Armament: $4 \times$ homing torpedoes or $2 \times$ AM39 *Exocet* missiles
Service dates: 1963–

The *Super Frelon* is the largest helicopter manu-factured in Western Europe. It saw extensive service with the French navy and Israeli army and in a variety of capacities.

In 1959 the French military released specifica-tions for a large troop-carrying helicopter. Sud-Avia-tion (now Aerospatiale) responded with the *Frelon* (Hornet), a large machine with three motors that was briefly considered and finally rejected by 1963. That year the company entered into agreement with Sikorsky and Fiat for assistance in designing an even bigger craft. Sikorsky contributed to the six-blade rotor and watertight hull typical of its own machines, whereas Fiat was responsible for the gearbox and power transmission. The resulting SA 321 *Super Frelon* emerged as the biggest helicopter assembled by a Western European country. In 1963 the prototype established several distance and pay-load records. And like the Sikorsky S 61, it can oper-ate from water using sponsons and land with equal agility on ships. The French navy appreciated this latter quality and ordered 17 machines as advanced antisubmarine warfare helicopters. Operating in groups of four, usually one naval *Super Frelon* low-ers its dunking sonar while the other three vector in on contacts and unleash homing torpedoes. Later versions of this hefty machine can also be outfitted with the deadly *Exocet* antiship missile for maritime interdiction purposes.

The *Super Frelon* is so large that it can easily accommodate up to 30 fully equipped troops. The Is-raelis put this capacity to good use during the 1967 Six Day War, as well as in numerous commando raids against Egypt and Lebanon since then. Others have been exported for use by South Africa and Libya. China, meanwhile, was so impressed by the *Super Frelon* that it purchased 13 outright and sub-sequently obtained rights to manufacture them under license. The SA 321 has been continually up-dated with better engines and electronics, but it is at the twilight of a long and distinguished service ca-reer. A total of 99 were built, exclusive of Chinese versions. Several civilian variants have also been marketed abroad.

⭐ Aerospatiale SA 341/342 *Gazelle* ──────────────────── **France**

Type: Antitank; Reconnaissance

Dimensions: rotorspan, 34 feet, 4 inches; length, 39 feet, 3 inches; height, 10 feet, 2 inches
Weights: empty, 2,208 pounds; gross, 4,630 pounds
Power plant: 1 × 858–horsepower Turbomeca XIV M2 turboshaft engine
Performance: maximum speed, 193 miles per hour; ceiling, 16,405 feet; range, 416 miles
Armament: up to 1,540 pounds of rockets or gunpods
Service dates: 1971–

The ubiquitous *Gazelle* is a popular light observation helicopter that pioneered several novel technologies. Jointly built by France and Great Britain, it is now flown by 36 nations.

In the mid-1960s, the French army released specifications calling for a new observation helicopter to replace its aging *Alouette II*. Aerospatiale subsequently designed a machine that utilized many parts of the former machine but also incorporated new technology. The new *Gazelle* retained the same Astazou IIIA turboshaft engine but introduced a rigid main rotorhead, composite construction rotor blades, and the unique fenestron (shrouded) tail rotor. This last feature was essentially a fan unit that could run at lower power levels than the main rotor, thanks to shielding from air turbulence. More significant, the *Gazelle* employed a completely enclosed aerodynamic fuselage, seating two pilots and three passengers. This lithe, little craft usually landed on twin skids, but pontoons could also be fitted. While the helicopter was still in its developmental stages,

the British firm Westland agreed to become a partner in producing both the *Gazelle* and *Puma* designs.

The first production SA 341 *Gazelle* flew in 1971 and was completely successful at home and abroad. The craft enjoyed special popularity in England, serving as an observation and communications craft with the army and navy and as a trainer in the air force. Britain also employed several armed machines in the 1982 Falkland Islands War, and subsequently many French machines were outfitted with HOT wire-guided antitank missiles. The lively chopper ultimately served with 36 nations, making it one of the great export successes of the century. In an attempt to improve the performance of French *Gazelles*, a more powerful Astazou XIV engine, with twice the horsepower, was fitted in 1973. This version, which was not adopted by Britain, is known as the SA 342. It sees extensive use by the French army as an antitank aircraft and was outfitted for nighttime operations during the 1991 Gulf War. A total of 1,200 *Gazelles* have been built.

Type: Air/Sea Rescue; Antisubmarine; Light Bomber; Transport

Dimensions: rotorspan, 39 feet, 2 inches; length, 39 feet, 8 inches; height, 13 feet, 1 inch
Weights: empty, 4,987 pounds; gross, 9,370 pounds
Power plant: 2 × 749–horsepower Turbomeca Arriel I M1 turboshaft engines
Performance: maximum speed, 184 miles per hour; ceiling, 11,810 feet; range, 544 miles
Armament: none or various combinations of gunpods, missiles, or torpedoes
Service dates: 1986–

The *Dauphin/Panther* family is a large series of versatile and reliable light helicopters well-suited for multimission roles. Some have even been imported by the United States for use in the Coast Guard.

By the early 1970s the French military expressed the need for a more flexible helicopter to replace the aging *Alouette III*. Aerospatiale (now Eurocopter) originally built a single-engine prototype called the SA 360 *Dauphin* (Dolphin), which possessed a four-blade main rotor and a fenestron (fan) tail rotor. However, this was rejected in favor of a twin-engine version that was developed and flew in 1975 as the *Dauphin 2*. This craft sports a clean, aerodynamic fuselage and retractable tricycle landing gear. It also employs a large vertical rudder with twin horizontal stabilizers. The *Dauphin* is unique among helicopters in being built partly from lightweight composites like Kevlar, which save weight and enhance structural strength. Several military and naval versions have been developed for France, functioning as assault craft, antitank platforms,

troop carriers, and antisubmarine and antishipping helicopters. An Americanized version, the SA 366G1, was imported by the U.S. Coast Guard in 1987 to replace the aging Sikorsky HH 52s. They serve as dedicated air/sea rescue machines called HH 65 *Dolphins* and carry the latest digital radar and communications gear. Several hundred *Dauphins* have either been built or are on order. China has also obtained a license to construct its own version, the Harbin Z 9.

In 1984 an updated military version, the AS 365M *Panther*, debuted. It is externally similar to the *Dauphin* but contains an even higher percentage of construction composites. It is also particularly crashworthy, as both crew armor and reinforced fuel systems are fitted. For military purposes, the *Panther* can be employed as a troop carrier or heavily armed gunship. Naval variants are also configured for surveillance and antishipping functions. Brazil is the biggest importer at present, with 36 of these versatile, ultramodern machines on order.

Type: Antitank; Reconnaissance; Transport

Dimensions: rotorspan, 36 feet, 1 inch; length, 37 feet, 6 inches; height, 11 feet, 5 inches
Weights: empty, 3,517 pounds; gross, 6,283 pounds
Power plant: 2 × 700–horsepower Turbomeca Arriel turboshaft engines
Performance: maximum speed, 161 miles per hour; ceiling, 18,500 feet; range, 333 miles
Armament: 8 × TOW antitank missiles; various rocket and gunpods
Service dates: 1977–

The stylish *Hirundo* is the latest in a continuing series of modern multipurpose helicopters derived from commercial machines. It combines high performance and heavy firepower with the Italian panache for design.

Agusta is one of Italy's oldest helicopter manufacturers, with roots dating to 1952. Since that time the factory has assembled hundreds of Bell, Boeing, and Sikorsky machines under license for the Italian military. However, in 1965 Agusta performed a market analysis highlighting the need for a modern high-speed helicopter to meet growing commercial demands. The prototype A 109A *Hirundo* (Swallow) was rolled out for these reasons in 1971 and proved an immediate success. This machine, in fact, is probably the most attractive helicopter ever designed. It features a sleek pod-and-boom fuselage with an extreme pointed nose. Two powerful turbine engines have been carefully fared over the cabin. The tail section consists of two horizontal and two vertical stabilizers, all sharply swept. More important, the tricycle undercarriage

is fully retractable and withdraws into the fuselage, leaving it aerodynamically clean. In flight, the machine is reputedly viceless. The A 109 enjoyed considerable commercial success in Italy before the military placed several examples under evaluation in 1976.

Several military variants of the *Hirundo* exist. The A 106CM can be configured for a variety of missions, including transport, light strike, and antitank. For this last endeavor, *Hirundos* can accommodate up to eight deadly Hughes TOW wire-guided missiles. Numerous rocket and gunpods can also be added and removed simply and speedily. The Italian army purchased 60 for its own use, with another 30 being obtained by Belgium. Argentina also purchased several, two of which were captured during the 1982 Falkland Islands War and have since been incorporated into the British army. A more recent variant, the A 109KM, fulfills similar roles and is also capable of naval missions such as antishipping and reconnaissance. Some 500 of the racy *Hirundos* have been constructed.

Type: Antitank

Dimensions: rotorspan, 39 feet; length, 40 feet, 3 inches; height, 11 feet
Weights: empty, 5,575 pounds; gross, 9,039 pounds
Power plant: 2 × Rolls-Royce 1004D turboshaft engines
Performance: maximum speed, 183 miles per hour; ceiling, 14,900 feet; range, 120 miles
Armament: 8 × *Hellfire* antitank missiles; various gunpods
Service dates: 1990–

The mighty *Mangusta* is the first European attack helicopter and Italy's most effective antitank weapons system. It is also the first such machine to utilize a fully computerized, integrated management system to ease crew workload.

The utility of helicopters as antitank weapons greatly increased in the 1970s with deployment of such armored behemoths as the Mil Mi 24 *Hind* and the Hughes AH-64 *Apache*. In 1972 the Italian army followed suit by advancing specifications for a new light attack helicopter, the first such machine designed in Europe. This helicopter was intended to be unique from the start because of its highly automated nature. Once airborne, both flight and armament functions were to be monitored and controlled by an integrated computer system. Agusta, fresh from its success with the A 106 model, advanced a prototype in 1983. The new A 129 *Mangusta* (Mongoose) utilizes the rear half of the earlier A 106 with a totally redesigned front portion. It is heavily armored and highly angular, with stepped seating for the pilot and gunner. The

two high-powered engines are well protected and fed cold air to reduce infrared heat signatures. The main rotor has four blades and is made primarily from light composite materials. These are tough, able to withstand direct hits from Soviet-style 23mm cannon shells.

The A 129 is especially designed to function in a combat environment without excessively tiring the crew. For this reason the integrated flight system monitors and displays only seven basic functions to pilot and gunner so as not to distract them. The *Mangusta* is also capable of nighttime activity and mounts state-of-the-art night vision with infrared detection gear. For offensive purposes it usually carries eight *Hellfire* antitank missiles and a plethora of smaller rockets and gunpods. The Italian army has procured 60 of these hard-hitting machines, and they proved effective during UN peacekeeping efforts in Somalia. However, the *Mangusta* has yet to find customers abroad. They remain potent fighting systems, but the Soviet Union's collapse in 1991 may render them redundant in the antitank role.

Type: Dive-Bomber

Dimensions: wingspan, 47 feet, 2 inches; length, 33 feet, 7 inches; height, 10 feet, 11 inches
Weights: empty, 5,310 pounds; gross, 5,772 pounds
Power plant: 1 × 1,080–horsepower Mitsubishi Kinsei 44 radial engine
Performance: maximum speed, 242 miles per hour; ceiling, 30,050 feet; range, 970 miles
Armament: 3 × 7.7mm machine guns; 816 pounds of bombs
Service dates: 1938–1945

Despite its obsolete appearance, the *Val* was responsible for sinking more Allied warships than any other Axis aircraft during World War II. It was subsequently employed in great numbers as a suicide plane (the dreaded kamikazes).

In 1936 the Imperial Japanese Navy decided to replace its aging Aichi D1A biplane dive-bombers with a more modern craft. A competition was held among several firms, and Aichi entered the winning design. It was the first all-metal monoplane bomber employed by the Japanese navy and owed much to the earlier Heinkel He 70. The D3A was a radial-engine low-wing monoplane with spatted fix undercarriage. Like the He 70, the large wing was elliptically shaped and canted slightly upward past the midsection. Test flights indicated the need for enhanced stability, so production models were fitted with a lengthy dorsal fin. D3As became operational in 1938 and were popular with crews. They were robust, highly maneuverable, and could dogfight once bombs were dropped. After December 1941, D3As formed the front ranks of Japan's elite carrier-based aviation squadrons.

The D3A, or *Val*, as it was code-named, quickly emerged as the terror of Allied shipping. Commencing with the attack on Pearl Harbor, they accompanied the first wave, inflicting heavy damage on numerous U.S. battleships. D3As then ventured to the Indian Ocean, sinking the British carrier HMS *Hermes* and cruisers *Dorsetshire* and *Cornwall*. They proved uncannily accurate: No less than 82 percent of bombs dropped by *Vals* struck their intended victims! *Vals* remained a potent force through the first half of 1942 before sustaining heavy losses at the Battles of Coral Sea and Midway. Thereafter, Japanese naval aviation could not replace their highly trained aircrews, and efficiency waned. By 1943 an improved version, the D3A2, arrived, featuring a cleaner cowl and a spinner, but *Vals* suffered greatly at the hands of improved Allied fighters. Those not hacked down in combat spent their last days as kamikazes. A total of 1,495 of these impressive bombers were produced.

Type: Glider; Transport

Dimensions: wingspan, 88 feet; length, 67 feet; height, 19 feet, 6 inches
Weights: empty, 7,500 pounds; gross, 15,250 pounds
Power plant: none
Performance: maximum speed, 127 miles per hour
Armament: none
Service dates: 1942–1945

The *Horsa* was the most numerous and widely used British assault glider of World War II. It functioned well at Sicily and Normandy and at one point lifted an entire airborne division across the Rhine.

The striking success of German glider troops in 1940 dismayed British authorities, so that year the Air Ministry issued Specification X.26/40 calling for creation of similar forces. The Airspeed company responded with a prototype called the AS.51 *Horsa* (named after an ancient Saxon king) in September 1941. This was a high-wing monoplane with tricycle landing gear and provisions for 25 troops. The *Horsa* was built entirely of wood and was canvas-covered, so it creaked loudly while flying. It was also relatively sophisticated, possessing ailerons, split trailing edge flaps, and underwing dive brakes powered by compressed air. The craft was towed aloft by a twin-engine bomber and affixed by a rope fastened to the nose and nosewheel strut. Once airborne, the large wheeled gear were jettisoned; the glider landed on a large retractable skid. It handled well in the air, even

when crammed with men and supplies, and could touch down in relatively small areas. The *Horsa* entered production in 1941 and was initially used for clandestine operations in Norway. It witnessed its large-scale baptism of fire in July 1943, when 30 were successfully launched over Sicily.

In 1941 the Air Ministry decided to develop a specialized freight-carrying version of the *Horsa*, the AS.58, so that airborne forces could ferry greater supplies to the drop zone. It was similar to the previous version but also featured twin nosewheels and a hinged nose section to ease unloading. The entire rear section could also be jettisoned for that purpose. Both models were present during the massive airborne assault over Normandy on June 6, 1944. *Horsas* carried select detachments of special forces that captured and held several strategic bridges. In March 1945 440 *Horsas* transported the entire 6th Airborne Division in another large movement across the Rhine River. The U.S. Army also employed several hundred of these useful craft. A total of 3,655 were built.

Type: Trainer

Dimensions: wingspan, 53 feet, 4 inches; length, 34 feet, 6 inches; height, 11 feet, 1 inch
Weights: empty, 5,670 pounds; gross, 8,000 pounds
Power plant: 2 × 370–horsepower Armstrong-Siddeley Cheetah radial engines
Performance: maximum speed, 188 miles per hour; ceiling, 19,500 feet; range, 550 miles
Armament: 1 × .303–caliber machine gun
Service dates: 1937–1954

The beloved "Ox-box" was one of the unsung heroes of World War II. Built in huge numbers, it trained thousands of British and Commonwealth airmen in the nuances of flying, gunnery, navigation, and bombardment.

In 1936 the British Air Ministry issued, as part of the Royal Air Force expansion program, Specification T.23/36 to obtain its first twin-engine training airplane. This was essential because biplane technology was being superceded by newer monoplanes that were faster and more demanding to fly. It so happened that Airspeed was then marketing a twin-engine passenger craft called the *Envoy*, which could be easily modified for instructional purposes. The Air Ministry agreed and in 1937 submitted an order for 137 aircraft as the *Oxford*. The new craft was an all-wood, low-wing monoplane with retractable landing gear and attractive lines. The Mk I version was also fitted with a single-gun power turret for gunnery practice. In service the *Oxford* exhibited easy handling, but it proved tricky for novices to land and required

vigilance. This characteristic was considered more useful than not, for it prepared students for the less-forgiving aircraft they would eventually fly. When World War II commenced in September 1939, the RAF counted 400 *Oxford Is* in its training inventory.

The *Oxford* eventually became an essential component of the Commonwealth Air Training Scheme. By 1945 no less than 8,751 "Ox-boxes" had been built, and they were operated in large numbers by Great Britain, Australia, Canada, New Zealand, South Africa, and Rhodesia. As time passed, this versatile trainer's regimen was expanded to include bombardier, radio-operator, and navigation training. Literally thousands of Allied crewmen gained their wings or specializations while flying the *Oxford*. Many others were employed for ambulance, liaison, and communications purposes. After the war, many surplus *Oxfords* transferred over to the civilian sector. The RAF did not relinquish its last "Ox-box" until 1954, and this stately machine stands as one of the most important military trainers in aviation history.

Type: Reconnaissance

Dimensions: 47 feet, 2 inches; length, 29 feet; height, 10 feet, 8 inches
Weights: empty, 2,251 pounds; gross, 3,613 pounds
Power plant: 1 × 260–horsepower Mercedes D VIa liquid-cooled in-line engine
Performance: maximum speed, 109 miles per hour; ceiling, 16,405 feet; range, 300 miles
Armament: 2 × 7.92mm machine guns
Service dates: 1917–1918

The long-serving Albatros C class was among the finest and most adaptable reconnaissance aircraft of World War I. They combined good performance and reliability into an aesthetically pleasing airframe.

The Albatros family of two-seat reconnaissance aircraft grew out of the prewar unarmed B-series. The new C versions, introduced in 1915, were armed, more strongly built, and capable of defensive maneuvering. Successive models tended to be better armed and better powered, and in 1917 the trend culminated in the introduction of the C X model. This version mounted the new 260-horsepower Mercedes D IVa engine that gave it greater speed and altitude than previous versions. It capped a tendency in the reconnaissance family to incorporate more and more features of the famous D series of fighters. It also sported lengthened wings that housed flush-mounted radiators and double ailerons. The C X displayed good high-altitude performance and the two-man crew carried its own oxygen supply aloft along with a wireless

radio. The plane commenced field service in the summer of 1917 and proved entirely successful as a photo platform and artillery spotter. A total of 330 machines were constructed, and they served with distinction to war's end.

In time Albatros followed up with an improved model of the C X, the C XII. From an aesthetic standpoint, this was the most pleasing aircraft of the entire series. The C XII was the first reconnaissance machine to directly incorporate the trademark elliptical fuselage cross-section of the famous D-series fighters. It also employed an enlarged, curved tailfin strongly reminiscent of the scouts, along with a triangular ventral fin attached to the tail skid. However, the motor, wing, and landing gear of the previous aircraft were retained. The overall effect of the new machine was sleek and elegant. However, for all its refinement, the C XII boasted little improvement over the C X in terms of performance. It was nevertheless deployed in some numbers and served alongside earlier versions until the Armistice.

Type: Fighter

Dimensions: wingspan, 29 feet, 8 inches; length, 24 feet; height, 8 feet, 10 inches
Weights: empty, 1,511 pounds; gross, 2,066 pounds
Power plant: 1 × 185–horsepower Mercedes D IIIa liquid-cooled in-line engine
Performance: maximum speed, 116 miles per hour; ceiling, 20,500 feet; range, 200 miles
Armament: 2 × 7.92mm machine guns
Service dates: 1916–1918

The famous Albatros scouts were among the most beautiful and deadly fighters of World War I. By the spring of 1917 they had become so indelibly associated with fighting that the British christened this period "Bloody April."

The famous Fokker scourge of 1915 was summarily ended by the appearance of the Nieuport 11 and the de Havilland DH 2, and the Germans were hard-pressed to field an effective foil. In the spring of 1916 the Albatros Werke under chief engineer Robert Thelen conceived a fighter design unlike anything that had been seen in the skies of Western Europe. Dubbed the D I, it was extremely sleek and heavily armed, being the first German biplane fighter powerful enough to carry two synchronized machine guns. It debuted with great success that spring before a subsequent version, the infamous D III, appeared. This machine proved even deadlier. The D III combined many aeronautical refinements and incorporated features of the heretofore unbeatable Nieuport 17, including vee struts and a smaller lower wing. In the hands of aces like von Richthofen, Boelcke, and Voss, it quickly established superiority over opposing Allied aircraft. Consequently, the spring of 1917 became reviled as "Bloody April," and the prowess of Albatros scouts caused the life expectancies of British airmen to be measured in days.

One persistent problem with the D III, which it had ironically inherited from Nieuport fighters, was the inherent weakness of the lower wing. In combat it was liable to flutter and break off, with fatal consequences. An improved model, the D V, was accordingly introduced in May 1917 to correct this. It featured a deeper, elliptical fuselage, a more powerful engine, and more closely spaced wings. However, despite these refinements, the D V and its successor, the D Va, boasted few advantages over the aging D III. Throughout most of 1918, the D Vs constituted the bulk of German fighter strength, although they continually lost ground to newer Allied types such as the SPAD XIII and Sopwith *Camel*. An estimated 3,000 Albatroses, including Austrian versions, were manufactured.

Type: Medium Bomber

Dimensions: wingspan, 80 feet, 4 inches; length, 59 feet; height, 18 feet
Weights: empty, 13,448 pounds; gross, 21,385 pounds
Power plant: 2 × 870–horsepower Gnome-Rhone Mistral Major radial engines
Performance: maximum speed, 193 miles per hour; ceiling, 25,920 feet; range, 746 miles
Armament: 4 × 7.5mm machine guns; 1,764 pounds of bombs
Service dates: 1935–1942

The Amiot 143 was an ugly but functional French bomber of the 1930s. It was still in frontline service at the beginning of World War II and sustained heavy losses.

In 1928 the French government circulated new specifications for an all-metal, four-place bomber capable of operating day or night. Three years later the Amiot Avions company fielded the first Model 140 prototype, a craft more noted for ugliness than performance. The type underwent additional refinements, which did little to enhance its looks, but in 1934 a revised model, the 143, emerged. This was a cantilevered high-wing monoplane featuring a fully enclosed cockpit, two hand-powered gun turrets, and a lengthy greenhouse gondola on the underside of a narrow fuselage. The wing chords were very broad and the air foil so thick that crew members could reach and service the engines in flight. Finally, the type rested on fixed landing gear covered by streamlined spats 7 feet in length. The first Amiot 143 was acquired in 1935, and a total of 138 were manufactured. It certainly did little to alleviate France's reputation for designing unattractive aircraft.

The angular Amiot was marginally obsolete by the advent of World War II, but it was still a major bombing type in the Armee de l'Air, equipping five bomb groups. Commencing in 1939, they were primarily used to drop leaflets over Germany and for other propaganda functions. The Battle of France commenced in May 1940, and the lumbering craft began dispensing more lethal cargo. Given their slow speed and light armament, Amiot 143s were usually constrained to night attacks on factories and marshaling yards, dropping 528 tons of bombs. However, they are best remembered for the heroic May 14, 1940, attack on the Meuse River bridges near Sedan. Flying in broad daylight against heavily defended positions, 13 of 14 aircraft committed were lost. Following the French capitulation, many Amiot 143s made their way to Africa and internment while others served the new Vichy regime. All were basically scrapped by 1942.

Type: Reconnaissance

Dimensions: wingspan, 40 feet, 7 inches; length, 26 feet, 6 inches; height, 10 feet, 5 inches
Weights: empty, 1,906 pounds; gross, 2,566 pounds
Power plant: 1 × 150–horsepower Salmson Canton-Unne radial engine
Performance: maximum speed, 89 miles per hour; ceiling, 14,110 feet; range, 250 miles
Armament: 2 × 7.7mm machine guns
Service dates: 1916–1918

The Anatra was a mediocre aircraft and beset by shoddy construction. Nonetheless, it was continuously operated by long-suffering Russian airmen and managed to perform useful work.

The Anatra aircraft company was owned and operated by an Italian banker based in Odessa. In 1915, the company's first effort at making warplanes, a Russian copy of the Voisin LA S, proved disastrous. The machine suffered from very poor lateral control and crashed inexplicably. The following year the company fielded an original design, the Anatra D, which was inspired by some captured German Aviatiks. The Anatra was a two-bay biplane with slightly backswept, unstaggered wings. These were constructed of wood and fabric, and the upper ones sported ailerons. The fuselage was likewise made of wood, being covered in aluminum up to the first undercarriage strut, then finished in fabric. The tail surfaces were steel tubing covered by fabric and possessed rounded leading edges. This first version, known as the *Anade*, was powered by a 100-horsepower Gnome Monosoupape rotary engine, which

was notorious for unreliability. The aircraft handled well for its class but remained structurally weak. It was nevertheless placed in production, with roughly 200 built in 1916.

In combat the Anatra D proved highly unsatisfactory. It was nose-heavy and glided poorly without power. The engine was also subject to malfunctioning, and several unexplained crashes were attributed to poor construction. Worse yet, shortages of quality wood necessitated the factory to produce main wing spars that were spliced and wrapped in glued linen. On July 17, 1917, an Anatra D piloted by a Lieutenant Robinet and a passenger broke up in flight over Odessa during a demonstration flight, killing both men. It was then decided to introduce a newer version, the DS *Anasal*, which was powered by a Salmson Canton-Unne radial engine. This improved performance somewhat, but the close-fitting cowl caused overheating. About 380 of all versions were acquired during the war. It is a tribute to the stoicism of Russian airmen that they bravely flew whatever airplanes were available when so ordered.

Type: Reconnaissance

Dimensions: wingspan, 29 feet, 10 inches; length, 26 feet, 7 inches; height, 8 feet, 8 inches
Weights: empty, 1,521 pounds; gross, 2,072 pounds
Power plant: 1 × 265–horsepower SPA liquid-cooled in-line engine
Performance: maximum speed, 140 miles per hour; ceiling, 22,965 feet; range, 450 miles
Armament: 2 × 7.7mm machine guns
Service dates: 1918–1929

The handsome Ansaldo craft conducted some of the longest and most impressive reconnaissance flights of World War I. They continued this tradition after the war and established many long-distance records.

In 1916 the Ansaldo firm began constructing a new high-performance fighter craft as a private company venture. It fell upon Umberto Savoia and Rodolfo Verduzio to design the prototype, which flew in March 1917. The SVA 4 was a good-looking biplane that employed "W"-shaped Warren struts along the wings, thus dispensing with the need for bracing wires. The wings themselves were of slightly unequal length, with the top possessing rakish ailerons and the bottom several degrees of dihedral. The slender fuselage was plywood-covered and tapered to a point past the cockpit, affording the pilot excellent rearward vision. Flight trials revealed that the SVA 4 possessed good performance, but it was too stable for fighter tactics. It therefore entered production as a reconnaissance craft and, in slightly modified form, joined the service in March 1918 as the SVA 5 *Primo*.

The single-seat Ansaldo designs accumulated a brilliant wartime career and were among the best aircraft of their class in the world. This fact was borne out by the many dangerous long-range reconnaissance missions seemingly performed with ease. On May 21, 1918, a pair of *Primos* crossed the Alps at high altitude, successfully photographed military installations at Friedrichshafen, Germany, and completed a flight of 435 miles. But the most famous Ansaldo mission happened on August 9, 1918, when six modified aircraft, accompanied by the poet Gabrielle di Annunzio, flew 300 miles to Vienna, dropped leaflets for half an hour, and returned after a 620-mile sojourn. Many other such flights were recorded.

The SVA 5s remained in service long after the Armistice. In 1920 five set out on an across-the-world venture from Rome to Tokyo, covering 11,250 miles in 109 flying hours. Production concluded in 1927, following a run of 2,000 machines.

Antonov An 2

Russia

Type: Liaison; Transport

Dimensions: wingspan, 59 feet, 8 inches; length, 42 feet, 6 inches; height, 13 feet, 9 inches
Weights: empty, 7,605 pounds; gross, 12,125 pounds
Power plant: 1 × 1,000–horsepower Shvetsov Ash–621R radial engine
Performance: maximum speed, 157 miles per hour; ceiling, 14,425 feet; range, 562 miles
Armament: none
Service dates: 1947–

The ubiquitous An 2 was built in greater numbers than any aircraft since World War II. Antiquated looks belie incredible ruggedness and adaptability, and it still serves in no less than 30 countries around the world.

Oleg Antonov, who spent most of his youth designing gliders, finally established his own aviation design bureau in 1947. From the onset his desire was to manufacture multipurpose aircraft capable of operating anywhere. His first design, the An 2, was originally intended as an agricultural airplane for the Soviet Union's Ministry of Agriculture and Forestry. He deliberately chose a biplane because of the prodigious lifting qualities such machines possess, as well as ease of handling at low altitude. The big An 2 is built entirely of metal, save for fabric-covered control surfaces, and is unique among biplanes in that the fuselage completely fills in between the two wings. The wings themselves are joined to each other by use of a single "I" strut and utilize such advanced devices as slotted trailing flaps and ailerons that automatically droop at low

speed. Consequently, An 2s display superb STOL (short takeoff and landing) characteristics and are also rugged and easily maintained. The Antonov factory built "only" 5,000 An 2s in the Soviet Union before production halted. However, the torch was then passed to Poland's WSK-Mielec factory, which manufactured another 18,000. China has also built 1,500 for its own purposes. Total An 2 production, worldwide, is estimated in excess of 30,000! It remains the last mass-produced biplane.

This hulking aircraft was eventually employed by 30 air forces around the world and in a bewildering variety of tasks. Most military establishments employ it as a transport, but it has since been adopted to crop-spraying, glider-tugging, navigation training, and parachute transport. It can also be fitted with skis to operate from snow. The Soviets recommenced production of An 2Ms in 1964, which featured bigger control surfaces and a variable-pitch propeller. Antonov's homely prodigy remains one of the world's great transportation aircraft. The NATO designation is COLT.

Type: Transport; Reconnaissance

Dimensions: wingspan, 124 feet, 8 inches; length, 108 feet, 7 inches; height, 34 feet, 6 inches
Weights: empty, 61,728 pounds; gross, 134,480 pounds
Power plant: 4 × 4,000–horsepower ZMBD AI-20K turboprop engines
Performance: maximum speed, 482 miles per hour; ceiling, 33,465 feet; range, 3,542 miles
Armament: 2 × 23mm cannon
Service dates: 1960–

For many years, the An 12 constituted the backbone of Soviet heavy airlift forces. It still functions today in the guise of a reconnaissance and electronic intelligence-gathering platform.

The perfection of turboprop technology by the mid-1950s ushered in a new era of military transportation. Higher power levels at greater economy, in turn, led to larger airplanes being built. The first of these, Lockheed's famous C-130 *Hercules*, inspired the Antonov design bureau to provide the Soviet Union with a craft of equal utility. The An 12 was developed in 1958 and, like the *Hercules*, is a high-wing monoplane with an up-swept rear section. The pressurized fuselage is completely circular in cross-section and possesses large landing gear fairings on either side. But unlike the American craft, the An 12 sports an integral rear loading ramp that can be folded and stored. Antonov's machine is also unique in mounting a tailgun position immediately below the rudder. It was a powerful addition to the Red Air Force after

becoming operational in 1960, and it could lift up to 20 tons of light tanks and trucks or 100 paratroopers while operating from the crudest landing strips. The An 12 therefore gave the Red Army a strategic mobility never before possessed. An estimated 850 of these brutish transports, designated CUB by NATO, were built by 1973.

As would be expected, the An 12 saw widespread use among the Warsaw Pact and other nations sympathetic to the Soviet Union. In addition to transportation duties, it also made an ideal platform for electronic espionage, with three versions being built. The CUB A was an interim type with bladelike antennas on the forward fuselage. The CUB B was fitted with two prominent belly radomes in addition to blade antennas, and the CUB C, sporting the usual array of antennas, had the tail turret deleted in favor of a radome. Most Russian An 12s have since been retired on account of wing-spar fatigue. Other major users, like India, are looking for jet-powered replacements.

Type: **Transport**

Dimensions: wingspan, 211 feet, 4 inches; length, 190 feet; height, 41 feet, 1 inch
Weights: empty, 251,323 pounds; gross, 551,146 pounds
Power plant: 4 × 15,000–horsepower KKBM NK-12MA turboprop engines
Performance: maximum speed, 460 miles per hour; ceiling, 24,605 feet; range, 6,804 miles
Armament: none
Service dates: 1967–

The mighty *Antei* was once the world's largest airplane and established several weight and altitude records that still stand. Despite its sheer bulk, it handles well and operates easily from unprepared airstrips.

Russia is characterized geographically by huge distances and varied topographical features that can make surface travel difficult, if not impossible. Air transportation is a possible solution, but this means that equipment must ferry huge quantities of cargo and supplies in order to be meaningful. In 1962 the Antonov design bureau was tasked with constructing a huge transport plane to facilitate the shuttling of military goods and services around the country and the world. In only three years, a functioning prototype emerged that stunned Western authorities when unveiled at the Paris Air Salon in 1965. The massive An 22 *Antei* (Antheus, after a huge son of Neptune in Greek mythology) was a well-conceived enlargement of the previous An 12. Like its predecessor, it was circular in cross-section and possessed wheel fairings under the fuselage. It also sports a capacious cargo hold and a pressurized crew and passenger cabin. To facilitate operations off wet and unprepared airstrips, pressurization of the six pairs of wheels is controllable from the flight deck and can be changed in midair to suit any landing surface. The secret to the An 22's prodigious hauling ability is found in the trailing-edge flaps. These are designed to utilize the powerful prop wash flowing over the wing from the four contrarotating turboprop engines and provide added lift. Its military implications were obvious, and since 1969 an estimated 100 of the giant craft have been built and deployed. The NATO code name is COCK.

The An 22 was the world's biggest airplane following its debut and established many useful world records. The only Soviet transport capable of freighting a T-72 tank, it was employed by the USSR as a propaganda machine during many "humanitarian" flights abroad. This giant reigned supreme until 1968, when an even larger craft, Lockheed's C-5A *Galaxy*, premiered.

Type: Transport

Dimensions: wingspan, 240 feet, 5 inches; length, 226 feet, 8 inches; height, 68 feet, 2 inches
Weights: empty, 385,800 pounds; gross, 892,875 pounds
Power plant: 4 × 51,590–pound thrust Lotarev D-18T turbofan engines
Performance: maximum speed, 537 miles per hour; range, 10,523 miles
Armament: none
Service dates: 1987–

In 1985 the mighty *Ruslan* edged out Lockheed's C-5A to become the biggest airplane to achieve production status. Three years later it was surpassed by an even larger derivative, the An 225.

In 1968 the U.S. Air Force's acquisition of the giant C-5A *Galaxy* gave it unparalleled ability to ship military hardware anywhere on the globe. The Soviet Union needed similar capacities to keep pace with the West, so in 1974 the Antonov design bureau was instructed to cease production of the huge An 22 turboprop transport and commenced designing a jet-powered craft. The specifications established for the An 124 were mind-boggling: It had to carry a minimum cargo of 150 tons to any point within the Soviet empire without refueling. Antonov, drawing inspiration from previous designs and the C-5A, fielded a prototype in 1985. The new An 124 was 18 feet wider than the vaunted *Galaxy*, and it also possessed 53 percent greater hauling capacity. Like its competitor, which it greatly resembles, the *Ruslan* (named after Puskin's legendary giant) has nose and

tail cargo doors that allow vehicles to drive on and off. The spacious cargo hold is lined by a special titanium floor equipped with rollers, and roof-mounted hydraulic winches facilitate cargo-handling. It also has a pressurized passenger cabin for 88 people. Moreover, the giant craft can be made to "kneel" while unloading through retractable nose-wheels. Since 1987 an estimated 48 An 124s have been built, with half going to the air force and the remainder operated by the state airline Aeroflot. The NATO designation is CONDOR.

The reign of the An 124 was exceedingly short, for in 1988 it yielded the throne to an even bigger derivative, the An 225 *Mriya* (Dream). This is essentially a stretched *Ruslan* fitted with six turbofans that expel a combined total of 309,540 pounds of thrust! It was expressly designed to freight heavy components for the Russian space program, carrying large items like the space shuttle *Buran* piggyback. Only two of these giants have been built, and they remain the largest aircraft in world history.

Arado Ar 68

Type: Fighter

Dimensions: wingspan, 36 feet, 1 inch; length, 31 feet, 2 inches; height, 10 feet, 9 inches
Weights: empty, 4,057 pounds; gross, 5,457 pounds
Power plant: 1 × 690–horsepower Junkers Jumo 210 Da liquid-cooled in-line engine
Performance: maximum speed, 190 miles per hour; ceiling, 26,575 feet; range, 258 miles
Armament: 2 × 7.92mm machine guns
Service dates: 1936–1940

The Arado Ar 68 was the last biplane fighter of the German Luftwaffe. A capable performer, it briefly fulfilled a variety of duties, including training and nighttime fighting.

By the terms of the 1918 Armistice, Germany was forbidden to possess military aircraft of any kind. But even before the Nazi era commenced, the German war ministry began secretly developing warplanes in collusion with the Soviet Union. By 1933 the newly elected Nazi regime under Adolf Hitler scoffed at these treaty provisions and encouraged Arado to develop a new fighter to replace the unpopular Heinkel He 51. Arado had previously acquired much experience in Russia, so in 1935 it fielded the first prototype Ar 68. This was a single-bay biplane with an oval-section fuselage made of metal. The wings were constructed of wood and were fabric-covered. A distinctive feature was the rather high, thin rudder, which subsequently became an Arado trademark. Results were initially disappointing, and subsequent prototypes experimented with a variety of power plants. By 1936 a 750-horse-power BMW VI–powered Ar 86 was regarded as ready and commenced flight trials against the He 51. The Luftwaffe high command was reluctant to acquire another biplane, seeing how the monoplane Messerschmitt Bf 109 was on the verge of production. However, in the hands of Ernst Udet, the Ar 68 easily outflew its opponent, and the type entered production in 1937.

The Ar 68 was an efficient design, fast and forgiving, but also obsolete at the inception of its career. It flew well during test trials in Spain, but the Bf 109, also present, consistently outperformed it. Consequently, the type was acquired only in small numbers before the Messerschmitt emerged as the Luftwaffe's standard fighter. By the onset of World War II in 1939, most Ar 68s were functioning as advanced trainers. A naval version, the radial-engine Ar 167, was developed for possible deployment on the carrier *Graf Zeppelin*, but the project was scrapped. After brief service as emergency night fighters in 1940, all surviving Ar 68s were unceremoniously retired.

Type: Trainer

Dimensions: wingspan, 36 feet, 1 inch; length, 27 feet, 1 inch; height, 8 feet, 8 inches
Weights: empty, 2,854 pounds; gross, 3,858 pounds
Power plant: 1 × 485–horsepower Argus As 410MA-1 liquid-cooled in-line engine
Performance: maximum speed, 211 miles per hour; ceiling, 22,965 feet; range, 615 miles
Armament: 1 × 7.92mm machine gun
Service dates: 1940–1945

The Ar 96 was the Luftwaffe's most significant advanced trainer, for it instructed virtually all German pilots of World War II. It was built in greater number than any training craft of the period, save for the North American AT-6.

The Ar 96 was designed by Walter Blume in 1938 as a new advanced trainer for the Luftwaffe. It was a streamlined, low-wing monoplane constructed entirely of metal and stressed skin. Student and instructor were housed in tandem seats under a highly glazed canopy. The fuselage was oval-sectioned and monocoque in design, topped by a trademark Arado tail fin. The new craft was a delightful performer, with a 240-horsepower Argus As 10C in-line engine and a fixed, two-blade propeller. However, the undercarriage, which originally retracted outward toward the wings was totally redesigned. An inward, widetrack retracting system was subsequently adopted as better suited for rough student landings. The Ar 96 entered production in 1940, and over the next five years it was a common sight at Luftwaffe training schools.

In 1940 the Ar 96B prototype emerged. This differed from earlier models by having a more powerful Argus AS 410A engine, as well as a lengthened fuselage housing more fuel. It also featured a distinct, variable-pitch propeller spinner and a 7.9mm machine gun for gunnery training. This variant was built in large numbers throughout the war years by Arado, Ago, and the former Czech factories of Avia and Letov. By 1945 no less than 11,546 Ar 96s had rolled off the assembly lines. It constituted the mainstay of the Luftwaffe's advanced training force and, as such, bore a conspicuous role in the overall excellence of that force. Toward the end of the war, several Ar 96Bs were impressed into field service with machine guns and bombs for ground-attack purposes. Afterward, the type was continued in production by the French concern SIPA, which built a wooden version in 1946, followed by an all-metal one. Similar craft were also manufactured in Czechoslovakia until 1948.

Type: Reconnaissance

Dimensions: wingspan, 40 feet, 8 inches; length, 36 feet, 1 inch; height, 14 feet, 4 inches
Weights: empty, 6,580 pounds; gross, 8,223 pounds
Power plant: 1 × 960–horsepower BMW 132K radial engine
Performance: maximum speed, 193 miles per hour; ceiling, 23,000 feet; range, 670 miles
Armament: 3 × 7.92mm machine guns; 2 × 20mm cannons; 220 pounds of bombs
Service dates: 1939–1945

From Norway to the Mediterranean, the versatile Ar 196 served as the "eyes" of the German Kriegsmarine. Fast, well-armed, and solidly built, they were the best floatplanes of their class during World War II.

By 1936 it was envisioned that the newly reconstituted Kriegsmarine (German navy) was destined to serve as fast, hard-hitting commerce raiders. Because this required efficient aerial reconnaissance, the German Air Ministry issued specifications for a new floatplane to accompany all German capital ships. In 1937 Arado perfected its prototype Ar 196 floatplane to compete with a design proffered by Focke-Wulf, the Fw 62. Arado's craft was a radial-engine, low-wing monoplane with twin floats. It was of all-metal construction and stressed skin, save for the rear fuselage, which was fabric-covered. The trailing edges of the rounded wings were filled entirely with flaps and ailerons. Once fitted with a variable-pitch, three-blade propeller, the Ar 196 easily outperformed its rival and entered service in 1939. In time, it ultimately outfitted air units on board the

major warships *Bismark, Scharnhorst, Gneisenau, Prinz Eugen, Admiral Scheer, Graf Spee,* and *Lutzow.*

In service the Ar 196 proved to be among the most capable floatplanes of the war, one of few designs to serve outside the Pacific. Moreover, it exhibited better performance than contemporary British and U.S. machines like the Fairey *Sea Fox* and Curtiss *Seagull.* As spotting aircraft, Ar 196s would shadow enemy vessels and relay intercept coordinates back to their home ships. Those not stationed on warships flew from bases ringing the Bay of Biscay and the Mediterranean. And despite their floatplane configuration, they were well-armed and could put up a fight. On May 5, 1940, two Ar 196s under Lieutenant Gunther Mehrens spotted the damaged British submarine HMS *Seal* off Denmark and forced its surrender. Other Ar 196s provided escort duty for Axis convoys and occasionally shot up British patrol aircraft with their heavy armament. Ar 196s served in dwindling numbers until the war's end. A total of 593 were built.

Type: Reconnaissance; Light Bomber

Dimensions: wingspan, 46 feet, 3 inches; length, 41 feet, 5 inches; height, 14 feet, 1 inch
Weights: empty, 11,464 pounds; gross, 21,715 pounds
Power plant: 2 × 1,980–pound thrust Junkers Jumo 004B turbojet engines
Performance: maximum speed, 460 miles per hour; ceiling, 32,810 feet; range, 684 miles
Armament: 2 × 20mm cannons; 3,307 pounds of bombs
Service dates: 1944–1945

The beautiful *Blitz* was the world's first operational jet bomber. Appearing too late to affect events in World War II, it served as a technological precursor of things to come.

In 1940 the German Air Ministry laid down specifications for a fast reconnaissance craft powered by the new Junker Jumo jet engines, then undergoing bench tests. The Arado design team, headed by Walter Blume and Hans Rebeski, came up with an extremely handsome machine. The Ar 234 was a high-wing monoplane made entirely of metal. The pilot sat up front in a fully glazed nose section, and two podded jet engines were mounted under straight wings. To reduce drag, the fuselage was deliberately kept as narrow as possible, although this initially precluded the use of landing gear. In fact, the first six prototypes were fitted with detachable trolleys that fell away upon takeoff, leaving the craft to land on skids. Commencing with the seventh prototype, all subsequent Ar 234s received narrow-track landing gear. In flight the Ar 234 was extremely

fast and quite maneuverable; it also pioneered such novel technology as pressurized cabins, ejection seats, autopilots, and bombing computers. With the Nazi regime fading fast by 1944, the Ar 234 received priority production status, and 274 machines were assembled.

The *Blitz* commenced operational sorties over England in the fall of 1944, where its high speed rendered it immune from Allied interception. Given such good performance, it was decided to introduce a bomber version, the Ar 234 B-2, which carried bombs on its fuselage and engine pods. These were the world's first operational jet bombers. Their most celebrated action occurred in January 1945, when waves of Ar 234s hit the Remagen Bridge over the Rhine, collapsing it. The *Blitz* continued its little war of unstoppable pinprick raids until the last few weeks of the war, when jet fuel became unavailable. Had this amazing airplane been available in quantity, serious damage might have resulted. It nonetheless demonstrated the viability of jet bomber technology.

Type: Reconnaissance

Dimensions: wingspan, 43 feet, 6 inches; length, 31 feet, 5 inches; height, 10 feet, 11 inches
Weights: empty, 1,916 pounds; gross, 2,811 pounds
Power plant: 1 × 160–horsepower Beardmore liquid-cooled in-line engine
Performance: maximum speed, 95 miles per hour; ceiling, 13,000 feet; range, 250 miles
Armament: 2 × .303–inch machine guns
Service dates: 1917–1918

The FK 8 was one of the most numerous British observation aircraft of World War I. Fast, strong, and well-armed, it went by the chummy but unflattering appellation of "Big Ack."

In 1914 Dutch aircraft designer Fredrick Koolhoven submitted plans to the British air minister to replace its antiquated BE 2c with a more capable machine. The design was entrusted to the firm Armstrong-Whitworth, and in 1915 the FK 3 emerged. More than 500 of these machines, informally dubbed "Little Ack," were constructed and equipped several squadrons in the Middle East. The following year Koolhoven suggested an upgraded version based upon the previous machine, and thus was born the FK 8. This was a standard biplane with two bay wings, the top of which exhibited pronounced dihedral. The crew of two sat in a deep fuselage constructed from wood and fabric. One interesting feature was the presence of controls in both cockpits so that a gunner could fly the plane if the pilot became incapacitated. Early FK 8s were also fitted with an ugly central skid on the landing struts to prevent noseovers. Around 1,500 were manufactured.

In combat the "Big Ack" was a rugged machine and capable of defending itself. Although not speedy, it maneuvered well, absorbed great amounts of damage, and was considered superior to the contemporary Royal Aircraft Factory RE 8. One incident illustrates the combat career of the FK 8 above all others when, on March 27, 1918, Lieutenants Macleon and Hammond were jumped by eight of the formidable Fokker triplanes. In a running battle, the FK 8 managed to shoot down four of its opponents, even while burning and badly shot up. The two men survived a crash landing and subsequently received the Victoria Cross, Britain's highest honor. The FK 8s were retired immediately after the war, but eight ended up in Australia. There they helped form the nucleus of the Northern Territory Aerial Services, better known today as QUANTAS.

Type: Fighter

Dimensions: wingspan, 33 feet, 2 inches; length, 25 feet, 4 inches; height, 10 feet, 2 inches
Weights: empty, 2,061 pounds; gross, 3,012 pounds
Power plant: 1 450–horsepower Armstrong-Siddeley Jaguar IV radial engine
Performance: maximum speed, 156 miles per hour; ceiling, 27,000 feet; range, 150 miles
Armament: 2 × .303–inch machine guns
Service dates: 1927–1932

The *Siskin* was Britain's first post–World War I fighter and the first to possess an all-metal structure. It was phenomenally maneuverable and standard fare at air shows for many years.

Britain, although victorious in World War I, was beset by extreme economic hardship during the postwar period. Consequently, it was unable to procure new fighter craft for the Royal Air Force until 1924. That year the Royal Air Ministry authorized two models into production, the Gloster *Grebe* and the Armstrong-Whitworth *Siskin*. The latter originated in a company aircraft of the same name that had first been designed in 1918. This was a standard, wood-constructed biplane in most respects, save for being powered by an ABC Dragon radial engine. A fine performer, it was subsequently refitted with a 200-horsepower Armstrong-Siddeley Jaguar radial, and it went on to win the 1923 King's Cup Air Race with speeds of 149 miles per hour. The new prototype, christened the *Siskin III*, differed from its predecessor in several respects. First, both wing and

fuselage frames were constructed of metal and were fabric-covered. As a sesquiplane, the upper wings were longer than the lower ones. The new craft was also the first British biplane to utilize vee interplane struts between the wings. In service the *Siskin* was a smart performer with outstanding maneuverability. A total of 62 machines were built in 1926, supplanting aging Sopwith *Snipes* in two squadrons.

In 1927 a definitive variant, the *Siskin IIIA*, emerged. This version lacked both an auxiliary fin beneath the rear fuselage and the dihedral on the upper wing. Moreover, it was powered by the 450-horsepower Jaguar IVS engine, which endowed it with even greater performance. A total of 385 *Siskin IIIAs* were acquired, and they outfitted 11 fighter squadrons. Their handling was so outstanding that they frequently starred at the yearly Hendon Displays. There No. 43 Squadron pioneered formation acrobatics and featured stunts with several aircraft tied together. The fine-flying *Siskins* were eventually phased out in 1932 by Bristol *Bulldogs*.

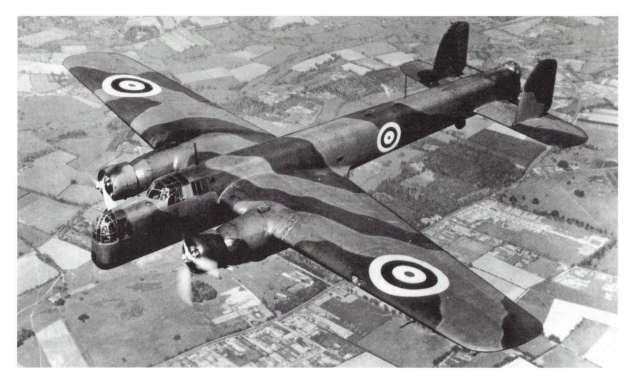

Type: Medium Bomber

Dimensions: wingspan, 84 feet; length, 69 feet, 3 inches; height, 15 feet
Weights: empty, 19,330 pounds; gross, 33,500 pounds
Power plant: 2 × 1,145–horsepower Rolls-Royce Merlin X liquid-cooled in-line engines
Performance: maximum speed, 222 miles per hour; ceiling, 17,600 feet; range, 1,650 miles
Armament: 2 × .303–inch machine guns; up to 7,000 pounds of bombs
Service dates: 1937–1945

The rugged *Whitley* was the principal British bomber during the early days of World War II. It was the first British aircraft to drop bombs on German soil since 1918 and saw extensive use up through the end of the war.

In 1935 Air Ministry Specification B.3/34 mandated replacing the aging Handley Page *Heyfords* with a more modern design. Armstrong-Whitworth responded with what would become its most numerous aircraft. The *Whitley* was a midwing monoplane whose construction was midway between contemporary designs and those of World War II. Constructed of metal, it possessed twin rudders, and sported a retractable undercarriage. The slab-sided fuselage was also sheeted with flushed metal skin, but the thick wing lacked dihedral and the ailerons were fabric-covered. The *Whitley* performed well in test flights, and its drooping nose gave it a distinct, jut-jawed appearance. The Royal Air Force decided to place orders in 1936, and the following year *Whitleys* began equipping various bomber squadrons. Subsequent versions were fitted with more power-

ful, in-line engines, and others were outfitted with radar and employed by the RAF Coastal Command. Production ran to 1,184 machines.

When World War II commenced in September 1939, *Whitleys* comprised the mainstay of RAF Bomber Command's frontline strength. It was marginally obsolete and overshadowed by the more modern *Wellingtons* and *Hampdens*, but in service it accomplished a number of aviation firsts. After spending the first year dropping leaflets over Germany, in August 1940 *Whitleys* became the first British aircraft to drop bombs on Berlin since World War I. The following February, they bombed the Tragino viaduct after Italy's declaration of war against Britain, the first such action against that country. Numerous *Whitleys* were then rigged for parachute operations, and in February 1942 the German radar installation at Bruneval was raided. They also sank their first U-boat in the Bay of Biscay on November 30, 1941. These unattractive, rugged aircraft finally performed training and patrolling activities up through the end of hostilities. The *Whitley* was a capable, underappreciated aircraft.

Type: Fighter

Dimensions: wingspan, 30 feet, 10 inches; length, 26 feet, 10 inches; height, 9 feet, 2 inches
Weights: empty, 3,218 pounds; loaded, 4,365 pounds
Power plant: 1 × 850–horsepower Hispano-Suiza 12Ydrs liquid-cooled in-line engine
Performance: maximum speed, 245 miles per hour; ceiling, 34,875 feet; range, 360 miles
Armament: 4 × 7.92mm machine guns
Service dates: 1934–1944

The beautiful Avia B 534 epitomized the very best of biplane technology. Although fast and maneuverable, it could not compete with modern monoplane fighters under development.

In 1932 the Avia firm under designer Frantisek Novotny substantially revised and updated its B 34 biplane fighter. Within a year a prototype emerged as the B 534, a machine as elegant in appearance as it was splendid in performance. Structurally, the B 534 was a single-bay biplane with wings of unequal length and highly staggered. Ailerons were placed on both the upper and lower wings to enhance maneuverability, while the whole craft was made of steel spars covered in fabric. The fuselage was streamlined and fitted with a beautifully wrought, close-fitting engine cowling. Moreover, it was heavily armed, mounting four machine guns. Two of these were originally wing-mounted, but when trials revealed unacceptable vibration when fired, they were relocated to the fuselage. The prototype was also fitted with a traditional open canopy, but subsequent production models were fully enclosed. Suf-

fice it to say that the Czechoslovakian Army Air Force now possessed the fastest, most maneuverable biplane fighter on the continent.

The B 534 was delightful to fly, fast, and responsive to controls. At the 1937 Zurich International Flying Meet, it dominated all events and categories until pitted against Germany's landmark monoplane fighter, the Messerschmitt Bf 109. Against this new breed of warrior, the Avia finished a close second, but the eclipse of biplane fighters was at hand. These craft might have put up tremendous resistance in 1938 when the Germans occupied western Czechoslovakia, but events transpired without a shot. A total of 446 Avia B 534s thus passed into German hands, and they were employed by the Luftwaffe as trainers and target tugs. Others were also similarly accorded to the puppet Slovak Air Force, which accompanied Hitler's 1941 invasion of the Soviet Union. Indifferently flown by unsympathetic pilots, they failed to distinguish themselves. A handful of B 534s eventually flew against Germany during the Slovak revolt of 1944.

Type: Reconnaissance

Dimensions: wingspan, 27 feet; length, 22 feet; height, 7 feet, 6 inches
Weights: empty, 1,440 pounds; gross, 2,152 pounds
Power plant: 1 × 160–horsepower Mercedes liquid-cooled engine
Performance: maximum speed, 111 miles per hour; ceiling, 8, 200 feet; range, 280 miles
Armament: 1 × 7.62mm machine gun; 40 pounds of bombs
Service dates: 1914–1918

The Aviatik series was mediocre and quickly withdrawn from the Western Front during World War I. However, the long range and dependability of these aircraft enabled them to serve in secondary theaters with distinction.

Following the onset of hostilities in August 1914, the Automobil und Aviatik AG company of Leipzig, Germany, commenced production of two-seat reconnaissance machines based upon its prewar P.15A models. An Austrian subsidiary, Osterreichische-Ungarische Flugzeugfabrik Aviatik of Vienna, also brought out slightly modified forms of the same craft. The first series, known as the Aviatik B I, was a conventional, fabric-covered, two-bay biplane with a slightly longer upper span. These craft were unusual in having the pilot placed in the rear seat while the gunner occupied the front. This seemingly absurd arrangement appreciably interfered with the latter's field of fire while also obstructing the pilot's view. Nonetheless, in the early days of aerial conflict, the long range and pleasant flying characteristics of the Aviatik made it popular with crews. It was also one of the few two-seaters that could be rigged with bombs for harassment raids. Two subsequent versions, the B II and B III were introduced with more powerful engines and more conventional seating. These machines could fly nearly half again as fast and as high as the first model, but by 1916 they suffered heavily at the hands of improved Allied fighters. Moreover, they were aerodynamically less stable than earlier versions. The Germans eventually deemed them unacceptable for the Western Front.

In an attempt to upgrade the performance of Austrian aircraft, a new version, the C I, was introduced in 1915. Modifications included a new 160-horsepower Mercedes engine, an exhaust stack piped over the top wing, and a streamlined spinner. However, this model reverted back to the awkward arrangement of placing the pilot in the rear seat, a feature corrected again in the subsequent C III model. For want of a better replacement, they remained in Austrian service on the Italian and Russian fronts up through the end of the war. A total of 167 C models were constructed.

Type: Fighter

Dimensions: 26 feet, 3 inches; length, 22 feet, 9 inches; height, 8 feet, 1 inch
Weights: empty, 1,345 pounds; gross, 1,878 pounds
Power plant: 1 × 200–horsepower Daimler liquid-cooled in-line engine
Performance: maximum speed, 115 miles per hour; ceiling, 20,177 feet; range, 250 miles
Armament: 2 × 7.92mm machine guns
Service dates: 1917–1918

The "Berg Scout" was the first fighter designed and mass-produced in Austria. Although fast-climbing and maneuverable, it was distrusted by pilots because of a reputation for frailty.

In the fall of 1916, the Osterreichische-Ungarische Flugzeugfabrik Aviatik of Vienna began constructing a single-seat version of its two-seater C I machine. The chief designer, Julius von Berg, incorporated many features of the previous model into the new craft, which became known as the "Berg Scout." The D I was a conventional biplane fighter with slightly staggered, single-bay wings. However, the fuselage was very deep, leaving only the pilot's head exposed. This provided considerable shelter against the elements but interfered with forward vision. Worse yet, the D I was armed with a single machine gun mounted on the top wing that fired above the propeller arc at an angle. Thus situated, pilots enjoyed clear shots only while diving upon a target. However, the D I was light and, propelled by a 185-horsepower Daimler motor, climbed like a rocket. It entered production in the spring of 1917 and joined the ranks of the hard-pressed Luftfahrtruppe (Austrian air service) that fall.

In service many pilots expressed displeasure with the D I's performance. Flight tests demonstrated that it could outclimb and outturn the Austrian-built Albatros (Oef) D III with ease, but several machines crashed after structural wing failures. Moreover, the new 200-horsepower Daimler engines were powerful but prone to overheating. An entire series of experimental radiators was eventually fitted, but these only further obstructed the already cramped front view. In an attempt to up-gun the D I, a pair of machine guns was also fitted with interrupter gear that fired through the propeller arc, but these were placed so far forward that pilots could not unjam them by hand. Despite long-standing deficiencies in the machine, Austrian pilots eventually adapted to the "Berg Scout," and it rendered respectable service against a host of Italian and Russian aircraft. Production orders totaled 1,200 aircraft, but only 700 had been delivered by the time of the Armistice.

Type: Reconnaissance; Light Bomber; Fighter; Trainer

Dimensions: wingspan, 36 feet; length, 29 feet, 5 inches; height, 10 feet, 5 inches
Weights: empty, 1,240 pounds; gross, 1,800 pounds
Power plant: 1 × 100–horsepower Gnome Monosoupape rotary engine
Performance: maximum speed, 82 miles per hour; ceiling, 10,000 feet; range, 250 miles
Armament: usually none, or 1 × .303–inch machine gun; up to 80 pounds of bombs
Service dates: 1913–1933

The gangly Avro 504 rates as one of the greatest airplanes ever. In a career spanning two decades it underwent many modifications and trained generations of pilots.

In 1913 Alliot Verdon Roe, a pioneer of tractor-propelled airplanes, demonstrated his latest creation, a rather modest-looking craft called the Avro 504. It was a standard two-seater biplane with four-bay wings and a large skid protruding from its landing gear. It was also immensely strong and exhibited docile handling qualities once airborne. Both the Royal Flying Corps and the Royal Navy ordered several copies on the eve of World War I. Not surprisingly, Avro 504s were among the many reconnaissance aircraft dispatched to France, and on August 22, 1914, one received the dubious distinction of becoming the first British airplane lost in combat. The Royal Navy, fortunately, had outfitted their 504s as light bombers, and on November 21, 1914, four of the little biplanes launched a daring and devastating raid upon the Zeppelin hangars at Friedrichshafen. During the course of the war, this handy craft received several modifications and one, the K version, was a single-seat fighter employed by home defense units until 1918!

However, it was as a trainer that the Avro 504 found its niche in aviation history. Commencing with the J model of 1916, it trained thousands of British and Allied pilots, including Prince Albert, the future King George VI. Moreover, it was the machine of choice at the famous School of Special Flying at Gosport. There the famous Major R. R. Smith-Barry used 504s to initiate his new and standardized system of flight instruction. After the war, it remained in production up through 1927 and was fitted with a bewildering variety of power plants. A total of 8,970 Avro 504s were built in England, with another 2,000 constructed in the Soviet Union. These remained in frontline service with the Royal Air Force until 1933 and flew many years thereafter with private owners.

Type: Reconnaissance; Trainer

Dimensions: wingspan, 56 feet, 6 inches; length, 42 feet, 3 inches; height, 13 feet, 1 inch
Weights: empty, 5,375 pounds; gross, 9,900 pounds
Power plant: 2 × 420–horsepower Cheetah XV radial engines
Performance: maximum speed, 188 miles per hour; ceiling, 19,200 feet; range, 700 miles
Armament: 2 × .303–inch machine guns; up to 360 pounds of bombs
Service dates: 1936–1968

The venerable *Anson* was one of the longest-serving types in Royal Air Force history. Ease of flying and great reliability garnered it the nickname "Faithful Annie."

In 1935 the British Air Ministry invited Avro to develop a twin-engine landplane for reconnaissance purposes. Avro drew upon its Model 652 commercial craft, two of which were sold to Imperial Airways in 1933. The prototype *Anson* was based upon this aircraft and first flew in 1935. It was a low-wing monoplane of mixed steel-tube, wood, and fabric construction. The fuselage was long and rectangular and sported a conspicuous dorsal gun turret. Having successfully concluded flight tests, *Ansons* entered service with the RAF in 1936. They were significant in being the first monoplane types accepted into service, and the first British warplane with retractable (if hand-cranked) landing gear. By the advent of World War II in 1939, *Ansons* equipped no less than 12 squadrons with the RAF Coastal Command. Its all-around utility and docile handling prompted the nickname "Faithful Annie."

The *Anson* was marginally obsolete at the commencement of hostilities yet gave a good account of itself before being replaced by Armstrong-Whitworth *Whitleys* and Lockheed *Hudsons*. Only two days after the declaration of war in September 1939, one dropped bombs on a U-boat, the first offensive action taken by a Coastal Command aircraft. In June 1940 a trio of *Ansons* was jumped by nine formidable Bf 109 fighters; the little cluster not only beat off the assailants but also shot down two and damaged a third! By 1942 they were replaced by more modern types, but *Ansons* continued to perform important work as trainers. Several versions were introduced during the war that instructed thousands of pilots, radio operators, and gunners throughout commonwealth air forces. *Ansons* remained in production until 1952; 11,020 had been constructed in Great Britain and Canada. The last six British aircraft served as communications aircraft until mustering out with great ceremony in 1968.

Type: Heavy Bomber

Dimensions: wingspan, 102 feet; length, 69 feet, 6 inches; height, 20 feet
Weights: empty, 36,900 pounds; gross, 68,000 pounds
Power plant: 4 × 1,460–horsepower Rolls-Royce Merlin XX liquid-cooled in-line engines
Performance: maximum speed, 287 miles per hour; ceiling, 24,500 feet; range, 660 miles
Armament: 8 × .303–inch machine guns; up to 2,000 pounds of bombs
Service dates: 1942–1954

The *Lancaster* overcame troubled beginnings to become Britain's legendary heavy bomber of World War II. Fitted with special ordnance, it gained special renown as the "Dam Buster."

In 1936 the British Air Ministry released Specification P.13/36 for a new twin-engine medium bomber. Avro originated the *Manchester*, which was a sound design but powered by totally unreliable Rolls-Royce Vulture engines. Two hundred of these unfortunate craft were built, but all left the service by 1942. However, the machine was refitted with an increased wingspan to accommodate four engines and rechristened the *Lancaster*. Thus was born the outstanding British night bomber of World War II. The *Lancaster* was an all-metal, high-wing monoplane with dual rudders. The fuselage was an oval-shaped, monocoque construction with a cavernous bomb bay extending half the length of the fuselage. This capacious feature could carry a variety of explosive and incendiary devices. The big bomber was rushed into production, with many *Manchesters* being converted while still on the production line. The new bomber commenced operations over Germany in March 1942, and within a

year *Lancasters* largely supplanted the Handley Page *Halifaxes* and Short *Stirlings* as the backbone of RAF Bomber Command. They proved instrumental in implementing the Royal Air Force policy of nighttime saturation bombing of German cities and industrial centers.

Lancasters distinguished themselves in the evening skies over Europe by delivering 608,612 tons of bombs in 156,000 sorties. However, they are best remembered for two very special attacks. The first, launched against the Mohne and Eder dams on May 17, 1943, utilized the famous Barnes Wallis "skipping bomb" that demolished its targets. The second fell upon the German battleship *Tirpitz* in Norway. On November 12, 1944, 31 *Lancasters* armed with 12,000-pound "Tallboy" bombs finally sank the dreaded raider in a fjord. By war's end, *Lancasters* had been modified to carry the 22,000-pound "Grand Slam" bomb. Many subsequently joined the RAF Coastal Command and performed maritime reconnaissance work until 1954. A total of 7,377 were built, and a handful remained in Canadian service until 1964.

Type: Patrol-Bomber; Early Warning

Dimensions: wingspan, 120 feet; length, 87 feet, 4 inches; height, 16 feet, 9 inches
Weights: empty, 57,000 pounds; gross, 98,000 pounds
Power plant: 4 × 9,820–horsepower Roll-Royce Griffon liquid cooled in-line engines
Performance: maximum speed, 273 miles per hour; ceiling, 20,000 feet; range, 2,900 miles
Armament: 2 × 20mm cannons; up to 20,00 pounds of bombs
Service dates: 1951–1991

The anachronistic *Shackleton* was the RAF's first dedicated maritime patrol-bomber. Fitted with decidedly third-rate radar, it also served as England's first distant-early-warning aircraft.

The *Shackleton* can trace its roots to the famous Avro *Lancaster* through an intermediary type, the *Lincoln* heavy bomber. In 1946 the Royal Air Force sought to replace its World War II–vintage patrol-bombers with a completely modern type. A standard *Lincoln* was accordingly modified into a prototype maritime patrol craft, and the differences were so pronounced that a new designation became necessary. The new *Shackleton* utilized the same wing and undercarriage as its forebear but employed an all-new fuselage that was narrower and taller. The first MR 1 version did not become operational with the RAF Coastal Command until 1951. The following year the MR 2 appeared with an extended and heavily modified nose section. The final version, the MR 3, finally debuted in 1955. This craft featured a nosewheel, tricycle landing gear, and

fixed wingtip tanks to boost the already impressive cruise range. The dorsal turret was also deleted in favor of additional space, and a clear-view cockpit canopy was fitted. Moreover, to alleviate the strain of extended patrols on the crew, it also possessed such creature comforts as a soundproof wardroom. These durable craft performed well, and all were retired from maritime duties in 1971 by the jet-powered Hawker-Siddeley *Nimrod*.

Defense cuts in the late 1960s led to the mothballing of several aircraft carriers and, with them, the distant-early-warning Fairey *Gannet* aircraft. As a completely stopgap effort, 12 of the obsolete MR 2 *Shackletons* were then dusted off, fitted with the *Gannet*'s World War II–vintage radar, and employed as the new AEW 2. This was a ramshackle affair at best, but the British government saw fit to employ these flying museum pieces until their replacement by infinitely superior Boeing E-3A *Sentries* in 1991. Thus ended an aircraft dynasty that had served Britain long and well for nearly half a century.

Avro *Vulcan* **Great Britain**

Type: Strategic Bomber

Dimensions: wingspan, 99 feet; length, 97 feet, 1 inch; height, 27 feet, 1 inch
Weights: empty, unknown; gross, 200,000 pounds
Power plant: 4 × 20,000–pound thrust Bristol Olympus 301 turbojet engines
Performance: maximum speed, 650 miles per hour; ceiling, 60,000 feet; range, 5,750 miles
Armament: up to 21,000 pounds of conventional or nuclear weapons
Service dates: 1957–1982

The hulking *Vulcan* was the second of Britain's famous "V" bombers and the first such craft outfitted with a delta wing. Although intended for a possible war with the Soviet Union, it fired its only shots in anger during the 1982 Falklands conflict.

A 1946 British air staff study recommended production of a trio of new strategic bombers that combined high speed, heavy payload, and great range. The Air Ministry then issued Specification B.35/46 to that effect, and an Avro design team under Roy Chadwick came up with a unique solution. They held that a large delta configuration was the best possible solution to all three requirements, especially in providing lift and, hence, range. A prototype of the huge craft was rolled out in August 1952 as the *Vulcan*. It was a very streamlined airplane, with the air intakes and engines buried within the wing and tricycle landing gear. The design was strong enough to be rolled in flight, and the prototype exhibited fighterlike qualities. The only major problem encountered was buffeting at high speeds,

which was corrected on production models by providing a kinked leading edge and a less swept-back wing. The *Vulcan* B.1 entered the service in 1957, and 45 were constructed. These were followed by 87 of the B.2 model in 1960, which had extensively modified flight-control surfaces and stronger engines. This version was also equipped to fire the nuclear-tipped *Blue Steel* standoff missile.

The *Vulcans* served capably in their roles as part of the West's nuclear deterrent. However, when the Soviet Union finally perfected surface-to-air missile technology, the big bomber's mission changed from high-altitude bombing to low-altitude penetration. New and better electronic countermeasures were installed, as well as an array of conventional bombs. The *Vulcans* were due to be phased out early in 1982 but earned a brief reprieve during the Falklands conflict with Argentina of that year, where a handful conducted very long-range bombing missions with mixed results. This memorable bomber's replacement was the Panavia *Tornado*.

Type: Fighter

Dimensions: wingspan, 58 feet; length, 54 feet, 1 inch; height, 15 feet, 7 inches
Weights: empty, 18,000 pounds; gross, 37,000 pounds
Power plant: 2 × 7,725–pound thrust Orenda turbojet engines
Performance: maximum speed, 650 miles per hour; ceiling, 54,000 feet; range, 2,500 miles
Armament: 8 × 12.7mm machine guns or 104 × 70mm unguided rockets
Service dates: 1953–1981

The capable *Canuck* was the first warplane entirely designed in Canada and was specifically tailored for the defense of that country's expansive reaches. It was also the first straight-wing jet fighter to exceed Mach 1, and enjoyed a career of considerable longevity.

In 1945 the Canadian Department of National Defense issued demanding requirements for a new jet-powered all-weather interceptor—Canada's first. Furthermore, any craft conforming to Specification AIR-7–1 would have to be optimized for operations at extreme latitudes off short, unprepared Arctic strips, as well as possess range in excess of 2,500 miles. With jet aviation technology then in its infancy, no such machine existed anywhere in the world. This obstacle did not deter an Avro Canada design team headed by John Frost, who conceived and built a functional prototype in January 1950. The new CF 100 was a large, all-metal monoplane with twin engines and nonswept wings. The engines were placed on either side of the capacious fuselage, where great amounts of fuel were stored.

There was also a high "T" tail arrangement to clear the jet efflux, and a crew of two was seated under a bubble canopy. The new craft flew well when Canadian-designed and -built Orenda engines were fitted. The CF 100 joined the Royal Canadian Air Force (RCAF) in 1953 as the world's most advanced jet interceptor, and it was nicknamed the *Canuck*. Despite its straight-wing configuration, it was fast and maneuverable, and on December 18, 1953, a CF 100 became the first such craft to exceed Mach 1 (the speed of sound) in a dive.

In November 1956, *Canucks* flew to France as NATO's first multiseat all-weather interceptor squadron. The initial versions were originally equipped with a retractable pack of eight machine guns, but later models forsook armament in favor of wingtip rocket pods. These were actuated by a special targeting and anticollision radar housed in the bulbous nose. The CF 100s enjoyed a long and largely problem-free service life with the Canadian and Belgian air forces. The last RCAF machines were finally retired in 1981.

Beriev Be 12 *Tchaika* — Russia

Type: Antisubmarine; Air/Sea Rescue

Dimensions: wingspan, 97 feet, 5 inches; length, 99 feet; height, 22 feet, 11 inches
Weights: empty, 47,840 pounds; gross, 68,342 pounds
Power plant: 2 × 4,190–horsepower ZMBD AI-20D turboprop engines
Performance: maximum speed, 378 miles per hour; ceiling, 37,000 feet; range, 4,660 miles
Armament: none
Service dates: 1964–

The gull-winged Be 12 is one of few amphibian aircraft still in service. At one time or another it held 44 international records for machines of its class, and it still plies the waves as an air/sea rescue craft.

Georgi M. Beriev is possibly the only designer in aviation history whose whole career centered around the production of flying boats. In 1949 he created the Be 6, a unique gull-wing design strongly reminiscent of the Martin PBM *Mariner.* These sturdy craft replaced all the antiquated flying boats of World War II and served well until 1967. A few years before, Beriev's design bureau was authorized to develop a successor aircraft to the venerable Be 6, one utilizing the very latest turboprop technology. His Be 12 *Tchaika* (Gull) amphibian of 1960 was widely recognized as a machine of considerable ingenuity. It bore superficial resemblance to the earlier machine, but it differed in mounting the engines on top of the gull wing to give the highest possible clearance for the propellers. The hull was also greatly modified into a single-step design that sported flared bow strakes to reduce sea spray upon takeoffs and landings. Rugged retractable landing gear was installed on the sides; as previously, twin rudders were also fitted. The Be 12 may have appeared as an ugly duckling, but it performed like a swan, being maneuverable, fast, and easy to operate on land, sea, or in the air. Production totals are estimated at 100 machines; they received the NATO code name MAIL.

Given their lengthy coastlines, Russia and Japan are the only nations that currently operate flying boats in any number. Like the ShinMaywa US 1, the Be 12 was originally outfitted for antisubmarine warfare, sporting a large nose radome and a sonar tailboom for detection purposes. It has since been slowly phased out by more capable land-based machines like the Ilyushin Il 38 and Tupolev Tu 142 in that role. However, Beriev's brainchild still performs air/sea rescue work and is expected to do so well into the twenty-first century.

Beriev MBR 2 **Russia**

Type: Reconnaissance; Patrol-Bomber; Antisubmarine

Dimensions: wingspan, 62 feet, 4 inches; length, 4 feet, 3 inches; height, 14 feet, 9 inches
Weights: empty, 5,456 pounds; gross, 9,039 pounds
Power plant: 1 × 680–horsepower M-17B air-cooled in-line engine
Performance: maximum speed, 124 miles per hour; ceiling, 14,435 feet; range, 404 miles
Armament: 2 × 7.62mm machine guns; up to 1,102 pounds of bombs or depth charges
Service dates: 1935–1965

The simple, rugged MBR 2 was built in large quantities and enjoyed a 30-year service life. At one time or another circumstances forced it to perform reconnaissance, bombing, and antisubmarine work.

In 1932 the talented designer Georgi M. Beriev submitted plans for his first flying boat, a machine intended for short-range maritime reconnaissance. Designated the MBR 2, it was a shoulder-wing monoplane with a pusher-mounted engine affixed by a pair of "N" struts. It had a wooden, two-step hull and a wing constructed of metal tubing covered by fabric. A crew of four was comfortably carried in open cockpits and gunnery stations, but subsequent versions introduced fully enclosed canopies and manually operated turrets. The new craft was simple and efficient from the onset, so in 1935 it entered service with Soviet naval units in the Black Sea and elsewhere. In service the MBR 2 established its designer's reputation for creating simple, robust aircraft that worked well on water and were easily maintained. Production ended in 1941 after a run of

1,300 machines. The MBR 2 was also popular with civilians, and in 1937 noted aviatrix Paulina Osipenka established several women's world records flying one of them.

The MBR 2 was marginally obsolete by 1939, but it served in considerable numbers throughout the war with Finland. When the Great Patriotic War commenced in June 1941, the MBR 2s were necessarily deployed everywhere that the Soviet navy fought and performed yeoman's work. In addition to maritime reconnaissance, the exigencies of combat required it to undertake night bombing and, in the absence of other machines, day bombing as well. Despite fierce German resistance, many MBR 2 simply absorbed great amounts of damage and returned home for more missions. In addition, the type's slow speed and long loitering ability made it an ideal antisubmarine platform. After the war, many MBR 2s found their way into fishery and air/sea rescue work. They remained so employed until being replaced by the newer Be 12 in the mid-1960s.

Type: Transport

Dimensions: wingspan, 162 feet; length, 99 feet, 5 inches; height, 38 feet, 9 inches
Weights: empty, 79,234 pounds; gross, 135,000 pounds
Power plant: 4 × 2,850–horsepower Bristol Centaurus radial engines
Performance: maximum speed, 238 miles per hour; ceiling, 16,000 feet; range, 1,300 miles
Armament: none
Service dates: 1956–1967

One of the bulkiest aircraft ever conceived, the *Beverly* was a dependable heavy-lifter that served capably for a decade. It had uncanny abilities to take off and land on very short strips, even when fully loaded.

In the immediate postwar era, the British Air Ministry issued Specification C.3/46 to secure a new and advanced tactical transport for the Royal Air Force (RAF). Such a plane had to be capable of carrying very large loads over medium distances. It so happened that the General Aircraft Corporation had conducted several studies of large freighter airplanes and had a design in hand. When a contract was authorized, the construction commenced and continued apace until 1949, when the company merged with Blackburn. The finished product finally flew as the GAL 60 *Universal* in June 1950. This was an odd bird, to say the least. The new plane centered around a large and capacious fuselage that was very deep if somewhat narrow. To this was connected a large tailboom sporting twin rudders, which could also hold cargo or troops. The shoulder-mounted wing also had four Bristol Hercules radial engines, while a pair of long, fixed landing gear were attached. Test flights revealed the craft lifted prodigious quantities of freight using very short runways and could touch down in even shorter spaces. With further modifications a newer craft, christened the *Beverly*, entered production in 1955. These became operational the following year; Blackburn ultimately constructed 47 machines.

In service the *Beverly* was the largest airplane operated by the RAF to that time. It could accommodate several light vehicles or up to 94 troops. It was also the first such craft equipped with clamshell rear doors for air-dropping supplies. In 1959 a *Beverly* tossed out a military load in excess of 40,000 pounds, then a national record. The big craft performed particularly useful service ferrying helicopters to the troubled island of Cyprus. They served RAF Transport Command well for a decade with little ceremony before finally being replaced in 1967 by the even more capable Lockheed C-130 *Hercules*.

Type: Light Bomber

Dimensions: wingspan, 44 feet; length, 63 feet, 5 inches; height, 16 feet, 3 inches
Weights: empty, 30,000 pounds; gross, 62,000 pounds
Power plant: 2 × 11,030–pound thrust Rolls-Royce Spey turbofan engines
Performance: maximum speed, 691 miles per hour; ceiling, 40,000 feet; range, 600 miles
Armament: up to 16,000 pounds of bombs or missiles
Service dates: 1962–1992

The massive *Buccaneer* was the world's first aircraft employed for high-speed low-altitude bombing. Nimble despite great bulk, *Buccaneers* could deliver a wide range of ordnance beneath enemy radar nets with remarkable accuracy.

In 1952 the Royal Navy issued Specification NA.39 calling for the creation of a two-seat, low-level strike aircraft capable of carrier operations. Such a machine would perform at high subsonic speed—a difficult proposition due to atmospheric density—yet possess considerable range. In 1955 Blackburn responded with a design that first flew in 1958. The *Buccaneer* was a large, portly aircraft with swept, midmounted wings and a high "T" tail. To facilitate high speed at low levels it utilized a unique boundary layer control system whereby hot gas was bled from the engines and ejected at certain points along the leading edges. This controlled the amount of air passing over the control surfaces and ensured a smooth ride. Other innovations included a rotary bomb bay, which turned inside the fuselage and thus did not

project doors into the slipstream. Finally, the fuselage incorporated area ruling, being pinched in toward the rear, again to ensure high speed. Flight trials were impressive, and the *Buccaneer* moved into production. The first S.1 models reached the Royal Navy carriers by 1961, and in service they proved fine bombing platforms, if somewhat underpowered. The S.2 versions, fitted with Rolls-Royce Spey engines with 30 percent more thrust and better fuel economy, arrived in 1964. Some 100 *Buccaneers* of both versions were built.

By 1969 British defense cuts had all but gutted the Fleet Air Arm of carrier aircraft, and surviving *Buccaneers* were passed along to the Royal Air Force (RAF). At first, the RAF looked askance at the brutish machines because they lacked supersonic capability, but the *Buccaneers*, once outfitted with better electronics, performed as formidable strike aircraft. These were slowly replaced by the newer Panavia *Tornadoes* beginning in 1984, but a handful flew missions during the 1991 Gulf War. They were superb interim machines.

Type: Reconnaissance; Torpedo-Bomber

Dimensions: wingspan, 46 feet; length, 35 feet, 3 inches; height, 12 feet, 1 inch
Weights: empty, 4,039 pounds; gross, 8,050 pounds
Power plant: 1 × 800–horsepower Bristol Pegasus radial engine
Performance: maximum speed, 150 miles per hour; ceiling, 16,000 feet; range, 625 miles
Armament: 2 × .303–inch machine guns; 1 × 1,550–pound torpedo
Service dates: 1935–1944

The *Shark* was the last in a long line of Blackburn torpedo planes and could operate as either a land plane or on floats. It had a relatively short service life, but lingered in reserve functions for many years.

In 1933 the Fleet Air Arm needed a new two- or three-seat torpedo-bomber to update its aging fleet of Blackburn *Darts*, *Ripons*, and *Baffins*. Blackburn responded with a prototype originally begun as a private venture, the M.1/30A, which first flew on February 24, 1933. It was a biplane with unequal wings, the top of which possessed a broad chord and a cut-out section over the pilot's canopy. The two wings were metal-framed, fabric-covered, and fastened by distinctive "N"-type struts. Interestingly, both spans possessed ailerons that could be lowered as flaps. Finally, the fuselage was round in cross-section, being an all-metal, semimonocoque structure with watertight compartments. Tests on board the carrier HMS *Courageous* proved satisfactory, and in 1934 16 aircraft were acquired as the *Shark I*. These

served with No. 820 Squadron, replacing their complement of Fairey *Seals*.

In 1935 a newer version, the *Shark II*, was developed that featured a new Armstrong-Whitworth VI Tiger radial engine developing 750-horsepower. The Royal Navy purchased 123 of this version for use in No. 810 and No. 821 Squadrons, supplanting their inventory of Fairey *Seals* and Blackburn *Baffins*. The *Shark II* was an efficient plane, but in 1938 it was replaced in turn by the newer Fairey *Swordfish* and assigned to training functions.

A final variant, the *Shark III*, emerged in 1937. This differed from the previous models in having a glazed sliding canopy and a three-blade wooden propeller. It was also powered by an 800-horsepower Bristol Pegasus radial engine. The navy acquired 95 *Shark IIIs* that year, and they served briefly before assuming training and target-towing duties. Several *Shark IIIs* still operated in the opening days of World War II, and a handful at Trinidad flew regular training missions until 1944. Production reached 238 machines.

Type: Fighter; Dive-Bomber

Dimensions: wingspan, 46 feet, 2 inches; length, 35 feet, 7 inches; height, 12 feet, 6 inches
Weights: empty, 5,490 pounds; gross, 8,228 pounds
Power plant: 1 × 890–horsepower Bristol Perseus XII radial engine
Performance: maximum speed, 225 miles per hour; ceiling, 20,200 feet; range, 760 miles
Armament: 5 × .303–inch machine guns; 500 pounds of bombs
Service dates: 1938–1942

The *Skua* is best remembered as the Fleet Air Arm's first carrier-based monoplane. Hopelessly outdated by World War II, it performed a few memorable tasks before being retired.

In 1934 the British Air Ministry, seeking a new aircraft to replace its Hawker *Ospreys* and *Nimrods*, issued Specification O.27/34, which called for an all-metal monoplane capable of being deck-handled on a carrier and flown as either a fighter or a dive-bomber. The prototype Blackburn *Skua* first flew in 1937 as a low-wing monoplane, the first Fleet Air Arm machine to possess a radial engine, retractable landing gear, and a variable-pitch propeller. The design was underpowered but pleasant to fly, so in 1938 it entered service aboard the carrier HMS *Ark Royal*. The advent of World War II clearly demonstrated the shortcomings of the *Skua* as a fighter, as it was too slow and underarmed to be effective. On September 25, 1939, a *Skua* managed—barely—to shoot down a lumbering Do 18 seaplane,

the first official kill by Fleet Air Arm aircraft. However, *Skuas* were better employed as dive-bombers, and they performed heroic work in the early campaigns around Norway. On April 10, 1940, 16 *Skuas* took off from Hatson in the Orkneys and flew directly to the Bergen Fjord. There they surprised and sank the German heavy cruiser *Konigsberg* at dawn and returned home with the loss of only one plane. *Skuas* remained in frontline service until 1941, when they were phased out by Fairey *Fulmars* and Hawker *Sea Hurricanes*. Many spent the rest of the war performing target-tug and training duties. A total of 192 were built.

In 1938 an attempt was made to convert the *Skua* into an effective turret-armed fighter, much in the manner of Bolton-Paul's *Defiant*. The resulting design was called the *Roc*, but it proved even slower and more incapable than its predecessor. Blackburn assembled 136 of these machines, but they saw no combat and very little active service.

Type: Reconnaissance

Dimensions: wingspan, 25 feet, 7 inches; length, 26 feet, 3 inches; height, 8 feet, 6 inches
Weights: empty, 769 pounds; gross, 1,378 pounds
Power plant: 1 × 70–horsepower Gnome rotary engine
Performance: maximum speed, 66 miles per hour; ceiling, 3,000 feet; range, 200 miles
Armament: up to 55 pounds of bombs
Service dates: 1910–1915

The fragile-looking Bleriot XI crossed the English Channel to tally one of history's most significant aviation firsts. In the early days of World War I, it was also operated by numerous French, British, and Italian squadrons.

Prior to 1908, Louis Bleriot had been an aviator of little consequence, that is, until he abandoned biplane pusher-type craft in favor of monoplane tractor designs. His greatest effort, the Bleriot XI, premiered at Paris in December 1908. This revolutionary craft consisted of steel tubing, wooden struts, a fabric-covered fuselage, and paper-covered wings. It possessed a conventional rudder but was assisted in turns by wing-warping, whereby the wing's trailing edges were bent during flight by wires. The craft landed on two bicycle tires suspended on struts and was initially powered by a coughing, 25-horsepower REP engine. The Bleriot XI seemed to epitomize the fragility of early flight, but in fact it was a well-conceived aircraft with high performance for its day. Bleriot underscored this fact on July 25, 1909, when he dramatically piloted his craft across the English

Channel—the first time such a feat had been accomplished. This act gained him international celebrity and dramatically signified that technology had ended England's isolation from continental Europe.

The French military acquired its first Bleriot XI in 1910 and went on to develop specialized versions with more powerful engines for reconnaissance and artillery-spotting. The craft was also acquired in large numbers by Italy, and on October 23, 1911, Captain Carlo Piazza conducted history's first reconnaissance mission by overflying Turkish positions in Libya. Following the onset of World War I in August 1914, the Bleriot was among the most numerous aircraft in a host of French, Italian, and British reconnaissance squadrons. In service it was slow and unarmed save for crew-carried rifles, but Bleriots could also carry small, hand-thrown bombs for harassment purposes. These pioneering craft rendered useful service well into 1915 before being withdrawn to serve as trainers. Prior to their removal, the Bleriots made history by demonstrating the utility of military aviation. About 800 were constructed.

Type: Fighter

Dimensions: wingspan, 29 feet; length, 24 feet, 5 inches; height, 12 feet, 2 inches
Weights: empty, 2,765 pounds; gross, 3,638 pounds
Power plant: 1 × 690–horsepower Hispano-Suiza 12Xbrs water-cooled in-line engine
Performance: maximum speed, 201 miles per hour; ceiling, 34,450 feet; range, 497 miles
Armament: 2 × 7.7mm machine guns
Service dates: 1937–1939

The handsome S 510 took six and a half years to develop before becoming the last biplane fighter to serve the French Armee de l'Air. Although superbly acrobatic, it was too outdated to see action in World War II.

In 1930 the French government announced competition for a new fighter. Three years later Andre Herbemont responded with the last biplane product to bear the old SPAD designation. His new craft was a single-bay biplane with fixed landing gear. The wings were equally long, but the upper was swept sharply back, and both were joined by single, faired "I" struts. Ailerons were present on the lower wing only. In contrast to the previous round-bodied fighters, the new design possessed an oval cross-section fuselage with the rear section forming a duralumin monocoque. The airplane frame was built entirely of metal, was fabric-covered, and sported an open cockpit. In a final touch, spatted wheel fairings gave it a sleek, modern look. The Bleriot-SPAD S 510 was certainly a handsome craft with outstanding ma-

neuverability and climb. However, in level flight it was slower than the Dewoitine D 510 all-metal monoplane, to which it lost the competition. The government then suggested that test models be lengthened to improve longitudinal stability. When Herbemont complied, 60 aircraft were ordered in 1936—six years after the design had been originated.

In service the S 510 proved delightful to fly, as were all SPAD fighters. However, even lengthened it was prone to spin, and at steep angles the engine could stall due to fuel starvation. Moreover, several accidents occurred as a result of undercarriage breakage. These deficiencies ensured that the S 510 enjoyed only brief service life, and by 1937 most had been transferred to regional (reserve) squadrons. Reputedly, a handful were clandestinely supplied to Spanish Republican forces during the Spanish Civil War. S 510s were still available in quantity when World War II commenced in September 1939, but none saw combat. If employed at all, the last French biplane fighter performed its final duties as a trainer.

Bloch MB 152 — France

Type: Fighter

Dimensions: wingspan, 34 feet, 7 inches; length, 29 feet, 10 inches; height, 12 feet, 11 inches
Weights: empty, 4,453 pounds; gross, 5,908 pounds
Power plant: 1 × 1,080–horsepower Gnome-Rhone 14N-25 radial engine
Performance: maximum speed, 320 miles per hour; ceiling, 32,810 feet; range, 373 miles
Armament: 2 × 7.5mm machine guns; 2 × 20mm cannon
Service dates: 1939–1942

The MB 152, having suffered a prolonged, troubled gestation, only entered service on the eve of World War II. It nonetheless formed a major part of French fighter strength and gave a good account of itself.

In 1934 the French Air Ministry issued specifications for a new monoplane fighter. Five companies responded and one, Marcel Bloch Avions, fielded the MB 150. This was an all-metal, low-wing monoplane with retractable undercarriage. However, the prototype was extremely underpowered, and on its first test hop it failed to leave the ground. A complete redesign became necessary, and it was not until May 4, 1937, that a test flight successfully concluded. Further modifications were required to make the craft suitable for mass production, and in 1939 the first MB 151 was accepted into service by the Armee de l'Air. Continued testing revealed their unsatisfactory nature as fighters, and the first 140 machines were used as trainers. Fortunately for Bloch a new version, the MB 152, was already under development. This was similar to the earlier version but enjoyed revised wings and a stronger GR 14N radial engine. In flight the MB 152 displayed good maneuverability, was a stable gun platform, and could outdive other fighters with ease. More political wrangling followed, but the government finally assented to procuring an additional 482 aircraft.

When World War II commenced in September 1939, the French possessed 140 MB 151s and 383 MB 152s, but the majority had been delivered without gun sights or propellers. Much valuable time was lost making them combat-worthy, and further efforts were expended correcting a tendency toward overheating. When Germany finally invaded France on May 10, 1940, no less than seven *groupes de chasse* (fighter groups) were equipped with MB 152s. Of these, only 80 were truly operational, but all were committed to combat against the mighty Luftwaffe. By the time fighting ceased, 270 of these attractive machines had been lost in action, but they accounted for 170 German aircraft. A total of 600 machines had been built.

Type: Reconnaissance; Light Bomber

Dimensions: wingspan, 58 feet, 8 inches; length, 40 feet, 2 inches; height, 11 feet, 7 inches
Weights: empty, 12,346 pounds; gross, 15,784 pounds
Power plant: 2 × 1,100–horsepower Gnome-Rhone 14N-48/49 radial engines
Performance: maximum speed, 329 miles per hour; ceiling, 36,090 feet; range, 1,025 miles
Armament: 7 × 7.5mm machine guns; up to 882 pounds of bombs
Service dates: 1939–1953

The elegant Bloch MB 174 was France's best reconnaissance aircraft of World War II. Fast enough to escape marauding Luftwaffe fighters, they had little opportunity to distinguish themselves.

In 1936 Bloch initiated work on a modern, two- or three-seat reconnaissance bomber for the French Armee de l'Air. The prototype first flew in February 1938 as an all-metal, twin-engine, low-wing monoplane. The craft was fitted with twin rudders, as well as retractable landing gear that buried itself in the engine nacelles. This first model possessed an elongated cupola under the fuselage to house a camera or an additional gun position, but this feature was deleted on subsequent models. By January 1939, the aircraft had evolved into the Bloch MB 174, with major modifications. It featured a lengthy greenhouse canopy set farther back along the fuselage than the prototypes. It also possessed an extensively glazed nose and a small bomb bay. Test flights revealed the craft to exhibit excellent performance at all altitudes, so in 1939 it entered production. Persis-

tent problems with overheating resulted in the adoption of smaller propeller spinners on most machines. A small number of bomber versions, the MB 175, had also been constructed. Around 80 machines were built in all.

Bloch MB 174s equipped three *groupes de reconnaissance* (reconnaissance groups) by the spring of 1940, shortly before the German invasion. At that time they were required to conduct dangerous missions deep into enemy territory, which were accomplished with little loss. With the imminent collapse of France, several MB 174s were flown to North Africa to escape, but most of these excellent craft were destroyed to prevent capture. The surviving machines were subsequently employed by Vichy air units in the defense of Tunisia. The Germans also kept the type in production, taking on 56 machines as trainers. During the immediate postwar period, an additional 80 MB 174Ts were constructed as torpedo-bombers for the French navy. These flew capably until being replaced in 1953 by more modern designs.

Type: Reconnaissance

Dimensions: wingspan, 88 feet, 4 inches; length, 65 feet, 1 inch; height, 19 feet, 4 inches
Weights: empty, 24,250 pounds; gross, 34,100 pounds
Power plant: 3 × 600–horsepower Junkers Jumo 205C liquid-cooled in-line engines
Performance: maximum speed, 170 miles per hour; ceiling, 18,700 feet; range, 2,500 miles
Armament: 2 × 20mm cannons; 1 × 13mm machine gun; up to 1,200 pounds of bombs or mines
Service dates: 1939–1945

Bizarre looks notwithstanding, the "Flying Clog" was an important part of the Luftwaffe's maritime reconnaissance program. It would frequently rendezvous with U-boats at sea, bringing them diesel fuel.

In 1933 the *Luftfahrtkommissariat* (part of the Air Ministry) issued specifications for a long-range reconnaissance flying boat. That year Dr. Richard Vogt of Hamburger Flugzeugbau GmbH, a subsidiary of the famous Blohm und Voss company, conceived an unusually configured design. Initially designated the Ha 138, this was a trimotor craft with dual booms. Moreover, the short fuselage also doubled as a watertight hull. The initial flight trials in 1937 revealed it to possess serious aerodynamic and hydrodynamic deficiencies, and so extensive modifications were undertaken to correct them. This entailed enlarging the fuselage by 50 percent, lengthening the booms, and redesigning the tail section. The craft was approved for production in 1939 under the revised designation Bv 138. The initial preproduction batch of 25 machines saw service in the Norwe-

gian campaign of 1940, where they were judged underpowered and restricted to transport duties.

Continual refinements resulted in appearance of the Bv 138B with stronger engines and greater armament. The open gun parts were fitted with power turrets mounting 20mm cannons. The final production version, the Bv 138C, arrived in the spring of 1941, featuring additional machine guns and more efficient propellers. By now the Bv 138 possessed fine flying and water characteristics and functioned well in its appointed role. Crews nicknamed it *Der Fliegende Holzschuh* or "Flying Clog," because of its distinct shape. In service these fine machines flew from bases along the North Sea and Norway, constantly shadowing Allied convoys and providing intercept coordinates for U-boats and surface raiders. Given its 18-hour endurance, Bv 138s would also alight next to U-boats far at sea, provisioning them with food and diesel fuel. A final version, the Bv 138MS, was equipped with a large degaussing ring for minesweeping. Production amounted to 279 units.

Type: Transport; Reconnaissance

Dimensions: wingspan, 150 feet, 11 inches; length, 121 feet, 4 inches; height, 35 feet, 9 inches
Weights: empty, 67,572 pounds; gross, 108,030 pounds
Power plant: 6 × 1,000–horsepower BMW Fafnir 323R radial engines
Performance: maximum speed, 242 miles per hour; ceiling, 23,950 feet; range, 3,787 miles
Armament: 3 × 20mm cannons; 5 × 13mm machine guns
Service dates: 1940–1945

The mighty *Wiking* was the largest flying boat to achieve operational status during World War II. It served extensively from Norway to the Mediterranean before heavy losses restricted its deployment.

In 1937 the airline Deutsche Lufthansa requested development of a new flying boat capable of nonstop service between Germany and New York. Such a craft would have to carry up to 24 passengers and remain airborne for 20 hours. A Blohm und Voss design team under Dr. Richard Vogt conceived such a craft in September 1940. It was a large, all-metal, high-wing monoplane with six engines. In typical Vogt fashion, the enormous wing mainspar functioned as both engine mount and fuel tank. The craft also possessed retractable stabilizing floats near the wingtips that drew up into recesses. The Bv 222 prototype originally flew in civilian markings, but by this time Germany was at war. Thereafter, it was pressed into service as an unarmed transport and flew on many occasions between Norway and the Mediterranean. As flying boats, Bv 222s were mar-

ginally larger than the Kawanishi H8K and Short *Sunderland.*

Continuous development of the Bv 222, called *Wiking* by its crews, resulted in an additional nine prototypes and four production models. These differed from the original version in being armed with an array of weapons. Several ended up in the hands of *Lufttranportstaffel See* (naval transport squadron) 222, which was organized to operate such large craft. Fully loaded, a *Wiking* could carry up to 92 fully equipped troops or 72 stretchers. Their tremendous range and endurance also made them ideal for maritime reconnaissance. One even managed to surprise and shoot down an Avro *Lancaster* at sea. However, the presence of British long-range fighters made unescorted *Wiking* missions hazardous, and several were lost in action. By 1944 the surviving six machines were restricted to medical evacuations in the Baltic region. After the war, two of these impressive flying boats were obtained by the United States for evaluation, while one remained in British service until 1947.

Type: Fighter; Night Fighter

Dimensions: wingspan, 39 feet, 4 inches; length, 35 feet, 4 inches; height, 12 feet, 2 inches
Weights: empty, 6,150 pounds; gross, 8,600 pounds
Power plant: 1 × 1,030–horsepower Rolls-Royce Merlin III liquid-cooled in-line engine
Performance: maximum speed, 303 miles per hour; ceiling, 31,800 feet; range, 480 miles
Armament: 4 × .303–inch machine guns
Service dates: 1940–1943

The turret-armed *Defiant* was hopelessly inept as a fighter craft, despite an impressive debut. It later performed useful work as a night fighter before ending up as a trainer.

By 1934 the British Air Ministry began toying with the notion of turret-armed fighters. These were envisioned as superior to the eight-gun aircraft then under development, the *Hurricane* and *Spitfire*, because pilots were theoretically free to concentrate on flying while the gunner remained focused upon shooting. Specification F.9/35 was consequently issued in 1935, and the Boulton-Paul company, which specialized in constructing aircraft turrets, entered a machine called the *Defiant*. This was an all-metal, low-wing monoplane with inward-retracting undercarriage. The armament consisted solely of four .303-inch machine guns housed in a large dorsal turret aft of the pilot's cockpit. No forward-firing weaponry was provided. In tests the *Defiant* flew well, though somewhat slower than other fighters owing to the weight and drag created by the gun turret. But the designers, as well as the Royal Air Force, held high expectations for the craft, and in May 1940 *Defiants* were committed to battle over France.

What followed was a near disaster for the RAF. On its first combat mission over the Low Countries in 1940, five of six *Defiants*, acting as bomber escorts, were shot down. They subsequently enjoyed better success during the British withdrawal from Dunkirk, however. In the heat of combat, German pilots mistook the lumbering craft for single-seat Hawker *Hurricanes* and, as Bf 109s locked on their tails, they were met by a withering fusillade of fire. *Defiants* managed to claim 65 kills in one week, with 38 Messerschmitts falling in one day. Naturally, the Germans quickly assessed the aircraft's weakness and attacked frontally or from below; the hapless *Defiants* were shot down in droves. Thereafter, they were fitted with radar and employed as night fighters with some success. Once replaced by more modern designs in 1942, all were either shunted aside into training and army cooperation duties or scrapped.

Type: Light Bomber; Reconnaissance

Dimensions: wingspan, 47 feet, 1 inch; length, 29 feet, 1 inch; height, 10 feet, 10 inches
Weights: empty, 2,271 pounds; gross, 3, 450 pounds
Power plant: 1 × 300–horsepower Renault liquid-cooled engine
Performance: maximum speed, 114 miles per hour; ceiling, 19,960 feet; range, 435 miles
Armament: 2 × 7.7mm machine guns; up to 661 pounds of bombs
Service dates: 1917–1932

The rugged Breguet 14 was the best French bomber of World War I, as well as an outstanding aircraft in general. It enjoyed a career of impressive longevity and established many aviation records throughout the postwar period.

In 1916 the talented aviation engineer Louis Breguet undertook designing a new bomber/observation plane for the Aviation Militaire (French air service). He deliberately disregarded specifications for a pusher-type aircraft and developed a conventional-looking machine that was years ahead of contemporaries. The Breguet Model 14 was a large, angular craft with square wings displaying a slightly negative stagger. The fuselage was constructed mostly of the metal duralumin, which contributed greatly to its lightness and strength. Moreover, to improve the aircraft's agility, ailerons were fitted on both upper and lower wings, along with automatic flaps—one of the earliest applications of this technology. Despite its size, the Breguet 14 was fast and strong, features that prompted the government to commence wholesale production in 1917. Within a

year, Breguet's magnificent design outfitted no less than 93 French bombardment and reconnaissance squadrons. It also went on to equip two Belgian formations and a number of units attached to the newly arrived American Expeditionary Force. By war's end, no less than 3,500 had been deployed, dropping 1,900 tons of bombs on German targets.

After the war, the mighty Breguet went on to distinguish itself in a number of nonmilitary applications. It was the first aircraft assigned to fly postal routes between Paris, Brussels, and London, and it registered several record-breaking endurance flights. In January 1919 a Breguet 14 flown by Captain Coli and Lieutenant Roget successfully crossed the Mediterranean twice, covering 1,000 miles without mishap. Throughout the 1920s, it was also widely used to fly the route between Toulouse, France, and Dakar, West Africa. The Breguet 14 underwent no less than 14 revisions and served with the French air force until 1932. It remained in production until 1927, with more than 8,000 being constructed.

Type: Reconnaissance; Light Bomber

Dimensions: wingspan, 48 feet, 8 inches; length, 31 feet, 2 inches; height, 10 feet, 11 inches
Weights: empty, 2,645 pounds; gross, 4,850 pounds
Power plant: 1 × 450–horsepower Lorraine water-cooled in-line engine
Performance: maximum speed, 137 miles per hour; ceiling, 22,970 feet; range, 497 miles
Armament: 2 × 7.7mm machine guns; up to 1,543 pounds of bombs
Service dates: 1924–1939

The Breguet 19 was one of the most successful machines of the interwar period, built in greater numbers than any contemporary. Throughout a lengthy military career it helped establish many world long-distance records.

Immediately after World War I, a design bureau under Louis Vullierme commenced work on a successor to the famous Breguet 14. The prototype was displayed at Paris in 1921 and flew the following year. The new Breguet 19 was a two-seat biplane with a structure built entirely of metal. The wings were unequal in length, with the top exhibiting greater span and twice the chord. Both were fabric-covered and fastened by a single interplane strut canting inward. Unlike its boxy predecessor, the new craft sported a circular cross-section and landed on two streamlined landing gears. It was initially powered by a 450-horsepower Breguet-Buggatti engine, and it was fast and maneuverable. Consequently, the French Armee de l'Air acquired more than 1,000 machines, equally divided between bomber and reconnaissance versions. These re-

mained in frontline units until 1939, rendering excellent service.

The Breguet 19 was proudly demonstrated in 1923 at the international fighter contest in Spain, where it made a profound impression. Orders from Yugoslavia soon followed, and Spain agreed to manufacture it under license. The 177 CASA-built machines subsequently served both sides during the Spanish Civil War, and many Yugoslavian Breguet 19s fought against German forces in 1940. The secret of the Breguet's success was its ability to be refitted with successively more powerful engines without extensive modifications. Several of these machines went on to establish impressive long-distance records. In 1927 the craft *Nungesser-Coli* flew around the world from Paris to Tokyo, covering 35,400 miles in 350 hours. Another famous Breguet 19, the *Point d' Interrogation* (Question Mark) also flew nonstop from Paris to Manchuria in 1929, a total distance of 4,912 miles. This same craft also flew nonstop from Paris to New York in 1930 and subsequently toured the United States amidst great fanfare.

Type: Light Bomber

Dimensions: wingspan, 50 feet, 5 inches; length, 31 feet, 8 inches; height, 10 feet, 5 inches
Weights: empty, 6,636 pounds; gross, 10,803 pounds
Power plant: 2 × 700–horsepower Gnome-Rhone 14M-6/7 radial engine
Performance: maximum speed, 304 miles per hour; ceiling, 27,885 feet; range, 840 miles
Armament: 4 × 7.7mm machine guns; 1 × 20mm cannon; 880 pounds of bombs
Service dates: 1939–1940

The Breguet 691 was among the best French aircraft of World War II. Fast and rugged, it was never available in sufficient numbers to have an impact.

A 1934 French Air Ministry announcement calling for a new three-seat fighter resulted in six contestants. The Breguet firm, however, felt the new specifications were restrictive, so it dropped out to experiment with a heavier, more adaptable design as a company project. The ensuing Model 690 of 1937 proved a radical departure from the company's angular, ugly biplanes. It was an all-metal, twin-engine, high-wing monoplane with extremely smooth lines. The puglike nose was rather short, not protruding beyond the propeller spinners, and the craft also mounted twin rudders. However, because the Model 690 was not officially sanctioned, it enjoyed little priority on engines and could not be flown until 1938. Flight results were excellent, and it demonstrated better performance than the Potez 63, the aircraft that won the earlier competition. It was also faster than the Morane-Saulnier MS 406, the stan-

dard French fighter, and easily kept apace with the new Dewoitine D 520. The usually indifferent French government was impressed, and in 1939 it finally authorized production.

Breguet soon spawned an entire family of related machines. The Breguet 691 was a two-seat ground attack version, of which 78 were constructed. These were followed by the Breguet 693, featuring bigger engines; production totaled 224 planes. The final version was the Breguet 695, again with differing engines, which amounted to 50 units. However, acute part shortages meant that only half of these excellent airplanes were combat-ready when the Germans invaded in May 1940. Breguet 691s engaged in heavy fighting around Belgium and distinguished themselves in low-level attacks on German troops. But because fighter escorts were unavailable, half of these fine machines were lost in combat. After France's capitulation, many surviving Breguet 691s were impressed into the Italian air service, but those confiscated by Germany had their engines removed and were scrapped.

Type: Fighter; Night Fighter; Torpedo-Bomber

Dimensions: wingspan, 57 feet, 10 inches; length, 41 feet, 8 inches; height, 15 feet, 10 inches
Weights: empty, 14,600 pounds; gross, 21,600 pounds
Power plant: 2 × 1,670–horsepower Bristol Hercules XVI radial engines
Performance: maximum speed, 333 miles per hour; ceiling, 26,500 feet; range, 1,480 miles
Armament: 4 × 20mm cannons; 6x .303–inch machine guns; 2,000 pounds of bombs or rockets
Service dates: 1940–1957

The mighty *Beaufighter* was the first dedicated night fighter employed by the Royal Air Force (RAF), and it helped pioneer radar-directed ground-controlled intercepts. It also functioned brilliantly as a torpedo-bomber, sinking scores of Axis vessels.

By 1938 the coming crisis in Europe highlighted Britain's deficiency in modern long-range fighters. That year Leslie Frise of Bristol commenced a company-funded project to design a large aircraft of unprecedented range and firepower. To save time, he utilized the tail and rear fuselage of the Bristol *Beaufort* then in production. The prototype *Beaufighter* first flew in September 1939 as a mid-wing, all-metal monoplane, with retractable undercarriage and hydraulically operated split flaps. Moreover, it was fitted with no less than four 20mm cannons in the belly and six .303-inch machine guns in the wings. Test flights proved that the *Beaufighter* was fast and maneuverable for its size, so the RAF decided to employ them as night fighters. Accordingly, they were fitted with the top-secret A/I radar system. These machines debuted in October 1940 and, guided by ground radar to their targets, destroyed many bombers. Losses proved so severe that the Germans were forced to cancel their nighttime blitz of January 1941. *Beaufighters* also served as long-range fighters in the Mediterranean and Western (Sahara) Desert until replaced by the even more capable de Havilland *Mosquito*.

Experiments in 1942 demonstrated that the *Beaufighter* could easily adapt to torpedo warfare. Consequently, RAF Coastal Command created several antiship strike wings of *Beaufighters* armed with torpedoes as well as rockets. They also carried the ASV Mk VII antishipping radar, housed in a unique thimble-shaped nose. These played havoc with Axis shipping, and one occasion the radar-equipped *Beaufighters* sank five U-boats in two days. In the Pacific, Japanese soldiers dubbed the big fighter "Whistling Death" on account of its quiet approach. By war's end, no less than 5,562 *Beaufighters* had been produced in England and Australia. The Aussie machines subsequently served as target tows and utility aircraft up through 1957.

Type: Torpedo-Bomber; Reconnaissance

Dimensions: wingspan, 57 feet, 10 inches; length, 44 feet, 3 inches; height, 14 feet, 3 inches
Weights: empty, 13,100 pounds; gross, 21,228 pounds
Power plant: 2 × 1,130–horsepower Bristol Taurus radial engines
Performance: maximum speed, 265 miles per hour; ceiling, 16,500 feet; range, 1,600 miles
Armament: 6 × .303–inch machine guns; 2,000 pounds of bombs or torpedoes
Service dates: 1940–1945

The *Beaufort* was the Royal Air Force's standard torpedo-bomber for most of World War II. It performed excellent service in many theaters and was also mass-produced in Australia.

In 1935 the British Air Ministry issued specifications for new aircraft to replace the aging Vickers *Vildebeest* as its standard torpedo-bomber. This announcement was later revised to include a similar craft to also serve as a reconnaissance bomber, but both versions were mandated to have crews of four. In 1938 Bristol, then engaged in manufacturing the *Blenheim*, flew a new prototype that mounted the new Taurus radial engines, prone to overheating. The new *Beaufort* was essentially an enlarged *Blenheim*, being an all-metal, midwing monoplane. Unlike its forebear, it had a high cabin roof ending in a semi-enclosed power turret. The bomb bay was also considerably enlarged to accommodate a torpedo. Tests were successful, and *Beauforts* starting arriving in the fall of 1939, but they were beset by engine problems. Consequently, most aircraft remained grounded until the spring of 1940. It was not

until that April that *Beauforts* successfully conducted their first mining operations. Soon after they also delivered 2,000-pound bombs for the first time, and gradually they acquired a reputation for reliability and strength. Perhaps their most celebrated action was the futile attempt on April 6, 1941, to prevent the German warships *Scharnhorst* and *Gneisenau* from escaping the English Channel, in which many *Beauforts* were sacrificed. A total of 1,429 were built.

Beauforts subsequently served with distinction throughout the Mediterranean, and squadrons based on Malta were especially effective at harassing Axis shipping. They remained so employed until 1944, when that task was assigned to new Bristol *Beaufighters*. In 1939 the Australian government also expressed interest in building the *Beaufort* under license. They were fitted with more powerful engines and, consequently, a taller tail fin. The 700 Australian-built *Beauforts* saw extensive service in the Pacific, bombing and torpedoing their way across New Guinea, New Britain, Rabaul, and the East Indies.

Type: Light Bomber; Night Fighter

Dimensions: wingspan, 56 feet, 4 inches; length, 42 feet, 7 inches; height, 9 feet, 10 inches
Weights: empty, 9,790 pounds; gross, 13,500 pounds
Power plant: 2 × 920–horsepower Bristol Mercury XV radial engines
Performance: maximum speed, 266 miles per hour; ceiling, 22,000 feet; range, 1,460 miles
Armament: 3 × .303–inch machine guns; 1,300 pounds of bombs
Service dates: 1937–1944

Ultramodern in its day, the *Blenheim* had grown obsolete by World War II. Despite sometimes heavy losses, it nonetheless saw widespread service with every branch of the Royal Air Force and in every theater.

The *Blenheim* had its origins in a commercial transport built for newspaper magnate Lord Rothmere of the London *Daily Mail*. Entitled Type 142, it was an all-metal, low-wing, snub-nosed monoplane with twin engines and U.S.-built variable-pitch propellers. The new craft caused a sensation by flying 50 miles per hour faster than the newest RAF biplane fighters. Naturally, the Air Ministry was acutely interested in the design, and it issued Specification B.28/35 in order to obtain it. The military version differed specifically in possessing a low wing, a bomb bay, and a power turret. It entered service in 1937 as the *Blenheim*, at the time the world's most advanced bombing aircraft. To accommodate additional fuel and range, a long-nosed version was test-flown in 1938.

Technology quickly overtook the *Blenheim* by the time World War II commenced in 1939, but it constituted the bulk of light bombers within RAF Bomber Command. Various subtypes also served with RAF Fighter Command, Coastal Command, Army Cooperation Command, and Training Command, becoming the only type to do so. On September 3, 1939, *Blenheims* conducted the first armed reconnaissance over Germany, and the following day they launched the first attack on the German fleet. It was subsequently active in daylight bombing raids but, in view of slow speed and weak armament, sustained heavy losses. The British, however, desperately needed aircraft of any kind, so in 1940 they outfitted *Blenheims* with top-secret A/I airborne radar, creating the first dedicated night fighter. That August *Blenheims* achieved the very first nighttime interception of a German bomber. Others served in the Mediterranean, Burma, and Singapore, where they did useful work but suffered heavily. Surviving aircraft were finally transferred to training duties by 1944. *Blenheim* production ceased at 4,440 machines.

Type: Fighter

Dimensions: wingspan, 33 feet, 10 inches; length, 25 feet, 2 inches; height, 8 feet, 9 inches
Weights: empty, 2,222 pounds; gross, 3,660 pounds
Power plant: 1 × 490–horsepower Bristol Jupiter VIIF radial engine
Performance: maximum speed, 174 miles per hour; ceiling, 29,300 feet; range, 300 miles
Armament: 2 × .303–inch machine guns; 80 pounds of bombs
Service dates: 1929–1937

The *Bulldog* was a mainstay of Royal Air Force fighter strength in the 1930s and represented a shift in Britain's philosophy toward fighter design. It served with distinction for several years and was also widely exported abroad.

By 1926 the appearance of high-speed bombers such as the Fairey *Fox*, which could outrun most fighters then in service, induced changes in British fighter philosophy. Thereafter, greater emphasis was placed on speed than maneuverability, although the latter trait still remained significant. The Air Ministry then issued Specification F.9/26, calling for new fighter designs to replace the Gloster *Gamecocks* and Armstrong-Whitworth *Siskins IIIAs* then deployed. Bristol fielded a new craft for the 1927 fighter competition that looked as pugnacious as its name implied: the *Bulldog*. This was a robust biplane of unequal wingspan whose wings and fuselage frames were constructed of stainless-steel strip for greater strength. Save for metal paneling in the engine area, it was entirely covered by fabric. The single-bay wings had pro-

nounced dihedral while the upper one sported a reduced center section to enhance pilot visibility. A variable-incidence tailplane was also fitted so that the craft could be trimmed in flight. The prototype successfully edged out competing designs and won a contract. The first batch, 95 machines, was constructed as *Bulldog IIs* in 1929 and was greeted with enthusiasm.

A newer version, the *Bulldog IIA*, evolved by 1930. This differed by the addition of a strengthened structure, higher weight, an improved oil system, and wider undercarriage. A total of 247 were procured, and they represented 70 percent of Britain's fighter strength over the next few years. In light of its fine performance, the *Bulldog* was also exported in quantity to Australia, Denmark, Estonia, Sweden, and Finland. Finland kept them in frontline service until 1940, and they fought actively during the Russo-Finnish War. These fine machines, a common sight at the Hendon Displays for many years, were gradually phased out of British service by Gloster *Gladiators* in 1937.

Type: Reconnaissance; Fighter

Dimensions: wingspan, 39 feet, 3 inches; length, 25 feet, 10 inches; height, 9 feet, 9 inches
Weights: empty, 2,150 pounds; gross, 3,250 pounds
Power plant: 1 × 275–horsepower Rolls-Royce Falcon III liquid-cooled in-line engine
Performance: maximum speed, 123 miles per hour; ceiling, 18,000 feet; range, 350 miles
Armament: 2 × .303–inch machine guns
Service dates: 1917–1932

The "Brisfit" was the best general-purpose warplane manufactured during World War I. Its combination of high speed, sound construction, and excellent maneuverability made it a formidable opponent.

By 1916 glaring deficiencies of the BE 2c reconnaissance aircraft necessitated a search for a suitable replacement. Frank Barnwell of Bristol originated such a machine, which first flew in October of that year. Designated the R.2A, it was a conventional, two-bay biplane with some distinguishing features. Foremost among them was a fuselage that sat midway between the two wings, by use of struts, to afford pilots a better forward view. Moreover, it also had a downward sweep toward the tail, which greatly enhanced the gunner's field of fire. Flight tests were encouraging, so the type entered production as the F.2A.

For such a promising craft, the F.2A had a disastrous combat debut. On April 5, 1917, a flight of six encountered Albatros D IIIs of Manfred von Richthofen's "Flying Circus," which promptly shot down four. Similar losses followed until it was discovered that tactics employed by F.2A crews were faulty, not the aircraft itself. Previously, F.2As were flown as reconnaissance craft, in straight lines and tight defensive formations. This made them easy prey for more agile German fighters. However, as pilots became better acquainted with the big "Brisfit" they adopted more aggressive tactics. The F.2A, flown offensively, soon emerged as one of the great fighters of the war. By year's end the improved F 2B was available in numbers and proved an even better dogfighter. For example, on May 7, 1918, two of the newer "Brisfits" were surprised by seven Fokkers yet promptly shot down four. Minutes later they encountered 15 more enemy craft and claimed another four without loss. The F 2B remained in production until 1927, after 5,252 had been constructed. The Royal Air Force employed the big craft in various army cooperation capacities until 1933, and it also saw service in air forces around the world.

Type: Reconnaissance

Dimensions: wingspan, 24 feet, 7 inches; length, 20 feet, 8 inches; height, 8 feet, 6 inches
Weights: empty, 760 pounds; gross, 925 pounds
Power plant: 1 × 100–horsepower Gnome rotary engine
Performance: maximum speed, 95 miles per hour; ceiling, 14,000; range, 200 miles
Armament: none, officially
Service dates: 1914–1916

Versatile Bristol Scouts were outstanding aircraft for their day but suffered from a lack of armament. They nonetheless saw varied, wide-ranging service, and one was even launched from the back of a seaplane!

In 1913 Frank Barnwell developed a fast single-seat biplane design with a view toward racing it. The prototype, called the *Baby*, first flew on February 23, 1914, and clocked a respectable 95 miles per hour. The *Baby*'s fine performance caught the attention of the military, and two additional craft, labeled Scout Bs, were delivered that August. By this time World War I had commenced, and both the Royal Flying Corps and the Royal Naval Air Service began placing orders for the sprightly machine.

The Scout C was the first production model, and it performed reconnaissance service for many months. That role was ironic, for the little Bristol craft was faster and more maneuverable than many German fighters opposing it. Many pilots thus lashed rifles to their Scouts and actively engaged the enemy.

On July 25, 1915, Captain L. G. Hawker won the Victoria Cross when he dispatched three machine gun–armed Albatros scouts with his rifle. That same year an improved version, the Scout D, which featured a more powerful engine and larger tail surfaces, arrived. It too was unarmed, but several squadrons jerry-rigged a wing-mounted Lewis machine gun on the upper wing to fire over the propeller arc. A total of 161 C and 210 D versions were constructed.

The Scouts were basically withdrawn from the Western Front in 1916, but attempts were made to convert it into an anti-Zeppelin device by mounting explosive Ranken darts. In an effort to increase range, two Scouts were nestled aboard the primitive carrier *Vindex*, and in November 1915 one became the first British aircraft launched from a ship. Experiments were also conducted with the large Porte *Baby* flying boat, which carried aloft a single Scout C on its wing. This piggyback arrangement proved perfectly functional, and on May 17, 1916, a Scout was successfully launched from an altitude of 1,000 feet.

Type: Fighter; Light Bomber

Dimensions: wingspan, 30 feet, 4 inch; length, 37 feet, 1 inch; height, 11 feet, 7 inches
Weights: empty, 15,542 pounds; gross, 31,000 pounds
Power plant: 1 × 21,750–pound thrust Rolls-Royce Pegasus turbofan engine
Performance: maximum speed, 601 miles per hour; ceiling, 51,000 feet; range, 932 miles
Armament: 2 × 30mm cannons; up to 8,000 pounds of bombs or rockets
Service dates: 1968–

The *Harrier* is the first vertical-takeoff fighter in history and among the most maneuverable. It performed sterling service as an interceptor during the 1982 Falkland Islands War and is continually upgraded.

The *Harrier* concept dates back to 1957 when Sir Sydney Camm of Hawker and Dr. Stanley Hooker of Bristol Siddeley teamed up to design the world's first vertical takeoff and landing (VTOL) fighter. They employed the new Bristol BS.53 turbofan engine, which directed thrust downward into four vectoring (movable) nozzles. In wartime, such an aircraft could dispense with runways and operate off of any level ground near the front, a tremendous tactical advantage. The prototype P 1127 first flew in October 1960 and was refined through a succession of stronger engines and vectoring configurations. This evolution culminated in 1968, when the first operational *Harrier* GR 1 appeared. This was a small craft with swept wings of negative dihedral and fuselage centerline landing gear. Four rotatable noz-

zles are located on the fuselage to control vertical assent and horizontal flight; two wingtip nozzles provide added stability. As a dogfighter, the *Harrier* is capable of vectoring in forward flight (vff, or "viffing"), literally stopping in midair and causing enemy aircraft to overshoot. *Harriers* are currently deployed in numbers by the Royal Air Force and U.S. Marine Corps and are operated by the Spanish navy as well.

In 1975 the Royal Navy also acquired its first *Sea Harriers*. These were initially based closely upon the RAF GR 3 model but were later refitted with a modified canopy and nose section. A total of 57 were purchased; they made aviation history during the 1982 Falkland Islands War with Argentina. Operating as interceptors, they bagged 22 enemy planes without loss, although three were lost to ground fire. These craft have since been superceded by the newer *Harrier F/A.2*, which utilizes the advanced *Blue Vixen* radar in a bulbous redesigned nose. India also operates this model in large numbers.

Type: Patrol-Bomber; Antisubmarine

Dimensions: wingspan, 142 feet, 3 inches; length, 128 feet, 9 inches; height, 38 feet, 8 inches
Weights: empty, 81,000 pounds; gross, 157,000 pounds
Power plant: 4 × 3,400–horsepower Wright R-3350-EA1 Cyclone radial engines
Performance: maximum speed, 315 miles per hour; ceiling, 25,000 feet; range, 5,900 miles
Armament: 8,000 pounds of internal ordnance; 3,800 pounds of wing-mounted ordnance
Service dates: 1957–1981

At the time of its debut, the all-seeing *Argus* was the world's most advanced antisubmarine patrol-bomber. Although partly based upon a commercial airliner, it flew for more than two decades with distinction.

By 1952 the Royal Canadian Air Force wished to replace its antiquated Avro *Lancasters* and Lockheed P2V *Neptunes* with a new craft better suited for antisubmarine (ASW) warfare. Such a machine would have to conduct lengthy patrols over open ocean and carry with the latest radar and sonar equipment. The RCAF consulted closely with Canadair and agreed that the most cost-effective solution for a new patrol-bomber would be to utilize an existing commercial craft. For that reason, Canadair selected the Bristol *Britannia* as the basis for its work. The tail unit, wings, and undercarriage of the *Britannia* were kept intact, but the fuselage was entirely redesigned to North American standards. It featured two capacious, 18-foot bomb bays, before and aft of the wings, that could house a vari-

ety of depth charges, sonobuoys, and homing torpedoes. Pressurization was also eliminated, as it was unnecessary for low-altitude maritime patrols. The first CL 28 rolled out in March 1957 and was successfully test-flown. That same year it entered production as the *Argus*, so named for the all-seeing, 100-eyed monster of Greek mythology. The first 12 units, designated *Argus Is*, utilized U.S.-built sonar and computers, but the subsequent version, the *Argus II*, operated more advanced British equipment. A total of 33 machines were constructed.

For many years the CL 28 functioned as the West's most advanced antisubmarine aircraft. It carried a crew of 15, who operated in shifts to ease the burden of long flights. Successive modifications also enabled the *Argus* to carry a complex variety of new weapons and equipment, which further enhanced its utility. The last of these useful machines was retired in 1981 by the more advanced Lockheed P-2C *Orion*, itself based on a commercial airliner. The *Argus* was a vital but little appreciated Canadian machine.

Type: Trainer; Light Bomber

Dimensions: wingspan, 36 feet, 6 inches; length, 32 feet; height, 9 feet, 4 inches
Weights: empty, 4,895 pounds; gross, 7,778 pounds
Power plant: 1 × 2,950–pound thrust Orenda J85-CAN J4 turbojet engine
Performance: maximum speed, 480 miles per hour; ceiling, 42,200 feet; range, 1,340 miles
Armament: none, or up to 4,000 pounds of bombs and rockets
Service dates: 1963–

The diminutive *Tutor* remains Canada's standard jet training craft. As part of the famed *Snowbirds* demonstration team, it has thrilled thousands of spectators with precision acrobatics.

In 1958 Canadair began investigating the possibly of constructing Canada's first jet trainer. This was regarded as essential for familiarizing students with the flight characteristics of jet aircraft then entering service in ever greater numbers. However, even when the Canadian government expressed no interest, Canadair continued with a private, company-funded project. The prototype CL 41 took flight in 1960 following a short gestation. It was a low-wing, all-metal monoplane with straight wings and an upward-opening canopy. Pilot and student were seated side by side in a spacious cockpit. The craft also employed a high "T" tail, retractable tricycle landing gear, and air brakes. The CL 41 performed well, and, in parallel with developments in the United States and England, the Canadian government acquired it in numbers. Since 1963, 190 CL 41s, under the official designation CT 114 *Tutor*, have

been purchased. These are all deployed at the No. 2 Flying School at Moosejaw, Saskatchewan, where pilots are trained up to wing standard and beyond. Other *Tutors* are employed by the Central Flying School, where instructor-pilots are taught. Their most famous unit, the *Snowbirds*, is an internationally renowned precision flying group composed entirely of instructors from that school. They operated stock but highly painted CL 41s outfitted with smoke generators for effect.

In the wake of various insurgency movements throughout Asia, the Malaysian government in 1967 needed to acquire an inexpensive strike aircraft. It approached Canadair to produce a militarized version of the *Tutor*, the CL 41G, which featured more powerful engines and hardpoints for hauling ordnance. Malaysia acquired 20 such machines as the *Tebuan* (Wasp), which have since been retired due to metal fatigue and corrosion. Canada maintains a fleet of about 100 machines, and they will remain its standard jet trainer well into the twenty-first century.

Type: Patrol-Bomber

Dimensions: wingspan, 73 feet, 10 inches; length, 46 feet, 10 inches; height, 14 feet, 6 inches
Weights: empty, 8,466 pounds; gross, 15,510 pounds
Power plant: 1 × 900–horsepower Isotta-Fraschini liquid-cooled inline engine
Performance: maximum speed, 171 miles per hour; ceiling, 22,965 feet; range, 1,490 miles
Armament: 3 × 7.7mm machine guns; up to 1,404 pounds of bombs
Service dates: 1936–1950

The Z 501 was a record-breaking flying boat that saw widespread service with Italian forces. Despite obvious obsolescence, it fought actively in World War II and was utilized by both sides.

Cantiere Navale Triestino (CANT) was formed in 1923 to design and build water-based aircraft for civilian and military applications. In 1931 fascist dictator Benito Mussolini dispatched his famous air marshal, Italo Balbo, to lure Filippo Zappata, one of Italy's finest aircraft designers, back from France. The entreaties worked, and in 1934 Zappata designed his first CANT aircraft—the Z 501. It was a single-engine flying boat constructed entirely of wood and fabric. A study in contrasts, its beautifully streamlined fuselage and gracefully elliptical wings were offset by unsightly bracing. It seated five crew members, including pilot and copilot in the cabin, two gunners, and a flight engineer stationed behind the nacelle to monitor the engine and man a machine gun. In 1934 noted pilot Mario Stoppani flew the prototype on a record-breaking 2,560-mile flight from Monfalcone to Eritrea. The French subsequently broke the record in 1935, but Stoppani won it back again when his Z 501 ranged 3,080 miles from Monfalcone to British-held Somalia. Such excellent performance pleased Italian authorities, and in 1936 the *Gabbiano* (Gull) entered production as the only flying boat in the Regia Aeronautica (Italian air force).

In service the Z 501 was well-liked, being easy to fly and maintain. It initially fought in the Spanish Civil War by conducting bombing missions from Majorca. The *Gabbiano* flew well, but as a wood and fabric machine it was hopelessly outclassed for the rigors of World War II. Z 501s flew missions throughout the Mediterranean and suffered heavy losses. The craft was also deployed in squadron strength by Romania, which operated on the Black Sea against Soviet forces. By the time of the 1943 Italian surrender, only a handful remained in service, equally divided between pro- and antifascist forces. Several surviving *Gabbianos* were maintained in service until 1950.

Type: Torpedo-Bomber; Reconnaissance

Dimensions: wingspan, 81 feet, 4 inches; length, 60 feet, 2 inches; height, 17 feet, 1 inch
Weights: empty, 19,338 pounds; gross, 30,029 pounds
Power plant: 3 × 1,000–horsepower Piaggio P.XI *bis* (improved) radial engines
Performance: maximum speed, 280 miles per hour; ceiling, 24,600 feet; range, 1,370 miles
Armament: 2 × 7.7mm or 12.7mm machine guns; up to 4,410 pounds of bombs or torpedoes
Service dates: 1937–1945

The Z 506 was one of the most versatile float-planes ever built and set several world records. It functioned throughout the Mediterranean in World War II as torpedo and reconnaissance craft.

In 1936 Filippo Zapata designed the CANT Z 506A, an all-wood trimotor float transport aircraft. Streamlined and ruggedly built, several were acquired by the airline Ala Littoria and established a reputation for good handling and reliability. That year test pilot Mario Stoppani helped establish 16 world distance and payload records in the Z 506A. Such excellent performance caught the attention of the Regia Aeronautica (Italian air force), and CANT was persuaded to develop a bomber/reconnaissance version for the military. The prototype emerged in 1937 sporting a long ventral gondola under the fuselage and a dorsal turret. Like its civilian counterpart, the new craft exhibited outstanding aerial and water characteristics. The large streamlined floats were specially designed to enable the craft to take off and land in water as rough as Force 5 conditions. These excellent seaplanes, designated the *Airone* (Heron), became operational in 1937, and several campaigned during the closing stages of the Spanish Civil War. By the time Italy entered World War II in 1940, Z 506Bs outfitted two reconnaissance groups.

Airones were initially employed as torpedo-bombers, and against relatively weak aerial opposition they attacked numerous French and Greek targets. They proved less successful facing determined resistance from the Royal Navy, and the slow-flying floatplanes sustained serious losses. Thereafter, most Z 506Bs conducted coastal reconnaissance, convoy escort, and antisubmarine operations. Once the Italian armistice was signed in 1943, 28 *Airones* managed to reach Allied lines. They were employed as rescue craft in southern Italy until the end of the war. A handful were also operated by the Luftwaffe, and it was a Z 506B that successfully evacuated Mussolini to safety. A total of 563 were built; a handful performed air/sea rescue operations until 1959.

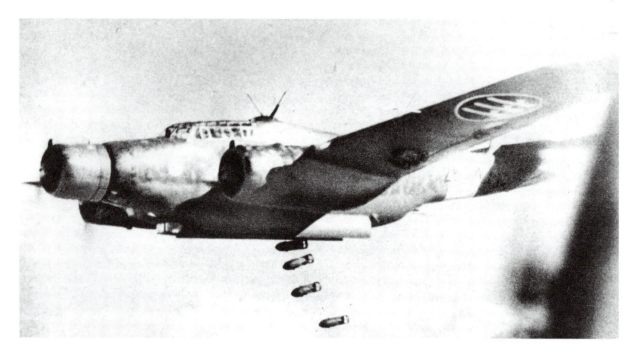

Type: Medium Bomber; Torpedo-Bomber

Dimensions: wingspan, 81 feet, 4 inches; length, 60 feet, 2 inches; height, 17 feet, 1 inch
Weights: empty, 19,338 pounds; gross, 30,029 pounds
Power plant: 3 × 1,000–horsepower Piaggio P.XI *bis* (improved) radial engine
Performance: maximum speed, 280 miles per hour; ceiling, 24,600 feet; range, 1,370 miles
Armament: 4 × 7.7mm or 12.7mm machine guns; up to 4,410 pounds of bombs or torpedoes
Service dates: 1939–1945

The graceful *Alcione* was Italy's second most important bomber of World War II. Despite wooden construction and weak defensive armament, it rendered useful service on many fronts.

In 1935 Filippo Zapata's success with the Z 506 floatplane inspired him to explore the possibility of a similar land-based bomber, the first such craft produced by CANT. Two years later the prototype Z 1007 flew as a low-wing monoplane of trimotor configuration. The reason for three motors was that Italian engines produced decidedly lower horsepower. In fact, a competing two-engine design, the Z 1011, was rejected by the Regia Aeronautica (Italian air force) as underpowered. The Z 1007 also employed outdated wooden construction, but that kept its overall weight down. One possible weakness was the armament, which was restricted to four 7.7mm machine guns in dorsal, ventral, and beam-hatch positions. Test pilots nonetheless enjoyed its fine flying characteristics, and in 1939 it entered production as the *Alcione* (Kingfisher). When

Italy joined World War II in 1940, only 55 Z 1007s were available. Many were the *bis* (improved) model, featuring heavier guns and better engines. Curiously, the *Alciones* were built in both single- and twin-rudder configurations, without differing designations, flying side by side in the same squadrons.

In service the *Alcione* was Italy's most important bomber after the SM 79 *Sparviero*. They ranged the length of the Mediterranean and performed bombing missions in Greece, France, North Africa, and Russia. The Z 1007 was also quite adept at anti-shipping functions and could be outfitted with a pair of 1,000-pound torpedoes. Even though a good basic design and easy to fly, the *Alcione* remained poorly defended and suffered heavy losses at the hands of Royal Air Force fighters. This resulted in curtailment of daylight operations over Malta in favor of night bombing. After the Italian surrender of 1943, *Alciones* continued serving both sides up through the end of the war. A total of 563 were constructed.

Type: Heavy Bomber

Dimensions: wingspan, 76 feet, 9 inches; length, 41 feet, 4 inches; height, 14 feet, 5 inches
Weights: empty, 5,512 pounds; gross, 11,685 pounds
Power plant: 3 × 300–horsepower Fiat A-12 liquid-cooled inline engines
Performance: maximum speed, 94 miles per hour; ceiling, 14,764 feet; range, 400 miles
Armament: 3 × 7.7mm machine guns; up to 3,000 pounds of bombs
Service dates: 1915–1928

Italy possessed the largest strategic bomber program of World War I, one that exceed contemporary British and German efforts both in size and capacity. The various Caproni aircraft involved were strong, functional machines and were well-suited to the tasks at hand.

Count Gianni Caproni founded his aircraft firm in 1908, and he manufactured successful civilian designs for several years. Italy, however, was unique among Western powers in that discussions pertaining to military applications of airpower were widespread. Caproni underscored this interest in 1913 when he constructed the world's first strategic bomber, the Ca 30. This was a large triplane with a single nacelle housing the crew and three pusher engines. Subsequent refinements culminated in the Ca 31, in which two of the pusher engines were mounted at the head of the booms in tractor configuration. This ungainly but practical machine entered production in 1914 as the Ca 1. Several were operational in August 1915 when, following Italy's declaration of war against

Austria, two Capronis dropped bombs on Aisovizza. The age of strategic warfare had dawned.

As the war progressed, Caproni continually introduced better engines and performance in his triplane bombers. Because most of the targets were at great distances, and mountain ranges had to be crossed, the company placed greater emphasis on more powerful engines, greater lift, and payload. The Ca 4 was a major subtype that featured 350-horsepower engines with varying arrangements of nose- and tailgunners. The latter position required gunners to stand upright—fully exposed to frigid mountain air. The final Caproni bomber of the war was the Ca 5, which maintained the same general layout as before but reverted back to biplane status. Like all aircraft of this design, it was rather slow and ponderous, but it was ruggedly built and easy to fly. By war's end, 740 of the giant craft had been assembled in various subtypes, and they did excellent work. Several were subsequently converted into civilian airliners, while others performed military service until 1928.

Type: Light Bomber; Torpedo-Bomber; Reconnaissance

Dimensions: wingspan, 53 feet, 2 inches; length, 40 feet; height, 11 feet, 7 inches
Weights: empty, 6,730 pounds; gross, 10,252 pounds
Power plant: 2 × 470–horsepower Piaggio P.VII radial engines
Performance: maximum speed, 227 miles per hour; ceiling, 22,956 feet; range, 1,025 miles
Armament: 2 × 7.7mm machine guns; 1,764 pounds of bombs
Service dates: 1938–1945

The versatile Ca 310 was progenitor of a wide-ranging family of reconnaissance and lighter bomber airplanes. They served Italian interests well during World War II and were widely exported abroad.

In 1936 Cesare Pallavincino of the Caproni firm unveiled his new Ca 309 *Ghibli* (Desert Wind) light bomber/reconnaissance aircraft. Its ancestry can be traced to the Ca 306 *Borea* (North Wind) of 1935, an extremely clean-lined commercial transport. Likes its forebear, the *Ghibli* was constructed of a metal-framework fuselage, wooden wings, and fabric covering. It also mounted fixed spatted landing gear, a glazed bombardier nose, and light armament. The Regia Aeronautica (Italian air force) acquired 165 for policing Italian possessions overseas. Given the success of the design, Pallavincino developed a more capable version, the Ca 310 *Libeccio* (Southwest Wind), with retractable landing gear, an extended nose, and all-around better performance. Like most Italian aircraft of the period, the Ca 310 was light and somewhat underpowered yet possessed delightful flying characteristics. The Regia

Aeronautica purchased 161 of these handsome craft by 1939, with several others being exported to Norway, Hungary, Spain, Yugoslavia, and Peru.

In service the Ca 310 proved to be versatile fighting machines, and they functioned as reconnaissance planes, light bombers, and torpedo-bombers. They were widely employed throughout the Mediterranean theater and saw extensive service in Russia. The utility and soundness of the basic design gave rise to numerous other versions. These included the Ca 311, which introduced a glazed bombardier nose and was ordered by France and Belgium (England even contemplated their purchase). The next model, the Ca 312, had a glazed nose, heavier armament, and different engines. Germany purchased 905 of these machines as crew trainers but received only a handful before the Armistice. A final version, the Ca 314, featured inline engines, a bank of windows along the fuselage; it was intended for convoy protection and naval reconnaissance. A total of 2,400 of all variants were produced, making them the most numerous Italian warplane of this period.

Type: Trainer; Light Bomber

Dimensions: wingspan, 34 feet, 9 inches; length, 41 feet; height, 13 feet, 11 inches
Weights: empty, 7,716 pounds; gross, 13,889 pounds
Power plant: 1 × 4,300–pound thrust Garrett TFE731 turbofan engine
Performance: maximum speed, 501 miles per hour; ceiling, 42,00 feet; range, 322 miles
Armament: none, or up to 4,960 pounds of gunpods, bombs, or rockets
Service dates: 1981–

The *Aviojet* is Spain's first indigenously designed and constructed jet aircraft. Small, underpowered, and unassuming, it nevertheless attracts buyers from South America and the Middle East.

Construcciones Aeronauticas SA (CASA) was founded in 1923 and is one of Europe's oldest airplane manufacturers. For many years it built foreign designs under license; in 1972 the firm absorbed Hispano Aviacion, a major competitor. Thus augmented, CASA was well positioned to fulfill a 1975 Spanish air force requirement for a new jet trainer to replace their outdated HA 200 *Saettas*. The main design emphasis was on simplicity and economy, not high performance. Yet the new machine also had to be capable of light strike missions. Faced with such varied specifications, CASA solicited technical advice from abroad. The U.S. firm Northrop was contracted to help design the wing and engine inlets, and Germany's MBB assisted with the rear fuselage and tail section. The prototype C 101 performed its maiden flight in June 1978 as a low-wing monoplane with unswept wings. To reduce costs, it employs modular construction, and the fuselage contains ample space capable of being retrofitted with different avionic systems as needed. The C 101 is powered by a commercial turbofan engine adapted for military use, which combines relatively good power with excellent fuel economy. A two-man crew is housed under a spacious canopy, with staggered seating to allow instructors a better view. For military applications a built-in bomb bay exists on the underside, and the wing also sports six pylons capable of holding weapons.

The *Aviojet*, although somewhat underpowered next to comparable French, British, and Italian machines, still possesses delightful characteristics at very affordable prices. As anticipated, the Spanish air force contracted for 88 machines under the designation *Mirlo* (Blackbird). Several of these were subsequently assigned to the national acrobatic squadron, *Team Aguila*. Such low-cost and good performance induced Chile, Honduras, and Jordan to place orders for trainers and attack craft. A dedicated attack version, the C 101DD, is currently under development.

Type: Reconnaissance; Trainer

Dimensions: wingspan, 43 feet; length, 22 feet; height, 8 feet, 6 inches
Weights: empty, 959 pounds; gross, 1,565 pounds
Power plant: 1 × 80–horsepower Le Rhone rotary engine
Performance: maximum speed, 67 miles per hour; ceiling, 13,000 feet; range, 240 miles
Armament: none
Service dates: 1914–1918

Despite its obsolete appearance, the Caudron G III was a popular French aircraft from the early days of World War I. Throughout its lengthy career it trained thousands of allied pilots.

The Caudron brothers, Gaston and Rene, were renowned as airplane builders long before the onset of hostilities in August 1914. Their first military design, the G III, was a development of an earlier civilian craft, the N.40, which was itself a frequent star at air shows across Europe. This Caudron machine was unique in being one of the few twin-boomed aircraft of its day. The crew of two sat in a short nacelle suspended between the two wings. To the rear, four booms supported a system of twin rudders; the craft was steered by wing-warping techniques. Despite its odd appearance, the G III was strongly built and possessed excellent climbing abilities. The French air force had only one squadron of G IIIs deployed when war broke out, but their excellent performance resulted in orders for more. In a display of patriotism and to facilitate rapid production, Caudron allowed other firms to construct the G III without a license.

The Caudron's climbing and handling made it valuable as a reconnaissance and artillery-spotting airplane. However, it was relatively slow and completely unarmed, so the advent of improved German fighters terminated its frontline usefulness by 1916. The G IIIs then rendered equally useful service as a trainer, for novice pilots appreciated its gentle and predicable qualities. They were also widely exported abroad, seeing service in the air forces of Italy, Great Britain, Belgium, and Russia. It gained considerable renown throughout 1917–1918, when G IIIs trained virtually every pilot attached to the American Expeditionary Force. Caudron and other companies ultimately assembled 2,450 of the ubiquitous G IIIs. In 1919 one plucky craft gained special notoriety in civilian hands when aviatrix Adrienne Bolland flew it over the Andes Mountains. That same year former French ace Jules Verdrines demonstrated its superb handling by successfully landing on the roof of the Galeries Lafayette department store in Paris!

Type: Reconnaissance; Light Bomber

Dimensions: wingspan, 56 feet, 5 inches; length, 23 feet, 7 inches; height, 8 feet, 6 inches
Weights: empty, 1,102 pounds; gross, 2,923 pounds
Power plant: 2 × 80–horsepower Le Rhone rotary engines
Performance: maximum speed, 82 miles per hour; ceiling, 14,108 feet; range, 250 miles
Armament: 2 × 7.7mm machine guns; 220 pounds of bombs
Service dates: 1915–1918

The Caudron G IV was the first twin-engine aircraft deployed by Allied air units in World War I. Like its predecessor, it was fast-climbing, easy to fly, and completely reliable.

The Caudron G III was a well-liked aircraft, but by 1915 it had reached the limits of development. The Aviation Militaire (French air service) therefore determined to capitalize on the successful design by authorizing an improved, scaled-up version. When the prototype G IV appeared in March 1915, it was similar to but much larger than its forebear. The new machine possessed a larger wingspan and was powered by two cowled engines suspended between the wings. Their placement, in close proximity to the crew nacelle, was fortunate, for it made the craft more easily handled in case of an engine failure. Like the G III, the G IV also had four booms stretching backward to the tail section, although the rudders had been increased to four. It was also armed with a machine gun in the forward nacelle, as well as one pointed backward over the top wing. Following successful test flights, the new Caudron entered French service in November 1915 and ultimately equipped 38 squadrons.

In the field, the G IV displayed many fine qualities reminiscent of the earlier craft. Delightful to fly, it climbed speedily and was easily maintained. As the Allies' first twin-engine bomber, it was sent in massed formations to German targets as distant as the Rhineland. Unfortunately, the slow, lightly armed G IVs were easy prey for newer and more heavily armed German fighters. Having sustained heavy losses, most G IVs were withdrawn from frontline service by August 1916. They continued in British and Russian service much longer, however, and Italians prized the awkward-looking craft for its quick climbing ability, an essential trait when flying in heavily mountainous terrain. Toward the end of the war, G IVs were employed as trainers by the newly arrived Americans, who also praised its docility. A total of 1,358 were built.

Caudron R 11 France

Type: Fighter

Dimensions: 58 feet, 9 inches; length, 36 feet, 9 inches; height, 9 feet, 2 inches
Weights: empty, 3,130 pounds; gross, 4,773 pounds
Power plant: 2 × 215–horsepower Hispano-Suiza liquid-cooled engines
Performance: maximum speed, 114 miles per hour; ceiling, 19,520 feet; range, 350 miles
Armament: 5 × 7.7mm machine guns
Service dates: 1918–1922

A big, impressive machine, the R 11 was the most successful escort fighter of World War I. In that role it shot down scores of German fighters while protecting vulnerable French bombers.

By 1917 the Aviation Militaire (French air service) required a new, three-seat aircraft for extended reconnaissance usage. The Caudron company decided to update its older R 4 bomber with a smaller, lighter, more heavily armed machine. Consequently, the prototype R 11 emerged in March 1917 as a sleek, imposing craft. It displayed a more pointed nose than its predecessor, along with two bays of wing braces and an elongated vertical stabilizer. The fuselage was also oval-shaped in cross-section, with provisions for a single pilot and forward and rear gunners. As an added measure of safety, the R 11 was outfitted with dual controls: If a pilot were killed or wounded, the rear gunner could land it safely.

The big craft exhibited sprightly performance during testing, and the decision was made to enter production. Troubles with the Hispano-Suiza geared

motors greatly slowed their acquisition, and it was not until the spring of 1918 that R 11s were acquired in quantity. At that time the French headquarters Service Aeronautique had modified the R 11's role from reconnaissance to escort fighter. The French reasoned that because the aircraft was fast and heavily armed, it provided a more stable gunnery platform compared to single-engine fighters. The R 11 consequently received the construction priorities usually reserved only for two other noted stalwarts, the Breguet 14 and the Salmson 2A2.

By the summer and fall of 1918, the big R 11s dutifully conducted massed formations of Breguet 14 bombers to and from targets in the Rhineland. Their heavy firepower accounted for the loss of many German fighters and saved several hundred French lives. Had the war continued another year, R 11s would have become one of the most import weapons in the French arsenal. Construction ended at 500 units, and the big fighters were retained in service until being declared obsolete in 1922.

Type: Trainer; Light Bomber

Dimensions: wingspan, 43 feet; length, 27 feet, 10 inches; height, 8 feet, 9 inches
Weights: empty, 3,992 pounds; gross, 6,595 pounds
Power plant: 1 × 600–horsepower Pratt & Whitney CAC R-1340 Wasp radial engine
Performance: maximum speed, 220 miles per hour; ceiling, 23,000 feet; range, 720 miles
Armament: 3 × .303–caliber machine guns; 500 pounds of bombs
Service dates: 1939–1958

The *Wirraway* was the first indigenous warplane produced in Australia and the first deployed by the Royal Australian Air Force. Despite severe design limitations, it was heroically employed during the perilous opening months of the Pacific War against Japan.

In 1936 the Australian government encouraged formation of the Commonwealth Aircraft Corporation (CAC). This was undertaken to lessen that country's dependency on outside sources for aircraft. The following year, CAC entered negotiations with North American Aviation and received permission to construct their BT-9 trainer under license. As such, the new CA 1 was a low-wing monoplane seating two crew members in a long, tandem cockpit. The wing and top fuselage were metal-plated, whereas the lower fuselage and control surfaces were fabric-covered. The Australian version was also outfitted with a larger engine, retractable landing gear, and armament consisting of two fixed machine guns for the pilot, and a single movable weapon for the gunner. Like the BT-9, the new craft, dubbed the *Wirraway*

(an aboriginal expression for "challenge"), was somewhat slow but handled well. At the onset of the Pacific War the *Wirraway* equipped several squadrons of Australia's fledgling air force.

Australia was woefully unprepared for this war, but the existing stocks of CA 1s were pressed into frontline service as an emergency stopgap. With no replacements in sight, *Wirraways* were employed as dive-bombers, scouts, reconnaissance craft and—on several hair-raising occasions—as interceptors. Bravely manned, CA 1s paid heavily for their obsolescence, but they were a contributing factor in helping to slow and ultimately stop the Japanese drive over New Guinea's Owen Stanley Mountains. In time, dangerous low-altitude flying above mountain jungles became something of an Australian specialty, and *Wirraways* spotted, marked, and dive-bombed targets to good effect. Eventually, these war-weary veterans were replaced by more modern aircraft, but several squadrons performed combat operations until 1945. CAC ultimately produced 755 *Wirraways*, and many of these stalwarts performed training duty until 1958.

Type: Fighter

Dimensions: wingspan, 36 feet, 3 inches; length, 25 feet, 6 inches; height, 11 feet, 6 inches
Weights: empty, 5,450 pounds; gross, 7,600 pounds
Power plant: 1 × 1,200–horsepower Pratt & Whitney R-1830 Twin Wasp radial engine
Performance: maximum speed, 296 miles per hour; ceiling, 29,000 feet; range, 930 miles
Armament: 4 × .303–inch machine guns; 2 × 20mm cannon
Service dates: 1943–1945

Pugnacious in appearance, this interim fighter was Australia's only indigenous warplane designed during World War II. Tough and agile, it did valuable ground-support work throughout New Guinea.

Commencement of the Pacific War in December 1941 caught the Royal Australian Air Force completely unprepared. Its combined fighter strength then consisted of two squadrons equipped with outdated Brewster F2A *Buffaloes*, and they were deployed at Singapore. Given the urgency of the situation, the government resolved to build a new fighter out of local materials and talent, rather than wait for replacements from the United States and Great Britain. Fortunately, the Commonwealth Aircraft Corporation was well situated to assist. Since 1938 it had been assembling *Wirraway* trainers and light bombers, which were based upon the excellent North American AT-6. It became necessary to construct a new craft using as many *Wirraway* components as possible. Laurence J. Wackett drew up the initial design in February 1942, and the first prototype flew that May. Christened the

CA 12 *Boomerang*, it bore a marked resemblance to the earlier *Wirraway* with major refinements. It was a low-wing, all-metal monoplane featuring a fully enclosed cockpit, retractable landing gear, and a three-blade propeller. The CA 12 was slower than the Japanese fighters it opposed, but it displayed great structural strength and maneuverability.

The first batch of *Boomerangs* arrived in the fall of 1942 and became operational in the spring of 1943. In service they proved themselves to be tough, agile customers. They never shot down a single Japanese aircraft but did outstanding ground-attack work in the mountain jungles of New Guinea. Using its exceptional maneuverability over rough terrain, CA 12s would identify Japanese troop concentrations at low altitude, strafe them, and mark their position with smoke bombs for incoming bombers. For two years they fought in this capacity, unheralded but loved by the infantrymen they assisted in this grinding campaign. All were retired by 1945 after a production run of 250 machines.

Type: Antisubmarine; Patrol-Bomber

Dimensions: wingspan, 122 feet, 9 inches; length, 110 feet, 4 inches; height, 35 feet, 8 inches
Weights: empty, 56, 659 pounds; gross, 101,850 pounds
Power plant: 2 × 6,100–horsepower Rolls-Royce Tyne Mk 21 turboprop engines
Performance: maximum speed, 368 miles per hour; ceiling, 30,000 feet; range, 1,150 miles
Armament: up to 7,716 pounds of rockets, bombs, or torpedoes
Service dates: 1989–

The *Atlantique 2* is Europe's latest and most modern antisubmarine warfare (ASW) aircraft. It combines state-of-the-art electronics with a robust, highly durable airframe.

Russian submarine construction of the 1950s sufficiently alarmed NATO into issuing requirements for a long-range maritime patrol aircraft to replace the aging Lockheed P2V *Neptune*. The new machine would have to conduct lengthy oceanic patrols and carry modern ASW equipment. In 1958 a contract was awarded to the French firm of Breguet, which by 1961 had constructed the first prototype *Atlantique*. This was a low-wing, all-metal monoplane with two engines and dual-wheel landing gear. It also featured a Thomson CSF search radar in a retractable radome. This aircraft differed conceptually from aircraft employed by the United States and Canada, as the Lockheed P-3 *Orion* and Canadair CL 28 *Argus* were essentially modified commercial airliners. The *Atlantique*, by comparison, was designed from the ground up as a dedicated ASW aircraft. A total of 87 were constructed and deployed

by France, Germany, the Netherlands, Italy, and Pakistan with considerable success.

By the 1970s a successor machine was needed, so Dassault (which had absorbed Breguet in 1971) suggested utilizing an improved airframe with greatly updated electronics. The first prototype *Atlantique 2* was derived from an existing *Atlantique* in 1981 and markedly resembles the earlier craft. However, it employs vastly improved engines and construction techniques, including better anticorrosion protection and better sealing between the panels. The new airframe now has a service-life expectancy of 30 years. The *Atlantique 2*'s electronic suite is a mind-boggling array of the very latest computer-enhanced sensory equipment. The new Thomson-CSF Iguane radar has an over-the-horizon sweep, tracks 100 targets simultaneously, and can reputedly pick out objects as small as a submarine snorkel at a distance of several miles! The plane also carries a lethal array of antishipping missiles, torpedoes, and depth charges that are electronically tethered to the radar. Currently France is the sole operator, with 42 machines on order.

Dassault *Mirage 2000* ───────────────────────────── **France** ─

Type: Fighter; Light Bomber; Strategic Bomber

Dimensions: wingspan, 30 feet; length, 47 feet, 1 inch; height, 17 feet, 1 inch
Weights: empty, 16,535 pounds; gross, 37,478 pounds
Power plant: 1 × 14,460–pound thrust SNECMA M53-P2 turbofan engine
Performance: maximum speed, 1,543 miles per hour; ceiling, 54,000 feet; range, 2,073 miles
Armament: 2 × 30mm cannons; up to 13,890 pounds of conventional or nuclear weapons
Service dates: 1983–

The *Mirage 2000* represents the third generation of a famous fighter design. Assisted by the latest fly-by-wire technologies, it enjoys all the advantages of delta configuration with none of the vices.

By the early 1970s, the Armee de l'Air was considering a new generation of fighters to serve as its *avion de combat futur* (future combat fighter) and eventual replacement for *Mirage IIIs* and *F 1s* then in service. Dassault originally advanced the very large *F 2 Super Mirage* design, which was rejected as too costly. The French government then stipulated a smaller, lighter machine along the lines of the General Dynamics F-16. In 1975 Dassault was authorized to proceed with plans for the *Mirage 2000*, a much tidier aircraft with an inherent 1:1 thrust-to-weight ratio. It revived the classic delta wing of old that, in this instance, was carefully blended into the roots for less drag. Moreover, by utilizing fly-by-wire technology—whereby computers assist and correct pilots while maneuvering—the fuselage was built

with its center of gravity farther back than usual. This makes for an intrinsically unstable aircraft that is highly maneuverable. The delta wing was also increased in overall area to allow for lower wing loading (pounds per square foot of wing area), which in turn resulted in superior low-altitude performance. The first *Mirage 2000* flew in 1978, with initial deliveries arriving in 1983. Around 440 have been built.

In 1979 Dassault was asked to come up with a two-seat version of the *Mirage 2000* as a possible replacement for the aging *Mirage IV* nuclear bombers. The resulting Model *2000N* (nuclear) first flew in 1991 with heavily revised avionics and a strengthened airframe for low-altitude work. This capable craft employs an Antilope radar that enables safe flying as low as 200 feet while barreling along at 700 miles per hour! Conventionally armed versions of the craft, the *Mirage 2000D* and *S*, are also being developed for the export market. Various versions are also operated by Egypt, Taiwan, India, and Peru.

Type: Fighter; Light Bomber

Dimensions: wingspan, 30 feet, 6 inches; length, 50 feet, 2 inches; height, 14 feet, 9 inches
Weights: empty, 16,314 pounds; gross, 35,715 pounds
Power plant: 1 × SNECMA Atar 9K-50 turbojet engine
Performance: maximum speed, 1,453 miles per hour; ceiling, 65,615 feet; range, 520 miles
Armament: 2 × 30mm cannons; up to 13,889 pounds of bombs, missiles, and rockets
Service dates: 1973–

The multipurpose F 1 was an attempt to expand the flexibility of Dassault's already capable *Mirage III*. It has taken the basic design to new levels of efficiency and, like its predecessor, is operated by many nations.

Responding to a 1964 Armee de l'Air requirement for a new all-weather interceptor, Dassault began work on a two-seat, 20-ton design—the F 2—which retained some similarities to the earlier *Mirage III* but was much larger. At length this machine was rejected, but a smaller design—the F 1—was developed as a company-funded project. Basically, it utilized the fuselage of the *Mirage III* but was fitted with a shoulder-mounted swept wing and tail surfaces. This more conventional layout yielded immediate advantage over the delta configuration, being less susceptible to energy loss during rapid maneuvering. The new F 1 also enjoyed a runway roll rate less than half that of the *Mirage III*. And because bladder tanks were superceded by in-

tegral fuel space, the F 1 possesses 40 percent greater range. The French military was very pleased with the new machine, which became operational in 1973 as the F 1C. As an interceptor, it is capable of lifting off with only two minutes' warning. The advanced Cyrano II radar then enables it to track and lock on incoming targets, regardless of low-altitude ground clutter. The F 1 also makes a better ground-attack craft than the *Mirage III* family, especially with regard to turbulence, as it handles better at low altitude.

The F 1C, like its forebear, was an outstanding success story in terms of export, for it is employed by no less than 11 nations. Its most notorious user was Iraq, which used them with good effect during the lengthy Iran-Iraq War. During the 1991 Gulf War, *Mirage F 1s* had the dubious distinction of serving on both sides. More than 900 have been manufactured, and these will continue on as a major service type for years to come.

Type: Fighter; Light Bomber

Dimensions: wingspan, 26 feet, 11 inches; length, 49 feet, 3 inches; height, 14 feet, 9 inches
Weights: empty, 15,542 pounds; gross, 21,164 pounds
Power plant: 1 × 9,436–pound thrust SNECMA Atar 9C-3 turbojet engine
Performance: maximum speed, 1,460 miles per hour; ceiling, 75,460 feet; range, 746 miles
Armament: 2 × 30mm cannons; up to 8,818 pounds of bombs or rockets
Service dates: 1961–

The sleek _Mirage III_ remains one of the classic fighter designs of all time and helped propel France to the forefront of military aviation. Through constant upgrades, many still fly in frontline service around the world.

In 1952 the Armee de l'Air sought an advanced lightweight interceptor to replace its aging Dassault _Mysteres_. The desired craft was intended to be built around two small turbojets and a small rocket booster. Dassault complied with a small delta design, the _Mirage I_, in 1953, but it was rejected as insufficiently powered. The firm then went on to develop the bigger _Mirage III_ as a company project; it was powered by a single turbojet engine. In 1956 this craft became the first European warplane to exceed Mach 2, and the French military immediately expressed interest. The _Mirage III_ was a conventional delta design, with a relatively small wing and a sharp, pointed profile. It was highly maneuverable and handled well, but like all delta designs it suffered from

high landing speeds and a prolonged takeoff. Nonetheless, the first _Mirage III_ entered service in 1961 and was followed by numerous multimission variants. It was also widely exported abroad, especially to Israel, which used them with decisive effect in the 1967 war. Most French machines have since been retired, but _Mirage IIIs_ are continually upgraded and flown by several air forces, including Australia, Argentina, Brazil, and South Africa.

In 1967 Israel asked Dassault to design a cheaper ground-attack version, which subsequently emerged as the _Mirage 5_. This model lacked advanced radar systems in exchange for more fuel and greater payload. It too was an export success. The final development was the _Mirage 50_ of 1979, which utilizes the _Mirage 5_ airframe in concert with a more powerful engine and advanced avionics. It is currently utilized by more than 20 nations and will continue flying well into the twenty-first century. A total of 1,400 _Mirages_ of all variants has been constructed.

Type: Fighter

Dimensions: wingspan, 31 feet, 6 inches; length, 46 feet, 11 inches; height, 12 feet, 8 inches
Weights: empty, 14,220 pounds; gross, 25,353 pounds
Power plant: 1 × 11,025–pound thrust SNECMA Atar turbojet engine
Performance: maximum speed, 749 miles per hour; ceiling, 44,950 feet; range, 404 miles
Armament: 2 × 30mm cannons; 1 × AM39 *Exocet* missile
Service dates: 1978–

The *Super Etendard* is a modest strike fighter with transonic capabilities. However, once armed with the deadly *Exocet* antishipping missile, they sank two British ships during the 1982 Falkland Islands War.

In the early 1950s, NATO began seeking light, low-cost attack craft as alternatives to more expensive conventional jet fighters. In 1956 Dassault fielded its prototype *Etendard IV* (*etendard* meaning "standard" or "flag") as a competitor. It was a relatively small machine with sweptback wings and a pronounced fence under the chin. Being somewhat underpowered, it lost out to the Fiat G 91, but Dassault privately developed a navalized version with stronger landing gear and an arrester hook. In 1958 the French navy authorized production, and the first *Etendard IVs* joined the fleet in 1962 as reconnaissance/strike fighters. By 1971 a more modern replacement was needed, and the French government announced its intention to procure navalized *Jaguar M* aircraft. When that project unraveled because of spiraling cost overruns, Dassault again proposed a refurbished

Etendard machine. By the time they were deployed in 1982, they bore little commonality with the original craft and received the designation *Super Etendard*. The new machine boasts a bigger engine, greater fuel capacity, and a redesigned wing. It also possesses an advanced navigation/attack radar and can be refueled during flight. Although somewhat modest in performance compared to U.S. and British carrier aircraft, the *Super Etendard* is fully capable of deploying the very accurate *Exocet* antishipping missile.

In the spring of 1982, Argentina, which operated five *Super Etendards*, made world headlines when pilots sank the British destroyer HMS *Sheffield* and cargo ship *Atlantic Conveyor* off the Falkland Islands. The next customer to employ them was Iraq, then in a protracted struggle with Iran over control of the Persian Gulf. Iraqi pilots attacked several Iranian tankers and even badly damaged a U.S. destroyer—allegedly by mistake. These aircraft returned to France in 1985 in exchange for *Mirage F 1s*. Despite continual upgrades, the *Super Etendard* will be phased out by Dassault *Rafael Cs* in 2008.

Type: Trainer; Light Bomber

Dimensions: wingspan, 29 feet, 10 inches; length, 38 feet, 6 inches; height, 14 feet, 2 inches
Weights: empty, 7,374 pounds; gross, 17,637 pounds
Power plant: 2 × 2,976–pound thrust SNECMA/Turbomeca Larzac turbojet engines
Performance: maximum speed, 621 miles per hour; ceiling, 14,630 feet; range, 764 miles
Armament: none, or up to 5,511 pounds of bombs, rockets, or gunpods
Service dates: 1978–

The *Alphajet* was a Franco-German effort to build a modern jet trainer easily adapted to ground-attack missions. The design functioned well and continues to serve with the air forces of several nations.

By 1968 the rising expense associated with modern military aircraft induced two former enemies, France and Germany, to undertake joint development of an advanced trainer/light strike aircraft for their respective air forces. The new craft was intended to replace a host of aging Fouga *Magisters*, Lockheed T-33s, and Fiat G 91s. Two highly respected firms, Dassault and Dornier, then spent several years working out the final details before developing a prototype. The first *Alphajet* flew in 1975 as a modern shoulder-wing jet seating two crew members under a lengthy canopy. The rear seat is also staggered above the front one to afford instructors better forward vision. The wings and tail surfaces are all highly swept, and the final product compact yet attractive. The craft also possesses twin engines—a Luftwaffe requirement resulting from its unsavory experience with single-en-

gine Lockheed F-104 *Starfighters*. Given their dual function, the French and German versions differ widely as to avionics. The French use them as dedicated advanced trainers with less powerful systems. The Germans, meanwhile, fly theirs with the backseat removed and mount highly sophisticated radar, targeting, and communications equipment. Curiously, either version of the *Alphajet* can be rigged for ground attack with the addition of weapons pods and bombs. A total of 600 were built by 1982.

This high-performance package naturally aroused the interest of poorer nations, which sought increased firepower at bargain prices. Belgium, Egypt, Ivory Coast, Morocco, Nigeria, Qatar, Cameroon, and Togo all have purchased the diminutive craft and arrayed them with various weapons arrangements. After the collapse of the Soviet Union, Germany decided to mothball its fleet of *Alphajets* and has since sold 80 refurbished machines to Portugal. France, meanwhile, continues to upgrade its trainers, calling the new machines *Lanciers*.

Type: Fighter

Dimensions: wingspan, 28 feet, 3 inches; length, 25 feet, 2 inches; height, 9 feet, 6 inches
Weights: empty, 943 pounds; gross, 1,441 pounds
Power plant: 1 × 100–horsepower Gnome Monosoupape rotary engine
Performance: maximum speed, 93 miles per hour; ceiling, 14,000 feet; range, 250 miles
Armament: 1 × .303–inch machine gun
Service dates: 1916–1917

The fragile-looking DH 2 was the Royal Flying Corps's first true fighter plane. Tough and maneuverable, its appearance signified the end of Germany's "Fokker scourge."

The DH 2 single-seat fighter craft evolved from Geoffrey de Havilland's earlier DH 1 two-seat reconnaissance craft in 1915. Like its predecessor, the pilot sat in a central nacelle well forward of the two-bay wings, enjoying unrestricted frontal vision. The rotary pusher engine was immediately to his rear. The wings were conventional wood and canvas affairs, and four tail booms jutted rearward and attached to a vee-shaped structure fastening the tail. De Havilland opted for a pusher design because the British still lacked synchronization technology that permitted firing machine guns through a propeller arc. Therefore, the DH 2 possessed a single drum-fed Lewis machine gun mounted in the pilot's nacelle. In flight the craft flew only moderately fast, but it climbed well and was completely acrobatic.

The first DH 2s were deployed to France in January 1916 with No. 24 Squadron—the first purely conceived fighter unit ever operated by the Royal Flying Corps. Prior to this, British formations were mixed bags of various kinds of aircraft. Air superiority at this time had passed completely into German hands because of the notorious, machine gun–armed Fokker *Eindekker.* But the DH 2s, despite their unconventional appearance, proved first-class dogfighters and swept the sky of German opposition. On one occasion, a single pusher flown by Major L.W.B. Rees mistakenly joined what he thought were 10 British bombers returning from a raid. They turned out to be German, and in the ensuing scrape his DH 2 dispatched two of the enemy and scattered the rest. Rees subsequently received the Victoria Cross.

In the fall of 1916 the first Albatros D Is and D IIs appeared, and de Havilland's little pushers became completely outclassed. They sustained heavy losses before withdrawing from frontline service in 1917. Nonetheless, the DH 2 had made its mark as Britain's first successful fighter.

Type: Light Bomber

Dimensions: wingspan, 42 feet, 5 inches; length, 30 feet, 8 inches; height, 11 feet
Weights: empty, 2,300 pounds; gross, 3,472 pounds
Power plant: 1 × 375–horsepower Rolls-Royce Eagle liquid-cooled in-line engine
Performance: maximum speed, 136 miles per hour; ceiling, 20,000 feet; range, 420 miles
Armament: up to 4 × .303–inch machine guns; 460 pounds of bombs
Service dates: 1917–1932

The DH 4 was the first British aircraft specifically designed for daylight bombing and among the best of its kind in World War I. It was built in even greater numbers by the United States and enjoyed considerable longevity there.

The DH 4 was designed in response to a 1916 Air Ministry specification for a new daylight-bombing aircraft, the first acquired by the Royal Flying Corps. A prototype was flown in August of that year and proved entirely successful. The DH 4 was a standard two-bay biplane constructed of wood and fabric. The fuselage consisted of two complete halves bolted together, with the forward half covered in plywood for greater strength. Another distinguishing feature was the widely spaced cockpits, between which sat a large fuel tank. Such placement facilitated better views for the pilot and gunner but rather hindered close cooperation. It was also fitted with dual flight controls for both crew members. The DH 4 was originally supposed to be powered by the splendid Rolls-Royce Eagle engine but they proved unavailable, so several other power plants were employed.

In service the DH 4 was a superb airplane. Fully loaded, it was as fast as most fighters and could absorb considerable damage. Great numbers were employed by both the Royal Flying Corps and its naval equivalent, and it enjoyed a wide-ranging career from France to Palestine. As such, DH 4s were successfully employed in bombing, reconnaissance, and antisubmarine patrols. In August 1918 a Royal Navy DH 4 even managed to shoot down a Zeppelin L 70. The DH 4 was also the only British warplane to be manufactured in great numbers by the United States; the U.S.-built machines were powered by the famous Liberty in-line engine. By 1918 DH 4s equipped no less that 11 American and nine Royal Air Force squadrons. The British, who built 1,449 examples, discarded them after the war, but the Americans went on to construct an additional 4,686 machines. They underwent constant modifications and remained in service until 1932.

Type: Light Bomber

Dimensions: wingspan, 45 feet, 11 inches; length, 30 feet, 3 inches; height, 11 feet, 4 inches
Weights: empty, 2,800 pounds; gross, 4,645 pounds
Power plant: 1 × 400–horsepower Packard Liberty liquid-cooled in-line engine
Performance: maximum speed, 123 miles per hour; ceiling, 16,750 feet; range, 600 miles
Armament: 3 × .303–inch machine guns; 660 pounds of bombs
Service dates: 1918–1931

The original DH 9, which suffered from a poor engine, had been foisted upon the Royal Flying Corps through governmental bureaucracy and proved a disaster. Fortunately, the much improved DH 9a became a splendid bomber it its own right and subsequently accrued a distinguished service record.

By 1917 the rising tempo of German raids against England forced the British High Command to increase its own bomber force for retaliatory purposes. The government then decided to replace the excellent DH 4 with an updated version, christened the DH 9. This new machine utilized the same wing and empennage as the DH 4, but it enjoyed closer cockpits and a new—and theoretically more powerful—BHP engine. However, in service the BHP was underpowered and completely unreliable, making the DH 9's performance inferior to the craft it was meant to replace. Also, their low-ceiling performance subjected them to attacks by both fighters and antiaircraft batteries; in time losses grew prohibitive. Despite appeals from General Hugh Tren-

chard to get rid of the DH 9 altogether, the government had other priorities, and full-scale production was maintained. A total of 4,000 were acquired.

In view of the DH 9's poor performance, a new version, the DH 9a, was developed. This appeared very similar to the old craft, although it employed greater wingspan and a stronger fuselage. Shortages of the splendid Rolls-Royce Eagle engine forced it to employ the 400-horsepower Liberty engine, built in the United States. The result of coupling a good engine to a fine airframe was an excellent aircraft that went by the sobriquet of "Nine-ack." DH 9as fought with distinction toward the end of World War I and remained in production after the Armistice. No less than 2,500 were built during the postwar period, and they continued in frontline service until 1931. Nine-acks were best remembered for the policing role they fulfilled across the British Empire, particularly along the North-West Frontier of India. Their reliable performance was greatly appreciated by crews, because crash-landing usually meant death at the hands of hostile tribesmen.

Type: Heavy Bomber

Dimensions: wingspan, 65 feet, 6 inches; length, 39 feet, 7 inches; height, 14 feet, 6 inches
Weights: empty, 5,585 pounds; gross, 9,000 pounds
Power plant: 2 × 400–horsepower Packard Liberty liquid-cooled in-line engines
Performance: maximum speed, 112 miles per hour; ceiling, 17,000 feet; range, 600 miles
Armament: 2 × .303–inch machine guns; 1,280 pounds of bombs
Service dates: 1918–1922

The jut-jawed DH 10 was one of the finest bomber designs of World War I, but it arrived too late for combat. It is best remembered as a postwar mail carrier that pioneered vital air routes in Europe, Egypt, and India.

In 1916 Geoffrey de Havilland designed a twin-engine pusher-type bomber known informally as the DH 3. It was a proficient design, and the Air Ministry placed an order for 50 machines. When production was canceled before the first example could be built, the project was summarily shelved until 1917. That year a new specification for heavy bombers was circulated, and de Havilland decided to upgrade his previous design. The resulting craft was named the DH 10, a three-seat, three-bay biplane pusher. It was distinct in that the fuselage was slung low, partially covered in plywood, and it employed a wide-track undercarriage. An ongoing shortage of Rolls-Royce engines prompted switching to the reliable American Liberty model, which were ultimately mounted in tractor position. As a bomber the DH 10 hoisted twice the bomb load of the DH 9a at higher speed and altitude. In the summer of 1918 a contract for 1,275 machines was placed.

The DH 10 was an excellent bomber for its day, strongly built and easy to fly. Had the war continued it would have become very numerous, but only eight had arrived in France by the time of the Armistice. Production then ceased at 223 machines, which were dispersed among various squadrons in Europe, Africa, and India. The DH 10 spent the rest of its days as a utility craft, most notably as a mail carrier. In 1919 the machines of No. 120 Squadron commenced the first night service between Hawkinge, England, and Cologne, Germany. Similar work was performed by DH 10s of No. 216 Squadron along the Cairo-to-Baghdad route. It finally had an opportunity to drop bombs in 1920–1922, during a revolt of rebel tribesmen along India's North-West Frontier.

Type: Trainer

Dimensions: wingspan, 29 feet, 4 inches; length, 23 feet, 11 inches; height, 8 feet, 9 inches
Weights: empty, 1,200 pounds; gross, 1,825 pounds
Power plant: 1 × 120–horsepower DH Gypsy liquid-cooled in-line engine
Performance: maximum speed, 109 miles per hour; ceiling, 13,600 feet; range, 300 miles
Armament: none
Service dates: 1932–1947

The ubiquitous _Tiger Moth_ was the last biplane trainer of the Royal Air Force and among the most numerous. During World War II it trained thousands of British and Commonwealth pilots from around the globe.

The great commercial and acrobatic success of de Havilland's _Moth_ aircraft in the late 1920s caused military circles to consider its adoption as a trainer. Around that time the RAF began employing the popular DH 60T _Gypsy Moth_ variant, which had been modified to allow pilots easier escape from the front cockpit while wearing a parachute. This meant staggering the top wing forward and providing it with several degrees of sweep. After several more refinements, it was introduced into the service as the DH 82 _Tiger Moth_, quite possibly the greatest biplane trainer of all time. This fabric-covered, compact little craft had single-bay wings and an inverted engine to improve the frontal view. As airplanes, _Tiger Moths_ were gentle and forgiving—perfect for training inexperienced pilots. However, they were also strong,

completely acrobatic, and could be literally thrown around the sky with abandon. A second model, the DH 82A _Tiger Moth II_, mounted a canvas hood over the rear cockpit to teach instrument flying.

By the advent of World War II in 1939, 1,611 _Tiger Moths_ were in use at 28 Elementary Flying Schools across Britain. During the war the number of machines increased exponentially, with more than 8,000 being manufactured in England, Canada, Australia, and New Zealand. Literally thousands of Commonwealth pilots took the first step toward winning their wings by strapping themselves into _Tiger Moths!_ During the war, several DH 82s were impressed into service as communications aircraft and flying ambulances. The threatened invasion of England in 1940 prompted others to be fitted with bomb racks. A radio-controlled version, the _Queen Bee_, also served as a flying drone for aerial gunnery. After the war, _Tiger Moths_ remained frontline trainers until 1947. Hundreds still fly today in private hands, and they remain beloved machines.

Type: Reconnaissance; Light Bomber; Fighter; Night Fighter

Dimensions: wingspan, 54 feet, 2 inches; length, 41 feet, 6 inches; height, 15 feet, 3 inches
Weights: empty, 16,631 pounds; gross, 25,500 pounds
Power plant: 2 × 1,710–horsepower Rolls-Royce Merlin 76 liquid-cooled in-line engines
Performance: maximum speed, 425 miles per hour; ceiling, 36,000 feet; range, 3,500 miles
Armament: 4 × 20mm cannons; 4 × .303–inch machine guns; up to 4,000 pounds of bombs
Service dates: 1941–1955

Hailed as the "Wooden Wonder," the *Mosquito* was among the most versatile and proficient warplanes of World War II. It saw service in a countless variety of roles and enjoyed the lowest loss rate of any Royal Air Force aircraft.

In 1938 the de Havilland company proposed a high-speed reconnaissance aircraft flown by only two men. The new craft would be totally unarmed, relying solely upon speed for survival. Moreover, to de-emphasize use of strategic resources like metal, de Havilland wanted the plane entirely made from wood. Understandably, officials at the Air Ministry simply scoffed at the proposal. The company nonetheless proceeded to construct several prototypes that first flew in 1940. The country was at war with Germany then, and severely hard-pressed, but ministry officials remained hostile to the notion of wooden warplanes. Their minds completely changed when the first *Mosquitos* demonstrated speeds and maneuverability usually associated with single-engine fighters. The aircraft was then rushed into production and flew its first daylight reconnais-

sance mission over Paris in 1941. When the "Mossies" easily outpaced pursuing German fighters, a legend was born.

During the next four years, de Havilland produced great quantities of *Mosquitos* in a bewildering variety of types. They capably performed several roles with distinction: reconnaissance, night fighter, day fighter, and light bomber. Fast and almost unstoppable, *Mosquitos* were also famous for their pinpoint accurate bombing raids. In January 1943 they interrupted a speech given by Luftwaffe chief Hermann Göring—then returned later that day to drop bombs on a rally given by propaganda chief Joseph Goebbels. Lightning raids against Gestapo headquarters in The Hague and Copenhagen were also a specialty. *Mosquitos* served in Europe, the Mediterranean, and the Pacific, suffering the lowest loss rate of any British aircraft. After the war they remained the fastest machines in RAF Bomber Command inventory until overtaken by *Canberra* jet bombers in 1951. A total of 7,781 *Mosquitos* were built—truly one of the world's greatest warplanes.

Type: Fighter; Light Bomber; Trainer

Dimensions: wingspan, 38 feet; length, 30 feet, 9 inches; height, 8 feet, 10 inches
Weights: empty, 7,283 pounds; gross, 12,390 pounds
Power plant: 1 × 3,350–pound thrust de Havilland Goblin turbojet engine
Performance: maximum speed, 548 miles per hour; ceiling, 42,800 feet; range, 1,220 miles
Armament: 4 × 20mm cannons; 2,000 pounds of bombs or rockets
Service dates: 1946–1990

The diminutive *Vampire* was England's second jet fighter and spawned a large number of subtypes. It enjoyed a lengthy career and was exported to no less than 25 nations.

The British Air Ministry issued Specification E.6/41 in 1941 to obtain a jet fighter built around a single de Havilland Goblin centrifugal-flow turbojet. The relatively low thrust of this early engine virtually dictated the design because of the necessity to keep the tailpipe as short as possible. De Havilland responded with a unique twin-boomed approach. The fuselage was a bulbous pod housing the pilot, engine, nosewheel, and armament. The pilot sat in a cockpit close to the nose and under a bubble canopy that afforded excellent vision. The all-metal wing was mid-mounted and affixed by twin booms extending rearward, themselves joined by a single stabilizer. The prototype first flew in September 1943, with Geoffrey de Havilland Jr. at the controls. He reported excellent flight characteristics, even at breathtaking

speeds of 500 miles per hour. In 1946 the aircraft entered the service as the DH 100 *Vampire* (the original designation was *Spider Crab*). Subsequent modifications yielded the Mk III, which had larger fuel tanks and a redesigned tail. However, it was not until 1949 that the major production version, the FB Mk 5, arrived. It featured clipped wings, longer undercarriage, and the ability to carry rockets and bombs.

The *Vampire* exhibited such docile handling in flight that it was an ideal trainer. It was also exported around the world and saw extensive service with 25 air forces. Switzerland operated its *Vampires* with little interruption until 1991. On December 3, 1945, a Royal Navy *Sea Vampire* also became the first pure jet to operate off a carrier deck. This version, naturally, was stressed for catapulting and used an arrester hook. One final model, the NF Mk 10, was a two-seat night fighter version with radar. The total number of *Vampires* manufactured was around 2,000. It was a classic early jet design.

Type: Fighter; Light Bomber

Dimensions: wingspan, 50 feet; length, 55 feet, 7 inches; height, 10 feet, 9 inches
Weights: empty, 22,000; gross, 36,000 pounds
Power plant: 2 × 11,250–pound thrust Rolls-Royce Avon turbojet engines
Performance: maximum speed, 650 miles per hour; ceiling, 48,000 feet; range, 600 miles
Armament: 4 × *Firestreak*, *Red Top*, or *Bullpup* missiles
Service dates: 1959–1972

The formidable *Sea Vixen* compiled a litany of firsts for the Fleet Air Arm. It was the Royal Navy's first all-weather interceptor, the first designed as an integrated weapons system, and the first armed solely with missiles.

In 1946 the British Admiralty issued Specification N.40/46, later upgraded to N.14/49, which instigated development of a twin-engine radar-equipped jet fighter. De Havilland, which had pioneered twin-boomed jet fighters, advanced the DH 110 design, but initially the navy rejected it in favor of the lower-powered *Sea Venom*. When the Royal Air Force also passed on it for what ultimately become the Gloster *Javelin*, the Fleet Air Arm took a second look and decided the craft was worth pursuing after all. The prototype debuted in 1951 as a most impressive warplane. The DH 110 was a large machine with the crew compartment and twin engines mounted within a central, streamlined pod. The twin booms streamed back from the highly swept wing and were joined farther aft by a single control surface. The pilot and radar operator sat side by side, but only the pilot was provided with a canopy, offset to the left. The DH 110 was a powerful flier, and during early testing it became the first British aircraft to break the sound barrier in a dive. When the prototype subsequently broke up in flight, development halted and several years of bureaucratic indecision ensued. Consequently, the first FAW.1 *Sea Vixens* did not reach the fleet until 1959.

In service the *Sea Vixen* proved itself a powerful addition to the fleet, both as an interceptor and a ground-attack plane (mounting U.S.-made *Bullpup* guided missiles). By 1961 a new version, the FAW.2, appeared, featuring revised booms extending over the front wing to carry additional fuel. This model also was the first navy fighter to dispense with cannons entirely in favor of four *Firestreak* or *Red Top* missiles. A total of 148 *Sea Vixens* were built, with the last retiring in 1972.

Type: Fighter; Light Bomber; Night Fighter

Dimensions: wingspan, 41 feet, 8 inches; length, 33 feet; height, 6 feet, 8 inches
Weights: empty, 8,100 pounds; gross, 15,310 pounds
Power plant: 1 × 4,850–pound thrust de Havilland Ghost turbojet engine
Performance: maximum speed, 640 miles per hour; ceiling, 45,000 feet; range, 1,075 miles
Armament: 4 × 20mm cannons; up to 2,000 pounds of bombs and rockets
Service dates: 1952–1990

The *Venom* was a successor to the earlier *Vampire*, but not nearly as popular. It nonetheless filled a critical niche in several areas until more advanced machines could be deployed.

Continuing refinement of the de Havilland Goblin engine resulted in a totally new version, the Ghost, which featured 50 percent more thrust. This power plant was fitted into a heavily redesigned DH 100 *Vampire* in 1949, and the resulting hybrid gained a new designation as the DH 112 *Venom*. It bore striking similarity to its forebear, but it enjoyed the advantage of a wholly redesigned, thinner wing of broader chord. Consequently, the *Venom* possessed much higher performance than the *Vampire*. The Royal Air Force immediately ordered the type into production, and it became operational in 1952. The *Venom* was employed initially as a fighter-bomber, and the FB.1s and FB.4s could carry useful payloads. Both France and Switzerland obtained license to manufacture the craft domestically; the Swiss

models flew regularly in frontline service up to 1990. Two night-fighter versions, the NF.2 and NF.3 were also developed that sat a crew of two side by side. These superceded the *Vampire* NF 10s after 1953 and rendered useful service until being replaced by Gloster *Javelins* in 1957.

The Fleet Air Arm was naturally interested in such good performance, and in 1954 it accepted deliveries of the *Sea Venom* FAW. These were the Royal Navy's first all-weather interceptor and featured arrester hooks, folding wings, and other naval equipment. They also sat a crew of two in side-by-side configuration. In 1956 *Sea Venoms* were at the forefront of the Anglo-French intervention during the Suez Crisis, making large-scale ground attacks in support of army units. Two years later *Sea Venoms* pioneered the use of *Firestreak* guided missiles as standard Fleet Air Arm armament. They served well until the arrival of the de Havilland DH 110 *Sea Vixen* in 1959. Around 500 of all types were built.

⭐ de Havilland Canada DHC 1 *Chipmunk* ———————————————— Canada

Type: Trainer

Dimensions: wingspan, 34 feet, 4 inches; length, 25 feet, 5 inches; height, 7 feet
Weights: empty, 1,425 pounds; gross, 2,014 pounds
Power plant: 1 × 145–horsepower de Havilland Gypsy air-cooled in-line engine
Performance: maximum speed, 138 miles per hour; ceiling, 15,800 feet; range, 280 miles
Armament: none
Service dates: 1946–1996

The famous *Chipmunk* was de Havilland Canada's first product and a very successful one at that. Built in large numbers, it trained pilots in Canada, England, and countries across the world.

Even before World War II had concluded, de Havilland and its Canadian subsidiary began negotiating for a new postwar trainer. Such a craft would be invariably compared against the immortal *Tiger Moth*, one of the greatest training machines of all time. If successful, the parent company even offered help in marketing it abroad. By 1946 a design team headed by W. J. Jakimiuk created a simple, robust machine that they dubbed the *Chipmunk*. It was a low-wing monoplane constructed entirely of metal, save for the control surfaces, which were fabric-covered. Under a braced canopy sat pupil and instructor in tandem, and the craft also employed fixed landing gear. Intended as a primary trainer, the first DHC 1 *Chipmunks* accepted into Canadian service were not stressed and, consequently, not entirely acrobatic. They were, however, gentle, responsive airplanes and quite popular in their intended role. By

1951 de Havilland Canada manufactured 218 *Chipmunks*. Many were subsequently fitted with a blown bubble canopy for better all-around vision.

In 1951 several DHC 1s were dispatched to England for evaluation as a standard Royal Air Force trainer. Flight tests were successful, but the RAF insisted on certain modifications to bring the machine up to their more rigorous standards. These included a variable-pitch propeller, all-around stressing, landing lights, antispin stakes, and landing gear that were moved forward. This done, the parent de Havilland company produced an additional 740 *Chipmunks* for the RAF. These machines fleshed out virtually every training squadron in the service for several years. Others were taken to Germany, stripped of their rear seat, and employed as light communications aircraft. A handful were also employed in Cyprus for internal security duties during difficulties there in 1958. Thereafter, several score found markets abroad. The venerable DHC 1s remained in declining numbers until 1996, when all were officially discharged. Several hundred still fly today in private hands.

– 92 –

Type: Fighter

Dimensions: wingspan, 39 feet, 8 inches; length, 26 feet; height, 8 feet, 10 inches
Weights: empty, 2,870; gross, 4,235 pounds
Power plant: 1 × 860–horsepower Hispano-Suiza 12Ycrs liquid-cooled in-line engine
Performance: maximum speed, 250 miles per hour; ceiling, 34,500 feet; range, 435 miles
Armament: 2 × 7.7mm machine guns, 1 × 20mm cannon
Service dates: 1935–1940

The Dewoitine 500 series represented the most modern, technically ambitious fighters of their day. They marked a transition phase between open-cockpit biplanes of the 1920s and the more modern aircraft of World War II.

In 1930 the French Aeronautique Militaire issued specifications for a new fighter to replace the aging Nieuport-Delage ND 62s then deployed. It fell upon designer Emile Dewoitine to conceive a revolutionary new concept that spelled the beginning of the end for biplanes. First flown in 1932, the Dewoitine 500 exuded modernity. It was a cantilevered, low-wing monoplane constructed entirely of metal. The craft was covered by stressed metal sheeting and completely devoid of drag-inducing struts and bracing wires. The only seemingly antiquated feature was fixed landing gear with conspicuous oblong spats. The in-line engine was closely covered by a pointed cowl, giving the craft an ultramodern, very sleek appearance. In the air, the Dewoitine was faster than its biplane contemporaries, more maneuverable, and, because of its metal construction,

much stronger. The Armee de l'Air was duly impressed by the new machine, and it entered production in 1933. Within two years a total of 143 were built, including a number of cannon-armed Model 501s.

In August 1934 Dewoitine fielded a more refined version, the Model 510. It mounted a larger rudder, an uprated engine, and other aerodynamic refinements. Consequently, it became the first French fighter to exceed 250 miles per hour in level flight. The French air service acquired an additional 120 of these sleek machines, with a further 30 being assigned to the Navy's Aviation Maritime (naval air arm). These craft also caught the attention of several governments and were exported abroad, with China acquiring 24 D 510s, Lithuania 14. The Dewoitine series still equipped several frontline units as late as 1940, at which time they had been overtaken and rendered obsolete by the newer Messerschmitt Bf 109. Nonetheless, the D 500 series made history by anticipating modern design trends by several years.

Type: Fighter

Dimensions: wingspan, 33 feet, 5 inches; length, 28 feet, 8 inches; height, 8 feet, 5 inches
Weights: empty, 4,685 pounds; gross, 5,897 pounds
Power plant: 1 × 930–horsepower Hispano-Suiza 12Y45 liquid-cooled in-line engine
Performance: maximum speed, 332 miles per hour; ceiling, 33,620 feet; range, 553 miles
Armament: 4 × 7.5mm machine guns; 1 × 20mm cannon
Service dates: 1939–1947

Dewoitine's racy D 520 was the most modern and capable French fighter of World War II. It fought with distinction in 1940 and went on to serve Vichy forces in Syria and North Africa.

By 1937 the French government felt pressing needs for new and more modern fighter aircraft. That year the Morane-Saulnier MS 405 won the competition when Dewoitine's entry, the D 513, proved inferior. The company subsequently went back to the drawing board under Emile Dewoitine, Robert Castello, and Jacques Henrat to redesign a totally new machine. The D 520 prototype first flew in October 1938 and was completely successful. It was an all-metal, low-wing monoplane fighter with stressed skin and retractable undercarriage. It was also heavily armed, possessing up to four machine guns and an engine-mounted 20mm cannon firing through the propeller hub. Moreover, the fighter plane proved impressively maneuverable and responsive, and it was faster than the MS 405. In 1939 the French government decided to purchase it in quantity.

The commencement of World War II in September 1939 did little to shake off the bureaucratic lethargy that plagued the French arms industry throughout the 1930s. Consequently, only one *group de chasse* (fighter group) was equipped with D 520s when the Germans invaded France in May 1940. Aircraft and pilots fought splendidly, claiming 147 enemy craft with a loss of 44 fighters, but France was nonetheless overwhelmed. Throughout the ensuing Vichy period, Germany allowed the D 520 to remain in production, and a total of 786 machines were built. They went on to reequip French forces in Syria and North Africa as Axis allies. In this capacity D 520s shot down numerous English airplanes while sustaining heavy losses of their own. In November 1942 Germany occupied Vichy France and impressed the surviving D 520s as trainers. After the Allied liberation of 1944, many Dewoitine fighters again passed into French hands and delivered parting shots against the retreating Germans. Several D 520s were subsequently converted into two-seat trainers and flown until 1947.

Type: Glider; Transport

Dimensions: wingspan, 68 feet, 5 inches; length, 36 feet, 10 inches; height, 9 feet
Weights: empty, 1,896 pounds; gross, 4,630 pounds
Power plant: none
Performance: maximum speed, 180 miles per hour
Armament: 1 × 7.92mm machine gun
Service dates: 1938–1945

The DFS 230 undertook the world's first, successful glider assault in 1940. Thereafter it was widely employed in less glamorous work of a supply transport.

In 1932 an experimental glider had been designed by the Rhon-Rossitten Gesellschaft agency for meteorological research. Soon it came to the attention of Luftwaffe leader Ernst Udet, who envisioned military potential for such craft. Accordingly, a prototype was constructed by the firm Deutsches Forschunginstitut fur Segelflug and tested in 1937 before a large gathering of senior officers. The DFS 230 was a high-wing design with a boxlike fuselage that took off under tow, jettisoned its wheeled undercarriage, and landed on a belly skid. It was flown by a crew of two and could hold up to eight soldiers. In the hands of noted aviatrix Hanna Reitsch, the prototype landed within a few feet of the generals and quickly disgorged its passengers. Following this impressive display, the glider entered into production, and by 1938 Germany possessed the world's first glider assault force.

In battle, the DFS 230s were usually towed by Junkers Ju 52 transports and released over a target, arriving silently and unannounced to the surprise of defenders. This is exactly what transpired on May 10, 1940, when 41 DFS 230s were assigned to take strategic Fort Eben-Emael on the Prince Albert Canal in Belgium. Nine gliders landed directly on target, stormed the fort, and held it against Belgian forces until the main German army arrived the following day. In May 1941 an even bigger force of 53 DFS 230s was towed in broad daylight over the British-held island of Crete. Resistance was fierce and losses heavy, but the island eventually succumbed to what was then the world's largest airborne assault. Thereafter, most DFS 230s were employed in Russia, ferrying much-needed supplies to troops at the front. But perhaps their most notorious mission occurred on September 12, 1943, in Abruzzi, Italy. There a glider force under legendary commando Otto Skorzeny put down on mountainous terrain just outside the Rifugio Hotel and rescued Italian dictator Benito Mussolini. A total of 1,022 of these useful gliders were built.

Type: Reconnaissance

Dimensions: wingspan, 43 feet, 7 inches; length, 25 feet, 10 inches; height, 19 feet, 8 inches
Weights: empty, 2,143 pounds; gross, 3,146 pounds
Power plant: 1 × 200–horsepower Benz Bz IV liquid-cooled in-line engine
Performance: maximum speed, 97 miles per hour; ceiling, 16,400 feet; range, 350 miles
Armament: 2 × 7.92mm machine guns
Service dates: 1916–1918

The ubiquitous DFW C series was built in greater numbers than any other German aircraft of World War I. Amazingly acrobatic, it frequently outmaneuvered the latest Allied fighters.

Throughout 1914–1916 Deutsche Flugzeug-Werke manufactured an unarmed two-seat reconnaissance aircraft called the B I. Once outmoded by more advanced allied fighters, it spent the rest of the war in training capacities. Meanwhile, DFW moved ahead on newer two-seaters—the C series, which was both armed and more maneuverable than the earlier machines. The most important was the C IV, which appeared at the front in the spring of 1916. It was a conventional two-bay biplane constructed of wood and fabric. The 150-horsepower Benz III engine was semi-cowled in Germanic fashion to facilitate cooling, and it sported a typical "rhinoceros"-type exhaust pipe. In service the C IV demonstrated excellent qualities, but the introduction of better enemy fighters again prompted DFW to update the basic design.

A new machine—the C V—emerged in the summer of 1916. It was outwardly very similar to the C IV but possessed a more powerful Benz IV engine and other aeronautical refinements. Among them were rounded tail contours, balanced tail surfaces, and side radiators. This last item was subject to considerable revision once the machine was mass-produced, and later-model C Vs were fitted with a box-type leading-edge device. The C V was well adapted for photographic and artillery-spotting roles and retained all the maneuverability of earlier models. Moreover, it could easily outturn the latest French and British fighters in pursuit. DFW ultimately constructed 2,340 C types, making them the most numerous German aircraft of this conflict. C Vs constituted the largest variant produced and were manufactured by DFW, Aviatik, and Halberstadt. More than 600 C Vs remained in frontline service by war's end. On June 17, 1919, a C V established a world altitude record of 31,561 feet.

Type: Reconnaissance

Dimensions: wingspan, 77 feet, 9 inches; length, 63 feet, 2 inches; height, 17 feet, 6 inches
Weights: empty, 12,897 pounds; gross, 22,046 pounds
Power plant: 2 × 880–horsepower Junkers Jumo 205D liquid-cooled in-line engines
Performance: maximum speed, 162 miles per hour; ceiling, 13,780 feet; range, 2,175 miles
Armament: 1 × 13mm machine gun; 1 × 20mm cannon; 220 pounds of bombs
Service dates: 1939–1942

Graceful Do 18s formed the bulk of Luftwaffe maritime reconnaissance units in the early days of World War II. One of them suffered the indignity of becoming the first German aircraft lost to British forces.

Throughout the late 1920s, Deutsche Lufthansa transatlantic business was conducted on the Dornier Do 15 *Wal* (Whale) flying boat, which established several record flights. In 1934 its successor, the Do 18, first appeared. This craft incorporated many characteristics of the previous design, having retained the two large sponsons on either side of the midfuselage. These features endowed it with stability in the water and also provided additional lift while in flight. The Do 18 was powered by two engines in tandem arrangement, one pulling and one pushing, atop of the wing. Several were acquired by Lufthansa in 1936, and within two years one Do 18 established a world record by flying 5,214 miles nonstop from Germany to Brazil. The Luftwaffe, which had also employed the older Do 15, began utilizing

Do 18s as of 1939. These differed from civilian versions by having more powerful engines and gunner positions in the bow and midships.

Do 18s ultimately equipped five squadrons in the *Kustenfliegergruppen* (coastal reconnaissance groups) by the advent of World War II. They served primarily over the Baltic and North Sea, keeping a wary eye on British naval movements. On September 26, 1939, three Do 18s were shadowing the British fleet when they were suddenly attacked by Blackburn *Skuas* from the carrier HMS *Ark Royal*. One of the stately flying boats was shot down, becoming the first German plane lost in combat to Britain. After 1940 the Do 18s were slowly withdrawn from maritime reconnaissance in favor of air/sea rescue missions. These craft were subsequently painted all white with large red crosses and largely ignored until the British discovered them conducting electronic surveillance. By 1942 the handful of Do 18s still in service functioned as trainers.

Type: Medium Bomber

Dimensions: wingspan, 84 feet; length, 61 feet, 8 inches; height, 18 feet
Weights: empty, 14,080 pounds; gross, 20,240 pounds
Power plant: 2 × 750–horsepower BMW VIU liquid-cooled in-line engines
Performance: maximum speed, 161 miles per hour; ceiling, 13,776 feet; range, 840 miles
Armament: 3 × 7.92mm machine guns; 2,205 pounds of bombs
Service dates: 1935–1940

The Do 23, Germany's first large bomber aircraft since World War I, was by most aviation standards an operational flop. However, it played a major role in helping reconstitute the Luftwaffe bomber force.

By 1930 Germany was increasingly disposed to ignore provisions of the 1918 Armistice, which forbade the nation from possessing combat aircraft. A number of firms, such as Dornier, had opened subsidiaries in Switzerland and other places to clandestinely develop such weapons. In this instance, Dornier had been entrusted to design Germany's first large bomber since World War I. The prototype Do F was constructed at the company's Swiss Altenhein factory in 1929, where it was marketed as a cargo transport intended for the German rail service. It was a twin-engine, high-wing monoplane design of metal construction. The fuselage was rectangular in cross-section, and the lengthy wings possessed a long chord. The big craft also possessed rudimentary retractable landing gear. The Do F was employed exactly as advertised, despite its uncanny

resemblance to a bomber. Moreover, its crews were actually military personnel being clandestinely trained in the rudiments of aerial warfare. From this was developed a more refined version, the Do 11, in 1933. With Adolf Hitler now in power, all pretense toward civilian applications was dropped.

The Do 11 bomber appeared very similar to the Do F, save for a glazed bombardier section in the nose. It entered production as the Luftwaffe's first bomber but was unpopular due to bad landing characteristics; only 79 were produced. Another failed version, the Do 13, was also made in small numbers. When these were subsequently modified with revised wing and tail surfaces in 1936, the type was reintroduced as the Do 23. A total of 273 units were built, fleshing out the first Luftwaffe bomber groups. The airplane performed well as a trainer, but its shortcomings as a bomber meant early retirement from frontline service in 1937. A handful survived during World War II and were outfitted with degaussing equipment for oceanic minefield work.

Type: Reconnaissance

Dimensions: wingspan, 88 feet, 7 inches; length, 72 feet, 2 inches; height, 17 feet, 10 inches
Weights: empty, 29,700 pounds; gross, 40,565 pounds
Power plant: 3 × 1,000–horsepower Bramo Fafnir radial engines
Performance: maximum speed, 211 miles per hour; ceiling, 19,360 feet; range, 2,950 miles
Armament: 2 × 7.92mm machine guns; 1 × 20mm cannon; 1,200 pounds of bombs
Service dates: 1939–1945

The Do 24 saw widespread service with the Luftwaffe as a reconnaissance and air/sea rescue craft. Throughout this same period it found similar employment with the Dutch and later Spanish navies.

In 1935 the Dutch government approached Dornier to build a new flying boat for use in the Royal Netherlands Naval Air Service. Because work on the Do 18 had just completed, the new airplane incorporated many features of its predecessor. The Do 24 was an all-metal, high-wing monoplane that utilized a typical two-step Dornier hull with large flotation sponsons on either side of the fuselage. The sizable tapered wing was fastened above the hull with struts and mounted three engines. A large twin rudder system was also employed. Service trials were excellent, and in 1939 the Do 24 entered Dutch service as part of the East Indies Air Forces. Several were also constructed in Holland under license.

In December 1941 the Japanese attack on the Dutch East Indies destroyed no less than nine Do 24s. The remainder then fled to Australia, where another four succumbed to strafing. The surviving six Do 24s subsequently served with the Royal Australian Air Force in intelligence capacities until 1945. Following the German occupation of the Low Countries in 1940, all Do 24s then under production were seized and impressed by the Luftwaffe. These machines were outfitted as air/sea rescue craft and extensively flown in the Arctic, the Mediterranean, the North Sea, and the Atlantic. The Do 24 distinguished itself in this capacity, being stoutly built and able to operate in rough water conditions. In one instance a Do 24 lost its tail section in high seas, so the crew simply sealed off the leak and taxied several hundred miles to land! Production of this useful craft was maintained in France and Holland, with a total of 294 being built. As a goodwill gesture to Spain, several Do 24s were sold in 1944, and they operated as air/sea rescue craft up through the 1970s.

Type: Liaison; Trainer

Dimensions: wingspan, 39 feet, 4 inches; length, 31 feet, 4 inches; height, 8 feet, 10 inches
Weights: empty, 2,167 pounds; gross, 3,460 pounds
Power plant: 1 × 275–horsepower Lycoming GO-480 air-cooled engine
Performance: maximum speed, 155 miles per hour; ceiling, 10,825 feet; range, 685 miles
Armament: none
Service dates: 1957–

The Do 27 was a successful postwar design and marked Germany's reentry into military aviation. It was a functional, rugged aircraft with an exceptionally varied and lengthy service life.

In the aftermath of World War II, Germany was forbidden to possess or manufacture military aircraft of any kind. Consequently, Dr. Claude Dornier was forced to set up his office in Spain to continue working. In 1954 he received from the Spanish government specifications for a new light utility craft with STOL (short takeoff and landing) capabilities. That year the first prototype Do 25 flew as a high-wing, unbraced monoplane with fixed undercarriage and a spacious cabin. It was equipped with oversize flaps for good STOL performance. Another notable feature was the wide wraparound windscreen, which allowed for excellent vision. The machine displayed impressive qualities and was ordered in numbers by the government. In light of existing restrictions, however, they were constructed by CASA in Spain as Do 27s.

The changing political climate of Central Europe was then becoming transfixed over East-West confrontation as NATO under the United States faced off against the Warsaw Pact headed by the Soviet Union. The Americans were determined to make Germany a full-fledged military partner and allowed it to rearm. It was against this background that Dr. Dornier offered his new plane to the newly formed Luftwaffe (air force) and *Heersflieger* (army air force) of the Federal Republic of Germany. The Do 27, by virtue of its excellent ability to operate from short, unprepared strips became much in demand as an all-purpose liaison and general utility craft. Dornier then relocated back to Germany, where he constructed 428 of his rugged little airplanes. A second version, the Do 27B, was fitted with dual controls and operated as a trainer. Production concluded by 1966 after a run of 571 units. Given the great versatility of the Do 27, it was widely exported overseas to Israel, Nigeria, Belgium, Turkey, and Congo. Germany gradually replaced its Do 27s with helicopters in the late 1980s, and many were transferred to Portugal.

Type: Medium Bomber; Night Fighter

Dimensions: wingspan, 62 feet, 4 inches; length, 55 feet, 9 inches; height, 16 feet, 4 inches
Weights: empty, 19,985 pounds; gross, 36,817 pounds
Power plant: 2 × 1,700–horsepower BMW 810D radial engines
Performance: maximum speed, 348 miles per hour; ceiling, 24,170 feet; range, 1,550 miles
Armament: 4 × 7.9mm machine guns; 2 × 13mm machine guns; up to 8,818 pounds of bombs
Service dates: 1937–1945

The "Flying Pencil" was a Luftwaffe workhorse throughout World War II. Although less numerous than competing Heinkel and Junker designs, it performed useful work in a wide variety of missions.

The Dornier Do 17 originated in a 1933 request by Deutsche Lufthansa for a modern high-speed carrier for mail and passengers. The prototype flew in 1934 as an all-metal, high-wing monoplane with a single fin. The new machine was fast, but the airline rejected it on account of its very narrow fuselage, which led to the name "Flying Pencil." Then the Luftwaffe expressed interest in developing the craft as a bomber. Fitted with a twin rudder assembly, the new Do 17s made a splash at the 1937 Military Aircraft Competition at Zurich, where they proved faster than any fighter present. By 1938 several bombers had been committed to combat in Spain, where it was decided to provide the front cabin with the trademark "beetle-eye" canopy and heavier armament. More than

1,200 Do 17s were built, and in the early years of World War II they formed a vital part of the Luftwaffe bomber arm, along with He 111s and Ju 88s. Most were phased out by 1942.

In 1938 the Dornier design team conceived a progressive development, the Do 217. Despite outward similarities to the Do 17, this was an entirely new and more capable machine. Equipped with radial engines, it served throughout the war years as a day bomber, a night fighter, and a dive-bomber. Like its predecessor, the Do 217 was fast, easy to fly, and very adaptable. By 1944 Model M and Model K versions were equipped to handle *Fritz X* guided anti-ship missiles during the Italian campaign. In this capacity Do 217s sank the British cruiser HMS *Janus* and also the Italian battleship *Roma* as it fled to join the Allies. Others were successfully rigged as night fighters. A final reconnaissance version, the Do 217P, could reach altitudes of 50,000 feet. More than 1,700 Do 217s were built.

Type: Trainer

Dimensions: wingspan, 36 feet, 7 inches; length, 32 feet, 4 inches; height, 11 feet, 2 inches
Weights: empty, 3,990 pounds; gross, 7,000 pounds
Power plant: 1 × 750–horsepower Pratt & Whitney Canada PT6A-25C turboprop engine
Performance: maximum speed, 278 miles per hour; ceiling, 30,000 feet; range, 1,145 miles
Armament: none
Service dates: 1983–

The racy *Tucano* is South America's first and most successful advanced training aircraft. It continues to be widely exported abroad in a number of versions.

In 1978 the Brazilian government approached Embraer to design a new trainer to replace its aging fleet of Cessna T-37s. The new craft would not only have to be cost-effective but also closely mimic jet flight characteristics. That year a design team under Joseph Kovacs began work on a prototype that was unveiled in August 1980. The EMB 312 *Tucano* (Toucan) is a low-wing, turboprop monoplane with exceedingly sleek lines. It seats two crew members in tandem under a spacious staggered canopy and is the only aircraft of its class fitted with ejection seats. The *Tucano* derives its name from a long and distinct cowling, which houses a powerful Pratt & Whitney Canada turboprop engine. To better mimic the handling characteristics of jet flight, it also features a throttle control that simultaneously synchronizes the propeller pitch. This assures smooth and rapid acceleration and deceleration. The plane exhibited delightful flying characteristics, so in 1983 the first EMB 312 was delivered to the Air Force Academy near São Paulo. Such high performance and low operating costs also attracted outside attention, with Egypt purchasing no less than 54 of these fine machines. In short order, Argentina, Columbia, Honduras, Paraguay, and Venezuela all purchased *Tucanos* for their cadets. The latest customer is France, which in 1994 ordered 80 examples with air brakes and deicing equipment.

By far the most significant user of the EMB 312 is Great Britain, which in 1985 sought to replace its BAe *Jet Prevost* trainers. Choosing the *Tucano* was significant because it represents the first trainer since the de Havilland *Chipmunk* of 1950 to seat pilots in tandem, not side by side. The British *Tucanos* are manufactured in Belfast by Shorts and are fitted with a more powerful Garrett turboprop engine and other advanced avionics. Thus far, more than 600 *Tucanos* have been built and exported around the world. A Brazilian success story!

Type: Light Bomber; Reconnaissance

Dimensions: wingspan, 63 feet, 11 inches; length, 65 feet, 6 inches; height, 15 feet, 8 inches
Weights: empty, 27,950 pounds; gross, 54,950 pounds
Power plant: 2 × 7,400–pound thrust Rolls-Royce Avon turbo jet engines
Performance: maximum speed, 541 miles per hour; ceiling, 48,000 feet; range, 806 miles
Armament: 4 × 20mm cannons; up to 5,000 pounds of bombs
Service dates: 1951–

The legendary *Canberra* was originally designed as a light bomber, but it also gained renown as a high-altitude spyplane. This superb machine was one of the most versatile aircraft ever constructed, and a handful still operate today—half a century after initial deployment.

The high performance of German jets in World War II prompted the British Air Ministry to release Specification B.3/45 in 1945 to acquire Britain's first jet bomber. At length designer W.E.W. "Teddy" Petter of English Electric decided against the very latest swept-wing philosophies then in vogue in favor of a conventional straight-wing design. He selected a very low-aspect wing, which was thin, broad, and ensured good fuel economy at very high cruising altitudes. The first *Canberra* debuted in 1949 to the astonishment and delight of the Royal Air Force. It was a streamlined machine with two engines mounted midway in-between the wings. The fuselage was smooth and monocoque in construction,

seating two pilots under a large bubble canopy near the nose. From the onset, the new craft was amazingly fast and agile at low altitude. In 1951 the first *Canberra B.2s* were deployed, the first of 27 distinct marks that were produced over a decade. *Canberras* were also highly successful as an export machine, and they served in great numbers with Argentina, South Africa, Australia, Germany, Kuwait, India, Sweden, the United States, and France. A total of 1,352 of these classic jet bombers were built.

It is not always appreciated that RAF *Canberras* conducted some of the earliest high-altitude overflights of the Soviet Union in the early to mid-1950s. In concert with Martin RB-57s—the U.S. version—these were some of the earliest spy flights of the Cold War. The advent of Soviet surface-to-air missiles curtailed these activities by 1960, and RAF machines reverted back to bombers and tactical reconnaissance until the 1980s. However, India still maintains and operates a large refurbished fleet of 65 *Canberras*.

Type: Fighter

Dimensions: wingspan, 34 feet, 10 inches; length, 55 feet, 3 inches; height, 19 feet, 7 inches
Weights: empty, 28,000 pounds; gross, 50,000 pounds
Power plant: 2 × 15,680–pound thrust Rolls-Royce Avon 302 turbojet engines
Performance: maximum speed, 1,500 miles per hour; ceiling, 40,000 feet; range, 800 miles
Armament: 2 × 30mm cannons; 2 × *Red Top* or *Firestreak* missiles
Service dates: 1961–1988

The fabulous *Lightning* was England's first supersonic fighter, as well as the first designed as an integrated weapons system. Despite maintenance headaches, it gave the Royal Air Force world-class interception capability.

The Air Ministry announced Specification F.23/49 in 1949 to stimulate production of a fighter that could operate faster than the speed of sound in level flight. W.E.W. "Teddy" Petter of English Electric had already designed a research craft called the P.1A, which was being constructed for that purpose. The prototype first flew in August 1954 with good results, but further development yielded the P.1B, a dramatically different aircraft. The most unusual feature was the engine arrangement—one stacked atop the other—which eliminated the need for a greater frontal area. The wings were also unusual in that they, as well as the tail surfaces, terminated at right angles to the flow of air. The P.1B became the first British aircraft to fly at twice the speed of sound in March 1958, and the government decided to enter it

into production as the *Lightning*. The first machines became operational in 1961 and differed from the prototype in having a faired bulge on the bottom of the fuselage for housing additional fuel. In service the *Lightning* was fast, highly agile, and possessed twice the performance of the aging Hawker *Hunters*. In time it developed into a world-class interceptor. However, with high speed came high fuel consumption, and the first F.1s were somewhat short-ranged. They were also dogged by recurrent maintenance problems, as technology this complex was a novelty.

The *Lightning* was also the first British fighter to serve as an integrated weapons system and not simply as a gunnery platform. It was equipped with an advanced fire control radar that simultaneously tracked targets and fired weapons at optimum range. A total of 338 of these impressive machines were built, and they remained in service until replaced by Panavia *Tornados* in 1988. Several were also exported to Saudi Arabia and Kuwait. This was a superb interceptor in its day.

Type: Reconnaissance

Dimensions: wingspan, 47 feet, 1 inch; length, 32 feet, 3 inches; height, 10 feet, 4 inches
Weights: empty, 1,323 pounds; gross, 1,918 pounds
Power plant: 1 × 100–horsepower Mercedes-Benz liquid-cooled engine
Performance: maximum speed, 71 miles per hour; ceiling, 9,840 feet; range, 240 miles
Armament: none, but small bombs could be carried
Service dates: 1914–1915

The beautiful *Taube* (Dove) was one of the world's earliest effective warplanes. Despite a seemingly frail persona, it was among the very first aircraft to conduct bombing runs.

Since its inception in 1903, aviation technology continued advancing and improving in leaps and bounds. In 1910 Austrian designer Igo Etrich designed what was to become the first of an entire series of famous warplanes. Christened the *Taube*, it was a sizable monoplane whose wingtips flared back in the shape of a large bird's wing. Because ailerons had not yet been invented, the craft was turned by a process known as wing-warping in which lateral control during flight was achieved by bending the rudder and wingtips using wires. The resulting craft proved pleasant to fly, and in July 1914 a *Taube* broke the world altitude record by reaching 21,600 feet. Knowledge of Etrich's invention led to its exportation to Italy, Turkey, and Japan. The design proved so popular that the firm Rumpler also obtained a license to manufacture it in Germany.

Despite its lovely appearance and gentle characteristics, the *Taube* was immediately pressed into military service. On November 1, 1911, Lieutenant Giulio Gavotti conducted the first bombing raid in history when he tossed hand grenades out of his cockpit during the Italian-Turkish War in Libya. On August 13, 1914, Lieutenant Franz von Hiddeson flew from the Marne River and unloaded four small bombs on Paris for the first time. This was followed up by a *Taube* flown by Max Immelmann, a future ace, who dropped leaflets on the city demanding its immediate surrender! On the other side of the world, a *Taube* formed part of the German garrison defending Tsingtao (Qingdao), China, during a siege by Japanese and British forces. In that instance Lieutenant Gunther Plutschow dropped several bombs and fought off attacks by Japanese-manned Nieuport and Farman fighters. Despite this auspicious combat debut, the *Taube* had been replaced in 1915 by better machines and relegated to training functions. Around 500 had been constructed by six different firms.

Type: Torpedo-Bomber; Dive-Bomber

Dimensions: wingspan, 49 feet, 2 inches; length, 39 feet, 9 inches; height, 12 feet, 3 inches
Weights: empty, 10,818 pounds; gross, 14,250 pounds
Power plant: 1 × 1,640–horsepower Rolls-Royce Merlin 32 liquid-cooled in-line engine
Performance: maximum speed, 240 miles per hour; ceiling, 16,600 feet; range, 1,150 miles
Armament: 2 × .303–inch machine guns; up to 1,600 pounds of bombs or torpedoes
Service dates: 1943–1953

The *Barracuda* was the Royal Navy's first monoplane torpedo-bomber. Underpowered and somewhat ungainly in appearance, it nonetheless fulfilled a wide variety of missions.

In 1937 the Air Ministry issued Specification S.24/37 to secure a new torpedo-bomber to replace the seemingly obsolete Fairey *Swordfish* biplanes. The new craft was envisioned as a three-seat, all-metal monoplane with good speed and carrying capacity. Fairey drew up plans for such a craft early on, but developmental problems with the new Rolls-Royce Exe engine delayed production by three years. Eventually, another low-powered substitute had to be fitted, and the prototype *Barracuda* did not take flight until December 1940. It emerged as a distinctive-looking machine with shoulder wings that sported broad Youngman flaps on the trailing edge and a very high tail. For its size and weight, the craft handled exceedingly well. But when additional production delays ensued, the first *Barracudas* did not reach the Fleet Air Arm until the spring of 1943. Nonetheless, they represented the first monoplane torpedo-bombers employed by that service.

The *Barracuda* was a welcome addition to the fleet, for it proved extremely adaptable when fitted with a succession of stronger power plants. In service they were mounted with a bewildering array of radars, weapons, and other devices. And although the *Barracuda* was designed as a torpedo-bomber, the lack of Axis shipping meant they were more actively deployed as dive-bombers. Their most famous action occurred on April 3, 1944, when 42 *Barracudas* were launched against the German battleship *Tirpitz* at Kaafiord, Norway. Appearing suddenly at dawn, they successfully negotiated the steep-sided fjord, scoring 15 direct hits. Subsequent strikes were also orchestrated throughout May–August of that year. The *Barracuda* received its Pacific-theater baptism of fire on April 21, 1944, when several raided Japanese-held islands in Sumatra. Most *Barracudas* were retired immediately after the war, but several were retained for antisubmarine duty until replaced by Grumman *Avengers* in 1953. Production totaled 2,602 machines.

Type: Light Bomber

Dimensions: wingspan, 54 feet; length, 42 feet, 4 inches; height, 15 feet, 6 inches
Weights: empty, 6,647 pounds; gross, 10,792 pounds
Power plant: 1 × 1,030–horsepower Rolls-Royce Merlin I liquid-cooled in-line engine
Performance: maximum speed, 257 miles per hour; ceiling, 25,000 feet; range, 1,000 miles
Armament: 2 × .303–inch machine guns; 1,000 pounds of bombs
Service dates: 1937–1945

The _Battle_ marked great aeronautical advances and was vastly superior to biplane contemporaries. However, it was hopelessly outdated in World War II and suffered severely during the Battle of France.

The Fairey _Battle_ evolved out of Specification P.27/32, which was issued in 1932 to replace older Hawker _Harts_ and _Hind_ biplane bombers with more modern aircraft. The prototype _Battle_ debuted in 1936, the very model of aerodynamic efficiency. It was a streamlined, all-metal, low-wing monoplane with retractable undercarriage and sheeted skin. A crew of three sat in a long greenhouse canopy. Test flights revealed that it carried twice the bomb load of the older planes at 50 percent higher speeds. Appreciably, the Air Ministry accepted it gleefully, and the first _Battle_ squadrons began forming in 1937. It became one of the major types produced during expansion of the RAF in the late 1930s. By the advent of World War II, the RAF possessed more than 1,000 _Battles_ in frontline service.

The _Battle_ enjoyed a brief and rather tragic wartime career with the Advanced Air Striking Force in France. There, on September 20, 1939, a _Battle_ tailgunner shot down the first German aircraft claimed in the West. However, this jubilation dissipated 10 days later when five _Battles_ on a reconnaissance flight were jumped by Bf 109s and only one survived. The German invasion of France then commenced in May 1940, and casualties increased exponentially. On a daylight mission against the Maastricht bridges on May 10, 1940, the _Battles_ lost 13 of 32 unescorted aircraft. This tragedy also occasioned the first Victoria Cross awarded, posthumously, to an RAF crew. An even bigger disaster occurred four days later when German fighters clawed down 32 of 63 _Battles_ intent on hitting bridgeheads at Sedan. The surviving craft were immediately withdrawn from service and spent the rest of the war in training duties. Others performed useful service as target tugs in Canada and Australia.

Type: Fighter; Reconnaissance

Dimensions: wingspan, 44 feet, 6 inches; length, 37 feet, 7 inches; height, 13 feet, 7 inches
Weights: empty, 9,750 pounds; gross, 14,020 pounds
Power plant: 1 × 1,730–horsepower Rolls-Royce Griffon IIIB liquid-cooled in-line engine
Performance: maximum speed, 316 miles per hour; ceiling, 28,000 feet; range, 1,300 miles
Armament: 4 × 20mm cannons; up to 2,000 pounds of bombs or rockets
Service dates: 1943–1956

The fearsome *Firefly* was the Royal Navy's most capable two-seat fighter of World War II. It was the first British plane to overfly Japan and later saw service during the Korean War.

Designed to fulfill Naval Specification N.5/50, the Fairey *Firefly* arose from the need to replace the relatively modern yet obsolete *Fulmar* two-seat fighter. The prototype first flew in December 1941 and greatly resembled the earlier machine. The *Firefly* was a low-wing, all-metal monoplane, with folding wings for carrier storage. The pilot sat up front near the leading edge while the radio operator/observer was located some distance aft. Like the earlier *Barracuda*, it employed broad Youngman flaps on the wings' trailing edges, and these were mechanically recessed into the wing when not in use. The powerful Rolls-Royce Griffon 61 engine also required a large "chin" radiator that gave the craft a distinctly pugnacious profile. Tests were entirely successful, and the *Firefly* exhibited lively performance that belied its size. The first units

reached the Fleet Air Arm in the summer of 1943 and served with distinction in both the European and Pacific theaters. Its armament of four 20mm cannons was regarded as particularly hard-hitting.

Perhaps the *Firefly* is best remembered for a reconnaissance flight that resulted in the sinking of the German battleship *Tirpitz* in July 1944. It also harassed Japanese aircraft and ground installations throughout the East Indies, and in July 1945 a *Firefly* became the first British aircraft to overfly Tokyo. After the war a more powerful version was introduced, the Mk IV, which featured a Rolls-Royce Griffon 74 engine without the distinctive radiator; it had a four-blade propeller and clipped wings. This version fought in Korea with the Royal Navy and Australian forces. Successive modifications kept this craft in frontline service as an antisubmarine aircraft until the appearance of the Fairey *Gannet* in 1956. Over the course of a 13-year career, 1,638 *Fireflys* were built and operated by the navies of England, Australia, Canada, and the Netherlands.

Type: Fighter

Dimensions: wingspan, 29 feet; length, 22 feet, 10 inches; height, 10 feet
Weights: empty, 2,038 pounds; gross, 3,028 pounds
Power plant: 1 × 410–horsepower Armstrong-Siddeley Jaguar IV radial engine
Performance: maximum speed, 134 miles per hour; ceiling, 19,000 feet; range, 263 miles
Armament: 2 × .303–inch machine guns; up to 80 pounds of bombs
Service dates: 1923–1934

The homely but capable _Flycatcher_ was among the Fleet Air Arm's longest-serving airplanes. For nearly a decade it constituted the only fighter craft available to British carriers.

Designed to a 1922 Air Ministry specification, the Fairey _Flycatcher_ enjoyed an illustrious career unique in the annals of naval aviation. The prototype materialized as a single-bay biplane of singularly grotesque appearance. The wood and metal fuselage was covered in fabric and terminated in a long, low rudder. Significantly, it canted upward just aft of the cockpit, giving the craft a decidedly "bent" look. The two wings were of equal length, but the upper one displayed dihedral, and both were fitted with a device—the Fairey Patent Camber Gear—across the trailing edges, which was an extended flap that could be lowered for greater lift during takeoff and for braking upon the landing approach. The _Flycatcher_ was also the first British carrier aircraft to utilize hydraulic brakes. All told, it was an ugly but functional machine that was strong and could dive

steeply in complete safety. But what pilots remember most was its superlative maneuverability. The _Flycatcher_ was forgiving, easy to fly, and outturned anything with wings. This extraordinary aircraft joined the Fleet Air Arm in 1923 and remained its star performer for nearly 11 years.

During the 1920s, the rugged _Flycatchers_ demonstrated their utility as carrier aircraft by launching without the benefit of catapults. They alighted so readily that the 60-foot tapered runway situated _below_ the main carrier flight deck could be utilized to shoot out over the bow. _Flycatchers_ performed similar feats while flying off platforms attached to the turrets of capital ships. They also helped pioneer a tactic known as "converging bombing" whereby three aircraft simultaneously swooped down on a target from three different directions. The versatile _Flycatcher_ was a common sight on carrier decks until 1930, when it was gradually replaced by Hawker _Nimrods_. A total of 192 of these classic fighters were built.

Type: Fighter

Dimensions: wingspan, 46 feet, 4 inches; length, 40 feet, 2 inches; height, 10 feet, 8 inches
Weights: empty, 7,051 pounds; gross, 10,200 pounds
Power plant: 1 × 1,080–horsepower Rolls-Royce Merlin VIII liquid-cooled in-line engine
Performance: maximum speed, 272 miles per hour; ceiling, 27,200 feet; range, 780 miles
Armament: 8 × .303–inch machine guns; 500 pounds of bombs
Service dates: 1940–1945

The *Fulmar* was the Fleet Air Arm's first eight-gun fighter. Although slower than land-based German adversaries, it performed useful service against the Regia Aeronautica (Italian air force).

By 1938 the British Admiralty felt a pressing need for more modern fighter craft, one mounting eight machine guns like the Hawker *Hurricanes* and Supermarine *Spitfires* then coming into service. However, unlike the land-based fighters, Fleet Air Arm requirements necessitated inclusion of a second crew member to act as navigator. This was deemed essential for ensuring that the aircraft could safely return to a carrier at night or in bad weather. It was recognized from the onset that the basic attributes of the new machine would be range and firepower, not speed. In 1938 a Fairey deign team under Marcel Lobelle took the existing P.3/34 light bomber prototype and converted it into a two-seat fighter. The new *Fulmar* prototype first flew in 1940, exhibiting many fine qualities. It was maneuverable, easy to handle, and functioned well on the deck. But as anticipated, the added weight of a second crew member rendered its performance somewhat disappointing. Nevertheless, the Fleet Air Arm needed an immediate replacement for its aging Blackburn *Skuas* and *Rocs*, so the craft entered production that year.

Fulmars debuted aboard the carrier HMS *Ark Royal* in the summer of 1940 and fought extensively during the defense of Malta. Its somewhat slow speed was considered no great disadvantage while tangling with lower-powered Italian aircraft, and its heavy armament made it lethal to enemy bombers. In an attempt to improve performance a new version, the *Fulmar II*, was introduced in 1943, featuring the more powerful Merlin 32 engine. By this time, however, *Fulmars* were being replaced by infinitely better *Sea Hurricanes* and *Sea Spitfires*. They subsequently completed additional useful work as night fighters before being phased out by 1945. Despite their sometimes sluggish performance, *Fulmars* performed well on balance and frequently under trying circumstances.

Type: Reconnaissance; Liaison

Dimensions: wingspan, 45 feet, 9 inches; length, 35 feet, 6 inches; height, 14 feet
Weights: empty, 3,923 pounds; gross, 6,300 pounds
Power plant: 1 × 570–horsepower Napier Lion X1A liquid-cooled in-line engine
Performance: maximum speed, 130 miles per hour; ceiling, 20,000 feet; range, 400 miles
Armament: 2 × .303–inch machine guns; up to 550 pounds of bombs
Service dates: 1928–1940

The venerable Fairey IIIF was the most numerous aircraft of the Fleet Air Arm between the wars. Deployed from every British carrier, it served extensively around the world.

The famous Fairey III series first flew in 1917, although it was developed too late for combat in World War I. For 10 years thereafter, these capable aircraft, built in both land and seaplane configurations, saw widespread service with the Royal Navy and Royal Air Force.

In 1924 the Air Ministry announced Specification 19/24, which called for a new two-seat general purpose aircraft for the RAF and a three-seat version of the Fleet Air Arm. Consequently, Fairey took a standard IIID model and made numerous modifications to the point where it was virtually a new airplane. Like all Fairey IIIs, this craft was a conventional biplane with equal-span two-bay wings made of wood and fabric. The IIIF version differed by having a metal-framed fuselage, covered in fabric as before but also sporting an extremely tight-fitting, streamlined cowling. The various changes greatly

enhanced its performance, and in 1927 the first Fairey IIIFs became operational.

The RAF employed Fairey IIIFs as general-purpose communications aircraft, and they were also capable of long, record-breaking flights. As an example, several Capetown-to-Cairo flights were performed throughout the early 1930s, including one headed by Lieutenant Commander A. T. Harris (who later became famous as "Bomber Harris"). In naval service, many Fairey IIIFs were fitted with twin floats and operated off of capital ships. Others, with landing gear, were flown from every carrier in the Royal Navy, with service as far afield as Hong Kong. They also supplanted the aging fleet of Avro *Bisons*, Blackburn *Blackburns*, and Blackburn *Ripons* stationed there. Toward the end of a long service life, three Fairey IIFs were converted into radio-controlled target drones known as *Fairey Queens*. The RAF machines were phased out of service beginning in 1935, but naval versions were not declared obsolete in 1941. A total of 622 of these efficient aircraft were constructed.

Type: Torpedo-Bomber; Reconnaissance

Dimensions: wingspan, 45 feet, 6 inches; length, 35 feet, 8 inches; height, 12 feet, 4 inches
Weights: empty, 4,700 pounds; gross, 7,510 pounds
Power plant: 1 × 750–horsepower Bristol Pegasus radial engine
Performance: maximum speed, 138 miles per hour; ceiling, 10,700 feet; range, 1,030 miles
Armament: 2 × .303–inch machine guns; up to 1,680 pounds of bombs, rockets, or mines
Service dates: 1936–1945

During World War II, the archaic-looking "Stringbag" sank more Axis tonnage than any other British aircraft. It successfully accomplished a wide variety of tasks and actually outlived the aircraft intended to replace it.

The legendary *Swordfish* evolved in response to a 1933 Air Ministry specification calling for a new torpedo/reconnaissance aircraft. Fairey Aviation enjoyed a long tradition of building excellent naval machines, and its prototype TSR 2 was no exception. It was a two-bay biplane of metal structure, covered in fabric throughout. The upper wing was slightly swept back, and provisions were made for a crew of three in open cockpits. When accepted for service in 1936, the *Swordfish* looked somewhat out of place— even obsolete—in an age where monoplanes were the future. The new craft, however, was strong, easily handled, and could accurately deliver a torpedo. By the time World War II erupted in 1939, *Swordfish* equipped no less than 13 Fleet Air Arm squadrons.

Nobody in aviation circles could have anticipated what happened next, for the anachronistic Stringbags emerged as one of the outstanding warplanes of aviation history. Commencing with action in Norwegian waters, *Swordfish* successfully directed naval gunfire and even scored the first U-boat sinking credited to the Fleet Air Arm. On November 11, 1940, 20 *Swordfish* made a surprise attack on the Italian fleet anchored at Taranto Harbor, severely damaging three battleships and sinking a host of lesser vessels. In May 1941, these aircraft also scored a damaging hit on the German superbattleship *Bismark* that resulted in its eventual destruction. Moreover, a handful of *Swordfish* operating out of Malta destroyed an average 50,000 tons of enemy shipping throughout most of 1942. These impressive tallies continued throughout the war. A new aircraft, the Fairey *Albacore*, arrived in 1942 to replace the old warrior, but it proved inferior in performance and popularity. The *Swordfish* was finally mustered out after 1945 with a production run of 2,391 machines. The *Swordfish* was a legendary warplane in every respect.

Type: Heavy Bomber

Dimensions: wingspan, 118 feet, 1 inch; length, 70 feet, 8 inches; height, 16 feet, 9 inches
Weights: empty, 23,122 pounds; gross, 39,242 pounds
Power plant: 4 × 860–horsepower Gnome-Rhone GR1Kbrs radial engines
Performance: maximum speed, 199 miles per hour; ceiling, 26,250 feet; range, 1,240 miles
Armament: 3 × 7.5mm machine guns; 9,240 pounds of bombs
Service dates: 1935–1944

The ugly Farman F 222 was the largest French bomber of the interwar period. Its service was undistinguished, but the type mounted the first Allied air raid against Berlin.

The design concept for the Farman family of heavy bombers originated with a 1929 requirement calling for a five-seat aircraft to replace the obsolete LeO 20s. The prototype, designated the F 220, first flew in May 1932 and had all the trappings of a French bomber of this period. It was a high-wing monoplane with wings of considerable chord and thickness, braced by large struts canting inward toward the fuselage. The fuselage itself was very boxy and angular, sporting pronounced nose and dorsal turrets and a smaller ventral position. The four engines were mounted in tandem pods below the wing in pusher/tractor configuration and secured to the fuselage by means of a pair of small winglets. The overall effect was an unattractive, if capable, craft and, being entirely constructed from metal, a signal improvement over earlier bombers. With some re-

finements it entered production as the F 221 in 1934 and was acquired in small batches. These represented the first four-engine bombers produced by the West at that time.

Looks aside, the Farman F 220 series was strong, reliable, and continually acquired in a series of updated models. The most important was the F 222 of 1938, which featured a redesigned nose section, dihedral on the outer wing sections, and retractable landing gear. However, the Farman aircraft were readily overtaken by aviation technology and rendered obsolete by 1939. They spent the first year of World War II dropping propaganda leaflets over Germany. After the Battle of France commenced in May 1940, several groups of Farman aircraft made numerous nighttime raids against industrial targets in Germany and Italy. It was a Navy F 223, the *Jules Verne*, that conducted the first Allied raid on Berlin that June. Many subsequently escaped to North Africa and were employed as transports by various regimes until 1944. Total production reached 45 units.

Type: Patrol-Bomber

Dimensions: wingspan, 95 feet, 7 inches; length, 46 feet, 3 inches; height, 17 feet, 6 inches
Weights: empty, 7,900 pounds; gross, 10,978 pounds
Power plant: 2 × 345–horsepower Rolls-Royce Eagle VIII liquid-cooled in-line engines
Performance: maximum speed, 95 miles per hour; ceiling, 9,600 feet; range, 700 miles
Armament: 4 × .303–inch machine guns; 920 pounds of bombs
Service dates: 1917–1927

The F2A was a British-American hybrid design and highly effective as a patrol craft. Its career closely paralleled the Short *Sunderland* of a later date and firmly established the reputation of flying boats as weapons.

Commander John C. Porte of the Royal Navy was a longtime advocate of flying boats for naval service. In 1914 he ventured to the United States at the behest of aircraft builder Glenn Curtiss to work on American designs. Following the onset of World War I he returned home, firmly convinced that England could benefit by such craft. However, as commander of the Felixstowe station, he found Curtiss H.4s operating there unsatisfactory and set about modifying them. His subsequent F1 was found to be a better performer, so in 1917 he scaled up the new hull and fit it to the wings of a very large Curtiss H-12 *Large America*. The resulting hybrid was a superb aircraft for the time. It easily operated off the rough water conditions inherent in Northern Europe and, despite its bulk, was relatively maneuverable once airborne. This new craft was christened the Felixstowe F2A, and it arrived in the spring of 1917 just as Germany's infamous U-boat campaign was peaking.

The Felixstowe flying boat acquired a well-earned reputation as the best flying-boat design of the war. Heavily armed with bombs and machine guns, it destroyed submarines and Zeppelins on several occasions. Moreover, it could readily defend itself against the numerous German floatplane fighters encountered over the North Sea. This fact was underscored on June 4, 1918, when four F2As beat off an attack by 14 Hansa-Brandenburg W.29s, shooting down six with no loss to themselves. In an attempt to improve the Felixstowe's performance, a new version, the F3, was developed. It featured longer wings and twice the bomb load but handled poorly and was never popular. The excellent F2As, meanwhile, remained on active duty for a decade following the war.

Type: Medium Bomber

Dimensions: wingspan, 70 feet, 9 inches; length, 52 feet, 9 inches; height, 15 feet, 7 inches
Weights: empty, 14,770 pounds; gross, 22,046 pounds
Power plant: 2 × 1,000–horsepower Fiat A.80 radial engines
Performance: maximum speed, 264 miles per hour; ceiling, 22,145 feet; range, 1,710 miles
Armament: 4 × 7.7mm machine guns; up to 3,527 pounds of bombs
Service dates: 1936–1943

The lumbering *Cignona* was the best-known Italian bomber of the 1930s and a potent symbol of fascist rearmament. Slow and poorly armed, it suffered heavy losses in World War II.

During the early 1930s, the fascist regime under Benito Mussolini strove mightily to acquire a first-rate air force for military as well as propaganda purposes. In 1935 the invasion of Ethiopia highlighted Italy's great need for modern bombers. The following year, noted engineer Celestino Rosatelli conceived a new design that, at the time it appeared, was the most advanced in the world. The BR 20 was a low-wing, twin-engine monoplane featuring a metal framework fuselage and wings, twin rudders, and retractable undercarriage. The craft employed stressed skin throughout save for the aft fuselage, which retained a fabric covering. Given the name *Cignona* (Stork), it became operational in 1936, and several were dispatched to Spain to fight alongside Franco's Nationalist forces. The BR 20s gave a good account of themselves, but glaring weaknesses in armament were addressed in subsequent versions. Cu-

riously, Japan purchased 100 *Cignonas* to serve as an interim bomber until the Mitsubishi K 21 arrived. Their performance in China confirmed earlier deficiencies, and they were quickly phased out. In 1939 the BR 20M (*Modificato*) appeared and introduced a cleaned-up fuselage, broader wings, and heavier defensive armament. Several hundred were deployed by June 1940, when Italy declared war on France and Great Britain.

Despite its prior celebrity, the service record of the BR 20 in World War II was mediocre at best. Two groups were dispatched to Belgium that fall with the Corpo Aereo Italiano (the Italian air corps) and participated in latter phases of the Battle of Britain. They suffered heavy losses at the hands of Royal Air Force fighters and were withdrawn in weeks. BR 20s next fought in Greece, Malta, Yugoslavia, and North Africa and performed well when unopposed. Unfortunately, they remained vulnerable in the face of determined resistance. By 1943 only a handful remained in service. A total of 602 were constructed.

Type: Fighter

Dimensions: wingspan, 31 feet, 1 inch; length, 24 feet, 5 inches; height, 8 feet, 7 inches
Weights: empty, 3,086 pounds; gross, 4,343 pounds
Power plant: 1 × 800–horsepower Fiat RA *bis* (improved) liquid-cooled in-line engine
Performance: maximum speed, 205 miles per hour; ceiling, 26,245 feet; range, 485 miles
Armament: 2 × 12.5mm machine guns; 2 × 7.7mm machine guns
Service dates: 1935–1941

The *Chirri* was one of the finest biplane fighters ever designed. It proved so good that Italian aviators were reluctant to abandon such craft long after they had become obsolete elsewhere.

In 1932 Italian aircraft designer Celestino Rosatelli unveiled his CR 30, a defining moment in biplane evolution. As a fighter, the CR 30 was breathlessly acrobatic for its day, but Rosatelli was determined to wring out even better performance with continuing refinement. The ensuing CR 32 was a slightly smaller, cleaned-up version of the earlier craft and the most significant Italian fighter plane of the 1930s. Like its predecessor, the CR 32 was a metal-framed, fabric design with a distinctive chin-type radiator. The wings were strongly fastened by "W"-shaped Warren interplane struts and trusses throughout. Consequently, the CR 32 could literally be thrown about the sky and was capable of the most violent acrobatics. This rendered it superbly adapted as a dogfighter, a point well taken by Italian pilots. In 1936 CR 32s entered into service and by

1939 a total of 1,212 machines had been built in four versions.

The *Chirri*, as it became known, was instantly popular with fighter pilots around the world. The Chinese imported several and used them effectively against the Japanese in 1937. Hungary also bought them for its air force, but the most important customer was Spain. CR 32s were flown by both Spanish and Italians during the Spanish Civil War (1936–1938), and they proved formidable adversaries to the Russian-supplied Polikarpov I 15 biplanes and I 16 monoplanes. However, success carried a price. Because of their experience with the *Chirri*, Italians became so enamored of biplane dogfighters that they continued producing them long after they were obsolete. By the time Italy entered World War II in 1940, the CR 32 and CR 42 biplanes constituted nearly 70 percent of Italian fighter strength. Nevertheless, some CR 32s were successfully employed in East Africa before assuming trainer functions in 1941.

Type: Fighter; Light Bomber

Dimensions: wingspan, 31 feet, 10 inches; length, 27 feet, 1 inch; height, 11 feet, 9 inches
Weights: empty, 3,929 pounds; gross, 5,060 pounds
Power plant: 1 × 840–horsepower Fiat A.74 RC.38 radial engine
Performance: maximum speed, 267 miles per hour; ceiling, 33,465 feet; range, 482 miles
Armament: 2 × 12.7mm machine guns
Service dates: 1939–1945

The superb-handling *Falco* (Falcon) was the last military biplane manufactured in quantity and the last to see wartime service. Despite obvious obsolescence, it was actively employed throughout World War II.

Celestino Rosatelli's successful CR 32 biplane fighter prompted him to extend the life of the series with a newer version. This was undertaken at a time when most nations were discarding biplanes in favor of faster monoplane aircraft. Nevertheless, in 1939 Fiat unveiled the CR 42, possibly the finest expression of biplane technology ever constructed. Like the CR 32, the new craft consisted of metal frames and fabric covering. It was also the first Rosatelli design to use a radial engine, which was covered in a long chord cowling. The usual Warren struts were present, as were fixed, spatted landing gear. Unquestionably, the CR 42 continued Fiat's tradition of robust fighters, being fast for a biplane, wonderfully acrobatic, and delightful to fly. The Regia Aeronautica (Italian air force) adopted it as its last biplane fighter, and by 1940 the *Falcos* were a major service type. The prevailing prejudice against biplanes notwithstanding, CR 42s were also exported abroad to Belgium, Hungary, and Sweden.

The CR 42 was history's last combat biplane, and it campaigned extensively throughout World War II. They were initially engaged in the defense of Belgium and, after Italian entry into the war by 1940, flew missions against southern France. A large number subsequently arrived in Belgium to participate in the Battle of Britain, where they took heavy losses and were withdrawn. In secondary theaters the *Falcos* had better success, and they fought well in the Greek campaign, over Crete, and against a host of obsolete British aircraft in East Africa.

CR 42s formed the bulk of Italian fighter strength throughout the North African campaign and, although failing as fighters, performed useful work in ground support. Only a handful survived the Italian surrender in 1943, and Germans operated them as night intruders in northern Italy until 1945.

Type: Fighter

Dimensions: wingspan, 36 feet, 1 inch; length, 27 feet, 2 inches; height, 11 feet, 9 inches
Weights: empty, 4,442 pounds; gross, 5,511 pounds
Power plant: 1 × 840–horsepower Fiat A.74 RC.38 radial engine
Performance: maximum speed, 302 miles per hour; ceiling, 35,269 feet; range, 621 miles
Armament: 2 × 12.7mm machine guns
Service dates: 1938–1943

The much-maligned *Freccia* was Italy's first all-metal monoplane fighter. Like many contemporaries, it was underpowered, underarmed, and outclassed by competing British and German designs.

By the mid-1930s Italy's aircraft industry felt increasing pressure to develop new and more modern aircraft. In 1935 Giuseppe Gabrielli of Fiat conceived that country's first all-metal monoplane fighter, the G 50 *Freccia* (Arrow). It was a midsized machine with a fully enclosed canopy, retractable landing gear, and rather appealing lines. However, it was powered by a bulky radial engine because suitable in-line power plants were unavailable. Tests successfully concluded by 1937, and the following year a preproduction batch of 12 machines was deployed to fight in the Spanish Civil War. There pilots enjoyed the G 50's outstanding maneuverability but disliked the closed canopy, which impeded all-around vision. Subsequent models featured an open cockpit reminiscent of World War I–era fighters. The *Freccia* entered production in 1939 with the Regia Aeronautica (Italian air force), and several were also obtained by Finland. Production remained

slow, and when Italy entered World War II in June 1940, only 97 G 50s were on hand.

The decision to build the *Freccia* seems even more absurd in light of events that followed. As a fighting platform, it offered performance nowhere comparable to the *Spitfire, Hurricane*, or Me 109, being slower and underarmed. Accordingly, when the first G 50s were deployed in Belgium to fight in the Battle of Britain, most fighter pilots deliberately avoided combat against their better English counterparts. In September 1940 the G 50 *bis* (improved) appeared, featuring increased fuel capacity, a redesigned tail, and glazed cockpit side panels but otherwise little enhancement of performance. Others were fitted with bomb racks and fulfilled ground-attack missions. *Freccias* fought throughout the Greek and North African campaigns with mediocre results and were largely discarded following the September 1943 Italian surrender. Curiously, in Finnish hands the aging fighters did valuable work against Soviet forces and remained in frontline service until 1947! A total of 774 *Freccias* were built.

Type: Fighter; Light Bomber

Dimensions: wingspan, 29 feet, 6 inches; length, 38 feet, 3 inches; height, 14 feet, 6 inches
Weights: empty, 8,117 pounds; gross, 17,196 pounds
Power plant: 2 × 2,725–pound thrust General Electric J85 turbojet engines
Performance: maximum speed, 690 miles per hour; ceiling, 41,000 feet; range, 740 miles
Armament: 2 × 30mm cannons; up to 4,000 pounds of bombs or rockets
Service dates: 1959–1998

The G 91 was the North Atlantic Treaty Organization's first attempt to build and deploy a standard warplane for use by member nations. Small and easy to operate, it served as a frontline strike fighter for many years.

In 1954 NATO announced competition for a modern tactical strike aircraft. The new machine had to be fast, well-armed, and capable of operating off short, unprepared landing strips. Moreover, it was to be built and deployed by NATO member nations in an attempt to standardize equipment and capabilities. In 1956 a Fiat design team headed by Giuseppe Gabrielli unveiled the prototype G 91, which bore strong resemblance to the larger F-86Ks then built under license. It was modestly sized with swept wings, tricycle gear, and a spacious bubble canopy. In flight the G 91 was light, responsive, and could carry a variety of weapons. Evaluation trials held in 1957 demonstrated that it was superior to several French contenders, so the decision was made to adopt the craft for German and Italian forces. France angrily refused to have anything to do with the diminutive craft, but 756 G 91s were ultimately produced. For Germany, G 91s were the first fighters manufactured in that country since 1945. Moreover, whatever G 91s lacked as dogfighters, they more than compensated for as strike aircraft.

By 1965 the original G 91 design had grown somewhat long in the tooth, so an updated version was proposed. This was the G 91Y, or *Yankee*, which differed from earlier models by having two General Electric engines instead of the single Orpheus turbojet. The result was nearly 60 percent more thrust and very little additional weight. The G 91Y was a far more capable attack craft and could carry all the latest NATO ordnance, including nuclear weapons. A total of 75 were built for the Italian air force, and they were widely employed in their intended role until 1998. The German machines had been retired a decade earlier by the Dassault/Dornier *Alphajet*.

Type: Liaison; Reconnaissance

Dimensions: wingspan, 46 feet, 9 inches; length, 32 feet, 5 inches; height, 9 feet, 10 inches
Weights: empty, 2,500 pounds; gross, 2,910 pounds
Power plant: 1 × 240–horsepower Argus As 10C liquid-cooled in-line engine
Performance: maximum speed, 109 miles per hour; ceiling, 17,060 feet; range, 205 miles
Armament: 1 × 7.92mm machine gun
Service dates: 1937–1945

The ungainly *Storch* was one of the earliest STOL (short takeoff and landing) airplanes. It served in large numbers across Europe and Africa wherever the German army fought.

In 1935 the German Air Ministry announced competition for an army cooperation aircraft, one specifically designed to operate from very confined areas. A prototype entered by Fieseler beat out two airplanes and a helicopter to win the contest in 1936. The Fi 156 was a high-wing, cabin monoplane with exceptionally long undercarriage to kept the nose highly elevated. It was conventionally constructed of steel tube, wood, and fabric covering. The wing surfaces were also braced and the cabin extensively glazed to afford the crew of two excellent vision. But the secret of the *Storch* (Stork) lay in the configuration of its main wing. The front portion sported full-span Handley Page wing slats while the trailing edge had slotted flaps and ailerons. Fully deployed, this arrangement allowed the diminutive craft to lift off in only 200 feet. Army officials were very im-

pressed with the Fi 156 and in 1937 production commenced. By 1945 a total of 2,834 had been built.

In service the *Storch* acquired a legendary reputation for its uncanny ability to operate where most aircraft could not. The slow-flying craft could even hover motionless while flying into a gentle headwind! This made it an ideal army cooperation craft, and hundreds were deployed with military units from the frozen fringes of the Arctic to the burning sands of North Africa. *Storches* were also widely employed to serve as medevac, liaison, reconnaissance, and staff transport. Moreover, Field Marshals Erwin Rommel and Albert Kesselring employed Fi 156s as personal transports throughout campaigns in North Africa and Italy. Perhaps its most notorious episode was in helping rescue Benito Mussolini from his mountainous prison in September 1943. Two years later, noted aviatrix Hanna Reitsch flew one of the *Storch's* last missions by touching down in the ruins of Berlin with General Robert Ritter von Greim, newly appointed head of the nearly defunct Luftwaffe.

Type: Reconnaissance

Dimensions: rotorspan, 39 feet, 4 inches; length, 21 feet, 6 inches; height, 7 feet, 2 inches
Weights: empty, 1,411 pounds; gross, 2,205 pounds
Power plant: 1 × 140–horsepower Siemens-Halske air-cooled engine
Performance: maximum speed, 68 miles per hour; ceiling, 12,992 feet; range, 106 miles
Armament: none
Service dates: 1943–1944

The diminutive *Kolibri* was the first combat-capable helicopter to reach mass production. Despite primitive appearances, it was perfectly functional and a harbinger of things to come.

Anton Flettner, one of Europe's most accomplished helicopter pioneers, built his first functioning machine in 1932. A succession of prototypes culminated in his Fl 184 autogyro of 1935, which was ordered by the German Kriegsmarine (navy) for evaluation. It was driven by a single three-blade rotor, with two smaller antitorque propellers on either side. Around this time, however, Flettner developed interest in counter-rotating, intermeshed, twin-rotor designs. Such a machine would cancel out the effects of torque and the need for other stability devices. In 1939 he perfected his Fl 265 *Kolibri* (Hummingbird), which was a small yet perfectly functional helicopter. The fuselage was made of steel tubing covered with metal skin and possessed a large rudder with dihedral tailplanes. The craft was driven by two shafts, spread apart from each other at divergent angles behind the pilot's seat. Both blades, made from steel

tube and plywood covering, were closely intermeshed with each other at all speeds for greater stability. Reputedly, a pilot could hover indefinitely with his hands off the controls. The Fl 282—designed with maritime reconnaissance in mind—carried a backward-facing observer behind the shafts. By 1941 several prototypes had flown with impressive results, and that year it entered into production.

It was the Kriegsmarine's intention to obtain up to 1,000 Fl 282s for antisubmarine work from the decks of warships. However, less than two dozen were actually completed, but they saw extensive service in the Baltic and Mediterranean Seas. As flying platforms, the tiny helicopters were impressive because they could alight safely in all kinds of weather conditions. One even landed on a pitching turret top of the cruiser *Koln* during a storm. By war's end, only three examples of the Fl 282 survived intact. Two of these visionary machines were shipped off to the United States for evaluation, and one remains on display at the U.S. Air Force Museum in Dayton, Ohio.

Type: Light Bomber

Dimensions: wingspan, 47 feet, 7 inches; length, 46 feet, 9 inches; height, 17 feet, 7 inches
Weights: empty, 8,900 pounds; gross, 14,991 pounds
Power plant: 2 × 988–horsepower Turbomeca XVIG turboprop engines
Performance: maximum speed, 311 miles per hour; ceiling, 31,825 feet; range, 2,305 miles
Armament: 4 × .30–caliber machine guns; 2 × 20mm cannons; 3,307 pounds of ordnance
Service dates: 1976–

The famous *Pucara* is a versatile counterinsurgency aircraft and the first to originate from a Latin American country. It failed to accrue distinction during the 1982 Falkland Islands War and has since been declared surplus.

During the late 1960s, South America was rocked by numerous revolutionary groups, inspired and frequently financed by the communist bloc. In 1969 the Argentine government approached Fabrica Militar de Aviones in Cordoba to devise a heavily armed light strike aircraft capable of dealing with fast-moving guerillas. After some preliminary testing with glider models, the first prototype lifted off in August 1969, at which point the Fuerza Aerea Argentina (Argentine air force) ordered it into production as the FMA IA 58 *Pucara*. The name refers to a stone stronghold erected by indigenous Indians of the Andes. The *Pucara* is an extremely handsome craft with a low-mounted wing and a high-"T" tail section. It is entirely made of metal and seats two crew members under a spacious canopy, with the pilot enjoying excellent frontal vision over a sharply downswept nose. It is also heavily armed, mounting two cannons, four machine guns, and a host of underwing ordnance. The first IA 58s became operational in 1974 and were deployed with good effect against communist guerillas operating in the Tucuman region of the country. Its impressive performance led to small orders from neighboring Columbia and Paraguay for similar purposes.

The *Pucara* is best known for the limited role it played during the 1982 Falkland Islands War with England. Once those islands had been seized in 1981, a force of no less than 24 IA 58s was deployed there to defend them. However, counterattacking British forces shot down several, and more were destroyed in nighttime raids by the Special Air Service. One *Pucara* was captured intact and is currently displayed at the Imperial War Museum in London. After this episode, Argentina lost interest in the craft, and most have been laid up in surplus. Around 100 have been built.

Type: Reconnaissance

Dimensions: wingspan, 60 feet, 4 inches; length, 39 feet, 4 inches; height, 10 feet, 2 inches
Weights: empty, 5,930 pounds; gross, 8,708 pounds
Power plant: 2 × 465–horsepower Argus air-cooled engines
Performance: maximum speed, 217 miles per hour; ceiling, 23,950 feet; range, 416 miles
Armament: 3 × 7.92mm machine guns; up to 440 pounds of bombs
Service dates: 1940–1945

The unattractive *Uhu* was the "eyes" of the German army in campaigns from Finland to Africa. Despite appearances, the craft was strong, maneuverable, and difficult to shoot down.

Since its inception, the Luftwaffe was basically viewed as a tactical appendage to the Wehrmacht, and reconnaissance aircraft were consequently an essential commodity. In 1937 the German Air Ministry issued specifications for a new short-range reconnaissance craft to replace its aging fleet of Heinkel He 46s. Of three firms to respond, the Focke-Wulf Flugzeugbau firm under Dr. Kurt Tank submitted an unorthodox design that was initially greeted with skepticism. The Fw 189 was a low-wing, twin-boom design of metal construction. A crew of three sat in a spacious, glazed fuselage pod affording them excellent visibility. Each of the thin booms mounted a single engine, and they were joined together aft by a single tailplane. Twin-boomed aircraft were not unknown in military circles, but German authorities initially viewed Tank's creation with suspicion. However, flight-testing proved extremely successful, and

the big craft demonstrated ample strength and maneuverability for the tasks at hand. Production commenced in 1939, and a total of 846 Fw 189s were built. Crew members unofficially dubbed it the *Uhu* (Owl), but Nazi propagandists touted it as *Die Fliegender Auge*, or "The Flying Eye."

In 1940 the Fw 189 saw its baptism of fire along the Eastern Front, where most were stationed. At least one squadron of *Uhus* also served in North Africa. The big craft was completely successful as a reconnaissance platform, possessing range, stability, and ease of handling to facilitate its tasks. Not particularly fast, the Fw 189 was extremely agile and, at low altitude, could outturn most fighters with ease. Failing this, it could also absorb considerable damage, and was known to survive direct ramming attacks by Russian aircraft. By war's end, improved Allied fighters made reconnaissance work untenable, so Fw 189s were reassigned to liaison and casualty evacuation work. A handful also flew with Hungarian and Slovakian forces for similar purposes.

Focke-Wulf Fw 190 ———————————————— **Germany**

Type: Fighter; Light Bomber

Dimensions: wingspan, 34 feet, 5 inches; length, 28 feet, 10 inches; height, 12 feet, 11 inches
Weights: empty, 6,393 pounds; gross, 8,700 pounds
Power plant: 1 × 1,700–horsepower BMW 801 radial engine
Performance: maximum speed, 391 miles per hour; ceiling, 34,775 feet; range, 497 miles
Armament: 2 × 7.92mm machine guns; 2 × 20mm cannons; up to 2,200 pounds of bombs
Service dates: 1940–1945

The aptly named "Butcher Bird" was one of the deadliest German fighters of World War II and, possibly, of all time. It was produced in huge numbers and became the chosen mount of many high-ranking aces.

In 1937 the German Air Ministry issued specifications for a new fighter as a hedge against the new and heretofore untried Messerschmitt Bf 109 fighter. Dr. Kurt Tank of the Focke-Wulf Flugzeugbau firm broke with tradition by conceiving a radial-engine design. This was a dicey departure from aerodynamic norms, given the Luftwaffe's stated preferences for in-line liquid-cooled motors. Tank, however, expertly streamlined the craft with a close-fitting cowl, a spacious canopy, and wide-track landing gear. The new Fw 190 underwent test flights throughout 1939, where it demonstrated marked superiority in handling over the Bf 109 and virtually every fighter then extant. It was fast, highly maneuverable, and ruggedly built and entered production in 1940. When first encountered over the English Channel in the summer of 1941,

Fw 190s had little trouble mastering the opposing *Spitfire Vs*. For once, German pilots enjoyed a qualitative—if short-lived—superiority over their enemies. But the Fw 190 also proved adept as a ground-attack craft and a dive-bomber. By 1944 they had almost completely displaced the previously vaunted *Stuka* in those roles.

Because the Fw 190's performance faltered at high altitude, in 1943 Tank began development of a radically different version. The new Fw 190D was powered by a liquid-cooled in-line engine, although its annular radiator preserved the radial appearance of the series. The fuselage was also lengthened and heavier armament fitted. "Long-nose Dora," as it was called, became the best German fighter of the war, easily capable of tangling on equal terms with P-51D *Mustangs* and late-model *Spitfires*. An even better high-altitude version, christened the Ta 152, exhibited superb performance, but only a handful were constructed, and none saw combat. By war's end, no less than 20,087 Fw 190s were constructed in various models.

Focke-Wulf Fw 200 *Condor* ——————————— **Germany**

Type: Patrol-Bomber; Transport

Dimensions: wingspan, 107 feet, 9 inches; length, 76 feet, 11 inches; height, 20 feet, 8 inches
Weights: empty, 37,478 pounds; gross, 50,044 pounds
Power plant: 4 × 1,000–horsepower BMW 323R-2 radial engines
Performance: maximum speed, 224 miles per hour; ceiling, 19,685 feet; range, 2,211 miles
Armament: 4 × 13mm machine guns; 1 × 20mm cannon; up to 4,630 pounds of bombs
Service dates: 1940–1945

Lumbering *Condors* were so adept at sinking ships that Winston Churchill dubbed them the "scourge of the Atlantic." Their success is even more remarkable considering that they were commercial aircraft adopted for military purposes.

In 1936 Deutsche Lufthansa requested designs for a 26-passenger airliner capable of nonstop service between Berlin and New York. Dr. Kurt Tank complied in 1937 with his beautiful Fw 200, an all-metal, low-wing monoplane with double wheels that retracted into streamlined nacelles. That year the Fw 200 established many world records for distance, including a 48-hour flight to Tokyo. The Japanese were so impressed that they requested a maritime reconnaissance version to be developed for their military. The onset of World War II in 1939 forestalled any such development, and various prototype and commercial Fw 200s were hastily impressed into service as transports. In this capacity they achieved only limited success as, being nonstressed for military service, they proved structurally weak. In fact, they acquired a bad reputation

for breaking their backs after a hard landing. But by 1940 the Fw 200 found its niche as a long-range anti-shipping bomber.

The Fw 200 *Condor* frequently operated in close cooperation with roving packs of U-boats. These machines had been refitted with a long ventral gondola beneath the fuselage, where bombs were housed. Having identified an enemy convoy, *Condors* would attack and cripple merchant vessels, leaving the submarines to finish them off. Within a year Fw 200s accounted for several thousand tons of Allied shipping and were justly feared as the "scourge of the Atlantic." Eventually, the development of long-range fighters like the Bristol *Beaufighter* and ship-launched disposable Hawker *Hurricanes* spelled the end of its maritime roles. The Fw 200s next pioneered antishipping missiles, but success proved elusive, and by 1944 most had been reconverted back into transports. Significantly, both Adolf Hitler and Heinrich Himmler used *Condors* as their personal transports. A total of 276 were constructed.

Fokker C V

Type: Fighter; Light Bomber

Dimensions: wingspan, 41 feet; length, 31 feet, 2 inches; height, 11 feet, 5 inches
Weights: empty, 2,756 pounds; gross, 4,079 pounds
Power plant: 1 × 336–horsepower Hispano-Suiza liquid-cooled in-line engine
Performance: maximum speed, 140 miles per hour; ceiling, 18,045 feet; range, 478 miles
Armament: 2 × 7.92mm machine guns; up to 441 pounds of bombs
Service dates: 1924–1940

The Fokker C V was one of the most popular and widely exported aircraft of the interwar period. It could be fitted with a wide variety of engines or wingspans depending upon its intended use.

In 1924 Anthony Fokker's genius for innovation was never more evident than in his C V aircraft. Outwardly, it was a conventional biplane with unequal wings, fixed landing gear, and a highly streamlined nose. The fuselage was constructed of steel tubing and fabric-covered throughout, while the wings employed wood in their construction. It flew exceptionally well, was fast for its day, and, in the tradition of Fokker airplanes, proved exceptionally rugged. The C V was marketed to the Dutch military as a light bomber, but Fokker had in mind a multipurpose aircraft. He accomplished this by enabling the C V to be fitted with differing sets of wing shapes and spans according to the mission desired, and all could be interchanged in under an hour. Engines were also easily replaced for the same purpose. The C V en-

tered the Dutch air force in 1924 and was immediately popular with both flight and ground crews. For almost a decade and a half it reigned as the most successful aircraft of its class. Fokker constructed more than 400 machines, which proved so well built that few ever returned for reconditioning. He later complained that this happy predicament led to acute work shortages at his factory!

The high performance, reliability, and supreme flexibility of the C V made it ideal for export purposes, and it was acquired by Bolivia, Denmark, Finland, Norway, Sweden, Italy, Hungary, and Switzerland. Once manufacturing licenses were granted, total production of C Vs worldwide exceeded 1,000 machines. The most popular variants proved the C V-D and C V-E, which functioned as fighters and light bombers, respectively. In 1928 it was a Swedish C V skiplane that rescued Admiral Umberto Nobile when his airship crashed in the Arctic. Several Dutch machines were still in service and actively flown during the German invasion of 1940.

Type: Fighter

Dimensions: wingspan, 29 feet, 2 inches; length, 22 feet, 9 inches; height, 9 feet
Weights: empty, 1,477 pounds; gross, 1,984 pounds
Power plant: 1 × 185–horsepower BMW IIIa liquid-cooled in-line engine
Performance: maximum speed, 117 miles per hour; ceiling, 19,685 feet; range, 200 miles
Armament: 2 × 7.62mm machine guns
Service dates: 1918–1926

The legendary Fokker D VII was one of history's greatest fighter aircraft. Its reputation was so formidable that the 1918 Armistice terms specifically authorized confiscation of all D VIIs by Allied forces.

By December 1917 the German High Command witnessed control of the air slipping irrevocably back into Allied hands. The following January they announced competition for a new fighter craft to employ the excellent Mercedes D III engine. No less than 60 prototypes appeared at Aldershof as planned, but events were dominated by a machine entered by Anthony Fokker. His D VII model, designed by Reinhold Platz, was a conventional biplane of exceptionally graceful lines. Its wings were constructed from wood, and the fuselage consisted of a tube steel structure covered by fabric. But first and foremost, the D VII was extremely maneuverable, especially at high altitudes. With such striking performance, it was decided to rush Fokker's invention immediately into production without further delay. An estimated 1,000 were constructed by Fokker, in concert with Albatros and AEG.

The first Fokker D VIIs appeared over the front in the spring of 1918 and were an unpleasant surprise to Allied pilots. Although slower than many adversaries, D VIIs could outturn and outclimb a host of excellent airplanes, including the SE 5a, Sopwith *Camel*, and SPAD XIII. Moreover, it had a remarkable ability to briefly "hang" on its propeller, firing upward. Allied casualties soared correspondingly, and it looked like the formidable Fokker might single-handedly regain control of the skies for Germany. The war ended in November 1918 before that transpired, but the Allies acknowledged the D VII's formidable reputation with a direct compliment. They demanded outright confiscation of all surviving D VII's as part of the Armistice conditions!

No sooner had hostilities ceased than Anthony Fokker smuggled about 160 D VIIs over the border into neutral Holland, where he sold them to the Dutch air force. These fine aircraft were subsequently exported globally and remained in the Belgian service until 1926. The D VII was a classic fighter design.

Type: Fighter

Dimensions: wingspan, 27 feet, 6 inches; length, 19 feet, 3 inches; height, 9 feet, 3 inches
Weights: empty, 848 pounds; gross, 1,238 pounds
Power plant: 1 × 110–horsepower Oberursel UR II rotary engine
Performance: maximum speed, 115 miles per hour; ceiling, 20,669 feet; range, 150 miles
Armament: 2 × 7.92mm machine guns
Service dates: 1918

The "Flying Razor" was the last and among the finest German fighters to appear in World War I. Had fighting continued into 1919, it would have ultimately replaced the already formidable Fokker D VII.

In the spring of 1918, the German High Command authorized a second fighter flyoff at Aldershof. Among the many prototypes represented was a new monoplane designed by Reinhold Platz, the Fokker V 26/28. From an appearance standpoint, it possessed a steel-tube and fabric-covered fuselage, a cowling borrowed from the Dr I triplane, and the tail section of the D VII. The single wing was made from wood and possessed a thick chord with tapering tips, and numerous struts secured it to the fuselage. This parasol machine represented the last German application of rotary-engine technology since the obsolete *Eindekker* of 1915. More important, it was fast and extremely agile, and for a second time the Fokker design totally dominated the competition. Consequently, it was decided to rush the new craft immediately into production as the Fokker E V. An

estimated 400 of these machines, subsequently redesignated D VIIIs, were constructed over the intervening months.

The first batches of D VIIIs reached the front in April 1918 for further evaluation. Pilots marveled at the new fighter's climb and maneuverability, but when three were lost to unexplained crashes, the program was suspended. Investigations revealed that poor workmanship and imperfect timber were the cause, which were corrected, but much valuable time had been lost. It was not until September 1918 that production could resume. The first combat-ready D VIII's arrived at the front in late October, just three weeks prior to the end of the war. Nevertheless, they fully upheld the formidable reputation acquired by the famous Fokker D VIIs and were flown with considerable success. In one skirmish on November 6, 1918, Flying Razors claimed three SPAD XIIIs in a matter of minutes. The war concluded in November before the D VIIIs had a chance for further distinction, but they were the last combat aircraft fielded by Imperial Germany.

Type: Fighter

Dimensions: wingspan, 36 feet, 1 inch; length, 26 feet, 10 inches; height, 9 feet, 8 inches
Weights: empty, 3,197 pounds; gross, 4,519 pounds
Power plant: 1 × 830–horsepower Bristol Mercury VIII radial engine
Performance: maximum speed, 286 miles per hour; ceiling, 36,090 feet; range, 590 miles
Armament: 4 × 7.92mm machine guns
Service dates: 1938–1944

The Fokker D XXI saw widespread service in three European air forces before and during World War II. It marked a transitional stage between fabric-covered biplanes and stress-skinned monoplanes.

The Fokker D XXI evolved in response to a 1935 specification laid out by the Netherlands East Indies Army Air Service, which sought a new monoplane fighter to replace the antiquated biplanes then employed. Fokker, which enjoyed a tremendous international reputation for effective and innovative designs, responded with a rather conservative machine, but it was well-suited to simplicity and ease of operation. The Fokker D XXI first flew in 1938 as a low-wing monoplane with fixed, spatted undercarriage. True to company tradition, it consisted of steel tubing and wooden wings and was covered by fabric. The only modern aspect was the fully enclosed cockpit. Test flights revealed the craft to be underpowered but also responsive and highly maneuverable. During one flight an altitude of 37,250 feet was reached—a Dutch record. In 1938 the Dutch air force obtained 36 examples. These were

followed by two imported by Denmark, which constructed another 10 under license, and 40 for Finland. The Republican government in Spain also expressed interest in the D XXI as its standard fighter, but Nationalist forces overran the factory intended to produce them. Worse still, the D XXI was verging on obsolescence when World War II broke out in September 1939.

Dutch Fokkers enjoyed a brief but useful wartime career. On May 10, 1940, they intercepted a formation of 55 Junkers Ju 52 transports, shooting down 37 with heavy loss of life. Several Me 109s were also claimed before ammunition stocks were exhausted and the planes grounded. Denmark, which had been experimenting with a 20mm cannon–armed version, offered no resistance, and its D XXIs were confiscated by Germany. However, Finland put the fighter to excellent use during the 1939 Soviet invasion, and D XXIs scored the first aerial kill of that conflict. When war resumed in 1941, Finland constructed an additional 50 D XXIs and flew them with great effect until 1944.

Type: Fighter

Dimensions: wingspan, 23 feet, 7 inches; length, 18 feet, 11 inches; height, 9 feet, 8 inches
Weights: empty, 904 pounds; gross, 1,289 pounds
Power plant: 1 × 110–horsepower Oberursel rotary engine
Performance: maximum speed, 103 miles per hour; ceiling, 20,013 feet; range, 150 miles
Armament: 2 × 7.92mm machine guns
Service dates: 1917–1918

The career of the famous triplane is indelibly linked to that of Manfred von Richthofen, the infamous "Red Baron." In his hands the diminutive Fokker was a deadly weapon whose reputation long survived his passing.

German authorities were shocked by the appearance of the Sopwith Triplane in the spring of 1917, which induced them to develop aircraft of similar design. A total of 14 different machines were eventually constructed and flown, but the most effective proved Fokker's Dr I *Dreidecker*, designed by Reinhold Platz. The resulting prototype was compact and initially lacked interplane struts. The surface area of three wings afforded it marvelous powers of maneuver and climb. The middle section vibrated excessively in a dive, however, so struts were subsequently added between them. Several preproduction craft were then dispatched to be evaluated under combat conditions. One of them was flown by leading ace Werner Voss, who scored 20 victories in only 24 days. In fact, the Dr I was a dangerous weapon in the hands of experienced pilots—

and equally dangerous and unforgiving for the novice. Nonetheless, in the summer of 1917 Fokker commenced full-scale production of the Dr I, which terminated at 320 machines.

One of the earliest *Jadgeschwaders* (fighter groups) to receive the diminutive craft was the famous "Flying Circus" of Manfred von Richthofen. The Red Baron excelled in flying the Fokker Dr I, and increased his already impressive tally to 80 kills before he himself was killed in action on April 21, 1918. The other leading *Dreidecker* ace, Voss, met his demise earlier, on September 23, 1917, when he dramatically and single-handedly dueled an entire patrol of British SE 5s. Despite uniform success in combat, several unexplained crashes were attributed to structural weaknesses. The Dr I was consequently grounded for several months pending repairs and did not return to combat until late 1917. Thereafter newer allied aircraft minimized its effectiveness, and by the spring of 1918 the heyday of the triplane had passed. The Dr I was superceded by Fokker's other superb design, the D VII.

Fokker E III ——————————————————————— **Germany**

Type: Fighter

Dimensions: wingspan, 31 feet, 4 inches; length, 23 feet, 7 inches; height, 9 feet, 2 inches
Weights: empty, 878 pounds; gross, 1,342 pounds
Power plant: 1 × 100–horsepower Oberursel U.I rotary engine
Performance: maximum speed, 81 miles per hour; ceiling, 11,500 feet; range, 100 miles
Armament: 1 × 7.92mm machine gun
Service dates: 1915–1916

In the autumn of 1915, the anachronistic-looking *Eindekker* reigned as the world's best fighter aircraft. Its superiority over contemporary French and English machines ushered in a period known as the "Fokker scourge"—and the dawn of modern aerial warfare.

April 19, 1915, signified a turning point in the history of military aviation when the French-built Morane-Saulnier L aircraft piloted by Roland Garros crashed behind German lines. German investigators combing through the wreckage discovered that Garros had clandestinely mounted a machine gun fixed so as to fire through the propeller arc. The propeller itself was fitted with metal wedges to deflect any unsynchronized projectiles, but the Germans recognized the advantages an improved system would bring. The brilliant aircraft designer Anthony Fokker was contacted, whose firm was familiar with the concept, and within two weeks a completely synchronized interrupter gear was devised. This allowed bullets to shoot through a moving propeller by being deliberately timed to miss it. This technol-

ogy was then grafted onto a Fokker M 5 monoplane, a design that had been flying since 1913, for trials. Thus was born the Fokker E I, the world's first true fighter craft. A total of 400 of all models were built, and their tactical implication was immense.

At a time when Allied craft were either unarmed or simply carried rifles and other sidearms for defense, the new Fokker *Eindekkers* represented a quantum leap in firepower. Throughout the fall and winter of 1915, they sawed through nearly 1,000 allied reconnaissance craft, chiefly lumbering British Be 2cs. The Fokkers also stimulated the evolution of new fighter tactics as pioneered by Germans aces like Max Immelmann and Oswald Boelcke. For several months the "Fokker scourge" dominated the skies of Western Europe until the spring of 1916, when superior fighters like the Nieuport 11 *Bebe* and the de Havilland DH 2 pusher debuted. The days of the ugly, ungainly *Eindekkers* were numbered in weeks, but a corner had been turned. Hereafter, warplanes ceased being frail-looking contraptions and evolved into machines of increasing deadliness.

Type: Fighter; Light Bomber

Dimensions: wingspan, 56 feet, 3 inches; length, 37 feet, 9 inches; height, 11 feet, 2 inches
Weights: empty, 7,410 pounds; gross, 10,582 pounds
Power plant: 2 × 830–horsepower Bristol Mercury VIII radial engines
Performance: maximum speed, 295 miles per hour; ceiling, 30,500 feet; range, 870 miles
Armament: 9 × 7.92mm machine guns; up to 882 pounds of bombs
Service dates: 1938–1940

The hulking G I was the Netherlands's most combat-capable aircraft of World War II. Despite great potential, nearly all were destroyed after heroic and futile resistance.

In 1935 Fokker initiated a company-funded project to produce a large interceptor that could also double as a ground-attack craft. Christened the G I, it was secretly developed and not publicly unveiled until the 1936 Paris Salon. The G I was unlike any aircraft previously seen and generated considerable interest. It was a twin-boomed craft with pilot, crew, and armament housed in a large central nacelle. The two booms mounted Hispano-Suiza radial engines and were joined aft of the fuselage by a single stabilizer. Construction was mixed, consisting of steel tubing and fabric covering. But the most significant feature was the armament: no less than eight 7.92mm machine guns were concentrated in the nose while the tailgunner operated a single weapon. The G I first flew in March 1937 to the satisfaction of company officials, and it was

next offered to the *Luchtvaartafdeling* (army air service). An order for 36 machines resulted, with initial deliveries arriving the following year. In the quest for engine standardization, however, the army required that the more common Bristol Mercury radial engine be mounted. At the time of its appearance, the G I was probably the most advanced warplane of its kind in the world. It seemed so promising that orders from Sweden, Spain, and Denmark were also forthcoming. Given its formidable armament, the G I was unofficially dubbed the *Faucheur* (Mower).

When Germany attacked the Netherlands in May 1940, only 23 G Is had been deployed, and these were assigned to the 3rd and 4th Fighter Groups of the 1st Air Regiment. Several were caught on the ground and destroyed during the initial onslaught, but a handful continued fighting over the next several days. All were destroyed save one. The Germans then confiscated several G Is still on the assembly line for completion and use as trainers.

Folland *Gnat* ———————————————————————— **Great Britain**

Type: Fighter; Light Bomber; Trainer

Dimensions: wingspan, 24 feet; length, 31 feet, 9 inches; height, 9 feet, 7 inches
Weights: empty, 5,140 pounds; gross, 8,630 pounds
Power plant: 1 × 4,230–pound thrust Hawker-Siddeley Orpheus turbojet engine
Performance: maximum speed, 636 miles per hour; ceiling, 48,000 feet; range, 1,151 miles
Armament: none
Service dates: 1962–1979

The lively little *Gnats* would have made excellent low-cost fighters, but the Royal Air Force preferred them as trainers instead. For many years they thrilled thousands as part of the *Red Arrows* precision acrobatic team.

The rising costs inherent to modern jet technology persuaded W.E.W. Petter to develop a new lightweight fighter. By 1955 this had become practical with the advent of smaller, more powerful jet engines, and the concept was pursued as a company-funded venture. That year Folland unveiled the *Midge*, a high-performance aircraft that was a foot shorter and 1,000 pounds lighter than the Messerschmitt Me 109! This was a high-wing monoplane with highly swept wings and control surfaces. The RAF, however, expressed no interest in the *Midge* as a combat aircraft, and they entreated Petter to develop a similar craft for training purposes. The prototype flew in 1956 and was similar to the *Midge*, save for an extended nose to house an additional pilot and broader wings to slow down landing speeds. The RAF was impressed by the little craft

and authorized a preproduction batch of six machines. By 1965 it had acquired no less than 105 *Gnats* for their inventory.

The *Gnat* was destined to replaced the *Vampire* T.11 as an advanced jet trainer and be the next instructional step after the slower Hunting *Jet Provost*. In service it possessed all the flight characteristics of modern jet fighters and could break the sound barrier in a shallow dive. *Gnats* also proved overly complex and difficult to maintain, but they nonetheless rendered useful service for nearly two decades before being replaced by BAe *Hawks*. They also performed useful recruiting service in the thrilling exhibitions by the famous *Red Arrow* acrobatic team. The *Gnat* also received friendly reception from Finland and India. The former bought a handful rigged as fighters and operated them as such until 1972. India, meanwhile, manufactured several hundred under license as the HAL *Ajeet*. In numerous wars with Pakistan they proved to be agile targets and difficult to hit. Many *Gnats* remain operational to this day.

Friedrichshafen G III ———————————————————— **Germany** —

Type: Heavy Bomber

Dimensions: wingspan, 77 feet, 11 inches; length, 42 feet, 1 inch; height, 12 feet
Weights: empty, 5,929 pounds; gross, 8,646 pounds
Power plant: 2 × 260–horsepower Mercedes D IVa liquid-cooled in-line engines
Performance: maximum speed, 87 miles per hour; ceiling, 14,764 feet; range, 400 miles
Armament: 2 × 7.92mm machine guns; 1,102 pounds of bombs
Service dates: 1916–1918

The Friedrichshafen G III was a capable German heavy bomber that combined good range with respectable bomb loads. In concert with the Gotha V, it ranged across the Western Front and inflicted considerable damage.

The firm Flugzeugbau Friedrichshafen had been founded by the famous Count Ferdinand Zeppelin prior to World War I and was best known for producing naval seaplanes. In 1914 chief engineer Theodor Kober began designing the company's first heavy bomber for the land service. The G I emerged in 1915 as a twin-engine, three-bay biplane of pusher configuration. It failed to go into production, and the following year a second variant, the G II, was constructed. This was a two-bay pusher design whose wings contained steel center-section spars for added strength. It also carried a pilot and two gunners who sat in the fore and aft positions. The G II was deployed in 1916, but because of limited range and payload it served only in small numbers.

The final Friedrichshafen bomber of the war was the G III. Like the earlier G I, it was a three-bay biplane pusher whose lengthy wings also sported double ailerons. The fuselage was constructed of wood, covered by fabric, and unique in that the central section served as an integral unit housing the crew, fuel, engines, and bombs. The landing gear were large, set in pairs, and also contained a large nosewheel to prevent overturning on rough terrain. The final product functioned well and entered production in 1917. Precise figures are not known, but at least 330 machines were assembled by various contractors.

In service the G III flew mostly from bases in Northwestern Europe and conducted long-range bombing raids against British positions at Dunkirk, along with several nighttime raids against Paris. There is, however, no proof that they raided England alongside the more famous Gotha Vs. In 1918 a final version, the G IV, was deployed, which differed from earlier variants in being snub-nosed and having engines mounted in tractor configuration. All were tough, reliable machines.

Type: Glider; Transport

Dimensions: wingspan, 110 feet; length, 68 feet; height, 20 feet, 3 inches
Weights: empty, 18,400 pounds; gross, 36,000 pounds
Power plant: none
Performance: maximum speed, 150 miles per hour
Armament: none
Service dates: 1944–1945

The giant *Hamilcar* was the largest transport glider employed by Allied forces in World War II. It was the first such craft to convey tanks and other armored vehicles directly into combat.

The development of airborne forces by 1940 gave armies unprecedented mobility and tactical surprise. Now it was possible to insert military power at any point on a map. However, paratroopers remained essentially light infantry because all their requisite supplies were carried on their backs. They were thus at a disadvantage when fighting well-armed ground forces possessing greater firepower and ammunition. The British Air Ministry contemplated this fact in 1940 when it undertook development of airborne forces in the wake of Germany's dazzling successes in Belgium. It also issued Specification X.27/40, calling for creation of a large glider craft capable of hoisting small tanks, trucks, or artillery pieces to assist parachutists wherever they landed.

In March 1942 General Aircraft responded with a glider transport called the *Hamilcar*, a huge and rather sophisticated craft. This was a high-wing monoplane of all-wood construction flown by a crew of two. The canopy was placed on top of the fuselage just forward of the wing's leading edge and was accessed by ladder. The wing itself was fitted with pneumatically actuated slotted trailing edges and slotted ailerons to facilitate short landings. The fuselage, meanwhile, was a boxy, rectangular affair with a cavernous cargo hold measuring 25 feet by 8 feet. No less than two armored Bren-gun carriers, a 40mm Bofors gun and a tow truck, or a seven-ton *Locust* or *Tetrarch* tank, could easily be accommodated. Furthermore, the entire nose of the craft was hinged to afford ease of loading and unloading. Up to 17,600 pounds of cargo could be towed aloft by a *Halifax* bomber and landed safely where needed.

Hamilcars experienced their baptism of fire on June 6, 1944, when 70 of these huge planes were successfully launched over Normandy in support of Allied paratroopers. They subsequently rendered useful service at Arnhem that fall, and during the Rhine crossings in 1945. A total of 390 were manufactured, including several powered Mk X versions intended for eventual use against Japan.

Type: Fighter

Dimensions: wingspan, 32 feet, 9 inches; length, 26 feet, 2 inches; height, 10 feet, 4 inches
Weights: empty, 2,775 pounds; gross, 3,970 pounds
Power plant: 1 × 645–horsepower Bristol Mercury radial engine
Performance: maximum speed, 230 miles per hour; ceiling, 33,500 feet; range, 460 miles
Armament: 2 × .303–inch machine guns
Service dates: 1934–1943

Last of the open-cockpit British biplanes, the *Gauntlet* was probably the world's best fighter of its day. Fast and maneuverable, it even conducted the first-ever radio-controlled intercept.

In 1929 the unexpected performance of the Fairey *Fox* bomber, which could outpace any British fighter then in service, was disconcerting to the Air Ministry. Consequently, it released specifications for a new craft capable of exceeding 250 miles per hour in level flight.

In 1933 a Gloster design team under H. P. Folland responded with Model SS.19B, the updated version of an aircraft first flown in 1928. This machine had earlier lost out to the superb Bristol *Bulldog*, but the company refined it over time at its own expense. The new design was a two-bay biplane with staggered wings, and extreme attention being paid to streamlining. For example, all bracing-wire fittings were carefully sunk into the wings, leaving only the wires themselves exposed, and these, too, were specially streamlined. Moreover, all external control levers were deleted, and the bottom wing was carefully faired into the fuselage. The fuselage itself was oval in cross-section, constructed of metal frames, and covered in fabric. The new machine was highly maneuverable and demonstrated a 40 mile-per-hour advantage over the same *Bulldog* that had bested it five years earlier. In 1934 it entered production as the *Gauntlet I*; 24 machines were purchased.

In 1935 a new version, the *Gauntlet II*, arrived. These differed mainly in construction techniques, as the Hawker firm had absorbed Gloster and imposed its own design philosophy. Some of these craft sported a new three-blade metal propeller in place of the standard two-blade wooden one. They were also built in relatively large numbers—204 machines—and equipped no less than 14 squadrons of RAF Fighter Command. In 1937 three *Gauntlets* were successfully vectored to an oncoming civilian airliner, thereby concluding history's first radio-controlled intercept. These versatile fighters were superseded by Hawker *Hurricanes* and Gloster *Gladiators* by 1938, although some flew combat missions in East Africa as late as 1943.

Gloster *Gladiator* — Great Britain

Type: Fighter

Dimensions: wingspan, 32 feet, 3 inches; length, 27 feet, 5 inches; height, 11 feet, 7 inches
Weights: empty, 3,444 pounds; gross, 4,864 pounds
Power plant: 1 × 830–horsepower Bristol Mercury IX radial engine
Performance: maximum speed, 257 miles per hour; ceiling, 33,500 feet; range, 440 miles
Armament: 4 × .303–inch machine guns
Service dates: 1937–1944

The doughty *Gladiator* was the last biplane fighter operated by the Royal Air Force and the Fleet Air Arm. More temperamental than the *Gauntlet*, it nonetheless gave a good account of itself during the early days of World War II.

The *Gladiator* began as a Gloster-funded company venture to improve its existing *Gauntlet* fighter. Using that aircraft as the basis, a new, more refined version was constructed and flown in 1934. It was a single-bay biplane with fixed landing gear; the fuselage was of an oval cross-section. The basic outlines of its predecessor were present, being metal-framed and fabric-covered, but it sported a number of refinements more associated with monoplanes. These included a fully enclosed cockpit, hydraulically operated flaps, and four machine guns. The new craft was faster than the *Gauntlet* but also less forgiving to fly, and it displayed a tendency to spin. Nonetheless, the Air Ministry authorized production to commence in 1936, and the first *Gladiator Is* arrived in 1937. They were followed by the *Gladiator II*, possessing a stronger engine and a three-blade propeller. A total of 747 were constructed.

When it debuted, the *Gladiator* represented the culmination of three decades of biplane evolution. However, it was a tactical anachronism once the newer, more capable monoplanes began to arrive. By 1939 most *Gladiators* had been supplanted by infinitely better Hawker *Hurricanes* and Supermarine *Spitfires*. However, several were actively engaged in the early days of World War II and gained a public reputation rivaling another biplane holdover, the Fairey *Swordfish*. *Gladiators* performed well in Norway by operating off of frozen lakes. They also gained a measure of immortality when four Royal Navy machines (three of them named *Faith*, *Hope*, and *Charity*) briefly defended Malta against the Italian Regia Aeronautica (Italian air force) in June 1940. Others performed useful work in the Western Desert before fading from the combat scene entirely. By 1944 only a handful of *Gladiators* survived, being restricted to communications and meteorological work. They were capable machines but unable to adapt to modern times.

Type: Fighter; Night Fighter

Dimensions: wingspan, 52 feet; length, 56 feet, 9 inches; height, 16 feet
Weights: empty, 38,100; gross, 43,165 pounds
Power plant: 2 × 12,300–pound thrust Armstrong/Siddeley Sapphire turbojet engines
Performance: maximum speed, 702 miles per hour; ceiling, 52,000 feet; range, 930 miles
Armament: 4 × 30mm cannons; 4 × *Firestreak* missiles
Service dates: 1956–1968

The mighty *Javelin* was the world's first twin-jet delta fighter and also the Royal Air Force's first all-weather interceptor. Mounting numerous radars and computer systems, it operated at day and night under any weather conditions.

Technological strides made during World War II badly blurred the distinction between daytime and nighttime fighters. By 1945 the state of bombardment aviation allowed such craft to perform military missions in any kind of weather or time of day. Clearly, new all-weather fighters, equipped with radar to peer through the overcast, were becoming necessary to intercept them. In 1948 the British Air Ministry proclaimed Specification F.4/48 to obtain a swept-wing jet-powered interceptor. The new machine was required to operate at great heights under all meteorological conditions and in the dark. A Gloster design team under Richard W. Walker then submitted plans for the world's first twin-engine delta fighter. After lengthy gestation, the prototype emerged in November 1951 with a spectacular appearance. The Gloster craft was a large delta configuration, with its twin engines

buried in the flattened fuselage. A crew of two sat in a teardrop canopy behind an extremely pointed nose housing a large radar system. Delta wings promised good performance at high speeds and high altitudes, but they were inherently dangerous to land owing to the high angle of attack on approach (that is, it approached the runway with its nose in the air). Because this was impractical for nighttime and poor-weather operations, the new craft was consequently fitted with a high "T" tail to allow landing at safer angles. After additional testing, the machine finally became operational in 1956 as the *Javelin*. It was England's first attempt at building a modern all-weather fighter.

During the next decade the *Javelin* passed through seven distinct models, each offering successive improvements in performance and capability. The most significant of these was the FAW.7, which deleted cannon armament in favor of *Firestreak* missiles for the first time. A total of 428 *Javelins* were built, equipping no less than 14 squadrons. Excellent craft all, they were finally mustered out by 1968 after a distinguished service career.

Gloster _Meteor_ ———————————————————————————————— **Great Britain**

Type: Fighter; Night Fighter

Dimensions: wingspan, 37 feet, 2 inches; length, 44 feet, 7 inches; height, 13 feet
Weights: empty, 8,140 pounds; gross, 15,700 pounds
Power plant: 2 × 3,500–pound thrust Rolls-Royce Derwent 8 turbojet engines
Performance: maximum speed, 598 miles per hour; ceiling, 43,000 feet; range, 980 miles
Armament: 4 × 20mm cannon
Service dates: 1944–1957

The _Meteor_ was the first jet operated by the Royal Air Force and the only Allied jet to see action during World War II. It proved surprisingly adaptable and spawned several postwar variants.

By 1940 the nascent technology of jet propulsion seemed promising, so the British Air Ministry issued Specification F.9/40, calling for the creation of a functioning jet fighter. Gloster, which had designed and operated the G.40, Britain's first jet, was selected for the task. A design team under George Carter constructed a prototype that first flew in March 1943. This craft, the _Meteor_, was a twin-engine machine with straight wings, a bubble canopy, and tricycle landing gear. Two engines were chosen over one due to the relatively weak thrust of British engines at that time. The plane was otherwise conventionally constructed of sheeted metal skin and flew surprising well. The first _Meteors_ became operational in July 1944, only weeks after the German Messerschmitt Me 262 had debuted, and commenced downing V-1 rocket bombs. Several improved Mk IIIs, with Rolls-

Royce Derwent engines, were also committed to Europe during the last weeks of the war, performing ground-attack missions. Afterward better engines became available, and in 1946 _Meteors_ established two absolute speed records of 606 and 616 miles per hour respectively.

The _Meteor_'s basic design was sound and rather adaptable, which gave rise to several versions throughout the postwar era. These included two-seat trainer, photo-reconnaissance, and night-fighting variants. The most numerous fighter, the Mk 8, flew in 1947 and constituted the bulk of RAF jet strength through the early 1950s. Several fought in the Korean War with Australian forces, although they were outclassed by Russia's more modern MiG 15s. The most important night fighter, the NF 11, was built by Armstrong-Whitworth in 1950. This craft employed two crew members and a totally redesigned and lengthened nose section. _Meteors_ of every stripe served with impressive longevity and rendered excellent service with the RAF and other air forces up through the late 1950s.

Type: Heavy Bomber

Dimensions: wingspan, 77 feet, 10 inches; length, 40 feet; height, 12 feet, 8 inches
Weights: empty, 6,041 pounds; gross, 8,763 pounds
Power plant: 2 × 260–horsepower Mercedes D IVa liquid-cooled in-line engines
Performance: maximum speed, 87 miles per hour; ceiling, 21,325 feet; range, 311 miles
Armament: 2 × 7.92mm machine guns; up to 1,061 pounds of bombs
Service dates: 1917–1918

The mighty Gotha symbolized German strategic bombing in World War I. Their attacks on London did relatively little damage but great psychological harm and were harbingers of what would transpire two decades later.

By 1916 Zeppelin attacks on England could not be mounted without intolerable losses to those giant lighter-than-air craft. The German High Command thereupon announced specifications for a *Grossflugzeug* (large bomber) capable of hitting these same targets. It so happened that the firm Gothaer Waggonfabrik had been experimenting with a series of large aircraft for such purposes. The first three models, G I through G III, were variations on a basic theme and suffered from inadequate range and bomb loads. The first production version, the G IV, proved an entirely different matter. This was a large, three-bay, twin-engine aircraft, with propellers mounted in pusher configuration. A crew of three was required, consisting of a pilot and two gunners. Made entirely of wood and fabric-covered, the G IVs were some-

what fatiguing to fly, owing to a poorly located center of gravity, and were also prone to damage if roughly landed. About 230 Gotha G IVs were acquired in 1917.

The first daylight Gotha raid against England occurred on May 25, 1915, when the city of Folkestone suffered 95 casualties. This was followed by a major attack against London on June 13, 1917, whereby 162 people were killed and 432 injured. From a strategic standpoint these raids were mere pinpricks, but public outrage necessitated redeploying several fighter squadrons from France for home defense. When the Gothas began taking losses, they switched to night attacks after August 1917. The British initially experienced difficulty coping with such tactics, but by dint of searchlights and pluck they managed to bring down several more bombers. Consequently, Gotha night raids were suspended after May 1918. A more powerful model, the G V, was in service by then, and surviving Gothas restricted their activities to bombing targets on the continent.

Type: Glider

Dimensions: wingspan, 80 feet, 4 inches; length, 51 feet, 10 inches; height, 15 feet, 5 inches
Weights: empty, 11,243 pounds; gross, 17,196 pounds
Power plant: none or 2 × 700–horsepower Gnome-Rhone 14M radial engines
Performance: maximum speed, 180 miles per hour; ceiling, 24,605 feet; range, 373 miles
Armament: 4 × 7.92mm machine guns
Service dates: 1942–1944

The Go 242 was the most widely used German glider during the letter half of World War II. It saw active use in the Mediterranean and Russian theaters, and a powered version also became available.

In 1941 the startling success of the DFS 230 assault glider prompted the German Air Ministry to request larger, more capable craft. It devolved upon Albert Kalkert of the Gothaer Waggonfabrik firm to design a radical solution to the problem of bigger gliders. His Go 242 was unique in being a high-winged craft with three times the troop-carrying capacity as the DFS 230. Constructed of metal framework, wood, and fabric, the Go 242 consisted of a large fuselage pod with a hinged rear section to permit ease of entry and exit. It was centered between twin booms joined together by a single tailplane and twin rudders. While being towed for takeoff, the Go 242 would drop a jettisonable wheeled dolly and land on a semiretractable noseskid and fixed rear wheels. Jeep-type vehicles could easily be accommodated in its capacious fuselage. German authori-

ties were highly pleased with the prototype, so in 1941 they authorized immediate production. A total of 1,528 were constructed.

The Go 242 became operational in the spring of 1941 and was initially deployed in the Aegean and Mediterranean theaters. However, they were used heavily along the Russian front and specialized in bringing supplies and reinforcements to isolated German detachments. An amphibious version, the Go 242C, was specially developed for an attack upon the British battle fleet at Scapa Flow. This craft possessed a watertight hull with flotation bags and carried small powered assault boats. Once landed, the boats would disgorge, move alongside a moored warship, and attach a 2,600-pound charge to the hull. This intriguing plan never materialized owing to a lack of aviation fuel. The final version was the Go 244, unique in being powered by captured Gnome-Rhone radial engines. A total of 144 machines were converted to this standard but, slow and vulnerable, were withdrawn from combat and assigned training duties.

Type: Reconnaissance

Dimensions: 44 feet, 8 inches; length, 22 feet, 8 inches; height, 11 feet
Weights: empty, 2,046 pounds; gross, 2,730 pounds
Power plant: 1 × 220–horsepower Benz Bx.IV liquid-cooled in-line engine
Performance: maximum speed, 106 miles per hour; ceiling, 16,405 feet; range, 350 miles
Armament: 2 × 7.92mm machine guns
Service dates: 1918

The Halberstadt C V was among the last reconnaissance aircraft acquired by Germany during World War I. It possessed excellent high-altitude performance and performed doggedly until the end of hostilities.

In 1916 the firm Halberstadter Flugzeugwerke manufactured its first two-seat aircraft, the C I, which was rotary-powered and failed to enter production. However, the firm enjoyed greater success the following year by introducing the C III, designed by Karl Theiss, as a *Fernerkunder* (long-range reconnaissance craft). It possessed the familiar traits of most Halberstadt machines: sleek lines, rounded, almost elliptical tail surfaces, and a fuselage short in relation to the wingspan. The lower wings were also somewhat unique in being attached to a large keel along the fuselage bottom. A 200-horsepower Benz Bz.IV engine provided adequate power and respectable speed, and the C III was successfully employed for many months. By the spring of 1918, the onset of faster Allied fighters prompted the company to develop a more powerful, aerodynamically refined version.

The C V was a new craft that appeared very much in the mold of Halberstadt two-seaters. For better performance at high altitude there were high-aspect wings of considerable length, as well as a proportionally longer fuselage. It also differed from the C II in discarding the large communal cockpit in favor of separate seats for pilot and gunner. The craft utilized a stronger, higher-compression version of the Benz Bz.IV motor, developing 220-horsepower. Consequently, the C V displayed even better high-altitude performance than its lighter forebear, an essential defensive trait in the waning days of the war.

This final Halberstadt aircraft reached forward units in late summer. Its arrival coincided with the final overland drive by Allied forces, and the aircraft was constantly employed in photography to keep headquarters abreast of the latest enemy movements. Throughout a rather brief service life, the C V upheld the Halberstadt tradition for excellent and reliable two-seaters. After the war many of them ended up in the Swiss air force as trainers.

Halberstadt CL IV ————————————— Germany

Type: Fighter; Light Bomber

Dimensions: wingspan, 35 feet, 4 inches; length, 24 feet; height, 9 feet
Weights: empty, 1,701 pounds; gross, 2,493 pounds
Power plant: 1 × 160–horsepower Mercedes D III liquid-cooled in-line engine
Performance: maximum speed, 103 miles per hour; ceiling, 16,730 feet; range, 300 miles
Armament: 3 × 7.92mm machine guns; up to 100 pounds of bombs or grenades
Service dates: 1917–1918

The Halberstadt CLs were the first machine constructed for the new Germany category of multipurpose aircraft. Although intended as an escort fighter, they found their niche as a ground-attack plane.

By 1917 the expanding size of C-series reconnaissance aircraft rendered them more vulnerable to enemy aircraft, so a new category—CL (for "light C")—was adopted. These two-seaters were intended to act as speedy, lightweight escort fighters for the slower C class and to fulfill reconnaissance duties if necessary. The first aircraft so designated was the Halberstadt CL II, an equal-span, two-bay biplane of exceptionally streamlined design. It was conventionally constructed from wood and fabric but differed from most German two-seaters by having a communal cockpit housing both pilot and gunner. The CL II was powered by the excellent 160-horsepower Mercedes D III engine, and the resulting craft was both fast and maneuverable.

The CL II saw its baptism of fire in the summer of 1917 and rendered useful service in its appointed

role. However, the craft also demonstrated suitability for the more dangerous business of ground attack, which entailed flying over enemy trenches at low altitude, strafing positions, and lobbing small bomblets. The CL II's fast speed, robust construction, and relatively compact size rendered it difficult to shoot down, despite the fact it was totally unarmored. CL IIs distinguished themselves in fighting around Cambrai and greatly assisted the successful German counterattack of November 30, 1917. These handsome machines remained in service until the end of the war.

At length it was decided to introduce an improved version of the CL II, the CL IV. This new craft sported similar lines to its predecessor but was three feet shorter, had repositioned wings closer to the fuselage, and sported totally redesigned tail surfaces. Consequently, it possessed even greater agility at low altitudes and admirably fulfilled its escort and attack missions. Eventually both types were culled into special formations called *Schlactstaffeln* (battle flights) that specialized in close-support missions.

Type: Fighter

Dimensions: wingspan, 28 feet, 10 inches; length, 23 feet, 11 inches; height, 8 feet, 9 inches
Weights: empty, 1,234 pounds; gross, 1,696 pounds
Power plant: 1 × 120–horsepower Mercedes D II liquid-cooled in-line engine
Performance: maximum speed, 90 miles per hour; ceiling, 13,000 feet; range, 155 miles
Armament: 1 × 7.92mm machine guns
Service dates: 1916–1917

The distinctive Halberstadt D II was Germany's first biplane fighter and the first equipped with a synchronized machine gun. An interim design at best, it fought well for several months before transferring to secondary theaters.

By the end of 1915, the balance of aerial power above the Western Front had shifted to the Allies due to the appearance of de Havilland's DH 2 pusher fighters. These proved superior to the heretofore unstoppable Fokker E III monoplanes and sent the Germans scrambling for superior designs of their own. By the spring of 1916 a design team under Karl Theiss began lightening and modifying a Halberstadt B II two-seater into a single-seat biplane fighter—Germany's first. The new D II was quite unlike any previous fighter to appear thus far. It possessed an extremely tapered fuselage made of wood and metal tubing. The two bay wings were highly staggered and nearly oblong in shape, with straight trailing edges. But the craft's most distinctive feature was the tail unit: The rudder was triangular, the horizontal stabi-

lizers square. Moreover, neither of these control surfaces was directly affixed to the fuselage; instead, they were joined together by tubing and braced for greater strength. The D II's seemingly frail appearance belied its robustness and maneuverability. Although lightly armed with one machine gun, it proved more than a match for the redoubtable DH 2.

Throughout the spring of 1916, the Halberstadt D II, alongside the equally new Albatros D IIs, wrested aerial supremacy back to the Central Powers. In combat, this small scout was an agile performer and displayed an uncanny ability to survive long, steep dives. This maneuver was unthinkable for most aircraft at that time. In 1916 D IIs also became the first German fighters equipped with small rockets for balloon-busting. However, within a year the lightly armed yet nimble Halberstadts were superceded by newer Albatros scouts and Allied designs. Only 100 were built, and most spent their final year of operations over Macedonia, Palestine, and other secondary theaters.

Type: Heavy Bomber; Reconnaissance

Dimensions: wingspan, 104 feet, 2 inches; length, 71 feet, 7 inches; height, 20 feet, 9 inches
Weights: empty, 39,000 pounds; gross, 68,000 pounds
Power plant: 4 × 1,800–horsepower Bristol Hercules radial engines
Performance: maximum speed, 312 miles per hour; ceiling, 24,000 feet; range, 1,260 miles
Armament: 9 × .303–inch machine guns; 13,000 pounds of bombs
Service dates: 1941–1952

The _Halifax_ was the second member of Britain's famous trio of "heavies." Like its famous _Lancaster_ rival, it began as a twin-engine design and underwent extensive modifications throughout a long service life.

The _Halifax_ originated with Air Ministry Specification B.13/36, issued for a new twin-engine bomber to be powered by the Rolls-Royce Vulture engines. When it became apparent that better power sources were needed, Handley Page extended the wingspan of its prototype to accommodate four Rolls-Royce Merlin engines. The _Halifax_ first flew in October 1939, and it succeeded completely for such a large craft hastily assembled. It was a midwing bomber of all-metal construction with three powered gun turrets. The _Halifax_ was not quite the racehorse that the latter Avro _Lancaster_ became, but it was a marked improvement over the earlier Short _Stirling_ in terms of altitude and payload. _Halifaxes_ commenced active operations in the spring of 1941 and soon jointly formed the backbone of England's nighttime strategic offensive against Germany. By 1945 it had flown 75,532 sorties and dropped 255,000 tons of bombs.

In service the _Halifax_ was nominally a heavy bomber, but it proved itself extremely adaptable to other chores. These included maritime patrol, radar-mapping, and transportation duties. _Halifaxes_ were also responsible for destroying Germany's V-1 launching sites, dropping off agents in Central Europe, and becoming the only heavy bomber assigned duty in the Middle East. Rounding out this impressive service record was parachute-dropping and long-range reconnaissance. Moreover, it was the only airplane capable of towing the large General Aircraft _Hamilcar_ transport glider and did so in large numbers by 1945. To upgrade overall performance, the new Mk III version featured four Bristol Hercules radial engines, extended wingspan, and a totally redesigned nose section. Several models were also fitted with large radomes on their bellies and performed the first radar-based ground-mapping missions. After the war, this useful plane remained in service with the RAF Coastal Command until 1952. A total of 6,176 were built.

Type: Medium Bomber; Torpedo-Bomber

Dimensions: wingspan, 69 feet, 2 inches; length, 53 feet, 7 inches; height, 14 feet, 11 inches
Weights: empty, 11,780 pounds; gross, 18,756 pounds
Power plant: 2 × 1,000–horsepower Bristol Pegasus radial engines
Performance: maximum speed, 254 miles per hour; ceiling, 19,000 feet; range, 1,885 miles
Armament: 6 × .303–inch machine guns; up to 4,000 pounds of bombs or torpedoes
Service dates: 1938–1942

The unsung *Hampden* was an outstanding medium bomber during the early campaigns of World War II. Although vulnerable to fighters, it was faster and carried nearly as many bombs as competing designs.

The *Hampden* design arose in response to Air Ministry Specification B.9/32 for a twin-engine bomber. Both Handley Page and Vickers submitted winning designs, with the former prototype becoming the *Hampden* and the latter the *Wellington*. The Handley Page creation was one of the most unique looking bombers ever flown. It possessed a deep forward fuselage joined to an extremely narrow aft section. The arrangement invariably led to nicknames like "Frying Pan" and "Tadpole." Looks aside, however, the *Hampden* proved itself a most capable aircraft. Being fitted with Handley Page leading-edge slats, it could touch down at extremely low speeds. Moreover, it was faster than its two main rivals, the *Wellington* and the Armstrong-Whitworth *Whitley*, and could carry nearly as heavy a bomb load over the same distance. As combat would demonstrate, the main deficiency of the *Hamp-* *ton* was its weak defenses. Nonetheless, by the advent of World War II in 1939, they constituted a major part of RAF Bomber Command.

Initial operations by *Hampdens* were restricted to reconnaissance and naval interdiction, as bombing Germany was forbidden. When a flight of 11 *Hampdens* was roughly handled on September 29, 1939, and five aircraft more were shot down on a reconnaissance mission, the craft were restricted to nighttime leaflet dropping. *Hampdens* were also utilized for mining operations off the German coast and made respectable torpedo-bombers. By 1940, however, daylight bombing missions were resumed during the Battle of France, and serious loss ensued. *Hampdens* were consequently fitted with heavier defensive armament and committed to nighttime bombing of German targets. Two squadrons were then dispatched to Murmansk for that purpose as well and were ultimately turned over to the Russians. Hampdens also managed to bomb Berlin on several occasions and successfully fulfilled various secondary capacities before retiring in 1942.

Type: Heavy Bombers

Dimensions: wingspan, 75 feet; length, 58 feet; height, 17 feet, 6 inches
Weights: empty, 9,200 pounds; gross, 16,900 pounds
Power plant: 2 × 550–horsepower Rolls-Royce Kestrel liquid-cooled in-line engines
Performance: maximum speed, 142 miles per hour; ceiling, 21,000 feet; range, 920 miles
Armament: 3 × .303–inch machine guns; 3,500 pounds of bombs
Service dates: 1933–1939

One of the stranger sights in the sky, the ungainly *Heyford* was the Royal Air Force's last biplane bomber. It proved a fine machine and constituted a link between lumbering giants of the 1930s and the fast monoplane weapons of World War II.

In 1927 the Air Ministry issued Specification B.19/27, calling for a new heavy night bomber to replace the rapidly aging Vickers *Virginia*. Handley Page, where heavy bombers were a company specialty, submitted one of the most usual designs ever flown by any air force in the world. Simultaneously elegant yet grotesque, the *Heyford* was a biplane configuration with two wings of equal length fitted to a long, attenuated fuselage, with the tail unit sporting double rudders. What made the craft so unique was placement of the fuselage under the top wing, while the bottom span sat several feet below on struts! The center section of the bottom wing was also twice the thickness of the outboard ones to accommodate the bomb bay. Being low to the ground, this placement facilitated access by ground crews, and the entire

plane could be rearmed in under 30 minutes. It also featured a retractable "dustbin" turret to protect the underbelly. The *Heyford* was otherwise conventionally constructed of metal framework and canvas covering. The big craft flew well and proved easy to operate. Accordingly, in 1933 *Heyfords* entered the service as the last biplane bombers of the RAF.

At length 124 *Heyfords* were constructed in three models, and they equipped a total of 11 bombardment squadrons. They proved popular craft, strongly built, and during the 1935 RAF display at Hendon, one was actually looped! Commencing in 1937, following the appearance of Armstrong-Whitworth *Whitleys*, the gangly *Heyfords* were slowly phased out of frontline service. By 1939 they had been completely displaced by Vickers *Wellingtons*, although several performed secondary functions like training and gilder-towing. The surviving machines were finally struck off the active list in 1941. Just prior to that, *Heyfords* served as testbeds for autopilots and experiments with radar navigation.

Type: Heavy Bomber

Dimensions: wingspan, 100 feet; length, 62 feet; height, 22 feet
Weights: empty, 8,502 pounds; gross, 13,360 pounds
Power plant: 2 × 250–horsepower Rolls-Royce Mk II liquid-cooled in-line engines
Performance: maximum speed, 97 miles an hour; ceiling, 8,500 feet; range, 800 miles
Armament: 3 × .303–inch machine guns; up to 2,000 pounds of bombs
Service dates: 1916–1920

The O/400 was Britain's first strategic bomber and, for many months, the largest aircraft assembled on the British Isles. It flew successful missions over Germany and also dropped the largest Allied bombs of the war.

Sir Frederick Handley Page established the first English factory solely dedicated to manufacturing airplanes in 1909. Six years later, the Admiralty issued specifications for a large two-engine patrol-bomber, which they deemed "a bloody paralyzer." In the spring of 1916, Handley Page responded with his model O/100. This giant craft was a three-bay biplane and powered by two tractor engines mounted in nacelles between the wings. The long, boxy fuselage was of conventional construction but featured a large biplane tail section. The craft was also unique for its time in that bombs were carried in a rudimentary bomb bay. That summer the O/100 entered production, with 42 being built. The Royal Navy initially employed them for maritime reconnaissance, but losses forced them to switch to nighttime bombing.

In the spring of 1917 a more refined version, the O/400, was introduced. This differed mainly in possessing more powerful engines and a fuel system that was relocated from the nacelles to the fuselage. This version was issued to the RAF's Independent Force and equipped its very first strategic bomber units. In response to the various Gotha raids over London, the Air Board ordered the O/400s to hit back at the German mainland. On the evening of August 25, 1918, two machines from No. 215 Squadron did exactly that by staging a successful low-altitude (200 feet) raid that severely damaged a chemical factory in Mannheim.

Commencing that September, O/400s were dispatched over German targets in groups of 40 or so, both at day and night, with good effect. Some of these aircraft unloaded a 1,650-pound bomb—England's biggest—on industrial targets in the Rhineland. By the time of the Armistice, 440 O/400s had been manufactured and were being supplanted by an even bigger craft, the V/1500. Both were replaced in turn by Vickers *Vimys* during the 1920s.

Type: Strategic Bomber; Tanker; Reconnaissance

Dimensions: wingspan, 120 feet; length, 114 feet, 11 inches; height, 28 feet, 1 inch
Weights: empty, 91,000 pounds; gross, 233,000 pounds
Power plant: 4 × 20,600–pound thrust Rolls-Royce Conway turbofan engines
Performance: maximum speed, 640 miles per hour; ceiling, 55,000 feet; range, 2,300 miles
Armament: 35,000 pounds of conventional or nuclear bombs or missiles
Service dates: 1958–1984

The graceful *Victor* was the last of Britain's famous V-bombers. Technologically advanced when conceived, it was quickly outdated and performed more useful service in tanker and reconnaissance roles.

After World War II, and anticipating the technological trends of the day, Britain determined to maintain a strategic bombing force that would be jet-powered and carry atomic weapons. Specification B.35/46 was thus issued in 1946 to secure such aircraft, and Handley Page responded with a unique design quite different from its competitor, the Avro *Vulcan*. First flown in 1952, the *Victor* was a graceful, high-wing monoplane of rather sophisticated lines. The wing was crescent-shaped with decreasing degrees of sweep toward the tips. This arrangement allowed a constant critical Mach number over the wing for fast speed and high-altitude performance. The front fuselage was also unusual in that the front cabin was slightly podded and drooping while the rear was crowned by a high "T" tail, also of crescent design. The object of the *Victor*'s construction was to enable higher speed and altitude than contemporary fighters. However, by the time it debuted in 1958, the Russians had perfected Mach 2 fighters and surface-to-air missiles. Thus, the first-model *Victor*, the B Mk 1, was obsolete as a nuclear strike craft from the onset. By 1964 several had been converted into K Mk 1 tankers to replace the aging and ailing Vickers *Valiant*.

The final version of the *Victor*, the B Mk 2, was redesigned as a low-altitude bomber and, hence, was fitted with a stronger, redesigned wing. It also possessed trailing-edge fairings to improve low-altitude maneuvering. With manned bombers being supplanted by guided missiles, however, it was decided to convert these aircraft into tankers as well. Several were also subsequently modified into SR Mk 2 strategic reconnaissance craft capable of photographing the entire Mediterranean in only seven hours. Four such craft could also cover the entire North Sea region in only six hours! These graceful machines were finally withdrawn from service in 1994.

Type: Fighter; Light Bomber

Dimensions: wingspan, 38 feet, 5 inches; length, 24 feet, 10 inches; height, 9 feet, 2 inches
Weights: empty, 1,581 pounds; gross, 2,381 pounds
Power plant: 1 × 180–horsepower Argus As III liquid-cooled in-line engine
Performance: maximum speed, 103 miles per hour; ceiling, 24,600 feet; range, 300 miles
Armament: 2 × 7.92mm machine guns
Service dates: 1918

During the final stages of World War I, the Hannover CL III was one of Germany's best ground-attack aircraft. A distinctive biplane tail unit gave its gunner a wide field of fire, making it extremely dangerous to approach.

The firm Hannoversche Waggonfabrik AG was long employed in the manufacture of wooden rolling stock for railroads. Consequently, the firm was well situated to commence building wooden airplanes when so instructed by the German government in 1915. At first it manufactured Aviatik, Rumpler, and Halberstadt designs under license, but in 1917 lead engineer Hermann Dorner initiated the company's first two-seat aircraft. This came in response to a new classification of aircraft, the CL, intended to act as fighter escorts to the slower, vulnerable C-series machines. This was undertaken in response to the growing effectiveness of Allied fighters.

The new aircraft, the Hannover CL III, was among the most unique German two-seaters deployed in the war. Constructed of wood and fabric, it featured a deep, plywood-covered fuselage that ta-

pered to a knife-edge. The wings were of average span but closely placed to the fuselage, so the pilot enjoyed excellent vision forward and upward. Pilot and gunner sat in closely spaced tandem cockpits to facilitate communication. However, the CL III's most notable asset was the unique biplane tail. This feature was usually associated with multiengine aircraft, but here it served a distinct purpose. The biplane structure enabled smaller tail surfaces to be utilized, granting the gunner unobstructed fields of fire.

The CL III entered service in the spring of 1918 and was extremely successful as an escort fighter and a ground-attack craft. It was fast, maneuverable, and could absorb tremendous damage. Moreover, the "Hannoveranas," as they were dubbed by the British, were extremely tough customers to tackle. Being small and compact, they were frequently mistaken for single-seat fighters—until the gunner popped up and unleashed a hail of bullets. Nearly 1,000 of these excellent machines were constructed in three slightly differing versions before hostilities ceased.

Type: Fighter

Dimensions: wingspan, 28 feet, 6 inches; length, 19 feet, 2 inches; height, 8 feet, 4 inches
Weights: empty, 882 pounds; gross, 1,334 pounds
Power plant: 1 × 120–horsepower Le Rhone rotary engine
Performance: maximum speed, 114 miles per hour; ceiling, 20,670 feet; range, 250 miles
Armament: 1 × 7.7mm machine gun
Service dates: 1917–1926

The nifty, compact HD 1 was one of World War I's most agile fighters. Overlooked in France, it found fame in the service of Belgian and Italian forces.

Pierre Dupont had manufactured airplanes for several years prior to World War I and subsequently spent several months building Sopwith 1 1/2 *Strutters* under license. In 1916 he teamed with chief engineer Emile Dupont to design a new fighter to replace the aging French Nieuport scouts. The HD 1 emerged as a trim, handsome design with decidedly Sopwith overtones. It sported highly staggered wings, the top one exhibiting a pronounced dihedral. The fuselage was rectangular in cross-section, being made of wood and fabric-covered. This was then faired into a round metal cowling that housed a 120-horsepower rotary engine. The resulting craft was extremely maneuverable and highly responsive to controls. A potential weakness of the design was the armament, restricted to a single machine gun to save weight.

The French military liked the HD 1 but was already committed to building the bigger, more powerful SPAD VII and displayed no interest. Fortunately, an Italian military deputation tested it during the winter of 1916 and, delighted by its performance, placed an immediate order for 100 machines. As demand for HD 1s proved insatiable, the Italian firm Nieuport-Macchi began producing them under license. The little fighter enjoyed tremendous success along the Italian front, and a leading ace, Tenente Scaroni, scored most of his victories flying it. HD 1s were also exported to Belgium, where they likewise became highly popular. Noted Belgian ace Willy Coppens scored most of his 37 kills in an HD 1. Moreover, when the British offered to replace them with formidable Sopwith *Camels* in 1918, the Belgian pilots refused. Their beloved HD 1s remained in frontline service until 1927. Several were also exported to the United States and Switzerland, where they functioned as trainers. A total of 1,145 of these nimble aircraft were produced in France and Italy.

Type: Reconnaissance; Light Bomber

Dimensions: wingspan, 40 feet, 2 inches; length, 27 feet, 9 inches; height, 10 feet, 11 inches
Weights: empty, 1,808 pounds; gross, 2,910 pounds
Power plant: 1 × 220–horsepower Benz liquid-cooled engine
Performance: maximum speed, 87 miles per hour; ceiling, 19,029 feet; range, 210 miles
Armament: 2 × 7.62mm machine guns; 200 pounds of bombs
Service dates: 1916–1917

For two years the Hansa-Brandenburg C I formed the backbone of Austrian World War I reconnaissance aviation. An exemplary design, it was rugged, long-ranged, and well-liked by its pilots.

In 1915 German aircraft designer Ernst Heinkel was commissioned to design a new two-seat reconnaissance craft for the Austro-Hungarian air service. His response was a sleek, modern design that could accept increasingly powerful engines without major modifications. The C I was a standard biplane in appearance, save for the two bay struts that canted inward. In what had become standard practice for the Austrian service, both pilot and gunner were housed in a spacious "tub" that kept the men in close proximity to facilitate cooperation. The C I first flew in 1916 and displayed exceptional takeoff, speed, and flying capabilities. The need for such a craft proved so great to Germany's ally that two Austrian firms, Phonix and Ufag, were authorized to construct it under license. Eventually, 18 series of the craft, all slightly different, were delivered.

In the field, the C I was a welcome change from the earlier Aviatik airplanes. Austria now possessed a robust craft that could operate easily from airfields located in cramped mountain regions. Fast and high-flying, it could also readily defend itself against swarms of Italian fighters. In one instance, a C I piloted by *Stabsfeldwebel* Julius Arigi downed five Italian Farmans sent to engage him. Moreover, the sturdy craft could accept up to 200 pounds of bombs without noticeable degradation of performance. This ability was underscored on July 11, 1916, when a C I flown by Sergeant Major Joseph Siegal crossed the Apennines Mountains to La Spenzia, southeast of Genoa, dropped his bombs, evaded enemy fighters, and safely completed the 248-mile mission. The C I's potential subsequently improved as it received additional guns, bigger engines, and a swept-back upper wing. Heinkel's excellent craft continued to provide sterling service to the hard-pressed Austrian army until its replacement by faster Phonix and Ufag machines of 1917. A total of 1,258 had been manufactured.

Type: Fighter

Dimensions: wingspan, 27 feet, 10 inches; length, 21 feet, 10 inches; height, 9 feet, two inches
Weights: empty, 1,482 pounds; gross, 2,073 pounds
Power plant: 1 × 150–horsepower Daimler liquid-cooled engine
Performance: maximum speed, 111 miles per hour; ceiling, 16,404 feet; range, 260 miles
Armament: 1 × 7.92mm machine gun
Service dates: 1916–1917

The infamous "Star-strutter" was one arguably of the worst fighter planes ever designed. Its slow climb, poor forward vision, and unpredictable stalls earned it an ignominious nickname: "The Flying Coffin."

By 1916 the Austrian Luftfahrtruppe (Austrian air service) was in urgent need for new fighter craft to counter more modern French and Italian designs. It fell upon Ernst Heinkel of the German firm Hansa und Brandenberg Flugzeugwerke to provide a prototype, as the company's owner was an Austrian national. Initially christened the KD *Spinne* (Spider), Heinkel's new craft was both bizarre and ugly. It was outwardly a standard biplane configuration, its squarish wings sporting a positive stagger, with a relatively small rudder buried deep in the fuselage. What made the craft unique was the arrangement of the bracing struts, namely, four sets of vees converging between the two wings in a star arrangement. This innovation enabled the KD to dispense with the usual wire rigging but did little to enhance its performance. Tests flights further revealed that the plane, dubbed "Star-strutter" by the press, was slow and unstable. More important, the placement of the radiator directly over the engine nearly obstructed the pilot's frontal view. Yet the pressing need for new fighters left Austria little recourse but to allow Heinkel's abomination to enter production. In the spring of 1916 these unsightly machines were deployed to field units as the D I.

Predictably, pilots immediately disliked the Star-strutter on account of its strange appearance and poor handling. Although relatively fast for its day, the D I possessed vicious stall characteristics, and several were lost to crashes. Moreover, its single machine gun, housed in a conspicuous fairing above the top wing, was inaccessible to the pilot and further denigrated its marginal handling. At length, the D I acquired the nickname *Die Fliegender Sarg* (The Flying Coffin). The Ufag and Phonix companies tried improving the craft with modified tail configurations, with little success. The hated D Is remained in frontline service until their welcome replacement by Aviatik D Is in mid-1917.

Type: Fighter

Dimensions: wingspan, 44 feet, 3 inches; length, 30 feet, 3 inches; height, 9 feet, 10 inches
Weights: empty, 2,205 pounds; gross, 3,296 pounds
Power plant: 1 × 150–horsepower Benz Bz III liquid-cooled in-line engine
Performance: maximum speed, 109 miles per hour; ceiling, 16,405 feet; range, 400 miles
Armament: 3 × 7.92mm machine guns
Service dates: 1918–1926

The fast, maneuverable W 29 was one of World War I's best floatplane fighters. From numerous stations along the Northern European coast, it continually menaced British shipping and aircraft with great effect.

In the early days of World War I, German naval installations along the North Sea shore were constantly raided by numerous well-armed British flying boats. The lack of an effective naval fighter prompted Hansa-Brandenburg's talented engineer, Ernst Heinkel, to develop a series of floatplane fighters to counter them. The first, the W 12 of 1917, was a uniquely shaped biplane fitted with pontoons, and it rendered effective service. By the spring of 1918, however, Heinkel realized that biplane fighters encumbered by floatation gear were unequal to the task of fending off the latest Allied seaplanes. The only solution was to develop a monoplane fighter with less drag and more performance.

The new Hansa-Brandenburg machine was designated the W 29 and among the finest deployed during the war. It was essentially a modified W 12

fitted with an enlarged, low-mounted wing whose surface area nearly equaled that of the biplane. Like all aircraft of this series, the W 29's fuselage formed a knife-edge rearward and canted upward. A rather small rudder was placed on the very end and partially drooped down under the fuselage. It was powered by a 150-horsepower Benz BZ III engine, which gave it excellent speed, and the overall design displayed great agility. The W 29 subsequently entered into production, and a total of 75 were completed.

In service the W 29 proved itself the terror of the North Sea. The detachment commanded by *Oberleutnant* Friedrich Christiensen routinely engaged and shot up numerous Felixstowe F2A flying boats. His W 29s were also responsible for sinking three British patrol boats in a single action, and Christiensen himself seriously damaged a British submarine. After the war, these superlative floatplanes were utilized by Denmark and Finland until 1926. Its basic features were also incorporated into similar designs throughout the postwar period.

Type: Fighter

Dimensions: wingspan, 30 feet; length, 26 feet, 9 inches; height, 10 feet, 2 inches
Weights: empty, 2,734 pounds; gross, 3,609 pounds
Power plant: 1 × 640–horsepower Rolls-Royce Kestrel VI water-cooled in-line engine
Performance: maximum speed, 223 miles per hour; ceiling, 29,500 feet; range, 270 miles
Armament: 2 × .303–inch machine guns
Service dates: 1931–1939

The Hawker *Fury* was the first British warplane to exceed 200 miles per hour in level flight. It united the virtues of beautiful design, high performance, and great maneuverability into one formidable machine.

Sydney Camm began working on the Hawker *Fury* in 1927 with an initial design called the *Hornet*. The Air Ministry at that time had been calling for fighters with superior speed and climbing capabilities, even at the expense of range. Camm took it upon himself to disregard ministry specifications favoring radial engines and fitted a new Rolls-Royce Kestrel in-line engine to the old *Hornet* body. The result was a masterpiece of aeronautical engineering: the *Fury I*. It was an unequal-span, single-bay biplane with wings supported by "N" struts splaying outward. The fuselage was oval in cross-section and covered in fabric save for a sharply pointed engine area, enclosed by metal. The result was a sleek-looking craft of particularly pleasing lines. Test flights demonstrated it was 30 miles per hour faster than the Bristol *Bulldog* and climbed faster as well. The

ministry was so impressed that it rewrote new specifications around this craft! In 1931 the first *Fury Is* were deployed; 146 were built. Pilots immediately took a liking to this aerodynamic doyen, which was both fast and nimble.

In 1936 the *Fury II* appeared, sporting a larger engine and more fuel capacity. This version climbed 30 percent faster than the original model but at the cost of shortened range. Pilots also reported that it was inferior at high altitudes to the Gloster *Gauntlet*. Nevertheless, the Royal Air Force acquired an additional 118 machines. The airplane's sparkling performance naturally attracted foreign governments, and about 50 were exported to Norway, Persia, Portugal, Yugoslavia, and South Africa. Three even clandestinely found their way to Spain during the Spanish Civil War (1936–1938). One was captured by Nationalist forces, and another was rebuilt by Republicans from wreckage of the original two, so the *Fury* ended up fighting for both sides! By 1939 these elegant biplanes had been supplanted by another Camm masterpiece: the Hawker *Hurricane*.

Type: Light Bomber

Dimensions: wingspan, 37 feet, 3 inches; length, 29 feet, 4 inches; height, 10 feet, 5 inches
Weights: empty, 2,530 pounds; gross, 4,554 pounds
Power plant: 1 × 525–horsepower Rolls-Royce Kestrel IB liquid-cooled in-line engine
Performance: maximum speed, 184 miles per hour; ceiling, 21,230 feet; range, 470 miles
Armament: 2 × .303–inch machine gun; up to 500 pounds of bombs
Service dates: 1930–1938

The successful *Hart* spawned more variants than any other British design of the 1930s. It became one of the most advanced and significant bomber aircraft of the interwar period.

The adaptable Hawker *Hart* evolved in response to Air Ministry Specification 12/26, which mandated creation of a day bomber with unprecedented speed. Hawker's Sydney Camm originated plans for such a craft in 1927, and when developed as a prototype it exerted profound military implications. The new craft was a standard single-bay biplane with unequal, staggered wings made of metal frame and covered in fabric. They were supported by "N"-type interplane struts that splayed outward. The fuselage was oval-sectioned, metal-framed, and canvas-covered. The most prominent characteristic of the *Hart* was its extremely pointed cowl and spinner, giving it a decidedly streamlined appearance. This was in complete contrast to the blunter, radial-engine machines of the day. The *Hart* flew well and extremely fast, so fast that it embarrassed all British

fighters then in production—none could catch it! The ministry was suitably impressed by Camm's brainchild, so in 1930 the Hawker *Hart* entered the service as a light bomber.

The overall excellence of Camm's creation can be gauged by the sheer number of variants spawned by his original design. The Fleet Air Arm went on to acquire the Hawker *Osprey*, a navalized version, in quantity. They were followed in short order by the Hawker *Audax*, built as an army cooperation type; the *Hardy*, a general-purpose type; and the *Hector*, another army cooperation craft. The *Hart* series also inspired its replacement, the Hawker *Hind*, which was just as striking and even more capable. The total number of *Harts* numbered roughly 1,000, exclusive of subtypes, making it one of the most numerous light bombers of the 1930s. They lingered in frontline service before being supplanted by Bristol *Blenheims* in 1938. Although best remembered as a light bomber, the *Hart* is more significant for having stimulated development of even faster British fighters.

Type: Fighter; Light Bomber

Dimensions: wingspan, 33 feet, 8 inches; length, 45 feet, 10 inches; height, 13 feet, 2 inches
Weights: empty, 14,400 pounds; gross, 24,600 pounds
Power plant: 1 × 10,150–pound thrust Rolls-Royce Avon turbojet engine
Performance: maximum speed, 620 miles per hour; ceiling, 50,000 feet; range, 443 miles
Armament: 4 × 30mm cannons; up to 6,000 pounds of bombs or rockets
Service dates: 1954–

Ostensibly the most beautiful jet fighter ever built, the rakish *Hunter* is also Britain's most successful postwar aircraft. At the half-century mark of its lifespan, several machines are still in active service.

By 1948 the British Air Ministry was looking for an updated aircraft to replace its Gloster *Meteors* and issued Specification F.4/48 for Britain's first swept-wing fighter. Sir Sydney Camm of Hawker, who had helped sire the *Hurricane, Tempest,* and *Sea Fury,* quickly promulgated a design of classic proportions and performance. The P 1967 made its first test flight in 1951 with great success. This was a midwing, stressed skin monoplane with wings of 40-degree sweep and a relatively high tail. The new craft exhibited sparkling performance in the transonic range and entered the service in 1954—much to the delight of Royal Air Force pilots. *Hunters* possessed world-class performance, were highly maneuverable, and proved very much the equal of any fighter then in production. However, an early prob-

lem encountered was engine failure after firing the four 30mm cannons positioned near the nose. The problem was traced to the ingestion of gun fumes, which induced a flameout, but this was corrected in subsequent versions. The most numerous of these was the FGA Mk 9, a dedicated ground-attack aircraft that could deliver a sizable load of bombs and rockets. By 1964 a total of 1,985 *Hunters* had been constructed.

The *Hunter* also proved itself one of the most outstanding export successes of the century. India, Iraq, Switzerland, Belgium, Sweden, and Jordan, among others, all imported the sleek fighter and employed it for years after its departure from the RAF stable. The various Indo-Pakistani wars of the 1970s proved that the aging fighter had lost none of its punch, and it was also flown against the redoubtable Israeli air force with good effect. The Swiss were so enamored of their beloved *Hunters* that they made no real attempt to replace them until 1991! A handful are still performing frontline service in Zimbabwe.

Type: Fighter; Light Bomber

Dimensions: wingspan, 40 feet; length, 32 feet; height, 13 feet, 1 inch
Weights: empty, 5,800 pounds; gross, 8,100 pounds
Power plant: 1 × 1,280–horsepower Rolls-Royce Merlin XX liquid-cooled in-line engine
Performance: maximum speed, 336 miles per hour; ceiling, 35,600 feet; range, 460 miles
Armament: 8 × .303–inch machine guns; up to 1,000 pounds of bombs or rockets
Service dates: 1938–1945

Few aircraft were as significant to England's survival as the famous _Hurricane_. During the Battle of Britain it shot down more aircraft than the vaunted _Spitfire_, and later rendered distinguished service in the Mediterranean and Pacific theaters.

Upon receipt of Air Ministry Specification F.7/30 in 1930, Sydney Camm decided to leapfrog existing biplane technologies by designing a monoplane fighter. He did this by incorporating lessons learned from the excellent but aging Hawker _Fury_ biplanes then extant. The prototype _Hurricane_ first flew in November 1935 to great applause. From a construction standpoint, it employed arcane features such as metal tubing structure and fabric covering, but this rendered the craft strong and easily repaired. The _Hurricane_ was also very streamlined for its day, possessed retractable landing gear, and carried no less than eight machine guns, the first British fighter so armed. The design exuded great promise, so in 1934 the Air Ministry issued Specification F.36/34, even before flight-testing concluded, to obtain them as quickly as possible. The urgency was

well justified, and by the advent of World War II, in 1939, _Hurricanes_ constituted 60 percent of RAF Fighter Command's strength.

The 1940 Battle of France proved that _Hurricanes_ were marginally outclassed by Bf 109Es, so throughout the ensuing Battle of Britain they were usually pitted against bombers.

Their great stability and heavy armament allowed them to claim more German aircraft than all other British defenses combined. Successive modifications next turned the _Hurricane_ into a formidable ground-attack aircraft and tankbuster in North Africa and Burma. Some versions sported two 40mm cannons or rockets in addition to 12 machine guns! By 1941 the Fw 200 _Condors_ were threatening Britain's sea-lanes, so expendable _Hurricanes_ were adapted to being catapulted off of merchant ships to defend them. These were then ditched after usage. By 1942 a navalized version, the _Sea Hurricane_, had also been developed. _Hurricanes_ saw active service in every theater up through 1945 before retiring as one of history's greatest warplanes. Production amounted to 14,449 machines.

Type: Fighter; Light Bomber

Dimensions: wingspan, 38 feet, 4 inches; length, 34 feet, 8 inches; height, 15 feet, 10 inches
Weights: empty, 8,977 pounds; gross, 12,114 pounds
Power plant: 1 × 2,470–horsepower Bristol Centaurus radial engine
Performance: maximum speed, 460 miles per hour; ceiling, 36,000 feet; range, 760 miles
Armament: 4 × 20mm cannons; up to 2,000 pounds of bombs or rockets
Service dates: 1946–1953

The *Sea Fury* was the Fleet Air Arm's ultimate piston-powered aircraft, probably the best of its class in the world. It served with distinction in Korea and counted among its many victims several MiG 15 jet fighters.

Origins of the mighty *Sea Fury* trace back to June 1942, when a German Focke-Wulf Fw 190 fighter mistakenly landed in England. Heretofore, radial engines had been dismissed as inferior to more complicated in-line types, but the streamlining and efficiency of the German craft surprised the British. Accordingly, the Air Ministry issued several specifications in 1943 for a lightened Hawker *Tempest* to equip both the Royal Air Force and Fleet Air Arm. Sir Sydney Camm then developed an entirely new monocoque fuselage, fitted it to *Tempest* wings, and mounted a powerful Bristol Centaurus radial engine. The resulting craft was called the *Fury*, a compact, low-wing fighter of great speed and strength. However, when World War II ended the RAF summarily canceled its contract, and the 100 or so *Furies* were

sent to Egypt, India, and Pakistan. The Royal Navy, meanwhile, continued development of the *Sea Fury*, which became operational in 1947. Being a naval aircraft, it was fitted with folding wings and an arrester hook. The big craft was nonetheless supremely agile for its size and popular with pilots. A grand total of 615 were ultimately acquired by the Fleet Air Arm, with several of these being farmed out to Commonwealth navies.

Commencing in 1950, several squadrons of *Sea Furies* participated in the Korean War (1950–1953). They carried prodigious ordnance loads, made excellent bombing platforms, and extensively flew interdiction strikes against communist supply lines. *Sea Furies* also destroyed more communist aircraft than any other non-American type and demonstrated their prowess by shooting down at least two MiG 15 jet fighters. *Sea Furies* were quickly phased out after 1953, for with the age of jets the end of propeller-driven fighters was nigh. Pakistan nevertheless operated their cherished machines until 1973.

Type: Fighter; Light Bomber

Dimensions: wingspan, 41 feet; length, 33 feet, 8 inches; height, 16 feet, 1 inch
Weights: empty, 9,250 pounds; gross, 13,640 pounds
Power plant: 1 × 2,180–horsepower Napier Sabre II liquid-cooled in-line engine
Performance: maximum speed, 435 miles per hour; ceiling, 36,000 feet; range, 740 miles
Armament: 4 × 20mm cannons; up to 2,000 pounds of bombs or rockets
Service dates: 1944–1951

The *Tempest* was another fearsome machine unleashed by Hawker. It combined all the hard-hitting attributes of the earlier *Typhoon* with exceptional high-altitude performance.

Shortcomings of the Hawker *Typhoon* at higher altitudes led Sydney Camm to reconsider his design. The problem—unknown at the time—was compressibility, whereby air passed over airfoils at nearly the speed of sound. Because the *Typhoon* employed a particularly thick wing, it gave rise to constant buffeting at high speed. In 1941 Camm suggested fitting the aircraft with a thinner airfoil of elliptical design. A new engine, the radial Centaurus, was also proposed.

Design went ahead with the new *Typhoon II*, as it was called, which was continuously modified over time. The thinner wing necessitated the fuel tanks being transferred to the fuselage, which was lengthened 2 feet and given a dorsal spine. In light of these modifications, Hawker gave it an entirely new designation: *Tempest*. It was then decided to fit the

Mk V version with the tested Napier Sabre II engine because of delays with the Centaurus engine. The first deliveries of *Tempest Vs* were made in the fall of 1943, and these reached operational status the following summer.

In service the *Tempest* continued the ground-attack tradition of the *Typhoon*, for it easily handled 1,000-pound bombs and a host of rockets. However, because of its new wing, it also possessed superb high-altitude performance. The *Tempest* flew so fast that it became one of few Allied fighters able to intercept the German V-1 rocket bombs, claiming 638 of the 1,771 destroyed. The *Tempest* could also successfully tangle with the German Me 262 jets, destroying 20 of those formidable fighters. After the war, the Centaurus engine was finally perfected and a new version, the *Tempest II*, was introduced. This was the last piston-engine fighter-bomber flown by the Royal Air Force, and it served as the basis of the superb Hawker *Sea Fury*. A total of 1,418 *Tempests* of all models were constructed.

Type: Fighter; Light Bomber

Dimensions: wingspan, 41 feet, 7 inches; length, 31 feet, 11 inches; height, 15 feet, 3 inches
Weights: empty, 8,800 pounds; gross, 13,980 pounds
Power plant: 1 × 2,180–horsepower Napier Sabre II liquid-cooled in-line engine
Performance: maximum speed, 405 miles per hour; ceiling, 34,000 feet; range, 510 miles
Armament: 4 × 20mm cannons; up to 2,000 pounds of bombs or rockets
Service dates: 1942–1945

The formidable "Tiffy" overcame a troubled gestation to emerge as the best ground-attack aircraft of World War II. Attacking in waves, they devastated German armored formations at Normandy and elsewhere.

In 1937 Air Ministry Specification F.18/37 stipulated a future replacement for the Hawker *Hurricanes* then in service. Design began that year, but intermittent problems with the Roll-Royce Vulture engine greatly prolonged its development. The prototype did not fly until May 1941, and then it was powered by the unreliable Napier Sabre I engine. The *Typhoon* was a low-wing monoplane and the first Hawker product featuring stressed-skin construction. It also mounted widetrack landing gear, and initial models had a cabin-type cockpit with a side door. The aircraft flew well at low altitudes but demonstrated dismal climbing capacity. However, when Focke-Wulf Fw 190 fighter-bombers began playing havoc on England's southern coast, the *Typhoon* was rushed into production with minimal testing.

The first *Typhoons* arrived in service during the fall of 1941 with mixed results. The Sabre engine remained unpredictable, and the rear fuselage suffered from structural failure. At one point the Royal Air Force seriously considered canceling the entire project, but Hawker persisted in refining the basic design. Consequently, the airframe was beefed up and more reliable versions of the Sabre engine were mounted. By 1943 the major bugs had been eliminated, and the *Typhoon* found its niche as a low-altitude fighter and ground-attack craft. Being the first British aircraft to achieve 400 miles per hour in level flight, it successfully countered Fw 190 raids at lower altitudes. By 1944 *Typhoons* were also modified to carry two 1,000-pound bombs or a host of rocket projectiles. Attacking in waves, they proved particularly devastating against German Panzer divisions at Falaise, destroying 137 tanks in one day! They were all retired by 1945 as the most effective ground-attack aircraft of the war. A total of 3,330 had been built.

Type: Trainer; Light Bomber

Dimensions: wingspan, 30 feet, 9 inches; length, 38 feet, 4 inches; height, 13 feet
Weights: empty, 9,700 pounds; gross, 11,350 pounds
Power plant: 1 × 5,845–pound thrust Rolls-Royce Turbomeca Adour turbofan engine
Performance: maximum speed, 645 miles per hour; ceiling, 44,500 feet; range, 317 miles
Armament: none or 1 × 30mm cannon pod; up to 6,614 pounds of bombs and rockets
Service dates: 1976–

The *Hawk* is one of the world's most successful jet trainers and is widely exported abroad. It can be fitted with a variety of weapons and functions as a highly capable light strike aircraft.

A 1964 air staff study predicted that the forthcoming SEPECAT *Jaguar* trainers would be too expensive and too few in number to meet Royal Air Force training requirements. That year specifications were issued for a cheaper yet capable trainer to replace the *Gnats* and *Hunters* then operating. At length the Hawker-Siddeley group announced its Model HS 1182, a sleek, low-wing aircraft seating two under a long tandem canopy. Suitably impressed, the RAF in 1972 placed an initial order for 176 *Hawk T* Mk 1s, the first of which was delivered in 1976. This relatively low-powered aircraft turned out to be surprisingly successful. The *Hawk* is fast, maneuverable, and easy to fly. It can also be rigged for weapons training and is fitted with a centerline cannon pod under the fuselage, and the wings employ four hardpoints capable of launching missiles.

In this capacity, the *Hawk* affords multimission trainer/light strike capability as much less cost than conventional jets. More than 700 have been built and are operated by seven nations.

In an attempt to exploit the *Hawk*'s potential as a combat type, British Aerospace (BAe, which acquired Hawker-Siddeley) in April 1977 developed a dedicated ground-attack version, the *Hawk* 100. It differed from earlier models in possessing a modified combat wing better suited for heavy ordnance and high-G maneuvers. First flown in 1992, it was purchased by Abu Dhabi, Brunei, Indonesia, Malaysia, Oman, and Saudi Arabia. In 1986 BAe subsequently designed the *Hawk 200*, which is a single-seat dedicated strike fighter for the Third World. This model exhibits a redesigned front section, a more bulbous nose housing an advanced radar, and other digital systems. As before, it offers relatively high performance and firepower at affordable prices. Thus far, only Oman and Malaysia have placed orders.

Hawker-Siddeley *Nimrod* ———————————————— Great Britain

Type: Antisubmarine; Patrol-Bomber; Reconnaissance

Dimensions: wingspan, 114 feet; length, 126 feet, 9 inches; height, 29 feet, 8 inches
Weights: empty, 86,000 pounds; gross, 192,000 pounds
Power plant: 4 × 12,140–pound thrust Rolls-Royce Spey turbofan engines
Performance: maximum speed, 575 miles per hour; ceiling, 42,00 feet; range, 5,758 miles
Armament: up to 13,500 pounds of torpedoes, depth charges, or mines
Service dates: 1969–

The *Nimrod* is one of the most capable antisubmarine platforms currently in service, a union of advanced electronics with fine flying characteristics. A few also serve as secret electronic countermeasure platforms and intelligence-gatherers.

By 1964 the British Air Ministry wished to replace its Korean War–vintage Avro *Shackletons* with a more advanced machine for antisubmarine warfare (ASW). Specifications were initially drawn around the existing Dassault *Atlantique*, but the British government intervened and requested that the existing *Comet 4* civilian airliner be adopted. This was an aircraft renowned for good cruising and flying abilities and had been in Royal Air Force service since 1955 as a transport. Accordingly, in 1967 the first *Nimrod* prototype was flown. It shared some similarities with its forebears but, being fitted with a lengthy bomb bay, the fuselage acquired a "double-bubble" cross-section. The *Nimrod* also sports an electronic "football" atop the rudder and a long magnetic anomaly detector boom jutting from

the tail. Consistent with its ASW mission, the plane carries a variety of depth charges, sonobuoys, homing torpedoes, and related detection gear. A typical patrol might last up to 12 hours, and the *Nimrod* can extend its loiter time over a target by up to six hours by shutting down as many as three of its engines! A total of 45 *Nimrods* (named after the great hunter of the bible) have been acquired and are subject to constant electronic upgrades.

In 1971 three aircraft were deflected from the ASW program to be outfitted as *Nimrod R* Mk 1s. These are highly sensitive, top-secret intelligence-gathering platforms of which much is said but little is known. They are distinguished from other airplanes by the absence of radar tailbooms and the presence of external fuel tanks on the leading edges. In the hands of No. 51 Squadron, they were highly active during the 1982 Falkland Islands War with Argentina and garnered a battle citation. Both *Nimrod* versions are expected to actively serve well into the twenty-first century.

Type: Fighter; Light Bomber

Dimensions: wingspan, 36 feet, 1 inch; length, 27 feet, 6 inches; height, 10 feet, 6 inches
Weights: empty, 3,247 pounds; gross, 4,189 pounds
Power plant: 1 × 750–horsepower BMW VI liquid-cooled in-line engine
Performance: maximum speed, 205 miles per hour; ceiling, 25,260 feet; range, 345 miles
Armament: 2 × 7.92mm machine guns; 120 pounds of bombs
Service dates: 1935–1943

The shapely He 51 was the first Luftwaffe fighter constructed since the Armistice of 1918 and a potent symbol of German rearmament. It was outclassed as a dogfighter in Spain but helped pioneer the ground-attack tactics used in World War II.

Ernst Heinkel formed his own company in 1922 following the liquidation of the old Hansa-Brandenburg firm. He was ostensibly engaged in constructing floatplanes and civilian craft, but as the political climate in Germany hardened, his designs more and more resembled military aircraft. As Germany embarked on national rearmament in 1933, Heinkel was directed to develop a new fighter plane—the first since World War I. He responded with the He 51, an outgrowth of his earlier He 49 civilian machines. It was a handsome, single-bay biplane of mixed wood and metal construction, covered with fabric. It featured an attractive pointed cowl and streamlined, spatted landing gear. Flight tests revealed the He 51 to be fast and nimble, so it was accepted for service in 1935. That same year,

the existence of the previously secret Luftwaffe was defiantly announced to the world.

In service the He 51 proved somewhat troublesome. It was unforgiving by nature, and a tendency to "hop" while landing contributed to several accidents. Nonetheless, it was the only aircraft on hand when the Spanish Civil War erupted in 1936, and Hitler dispatched large numbers of them piloted by German "volunteers" of the Kondor Legion. Initial reports were favorable, for the He 51 easily dispatched a host of older French and British machines. But Heinkel's fighter was badly outclassed by the Russian-supplied Polikarpov I 15 and sustained heavy losses. Thereafter, it became necessary to restrict He 51s to ground attack, a role in which they performed admirably and helped pioneer the close-support tactics made famous in World War II. The introduction of Arado's Ar 68 in 1937 led to its withdrawal from frontline service. This neat biplane spent its last days as a training craft up through 1943. A total of 725 were built.

Type: Patrol-Bomber

Dimensions: wingspan, 77 feet, 9 inches; length, 57 feet, 1 inch; height, 23 feet, 3 inches
Weights: empty, 13,702 pounds; gross, 19,842 pounds
Power plant: 2 × 660–horsepower BMW VI liquid-cooled in-line engines
Performance: maximum speed, 134 miles per hour; ceiling, 11,480 feet; range, 1,087 miles
Armament: 3 × 7.92mm machine guns; 2,205 pounds of bombs
Service dates: 1932–1943

One of the first aircraft acquired by the Luftwaffe, the big He 59 was a versatile machine capable of many functions. It saw active service in World War II and even helped stage daring commando missions.

The He 59 was originally designed in 1930 as part of a clandestine program to equip Germany with military aircraft. Although posited as a twin-engine maritime rescue craft, it was in fact intended as a reconnaissance bomber capable of serving off both water and land. The first prototype, designed by Reinhold Mewes, flew in 1931 with large "trousered" wheel spats, but subsequent versions were all fitted with twin floats. Like many aircraft of this era, the He 59 was of mixed construction, having a fuselage made from steel tubing, wings of wood, and entirely covered by fabric. The bomber seated a crew of four comfortably and was well-armed with machine guns in nose, dorsal, and ventral positions. Both flight and water performance were adequate, so the German government ordered 105 machines built in several versions.

The He 59 first saw combat during the Spanish Civil War (1936–1938), where it functioned as a patrol-bomber. At night the big craft would glide over an intended target unannounced, then drop bombs upon astonished defenders. He 59s were pushing obsolescence in 1939 when World War II erupted, but for many months the lumbering craft performed useful work. Most He 59s equipped coastal reconnaissance groups, but others operated with the *Seenotdienststaffeln* (air/sea rescue squadrons). These craft were conspicuously painted white with large red crosses in the early days of the war and left unmolested by Royal Air Force fighters—until they were discovered directing German bombers by radio. But the most important service of the He 59 was in transporting *Staffel Schwilben* (special forces). On May 10, 1940, a dozen He 59s landed in the Maas River, Rotterdam, and disgorged 120 assault troops, who paddled ashore and stormed the strategic Willems bridge. They were all finally retired by 1943.

Type: Reconnaissance; Light Bomber; Liaison

Dimensions: wingspan, 48 feet, 6 inches; length, 38 feet, 4 inches; height, 10 feet, 2 inches
Weights: empty, 5,723 pounds; gross, 7,716 pounds
Power plant: 1 × 750–horsepower BMW VI water-cooled in-line engine
Performance: maximum speed, 220 miles per hour; ceiling, 19,685 feet; range, 500 miles
Armament: 1 × 7.92mm machine gun; up to 661 pounds of bombs
Service dates: 1933–1939

When it appeared in 1932, the futuristic He 70 was a marvel of streamlining and aerodynamic innovation. It enjoyed a relatively short service life but set significant trends in aircraft design for years to come.

With the acquisition of Lockheed *Orion* aircraft in 1932, Swiss Air became Europe's fastest passenger carrier. This development alarmed the German national airlines, Deutsche Lufthansa, which then approached Heinkel for a new and even faster aircraft. It fell upon two brothers, Siegfried and Walter Gunter, to conceive one of the most advanced yet beautiful aircraft of the decade. Christened the He 70 *Blitz* (Lightning), this was a single-engine, low-wing monoplane of extremely clean, aerodynamic lines. The broad wings were elliptically shaped and sported retractable landing gear. The fuselage, meanwhile, was oval in cross-section and semimonocoque in construction with a low-profile windscreen to cut drag. Moreover, the engine utilized ethylene glycol as a coolant, which allowed a smaller radiator and overall frontal area. To reduce

drag even further, the stressed metal skin was secured in place by countersunk riveting. The net result was a strikingly beautiful airplane that anticipated the features of monoplane fighters by several years.

In test flights the He 70 easily outpaced the He 51 biplane, a craft possessing a more powerful engine, while weighing half as much! In 1933 the prototype alone went on to establish eight world speed records and bolstered Lufthansa's reputation as the fastest airline on the continent. Naturally, such high performance caught the military's attention, so several models were built for the Luftwaffe. These included both light attack and reconnaissance versions, 18 of which served in the Spanish Civil War. Flown by the Kondor Legion, they performed with distinction and easily outflew all opposition. A total of 296 He 70s had been manufactured by the time production ceased in 1937, and most were employed as courier/liaison craft. Heinkel's masterpiece enjoyed a short, undistinguished career but is best remembered as a harbinger of things to come.

Heinkel He 111 ———————————————————————— **Germany**

Type: Medium Bomber

Dimensions: wingspan, 74 feet, 1 inch; length, 53 feet, 9 inches; height, 13 feet, 1 inch
Weights: empty, 19,136 pounds; gross, 30,865 pounds
Power plant: 2 × 1,350–horsepower Junkers Jumo liquid-cooled in-line engines
Performance: maximum speed, 227 miles per hour; ceiling, 21,980 feet; range, 1,212 miles
Armament: 4 × 7.92mm machine guns; 1 × 20mm cannon; up to 4,409 pounds of bombs
Service dates: 1936–1945

The long-serving He 111 was a mainstay of the Luftwaffe bomber force, as well as a successful tactical machine. However, the lack of a suitable successor kept it in production long after becoming obsolete.

In the early 1930s the Germans resorted to clandestine measures to obtain modern military aircraft. Accordingly, the Heinkel He 111 had been ostensibly designed by Walter and Siegfried Gunter as a fast commercial transport for the German airline Lufthansa. Like the famous He 70, it was a radically streamlined, all-metal aircraft with smooth skin and elliptical wings. Early models, both civil and military, also featured a stepped cabin with a separate cockpit enclosure. The new bomber proved fast and maneuverable, so in 1937 several were shipped off to the Spanish Civil War for evaluation. Not surprisingly, the He 111s outclassed weak fighter opposition and flew many successful missions unescorted. Thereafter, German bomber doctrine called for fast, lightly armed aircraft that could survive on speed alone. That decision proved

a costly mistake in World War II. In 1939 the Model P arrived, introducing the trademark glazed cockpit canopy that appeared on all subsequent versions. When war finally erupted that fall, the fast, graceful Heinkels constituted the bulk of Germany's bomber forces.

After deceptively easy campaigning in Poland and France, He 111s suffered heavily at the hands of British fighters during the 1940 Battle of Britain. This caused later editions to carry more armor and weapons, which in turn degraded performance. And because its designated successor, the He 177, proved a failure, the He 111 was kept in production despite mounting obsolescence. For the rest of the war, the lumbering craft functioned as torpedo-bombers, cable-cutters, pathfinders, and glider tugs. A final variant, the He 111Z (for *Zwilling*, or "twin"), consisted of two bombers connected at midwing with a fifth engine. These were designed to tow massive Messerschmitt Me 323 *Gigant* gliders into action. By war's end, more than 7,000 of these venerable workhorses had been produced.

Type: Reconnaissance; Torpedo-Bomber

Dimensions: wingspan, 72 feet, 2 inches; length, 56 feet, 9 inches; height, 21 feet, 8 inches
Weights: empty, 11,684 pounds; gross, 22,928 pounds
Power plant: 2 × 865–horsepower BMW 132N radial engines
Performance: maximum speed, 220 miles per hour; ceiling, 18,045 feet; range, 2,082 miles
Armament: 2 × 7.92mm machine guns; 2,765 pounds of bombs, torpedoes, or mines
Service dates: 1937–1945

The Heinkel He 115 was the Luftwaffe's most versatile floatplane reconnaissance craft. It performed so successfully that production was resumed in midwar.

In 1936 the prototype He 115 was flown as the successor to the aging He 59. It was a standard, all-metal, midwing monoplane whose broad wing possessed tapering outer sections. A crew of three was housed in an elongated greenhouse canopy, and the craft rested upon two floats secured in place by struts. The prototype was fast, handled well, and quickly broke eight floatplane records in 1938. Such impressive performance resulted in orders from overseas, and both Norway and Sweden purchased several machines. The He 115 also entered production with the Luftwaffe *Seeflieger* (coastal reconnaissance forces). In 1939 the B model appeared, featuring greater fuel capacity and reinforced floats for operating in snow and ice.

When World War II commenced, the He 115s partook of routine maritime patrolling and mining of English waters. They were the first German craft adapted to drop the new and deadly acoustic sea mines from the air, which inflicted great damage upon British shipping. They also proved quite adept at torpedo-bombing and as long-range reconnaissance craft. Curiously, the 1940 invasion of Norway found He 115s closely engaged on both sides of the conflict. The six Norwegian machines put up stout resistance, with three survivors and a captured German machine escaping to Britain. These were subsequently given German markings and employed for clandestine operations ranging from Norway to Malta. These activities were subsequently suspended after 1943 for fear of attacks by Allied aircraft. The high point of He 115 operations with German forces occurred in 1942, when they shadowed ill-fated Convoy PQ-17 in the Arctic Circle and assisted in its destruction. Production of He 115s ceased in 1941, but their services were so highly regarded that it resumed in 1943! A total of 450 machines were built, and most performed capably up to the end of hostilities.

Type: Heavy Bomber

Dimensions: wingspan, 103 feet, 1 inch; length, 72 feet, 2 inches; height, 20 feet, 11 inches
Weights: empty, 37,038 pounds; gross, 68,343 pounds
Power plant: 4 × 950–horsepower Daimler-Benz 610 A-1 in-line engines
Performance: maximum speed, 304 miles per hour; ceiling, 26,245 feet; range, 3,417 miles
Armament: 6 × 7.92mm or 13mm machine guns; 1 × 20mm cannon; 2,205 pounds of bombs
Service dates: 1942–1945

The He 177 was the Luftwaffe's sole heavy bomber type of World War II, but it remained a minor player. Considering the quantity of resources squandered, the *Greif* (Griffon) was Germany's most conspicuous aeronautical failure.

The 1936 death of General Walter Wever, the Luftwaffe's vocal proponent of heavy bombers, seriously compromised Germany's attempt to obtain strategic weapons. Two years later the Air Ministry contacted Heinkel to build a long-range bomber, despite that firm's unfamiliarity with such craft. The prototype He 177 *Greif* emerged in 1939 as a modern, all-metal, high-wing monoplane. Curiously, it was propelled by four engines, but to reduce drag two power plants were coupled together in each nacelle, attached to a single propeller. As an indication of how disoriented German war planners had become, the giant craft was also expected to be capable of dive-bombing! Consequently, the much-maligned He 177 suffered a litany of insurmountable technical problems, especially engine fires. Several

prototypes were built and crashed before the first He 177s could become operational in March 1942.

From the onset, the *Greif* was an unsatisfactory aircraft, one that wasted huge quantities of scarce resources and manpower. Operations on the Eastern Front proved sporadic owing to the constant engine fires, as well as structural failure arising from dive-bombing attacks. Crews, although admiring the fine flying qualities of the craft, came to regard it as the "Flaming Coffin." In the West, He 177s conducted Operation *Steinbock*, also known as the "Little Blitz" of January 1944. Those few machines able to get airborne climbed to their maximum height over Germany, then commenced long, shallow dives over London. Ensuing speeds of more than 400 miles per hour prevented their interception but did little to ensure bombing accuracy. With greater emphasis on research and development, the He 177 might have evolved into a formidable weapon. As it was, most were abandoned by late 1944 because of fuel and parts shortages. Around 1,000 were built.

Type: Night Fighter

Dimensions: wingspan, 60 feet, 8 inches; length, 50 feet, 11 inches; height, 13 feet, 5 inches
Weights: empty, 25,691 pounds; gross, 33,370 pounds
Power plant: 2 × 1,800–horsepower Daimler-Benz 603E radial engines
Performance: maximum speed, 416 miles per hour; ceiling, 41,665 feet; range, 1,243 miles
Armament: 6 × 30mm cannons; 2 × 20mm cannon
Service dates: 1944–1945

The mighty *Uhu* was Germany's best operational night fighter of World War II. Fast and heavily armed, it was one of few aircraft capable of engaging the formidable British *Mosquito* on equal terms.

Ernest Heinkel began developing the He 219 in 1940 as a private venture to create a long-range fighter-bomber. The Luftwaffe leadership expressed no interest in the project until 1941, when large-scale night bombing by the Royal Air Force commenced. They then requested Heinkel to modify his design into a dedicated night fighter, and the prototype flew in 1943 with impressive results. The new He 219 was a big, high-wing, twin-engine monoplane with a nose-wheel and double rudders. It was also the first production airplane to be equipped with ejection seats. The crew sat back-to-back under a spacious canopy that granted excellent visibility. Moreover, the armament of four cannons was buried in the fuselage belly so that muzzle flashes did not blind the operators. Flight tests were concluded after a preliminary order for 300 machines was received. The first

He 219s, called *Uhu* (Owl) by their crews, were initially deployed at Venlo, Holland. On his first night-time sortie, Major Werner Streib shot down five *Lancaster* bombers, and after only six operational sorties the unit tally stood at 20 victories. Six of these were the heretofore unstoppable *Mosquitos*.

Production of the He 219 commenced in 1943 but remained slow and amounted to only 288 aircraft. This proved fortunate for the Allies, as successive versions of the *Uhu* grew increasingly lethal to bombers. One reason was adoption of the *Schrage Musik* ("slanted music," or jazz) installation, whereby heavy cannons were mounted on top of the fuselage at an angle. This enabled He 219s to slip below the bomber stream in level flight and pour heavy fire directly into their bellies. The handful of He 219s constructed and deployed were responsible for thousands of Allied casualties. But in 1944 General Edward Milch canceled the entire project in favor of the unsuccessful Focke-Wulf Ta 154 and Junkers Ju 388 projects.

Type: Dive-Bomber; Light Bomber

Dimensions: wingspan, 34 feet, 5 inches; length, 27 feet, 4 inches; height, 10 feet, 6 inches
Weights: empty, 3,361 pounds; gross, 4,888 pounds
Power plant: 1 × 880–horsepower BMW 132Dc radial engine
Performance: maximum speed, 214 miles per hour; ceiling, 29,530 feet; range, 530 miles
Armament: 2 × 7.92mm machine guns; 440 pounds of bombs
Service dates: 1936–1944

The antiquated-looking Hs 123 was the Luftwaffe's first dive-bomber. Although eclipsed by the legendary Ju 87 *Stuka*, it rendered impressive service during World War II and gained a reputation for toughness.

One of the first requirements espoused by the newly established Luftwaffe in 1933 was the need for dive-bombers. Henschel consequently fielded the Hs 123, a single-bay sesquiplane (two wings of unequal length) with an open canopy, a large radial cowling, and streamlined, spatted landing gear. The craft was of all-metal construction, save for fabric-covered control surfaces, and the pilot enjoyed excellent all-around vision. Noted pilot Ernst Udet test-flew the prototype in the spring of 1935 with great success, and the government determined to acquire it as an interim type until the Junkers Ju 87 *Stuka* became available. Accordingly, the first Hs 123s rolled off the production lines in 1936 and were sent to Spain for evaluation under combat conditions. At high altitude they proved vulnerable to attacks by Russian-supplied Polikarpov I 15 fighters, so they were subsequently employed as ground-attack aircraft. Here the Hs 123s enjoyed remarkable success for such an allegedly obsolete design, dropping bombs and strafing enemy troops with great precision. By 1938, however, the *Stuka* became the standard Luftwaffe dive-bomber, and the handful of Hs 123s still in service equipped only one squadron.

The onset of World War II in September 1939 garnered additional luster for the little biplane's reputation. They served with great success in the Polish campaign where, flying low with throttles wide open, their deafening howl terrorized men and horses alike. The craft also established a legendary reputation for absorbing tremendous damage. Hs 123s then bore prominent roles in the 1940 campaigns in Belgium and France, where they readily broke up concentrations of troops and tanks. Despite the growing obsolescence of its equipment, the squadron distinguished itself further during the Balkan and Russian campaigns of 1941. They were finally withdrawn from combat in 1944, one of the world's great fighting biplanes.

Type: Antitank; Light Bomber

Dimensions: wingspan, 46 feet, 7 inches; length, 31 feet, 11 inches; height, 10 feet, 8 inches
Weights: empty, 8,400 pounds; gross, 11,574 pounds
Power plant: 2 × 700–horsepower Gnome-Rhone 14M radial engines
Performance: maximum speed, 253 miles per hour; ceiling, 29,540 feet; range, 429 miles
Armament: 2 × 7.92mm machine guns; 2 × 20mm cannons; up to 551 pounds of bombs
Service dates: 1942–1945

Despite its small size, the Hs 129 was the most successful German tankbuster of World War II. It flew persistently throughout the Eastern Front, exacting a heavy toll from Russian armor.

One lesson learned from the Spanish Civil War was the need for dedicated ground-attack aircraft. Consequently, in 1937 the German Air Ministry issued specifications for a well-armored, single-seat machine powered by two engines. Henschel responded in 1939 with a unique prototype designed by Friedrich Nicolaus. It was an all-metal, midwing craft with an extremely blunt nose and wings possessing a tapered trailing edge. Moreover, the relatively small cockpit was shielded by bulletproof glass and so cramped that several engine instruments were by necessity relocated to the inboard engine nacelles! Power was provided by two Argus As 410A-1 inverted in-line engines. Test flights, unfortunately, were disappointing, as the Hs 129 proved underpowered and sluggish. The Luftwaffe authorized several preproduction examples as a

hedge, but they were subsequently passed off to the Romanian air force.

By 1940 Nicolaus had sufficiently revamped his creation, the Hs 219B, and submitted it for flight trials. This time it was powered by captured French Gnome-Rhone 14M radial engines and assisted in flight by electric trim tabs. Results were better, so the Hs 129B entered into production; 870 were eventually built. These craft also were fitted with an amazing array of heavy weapons for antitank warfare, particularly along the Eastern Front. Eventually, Hs 129s proved themselves the scourge of Soviet armor, and during the 1943 engagement at Kursk they destroyed several hundred tanks. Attempts were then made to upgrade the Hs 129s firepower, and several were fitted with a huge 75mm Pak40 antitank gun. This weapon could destroy a tank from any angle, but it recoiled so strongly that the Hs 129s usually stalled. These "Flying Can-openers" remained the bane of Russian armor until the end of 1944, when most were grounded due to lack of fuel and spare parts.

Type: Fighter; Light Bomber

Dimensions: wingspan, 29 feet, 6 inches; length, 52 feet, 3 inches; height, 11 feet, 9 inches
Weights: empty, 13,658; gross, 24,048 pounds
Power plant: 2 × 4,850–pound thrust Rolls-Royce Orpheus turbojet engines
Performance: maximum speed, 675 miles per hour; ceiling, 40,000 feet; range, 898 miles
Armament: 4 × 30mm cannons; 54 unguided rockets in a retractable pack; 4,00 pounds of bombs
Service dates: 1968–1985

The *Marut* was the first and only indigenous jet fighter constructed in India. Although designed by the famous Dr. Kurt Tank, it was continually hindered by lack of adequate power and so never fulfilled its obvious potential.

In 1950 the newly independent government of India sought to break its traditional reliance on European aircraft by developing warplanes of its own. Necessity required them to replace the aging fleet of Dassault *Mysteres* and *Ouragans* then in service as well. In 1956 Hindustan Aircraft Limited tasked a German engineering staff headed by the brilliant Dr. Kurt Tank, formerly of Focke-Wulf, with designing a multipurpose jet fighter with supersonic performance. With the aid of Indian engineers, a full-scale glider was tested in 1959, followed two years later by a functioning prototype. The new HF 24 *Marut* (the Wind Spirit in Hindu mythology) was a sleek, twin-engine design with a highly pointed profile and a low-mounted wing. It flew in 1961 powered by two Bristol-Siddeley Orpheus 703 turbojets, but nearly a year lapsed before a

second prototype emerged. In 1964 16 preproduction *Maruts* followed, but they were not equipped with afterburners. This deficiency ensured that HF 24s would never approach Mach 2. Work continued on a succession of different power plants and a locally designed afterburner for several years, and it was not until 1967 that full-scale production of the HF 24 resumed. This concluded after 145 machines were built; an additional 18 Mk IT two-seat trainers were added in 1970.

Despite its low power, the *Marut* handled fine and proved a capable fighter-bomber when so armed. Their combat initiation occurred during the 1971 war with Pakistan and three squadrons acquitted themselves well with few losses. After this a variety of new engines was fitted, none of which nudged the aging HF 24 toward supersonic speed. The scheme was ultimately abandoned, and by 1995 most *Maruts* were replaced in service by MiG 23s and SEPECAT *Jaguars*. The HF 24s were fine aircraft, but their passing confirms India's continuing dependence on foreign technology.

IAI _Kfir_ **Israel**

Type: Fighter; Light Bomber

Dimensions: wingspan, 26 feet, 11 inches; length, 54 feet; height, 13 feet, 11 inches
Weights: empty, 16,06 pounds; gross, 36,376 pounds
Power plant: 1 18,750–pound thrust General Electric J-79 turbojet engine
Performance: maximum speed, 1,516 miles per hour; ceiling, 58,000 feet; range, 548 miles
Armament: 2 × 30mm cannons; up to 13,415 pounds of bombs or rockets
Service dates: 1975–

The _Kfir_ resulted from Israel's attempt to sever its traditional dependency upon France for military aircraft. It was a feat of considerable engineering and placed that country in the forefront of aviation technology.

Since acquiring independence in 1947, the state of Israel relied heavily upon French patronage for modern weapons to defend itself against its Arab neighbors. In the early 1960s Israel acquired the relatively sophisticated Dassault _Mirage IIIs_, which were superbly utilized in the 1967 Six Day War. Israel had also ordered 50 of the less-expensive _Mirage 5_ ground-attack craft, fully paid for, when French President Charles de Gaulle ordered an arms embargo. Cut off from its main supplier of aircraft, and faced with the specter of the Soviets arming Arab states with sophisticated MiG fighters, the Jewish state resolved to develop indigenous fighters. This required imaginative engineering of a very high order.

Israeli Aircraft Industries (IAI) initially began by marketing its own version of the _Mirage 5_, which

it called the _Nesher_ (Eagle). This was a potent craft but possessed all the shortcomings of the original _Mirage III_ design. But having purchased McDonnell-Douglas F-4 _Phantoms_ from the United States, the firm hit upon squeezing the powerful J-79 turbojet engine into the _Mirage 5_ fuselage. This feat required engineering skills and was resolved only after much difficulty. However, the resulting new craft, the _Kfir_ (Lion Cub), was revealed to the world in 1975. This was still a _Mirage_ in outline, but it possessed an expanded fuselage to accommodate the bigger engine. The rear was also consequently shortened and the front extended in comparison with the _Mirage 5_. And because the J-79 runs hotter than the original French power plant, four additional airscoops were installed. Newer versions of the _Kfir_, the C2, feature removable canards just aft of the canopy to improve maneuverability at low speed. The _Kfir_ remains a potent weapon in Israeli hands and has also been exported to Colombia and Ecuador.

Type: Antitank; Light Bomber

Dimensions: wingspan, 48 feet; length, 36 feet; height, 11 feet, 1 inch
Weights: empty, 9,590 pound; gross, 14,021
Power plant: 1 × 1,770–horsepower AM-38F liquid-cooled in-line engine
Performance: maximum speed, 251 miles per hour; ceiling, 19,685 feet; range, 373 miles
Armament: 2 × 7.62mm machine guns; 2 × 30mm cannons; 1,321 pounds of bombs or rockets
Service dates: 1941–1955

The famous *Shturmovik* was the most important Russian aircraft of World War II. Built in massive quantities, it proved instrumental in defeating German armor and preserving the Soviet Union. The Il 2 is also among the most numerous warplanes ever built.

The Red Air Force was conceived as a tactical adjunct to the Red Army and, as such, bore responsibility for removing tanks and fortifications in its path. Throughout the 1930s several experimental craft were tested that were heavily armored and intended to function as *bronirovanni shturmovik* (armored attackers). In 1939 Sergei Ilyushin developed a prototype that was to exert profound influence on the military history of the world. His Il 2 was a relatively sleek, all-metal, low-wing monoplane with retractable undercarriage that withdrew into wing nacelles. The most distinguishing feature was the highly armored "tub," an integral metal structure holding the engine, pilot, and fuel. It was impervious to ground fire and gave the aircraft great structural integrity. Test flights were encouraging, so the first

Il 2s became operational in May 1941. Their appearance was fortuitous, for the following month Nazi Germany invaded the Soviet Union.

From the onset, the Il 2 proved itself the bane of German tanks. Flying low at treetop level, it swooped upon them from behind, where their defenses were weakest, delivering lethal blows. Many Il 2s were lost for want of a tailgunner, so in 1942 a two-seat version was introduced with even heavier weapons, including the world's first air-to-ground rockets. These performed essential work during the 1943 battle at Kursk, knocking out many of Germany's latest Tiger tanks with ease. The Il 2 was so important that Stalin himself declared it "as essential to the Red Army as bread and water"—and warned factory officials to produce them faster. With some justification, Germans regarded the Il 2 as the *Schwartz Tod* (Black Death). This landmark Russian design remained in production until 1955 after 36,000 had been built. Only the vaunted Polikarpov Po 2 was obtained in greater quantity.

Type: Medium Bomber; Torpedo-Bomber

Dimensions: wingspan, 70 feet, 4 inches; length, 48 feet, 6 inches; height, 13 feet, 5 inches
Weights: empty, 13,228 pounds; gross, 22,046 pounds
Power plant: 2 × 1,100–horsepower M-88B radial engines
Performance: maximum speed, 255 miles per hour; ceiling, 32,810 feet; range, 1,616 miles
Armament: 3 × 12.7mm machine guns; up to 2,205 pounds of bombs or torpedoes
Service dates: 1937–1945

The Il 4 was another simple, exceedingly tough design that saw widespread use during World War II. It gained notoriety for becoming the first Soviet bomber to raid Berlin in 1941.

In 1936 Sergei Ilyushin delighted Soviet authorities by designing the DB 3 medium bomber. This was an all-metal, low-wing, twin-engine craft with a peculiarly blunt nose turret. More important, the craft boasted outstanding performance for its day and established several payload and altitude records. DB 3s became operational in 1937, and the following year Ilyushin began developing an improved variant, the DB 3F. This plane differed from its pug-nosed predecessor by sporting a redesigned, streamlined nose that was highly glazed. Other refinements included greater internal capacity for fuel—in this instance up to 27 percent of its loaded weight—and an autopilot. The DB 3F consequently enjoyed excellent long-range capability for a relatively small bomber. In addition to carrying a useful payload, it could also be fitted with a torpedo for an-

tishipping work. DB 3Fs became operational in 1939 with both Red Air Force and Red Navy bomber regiments. The following year it was redesignated Il 4 after the new Soviet system of employing designers' initials. Ultimately, 5,520 were constructed.

Il 4s were the most numerous bomber in the Soviet inventory when Nazi Germany invaded Russia in June 1941. They gained international notoriety on the evening of August 8, 1941, when several navy Il 4s staged the first Russian bombing raid on Berlin. German advances, meanwhile, forced Ilyushin to relocate his factories beyond the Ural Mountains. There he faced critical shortages of strategic metals, and so many Il 4s were partially constructed of wood. This did not detract from the basic robustness of the design, although Il 4s continually suffered from weak defensive armament. This unsung aircraft, largely unknown to the West, fought hard, absorbed staggering losses, and performed well up through the end of the war. It remains an unsung hero of the Soviet Union.

Type: Light Bomber

Dimensions: wingspan, 70 feet, 4 inches; length, 57 feet, 11 inches; height, 22 feet
Weights: empty, 26,455 pounds; gross, 46,300 pounds
Power plant: 2 × 6,040–pound thrust Klimov VK-1 turbojet engines
Performance: maximum speed, 560 miles per hour; ceiling, 40,350 feet; range, 684 miles
Armament: 4 × 23mm cannons; up to 2,205 pounds of bombs
Service dates: 1950–

The Il 28 was the first Soviet jet bomber and a direct counterpart of the North American B-45 *Tornado* and British *Canberra*. Less capable than either, it nonetheless enjoyed a service career of great longevity and still flies in China.

After World War II a race commenced to evaluate captured German jet technology and incorporate it into new generations of warplanes. For the Soviet Union, this meant development of a practical jet bomber that would eventually carry atomic weapons. The Ilyushin design bureau constructed the Il 28 prototype in 1948 as a high-wing, twin-jet design with swept tail surfaces. Curiously, the main wing was straight with a tapered trailing edge. A crew of three was housed in a streamlined, attractive fuselage. The bombardier sat in a glazed nose section while the pilot was sequestered under a handsome canopy, and the tailgunner reposed in a turret reminiscent of the Boeing B-29, from which it had been copied. The Il 28 was powered by two VK-1 engines, mounted far forward beneath the wings.

The craft was originally flown with weak Junkers Jumo engines, but due to the shortsightedness of the British Labor government, the Soviets obtained examples of the latest Rolls-Royce Nene—then the world's finest. The prototype flew well on these copied engines, and the design entered production in 1949. However, Stalin insisted that at least 25 Il 28s be utilized in the 1950 May Day flyover, and the company strained every resource to successfully meet his demand. At length 6,317 Il 28s were constructed and received the NATO designation BEAGLE.

The Il 28 enjoyed a long service record with Russian and numerous Warsaw Pact air forces. The type was also widely exported abroad to several communist client states. Il 28s were primitive machines and carried a relatively light payload, but they displayed rugged construction and ease of maintenance. Russian and Eastern European Il 28s have long been retired, but China retains and operates a number as trainers.

Type: Antisubmarine; Reconnaissance

Dimensions: wingspan, 122 feet, 9 inches; length, 129 feet, 10 inches; ceiling, 33 feet, 4 inches
Weights: empty, 79,365 pounds; gross, 139,991 pounds
Power plant: 4 × 4,250–horsepower ZMD AI-20 turboprop engines
Performance: maximum speed, 448 miles per hour; ceiling, 32,810 feet; range, 2,299 miles
Armament: unknown
Service dates: 1967–

The far-ranging Il 38 was the Soviet Union's first long-range antisubmarine aircraft. It is also encountered while performing reconnaissance and electronic intelligence-gathering missions.

During World War II, the Allies acquired tremendous experience in the field of antisubmarine warfare (ASW) throughout the Atlantic and Pacific theaters. Afterward, they parleyed this expertise into several specifically designed ASW aircraft like Lockheed's P2V *Neptune*. Russia, primarily a land power, felt no such necessity and was content to deploy short-range platforms like the Beriev Be 12 for coastal patrol work. However, the advent of missile-firing submarines in the 1960s interjected new urgency to the development of such aircraft. Because nuclear-tipped submarine-launched missiles constituted a vital threat to Russia, they had to be engaged far away from coastal waters to be defeated. It was not until 1967 that the Soviets fielded their first dedicated ASW aircraft, the Ilyushin Il 38, known by the NATO code name MAY. This was essentially a highly modified Il 18 commercial airliner adapted for long-

range maritime reconnaissance. The West had previously set a precedent by developing two similar craft, the Lockheed P-3 *Orion* and BAe *Nimrod*, also from civilian craft. The most notable difference from the Il 18 is the forward positioning of the wing, which suggests that the center of gravity has been altered by the presence of heavy equipment in the front fuselage. The Il 38 also displays a very prominent chin radome, along with the numerous protuberances and airducts typical of ASW designs.

Little is known of the capability or armament of the Il 38, but certainly it cannot be slighted. Two spacious bomb bays, before and after the wing, are undoubtedly crammed with a huge array of sonobuoys, depth charges, homing torpedoes, and other tools of the ASW trade. But its procurement in small numbers (around 60) suggests that the more numerous Tu 142 BEAR is actually the preferred machine for this role. The only other operator is India, which maintains its own five-plane squadron of Il 38s. Operationally, the craft appears slated for replacement soon.

Type: Transport; Early Warning

Dimensions: wingspan, 165 feet, 8 inches; length, 152 feet, 10 inches; height, 48 feet, 5 inches
Weights: empty, 216,050 pounds; gross, 374,780 pounds
Power plant: 4 × 26,455–pound thrust Soloviev D-30KP turbojet engines
Performance: maximum speed, 528 miles per hour; ceiling, 50,855 feet; range, 3,107 miles
Armament: 2 × 23mm cannon
Service dates: 1974–

The Il 76 is a standard Russian heavy air transport capable of carrying heavy loads to remote, unprepared landing strips throughout Siberia. Modern variants also serve as that nation's most advanced airborne warning command center.

The advent of Lockheed's C-141 *Starlifter* in 1965 demonstrated the viability of large jet transports. Its great range and lifting capacity certainly inspired the Soviet government to acquire a similar machine for its own use. Such a craft would be especially useful in helping to develop remote parts of Russia like Siberia, where adverse operating conditions are routine. The government then instructed the Antonov design bureau to create such a beast; of course, it had to be bigger and better than its capitalist counterpart. In 1971 Antonov complied with the prototype Il 76, which bore great similarity to the *Starlifter.* It possessed a high-mounted wing fitted with leading-edge slats and trailing-edge slotted flaps for quick takeoffs. The spacious fuselage was circular in cross-section with streamlined fairings on either side to house the landing gear. As with most Soviet airplanes, the tire pressure can be adjusted in flight for landing on any kind of surface. The Il 76 became operational in 1974 and broke several altitude and payload records. Around 750 have been built, making it among the most numerous aircraft of its class in the world. The NATO designation is CANDID.

Around this time the United States began manufacturing self-guided cruise missiles, which are small, fast, and designed to operate at altitudes below a radar net. The Soviets responded by converting several Il 76s into airborne early warning and control (AWACS) aircraft. The AWACS version of the Il 76, called the A 50, is fitted with a rotating radome that scans downward and picks out missiles from the ground clutter. This information is then relayed by computer to MiG 31 interceptors, which then maneuver to engage the missiles. This version, built by Beriev, received the NATO designation MAINSTAY and will probably see frontline service for years to come.

Type: Light Bomber

Dimensions: wingspan, 39 feet, 6 inches; length, 25 feet, 11 inches; height, 7 feet, 9 inches
Weights: empty, 1,562 pounds; gross, 2,310 pounds
Power plant: 1 × 180–horsepower Mercedes D IIIa liquid-cooled in-line engine
Performance: maximum speed, 100 miles per hour; ceiling, 19,685 feet; range, 200 miles
Armament: 3 × 7.92mm machine guns
Service dates: 1918–1919

The angular, futuristic CL I was probably the best attack aircraft of World War I. It was certainly the most sophisticated of its day and pioneered building techniques that were years ahead of the time.

In the spring of 1918, the Junkers firm sought to replace the Halberstadt CL attack planes with a derivative of its ultramodern D I fighter. The new craft flew on May 4, 1918, and, like its predecessor, was built entirely of metal. It consisted of a steel-tube structure covered by corrugated metal skinning, buttressed by extensive internal bracing. This combination provided the craft with both strength and lightness. The fuselage employed a carlike radiator placed in front of the engine and just above the thrust line. A crew of two was also provided with separate cockpits. The gunner's position, in particular, was elevated and granted an unimpeded field of fire. In the air, the CL I was speedy, agile, and virtually impervious to small-arms fire. These traits made

it ideal for low-level ground attacks, so CL Is were outfitted with bomb racks, hand grenades, and other antipersonnel devices. For strafing duties, the pilot also operated two fixed machine guns.

Production of the CL I commenced in the summer of 1918, and 47 machines arrived at the front before the war ended. They were certainly the most advanced attack craft deployed by either side, years ahead of competing designs. Although there is no record of CL Is being used on the Western Front, they most certainly operated against Bolshevik forces in Finland, Estonia, and Latvia throughout 1919. Flown by veteran German pilots, CL Is were credited with excellent results. An interesting derivation was the CLS, a floatplane created for reconnaissance duties. Three examples were delivered to the navy, but no orders were forthcoming. After the war, a single CL I was also fitted with a canopy over the rear seat, thus becoming the first-ever all-metal airliner.

Type: Fighter

Dimensions: wingspan, 29 feet, 6 inches; length, 23 feet, 9 inches; height, 7 feet, 4 inches
Weights: empty, 1,439 pounds; gross, 1,835 pounds
Power plant: 1 × 185–horsepower BMW liquid-cooled in-line engine
Performance: maximum speed, 118 miles per hour; ceiling, 19,685 feet; range, 150 miles
Armament: 2 × 7.92mm machine guns
Service dates: 1918–1919

The diminutive Junkers D I was the first all-metal fighter plane produced in quantity. Deployed but never tested in battle, it dramatically foreshadowed events to come.

Hugo Junkers had conceived and constructed the first all-metal aircraft as early as 1915. This was the J I, a compact monoplane with relatively high performance. However, the conservative-minded German military greeted such futuristic contraptions with suspicion and manifested no official interest. Junkers persisted with several intervening designs, and he arrived at the J 7 in October 1917. This was another monoplane aircraft, exceptional in being fitted with pivoting wingtips, instead of ailerons, for longitudinal control. When these were found to cause wing flutter, more conventional arrangements were affixed. However, one feature that could not be overlooked was the radiator, which bizarrely sat astride the engine, directly blocking the pilot's view! Subsequent revisions relocated it toward the front of the fuselage. It was not

until March 1918 that Junkers fielded his most refined effort, the J 9. As before, this was a low-wing cantilever monoplane with considerable military promise. It flew effectively during the D-class fighter trails at Aldershof, and authorities finally decided to authorize production that spring.

The new craft entered the military service as the Junkers D I in the summer of 1918. It differed from the prototype in only minor details, but the most obvious was the large ailerons of unequal chord on each wing. A rollbar to protect the pilot in the event of an overturned landing was also fitted. The D I's metal construction rendered it light and strong, and once airborne it was fast and agile. Junkers's invention might have wielded considerable influence in the waning weeks of World War I, but because the construction techniques employed were so novel, only 41 machines were delivered before the Armistice that November. After the war, several were exported to the Baltic states and flown by German pilots against Bolshevik forces there.

Type: Light Bomber

Dimensions: wingspan, 52 feet, 5 inches; length, 29 feet, 10 inches; height, 11 feet, 1 inch
Weights: empty, 3,885 pounds; gross, 4,795 pounds
Power plant: 1 × 200–horsepower Benz BZ IV liquid-cooled in-line engine
Performance: maximum speed, 96 miles per hour; ceiling, 13,100 feet; range, 193 miles
Armament: 3 × 7.92mm machine guns
Service dates: 1918

The big J I appeared so ungainly to crew members that it was unofficially known as the "Moving Van." However, it was heavily armored and ideally configured for the dangerous work of ground support.

For many years Hugo Junkers proffered the idea of all-metal airplanes to a skeptical German High Command. Commencing in 1915, when he constructed the first metallic monoplane, Junkers developed a succession of viable designs that had obvious military applications. His perseverance paid off in 1917, when the government finally approached him to design and develop an armored biplane for the *Infanterieflieger* (ground-support units). The ensuing Junkers J I turned out to be one of the most unusual, if not outright ugly, aircraft employed by the German air arm during this conflict.

Despite a conventional biplane configuration, the J I was unique in several aspects. Its most prominent feature was the enormous top wing, spanning more than 50 feet tip to tip. It possessed a thick airfoil section and cantilevered construction and was made entirely of metal frames with corrugated covering. The lower wing was of identical planform but nearly a third smaller. The intrinsic strength of these units meant that they were fastened to the fuselage only by a series of inboard struts. The J I's fuselage, meanwhile, possessed an unusual octagonal cross-section. Its front half consisted of a completely armored "tub" that housed the motor, fuel, pilot, and gunner. To the rear were large, almost rectangular tail surfaces, also covered in metal. In service the J I was heavy to fly, required a long runway for takeoff, and was difficult to land on short strips. It was so ungainly in bulk that crew members christened it the *Mobelwagen* (Moving Van).

Despite appearances, Junkers's design was superbly adapted for infantry close-support missions. Its heavy armor made it nearly invulnerable to small-arms fire from below, and it also exhibited good low-altitude characteristics. No less than 227 of these rugged craft were built, and they served with distinction along the Western Front throughout 1918.

Type: Transport

Dimensions: wingspan, 95 feet, 11 inches; length, 62 feet; height, 18 feet, 2 inches
Weights: empty, 12,610 pounds; gross, 23,149 pounds
Power plant: 3 × 725–horsepower BMW 132A-3 radial engines
Performance: maximum speed, 171 miles per hour; ceiling, 19,360 feet; range, 808 miles
Armament: 2 × 7.92mm machine guns; up to 1,102 pounds of bombs
Service dates: 1935–1945

Beloved "Tante Ju" (Auntie Ju) was the most numerous European transport aircraft in history. As versatile as they were ungainly, Ju 52s participated in every German campaign during World War II.

In 1931 a design team under Ernst Zindel converted a single-motor Ju 52 passenger transport into a trimotor aircraft. The original version was a boxy, low-wing, all-metal machine with corrugated skin and fixed landing gear. It also employed a double set of flaps and ailerons along the trailing edges for better STOL (short takeoff and landing) performance. When the two engines were added to the wings, they were sharply canted outward to offset asymmetric power in the event of engine failure. The revised Ju 52 was a startling success and sold in great numbers to the airline Deutsche Lufthansa. By 1940 they comprised 75 percent of its inventory and won plaudits for safety and reliability. In the early 1930s the Luftwaffe was also clandestinely seeking military aircraft, so it adopted the Ju 52 as an interim bomber. In 1936 several were dispatched to fight in the Spanish Civil War and served effectively, dropping 6,000 tons of bombs and ferrying 13,000 Moroccan troops without loss. By the eve of World War II, the angular Ju 52 was the most numerous and important Luftwaffe transport, with more than 500 in service.

World War II only enhanced Auntie Ju's reputation for ruggedness. They were initially employed during the 1940 assault on Norway, the first military campaign to utilize air transport on a huge scale. They then flew against France and the Low Countries, and in 1941 Ju 52s played a conspicuous role in Operation Mercury, the airborne assault on Crete. At the time, this was the largest aerial assault in history, and losses were staggering. However, Ju 52s subsequently did meritorious work in Russia, where they ferried supplies, dropped parachute troopers, and evacuated casualties. Total wartime production of this rugged craft peaked at 4,845 machines. Spain also constructed several hundred transports that remained in service through the 1970s. The Ju 52 was a legendary aircraft.

Type: Medium Bomber; Reconnaissance

Dimensions: wingspan, 73 feet, 9 inches; length, 58 feet, 7 inches; height, 16 feet, 7 inches
Weights: empty, 11,354 pounds; gross, 18,078 pounds
Power plant: 2 × 600–horsepower Junkers Jumo 205C-4 diesel engines
Performance: maximum speed, 202 miles per hour; ceiling, 19,360 feet; range, 932 miles
Armament: 3 × 7.92mm machine guns; up to 1,764 pounds of bombs
Service dates: 1936–1941

The Ju 86 suffered from abysmally bad power plants that compromised its service career in Spain and elsewhere. However, several specially modified craft were among the highest-flying reconnaissance aircraft of World War II.

In 1933 the German government issued requirements for a new commercial airliner that could simultaneously function as a bomber. Heinkel responded by fielding the He 111 while Junkers originated the Ju 86; prototypes were ordered for both. Unlike the gracefully elliptical Heinkel design, the Junkers entry looked brusquely angular. It was an all-metal, low-wing monoplane with twin rudders and retractable landing gear that folded outward from the fuselage to the engines. It was to be powered by Junker Jumo diesel engines, an unproven form of technology at that time. The prototype first flew in November 1934, exhibiting sluggish performance and instability at low speeds. Its narrow-track landing gear, when combined with poor forward vision from the canopy, made it difficult to taxi as well as land. Nonetheless, the type was ordered into pro-

duction that year, and with better engines it enjoyed considerable overseas success as a passenger airliner. Several diesel-equipped bombers were sent to Spain in 1936, but they proved unreliable and unsatisfactory in combat. It was not until the Ju 86E version of 1937 that the plane received conventional motors. The follow-on Ju 86G also introduced a redesigned nose for improved pilot vision.

The Ju 86's inferior performance to the He 111 mandated its retirement from frontline service by 1939 and relegation to training duties. At length, Junkers decided to convert several machines into high-flying reconnaissance platforms. This was accomplished by extending the wingspan, employing new engines, and installing a pressurized cabin. The new Ju 86Ps could reach altitudes upward of 40,000 feet and were active during the Battle of Britain. They also flew with impunity in Africa until August 1942, when one was shot down by a specially equipped, stripped-down *Spitfire V.* By 1943 most Ju 86s had been scrapped following a production run of around 800 machines.

Type: Dive-Bomber

Dimensions: wingspan, 49 feet, 2 inches; length, 37 feet, 8 inches; height, 12 feet, 9 inches
Weights: empty, 8,686 pounds; gross, 14,550 pounds
Power plant: 1 × 1,500–horsepower Junkers Jumo 211P liquid-cooled in-line engine
Performance: maximum speed, 248 miles per hour; ceiling, 27,885 feet; range, 410 miles
Armament: 2 × 7.92mm machine guns; 2 × 20mm cannons; up to 6,000 pounds of bombs
Service dates: 1936–1945

Few aircraft projected such an evil intent as the unattractive, angular *Stuka*. It nevertheless personified Nazi blitzkrieg warfare and was an effective dive-bomber when unopposed, but it wilted quickly in the face of fighter opposition.

In 1933 German aerial expert Ernst Udet witnessed dive-bombing in the United States, which convinced him of similar applications for Europe. The embryonic Luftwaffe had been envisioned as aerial artillery for Wehrmacht land forces, and Udet urged creation of a new *Sturzkampfflugzeug* (*Stuka*) forces. A Junkers design team under Hans Pohlmann fielded a prototype in 1935, which was unlike any airplane ever built. Angular and ugly, the Ju 87 was an all-metal monoplane with unmistakable "cranked" wings and trousered landing gear. A crew of two sat back-to-back in a short greenhouse canopy. Test flights proved the new craft to be somewhat slow and sluggish yet highly accurate while diving. Several saw combat during the Spanish Civil War, where they operated with great effect against weak enemy opposition. When World War II commenced, only 500 Ju 87s were in the Luftwaffe inventory, but they wielded a tactical and psychological impact far greater than mere numbers suggested.

The screaming, precision-bombing *Stukas* epitomized blitzkrieg warfare as they blasted a path for oncoming German tanks and infantry. Their effect upon unarmed civilians was terrifying, for *Stukas* emitted a loud, high-pitched howl as they nosed over, giving the impression of giant birds of prey. The Ju 87s functioned brilliantly until the Battle of Britain in 1940, where effective fighter opposition caused heavy losses. Thereafter, *Stukas* were assigned to secondary theaters like the Aegean and Mediterranean with good results. They also enjoyed startling success against Russia, where on September 23, 1941, Hans-Ulrich Rudel destroyed the battleship *Marat* with a single 2,200-pound bomb, and ultimately accounted for 511 tanks. *Stukas* rendered good work wherever the Luftwaffe enjoyed air superiority, but by late 1944 they had faded from the scene entirely. More than 5,000 had been constructed.

Type: Medium Bomber; Night Fighter; Fighter

Dimensions: wingspan, 65 feet, 7 inches; length, 48 feet, 2 inches; height, 15 feet, 8 inches
Weights: empty, 18,250 pounds; gross, 30,400 pounds
Power plant: 2 × 1,730–horsepower BMW 801G-2 radial engines
Performance: maximum speed, 340 miles per hour; ceiling, 32,800 feet; range, 2,130 miles
Armament: 6 × 20mm cannons; 1 × 13mm machine gun; up to 4,409 pounds of bombs
Service dates: 1939–1945

The Ju 88 was the most numerous and versatile German bomber of World War II. It was grafted to every conceivable purpose, and even served as the lower half of a primitive guide missile!

In 1935 the German Air Ministry announced specifications for a new, twin-engine *Schnellbomber* (fast bomber). One year later Junkers beat out two other contenders with the Ju 88, a highly streamlined, smoothed-skinned airplane with midmounted wings. A crew of four sat under a large glazed canopy while a bombardier gondola, offset to the left, ran back from the nose. Test results were excellent, but Luftwaffe priorities were skewed to other craft, and production remained slow. By the time World War II erupted in September 1939, only about 50 Ju 88s had reached Luftwaffe units.

In combat the Junkers design was fast, carried a good bomb load, and could absorb great amounts of damage. Moreover, although originally intended as a bomber, it could be adapted to virtually every mis-

sion assigned to it: mine-laying, nighttime fighting, reconnaissance, antiship patrols, heavy fighter, ground attack, and dive-bombing. Ju 88s accordingly distinguished themselves in combat from England to Russia, Norway to North Africa. As the Allied ring began closing in on Germany, several dedicated night-fighter versions were developed with radar and heavy armament, such as the Ju 88G. These were among the best such craft deployed, and they accounted for hundreds of Allied bomber kills. The Ju 88S was a stripped-down high-speed bomber that appeared in 1943. It was as fast or faster than most contemporary fighters and therefore only lightly armed. One final version of note was the *Mistal*, which consisted of a radio-controlled Ju 88 carrying a piggyback Bf 109 or Fw 190 fighter. Once launched, it would be guided to a target like a primitive air-to-ground missile. Ju 88s of every stripe fought with distinction until the very end. Total production of this amazingly versatile machine reached 14,676 units.

Type: Medium Bomber; Reconnaissance; Torpedo-Bomber

Dimensions: wingspan, 72 feet, 2 inches; length, 49 feet; height, 14 feet, 7 inches
Weights: empty, 21,825 pounds; gross, 31,898 pounds
Power plant: 2 × 1,776–horsepower Junkers Jumo 213A radial engines
Performance: maximum speed, 325 miles per hour; ceiling, 30,665 feet; range, 1,210 miles
Armament: 3 × 7.92mm machine guns; 1 × 20mm cannon; up to 6,614 pounds of bombs
Service dates: 1943–1945

Appearing in the wake of the superlative Ju 88, the Ju 188 proved itself an even better aircraft. It excelled as a bomber, torpedo plane, and reconnaissance platform but came too late and in too few numbers to have an impact.

In 1939 the German Air Ministry announced specifications for a new high-speed bomber to replace the Do 17s and He 111s then in service. Junkers proposed a radical new design, the Ju 288, which was plagued with technical obstacles from the onset and never materialized. Meanwhile, the company also worked on the Ju 188 as a private venture in a logical progression from the already successful Ju 88. The new craft bore marked resemblance to its forebear, but it differed in having a new bulbous canopy section and longer, tapering wings. It also sported a power turret and squared-off tail surfaces. The first Ju 188 was test-flown in 1940 with excellent results, although its initial payload was the same as the earlier craft's. Nonetheless, production commenced in 1942, and by war's end 1,076 machines had been delivered.

The Ju 188E was the first production variant and was employed as a radar-equipped torpedo-bomber. It functioned well and was possibly the best of its type during the war. They were followed by the Ju 188F, a high-altitude long-range reconnaissance version that performed useful work in Russia. By 1943 the bugs had been shaken out of the new Jumo 213A engines, and they were fitted to the dedicated bomber variant, the Ju 188A. These proved even faster and more versatile than the already legendary Ju 88s and were very popular with crews. Many were employed as pathfinders during the January 1944 "Little Blitz" against London. The final version, the Ju 188T, was a stripped-down reconnaissance machine that could reach 435 miles per hour at very high altitude. The Ju 188s were excellent machines but appeared too late and in too small numbers to improve Germany's fortunes.

Type: Patrol-Bomber; Reconnaissance; Transport

Dimensions: wingspan, 137 feet, 9 inches; length, 95 feet, 7 inches; height, 22 feet, 4 inches
Weights: empty, 72,764 pounds; gross, 101,413 pounds
Power plant: 4 × 1,700–horsepower BMW 801D radial engines
Performance: maximum speed, 273 miles per hour; ceiling, 19,685 feet; range, 3,784 miles
Armament: 7 × 20mm cannons; up to 6,614 pounds of bombs or missiles
Service dates: 1943–1945

The huge Ju 290 transport was successfully adapted as a patrol-bomber but served in only limited numbers. One variant, the six-engine Ju 390, was designed to reach New York City and return.

In 1936 Junkers constructed the Ju 89, a practical, four-engine strategic bomber, but Luftwaffe authorities expressed little official interest. The company subsequently developed the aircraft into a civil version, the Ju 90, for the benefit of Deutsche Lufthansa. Eight were built and functioned as the pride of Lufthansa until 1939, when all were impressed into military service. At that time, the Luftwaffe desired a new bomber as an eventual replacement for the Focke-Wulf Fw 200 *Kondor*, and Junkers complied with the Ju 290. This was essentially a Ju 90 with redesigned wings and better engines. Flight tests were encouraging, so the aircraft entered production in 1942. A total of 66 of the lumbering giants were built.

The Ju 290s were variously employed in maritime patrol and as military transports. They were excellent machines and well-liked by crews but were never available in sufficient number to affect much. From their bases in France they would arc out over the Atlantic, relaying convoy locations to a dwindling number of U-boats. Others found work during the siege of Stalingrad, ferrying supplies and evacuating wounded, with several being lost. Subsequent models of the Ju 290 bristled with increasingly heavier armament, radar, and antishipping missiles, but they failed to surmount Allied control of the air. Nonetheless, in the fall of 1944 a pair of Ju 290s staged an impressive round-trip flight, 5,000 miles, to Manchuria and back.

In 1940 the Luftwaffe called for creation of an even bigger machine, the so-called *Amerika Bomber*, in the event of war with the United States. Junkers then conceived the Ju 390, which had a lengthened fuselage, wings, and six engines. Only two of these capable craft were built, and they did not proceed beyond a few test flights.

Kamov Ka 27 — Russia

Type: Antisubmarine; Transport

Dimensions: rotorspan, 52 feet, 2 inches; length, 37 feet, 1 inch; height, 17 feet, 9 inches
Weights: empty, 13,338 pounds; gross, 27,778 pounds
Power plant: 2 × 2,205–horsepower Klimov TV3–117V turboshaft engines
Performance: maximum speed, 155 miles per hour; ceiling, 16,405 feet; range, 497 miles
Armament: torpedoes or depth charges
Service dates: 1981–

The tubby Ka 27 (NATO code name HELIX) is the latest member of a long-serving and successful series of Russian naval helicopters. In addition to antisubmarine warfare (ASW) versions, other models can perform assault and radar picket work.

In 1956 the Soviet navy issued requirements for a new and capable helicopter for ASW purposes. Such a machine would also have to be compact, owning to the cramped storage facilities aboard many Russian naval vessels. Nikolai Kamov's design bureau confronted the problem with great imagination and engineering skill by producing the first Ka 25 (NATO code name HORMONE) in 1960. This was a rotund, twin-engine helicopter utilizing what became the company trademark: counter-rotating coaxial rotors. This unique system offered many advantages over conventional layouts, with the most obvious being deletion of the long tailboom and dangerous tailrotor. Commencing in 1966, the Ka 25 became the standard Soviet ASW platform at sea, easily recognized by various sonar bugles and protuberances. More than

600 were built, and many still fly in former Soviet client state navies.

In 1981 Kamov was succeeded by Sergei Mikheyev, who continued the company tradition by designing the newer Ka 27. As before, the new machine was coaxial-powered, which allowed a stubby, compact design, although in this case somewhat bigger than the previous machine. The Ka 27 featured a crew of five, twin canted fins, and two engines with twice the power. Moreover, it is the first Kamov design capable of all-weather and nighttime ASW missions. At least 100 have been built and currently serve with the Russian navy.

In 1980 Kamov subsequently built upon its earlier success by designing two additional models. The Ka 39 is a tactical assault helicopter for Russian naval infantry, with an enlarged cabin and heavy armament in the form of machine guns and rocket pods. The similar Ka 31 is designed for radar picket work, with a large E-801 Oko radar bulge under the belly. Both were procured in small numbers before the collapse of the Soviet Union in 1991.

Type: Antitank

Dimensions: rotorspan, 45 feet; length, 52 feet, 5 inches; height, 17 feet, 8 inches
Weights: gross, 16,534 pounds
Power plant: 2 × Klimov TV3–11VK turboshaft engines
Performance: maximum speed, 217 miles per hour; ceiling, 13,125 feet; range, 155 miles
Armament: 1 × 30mm cannon; 16 × AT-9 *Vikhr* missiles; various gunpods
Service dates: 1992–

The futuristic Ka 50, nicknamed "Black Shark" by the Russians, is the world's first single-seat attack helicopter. It retains many trademark features of the Kamov design bureau and is currently awaiting export orders.

In the 1970s Western mania for large and sophisticated attack helicopters like the Hughes AH-64 *Apache* convinced Soviet authorities that they should emulate such tactical thinking. In 1977 Kamov design bureau chief Sergei Mikheyev advanced a new machine based upon proven company concepts. The Ka 50 is the world's first single-seat attack helicopter design, so chosen to enhance its survivability over larger two-seat machines. It is also unique in employing the coaxial rotor configuration that is a Kamov trademark. The reason behind this adaptation is that single rotors were perceived as too vulnerable to damage in low-level ground-attack work. The fuselage is attenuated, heavily armored, and ends in a long, blunt snout. It is also partially made from lightweight composite materials that add

greatly to overall strength. Moreover, to assist the pilot, the cockpit is completely computerized and employs the Kamov autoland, autohover, and auto–formation-flying equipment pioneered in naval helicopters. Finally, this craft is the first helicopter in the world to boast an ejection system for the pilot. The sequence begins when explosive bolts shed the rotor blades, and then a rocket pack drags the helpless operator out of his cockpit!

To fulfill its mission as an antitank attack helicopter, the Ka 50 is extremely well armed. It sports no less than 16 *Vikhr* antitank missiles, which are supersonic and capable of penetrating reactive armor up to a thickness of 35 inches. A 30mm high velocity cannon is also fitted to the starboard side of the fuselage, and the choice of either explosive or armor-piercing ammunition can be made in flight. In sum, the Ka 50 is a formidable adversary and goes by the NATO designation HOKUM. The precise number of Ka 50s in service since the collapse of the Soviet Union has not been determined.

Kawanishi H6K — Japan

Type: Reconnaissance; Transport

Dimensions: wingspan, 131 feet, 2 inches; length, 84 feet, 1 inch; height, 20 feet, 6 inches
Weights: empty, 27,293 pounds; gross, 50,706 pounds
Power plant: 4 × 1,300–horsepower Mitsubishi Kinsei 53 radial engines
Performance: maximum speed, 239 miles per hour; ceiling, 31,365 feet; range, 4,210 miles
Armament: 4 × 7.7mm machine guns; 1 × 20mm cannon; up to 2,205 pounds of torpedoes
Service dates: 1938–1945

The graceful H6K was among the best flying boats during the early stages of the Pacific war. It boasted greater range and endurance than its American and British counterparts.

The Japanese navy first gained experience with flying boats with the assistance of a team of engineers from the British Short firm in 1930. Within five years Japan had accumulated sufficient experience to manufacture similar craft on its own. Such was the case when the navy issued a *9-Shi* (1934) specification to Kawanishi for a large flying boat of unprecedented range and endurance. Fortuitously, the Japanese had recently purchased an example of the Consolidated P2Y *Ranger* from the United States, and Kawanishi design teams under Yoshio Hashiguchi and Shizuo Kikuhara set about adapting it for their own purposes. The prototype H6K first flew in 1936 as a large four-engine aircraft with particularly pleasing lines. The streamlined two-step hull mounted a parasol wing on struts and pylons, and two stabilizing floats were placed outboard of midspan. The first H6Ks rolled off the assembly lines in 1938 and, by virtue of their excellent air and water handling, were among the best flying boats in the world. When the Pacific war commenced in December 1941, the Imperial Japanese Navy possessed 64 of these impressive giants, soon to be known to the Allies as *Mavis.*

The H6K was heavily employed throughout extensive reaches of the Southwest Pacific. In addition to reconnaissance work, they carried a variety of bombs or torpedoes, and on several occasions they raided Rabaul and northern Australia. However, a major weak point was the lack of self-sealing fuel tanks, which rendered them very vulnerable to enemy fighters. By 1943, as Allied defenses improved, losses had grown untenable, and the *Mavis* became restricted to nighttime flying and transportation work. They were well suited to this role, having been operated by Japan Air Lines in this manner for several months prior to hostilities. A total of 217 H6Ks were built.

Type: Reconnaissance; Transport

Dimensions: wingspan, 124 feet, 8 inches; length, 92 feet, 4 inches; height, 30 feet
Weights: empty, 40,521 pounds; gross, 71,650 pounds
Power plant: 4 × 1,530–horsepower Mitsubishi MK4B Kasei radial engines
Performance: maximum speed, 290 miles per hour; ceiling, 28,740 feet; range, 4,460 miles
Armament: 5 × 20mm cannons; 4 × 7.7mm machine guns; up to 4,408 pounds of bombs
Service dates: 1942–1945

The mighty *H8K* was the best all-around flying boat of World War II, superior in many respects to all other British, American, and German designs. Fast and heavily armed, it was difficult to shoot down and treated respectfully by enemy fighters.

By 1938 Japanese naval planners realized that it would take three years to produce a more modern replacement for the H6K flying boat. They then issued a *14-Shi* specification calling for a craft with performance superior to that of the contemporary Short *Sunderland*. Accordingly, a design team headed by Shizuo Kikuhara set about conceiving what evolved into the world's best flying boat. The prototype flew in 1940 as a high-wing, all-metal monoplane with a rather narrow hull and extremely clean lines. Unfortunately, this version proved unstable during water taxiing tests and prone to porpoising uncontrollably. Consequently, a revised model was built featuring a deepened two-step hull and modified flaps, both of which cured the problem. The new craft, designated the H8K 1, was also heavily

armed, mounting no less than five 20mm cannons and four 7.7mm machine guns. Moreover, unlike traditional Japanese warplanes, it also featured self-sealing fuel tanks and considerable armor plating for the crew. During World War II this massive craft came to be known to the Allies as *Emily*.

The H8K was a formidable war machine. With a range over 4,000 miles, it was fast, maneuverable, and could cruise 27 hours without refueling. Well-armed and armored, it was also extremely difficult to shoot down and had to be approached gingerly. The combat debut of the H8K occurred in March 1942 when a pair of *Emilys* flew several hundred miles from French Frigate Shoals to Pearl Harbor, only to discover the target was obscured by cloud cover. Thereafter, the big flying boat was encountered throughout the Pacific while performing maritime reconnaissance. In 1943 a transport version, the H8K2 *Seika* (Clear Sky), was developed that could carry 64 fully armed troops. A total of 175 were constructed.

Type: Fighter

Dimensions: wingspan, 39 feet, 4 inches; length, 30 feet, 8 inches; height, 13 feet
Weights: empty, 5,858 pounds; gross, 8,818 pounds
Power plant: 1 × 1,990–horsepower Nakajima NK9H Homare radial engine
Performance: maximum speed, 369 miles per hour; ceiling, 35,300 feet; range, 1,488 miles
Armament: 4 × 20mm cannon
Service dates: 1944–1945

The *Shiden Kai* was one of the best all-around fighters deployed by Japan in World War II. Its success is even more surprising considering that it evolved from a floatplane.

In 1940 the Imperial Japanese Navy sought possession of a capable floatplane fighter to be used in conjunction with the tactic of island hopping. Kawanishi responded with the N1K1 *Kyofu* (Mighty Wind), a streamlined and powerful aircraft. By 1943, however, Japan was on the defensive and needed newer, land-based fighters. A design team subsequently overhauled the *Kyofu* by eliminating the floats, and thus the N1K1-J was born. This was a heavily armed, mid-wing fighter of great strength and maneuverability. It carried no less than four 20mm cannons and two 7.7mm machine guns, in addition to armor for the pilot. Called the *Shiden* (Violet Lightning), it proved a formidable fighter and very much equal to Grumman F6F *Hellcats* and Vought F4U *Corsairs*. And unlike most Japanese fighters, it was rugged and difficult to shoot down. However, *Shidens* suffered from unreliable Homare radial engines and problems associated with the long, telescopic landing gear inherent in mid-wing configurations. Kawanishi nonetheless produced 1,001 of these excellent machines, which received the Allied code name *George 11*.

In the fall of 1943, the Kawanishi design teams took another look at their promising fighter in an attempt to simplify and improve it. The biggest changes involved adapting a low-wing construction, along with revised tail surfaces and a cleaned-up cowl. Shorter, more conventional landing gear were also fitted. The result was the N1K2-J *Shiden Kai* (Modified Violet Lightning). It boasted higher performance using the same engine and one-third fewer parts than the original design. This craft, known to the Allies as *George 21*, was an even better dog-fighter than the legendary *Zero*. On February 6, 1945, a single N1K2 flown by the noted ace Kaneyoshi Muto single-handedly engaged 12 Grumman F6F *Hellcats*, shooting down four and driving the remainder off! Unfortunately for Japan, this excellent fighter was never available in sufficient quantity to turn the tide of events. Only 428 were built.

Kawasaki Ki 45 *Toryu* — Japan

Type: Fighter; Night Fighter

Dimensions: wingspan, 49 feet, 4 inches; length, 36 feet, 1 inch; height, 12 feet, 1 inch
Weights: empty, 8,818 pounds; gross, 12,125 pounds
Power plant: 2 × 1,080–horsepower Mitsubishi Ha–102 radial engines
Performance: maximum speed, 339 miles per hour; ceiling, 32,810 feet; range, 1,243 miles
Armament: 1 × 37mm cannon; 2 × 20mm cannon, 1 × 7.7mm machine gun
Service dates: 1942–1945

The Ki 45 was Japan's first twin-engine fighter and its most successful night fighter. It also served capably in a variety of missions, including ground attack, antishipping, and kamikaze.

By 1937 the notion of long-range strategic fighters, capable of escorting bomber fleets to targets and back, was becoming prevalent. Germany began successfully experimenting with its Messerschmitt Bf 110, which prompted the Imperial Japanese Army to adopt similar craft. That year it invited several companies into a competition, and Kawasaki, after many trials and prototypes, originated the Ki 45 *Toryu* (Dragon Slayer). This was a handsome, low-wing design with a pointed nose and a long, tandem cabin housing pilot and gunner. Initial flights revealed that the craft was underpowered, so a succession of better engines ensued until the Nakajima Ha–25 was utilized. Other problems centered around the landing gear, which were weak and hand-cranked in flight. With better motors and powered undercarriage, the Ki 45 showed promise,

so in 1941 it entered production. A total of 1,701 were ultimately built, and they received the code name *Nick* during World War II.

The first Ki 45s were deployed in Southeast Asia and, despite exceptional maneuverability for their size, were at a disadvantage fighting single-engine opponents. Given their speed and heavy armament, however, they proved ideal for ground attacks and antishipping strikes. Moreover, the Ki 45 was also an effective bomber interceptor and played havoc with American B-24 formations throughout Burma and Indochina. When the B-24s switched to night attacks, the Ki 45 was converted into a night fighter by mounting heavy cannons on top of the fuselage in slanted fashion. Considerable success was achieved, which gave rise to the Ki 45 KAIc, a dedicated night-fighter version, in 1944. These machines also performed useful work against high-flying B-29s over Japan toward the end of the war. More ominously, on May 27, 1944, it fell upon four *Nicks* to perform the first army kamikaze attacks against American warships off Biak.

Type: Light Bomber

Dimensions: wingspan, 57 feet, 3 inches; length, 41 feet, 10 inches; height, 12 feet, 5 inches
Weights: empty, 10,031 pounds; gross, 14,881 pounds
Power plant: 2 × 1,150–horsepower Nakajima Ha–115 radial engines
Performance: maximum speed, 314 miles per hour; ceiling, 33,135 feet; range, 1,491 miles
Armament: 3 × 7.7mm machine guns; up to 1,764 pounds of bombs
Service dates: 1940–1945

At the beginning of World War II, the Ki 48 was Japan's most important light bomber. Slow and underarmed, it was never much of a threat against improving Allied defenses.

By 1938 Japanese forces operating in China began encountering numbers of Soviet-supplied Tupolev SB 2 light bombers. These proved so fast that Japan's most modern interceptor, the Nakajima Ki 27, could scarcely intercept them. Naturally, the Imperial Japanese Army sought possession of a light bombardment aircraft with similar capabilities. A Kawasaki design team under Takeo Doi then commenced work on a prototype that emerged in 1939. The new Ki 48 was a modern-looking, midwing bomber with a crew of four and an internal bomb bay. Variable-pitch propellers were also fitted to the two Nakajima Ha–25 radial engines for improved performance. The new craft flew fast and handled very well, so it entered production in 1940. That fall the first units equipped with Ki 48s arrived in northern China and commenced combat operations. As

expected, the new bomber simply outflew weak Chinese defenses and established a reputation for reliability and ease of maintenance. By the advent of the Pacific war in December 1941, the Ki 48 was the most numerous light bomber in the Japanese arsenal. It received the Allied designation *Lilly*.

During the opening phases of war, Ki 48s performed useful work against British forces in Southeast Asia and the U.S. installations in the Philippines. This, however, was accomplished largely in the presence of Japanese air superiority. Advancing next upon the Dutch East Indies and New Guinea, Ki 48s began taking heavy losses over Australia as defenses consolidated and resistance stiffened. Kawasaki then introduced the Ki 48-II, which featured bigger engines, twice the bomb load, and slightly heavier armament. These, too, wilted in the face of newer Allied fighters, and by 1943 the *Lilly* was restricted to night bombing. By 1944 all were declared obsolete, and many ended their days as kamikazes. Production amounted to 1,977 machines.

Type: Fighter

Dimensions: wingspan, 39 feet, 4 inches; length, 29 feet, 4 inches; height, 12 feet, 1 inch
Weights: empty, 5,798 pounds; gross, 7,650 pounds
Power plant: 1 × 1,175–horsepower Kawasaki Ha–40 liquid-cooled in-line engine
Performance: maximum speed, 348 miles per hour; ceiling, 32,810 feet; range, 1,181 miles
Armament: 2 × 12.7mm machine guns; 2 × 20mm cannon
Service dates: 1943–1945

The streamlined *Hien* was a useful aircraft beset by troublesome power plants. Once outfitted with a new radial engine, however, it became Japan's finest fighter of World War II.

In 1937 Kawasaki obtained rights to manufacture the superb German Daimler-Benz DB 601A in-line engine. Three years later the Japanese army requested that Kawasaki design a fighter around this power plant. A team under Takeo Doi then constructed a prototype that initially flew in December 1941. In contrast with other radial-powered Japanese fighters, the Ki 61 possessed rakish lines reminiscent of the Messerschmitt Bf 109F. It was also heavily armed with four machine guns and possessed pilot armor in contrast to prevailing design philosophies. Moreover, mock combat trials between the Bf 109 and captured examples of the Curtiss P-40 revealed the Ki 61 superior to either warplane. The Imperial Japanese Army was then in great need to replace its aging Ki 43 *Hayabusa* fighters, so it authorized the new craft into production as the *Hien* (Swallow). Al-

lied forces gave it the code name *Tony;* production came to 2,654 machines

The Ki 61 debuted at New Guinea in the spring of 1943 and was relatively successful in combat. It was as fast as many Allied fighters and even more maneuverable. However, recurrent problems with the Ha–40 engine were never resolved. In 1943 an improved version, the Ki 61-II, mounted a bigger engine, but it suffered from even worse maintenance problems than earlier craft. Nonetheless, by 1945 the *Tony* was one of few Japanese aircraft able to attack American B-29 bombers at high altitude. When air raids finally destroyed the last stock of Ha–40 engines, Kawasaki was ordered to fit existing airframes with the Mitsubishi 112-II radial engine. This was engineered with considerable finesse, and the new fighter, christened the Ki 100, was the best Japanese fighter of the war. It easily outflew the F6F *Hellcats* and P-51 *Mustangs* encountered over Japan, but only 272 were built before the war ended.

Lavochkin La 5/7 —————————— **Russia**

Type: Fighter

Dimensions: wingspan, 32 feet, 2 inches; length, 28 feet, 2 inches; height, 9 feet, 3 inches
Weights: empty, 5,816 pounds; gross, 7,496 pounds
Power plant: 1 × 1,859–horsepower Shvetsov M-82FN radial engine
Performance: maximum speed, 413 miles per hour; ceiling, 35,435 feet; range, 395 miles
Armament: 3 × 20mm cannons; up to 441 pounds of bombs
Service dates: 1942–1945

The La 7 was among the best fighters produced during World War II. It was a superior dogfighter to both the Bf 109 and Fw 190 and the chosen mount of leading Soviet aces.

In the fall of 1941, as the German blitzkrieg rolled toward Moscow, the Soviet government began frantically scrambling to acquire more efficient weapons. Semyon Lavochkin, who had divested himself from his earlier partnership, began developing the inadequate LaGG 3 into a first-class fighter. He started by taking a basic LaGG frame, fitting it with a powerful M-82 radial engine, and the effects were startling. With additional refinements like a cut-down canopy and redesigned cowl, the new La 5 proved faster than the fabled Bf 109G in speed and maneuverability. These machines were first committed during the horrific Battle of Stalingrad in 1942 and acquitted themselves well. The following year, the La 5FN, with a fuel-injected engine, arrived during the Battle at Kursk, again with good results. Compared to the stopgap LaGG 3, Lavochkin's new

fighters were fast, responsive, and highly agile at low altitudes. In the hands of capable pilots like Ivan Kozhedub, the leading Allied ace with 62 kills, Russia slowly wrested air superiority away from the Germans.

Lavochkin's final wartime variant was the La 7. This was basically an La 5FN fitted with a more powerful engine and additional aeronautical refinements. These included metal wing spars (earlier craft being made entirely of wood) for greater strength and lighter weight. The armament was also increased to three 20mm cannons that spat out seven pounds of lead per second. In an attempt to shed even more weight, the fuel capacity was cut in half, reducing the fighter's operational radius to about an hour. However, because Soviet fighters were usually deployed right on the front lines, this was not viewed as detrimental. Lavochkin fighter craft were major contributors to the ultimate Soviet victory, and their designer received the prestigious Stalin Prize. Production totaled 21,975 of all models.

Type: Fighter

Dimensions: wingspan, 32 feet, 1 inch; length, 29 feet, 1 inch; height, 8 feet, 10 inches
Weights: empty, 5,776 pounds; gross, 7,275 pounds
Power plant: 1 × 1,240–horsepower M-105PF liquid-cooled in-line engine
Performance: maximum speed, 348 miles per hour; ceiling, 29,350 feet; range, 404 miles
Armament: 2 × 7.62mm machine guns; 2 × 12.7mm machine guns; 1 × 20mm cannon
Service dates: 1940–1945

The much-derided LaGG 3 was the most numerous Soviet fighter during the early days of the Great Patriotic War (the Soviet name for World War II). A robust design, it nonetheless exhibited marginal performance and suffered great losses.

In 1938 the Soviet government announced competition for a new single-seat fighter with optimal performance at medium to low altitudes. A design bureau headed by Semyon A. Lavochkin, assisted by engineers V. Gorbunov and M. Gudlov (hence the designation LaGG), designed and flew the prototype I 22 in 1939. It was a streamlined and conventional-appearing aircraft for its class but also unique in reverting to wooden construction. In fact, only the cowling and movable control surfaces employed metal. The wood itself was impregnated with plastic for added strength, but this added greatly to overall weight. The I 22 demonstrated serious performance deficiencies during flight-testing, but as Stalin demanded great amounts of fighters, Lavochkin was ordered to salvage his design rather than start over.

The I 22 entered production as the LaGG 1 in 1940 and, in a play upon the designer's initials, pilots nicknamed it the "Guaranteed Wooden Coffin." Further modifications eventually yielded the LaGG 3 in 1941, which was lighter and fitted with wing slats. These modifications cured the craft's most vicious characteristics, but climbing performance remained poor. By 1942, 6,258 LaGG 3s had been constructed.

The LaGG 3 was among the most numerous Soviet fighters when the Great Patriotic War erupted in June 1941. For many months they bore the brunt of Germany's aerial onslaught and, being inferior to the Messerschmitt Bf 109, suffered heavily. Many more craft would have been lost had it not been for the LaGG's amazing ability to absorb damage and keep flying. By 1943 most had been superceded by the radial-powered and far superior La 5. Many LaGGs were employed for the rest of the war as low-level escorts for the Il 2 ground-attack craft. It is best remembered as a sacrificial aircraft marking time until the arrival of better designs.

Type: Medium Bomber

Dimensions: wingspan, 73 feet; length, 45 feet, 3 inches; height, 13 feet, 11 inches
Weights: empty, 6,008 pounds; gross, 12,037 pounds
Power plant: 2 × 420–horsepower Gnome-Rhone 9 Ady radial engines
Performance: maximum speed, 123 miles per hour; ceiling, 18,900 feet; range, 621 miles
Armament: 5 × 7.7mm machine guns; 2,205 pounds of bombs
Service dates: 1928–1939

The LeO 20 was the standard French heavy night bomber for over a decade. Although slow and underpowered, it served admirably in a variety of functions.

The Liore et Olivier (LeO) firm was founded in 1912 at Levallois-Perret, and throughout World War I it manufactured various Nieuport, Morane-Saulnier, and Sopwith designs under license. The firm then established itself as a major force in French aviation design, specializing in large bombers. In 1924 specifications were issued for a new night bomber and the firm's prototype, the LeO 32, proved a rival to the bigger Farman *Goliath* and just as capable. This was followed by the LeO 122 of 1926, which was not produced but served as a model for a subsequent aircraft, the LeO 20 which was a conventional biplane bomber with three-bay, equal-span wings (a consistent LeO trait) melded to a deep, rather rectangular fuselage. The nose housed a gunner's cockpit while a bombardier's station was placed directly below him. Two radial engines sat in uncowled nacelles on the lower wings, to which were affixed large "trousered" landing gear. Despite its appearance, the LeO 20 was stable, handled well, and functioned capably as a night bomber. The French Armee de l'Air eventually acquired 320 of these cumbersome machines, and they formed the backbone of French nighttime attack squadrons for a decade. This functional design attracted overseas interest, and seven LeO 20s were exported to Romania.

The reliable LeOs underwent a number of experimental developments throughout their long service life. The LeO 206 was a four-engine variant that entered production in 1932 with a run of 40 machines. Less successful was the LeO 208, which featured narrow-chord lower wings, bigger engines, and retractable landing gear. It offered better performance than the stock LeO 20 but was not produced. Several machines, designated LeO 201s, were also outfitted for training of parachute forces in 1937. By the advent of World War II, nearly 100 LeO 20s were still employed as target tugs or trainers in North Africa.

Type: Medium Bomber

Dimensions: wingspan, 73 feet, 9 inches; length, 56 feet, 4 inches; height, 17 feet, 4 inches
Weights: empty, 17,229 pounds; gross, 25,133 pounds
Power plant: 2 × 1,140–horsepower Gnome-Rhone 14N 48/49 radial engines
Performance: maximum speed, 308 miles per hour; ceiling, 29,350 feet; range, 1,429 miles
Armament: 2 × 7.5mm machine guns; 1 × 20mm cannon; up to 3,307 pounds of bombs
Service dates: 1939–1945

The LeO 451 was the best French bomber of World War II and one of few available in quantity. It fought well during the Battle of France and also flew capably in the hands of Vichy French pilots.

No sooner had the Armee de l'Air become independent in April 1933 than it pressed for immediate expansion and modernization programs. Part of this entailed development of a new four-seat medium bomber capable of day and night operations. In 1937 the firm Liore et Olivier fielded its Model 451 prototype, which marked a breakthrough in French bomber design. It was an all-metal, midwing, twin-engine craft with a glazed nose and twin rudders. In contrast to the ungainly aircraft of the early 1930s, the LeO 451 was beautifully streamlined and performed as good as it looked. Operationally, however, the type suffered from technical detriments that were never fully corrected. It had been designed for 1,600-horsepower engines at a time when no such power plants were available. Hence, employing 1,000-horsepower motors, LeO 451s remained significantly un-

derpowered and never fulfilled their design potential. Worse still, when the French government decided to acquire the bomber in quantity, bureaucratic lethargy militated against mass production. By September 1939 only five LeO 451s had been delivered.

The German onslaught in Poland energized French aircraft production, and when the Battle of France commenced in May 1940 around 450 LeO 451s were available. They had been designed for medium-level bombing, but the speed of the German blitzkrieg necessitated their employment in low-level ground attacks. The bomber served well in that capacity, but, exposed to enemy fighters and antiaircraft fire, serious losses ensued. Yet the type remained in production after France's capitulation, with an additional 150 being acquired. These were actively flown against the Allies in North Africa before Vichy France was occupied by the Germans. They confiscated about 94 LeO 451s; stripped of armament, these were flown as transports. A handful survived into the postwar period as survey aircraft.

Letov S 328 ——————————————————————— **Czechoslovakia**

Type: Light Bomber; Reconnaissance

Dimensions: wingspan, 44 feet, 11 inches; length, 33 feet, 11 inches; height, 11 feet, 2 inches
Weights: empty, 3,704 pounds; gross, 5,820 pounds
Power plant: 1 × 635–horsepower Bristol Pegasus radial engine
Performance: maximum speed, 174 miles per hour; ceiling, 23,620 feet; range, 435 miles
Armament: 4 × 7.92mm machine guns; up to 1,102 pounds of bombs
Service dates: 1933–1944

A useful craft, the Letov S 328 was designed for Finland yet deployed by Czechoslovakia. Ironically, it flew actively during World War II in the hands of numerous belligerents.

In 1931 the Czechoslovakian Letov firm, which had manufactured airplanes since 1918, developed a two-seat reconnaissance/utility machine for Estonia called the S 228. It was a fine machine, and the following year the Finnish government asked for a similar craft. A team headed by Alois Smolik responded with the S 328, which borrowed heavily from the earlier design. It was a single-bay biplane with staggered wings of equal length. Both the wings and fuselage were made of metal framework and fabric-covered, although the engine area sported alloy panels. Provisions were made for two forward-firing machine guns up front, with a similar armament for the gunner/observer. Like all Letov products, the S 328 was a first-rate machine, but orders from Finland never materialized. The changing political climate of Europe, occasioned by Adolf Hitler's rise to power in 1933,

then induced the Czech government to acquire S 328s in quantity. A total of 445 machines were constructed, including several night-fighter and floatplane variants.

In March 1939 German forces occupied Bohemia/Moravia and acquired all existing stocks of S 328. Interestingly enough, the type was kept in production for another year. The excellent Letovs were subsequently impressed into Luftwaffe service as trainers, but others were doled out to the puppet Slovakian air force. Several S 328s accompanied the invasion of Poland that year and acquitted themselves well. Two years later S 328s were present during the German invasion of the Soviet Union, although many Slovak pilots defected along with their aircraft. Those remaining in German hands were employed as night fighters to foil the harassing raids of Polikarpov Po 2s. Finally, a small number of S 328s ended up with the Bulgarian air force for patrolling the Black Sea. The hardworking Letovs saw their final service during the 1944 Slovakian uprising against German forces.

Type: Reconnaissance

Dimensions: wingspan, 33 feet, 10 inches; length, 25 feet, 3 inches; height, 9 feet, 6 inches
Weights: empty, 1,680 pounds; gross, 2,824 pounds
Power plant: 1 × 160–horsepower Mercedes D III liquid-cooled in-line engine
Performance: maximum speed, 103 miles per hour; ceiling, 15,000 feet; range, 500 miles
Armament: 2 × 7.92mm machine guns
Service dates: 1916–1917

When it appeared in 1916, the LFG Roland C II was an unusual and effective German reconnaissance craft of World War I. Simultaneously streamlined yet rotund, it was affectionately known to crew members as the "Whale."

The firm Luftfahrzeug Gesellschaft was founded in 1906 with a view toward constructing airships. Shortly before the onset of World War I, it modified its name to LFG Roland to avoid confusion with another firm, LVG. For two years into the war, LFG manufactured Albatros fighters, but by 1916 the company was ready to field its own design.

The new craft debuted in the spring of 1916 as a two-seat reconnaissance vehicle of most unusual lines. In fact, compared to contemporary German observation craft, beset with numerous struts and wires, the LFG Roland C II represented a tremendous advance in the art of streamlining. The most obvious aspect of this was the plywood-covered monocoque fuselage, which was very deep and ta-

pered off to the rear. The two wings were wedded directly to it, thereby closing the interplane gap and giving both pilot and gunner unrestricted views up and forward. The highly staggered wings were also buttressed by a single "I" strut to minimize drag. The net result was an extremely modern design that anticipated the CL-class aircraft of the late war. In light of its somewhat tubby appearance, the C II was unofficially dubbed the *Walfisch* (Whale).

In service the C II proved itself to be fast, rugged, and difficult to shoot down. On occasion, the nimble craft was called upon to serve as an escort fighter to slower C-series reconnaissance airplanes. However, its peculiarly thin wings gave it mediocre climbing abilities, and the pilot's view downward was also poor, leading to a propensity for accidents while landing. Within a year the C II was withdrawn from service on the Western Front and relegated to secondary theaters and training functions. An estimated 250–300 had been constructed.

Type: Fighter

Dimensions: wingspan, 29 feet, 4 inches; length, 22 feet, 8 inches; height, 10 feet, 2 inches
Weights: empty, 1,397 pounds; gross, 1,749 pounds
Power plant: 1 × 180–horsepower Argus liquid-cooled in-line engine
Performance: maximum speed, 112 miles per hour; ceiling, 16,400 feet; range, 230 miles
Armament: 2 × 7.92mm machine guns
Service dates: 1917–1918

The LFG Roland D II was a failed attempt to modify the successful C II *Walfisch* (Whale) into a single-seat fighter. Despite an attractive appearance, it was tricky to fly, heavy on the controls, and inferior to contemporary Albatros fighters.

By 1916 the outstanding performance of the two-seat LFG Roland C II induced that company to develop a single-seat fighter along similar lines. The prototype first flew in July of that year and bore unmistakable resemblance to its predecessor. Like the C II, the new D I possessed a rather deep, fishlike outline. The cross-sectioned oval fuselage was constructed from a wooden monocoque shell that left the engine almost completely buried. The front end possessed metal engine-access panels, typical Roland cooling vents, and terminated in a large, bowl-shaped propeller spinner. Meanwhile, the two equal-chord wings were unstaggered and lacked dihedral. Moreover, the upper span attached directly to the fuselage, completely filling in the gap. A relatively small wooden rudder and broad, trapezoidal tailplanes outfitted the

rear quarter. In view of the D I's slimmer appearance, it was unofficially dubbed the *Haifisch* (Shark).

From the onset, unfortunately, the D I exhibited poor flying characteristics for a fighter. Both forward and downward views from the cockpit were obstructed by the wings, placing pilots at a serious disadvantage. In an attempt to rectify this deficiency, a new model, the D II, evolved with a modified center section for improved vision. This consisted of a long, narrow pylon and a cut-down cockpit. The aircraft, however, remained sluggish to maneuver, heavy on the controls, and clearly inferior to the Albatros scouts they were meant to replace. A total of 300 D IIs were manufactured, but in view of their inferior qualities they were confined mostly to secondary theaters like Macedonia and quiet sectors of the Western Front. A final version, the D III, emerged in late 1917 with more conventional struts affixing the upper wing, and 150 machines were eventually built, serving mostly as advanced trainers.

Type: Reconnaissance

Dimensions: wingspan, 45 feet, 11 inches; length, 29 feet, 6 inches; height, 11 feet, 1 inch
Weights: empty, 1,859 pounds; gross, 2,888 pounds
Power plant: 1 × 160–horsepower Daimler liquid-cooled engine
Performance: maximum speed, 85 miles per hour; ceiling, 9,843 feet; range, 180 miles
Armament: 2 × 7.92mm machine guns
Service dates: 1914–1917

Sleek-looking Lloyd biplanes were among the best of their kind in the early days of World War I. They performed useful field service before obsolescence relegated them to training duties.

The firm Ungarische Lloyd Flugzeug und Motorenfabrik AG fielded its first military biplane design in 1914, shortly before the commencement of World War I. Its C I was a streamlined design, unique in being entirely covered by wood, not fabric. It also possessed two-bay, swept-back wings whose trailing edges flared dramatically rearward. In 1914 a Model C I piloted by Henrik Bier set an altitude record of 20,243 feet, which brought it to the attention of the Austrian military. One day following the declaration of war against Serbia in August, Lloyd was immediately contracted to provide two-seat biplanes for reconnaissance purposes. The C I performed yeoman's work over the Italian front for nearly two years and was the sole Austrian craft that could safely negotiate the 13,000-foot mountain ranges there. Within a year a new model, the C II,

had been introduced, which mounted a stronger engine and a single Schwarzlose machine gun for the observer. In 1916 the most numerous model, the C III, was deployed. It featured a 160-horsepower Daimler engine and a fixed machine gun on the upper wing that fired above the propeller arc. Despite these changes, the Lloyd remained a docile machine, stable in rough weather and possessing excellent gliding characteristics.

As the Allies introduced better fighter planes, the leisurely, underpowered Lloyds began suffering disproportionate losses. The company countered with the Model C IV, which adopted a two-bay system of wing supports to save weight. The final version, the C V, was more drastically revised with a shorter wingspan and a 220-horsepower Benz engine. It was faster than previous marks but also inherently less stable and therefore less popular. By war's end, the remaining Lloyd aircraft still in service were retained for training purposes only. Nearly 500 of all versions had been acquired.

Lohner B VII ———————————————— **Austria-Hungary**

Type: Reconnaissance; Light Bomber

Dimensions: wingspan, 44 feet, 1 inch; length, 29 feet, 3 inches; height, 10 feet, 8 inches
Weights: empty, 2,075 pounds; gross, 3,069 pounds
Power plant: 1 × 160–horsepower Daimler liquid-cooled engine
Performance: maximum speed, 85 miles per hour; ceiling, 11,483 feet; range, 250 miles
Armament: 1 × 7.92mm machine gun; 485 pounds of bombs
Service dates: 1914–1917

The underpowered Lohner series was marginally obsolete throughout its service life. Nonetheless, these planes handled well in mountainous terrain and gave a good account of themselves.

In 1913 the firm Jakob Lohner Werke in Vienna constructed its first military land planes for the Austrian air service. The B I was a two-seat reconnaissance design built of wood, covered in fabric, and seated two crew members in a common cockpit. Its narrow fuselage, highly pointed cowling, and two-bay, swept-back wings gave it an exceptionally sleek appearance. As World War I progressed, the B II version was introduced in 1915 with minor refinements, followed by the B III a year later. This was the first Lohner to be armed, although it boasted but a single Schwarzlose machine gun for defense. A maximum of 485 pounds of bombs could also be carried aloft, which for the day was considered impressive.

In service the Lohners tended to be plodding, but they were rugged with excellent STOL (short takeoff and landing) characteristics. This made them ideal for operating in mountain valleys along the Italian front, and they gradually replaced the aging Lloyd C Is and C IIs that preceded them. Lohners frequently conducted air raids deep behind Italian lines, both singly and in formation, which could last five or six hours in duration. On February 14, 1916, the Austrians launched their most ambitious attack when 12 of the new 160-horsepower Daimler-powered Lohner B VII's successfully struck Milan's Porta Volta electrogeneration plant. This was accomplished by traversing 236 miles of dangerous mountain terrain and occasioned the loss of only two aircraft through mechanical failure. The Allies responded to such raids by deploying better air defenses, and the leisurely Lohners were eventually phased out by faster, more modern Hansa-Brandenburg C Is.

Lohner tried updating his basic design with the C I model, which featured reduced wing sweep and less bracing, but to no avail. By 1917 all surviving Lohners were consigned to training functions.

Type: Reconnaissance

Dimensions: wingspan, 42 feet, 7 inches; length, 24 feet, 5 inches; height, 9 feet, 2 inches
Weights: empty, 2,046 pounds; gross, 3,058 pounds
Power plant: 1 × 200–horsepower Benz BZ IV liquid-cooled in-line engine
Performance: maximum speed, 106 miles per hour; ceiling, 19, 680 feet; range, 350 miles
Armament: 2 × 7.92mm machine guns
Service dates: 1917–1918

Late model LVG C aircraft were the most numerous of their class and among the largest. They shared many design features of the contemporary DFW C V, having originated with the same engineer.

The firm Luft-Verkehrs Gesellschaft had produced numerous C-series aircraft for the German military since 1915, mostly designed by the Swiss engineer Franz Schneider. These were functional, solidly constructed craft and well-adapted for artillery-spotting and reconnaissance. In November 1916 an LVG C II became the first aircraft ever to drop bombs on London. As the war continued, it became apparent that more modern machines were necessary to keep apace of the latest Allied fighters. In 1917 it fell upon a new engineer, Sabersky-Mussigbrod, formerly of DFW, to initiate a new series of C-type airplanes.

In the autumn of 1917, LVG unveiled its new C V model, which boasted considerable improvements over earlier versions. It was a large airplane,

spanning 42 feet, but also neatly designed and compact for its size. In this respect, it also bore marked resemblance to the DFW C V, an earlier product of Sabersky-Mussigbrod. The new C V maintained the company's reputation for fine-looking, rugged airplanes, and it served with distinction along the Western Front. However, in service the exposed engine, radiator, and numerous struts seriously impeded the pilot's forward view.

To correct deficiencies associated with the C V, LVG developed a new model, the C VI, in 1918. At first glance the two machines appeared similar, but the C VI placed greater emphasis on practicality than aesthetics. The fancy spinner was eliminated in favor of a plain propeller hub, the wings acquired a slight positive stagger to afford the pilot a better view, and the entire craft was lightened to improve performance. The C VI was completely successful in the field, and more than 1,100 were constructed. They served alongside the C V versions up through the end of the war.

Type: Fighter

Dimensions: wingspan, 39 feet; length, 26 feet, 6 inches; height, 9 feet, 4 inches
Weights: empty, 1,587 pounds; gross, 2,183 pounds
Power plant: 1 × 160–horsepower Isotta-Fraschini water-cooled in-line engine
Performance: maximum speed, 117 miles per hour; ceiling, 20,340 feet; range, 300 miles
Armament: 2 × 7.7mm machine guns
Service dates: 1918–1923

The elegant Macchi M 5 was Italy's most numerous flying-boat fighter of World War I. Developed from a captured Austrian machine, they rendered excellent service in a variety of capacities.

Prior to World War I, the Societa Anonima Nieuport-Macchi firm of Varese was preoccupied with manufacturing fine coaches. It obtained licenses to build various Nieuport aircraft in 1912, an activity that expanded during the war years. The firm's expertise was limited to land planes until May 1915, when Italian forces captured an Austrian Lohner L I flying-boat fighter intact. The government authorized Macchi to build copies of the craft for its own use as the L 1. In 1916 a more refined version, the M 3, was introduced, featuring more powerful engines and aerodynamic streamlining. Macchi constructed 200 of these fine aircraft.

By 1917 the Austrians were employing Hansa-Brandenburg KDW flying-boat fighters with better performance than the M 3s, so Macchi undertook improving their design. The prototype M 5 was constructed in the spring of 1918. Like its forebear, it was a handsome airplane with obvious Nieuport influence. The two wings were of uneven length, with the top being longer in both length and chord, and both were secured in place by two sets of the famous Nieuport-type vee struts. A powerful Isotta-Fraschini motor was affixed to the bottom of the top wing, under which sat the pilot. From there he operated a pair of machine guns buried in the airplane's nose.

The Macchi M 5 was attractive, and it flew as good as it looked. The craft possessed high speed comparable to most land-based fighters and was fully acrobatic with a good rate of climb. M 5s were deployed throughout the spring of 1918 and saw active service against Austrian naval forces throughout the Adriatic. It was also flown by a small number of U.S. Navy pilots sent to Italy as observers. By 1918 the Macchi floatplane fighters vied with their bigger Caproni cousins as the most famous Italian aircraft of World War I.

Type: Fighter

Dimensions: wingspan. 34 feet, 8 inches; length, 26 feet, 10 inches; height, 11 feet, 6 inches
Weights: empty, 4,451 pounds; gross, 5,710 pounds
Power plant: 1 × 870–horsepower Fiat A.74 RC.38 radial engine
Performance: maximum speed, 312 miles per hour; ceiling, 29,200 feet; range, 540 miles
Armament: 2 × 12.7mm machine guns
Service dates: 1939–1945

Delightful to fly, the _Saetta_ (Lightning Bolt) was the most numerous Italian fighter of World War II. It suffered from the usual Italian attributes of being underpowered and underarmed yet gave a good account of itself.

The biggest handicap facing the Italian aviation industry in the 1930s was the lack of high-powered in-line engines. Thus, when the transition was made to all-metal monoplane fighters in 1935, these craft were inevitably equipped with bulky, high-drag radials. In 1936 Dr. Mario Castoldi, famed designer of the Macchi Schneider Cup racing planes, conceived what was then an excellent design around the 840-horsepower Fiat A.74 engine. It was an all-metal, low-wing machine with a fully enclosed cockpit, stressed skin, and two heavy machine guns for armament. A unique feature was the wings' trailing edge, which was completely hinged and interconnected with the ailerons. Test flights demonstrated that the new MC 202 possessed viceless characteristics, being highly maneuverable and responsive to controls. As good as it was, the _Saetta_ was still slower and possessed less fire-

power than contemporary British _Hurricanes_ and _Spitfires_ as well as German Bf 109s. Nonetheless, Italian dictator Benito Mussolini wanted modern-looking aircraft to replace the popular biplanes fighters still in use, so in 1938 the MC 200 entered production. After the first models were viewed suspiciously by conservative-minded Italian fighter pilots, an open cockpit was reinstalled.

When Italy entered World War II in June 1940, only 156 _Saettas_ were on hand. They witnessed their baptism of fire over Malta, suffering considerably at the hands of modern British fighters. Italian losses overall proved so disturbing that Germany's _X Fliegerkorps_ (air division) was moved down in support. The MC 200s were subsequently encountered in greater numbers throughout North Africa. Italians pilots did commendable work despite great odds but were finally outclassed as better opposition materialized. Curiously, several _Saettas_ operated against the Red Air Force in Russia until 1943, claiming 88 kills at a loss of only 15. Only a handful survived at war's end. A total of 1,153 were built.

Type: Fighter

Dimensions: wingspan, 34 feet, 8 inches; length, 29 feet; height, 9 feet, 11 inches
Weights: empty, 5,545 pounds; gross, 6,766 pounds
Power plant: 1 × 1,175–horsepower Daimler-Benz DB 601A liquid-cooled in-line engine
Performance: maximum speed, 372 miles per hour; ceiling, 37,730 feet; range, 475 miles
Armament: 2 × 7.7mm machine guns; 2 × 12.7mm machine guns
Service dates: 1941–1945

The sleek *Folgore* (Thunderbolt) was Italy's best all-around fighter of World War II. Fast and maneuverable, it arrived in too few numbers to alter the balance of power.

One of few advantages of an Italian alliance with Nazi Germany was access to advanced aviation engine technology. Once the superb Daimler-Benz DB 601A in-line engine was imported by Macchi, Dr. Mario Castoldi was convinced that the potential of his MC 200 design could finally be realized. He then melded the German engine to existing airframes to create the MC 202 *Folgore*, one of the best Italian fighters of World War II. The new fighter employed the basic outline of the earlier craft and almost the exact tooling, so production was greatly facilitated. In 1940 test flights revealed that the streamlined *Folgore* enjoyed a 60-mile-per-hour advantage over the earlier *Saetta*, with commensurate improvements in climb rate. Neither were any of the sweet flying characteristics adversely affected. It even enjoyed the advantage of an additional pair of wing-mounted

machine guns. The MC 202 was deployed in strength throughout 1941, and it demonstrated superiority to both the Hawker *Hurricane* and the Curtiss P-40 *Tomahawk* in the Western Desert. Had the craft been deployed in numbers a year earlier, Axis control of the air might have been established. Nonetheless, the *Folgore* distinguished itself along a number of fronts, including Russia, where it completely mastered the numerous MiGs and LaGGs opposing it. A total of 1,200 were built.

In 1943 Macchi unveiled its last and best fighter of the war, the MC 205 *Veltro* (Greyhound). This came about by marrying the MC 202 airframe to an even more powerful DB 605A engine. The resulting fighter easily matched North American P-51 *Mustangs* and late-model *Spitfires*. It was also more heavily armed than its ancestor, sporting a pair of 20mm cannons. After the 1943 Italian surrender, the Germans seized several examples and outfitted a Luftwaffe *Gruppe* that flew continuously until war's end. Only 289 *Veltros* were manufactured.

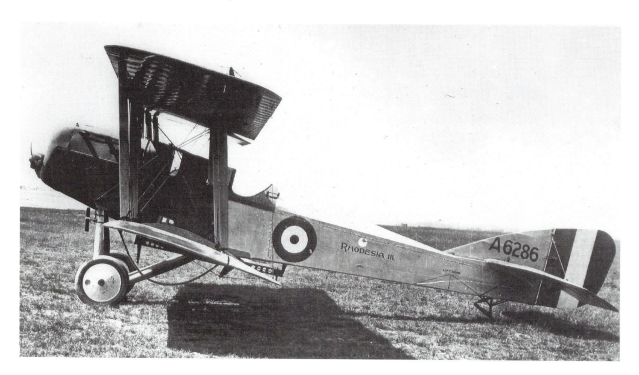

Type: Light Bomber

Dimensions: wingspan, 38 feet; length, 27 feet; height, 9 feet, 8 inches
Weights: empty, 1,793 pounds; gross, 2,458 pounds
Power plant: 1 × 160–horsepower Beardmore liquid-cooled in-line engine
Performance: maximum speed, 104 miles per hour; ceiling, 16,000 feet; range, 400 miles
Armament: 2 × .303–inch machine guns; 260 pounds of bombs
Service dates: 1916–1917

The aptly named *Elephant* was too large to serve as an effective escort fighter. Instead, it functioned better as a hard-hitting low-level bomber.

In the summer of 1915, Martinsyde engineer A. A. Fletcher conceived plans for a new and very modern escort fighter. The design was large by necessity, as it was required to hold sufficient fuel to complete missions lasting up to four hours. The resulting prototype then flew as a two-bay biplane fighter with staggered, broad-chord wings. It was of conventional wood-and-fabric construction, and the fuselage was fitted with a close-fitting metal cowling. A single Lewis machine gun sat on the top wing above the pilot, owing to the lack of interrupter gear, while a second gun was strangely situated behind him, firing backward, to ward off attacks from that quarter. Test results were encouraging, so the craft entered production as the Martinsyde G 100. In view of its large size for a fighter, pilots quickly dubbed it the *Elephant*.

The first G 100s reached France in the spring of 1916, and they were initially deployed in penny packets of two or three aircraft per reconnaissance squadron. The big plane flew well and possessed good range, but its sheer size precluded the agility necessary to combat nimble German fighters. However, in view of its excellent range and lift, *Elephants* quickly found work as light bombers with No. 27 Squadron, the only unit so equipped. In service the G 100s were strong and could handle great amounts of damage. Their payload was also considerable, and No. 27 Squadron conducted numerous effective raids on German positions. Several *Elephants* were also deployed to Palestine and Mesopotamia for bombing and strafing duties against the Turks. Production of G 100s reached 100, and they were followed by 171 slightly more powerful G 102s. The big craft were retired from service in mid-1917, although several carried on as trainers. Their memory is perpetuated by today's No. 27 Squadron, whose unit heraldry displays an elephant.

Type: Reconnaissance; Antitank Helicopter

Dimensions: rotorspan, 32 feet, 4 inches; length, 38 feet, 11 inches; height, 9 feet, 10 inches
Weights: empty, 2,820 pounds; gross, 5,290 pounds
Power plant: 2 × 429–horsepower Allison 250-C20B turboshaft engines
Performance: maximum speed, 150 miles per hour; ceiling, 17,000 feet; range, 388 miles
Armament: none, or 6 × HOT antitank missiles
Service dates: 1976–

The rotund BO 105 is Germany's first postwar helicopter and helped pioneer new rigid-rotor technology. It is renowned for high performance and agility at low altitude, especially as an antitank platform.

Design of the BO 105 was initiated in 1962 by Messerschmitt-Bolkow-Blohm (MBB) in response to a German government specification for new helicopters to replace the *Alouette IIs* in service. These would be the first such machines to originate in Germany since World War II. The prototype emerged in 1967 as a standard-looking pod-and-boom affair, but the BO 105 was designed from the onset to employ the radically different rigid-rotor technology. In most helicopters, the rotors are relatively loose so blade angle can be pitched downward during forward flight. This system allows for rapid climbing but is unable to sustain much in the way of negative-G forces—that is, rapid sinking. The new rigid rotor, as the name implies, was hingeless and kept the blades at right angles to the main rotor at all times. It was a very strong arrangement

and capable of resisting high negative-G forces. A helicopter thus equipped could rise quickly over obstacles in the conventional sense—and then sink past them with equal rapidity. Moreover, the BO 105 was fully acrobatic and maneuverable. Its military potential was immense, and the German army enthusiastically ordered 312 machines for the *Herresflieger* (army aviation).

In service the BO 105 received two designations. The first, VBH, is a dedicated reconnaissance/liaison craft for close work with field units. The PAH 1, meanwhile, is especially rigged as an antitank platform. It mounts up to six HOT wire-guided antitank missiles and carries a variety of sighting and imaging technology. Both versions are also equipped for nighttime operations and, by dint of their great maneuverability, can easily utilize terrain for cover at low altitude. A total of 1,200 BO 105s have been built and exported to 18 countries worldwide. With constant upgrades, they will remain potent weapons well into the twenty-first century.

Type: Fighter

Dimensions: wingspan, 32 feet, 6 inches; length, 29 feet; height, 8 feet, 2 inches
Weights: empty, 5,893 pounds; gross, 7,491 pounds
Power plant: 1 × 1,475–horsepower Daimler-Benz BD 605 liquid-cooled in-line engine
Performance: maximum speed, 386 miles per hour; ceiling, 37,890 feet; range, 350 miles
Armament: 1 × 20mm cannon; 2 × 13mm machine guns
Service dates: 1937–1945

The Bf 109 was one of history's greatest combat aircraft and the most widely produced German fighter of World War II. Small and angular, its very lines seemed to exude menace.

Willy Messerschmitt began developing his benchmark fighter in 1933 once the Luftwaffe desired to substitute its Arado Ar 68 and Heinkel He 51 biplanes. The prototype flew in 1935 as a rather angular, low-wing monoplane with a fully enclosed cockpit and narrow-track landing gear. Results were impressive, and in 1937 the new Bf 109B fighter outpaced all other rivals at the International Flying Meet in Zurich, Switzerland. By 1939 the first production model, the Bf 109E, was introduced, featuring a bigger engine and heavier armament. As a fighter, the diminutive craft flew fast and maneuvered well, features that helped secure German air superiority at the start of World War II. Simply put, Bf 109s annihilated all their outdated opposition until encountering Supermarine *Spitfires* during the 1940 Battle of Britain. Although speedier than its British opponent, Bf 109Es turned somewhat slower and never achieved superiority.

As the war ground on, successive new models were introduced to keep the five-year-old design solvent. The F model was aerodynamically refined, with rounder wings and tail surfaces, as well as a bigger engine. It was the best-handling variant, but in 1942 the most numerous version, the Bf 109G, made its appearance. It featured a stronger engine and heavier armament but sacrificed the sweet handling characteristics of earlier versions. Worse yet, German war planners failed to provide for new designs, so the Bf 109G remained in production long after its growth potential ceased. Late-model H and K versions tried interjecting better high-altitude performance into the old workhorse with some success, but they never became available in quantity. Nonetheless, leading German ace Eric Hartmann scored all 451 victories in his beloved Messerschmitt. By war's end, no less than 33,000 Bf 109s had been produced. Moreover, Spain continued constructing them up until 1956, and they also served in the postwar air forces of Israel and Czechoslovakia.

Type: Fighter; Night Fighter; Light Bomber

Dimensions: wingspan, 53 feet, 3 inches; length, 39 feet, 7 inches; height, 13 feet, 6 inches
Weights: empty, 12,346 pounds; gross, 15,873 pounds
Power plant: 2 × 1,110–horsepower Daimler-Benz liquid-cooled, in-line engines
Performance: maximum speed, 352 miles per hour; ceiling, 35,760 feet; range, 745 miles
Armament: 5 × 7.92mm machine guns; 2 × 20mm cannons; up to 2,205 pounds of bombs
Service dates: 1939–1945

The fearsome-looking Bf 110 was actually rather defenseless in the face of determined fighter opposition. However, it found its niche as a nocturnal predator and accounted for 60 percent of Germany's night-fighter defenses.

The notion of long-range strategic fighters arose simultaneously in several countries during the 1930s. In Germany, as elsewhere, they were envisioned as escorts for heavy bomber forces then under development. In 1936 Willy Messerschmitt fielded his second warplane design, the twin-engine Bf 110, for the task. It was an advanced, all-metal design with twin rudders and a long greenhouse canopy. Test flights showed that the airplane was extremely fast, but it handled sluggishly. Moreover, the death of General Walter Wever in 1936 led to the cancellation of Germany's heavy bomber program, hence the new craft was without a mission. The Bf 110 was nonetheless ordered into production as a heavy fighter and deployed in strength just prior to World War II. The Luftwaffe held high expectations for it.

In the early days of the war, the Bf 110s easily swept aside obsolete Polish and French machines, fully living up to its role as a *Zerstorer* (Destroyer). Thus, in the summer of 1940 they were confidently thrown into the Battle of Britain, but they took staggering losses at the hands of nimble *Spitfires* and *Hurricanes*. The Bf 110s were so outclassed that they required escorts of single-engine Bf 109 fighters! Thereafter, Bf 110s were deployed in secondary theaters as ground-attack craft. Production of the aging craft began to wane when, in 1943, the failure of the Me 210 caused production to be accelerated. This time the Bf 110 was outfitted as a night fighter and equipped with heavy cannons and radar systems. Fast and stable, it made an ideal platform for nocturnal warfare and destroyed several hundred British bombers. In sum, the Bf 110 exhibited many fine qualities, but it was simply not on par with modern single-engine fighters. By war's end, more than 6,000 machines had been constructed.

Type: Fighter

Dimensions: wingspan, 30 feet, 7 inches; length, 19 feet, 2 inches; height, 9 feet, 1 inch
Weights: empty, 4,206 pounds; gross, 9,502 pounds
Power plant: 1 × 3,750–pound thrust Walter liquid-fuel rocket motor
Performance: maximum speed, 593 miles per hour; ceiling, 39,500 feet; range, 50 miles
Armament: 2 × 30mm cannon
Service dates: 1944–1945

The revolutionary *Komet* was the world's first rocket-propelled fighter and the fastest aircraft of World War II. Fast and lethal-looking, it often posed greater hazards to its own pilots than the enemy.

The Me 163 had its origins in the work of Dr. Alexander Lippisch, the world's leading exponent of tailless gliders. He joined the Messerschmitt company in 1939 and, despite personal antipathy for Willy Messerschmitt, set about developing a rocket-powered glider. The prototype emerged in 1941 as a rather small, but very futuristic, swept-wing design. Built of metal and wood, the new craft dispensed with landing gear to save weight. Accordingly, it lifted off on a jettisonable dolly and landed on a retractable skid. But when rocket motors finally became available, even greater technical problems arose. The *Komet* was powered by a combination of two highly combustible fuels, C-Stoff (hydrazine hydrate and methyl alcohol) and T-Stoff (hydrogen peroxide and water). The two ignited when combined, providing tremendous thrust for about eight minutes. However, the practice of fueling the Me 163 was unpredictable, and the slightest misstep led to catastrophic explosions. Test flights were nonetheless successful, reaching unprecedented speeds of nearly 600 miles per hour. In 1944 the Me 163 entered production as a last-ditch weapon against the seemingly unstoppable Allied bomber streams. Around 350 were built.

In service the aptly named *Komet* (from the large flame it exuded) had a short but spectacular career. It skyrocketed to altitudes of 30,000 feet in only two minutes and traversed bomber formations so fast that gunners could scarcely draw a bead. However, closing speeds were tremendous and allowed for few bursts. Consequently, in nine months of combat, only 15 or so bombers were claimed by *Komets*. Moreover, many Me 163s were lost, mostly upon landing, when residual fuel left in the tanks exploded without warning. For all its shortcomings, the Me 163 possessed excellent performance for its day and reflects considerable German ingenuity. Had time existed for additional research, the *Komet* might have evolved into a formidable weapon.

Messerschmitt Me 262 **Germany**

Type: Fighter; Light Bomber

Dimensions: wingspan, 40 feet, 11 inches; length, 34 feet, 9 inches; height, 12 feet, 7 inches
Weights: empty, 8,378 pounds; gross, 14,110 pounds
Power plant: 2 × 1,984–pound thrust Junkers Jumo 004B turbojet engines
Performance: maximum speed, 540 miles per hour; ceiling, 37,565 feet; range, 652 miles
Armament: 4 × 30mm cannon
Service dates: 1944–1945

With its unmistakable sharklike lines, the Me 262 was the world's first operational jet fighter. It might have reestablished German aerial supremacy had sufficient jet engines been available.

In 1938 the German Air Ministry approached Willy Messerschmitt to create a radically different fighter craft, one powered by new turbojet engines then under development. The first prototype emerged in April 1941 but had to be flown with a conventional nose-mounted engine. The Me 262 was a low-wing, all-metal monoplane of stressed-skin construction. The wings were swept, and the first prototypes landed on tailwheels, but subsequent versions employed tricycle landing gear. However, the Luftwaffe displayed little interest initially, and the project received few construction priorities. It was not until July 1942 that the first jet-powered flight could be held, but the new craft was a marvel to behold. It was at least 100 miles per hour faster than the best Allied piston-powered fighters, and it handled extremely well. At this time the Third Reich

was being battered by enormous fleets of Allied heavy bombers, so it became imperative to deploy the Me 262 as an air-superiority weapon. However, when Adolf Hitler witnessed a test flight, he ordered that the craft be outfitted as a high-speed bomber! This did little to facilitate production, and efforts were further beset by a lack of engines.

The first Me 262s deployed in August 1944, less than a year before the war in Europe ended. There were ongoing problems with engine reliability and fuel shortages, but the vaunted *Schwalbe* (Swallow), as it was dubbed, created havoc with Allied bombers. On March 18, 1945, a force of 37 Me 262s attacked U.S. B-17s near Berlin, scything down 15 with a loss of two jets. The bomber version, known as the *Sturmvogel* (Storm Petrel), had also debuted, but it was tactically misused. Although 1,430 Me 262s were built, only a handful actually saw combat. They claimed 150 Allied aircraft—and may have shot down many more—save for Hitler's meddling and the Luftwaffe's initial indifference.

– 215 –

Type: Glider; Transport

Dimensions: wingspan, 180 feet, 5 inches; length, 93 feet, 6 inches; height, 31 feet, 6 inches
Weights: empty, 64,066 pounds; gross, 99,210 pounds
Power plant: 6 × 1,140–horsepower Gnome-Rhone 14N radial engines
Performance: maximum speed, 149 miles per hour; ceiling, 14,760 feet; range, 808 miles
Armament: 2 × 20mm cannons; 2 × 13mm machine guns
Service dates: 1942–1945

The lumbering *Gigants* were among the biggest aircraft used in World War II. They carried useful payloads but were highly vulnerable when confronted by Allied fighters.

The Me 321 evolved in October 1940 when the German invasion of Great Britain seemed imminent. The German Air Ministry requested development of giant glider craft to ferry troops and equipment across the English Channel by air. Willy Messerschmitt, who had designed gliders since childhood, readily complied, and within two weeks he conceived the Me 321 *Gigant* (Giant). This was a high-wing, braced monoplane featuring mixed construction. Both wing and fuselage were made from steel tubing, strengthened by wood, and then covered in fabric. The *Gigant* was also the first airplane to possess clamshell nose doors for ease of loading. Up to 22 tons of men and supplies could be hauled aloft and safely landed, making it the biggest transport of World War II. The prototype debuted in the spring of 1941 and, although somewhat fatiguing for a single

pilot to handle, flew well. Getting airborne was tricky, however, and usually meant being towed by three Bf 110s, or a single He 111Z (two bombers lashed together at midwing). The Me 321 entered production that year, and 211 were built. Most served along the Eastern Front ferrying supplies.

At length it was decided that a powered model, the Me 323, would be safer and offer more strategic flexibility. Accordingly, an Me 321 was fitted with six French Gnome-Rhone radial engines and fuel tanks. The added weight almost reduced the payload by half, and the giant craft still needed to be towed or employ rockets to assist takeoff. Nonetheless, the Me 323 entered production in 1943 and saw widespread service in Russia, North Africa, and the Mediterranean. The slow-moving transports proved easy prey for Allied fighters, and on one occasion British *Spitfires* annihilated 14 of 16 *Gigants* at sea. Given the hazards of interception, the lumbering behemoths were restricted to rear-area supply missions.

Type: Fighter; Light Bomber

Dimensions: wingspan, 53 feet, 7 inches; length, 40 feet, 11 inches; height, 14 feet
Weights: empty, 16,574 pounds; gross, 21,276 pounds
Power plant: 2 × 1,850–horsepower Daimler-Benz 603A liquid-cooled in-line engines
Performance: maximum speed, 364 miles per hour; ceiling, 32,180 feet; range, 1,050 miles
Armament: 2 × 7.92mm machine guns; 4 × 20mm cannons; up to 2,205 pounds of bombs
Service dates: 1943–1945

The formidable-looking Me 410 was an outgrowth of the earlier Me 210, an embarrassing failure. It was fast and capable but never fulfilled design expectations.

In 1937 the German Air Ministry began looking for a successor to the Bf 110 *Zerstorer* (Destroyer), the Luftwaffe's only strategic fighter. Willy Messerschmitt originated his second warplane design, the Me 210, which was heavily based upon the initial machine. Like its precursor, the new craft had twin engines and twin rudders, but it also sported tapered wings and lengthened engine nacelles. The effect was a handsome machine that proved very unstable in flight and prone to stalls and spins. Subsequent modifications introduced a single rudder, but Marshal Hermann Göring, the Luftwaffe chief, ordered 1,000 machines produced before the design was perfected. Consequently, when the Me 210 became operational in 1941, it still possessed all the old vices of the prototype. Several crashed due to bad handling, and the government canceled its contract after 300

machines. Several officials also demanded Messerschmitt's resignation from the company bureau.

In an attempt to save both the Me 210 and his own reputation, Messerschmitt tried revamping the balky craft. The resulting Me 410 appeared almost indistinguishable from its predecessor, but it had a lengthened fuselage and nacelles, along with automatic wing slots on the leading edges. Larger engines were also fitted, and the Me 410, when it appeared in 1943, was a significant improvement. Through most of 1944, the *Hornisse* (Hornet) was employed as a night bomber over England, where its high speed made interception difficult. It was also utilized to defend the Reich, where its heavy armament caused havoc with bomber formations. However, like all two-engine fighters, the Me 410 was at a severe disadvantage when opposing single-engine craft and suffered heavy losses. By the time production ceased in the fall of 1944, no less than 1,160 had been produced. Their contribution to the war effort proved negligible and constituted a waste of valuable resources.

Type: Fighter

Dimensions: wingspan, 33 feet, 9 inches; length, 26 feet, 9 inches; height, 8 feet, 9 inches
Weights: empty, 5,996 pounds; gross, 7,694 pounds
Power plant: 1 × 1,350–horsepower Mikulin liquid-cooled in-line engine
Performance: maximum speed, 398 miles per hour, ceiling, 39,370 feet; range, 777 miles
Armament: 2 × 7.62mm machine guns; 1 × 12.7mm machine gun; up to 440 pounds of bombs
Service dates: 1941–1943

The MiG 3 was an impressive high-altitude interceptor when it appeared in 1941 and won its designers the coveted Stalin Prize. However, it proved woefully inadequate at lower levels and could not compete with better German fighters.

In 1939 Artem Mikoyan and Mikhail Gurevich, veterans of the Polikarpov design bureau, proposed a high-altitude interceptor, the MiG 1. This was a highly streamlined, modern-looking craft with a long cowling, retractable landing gear, and an open cockpit. Constructed from steel tubing and covered with wood, the prototype flew in April 1940 with impressive speed and performance at high altitude. However, the extreme length of the nose—designed to accommodate the biggest possible engine around the smallest possible fuselage—rendered it inherently unstable. In fact, the MiG 1 displayed downright vicious handling characteristics, but the Soviet government needed fighters quickly, and so the design entered production. In 1941 the MiG bureau attempted to rectify earlier shortcomings with a new machine, the MiG 3. This was essentially a cleaned-up version of the earlier craft, with a fully enclosed canopy, a cut-down rear deck for better vision, and increased dihedral on the outer wing sections. The new design performed only marginally better, but the government awarded Mikoyan and Gurevich the prestigious Stalin Prize.

The onset of the German invasion of June 1941 only underscored the inadequacy of the MiG 3 as a fighter. Unstable and unforgiving, it was tiring to fly and could not engage nimble Messerschmitt Bf 109s at low altitudes, where the majority of battles were fought. It was also unsatisfactory as an interceptor, being too lightly armed with machine guns to inflict much harm upon bombers. Nonetheless, the Soviets, hard-pressed for aircraft of any kind, dutifully employed the MiG 3 in frontline service for nearly three years. Russian pilots accepted the assignment stoically—and suffered commensurately. By 1943 most MiG 3s had been withdrawn from combat functions and were restricted to high-speed reconnaissance missions. Total production exceeded 4,000 units.

Type: Fighter

Dimensions: wingspan, 33 feet, 1 inch; length, 35 feet, 7 inches; height, 11 feet, 2 inches
Weights: empty, 7,500 pounds; gross, 12,750 pounds
Power plant: 1 × 5,950–pound thrust Klimov VK-1 turbojet engine
Performance: maximum speed, 668 miles per hour; ceiling, 51,000 feet; range, 665 miles
Armament: 2 × 23mm cannons and 1 × 37mm cannon; up to 1,100 pounds of bombs
Service dates: 1950–

This classic design was the most successful of early Soviet jet fighters and a complete shock to the West. Its debut during the Korean War put the world on notice that Russian aircraft were among the best in the world.

At the end of World War II, the Soviets inherited a trove of advanced German technology, especially concerning jet aviation. Stalin, fearful of trailing the West in its use, demanded the creation of new jet-powered aircraft for the Red Air Force. In 1946 engineers Artem Mikoyan and Mikhail Gurevich conceived what was then a highly advanced fighter design. It was a midsize, fairly compact machine with swept midmounted wings and high tail surfaces. The MiG 15 also carried a bomber-killing three-cannon pack that lowered down on wires for ease of servicing. Up until then, Soviet attempts with jet aircraft largely failed on account of using weak German Jumo engines of insufficient thrust. However, Great Britain's shortsighted Labor government had fatefully arranged the export of several Rolls-Royce

Nene jet engines, then the world's best. This proved a technological windfall of the first order, and the engine was quickly copied by Soviet engines as the VK-1. Once installed in the MiG 15 prototype, the result was a world-class jet fighter that was faster and could outclimb and outturn almost any jet employed by the West. The MiG 15 entered mass production in 1949 and received the NATO designation FAGOT.

MiG 15s were an unwelcome surprise to UN forces when these fearsome new machines suddenly appeared over North Korea in November 1950. Only rapid deployment of equally advanced North American F-86 *Sabres* kept control of the skies from communist hands. These two adversaries were almost evenly matched, and in 1953 a defecting North Korean pilot, Ro Kim Suk, gave the West its first intact example. MiG 15s continued in production throughout the 1950s until an estimated 18,000 were made. They were employed by all Soviet allies and client states, with many two-seat trainer versions still in use.

Type: Fighter; Light Bomber

Dimensions: wingspan, 23 feet, 6 inches; length, 51 feet, 9 inches; height, 13 feet, 6 inches
Weights: empty, 12,051 pounds; gross, 21,605 pounds
Power plant: 1 × 15,653–pound thrust Tumansky R-25–300 turbojet engine
Performance: maximum speed, 1,385 miles per hour; ceiling, 62,336 feet; range, 600 miles
Armament: 1 × 23mm cannon; up to 4,409 pounds of bombs or rockets
Service dates: 1959–

The classic MiG 21 is the most extensively exported jet fighter in history. It has fought in several wars and continues in frontline service four decades after its appearance.

The experience of air combat in Korea forced the Mikoyan design bureau to draw up radical plans for a new air-superiority fighter. This machine would have to be lightweight, be relatively simple to build, and possess speed in excess of Mach 2. The prime design prerequisite entailed deletion of all unnecessary equipment not related to performance. No less than 30 test models were built and flown through the mid- to late 1950s before a tailed-delta configuration was settled upon. The first MiG 21s were deployed in 1959 and proved immediately popular with Red Air Force pilots. They were the first Russian aircraft to routinely operate at Mach 2 and were highly maneuverable. Moreover, the delta configuration enabled the craft to remain controllable up to high angles of attack and low air speed. One possible draw-

back, as with all deltas, was that high turn rates yielded a steep drag rise, so the MiG 21 lost energy and speed while maneuvering. This was considered a fair trade-off in terms of overall excellent performance. More than 11,000 MiG 21s were built in 14 distinct versions that spanned three generations of design. They are the most numerous fighters exported abroad, and no less than 50 air forces employ them worldwide. The NATO code name is FISHBED.

The MiG 21 debuted during the Vietnam War (1964–1974), during which they proved formidable opponents for bigger U.S. fighters like the McDonnell-Douglas F-4 *Phantom*. Successive modifications have since endowed them with greater range and formidable ground-attack capability, but at the expense of their previously spry performance. Russian production of the MiG 21 has ended, yet China and India build, refurbish, and deploy them in great numbers. These formidable machines will undoubtedly remain in service for many years to come.

✪ Mikoyan-Gurevich MiG 23/27 ————————————— **Russia**

Type: Fighter; Ground Attack

Dimensions: wingspan, up to 45 feet, 8 inches; length, 54 feet, 9 inches; height, 15 feet, 9 inches
Weights: empty, 22,487 pounds; gross, 39,242 pounds
Power plant: 1 × 18,849–pound thrust Soyuz turbojet engine
Performance: maximum speed, 1,553 miles per hour; ceiling, 60,695 feet; range, 715 miles
Armament: 1 × 23mm Gatling gun; up to 8,818 pounds of bombs or rockets
Service dates: 1970–

The MiG 23 was the first Soviet combat plane equipped with variable-wing geometry. Its success led to an equally capable ground-attack version, the MiG 27.

By the mid-1960s the Red Air Force wanted to supplement its vaunted MiG 21s with air-superiority fighters that could also perform ground-attack work. The new machine would have to approximate the formidable performance of such Western stalwarts as the F-4 *Phantom* and F-105 *Thunderchief*. Furthermore, excellent STOL (short takeoff and landing) ability from unfinished fields was also required. The Mikoyan design bureau initially toyed with revised delta configurations before settling upon a "swing-wing" version like the General Dynamics F-111. The new MiG 23 prototype first flew in 1967 as a high-wing jet with an extremely sharp profile. The wing could be deployed at three different angles for takeoff, cruise, and fighting mode and, when fully extended, would assist in achieving shorter landing distances. To ensure high performance at high speed, the craft also carried adjustable "splitters" at the front of each air intake. The first MiG 23s had no sooner been deployed in 1970 than it was determined to optimize them for air supremacy and forego ground-attack functions for a subsequent model.

The impracticality of endowing the MiG 23 with good tactical strike abilities led to development of a related design, the MiG 27. This was essentially a stripped-down MiG 23 refitted with a distinct flattened nose housing a laser range finder. The craft lost its intake splitters, as excessively high speed is considered unnecessary at low altitude. The afterburner was also simplified and lightened to compensate for weight lost at the front end. Not surprisingly, Russian pilots dubbed the MiG 27 *Utkonos* (Duck-nose) on account of its odd appearance. More than 3,000 of both versions have been built, and collectively they are identified by the NATO designation FLOGGER. Neither craft is considered a match for their Western equivalents.

Type: Fighter; Reconnaissance

Dimensions: wingspan, 46 feet; length, 78 feet, 2 inches; height, 20 feet
Weights: empty, 44,092 pounds; gross, 79,807 pounds
Power plant: 2 × 27,000–pound thrust Tumansky R-31 turbojet engines
Performance: maximum speed, 1,849 miles per hour; ceiling, 80,000 feet; range, 901 miles
Armament: 9,636 pounds of missiles
Service dates: 1973–

An ingenious design, the elusive MiG 25 was once the doyen of Soviet high-altitude reconnaissance. It continues on today as a formidable cruise-missile interceptor.

Toward the end of the 1950s the United States embarked upon developing a viable Mach 3 high-altitude bomber, the North American XB-70 *Valkyrie.* Such a craft would fly so high and fast that it appeared virtually immune to Soviet missiles and conventional jet aircraft. Aware of its weakness, the Red Air Force scrambled for a new, ultra–high speed interceptor to thwart such a menace. Mach 3 operations posed daunting operational difficulties, but the Mikoyan design bureau tackled them with characteristic aplomb. The first MiG 25 prototype flew in 1964 with complete success. This was a large, if squat, machine of futuristic appearance. Highly streamlined, it possessed a high-mounted, swept wing, an extremely pointed profile, and twin rudders that canted outward. It was powered by two huge Tumansky engines and mounted equally imposing airducts on either side of the fuselage. Because heat

arising from air friction at Mach 3 was intense, the MiG 25 was constructed mostly of expensive stainless steel and titanium—anything less would melt! Every design priority reflected an unyielding emphasis on speed and high-altitude performance, but outside of this regimen the MiG 25 maneuvered like a brick. It nonetheless became operational as a fighter and reconnaissance craft in 1973—a decade after the XB-70 program was canceled. The NATO code name is FOXBAT.

During the 1970s the MiG 25 performed considerable overflight activity in the Middle East and could not be intercepted by the redoubtable Israeli air force. The West got its first up-close look when MiG 25 pilot Viktor Belenko defected to Japan in September 1976. Engineers marveled at the ingenuity of design yet crudity of construction. Since then, FOXBATs have undergone considerable electronic and engine upgrades, making them even more formidable. Modern versions are equipped with the very latest look down/shoot down radar capable of detecting and destroying U.S. cruise missiles at any altitude.

 Mikoyan-Gurevich MiG 29 ——————————————————————— **Russia**

Type: Fighter; Light Bomber

Dimensions: wingspan, 37 feet, 3 inches; length, 56 feet, 9 inches; height, 15 feet, 6 inches
Weights: empty, 24,030 pounds; gross, 40,785 pounds
Power plant: 2 × 11,111–pound thrust Klimov/Leningrad RD-33 turbofan engines
Performance: maximum speed, 1,519 miles per hour; ceiling, 55,575 feet; range, 932 miles
Armament: 1 × 30mm cannon; up to 6,614 pounds of bombs and rockets
Service dates: 1984–

The MiG 29 is one of the most modern and capable fighter planes ever designed. It confirms Russia's ability to construct weapons of lethality equal to Western counterparts.

In 1972 the Soviet government issued demanding specifications for a new lightweight fighter with secondary ground-attack capability to offset the aging MiG 21s, MiG 23s, and Su 17s in service. In addition, such a machine would have to be capable of engaging and defeating the formidable Grumman F-14s and McDonnell-Douglas F-15s of the United States, as well as the forthcoming General Dynamics F-16 and McDonnell-Douglas F-18. As usual, the Mikoyan design bureau undertook the assignment with determination and originality. By 1977 it had arrived at a solution: the modest-sized MiG 29. This was an ultrasleek and futuristic-looking machine with a beautifully blended high-lift, low-drag wing and fuselage. The twin engines were widely spaced and outwardly canted; twin rudders were also provided. One of the most unusual features was the underwing air intakes.

Like all Russian warplanes, MiG 29s are expected to operate off of rough, unprepared airstrips. To minimize any chance that dirt or rocks might be ingested by an engine, they are covered by panel doors that open automatically when lifting off and close again upon touchdown. While these are shut, air is fed continuously to the engine through louvers near the wing roots. In terms of maneuverability, the MiG 29 is a sterling dogfighter, light on the controls and highly responsive. An estimated 1,350 have been built and deployed by Russia and former Soviet client states. The NATO designation is FULCRUM.

As expected, the MiG 29 was a popular addition to the Red Air Force stable, placing Russian pilots on equal footing with potential Western adversaries. A look down/shoot down fire-control system, helmet-actuated sights, and accurate missiles make it possibly the world's best interceptor. Its handling is even more impressive considering that all controls are hydraulic and devoid of fly-by-wire technology. The FULCRUM remains every fighter pilot's dream.

Type: Fighter

Dimensions: wingspan, 44 feet, 2 inches; length, 74 feet, 5 inches; height, 20 feet, 2 inches
Weights: empty, 48,115 pounds; gross, 101,859 pounds
Power plant: 2 × 34,170–pound thrust Aviavidgatel D-30F6 turbofan engines
Performance: maximum speed, 1,865 miles per hour; ceiling, 67,600 feet; range, 745 miles
Armament: 1 × 30mm cannon; up to six homing missiles
Service dates: 1982–

The MiG 31 is a heavily armed long-range interceptor designed to engage and destroy fast, low-flying targets. Linked by computer, four of these fearsome machines can effectively blanket 590 miles of airspace!

By the late 1980s Russia anticipated that the threat of strategic bombardment from the United States had undergone fundamental changes. Instead of subsonic, low-flying B-52s, Russia now faced the prospect of ultrasophisticated and stealthy B-1 *Lancers* backed my myriads of terrain-following cruise missiles. In 1975 the Mikoyan design bureau was tasked with creating a totally new machine to counter this new threat. After several studies, it elected to begin with a revamped version of the MiG 25 FOXBAT, a high-speed, high-altitude interceptor. Despite its international celebrity as an unstoppable spy plane, the FOXBAT was incapable of supersonic speed at low altitudes. Thus, the solution posed was to build a new craft: the MiG 31. It shared some common ancestry with the earlier machine but was, in fact, a much more capable interceptor. Like the

MiG 25, the MiG 31 (NATO code name, FOXHOUND) is a big, squat airplane with twin engines and twin tails. However, it differs by seating two crew members in tandem, possessing larger air intakes for low-altitude work, as well as extended afterburner nozzles. Moreover, its construction has dispensed with heavy stainless steel in favor of lighter titanium and nickel steel. All told, the MiG 31 displays lower absolute top speed than the MiG 25 but enjoys much better handling and maneuverability. Its role is to assist the faster Sukhoi Su 27s by plugging gaps in Russia's defensive radar net.

The biggest changes in the MiG 31 are electronic. It boasts state-of-the-art Zaslon phased-array nose radar, which can detect targets as far out as 125 miles. In addition, the computerized fire-control system can track up to 10 targets independently and engage four. The MiG 31 is also capable of linking to other aircraft via computer and their fire being coordinated by a team leader. To date a total of 280 FOXHOUNDS have been manufactured and deployed.

Type: Transport; Gunship

Dimensions: rotorspan, 69 feet, 10 inches; length, 59 feet, 7 inches; height, 18 feet, 6 inches
Weights: empty, 14,990 pounds; gross, 26,455 pounds
Power plant: 2 × Klimov TV3–117MT turboshaft engines
Performance: maximum speed, 155 miles per hour; ceiling, 14,760 feet; range, 289 miles
Armament: 2 × rocket or gunpods
Service dates: 1962–

For four decades, the Mi 17 has been among the most numerous large helicopters in the world. It was the workhorse of the former Soviet Union and continues in active service with many nations.

Toward the end of the 1950s, the Mil design bureau attempted to update and enlarge its existing Mi 4 helicopters with a view toward greater power and lifting capacity. By 1961 it had developed the Mi 8, which retained the transmission and tailboom of the earlier craft but relocated the engine overhead and the canopy forward. The new craft was much bigger internally but somewhat underpowered, so a second engine was added. When the Mi 8 became operational in 1962, it was among the world's foremost military helicopters. It could lift up to 28 fully armed troops and carry them to their objective with good reliability. As Soviet imperialism spread through client states in the 1970s, more often than not the Mi 8s were there. Cuban and East German advisers employed them to good effect in Ethiopia, Angola, and

Nigeria. However, the Mi 8s enjoyed far less success when they were outfitted as gunships and deployed in huge numbers during the Soviet invasion of Afghanistan. Muslim guerillas, equipped with CIA-supplied *Stinger* missiles, took a heavy toll on the lumbering giants. The craft still operates under the NATO designation HIP.

In 1981 the Mil bureau decided to update its basic design by introducing the Mi 17. This was a standard Mi 8 refitted with the more powerful engines and transmission from the naval Mi 14; the tailrotor was relocated to the port side. The craft also employs a unique system for maintaining engine synchronization. Should one engine lose power or fail completely, the other automatically reaches a contingency rating of 2,200 horsepower to ensure steady flight. The Mi 8/17 family is a rugged, dependable series of military machines with a long service life ahead. An estimated 13,000 have been built and are operated by 60, predominately Third World, nations.

Type: Attack Helicopter

Dimensions: rotorspan, 56 feet, 9 inches; length, 57 feet, 5 inches; height, 13 feet, 1 inch
Weights: empty, 18,078 pounds; gross, 26,455 pounds
Power plant: 2 × 2,190–horsepower Klimov TV3–117 turboshaft engines
Performance: maximum speed, 208 miles per hour; ceiling, 14,750 feet; range, 456 miles
Armament: 1 × 23mm Gatling gun; 4 × gun or rocket pods
Service dates: 1973–

Described as a "flying tank," the formidable Mi 24 is the world's biggest and most heavily armed helicopter gunship. It offers heavy firepower, good speed, and troop-carrying capacity in one lethal package.

The year 1967 witnessed introduction of the Bell AH-1 *Cobra*, the world's first dedicated helicopter gunship. It proved highly effective against unprotected infantry during the Vietnam War and added new dimensions of firepower into battlefield equations. Soviet planners watched such developments closely and decided they needed to counter this latest Western threat. It fell upon Mikhail Mil to design Russia's first gunship, drawing upon his earlier experiences with large machines like the Mi 8 transport helicopter. He utilized the engine and transmission of the earlier craft, melded to a somewhat smaller, heavily armored fuselage. This contained high proportions of steel and titanium, making it nearly imperious to small-arms fire. To this were fitted large anhedral winglets that produced added lift and acted as convenient platforms for carrying weapons.

A squad of eight fully armed soldiers could also be transported. Finally, the crew of two sat in a squared-off cabin with large glazed windows. The overall effect was impressive, and when the first Mi 24s were sighted in East Germany, NATO dubbed them HINDs.

Greater operational experience with the Mi 24 resulted in a total redesign of the forward portion. Henceforth, newer models sported two staggered canopies that granted better vision, along with a four-barrel machine gun in a chin turret. Tactically speaking, the HIND D was now more involved with battlefield firepower than in transporting troops. These behemoth gunships were employed in great numbers throughout the Soviet invasion of Afghanistan, sometimes with great success against lightly armed guerillas. It was not until the United States supplied *Stinger* antiaircraft missiles that the big helicopters sustained meaningful losses. Mil 24s are still regarded as formidable antitank platforms in more conventional modes of warfare. An estimated 2,300 have been built and are still flown by 20 nations.

Type: Transport

Dimensions: rotorspan, 105 feet; length, 110 feet, 8 inches; height, 26 feet, 9 inches
Weights: empty, 62,170 pounds; gross, 123,450 pounds
Power plant: 2 × 10,000–horsepower ZMKB D-136 turboshaft engines
Performance: maximum speed, 183 miles per hour; ceiling, 15,090 feet; range, 497 miles
Armament: none
Service dates: 1983–

By many measures, the giant Mi 26 is the world's most powerful helicopter. It has an internal storage capacity equivalent to the Lockheed C-130 *Hercules!*

By the early 1970s the Soviet government desired a heavy-lift replacement for its already impressive Mi 6 helicopters. The new machine was intended to possess twice the power and lifting ability of the older craft. These features were necessary for transporting great amounts of supplies to undeveloped regions of the country, like Siberia, to assist development there. The Mil design bureau under N. M. Tishchyenko settled for a slightly smaller version of the existing craft, one absolutely crammed with power and aeronautical efficiency. In 1977 the first Mil 26 took flight and went on to establish several world payload and altitude records. At first glance it was outwardly similar to the Mi 6 but was driven by the world's first eight-blade rotor. This device allowed the helicopter to absorb power from the massive, twin ZMKB engines, and it made for smooth, almost vibration-free flight. It also allowed the Mi 26 to dispense with the two pronounced winglets of the earlier craft. For loading purposes, the Mi 26 boasts an integral rear loading ramp and two powered clamshell cargo doors. It can carry up to 44,000 pounds of cargo or 100 fully equipped troops on a very strong titanium floor. It flies in both civilian and military guises with the NATO code name HALO.

Considerable ingenuity was expended in weight-saving measures. In fact, the Mi 26 is actually 2,200 pounds lighter that the less-capable Mi 6. Part of this comes from the rotor assembly, which is titanium; the huge rotor blades are made from steel spars and fiberglass. The big craft can be flown in any weather conditions using state-of-the-art navigation and computerized flight assistance. On autohover it can reputedly remain motionless only 5 feet off the ground! This triumph of aeronautical engineering is destined to be the world's chopper-lift champ for some time. A total of 70 have been built.

Type: Trainer

Dimensions: wingspan, 39 feet; length, 35 feet, 7 inches; height, 9 feet, 3 inches
Weights: empty, 4,293 pounds; gross, 5,573 pounds
Power plant: 1 × 870–horsepower Bristol Mercury XX radial engine
Performance: maximum speed, 242 mile per hour; ceiling, 25,100 feet; range, 393 miles
Armament: 1 × .303–inch machine gun
Service dates: 1939–1950

The *Master* was the most numerous advanced British trainer of World War II. In its original form it possessed performance almost rivaling the fabled *Hurricanes* and *Spitfires*.

By 1935 the advent of high-performance monoplanes necessitated adoption of training craft with similar flight characteristics. In 1937 M. G. Miles fielded his *Kestrel* design, a low-wing monoplane made of wood frames and covered in plywood. A crew of two was housed in a tandem cockpit, and the instructor's seat could be raised in flight for better view on takeoffs and landings. Powered by a 745-horsepower Rolls-Royce Kestrel engine, it reached 300 miles per hour, slightly slower than *Hurricanes* and *Spitfires* employing much more powerful engines. However, the Air Ministry remained disinterested, and the project subsided. The following year it reversed that decision, and Miles was required to modify the fuselage and reposition the radiator from the nose to the wing's center section. Moreover, a derated Kestrel XXX engine was utilized, which slowed the new craft down by 70 miles per hour. The *Master*, as it was christened, was still delightful to fly and handled very much like a fighter. In June 1938 the ministry adopted it under Specification 16/38 and ordered 500 copies. This was the largest order placed for a training plane to that date.

The first *Master Is* were not deployed at flight schools until the fall of 1939. Thereafter, they trained thousands of British pilots in the art of fighter tactics. As the war progressed, a shortage of Kestrel engines developed, so the *Master II* arose by mounting an 870-horsepower Bristol Mercury radial engine. This spoiled the airplane's fine lines but resulted in a 16-mile-per-hour increase in speed. When these stocks ran out, the *Master III* was fitted with a lower-rated 825-horsepower Pratt & Whitney Wasp Junior and suffered a commensurate decrease in top speed. By war's end, a total of 3,227 of the wonderfully agile *Masters* had been delivered. Many were retained as trainers until 1950.

Type: Fighter

Dimensions: wingspan, 36 feet, 1 inch; length, 24 feet, 9 inches; height, 10 feet, 6 inches
Weights: empty, 2,681 pounds; gross, 3,759 pounds
Power plant: 1 × 710–horsepower Nakajima Kotobuki radial engine
Performance: maximum speed, 273 miles per hour; ceiling, 32,150 feet; range, 746 miles
Armament: 2 × 7.7mm machine guns
Service dates: 1937–1945

The diminutive A5M set aviation standards as the world's first all-metal, carrier-based monoplane. Commencing in 1937 it helped secure Japanese control of the air during the war against China.

In 1934 the Imperial Japanese Navy issued new specifications for a monoplane fighter that could top 217 miles per hour in level flight and reach 6,000 feet in less than six minutes. It devolved upon a Mitsubishi design team under Jiro Horikoshi to devise an appropriate solution. He responded with a prototype that, at the time it appeared, was revolutionary for Japan's fledgling naval air arm. The new craft was an all-metal, low-wing monoplane with fixed, spatted wheels. It was totally covered in stressed metal and flush-riveted to reduce drag. During test flights in 1936 the prototype reached 280 miles per hour, 60 miles per hour faster than the specifications, but problems were encountered with the wing shape. It originally possessed a gull-shaped planform, but this subsequently gave way to a graceful, elliptical design. Once fitted to a more powerful engine, the new craft exhibited better speed and performance than contemporary Japanese biplanes, so in 1937 it entered the service as the A5M. It debuted as the world's most advanced carrier-based fighter, and during World War II Allied intelligence gave it the code name *Claude*.

No sooner were A5Ms built than they deployed from Japanese carriers operating off the Chinese coast. These demonstrated their mettle over Nanking in September 1937 by shooting down 10 Chinese-piloted Polikarpov I 16 monoplanes without loss. Thereafter, the *Claudes* facilitated Japanese control of the air over Chinese coastal regions. A fully enclosed cockpit was fitted to the second model in an attempt to improve the A5M, but the swashbuckling Japanese pilots objected, and later models reverted back to an open cockpit. In the early days of the Pacific war, *Claudes* were the most numerically important Japanese fighter, but they were rapidly outclassed by newer Allied fighters. Most were retired by the summer of 1942 to serve as trainers, but after 1945 many became kamikazes. Total production ran to 1,094 machines.

Type: Fighter

Dimensions: wingspan, 36 feet, 1 inch; length, 29 feet, 11 inches; height, 11 feet, 6 inches
Weights: empty, 4,136 pounds; gross, 6,508 pounds
Power plant: 1 × 1,130–horsepower Nakajima NK1F radial engine
Performance: maximum speed, 351 miles per hour; ceiling, 36,255 feet; range, 1,193 miles
Armament: 2 × 7.7mm machine guns; 2 × 20mm cannon
Service dates: 1940–1945

The legendary A6M (the dreaded *Zero*) was the first carrier-based fighter in history to outperform land-based equivalents, and it arrived in greater quantities than any other Japanese aircraft. Despite the *Zero*'s aura of invincibility, better Allied machines gradually rendered it obsolete.

As early as 1937 the Imperial Japanese Navy began searching for a craft to replace its A5M carrier-based fighters. That year it issued specifications so stringent that only Mitsubishi was willing to hazard a design. Specifically, the navy wanted a fighter of prodigious range and maneuverability, one able to defeat bigger land-based opponents. A design team headed by Jiro Horikoshi originated a prototype in 1939. The A6M was a study in aerodynamic cleanliness despite its bulky radial engine. It had widetrack undercarriage for easy landing and was heavily armed with two cannons and two machine guns. Tests proved it possessed phenomenal climbing and turning ability, so it entered production in 1940, the Japanese year 5700. Henceforth, the new fighter was known officially as the Type 0, but it passed into history as the *Reisen*, or *Zero*.

A small production batch of 30 *Zeroes* was sent to China in the summer of 1940 for evaluation, and they literally swept the sky of Chinese opposition. Such prowess was duly noted by Claire L. Chennault, future commander of the famed *Flying Tigers*, but his warnings were ignored. *Zeroes* subsequently spearheaded the Japanese attack on Pearl Harbor in December 1941, and over the next six months they ran roughshod over all Allied opposition. However, following the Japanese defeat at Midway in June 1942, the fabled fighter lost much of its ascendancy to new Allied fighters and a growing shortage of experienced pilots. New and more powerful versions of the *Zero* were introduced to stem the tide, but relatively weak construction could not withstand mounting Allied firepower. Furthermore, the additional weight of new weapons and equipment eroded its famous powers of maneuver. By 1945 most A6Ms had been converted into kamikazes in a futile attempt to halt the Allied surge toward the homeland. A total of 10,964 were constructed.

Type: Medium Bomber; Torpedo-Bomber

Dimensions: wingspan, 82 feet; length, 53 feet, 11 inches; height, 12 feet, 1 inch
Weights: empty, 11,552 pounds; gross, 17,637 pounds
Power plant: 2 × 1,300–horsepower Mitsubishi Kinsei radial engines
Performance: maximum speed, 258 miles per hour; ceiling, 33,725 feet; range, 3,871 miles
Armament: 4 × 7.7mm machine guns; 1 × 20mm cannon; 1,764 pounds of bombs or torpedoes
Service dates: 1937–1945

At the time of its appearance, the *Nell* was one of the world's most advanced long-range bombers. It participated in many famous actions in World War II before assuming transport duties.

In 1934 Admiral Isoroku Yamamoto, future head of the Japanese Combined Fleet, advocated development of long-range land-based naval bombers to compliment carrier-based aviation. That year Mitsubishi designed and flew the Ka 9, an unsightly but effective reconnaissance craft with great endurance. It owed more than a passing resemblance to Junkers's Ju 86, as that firm had assisted Mitsubishi with the design. Now a team headed by Dr. Kiro Honjo developed that craft into the even more capable Ka 15. It was a twin-engine, midwing design with stressed skin throughout, twin rudders, and distinctive, tapered wings. Following a succession of prototypes, it entered service in 1937 as the G3M. That year these bombers made history by launching the first transoceanic raids against the Chinese cities of Hankow and Nanking from their home island—convincing proof of Japan's

burgeoning aerial prowess. Moreover, the G3M could also function as an effective torpedo-bomber, adding even greater punch to Japanese naval aviation. By the time World War II erupted in the Pacific in December 1941, the G3M formed the bulk of Japanese naval medium bomber strength. At that time it acquired the Allied designation *Nell*.

Three days after Pearl Harbor, G3Ms made world headlines when a force of 60 bombers helped sink the British battleships HMS *Repulse* and HMS *Prince of Wales* off Malaysia. Several days later, *Nells* were among the first Japanese aircraft shot down by U.S. Navy fighters at Wake Island. The spring of 1942 then witnessed G3Ms functioning as parachute aircraft over the Dutch East Indies. Within months, however, revitalized Allied forces poured into the region, forcing the slow and under-armed *Nells* to sustain heavy losses. By 1942 most had ceased active combat operations and spent the rest of the war as transports. Production came to 1,048 machines.

Type: Medium Bomber; Torpedo-Bomber

Dimensions: wingspan, 82 feet; length, 63 feet, 11 inches; height, 19 feet, 8 inches
Weights: empty, 18,409 pounds; gross, 27,558 pounds
Power plant: 2 × 1,825–horsepower Mitsubishi MK4T Kaisei radial engines
Performance: maximum speed, 292 miles per hour; ceiling, 30,250 feet; range, 2,694 miles
Armament: 4 × 7.7mm machine guns; 1 × 20mm cannon; 2,205 pounds of bombs or torpedoes
Service dates: 1940–1945

The bulbous G4M was the most numerous and best-known Japanese medium bomber of World War II. It possessed incredible range, but its unarmored fuel tanks led to the unenviable nickname "Flying Lighter."

In 1937 the Imperial Japanese Navy issued an incredibly difficult specification mandating production of land-based bombers with even greater range than the superb G3M. Although such performance was usually attained by four-engine designs, the new craft was restricted to only two. That year Kiro Honjo commenced work on a machine whereby fuel capacity was emphasized to the exclusion of all other considerations. In 1939 the G4M prototype was flown as an all-metal, midwing design with rakish wings and tail surfaces melded to a rotund fuselage. As expected, the airplane performed well and possessed impressive range. However, this was achieved by stuffing as much fuel as possible into wing tanks that remained unarmored to save weight; crew armor was also deleted for the same reason. Nonetheless, the navy was highly pleased with the

G4M, and in 1940 it entered production. The following year they were baptized under fire in northern China, performing well against limited opposition. When the Pacific war broke out in December 1941, roughly 160 G4Ms were in service. Allied forces gave them the code name *Betty*.

The G4M came as quite a surprise to British and American forces, who believed themselves beyond the reach of medium bombers. But in quick succession, G4Ms helped sink the battleships HMS *Repulse* and *Prince of Wales*, and they plastered airfields throughout the Philippines. It was not until the spring of 1942 that the *Betty*'s weakness was revealed. The very attributes endowing it with such long range caused it be destroyed by a few tracer rounds. The G4Ms took staggering losses during the Guadalcanal campaign, and the Japanese finally introduced self-sealing tanks and crew armor in subsequent versions. One of the last roles of the G4M would be to carry the Yokosuka MXY 7 *Oka* suicide rocket. Production totaled 2,416 of all versions.

Type: Fighter

Dimensions: wingspan, 35 feet, 5 inches; length, 32 feet, 7 inches; height, 12 feet, 11 inches
Weights: empty, 5,423 pounds; gross, 8,695 pounds
Power plant: 1 × 1,820–horsepower Mitsubishi MK4R Kasei radial engine
Performance: maximum speed, 371 miles per hour; ceiling, 38,385 feet; range, 655 miles
Armament: 4 × 20mm cannon
Service dates: 1944–1945

The J2M was a radical departure from traditional Japanese fighter design precepts, emphasizing speed and climb over maneuverability. Despite persistent engine problems, it matured into an effective bomber interceptor.

A 1939 Japanese navy specification outlined creation of an interceptor-fighter, the first acquired by that service. Foremost among design considerations was an ability to reach 20,000 feet in only six minutes. Jiro Horikoshi subsequently led a team that created a machine that emphasized climb and speed above all other attributes. The prototype arrived in March 1942 and differed completely from Japanese fighters then in service. The new craft was exceedingly squat and compact, with stubby, laminar-flow wings and a long-chord cowl. The canopy section was extremely curved while the radial engine, which was rather broad, was fitted with a streamlined reduction assembly to reduce cowling surface area. The J2M's first flights proved disappointing, as it was slower than anticipated, hard to handle, and difficult to see from. A complete overhaul was enacted to

correct these problems, but the engine chosen, the Mitsubishi Kasei, remained a source of endless teething problems. It was not until late 1943 that the J2M's performance became acceptable, and it entered operations the following spring as the *Raiden* (Thunderbolt). Allies came to call the diminutive little powerhouse the *Jack*.

In service the *Raiden* was beset by continual technical problems, mostly arising from the Kasei engine. Unfortunately, thanks to U.S. bombing, no other power source could be made available. Thus, the *Raiden* never reached its full potential until the last months of the war, when the remaining bugs were worked out. It was then pitted against Boeing's formidable B-29. The J2M was one of few Japanese aircraft that could engage heavy bombers at high altitude, and by virtue of its heavy armament, several kills were scored. It was fortunate for the Allies that the *Jack's* development was prolonged, for postwar tests revealed it to be a formidable interceptor. Moreover, it could outclimb any Allied fighter extant. Only 476 J2Ms were constructed before the war ended.

Type: Medium Bomber

Dimensions: wingspan, 73 feet, 9 inches; length, 52 feet, 6 inches; height, 15 feet, 11 inches
Weights: empty, 13,382 pounds; gross, 23,391 pounds
Power plant: 2 × 1,500–horsepower Mitsubishi Ha–101 radial engines
Performance: maximum speed, 301 miles per hour; ceiling, 32,810 feet; range, 1,678 miles
Armament: 5 × 7.7mm machine guns; 1 × 12.7mm machine gun; up to 2,205 pounds of bombs
Service dates: 1938–1945

The Ki 21 was one of the world's best bombers when it appeared in 1938, combining good speed and range into an attractive airframe. However, by World War II it was rapidly overtaken by more modern designs.

In 1936 the Imperial Japanese Army issued demanding specifications for a new bomber with five hours' endurance and a cruising speed of 250 miles per hour. Mitsubishi accepted the challenge and in 1937 beat out a Nakajima competitor with the Ki 21. It was an extremely attractive, all-metal, midwing bomber with stressed skin. It featured retractable landing gear, and its most distinctive feature was a long greenhouse canopy for the rear gunner. In flight the Ki 21 was fast and very agile for its size. The army approved the Ki 21 as its new heavy bomber (although by Western standards it would be classified as a medium bomber), and by 1938 the first units were deployed in China. During the next three years, Ki 21s did sterling service against weak Chinese defenses, although crews realized that stronger defensives were needed. Mitsubishi then added a dorsal turret, ventral guns, and a remotely operated "tail stinger" in the rear. By 1941 the Ki 21 was the most important Japanese army bomber in service. Early in World War II it initially received the Allied designation *Jane*, a none-too-subtle reference to General Douglas MacArthur's wife, but this was subsequently changed to *Sally*.

The *Sally* performed useful work during the initial phases of the Pacific war against scattered and disorganized Allied defenses. It flew in great numbers against Burma, the Philippines, Java, and northern Australia. However, within a year more advanced British and American fighters began appearing, and lightly armed Ki 21s suffered disproportionate losses. Stronger engines and heavier armament were fitted on late-production models, but by 1943 the hardworking *Sally* had been surpassed by better machines. Thereafter and until the end of the war, it was employed in transport and training functions. A total of 2,062 were constructed.

Type: Reconnaissance; Fighter

Dimensions: wingspan, 48 feet, 2 inches; length, 36 feet, 1 inch; height, 12 feet, 8 inches
Weights: empty, 8,444 pounds; gross, 14,330 pounds
Power plant: 2 × 1,500–horsepower Mitsubishi Ha–112 II radial engines
Performance: maximum speed, 391 miles per hour; ceiling, 34,450 feet; range, 2,485 miles
Armament: none
Service dates: 1941–1945

The beautiful Ki 46 was the among the most capable reconnaissance aircraft of World War II. It performed critical intelligence work prior to the outbreak of hostilities by mapping invasion routes and Allied defenses.

Commencing in 1937, the Japanese army employed the Mitsubishi Ki 15 in China for reconnaissance purposes. This single-engine craft did extremely useful photographic work, although war planners realized a more modern airplane would be needed for a war with Western powers. Therefore, that same year they authorized Mitsubishi to commence research on a new twin-engine replacement for the Ki 15, with speed, altitude, and range taking precedence over all other considerations. A design team headed by Tomio Kubo then originated a prototype that first flew in November 1939. This new machine, the Ki 46, was startlingly beautiful to behold. It was a low-wing, all-metal affair with extremely rakish lines, a sharply pointed nose, and cleanly cowled engines. Test flights revealed it fell about 10 percent short of required performance, but it was still faster than any Japanese fighter in service. The following year more powerful motors were installed, and the Ki 46 easily reached 35,000 feet at 350 miles per hour, with endurance of seven hours. When the Ki 46 entered production in 1941, it was the most outstanding reconnaissance craft in the world. During World War II it received the Allied designation *Dinah*.

Prior to the Pacific war, the *Dinah* flew clandestine intelligence missions throughout Southeast Asia and the Pacific, carefully photographing Allied installations and the best invasion routes to reach them. It continued this work well into 1942, being so fast and high-flying that interception was virtually impossible. Eventually, improved Allied fighters began to take a toll on the earlier machines, so a new variant, the Ki 46 III, was introduced. It featured a front canopy that was completely fared into the fuselage. This model flew so high and fast that a special bomber-interceptor version was introduced late in 1944. *Dinahs* continued excellent reconnaissance work up through the end of hostilities. It was a truly outstanding aircraft for its time.

Type: Medium Bomber; Torpedo-Bomber

Dimensions: wingspan, 73 feet, 9 inches; length, 61 feet, 4 inches, height, 25 feet, 3 inches
Weights: empty, 19,070 pounds; gross, 30,347 pounds
Power plant: 2 × 1,900–horsepower Mitsubishi Ha–104 radial engines
Performance: maximum speed, 334 miles per hour; ceiling, 31,070 feet; range, 2,361 miles
Armament: 3 × 12.7mm machine guns; 1 × 20mm cannon; 2,350 pounds of bombs or torpedoes
Service dates: 1944–1945

The Ki 67 *Hiryu* was the best all-around Japanese bomber of World War II and possessed impressive speed and agility for its class. However, it arrived too late and in too few numbers to alter Japan's military fate.

A spate of border clashes with the Soviet Union during the late 1930s convinced the Japanese military that it needed bombers with greater speed, range, and payload than existing models. In 1940 the army drafted demanding specifications for a new tactical bomber, and Mitsubishi responded with a prototype that first flew in December 1942. The Ki 67 was an all-metal, midwing machine with tapering wings and tail surfaces not unlike the earlier G4M bomber. However, the fuselage was much slimmer and more aerodynamically refined. The new craft also boasted ample armament and armor for the crew, along with self-sealing fuel tanks. The Ki 67 performed extremely well during flight tests, being fast and maneuverable for its size; it could even be

looped! The army was delighted and ordered it into production as the *Hiryu* (Flying Dragon). Experiments had shown that it excelled as a torpedo-bomber, so the navy also acquired the plane in quantity. Soon the Allies came to know this formidable machine as the *Peggy*.

In 1944 the Ki 67 debuted with naval units during the Battle of the Philippine Sea. They performed capably, but their effectiveness was compromised by inexperienced pilots and swarms of U.S. fighters. At length it was decided to produce a specialized kamikaze model operated by three crew members and outfitted with a nose boom that ignited explosives on impact. By this time the homeland was being ravaged by massed B-29 raids, so a high-altitude fighter version, the Ki 109, was also developed. This version mounted a 75mm cannon in a solid nose but, given Japan's inability to obtain turbosuperchargers, it failed to reach the necessary altitudes. *Peggys* fought well until the end of the war; only 698 were built.

Type: Trainer; Light Bomber

Dimensions: wingspan, 25 feet, 10 inches; length, 58 feet, 7 inches; height, 14 feet, 5 inches
Weights: empty, 14,017 pounds; gross, 30,203 pounds
Power plant: 2 × 5,115–pound thrust Rolls-Royce/Turbomeca turbojet engines
Performance: maximum speed, 1,056 miles per hour; ceiling, 50,000 feet; range, 345 miles
Armament: 1 × 20mm Gatling gun; up to 6,000 pounds of bombs and rockets
Service dates: 1976–2000

The T 2/F 1 series was Japan's first foray into super- sonic technology and the first warplanes con- structed there since 1945. Given the defensive-minded outlook of Japan, these imposing machines are offi- cially designated as "anti–landing craft" airplanes.

By 1967 the Japan Self Defense Force desired modern supersonic equipment to replace its Korean War–vintage North American F-86 *Sabres*. It also needed a more capable trainer to facilitate easier transition to Lockheed F-104 *Starfighters* and Mc- Donnell-Douglas F-4 *Phantoms* then being acquired. Accordingly, a design team under Dr. Kenji Ikeda conceived an aircraft not dissimilar in appearance and performance to the Northrop T-38 *Talon* and SEPECAT *Jaguar* trainers. The prototype T 2 emerged in 1971 with marked similarity to the ear- lier *Jaguar* and, in fact, utilized the same engines. It was a streamlined, high-wing machine with an ex- tremely pointed profile. Lacking ailerons, it obtains lateral control through the use of differential spoil- ers mounted in front of the flaps. The T 2 also em-

ploys variable-geometry lateral air intakes to opti- mize performance at high altitude. The type entered production in 1976, and a total of 90 were com- pleted. The T 2 also displays the maneuverability and handling qualities long associated with Japa- nese airplanes.

The next stage of the program's evolution was to modify the T 2 into a high-performance strike fighter for antishipping/defensive purposes. This specification was precisely delineated, as the cur- rent Japanese constitution precludes offensive oper- ations and, hence, no attack aircraft are permitted. The first F 1 rolled out in 1975 as a machine very similar to the T 2. The most notable change was a fared-over rear canopy containing an advanced radar/navigation set. The first F 1s were delivered in 1977 and rapidly replaced the elderly F-86s. In ser- vice these aircraft proved themselves fast and reli- able strike platforms. A total of 77 were constructed, but they are eventually to be phased out by the more advanced FS-X.

Type: Fighter

Dimensions: wingspan, 27 feet, 11 inches; length, 18 feet, 6 inches; height, 7 feet, 10 inches
Weights: empty, 928 pounds; gross, 1,431 pounds
Power plant: 1 × 150–horsepower Gnome Monosoupape rotary engine
Performance: maximum speed, 129 miles per hour; ceiling, 22,965 feet; range, 200 miles
Armament: 1 or 2 × 7.7mm machine guns
Service dates: 1918

The A 1 was an attractive machine, but a reputation for structural weakness forestalled widespread service. However, it subsequently inspired a generation of French parasol fighters in the decades that followed.

In 1917 the firm of Morane-Saulnier decided to develop a new monoplane fighter to replace its novel but unsuccessful N model, or "Bullet." The new craft, christened the A 1, was a handsome parasol design with several unique features. The overhead wing was decidedly backswept and possessed large ailerons that cut forward into each wingtip. This assembly was then secured to the fuselage by an intricate series of bracing struts to withstand the stress of violent maneuvering. The fuselage itself possessed a circular cross-section and tapered rearward to a point. It was fabric-covered up to the distinct metal cowling, a beautifully contoured piece sporting seven ventilation slots around the opening. The A 1 looked and flew impressively, so in the fall of 1917 it was ordered into production. Three models were built; the MoS 27, which had one machine

gun; the MoS 29, which mounted two; and the MoS 30, an unarmed trainer.

The new fighter originally equipped three fighter *escadrilles* (squadrons) as of January 1918 but was withdrawn from combat a few months later. Apparently, several aircraft had been lost to structural failure, and it was also deemed underpowered. The 1,210 production machines consequently spent the remainder of the war as trainers. It was a standard French practice to take A 1s and strip large portions of their wing fabric, rendering them unflyable. Such craft, known as "Penguins," were employed for taxiing instruction only. Postwar service largely refuted the A 1's reputation for weakness. It became a favored stunt machine of French ace Charles Nungesser, and on February 25, 1928, Alfred Fronal consecutively looped his parasol fighter 1,111 times over a period of four hours without incident! But the greatest legacy of the A 1 was that it inspired Morane-Saulnier parasol fighters like the MS 130 and MS 230 in the 1920s and 1930s.

Type: Reconnaissance

Dimensions: wingspan, 33 feet, 9 inches; length, 20 feet, 9 inches; height, 10 feet, 4 inches
Weights: empty, 849 pounds; gross, 1,444 pounds
Power plant: 1 × 80–horsepower Gnome rotary engine
Performance: maximum speed, 71 miles per hour; ceiling, 13,123 feet; range, 280 miles
Armament: none, officially
Service dates: 1914–1915

The fragile-looking Type L, nominally a reconnaissance craft, became the world's first successful "fighter" without ever intending to do so. Among its many victims was a giant German Zeppelin.

In 1913 the Morane-Saulnier firm initiated what would become a two-decade long obsession with parasol aircraft by designing the Model L. It was a functional, if indisputably ugly, machine with a single wing mounted high over the rectangular fuselage. The Model L did, in fact, possess lively performance for its day, and that year the Turkish government ordered 50 copies. These machines were seized by the French government following the start of World War I and hastily impressed into service. The seemingly harmless two-seaters were originally intended for reconnaissance purposes until flight crews began arming themselves with rifles, pistols, and carbines. In this manner, several of the equally vulnerable German Albatros and Aviatik reconnaissance aircraft were shot down in primitive aerial combat. The Morane-Saulnier Ls gave a good account of themselves until forced into retirement by more advanced German fighters in 1915.

Two incidents stand out in the history of this pioneer warplane. Of the 600 Type Ls constructed, several were exported to England for service with the Royal Navy Air Service. On June 7, 1915, Sub-Lieutenant R.A.J. Warneford encountered a huge German Zeppelin while patrolling over Bruges, Belgium. He valiantly dodged heavy machine gun-fire until reaching an altitude of 11,000 feet, above his intended victim. He then dove straight down, dropping six small bomblets and setting it afire. For destroying the first Zeppelin of the war, Warneford received the Victoria Cross, Britain's highest honor. Another famous name indelibly associated with this craft was noted French aviator Roland Garros. Garros had installed a machine gun in his parasol that fired through the propeller arc in unsynchronized fashion. He claimed four German victims, but on April 19, 1915, Garros was himself shot down. The captured airplane inspired Anthony Fokker to invent a truly synchronized machine gun; thus was born the "Fokker scourge" of the following year.

Type: Fighter

Dimensions: wingspan, 34 feet, 9 inches; length, 26 feet, 9 inches; height, 9 feet, 9 inches
Weights: empty, 4,189 pounds; gross, 5,445 pounds
Power plant: 1 × 860–horsepower Hispano-Suiza 12Y-21 liquid-cooled in-line engine
Performance: maximum speed, 302 miles per hour; ceiling, 30,840 feet; range, 497 miles
Armament: 2 × 7.5mm machine guns; 1 × 20mm cannon
Service dates: 1939–1940

This mediocre design was the most numerous French fighter of World War II. Underpowered and underarmed, it subsequently saw service in the air forces of Switzerland, Croatia, and Finland.

In 1934 the Morane-Saulnier firm broke with its long practice of building parasol fighters by fielding the company's first monoplane aircraft. This was the prototype MS 405, a low-wing machine with fully retractable landing gear. It was the first French fighter to exceed 250 miles per hour in level flight, but retained many archaic features. Rather than breaking with tradition, the new craft employed steel-tube construction with fabric-covered control surfaces and aft fuselage. Its composite skin consisted of plymax—plywood bonded to aluminum, which covered the wings and forward fuselage. The braced tailplane and fixed tailskid also harkened back to an earlier age. The MS 405 first flew in 1935, but flight-testing was dreadfully slow, and three years lapsed before the craft entered production as the MS 406. Nonetheless, when World War II erupted in September 1939, it was the most important French fighter available and fully equipped 12 *groupes de chasse* (fighter groups).

From the onset, the MS 406 proved markedly inferior to nimble German Messerschmitt Bf 109Es. It was slower, less robust, and possessed weaker firepower in the form of a 20mm cannon firing through the propeller hub and two 7.5mm machine guns. In its favor, the MS 406 did handle pleasantly, but that alone could not transform it into an effective fighter. By the time of France's collapse, MS 406s claimed 175 German airplanes at a loss of 400. As an indication of its poor reputation, the newly imposed Vichy regime retained only one MS 406 unit in service and exported the remainder abroad. The biggest customers were Finland and Croatia, which refitted many MS 406s with more powerful Soviet engines for better performance. Total production amounted to 1,080 machines. The Swiss also subsequently developed it into a series of domestic fighters, the D 3800.

Type: Strategic Bomber; Tanker; Reconnaissance

Dimensions: wingspan, 174 feet, 4 inches; length, 169 feet, 7 inches; height, 46 feet, 3 inches
Weights: empty, 166,975 pounds; gross, 423,280 pounds
Power plant: 4 × 20,944–pound thrust Mikulin RD-3M-500A turbojet engines
Performance: maximum speed, 620 miles per hour; ceiling, 44,950 feet; range, 7,705 miles
Armament: 8 × 23mm cannons; up to 19,842 pounds of nuclear weapons
Service dates: 1956–

The impressive M 4, often touted as "Russia's B-52," was in fact a strategic white elephant. Incapable of bombing the United States, they found useful employment as tankers and reconnaissance craft.

Vladimir M. Myasishchev was a senior engineer with the Petlyakov design bureau until the end of World War II, when he was summarily told to retire. Having prior experience with the Soviet gulag system, he dutifully slipped into obscurity to teach aeronautics until 1949, when Stalin personally ordered him to create his own design bureau. Myasishchev suddenly found himself tasked with creating a huge intercontinental jet bomber capable of dropping atomic bombs on the United States and returning safely! Given the primitive nature of jet technology at that time, the Tupolev rival firm opted to utilize turboprop engines instead. However, Myasishchev performed as ordered, and in 1954 the prototype M 4 _Molot_ (Hammer) made its dramatic appearance during the annual May Day flyover. It was a sight calculated to send shivers down the spines of

Western observers. The M 4 was huge, possessed swept wings and tail surfaces, and mounted four gigantic Mikulin turbojet engines buried in the wing roots. By 1956 around 200 of the giant craft had been delivered and constituted the bulk of Soviet strategic aviation. For many years thereafter, U.S. defense experts strained over the prospect of countering the Soviets' intimidating "B-52." NATO code named it BISON.

In reality, the M 4 possessed only half the thrust and range of Boeing's B-52, a true intercontinental bomber, and was scarcely a strategic threat. The Soviets understood this perfectly and continued building seemingly obsolete Tu 95 turboprop bombers for many years thereafter. By the 1960s the aging Myasishchev giants were employed only as tankers and maritime reconnaissance craft. One example, the VM-T _Alant_, was given twin rudders and employed to haul oversized parts for the Soviet space program. A few M 4s remain in service as test vehicles. Literally—and figuratively—the massive _Molot_ was a big failure.

Type: Torpedo-Bomber; Light Bomber

Dimensions: wingspan, 48 feet, 10 inches; length, 34 feet; height, 12 feet, 6 inches
Weights: empty, 6,636 pounds; gross, 11,464 pounds
Power plant: 1 × 1,800–horsepower Nakajima Mamoru radial engine
Performance: maximum speed, 235 miles per hour; ceiling, 27,100 feet; range, 1,237 miles
Armament: 1 × 7.7mm machine gun; 1,764 pounds of bombs or torpedoes
Service dates: 1938–1945

The stately B5N was the world's best carrier-based torpedo-bomber during the initial phases of World War II. Although somewhat outdated, it sank several thousand tons of U.S. warships.

In 1935 the Imperial Japanese Navy sought quantum improvement in its torpedo-bombers, issuing specifications for a new all-metal monoplane. The new craft had to reflect stringent requirements: less than 50 feet in wingspan, capable of carrier storage, with at least four-hour endurance fully armed. The following year a Nakajima design team under Katsuji Nakamura conceived the B5N, which first flew in 1937. It was a low-wing monoplane with stressed skin and a long greenhouse canopy housing three crew members. It also possessed widetrack landing gear for ease of landing, and had extremely smooth lines. The B5N proved somewhat underpowered but entered production the following year. They performed well against weak Chinese defenses as a light bomber, but clearly a stronger engine was needed. By 1939 new versions with the Sakae 11 radial engine were produced, with little overall improvement. However, the gentle-handling B5N, once teamed with the *Long Lance* torpedo, a notorious shipkiller, was a weapon of great potential. At the onset of the Pacific war in December 1941, B5Ns formed the core of elite Japanese carrier aviation. They received the Allied code name *Kate*.

The deadly effectiveness of the B5N was underscored during the attack on Pearl Harbor when 146, flying as light bombers and torpedo craft, sank eight U.S. battleships. Thereafter, in a succession of naval engagements that ranged throughout the eastern Pacific, *Kates* were responsible for sinking or severely damaging the carriers USS *Lexington*, USS *Yorktown*, and USS *Hornet* by October 1942. But Japanese forces were severely pummeled in these affairs, and the Americans slowly acquired air superiority with better fighters. Thereafter, *Kates* became easy targets and suffered severe losses until 1944, when they finally withdrew from frontline service. Several were then fitted with radar and performed antisubmarine patrols until the war's end.

Type: Torpedo-Bomber

Dimensions: wingspan, 48 feet, 10 inches; length, 35 feet, 7 inches; height, 12 feet, 5 inches
Weights: empty, 6,636 pounds; gross, 12,456 pounds
Power plant: 1 × 1,850–horsepower Mitsubishi MK4T Kasei radial engine
Performance: maximum speed, 299 miles per hour; ceiling, 29,660 feet; range, 1,085 miles
Armament: 1 × 7.7mm machine gun; 1 × 12.7mm machine gun; 1 × 1,764 pound torpedo
Service dates: 1944–1945

The rugged *Jill*, as it was known to the Allies, was a tardy entry to World War II intended to replace the earlier and more famous *Kate*. A capable machine, it was continually beset by engine problems and inexperienced crews.

By 1939 the Imperial Japanese Navy realized that a replacement of the aging B5N torpedo-bomber was becoming a military necessity. The naval staff then approached Nakajima and suggested a new craft, based upon existing designs, that would employ the widely manufactured Mitsubishi Kasei radial engine. The ensuing B6N was then developed by Kenichi Matsumura, who took the liberty of powering it with the company's new and untested Mamoru engine. This airplane showed strong family resemblance to the B5N and sported its big engine in an oversized cowling. Another unique feature was the oil cooler, which was offset to the left so as not to interfere with torpedo-launching. Tests revealed the plane to be faster than the old *Kate* but less easily handled. Furthermore, the B6N suffered from prolonged development because

the Mamoru engine vibrated strongly and tended to overheat. It was not until 1943 that these teething problems were resolved and the B6N could enter production as the *Tenzan* (Heavenly Mountain). The B6N was superior in some technical aspects to the Grumman TBF *Avenger* and Fairey *Barracuda*, but by then the Japanese navy was in dire straits.

The B6N, code named *Jill*, was a fine torpedo platform, but it was deployed at a time when the Americans enjoyed total air superiority. Moreover, sheer size restricted it to operating from the biggest carriers, and it frequently went into battle bereft of fighter escort. Consequently, in a succession of battles ranging from Bougainville to Okinawa, most B6Ns were shot down before ever reaching their targets. Once all Japanese carriers were lost, they were further restricted to operating from land bases. By 1945 the tide of war had inexorably turned in America's favor, and many *Jills* were converted and flown as kamikazes. A total of 1,133 of these formidable machines were built.

Type: Reconnaissance; Night Fighter

Dimensions: wingspan, 55 feet, 8 inches; length, 39 feet, 11 inches; height, 14 feet, 11 inches
Weights: empty, 10,670 pounds; gross, 18,043 pounds
Power plant: 2 × 2,260–horsepower Nakajima NK1F Sakae radial engines
Performance: maximum speed, 315 miles per hour; ceiling, 30,580 feet; range, 2,330 miles
Armament: 4 × 20mm cannon
Service dates: 1943–1945

The J1N1 was a lumbering, unspectacular machine but did useful service as a high-speed reconnaissance craft. It was later crash-converted into a night fighter but flew too slowly to impact B-29 raids.

The ongoing war with China convinced Japanese naval officials of the need for a strategic fighter capable of escorting long-range bombers. By 1938 they could point to the French Potez 63 and German Me 110 as examples of what then seemed a promising new technology. Specifications were then issued for a three-seat aircraft possessing tremendous range and firepower while retaining maneuverability equal to single-seat fighters. Katsuji Nakamura of Nakajima conceived such a craft that first flew in 1941. Called the J1N1, it was a big twin-engine fighter with a low wing and a two-step fuselage to accommodate a pilot, observer/navigator, and tailgunner. Another unique feature was the remote-controlled twin barbettes mounting four machine guns. In flight the big craft demonstrated good speed and handling, but it was in no way comparable to a fighter. The navy then decided to strip it of excess equipment for use as a high-speed reconnaissance craft. Thus, in 1943 the J1N1 entered service as the *Gekko* (Moonlight); Nakajima manufactured 477.

The *Gekko* was first encountered during the later phases of the Solomon Islands campaign and failed to distinguish itself in its appointed role. The Americans, who perceived it as a fighter of some kind, bestowed the code name *Irving*. At length Commander Yasuna Kozono of the Rabaul garrison suggested fitting the big craft with oblique 20mm cannons to operate as a night fighter. Several aircraft were so modified and enjoyed some success against B-24 *Liberators*. Consequently, the majority of J1N1s were retrofitted to that standard. The fuselages were cut down to accommodate two crew members, and they were fitted with 20mm cannons and AI radar. Most *Irvings* flew in defense of the homeland but lacked the speed necessary to engage high-flying B-29s. Consequently, most spent their final days employed as kamikazes.

Type: Fighter

Dimensions: wingspan, 37 feet, 1 inch; length, 24 feet, 8 inches; height, 10 feet, 8 inches
Weights: empty, 2,447 pounds; gross, 3,946 pounds
Power plant: 1 × 710–horsepower Nakajima Ha–1*otsu* radial engine
Performance: maximum speed, 265 miles per hour; ceiling, 40,190 feet; range; 389 miles
Armament: 2 × 7.7mm machine guns
Service dates: 1937–1945

The lithe and comely Ki 27 was quite possibly the most maneuverable fighter plane of all time. It was built in greater quantities than any other Japanese prewar aircraft.

As in Italy, Japan's predilection for maneuverability in fighter craft outweighed all other tactical considerations. In 1935 the Imperial Japanese Army announced specifications for its first monoplane. Of three contenders, the Nakajima design triumphed based on its startling agility. It was an all-metal, low-wing aircraft employing stressed aluminum skin and flush-riveting. It also featured streamlined, spatted landing gear and the army's first fully enclosed canopy. The machine was also extremely compact, representing—literally—the smallest fuselage and biggest wing that could be designed around a Nakajima Kotobuki radial engine. Flight tests revealed it was highly responsive and even more acrobatic than existing Japanese biplanes. It was also somewhat slower than comparable Western machines, a fact that maneuver-oriented Japanese pilots chose to ignore. In 1937 the new machine entered into service

as the Ki 27. During World War II Allied intelligence assigned the code name *Nate*.

No sooner had Ki 27s arrived in China than they swept the skies of outdated Chinese aircraft. In 1939 fighting also flared up between Japan and the Soviet Union along the Mongolian border. Ki 27s saw much hard fighting against Polikarpov I 15 biplanes, usually with good results, but they were at a disadvantage when opposing faster I 16 monoplanes. To improve pilot vision, later models had a cut-down canopy. Production ceased in 1940 after a run of 3,999 machines. When the Pacific war commenced in 1941, Ki 27s were conspicuously engaged at Malaysia, the Philippines, and Burma. They easily mastered obsolete Allied machines in those theaters but were less successful against faster Curtiss P-40s of the *Flying Tigers*. After 1942 *Nates* were withdrawn from frontline service in favor of the more modern Ki 43 *Hayabusas*. Most were relegated to training and home defense squadrons, but after 1945 many surviving Ki 27s were impressed into kamikaze service.

Type: Fighter

Dimensions: wingspan, 35 feet, 6 inches; length, 29 feet, 3 inches; height, 10 feet, 8 inches
Weights: empty, 4,211 pounds; gross, 5,710 pounds
Power plant: 1 × Nakajima Ha–115 radial engine
Performance: maximum speed, 329 miles per hour; ceiling, 36,745 feet; range, 1,988 miles
Armament: 2 × 12.7mm machine guns; 551 pounds of bombs
Service dates: 1941–1945

The nimble Ki 43 was the most numerous Japanese army fighter despite an inherently limited design potential. Rendered obsolete by modern Allied fighters, it remained in frontline service to the bitter end of World War II.

In 1938 the Imperial Japanese Army staff began considering a replacement for the Nakajima Ki 27 fighter and asked Nakajima to comply. As before, they sought an aircraft with peerless maneuverability, even at the expense of speed, firepower, and pilot protection. A design team under Hideo Itokawa advanced plans for a craft based upon the Nakajima Ki 27, one that was thinner and possessed retractable landing gear. It was a handsome, low-wing monoplane of extremely light construction, but it was rather low-powered. Subsequent modifications included bigger wings and combat "butterfly flaps" that greatly enhanced performance and handling qualities. One notable weakness was the armament that, to save weight, was restricted to two rifle-caliber machine guns. Nevertheless, the Ki 43 entered the service in late 1941 as the *Hayabusa* (Peregrine Fal-

con), possibly the most maneuverable fighter in history. Only 50 Ki 43s were on hand when the Pacific war broke out in December 1941. They nevertheless proved quite an unpleasant surprise to the unsuspecting Allies, who christen it the *Oscar*.

The Ki 43 debuted during the successful Japanese conquest of Singapore and Burma and swept aside all the Hawker *Hurricanes* and Brewster *Buffaloes* it encountered. They had tougher going against Curtiss P-40s of the *Flying Tigers*, which refused to engage them in a suicidal contest of slow turns. Soon it became apparent that newer and more powerful versions of the fighter were needed, so the *Oscar II* employed a larger engine, two 12.7mm machine guns, and a three-blade propeller. These new versions retained all of the *Hayabusa*'s legendary maneuverability. However, by 1943 they were hopelessly outclassed in the face of new and better Allied machines. Lacking a replacement, *Oscars* remained in frontline service until 1945, the most numerous Japanese army fighter of the war. Production peaked at 5,919 machines.

Type: Fighter

Dimensions: wingspan, 31 feet; length, 28 feet, 10 inches; height, 10 feet, 8 inches
Weights: empty, 4,614 pounds; gross, 6,598 pounds
Power plant: 1 × 1,520–horsepower Nakajima Ha–109 radial engine
Performance: maximum speed, 376 miles per hour; ceiling, 36,745; range, 1,056 miles
Armament: 2 × 12.7mm machine guns; 2 × 20mm cannon
Service dates: 1942–1945

Like the J2M *Jack*, the Ki 44 was one of few Japanese aircraft designed specifically as an interceptor. It acquired limited success in that role but never enjoyed much popularity among its pilots.

In 1939 the Imperial Japanese Army staff broke with tradition by agitating for interceptor fighters that placed speed and climb over time-honored qualities of maneuverability. Nakajima complied with a prototype somewhat based upon its Ki 43 *Oscar*, which made its maiden flight in August 1940. The new machine, the Ki 44, was a low-wing monoplane as before, but it possessed stubby wings and a bulbous cowling over a large Nakajima Ha–41 radial engine. It was also heavily armed, carrying two light and two heavy machine guns. Flight tests proved that the Ki 44 climbed faster and higher than any Japanese fighter extant. In 1942 limited numbers arrived at the front as the *Shoki* (Demon Queller), but they were coolly received by pilots accustomed to pristine dogfighters. The *Shoki* did, in fact, display some dangerous characteristics, and extreme

maneuvers such as snap rolls and spins were forbidden. After a while, pilots came to appreciate the speed and ruggedness of the *Shoki* and developed a healthy respect for the plane. The same might be said for the Allies, who christened it the *Tojo* after Japan's prime minister. Interestingly, this was the only Japanese warplane identified by a non-Western code name.

The Ki 44 saw limited deployment in China and was latter based at Palembang in Sumatra for defense of valuable oil installations there. As newer Allied fighters were encountered, subsequent versions of the *Tojo* introduced stronger engines and greater armament. It was not until 1944, when fleets of U.S. B-29s began plastering Japanese cities, that the *Tojo* came into its own. Climbing quickly, they proved one of few Japanese fighters capable of engaging the giant bombers at high altitude. The Ki 44 enjoyed some success in this mode, but by 1944 production was halted in favor of the all-around better Ki 84 *Hayate*. A total of 1,233 were built.

Type: Medium Bomber

Dimensions: wingspan, 67 feet; length, 54 feet, 1 inch; height, 13 feet, 11 inches
Weights: empty, 14,396 pounds; gross, 25,133 pounds
Power plant: 2 × 1,500–horsepower Nakajima Ha–109 radial engines
Performance: maximum speed, 306 miles per hour; ceiling, 30,510 feet; range, 1,243 miles
Armament: 5 × 7.7mm machine guns; 1 × 20mm cannon; up to 2,205 pounds of bombs
Service dates: 1942–1945

The Ki 49 was intended as a much-needed replacement for the aging Ki 21 *Sally*. However, it conferred few advantages in terms of performance, and most crews actually preferred the older machine.

Deployment of the Mitsubishi Ki 21 bomber had no sooner begun in 1938 than the Japanese army began contemplating its successor. That year the army staff drafted specifications for a new aircraft featuring crew armor, self-sealing tanks, and the first-ever tail turret mounted in an army bomber. Nakajima, which had earlier lost out to Mitsubishi and ended up producing Ki 21s under license, gained firsthand knowledge about their competitor's product and sought to improve upon it. The prototype Ki 49 first flew in August 1939 as an all-metal, mid-wing aircraft with retractable undercarriage. Its inner wing possessed a wider chord than the outer sections to accommodate self-sealing fuel tanks. The trailing edge also mounted full-length Fowler flaps to enhance takeoff and climbing characteristics. The craft completed test flights, and pilots praised its handling qualities but otherwise deemed it underpowered. Nonetheless, production was authorized in 1941, and the first Ki 49 units were deployed in China. Known officially as the *Donryu* (Storm Dragon), it performed well enough against weak Chinese resistance but represented only marginal improvement over the earlier Ki 21. It eventually received the Allied code name *Helen*.

The Ki 49 saw extensive service along the Japanese Empire's southern fringes. It debuted during the February 1942 attack on Port Darwin, Australia, and was frequently encountered over New Guinea. But despite armor and heavy armament, the *Helen* proved vulnerable to fighters and lost heavily. Nakajima responded by fitting subsequent versions with bigger engines and more guns, but the type remained too underpowered to be effective. After the U.S. invasion of the Philippines in 1944, where Ki 49s were sacrificed in droves, they were finally withdrawn from frontline service. Most spent the rest of their days as antisubmarine craft, transports, or kamikazes. Only 819 were built.

Type: Fighter

Dimensions: wingspan, 36 feet, 10 inches; length, 32 feet, 6 inches; height, 11 feet, 1 inch
Weights: empty, 5,864; gross, 8,576 pounds
Power plant: 1 × 1,900–horsepower Nakajima Ha–45 radial engine
Performance: maximum speed, 392 miles per hour; ceiling, 34,450; range, 1,347 miles
Armament: 2 × 12.7mm machine guns; 2 × 20mm cannons; up to 1,100 pounds of bombs
Service dates: 1944–1945

The Ki 84 was the best Japanese army fighter of World War II to reach large-scale production. Fast, well-armed, and well-protected, it could easily outfly the formidable P-51 *Mustangs* and P-47 *Thunderbolts*.

By 1942 the attrition of experienced Japanese pilots forced the High Command to reconsider its philosophy of fighter design. By default, they concluded that maneuverability had lost ground to high performance, firepower, and pilot survivability. Accordingly, specifications were issued for a new machine to replace the aging Ki 43s in service. Nakajima subsequently fielded the prototype Ki 84 that flew in April 1943. This was a handsome, low-wing fighter with an extremely advanced power plant, the Nakajima Ha–45 radial. To the surprise of many, the new design possessed impressive qualities of speed and climb without sacrificing the cherished maneuverability of earlier machines. More important, it was also well-armed for a Japanese fighter, mounting two cannons and two heavy machine guns. The decision was made to pur-

sue production immediately, and the Ki 84 entered service as the *Hayate* (Gale) during the autumn of 1944. Allies gave it the code name *Frank*.

The first production batches of Ki 84s gave the 14th Air Force in China an extremely hard time, demonstrating marginal superiority over such stalwarts as the P-51 and P-47. As more became available, they fleshed out fighter units in the Philippines, where a major invasion was anticipated. In combat the *Frank* was an outstanding fighter plane, strong enough to be fitted with bombs for ground-attack purposes. However, its Achilles' heel was the Ha–45 direct-injection engine, which was complex, required constant maintenance, and was frequently unreliable. Japan was also experiencing an alarming decline in quality control, for vital parts such as landing gear began inexplicably snapping off during touchdown. The *Frank* nonetheless gave a good account of itself until war's end and confirmed Japan's ability to design first-rate warplanes. Production of these outstanding craft came to 3,514 machines.

Type: Light Bomber

Dimensions: wingspan, 31 feet, 10 inches; length, 53 feet, 4 inches; height, 14 feet, 10 inches
Weights: empty, 14,317 pounds; gross, 26,455 pounds
Power plant: 1 × 7,165–pound thrust Shenyang WP6 turbojet engine
Performance: maximum speed, 740 miles per hour; ceiling, 52,000 feet; range, 404 miles
Armament: 2 × 23mm cannons; up to 4,410 pounds of bombs or rockets
Service dates: 1965–

The Q 5 is built and marketed as a relatively simple and low-cost alternative to high-priced Western strike aircraft. Although based on outdated technology, it is capable and available in large numbers.

The history of the Nanchang Q 5 dates back to 1958, when the People's Republic of China began mass-producing copies of the Russian MiG 19 fighter. At that time, the People's Liberation Air Force sought a dedicated ground-attack craft with better performance than existing MiGs. The program was interrupted in 1961 by the Cultural Revolution and did not recommence until 1965. That June a prototype Q 5 flew for the first time as a highly modified airframe with overtones of the earlier craft. The biggest change was the nose section, which was highly pointed and replaced the frontal intake of the MiG 19 with ones on either side of the fuselage. Other changes included broader wings and an internal bomb bay. The tail control surfaces were apparently retained intact. Around 1970 the Q 5 entered produc-

tion and received the NATO designation FANTAN. Roughly 1,000 have been built and are deployed in three main versions. The variant associated with the People's Liberation Navy carries additional radar and torpedoes. It is also nuclear-capable.

The Q 5 continues to be regarded as a major tactical asset within the Chinese air force judging from the sheer number of machines fielded. The FANTAN is apparently a rugged, capable ground-attack aircraft that can be fitted with a variety of internal and external ordnance, including ground-to-air missiles and bomb clusters. It also mounts a pair of 23mm cannons for defensive purposes. Such cheap, effective machines have decided appeal for poorer Third World countries seeking to enhance their military capabilities. For this reason, Pakistan, North Korea, and Bangladesh all have imported small quantities of Q 5s. The newest version, the Q 5I, has deleted the bomb bay in favor of additional fuel and fuselage hardpoints.

Type: Fighter

Dimensions: wingspan, 24 feet, 9 inches; length, 19 feet; height, 8 feet
Weights: empty, 728 pounds; gross, 1,058 pounds
Power plant: 1 × 80–horsepower Gnome rotary engine
Performance: maximum speed, 97 miles per hour; ceiling, 15,090 feet; range, 200 miles
Armament: 1 × 7.7mm machine gun
Service dates: 1915–1916

The Nieuport 11 was one of the most famous aircraft of World War I. Light and maneuverable, it helped end the "Fokker scourge" and restore Allied control of the air.

In response to the 1914 Gordon Bennett Air Race, Gustave Delage of Nieuport undertook design of a new and relatively small machine. This craft, which he christened the *Bebe* (Baby) on account of its size, was built in only four months. It featured conventional wood-and-fabric construction with highly staggered, swept-back wings. The lower wing was slightly shorter than the top, possessed only half the surface area, and was secured by distinctive vee struts. The racer was fast and demonstrated a good rate of climb with superlative flying qualities. Because World War I canceled the air race, the Aviation Militaire (French air service) decided to adopt the airplane as the Nieuport 11 scout. For combat purposes it sported a single Lewis machine gun on the top wing that fired above the propeller arc.

The first Nieuport 11s arrived at the front in the summer of 1915—none too soon for the hard-pressed Allies. For six months previously the Fokker E III monoplanes had monopolized air combat over the Western Front, inflicting heavy losses. This latest French fighter could literally fly rings around its opponent and, in concert with the de Havilland DH 2 pusher, recaptured air supremacy for the Allies. The Italians were also singularly impressed by the design, and they obtained rights to manufacture it under license. By 1917 Nieuport 11s formed the mainstay of Italian fighter strength and were also widely exported to Belgium and Russia.

In 1916 Nieuport fitted the *Bebe* fuselage with a more powerful engine and additional armament. The ensuing Model 16 proved as popular as its predecessor, launching the careers of many French aces, including Georges Guynemer and Charles Nungesser. This model was also unique in being fitted with small Le Prieur rockets for shooting down observation balloons. More than 600 Nieuport 16s were constructed, and they remained actively employed until 1917.

Type: Fighter

Dimensions: wingspan, 26 feet, 11 inches; length, 18 feet, 10 inches; height, 7 feet, 7 inches
Weights: empty, 705 pounds; gross, 1,179 pounds
Power plant: 1 × 110–horsepower Le Rhone rotary engine
Performance: maximum speed, 109 miles per hour; ceiling, 17,388 feet; range, 186 miles
Armament: 1 × 7.7mm machine gun
Service dates: 1916–1917

The Nieuport 17 was one of the most famous warplanes in aviation history. Its dogfighting abilities were legendary, and German aircraft designers felt obliged to incorporate many of its technical aspects into their own craft.

In 1916 Gustave Delage sought to improve upon his existing Nieuport 16 to counteract a tendency toward nose-heaviness and structural failures in the lower wing. The result was a strengthened, lengthened design: the classic Nieuport 17. It featured additional wing area, cleaned-up lines, and a reinforced lower wing. A fully synchronized Vickers machine gun, installed in front of the pilot's position, also replaced the wing-mounted Lewis weapon. Consequently, the new craft displayed all the agility of older models with none of their vices.

The Nieuport 17 appeared at the front in the summer of 1916, just as the struggle against the Fokker E III monoplanes was climaxing. As with earlier models, it had little difficulty dispatching numerous German adversaries. It also was one of the few Allied aircraft that could hold its own against the new-model Albatros and Halberstadt D I fighters appearing that fall. Being propelled by a rotary engine, which exerted great torque forces while spinning inside the cowling, Nieuports easily outturned their faster opponents. The Italians were impressed by this compact dervish and obtained a license to manufacture it on their own. The type was also exported abroad to Belgium and Russia with similar results. Moreover, it formed the strength of the American volunteer squadron, the famous *Lafayette Escadrille.*

Few aircraft are so closely associated with a stable of aces as this legendary Nieuport design. It assisted the careers of such flying legends as Georges Guynemer, Rene Fonck, and Jean Navarre in France, Italy's Francesco Baracca, Edward Mannock of Great Britain, and William "Billy" Bishop of Canada. The great British ace Albert Ball was allegedly so attached to his Nieuport that he refused to trade it when ordered to do so! This superlative fighter plane remained in frontline service until 1917 before being superceded by the SPAD VII.

Type: Fighter

Dimensions: wingspan, 28 feet, 8 inches; length, 21 feet; height, 8 feet, 2 inches
Weights: empty, 1,047 pounds; gross, 1,625 pounds
Power plant: 1 × 160–horsepower Gnome Monosoupape rotary engine
Performance: maximum speed, 122 miles per hour; ceiling, 17,000 feet; range, 155 miles
Armament: 2 × .303–caliber machine guns
Service dates: 1918

The Nieuport 28 was among the most elegant fighters of World War I but inferior to earlier models. It nonetheless gained renown as the first combat aircraft piloted by newly-arrived Americans.

The appearance of new German fighters in the summer of 1917 prompted Gustave Delage to radically overhaul the design philosophy of his aging Nieuport scouts. A new craft, designated the Nieuport 28, dispensed with the familiar sesquiplane approach (with one wing longer than the other) and adopted wings of equal length. Moreover, in contrast to the square-tipped wings anchored by vee struts of earlier versions, the new craft sported rounded tips and two-bay, conventional strutting. The graceful fuselage was also circular in cross-section, with a highly streamlined metal cowling. The resulting craft exhibited delightfully stylish lines and proved highly maneuverable with a good rate of climb. Unfortunately, it was also structurally weak, as the leading edge tended to break up during dives. This could lead to the entire upper wing collapsing—with fatal results. In light of additional prob-

lems with the 160-horsepower Gnome Monosoupape rotary engine, the Aviation Militaire (French air service) decided to purchase the more rugged SPAD VII instead.

The Nieuport 28 might have lapsed into obscurity save for developments overseas. In 1917 the United States declared war against Germany and began dispatching the American Expeditionary Force to France. It arrived in the summer and fall of that year wholly destitute of aircraft and eager to purchase modern designs. Because the Nieuport 28 was the only available fighter at the time, 297 of these rejected machines outfitted the 27th, 94th, 95th, and 147th Aero Squadrons in the spring of 1918. Both Douglas Campbell, the first American ace, and Eddie Rickenbacker, the highest-scoring pilot, cut their teeth in these fragile fighters. Other noted fliers such as Raoul Lufbery and Quinten Roosevelt were killed flying them. After a service life of several months, the unpopular Nieuports were finally replaced by SPAD XIIIs. A handful lingered on as racing craft well into the 1920s.

Type: Fighter

Dimensions: wingspan, 31 feet, 10 inches; length, 21 feet, 3 inches; height, 8 feet, 5 inches
Weights: empty, 1,675 pounds; gross, 2,535 pounds
Power plant: 1 × 300–horsepower Hispano-Suiza 8Fb water-cooled in-line engine
Performance: maximum speed, 146 miles per hour; ceiling, 27,885 feet; range, 360 miles
Armament: 2 × 7.7mm machine guns
Service dates: 1922–1933

Too late to serve in World War I, the Ni-D 29 was one of the best fighters of the 1920s. It served many years in the air forces of France, Italy, Belgium, and Japan.

In 1918 Gustave Delage undertook design of a fighter to replace his less-than-successful Nieuport 28. In doing so he completely forsook the long-standing design norms of the Nieuport company. His new Ni-D 29 differed greatly from previous machines by mounting an in-line, not rotary, engine. It also dispensed with traditional vee struts associated with that company. The new craft was a two-bay biplane of conventional wood-and-canvas design. The wings were of equal length, slightly staggered, and both possessed ailerons. The fuselage was of streamlined monocoque construction with a close-fitting metal cowl over the engine. This necessitated twin radiators to be suspended below the engine and between the landing struts. Delage's latest creation first flew in June 1918, exhibiting high speed and great maneuverability. The second prototype even established a

world's altitude record of 29,931 feet in 1919. Having missed World War I, the Ni-D 29 entered production in 1921, with 250 units acquired by fighter squadrons. The craft proved immediately successful, and soon it was redesigned with longer wings and no upper ailerons. This version, the Ni-D 29 C.1, remained in frontline service until 1928.

The Ni-D 29 subsequently became one of the most important and numerous fighter aircraft of the postwar period. It was widely exported abroad, serving with the air forces of Belgium, Sweden, Argentina, and Spain; it was also built under license by Italy and Japan. The Japanese firm Nakajima supplied army air force units with no less than 608 machines (designated Ko 4), which remained in service until 1933. These aircraft saw extensive use during the Manchurian campaign, while French and Spanish Nieuports fought against rebels throughout North Africa. In 1927 a mock dogfight of Ni-D 29s was even staged over Paris between a French pilot and Charles Lindbergh!

Type: Light Bomber; Fighter

Dimensions: wingspan (swept) 28 feet; length, 61 feet, 3 inches; height, 19 feet, 6 inches
Weights: empty, 31,970 pounds; gross, 61,700 pounds
Power plant: 2 × 8,650–pound thrust Turbo-Union RB.199–34R Mk 104 turbofans
Performance: maximum speed, 921 miles per hour; ceiling, 50,000 feet; range, 863 miles
Armament: 2 × 27mm cannons; up to 19,841 pounds of rockets, bombs, or gunpods
Service dates: 1980–

The *Tornado* is possibly the most flexible multi-mission aircraft in history. Designed as a strike aircraft, it can also perform air-defense, antishipping, and reconnaissance missions with ease.

In the late 1960s Germany, Italy, and Great Britain joined hands to design a basic ground-attack aircraft that would be built and deployed by all three nations. The new machine would have to operate from short runways, deliver ordnance with pinpoint accuracy, and operate in any weather conditions. It would also be optimized for high-speed/low-level operations that are highly taxing to both crew and airframe alike. After extensive studies, the prototype Panavia *Tornado* IDS was flown in 1974. It was a compact yet highly complicated aircraft, the first European production design to employ variable-geometry wings. The wings are extremely complicated and designed around a number of high-lift technologies that enable it to become airborne quickly. The craft is characterized by a somewhat short, pointed nose, a long canopy seating two crew members, and a very tall stabilizer. Internally, the

Tornado utilizes advanced fly-by-wire technology, as well as highly sophisticated navigation/attack radar that combines search, ground-mapping, and terrain-following capabilities. Around 900 *Tornados* have been built and acquired by the manufacturing nations since 1980. Several dozen have also been exported to Saudi Arabia.

In 1976 Great Britain wanted to develop an air-defense version on its own accord to replace the aging inventory of English Electric *Lightnings* and McDonnell-Douglas *Phantoms*. It desired a fast, flexible interceptor to protect NATO's northern and western approaches. The new *Tornado* ADV rolled out in 1976 and is distinguished from the IDS variant by a lengthened nose. It houses the advanced Foxhound radar system, which can track up to 20 targets simultaneously at ranges up to 100 miles. The Royal Air Force currently operates 144 *Tornado* ADVs, and several have been exported to Saudi Arabia. Both versions saw active duty in the 1991 Gulf War and sustained the heaviest losses of any Allied type. They will continue to serve well into the twenty-first century.

Type: Medium Bomber; Dive-Bomber

Dimensions: wingspan, 56 feet, 3 inches; length, 41 feet, 6 inches; height, 11 feet, 6 inches
Weights: empty, 12,952 pounds; gross, 18,726 pounds
Power plant: 2 × 1,260–horsepower M-105PF liquid-cooled in-line engines
Performance: maximum speed, 360 miles per hour; ceiling, 28,870 feet; range, 721 miles
Armament: 2 × 7.62mm machine guns; 3 × 12.7mm machine guns; 6,614 pounds of bombs
Service dates: 1940–1945

The Pe 2 was Russia's outstanding tactical bomber of World War II and distinguished itself throughout that conflict. Even when fully loaded, it flew so fast that escorting fighters were hard-pressed to keep up.

In 1938 a design bureau under Vladimir Petlyakov responded to Soviet specifications for a high-altitude fighter with the VI 100. It was an all-metal, twin-engine machine with two rudders and streamlined engine nacelles. A crew of three sat in a spacious cockpit toward the front of the fuselage. In designing the VI 100, careful consideration was given to weight and drag reduction, so bulky radiators were located along the wings while the fuselage employed the smallest possible cross-section. Flight-testing commenced in 1939 with excellent results, but the government changed the role of the craft to high-level bombing. When this proved impractical due to inaccuracy, dive-bombing was substituted, and the plane was fitted with dive brakes. Petlyakov's design proved successful in this mode, and in 1940 it entered service as the Pe 2.

When war with Germany commenced in June 1941, Pe 2s distinguished themselves in hard-pressed attacks and flew faster than pursuing Bf 109E fighters. Pe 2s were so speedy that they frequently throttled back to allow Lend-Lease Hawker *Hurricane* escort fighters to keep up. The Pe 2 was also quite strong and could sustain major damage with few ill effects. Successive modifications and stronger engines improved performance and kept them slightly beyond the reach of the newer Bf 109F/Gs. The biggest modifications occurred in 1943, when the wing profile was modified, oil-cooler intakes were reshaped, and bomb mounts received streamlined fairings. The net result was a 25 percent increase in speed. Features to enhance crew survival were also incorporated, including a novel cold-gas bleeding system to suppress fires in the fuel tanks. No less than 11,400 of these impressive machines were constructed. In concert with the smaller Ilyushin Il 2, they were significant contributors to the final Russian victory.

Type: Heavy Bomber

Dimensions: wingspan, 128 feet, 3 inches; length, 77 feet, 4 inches; height, 20 feet, 4 inches
Weights: empty, 40,609 pounds; gross, 79,366 pounds
Power plant: 4 × 1,700–horsepower Shvetsov Ash–82FN radial engines
Performance: maximum speed, 280 miles per hour; ceiling, 29,525 feet; range, 2,920 miles
Armament: 2 × 7.62mm machine guns; 2 × 12.7mm machine guns; 8,818 pounds of bombs
Service dates: 1940–1950

The Pe 8 was an excellent heavy bomber, but the Soviet High Command had little regard for strategic bombing. Despite great range and a good payload, this potentially useful weapon remained a minor player in a very big war.

In 1934 the Soviet government announced specifications for a fast long-range bomber to replace the Tupolev TB 3s in service. It devolved upon the Tupolev design bureau to create such a craft, although under the aegis of Vladimir Petlyakov. The new machine, initially designated TB 7, first flew in December 1936 as an all-metal, midwing monoplane with power turrets and retractable landing gear. A unique feature was the peculiarly thick wings; these allowed crew members to crawl to the inboard engine nacelles and man rear-firing machine guns. Initial flights were also impressive, as the TB 7 reached 30,000 feet at speeds exceeding the latest German fighters. They entered production in 1937, but only 79 of these excellent machines were constructed.

This was because the Soviet High Command wanted great numbers of smaller two-engine tactical bombers to operate at low altitude in support of Red Army units. Thus, Soviet long-range bombardment aviation took a permanent backseat to battlefield considerations.

During the initial stages of World War II, the big Pe 8s were actively employed, but seldom in the capacity for which they were designed. On the night of August 11, 1941, several managed to bomb Berlin, and subsequent raids were conducted deep behind German lines. But compared to British and U.S. efforts, these were mere pinpricks. However, in May 1942 a Pe 8 made headlines when it flew by stages from Moscow to Washington, D.C., bearing Prime Minister V. M. Molotov. This successful round-trip flight, totaling over 11,000 miles, was a considerable achievement and eloquent testimony to the soundness of Petlyakov's design. After the war several Pe 8s remained employed as engine testbeds until 1950.

Type: Fighter

Dimensions: wingspan, 30 feet, 10 inches; length, 22 feet, 9 inches; height, 8 feet, 9 inches
Weights: empty, 1,653 pounds; gross, 2,056 pounds
Power plant: 1 × 180–horsepower Mercedes D III liquid-cooled in-line engine
Performance: maximum speed, 103 miles per hour; ceiling, 17,060 feet; range, 217 miles
Armament: 2 × 7.92mm machine guns
Service dates: 1917–1918

The sleek-looking Pfalz D IIIs were among the most streamlined fighters to appear in World War I. Its dogfighting abilities were marginally inferior to contemporary Fokkers and Albatroses, but as a balloon-buster it had no peer.

Pfalz Flugzeug-Werke of Bavaria spent the first three years of World War I building Roland D-series fighters and other craft under license. By 1917 chief engineer Rudolph Gehringer advanced plans for a new fighter possessing unmistakably sharklike lines. This new craft, the Pfalz D III, first flew in June of that year. It possessed a plywood-covered monocoque fuselage with a sharply pointed profile. The wings were slightly staggered with single-bay struts ending in raked, pointed wingtips and mounted as close to the fuselage as possible to afford good all-around view. The lower wing was somewhat shorter than the top and featured cutouts near the roots for enhanced downward vision. The German air service greatly needed a new fighter, so construction of the D III commenced in the summer of 1917.

For all its promise, the Pfalz D III proved something of a bust in combat. Good looks notwithstanding, the plane climbed more slowly and was judged inferior in maneuverability to the contemporary Albatros and Fokker triplane fighters then in service. Yet the Pfalz was fast in level flight, possessed pleasant handling characteristics, and could outdive any German fighter extant. This trait, coupled with robust construction, made it ideal for the dangerous business of balloon-busting. Observation balloons at this time were heavily defended by artillery batteries below and were surrounded by constant fighter patrols. Thus, they were extremely difficult targets to bring down. The great strength of the Pfalz allowed it to dive upon its quarry, absorb considerable damage, and return home safely. At length, the D IIIa version was introduced, which featured minor aerodynamic refinements, including rounder wingtips and bigger tail surfaces. Nearly 600 of both models were completed, and at least 350 were in service by war's end.

Type: Fighter

Dimensions: wingspan, 29 feet, 6 inches; length, 20 feet, 10 inches; height, 8 feet, 10 inches
Weights: empty, 1,579 pounds; gross, 1,984 pounds
Power plant: 1 × 160–horsepower Mercedes D IIIa liquid-cooled in-line engine
Performance: maximum speed, 106 miles per hour; ceiling, 18,500 feet; range, 200 miles
Armament: 2 × 7.92mm machine guns
Service dates: 1918

The Pfalz D XII was among the very last German fighters to appear in World War I. It was an excellent machine but always operated in the shadow of Fokker's superb D VII.

The lackluster performance of the earlier D III fighters induced the Pfalz company to design a better high-performance aircraft as a replacement. Several intermediary prototypes were built and flown, but it was not until the Aldershof fighter trials of June 1918 that the Pfalz D XII made its unheralded appearance. The new craft showed striking resemblance to the famous Fokker D VII already in service, but it was a completely original design. Like the earlier D III, it possessed a plywood monocoque fuselage that tapered rearward to a knife's edge. A 160-horsepower Mercedes engine was housed in a tight-fitting cowl section, with the top exposed and a radiator in front. The two-bay wings were of unequal length and heavily braced by wiring, while the top wing sported ailerons that flared out past the wingtips. But, given the applause surrounding Fok-

ker's marvel, skeptics assumed that a few select bribes by the Bavarian government accounted for the Pfalz's appearance. Nonetheless, several veteran pilots test-flew the craft and praised its many qualities. The government then decided to undertake production of the little-known craft to supplement the Fokkers, then in short supply.

In fact, the D XII proved an excellent design, if marginally inferior to its more famous stablemate. It was fast, immensely strong, and could outdive the D VII with complete safety. However, most pilots had their hearts set upon flying Fokkers, and when the Pfalz machine appeared at aerodromes in September 1918 pilots viewed it with disappointment and suspicion. Familiarization flights soon convinced them otherwise, and in combat it proved one of few German types able to withstand the Sopwith *Camel* and the SPAD XIII. The much-neglected fighter fought with distinction until the Armistice of November 1918. An estimated 200 Pfalz D XIIs had been constructed.

Type: Reconnaissance

Dimensions: wingspan, 36 feet, 1 inch; length, 24 feet, 8 inches; height, 9 feet, 8 inches
Weights: empty, 1,808 pounds; gross, 2,734 pounds
Power plant: 1 × 230–horsepower Hiero liquid-cooled engine
Performance: maximum speed, 112 miles per hour; ceiling, 17,715 feet; range, 350 miles
Armament: 2 × 7.92mm machines guns; 110 pounds of bombs
Service dates: 1918–1935

The ugly, angular Phonix C I was unquestionably the best Austrian two-seater of World War I. After a brief combat life, it capably served the Swedish air force for an additional two decades.

The advent of newer, more deadly Allied fighters toward the closing months of World War I induced Austria to seek better aircraft and replace its aging fleet of Hansa-Brandenburgs and Lohners. In the spring of 1917 the Phonix Flugzeug-Werke firm entered into competition with a rival firm, Ufag, to design the new craft. Both prototypes were based upon the Hansa-Brandenberg C I, a German two-seater of the "star-strutter" variety. When the Phonix machine emerged, it possessed unequal, positive-staggered wings with an unusual system of dual interplane vee struts. The fuselage was also very deep and placed close to the upper wing. This gave the pilot almost unrestricted frontal and upward view. Another distinctive feature was the very small rudder, which granted the gunner a near-perfect field of fire. The new craft, christened the Phonix C I, was

initially underpowered but demonstrated many useful qualities. Production commenced in the spring of 1918 following a prolonged gestation of nearly a year.

In combat, the Phonix C I proved itself one of the best warplanes of its class. Once retrofitted with a powerful, 230-horsepower motor, it exhibited excellent climbing and turning capabilities. In fact, C Is flew so well that they were easily mistaken for the single-seat Phonix D I fighter—often with fatal results. The noted Italian ace Francesco Baracca met his death at the hands of a C I tailgunner, as did scores of other unsuspecting Allied pilots. It was Austria's fate that this fine machine served only a few months before the Armistice concluded in November 1918. A total of 110 were built.

After the war, the C I's excellent reputation came to the attention of the newly founded Swedish air force. Between 1920 and 1932, an additional 32 C Is, known as *Dronts*, were built, remaining actively employed until 1935.

Type: Fighter

Dimensions: wingspan, 32 feet, 2 inches; length, 21 feet, 9 inches; height, 9 feet, 5 inches
Weights: empty, 1,510 pounds; gross, 2,097 pounds
Power plant: 1 × 230–horsepower Hiero liquid-cooled engine
Performance: maximum speed, 117 miles per hour; ceiling, 22,310 feet; range, 217 miles
Armament: 2 × 7.92mm machine guns
Service dates: 1918–1933

The Phonix D I was arguably the best Austrian fighter of World War I. Slow-climbing and hard to handle, it was fast in level flight, maneuverable, and served the Swedish air force for several years.

Previously, the Phonix Flugzeug-Werke firm had been contracted to produce the Hansa-Brandenburg D I fighter under license. When it became apparent by 1917 that the infamous *Star-strutter* could not be developed further, the company embarked on a new aircraft. The design eventually incorporated a fuselage similar to the D I and also sported wings of unequal span that ended in rounded wingtips and swept-back leading edges. It was also considerably more powerful than the earlier machine, being propelled by a 200-horsepower Hiero engine. One interesting innovation was locating the armament within the engine cowling. This enhanced streamlining but placed the guns beyond the pilot's reach if they jammed. The resulting craft was faster in level flight but somewhat unstable and slow-climbing. The Austrian government, hard-pressed on all fronts, nonetheless ordered the new craft into immediate production. In the spring of 1918

it entered service as the Phonix D I and was deployed with army and navy units.

The new machine was far from perfect, but it represented a dramatic improvement over the earlier *Star-strutter.* In capable hands the D I proved more than a match for the Italian Hanriots and SPADs. To enhance maneuverability, the new D II model introduced balanced elevators and other refinements, but the craft was judged too stable for violent acrobatics. On this basis, a few machines were fitted with cameras to pioneer single-seat high-speed reconnaissance work. Phonix then concocted the D III model shortly before hostilities concluded. It featured a more powerful engine and ailerons on all four wings, which greatly improved all-around maneuverability. The war ended before the D III could be deployed, but 158 examples of all versions were delivered.

After the war, Sweden expressed interest in obtaining several copies of the D III along with manufacturing rights. Seventeen were ultimately constructed, and they rendered useful service until 1933.

Type: Heavy Bomber

Dimensions: wingspan, 104 feet, 11 inches; length, 73 feet, 1 inch; height, 19 feet, 8 inches
Weights: empty, 38,195 pounds; gross, 65,885 pounds
Power plant: 4 × 1,500–horsepower Piaggio P.XII RC35 radial engines
Performance: maximum speed, 267 miles per hour; ceiling, 27,890 feet; range, 2,187 miles
Armament: 8 × 12.7mm machine guns; up to 7,716 pounds of bombs
Service dates: 1942–1943

The Piaggio P 108B was the only four-engine strategic bomber employed by Italian forces in World War II. It enjoyed performance comparable to early B-17s but was never produced in great quantity.

Italian aviation had demonstrated talent for strategic bombing, a fact clearly established during World War I. However, throughout the 1930s and until the beginning of World War II, the bulk of dictator Benito Mussolini's bombardment assets were tied up in short-ranged twin-engine aircraft. In 1939 designer Giovanni Casiraghi attempted a more modern solution when he conceived the Piaggio P 108B (*Bombardiere*). This was an ultramodern, all-metal, four-engine aircraft similar to the famous Boeing B-17, and it was constructed for identical purposes. The P 108B housed a crew of seven and could carry a good bomb load for respectable distances. It was also heavily armed, mounting no less than eight 12.7mm machine guns. Four weapons were placed at various fuselage points, but the remaining four were ingeniously mounted in two remote-controlled barbettes atop the outboard engines. Sighted and fired by gunners peering through transparent domes, this system anticipated by several years the system that would be utilized in Boeing B-29 *Superfortresses*. Despite its size, the big craft handled well in the air; it entered production in 1940. Nearly two years lapsed before the P 108B was available in squadron strength, and by that time Axis fortunes had waned considerably.

In service the P 108B proved rugged and dependable, especially when contrasted with Germany's ill-fated He 177 *Greif*. It conducted several nighttime raids against Gibraltar, being fitted with flame dampeners on the exhausts. The type also performed useful service in North Africa and Russia until the Italian surrender of 1943. Beforehand, Piaggio had also been working on a transport version of the craft, the P 108C, which featured a completely redesigned fuselage for seating 56 fully armed troops. Only 12 were built, and these were seized and used by the Luftwaffe. A total of 182 of all types were constructed.

Type: Fighter

Dimensions: wingspan, 32 feet, 9 inches; length, 20 feet, 3 inches; height, 9 feet, 2 inches
Weights: empty, 3,201 pounds; gross, 4,652 pounds
Power plant: 1 × 1,000–horsepower M-62 radial engine
Performance: maximum speed, 276 miles per hour; ceiling, 35,105 feet; range, 292 miles
Armament: 4 × 7.62mm machine guns; up to 441 pounds of bombs
Service dates: 1934–1943

The *Chaika* (Gull) was among the fastest and most maneuverable biplanes ever built. It performed active duty from Spain to Mongolia before taking heavy losses in World War II.

In 1934 the gifted Soviet designer Nikolai Polikarpov, recently released from the gulag, updated his successful I 5 fighter into an even more effective craft. The new I 15 shared some commonality with its predecessor, being constructed of wooden wings, steel tubing, and fabric covering. It differed, however, in possessing an inverted gull wing that melded into the fuselage near the roots. Despite a stubby appearance, the I 15 was rugged, relatively fast, and an excellent fighter. It entered production that year, and in 1936 large numbers were sent to assist Republican forces during the Spanish Civil War. There the *Chaika* proved demonstrably superior to the German Heinkel He 51, and it was a formidable opponent for the supremely agile Fiat CR 32 *Chirri*. By 1938 I 15s were also heavily engaged against Japanese forces in Mongolia, but they suffered at the hands of modern Nakajima Ki 27 monoplane fighters.

Russian authorities remained convinced that biplanes were still viable weapons, so they authorized Polikarpov to update his design again. In 1937 he responded with the I 15*ter*, later designated the I 153, which brought biplane performance on par with monoplane opponents. With a powerful engine and retractable landing gear, it climbed faster than many of its intended adversaries. After preliminary combat in Spain during 1938–1939, large numbers of I 153s arrived in Mongolia, where, after heavy losses to both sides, they finally mastered the nimble Japanese monoplanes. Consequently, the Soviets kept the I 153 in production long after it had become obsolete. In 1941 it represented a fair portion of Russian fighter strength and sustained great losses from German Messerschmitt Bf 109s. The rugged biplane then found a new lease on life as a ground-attack craft until being replaced by Ilyushin Il 2s in 1943. A total of 3,457 *Chaikas* had been built.

Type: Fighter

Dimensions: wingspan, 29 feet, 6 inches; length, 19 feet, 7 inches; height, 8 feet, 4 inches
Weights: empty, 2,976 pounds; gross, 3,781 pounds
Power plant: 1 × 775–horsepower Shvetsov M-52 radial engine
Performance: maximum speed, 242 miles per hour; ceiling, 16,405 feet; range, 497 miles
Armament: 4 × 7.62mm machine guns
Service dates: 1935–1943

The stubby I 16 heralded new concepts in fighter technology, becoming the first monoplane with retractable landing gear to enter squadron service. Obsolete by World War II, it gained further renown by pioneering ramming tactics.

The famous I 16 fighter evolved from attempts by Nikolai Polikarpov to wring greater performance from his already successful I 5 design. His engineers began tinkering with notions of a squat, powerful monoplane fighter, Russia's first. The resulting prototype was extremely advanced in concept, arguably superior to any fighter in existence. The I 16 was a low-wing, cantilevered monoplane with a metal frame, a wooden monocoque fuselage, and fabric-covered wings. More important, it was the first such Russian craft with fully retractable landing gear. The I 16 was extremely fast for its day, exhibiting a 60–75 mile-per-hour advantage over biplane fighters. It also possessed an excellent roll rate and was superbly capable of climbing and zooming. However, the stubby craft proved unforgiving and somewhat unstable along all three axes. Pilots had to carefully employ tactics emphasizing speed, not maneuverability, to survive.

I 16s were initially sent to Spain to assist Republican forces, who dubbed the little craft *Mosca* (Fly). It fought well enough but was never as highly regarded as the slower I 15 biplanes. I 16s were also fielded during the 1939 clash with Japan in Mongolia, rendering useful service against more nimble but slower adversaries. With international tensions on the rise, the Soviets decided to acquire large numbers of I 16s as quickly as possible. By the time production ceased in 1940, more than 7,000 had been produced, making it the most numerous fighter of the Red Air Force. In June 1941 German forces exacted a heavy toll from the obsolete I 16s, but their rugged construction was ideal for the desperate *taran* (ramming) attacks. Despite perils to both plane and pilot, Soviet fliers bravely adopted the new tactic, inflicting heavy damage on German aircraft. The I 16s were finally withdrawn from service in 1943.

Type: Light Bomber; Reconnaissance

Dimensions: wingspan, 50 feet, 10 inches; length, 34 feet, 7 inches; height, 11 feet, 9 inches
Weights: empty, 4,916 pounds; gross, 7,716 pounds
Power plant: 1 × 850–horsepower M-34N liquid-cooled in-line engine
Performance: maximum speed, 196 miles per hour; ceiling, 28,545 feet; range, 621 miles
Armament: 3 × 7.62mm machine guns; up to 882 pounds of bombs
Service dates: 1930–1943

The R 5 was a successful multipurpose Russian design of the 1930s and superior to similar machines in the West. Rugged and fast, it gained notoriety during the Spanish Civil War under the nickname *Natasha*.

The year 1927 was a banner one for Nikolai Polikarpov, for he introduced two exceptionally long-serving aircraft. The first was the famous U 2, destined to be the most numerous airplane of all time. The second was the R 5, conceived as a general-purpose plane/light bomber, the first of its kind for the Red Air Force. The R 5 was an unequal-wing biplane constructed mostly of wood and was fabric-covered. It had single-bay wings fastened by "N" struts canting outward toward the wingtips. The fuselage was rather streamlined and seated a crew of two in closely spaced tandem cockpits. The craft could be fitted with either wheels or skis, and test flights revealed the R 5 to be fast and strong. It entered service in 1930; by the time production halted in 1938,

more than 6,000 R 5s had been produced. They were the most numerous aircraft of their class in the world.

In service the R 5 was possibly the best light bomber of its day. During a 1930 international airplane meet in Teheran, Persia, it easily bested such notables as the Fokker CV and Westland *Wapiti* in a number of categories. During this period the craft also did useful work pioneering the art of in-flight refueling. In September 1930 three R 5s flew continuously for 61 hours, landing without incident after covering 6,526 miles. In 1938 the craft was dispatched in small numbers to fight in the Spanish Civil War on behalf of Republican forces. It did useful ground-attack work, earning the affectionate nickname *Natasha*. R 5s subsequently formed the bulk of Soviet light attack regiments up through the German invasion of 1941. Many were destroyed in that conflict, but others simply soldiered on until being replaced by Ilyushin Il 2s in 1943.

Type: Trainer; Light Bomber; Reconnaissance; Liaison

Dimensions: wingspan, 37 feet, 4 inches; length, 26 feet, 7 inches; height, 9 feet, 10 inches
Weights: empty, 1,350 pounds; gross, 2,167 pounds
Power plant: 1 × 110–horsepower Shvetsov M-11 radial engine
Performance: maximum speed, 93 miles per hour; ceiling, 10,827 feet; range, 342 miles
Armament: none
Service dates: 1928–

The amazingly versatile U 2 was built in greater numbers than any other aircraft. It proved equally useful as a trainer or transport, but it won a measure of immortality as a night bomber.

In 1927 the Soviet government expressed need for a new general-purpose biplane. It was intended as their first mass-produced trainer, so the new machine had to be easy to fly, simple to maintain, and able to operate under very primitive conditions. The Polikarpov design bureau was tasked with developing such a craft, but initial efforts proved halting. The first prototype featured rectangular, austere lines, wings, and tail surfaces. When first test-flown, it failed to become airborne. Polikarpov subsequently revamped the design with rounder wingtips and single-bay configuration. The resulting U 2 was completely successful, one of the most versatile aircraft ever flown. It entered production in 1928, and by 1941 an estimated 13,000 were flying. They fulfilled a staggering variety of roles, including agricultural, civilian, ambulance, transportation, glider tug,

and parachute training duties. In 1938 a U 2 made history by locating five Soviet scientists marooned on a floating iceberg for nine months. It seemed there was little that the easy-handling biplane could not do.

The onset of World War II brought additional luster to Polikarpov's masterpiece. Armed with bombs and small arms, they distinguished themselves as nighttime light bombers, or intruders. Flying low in the dark, the noisy U 2s dropped bombs on German soldiers to deny them sleep. Given their slow speed and great maneuverability, U 2s were also extremely hard to shoot down. When Nikolai Polikarpov died in 1943, Stalin ordered the airplane rechristened the Po 2 in his honor. By war's end, entire regiments of Po 2 night squadrons existed, many flown exclusively by women. The little plane continued in production up until 1952, after 40,000 had been constructed. Thousands of others were exported to former Soviet satellite countries and are still in use today.

Potez 63

Type: Fighter; Light Bomber; Reconnaissance

Dimensions: wingspan, 52 feet, 6 inches; length, 35 feet, 10 inches; height, 11 feet, 9 inches
Power plant: 2 × 700–horsepower Gnome-Rhone 14M radial engines
Performance: maximum speed, 276 miles per hour; ceiling, 27,890 feet; range, 932 miles
Armament: 5 × 7.5mm machine guns; 1,323 pounds of bombs
Service dates: 1938–1942

The Potez 63 represented a large multirole family of combat aircraft. Marginally obsolete by 1940, they suffered heavy losses and were later exported to Romania.

In 1934 the French Air Ministry issued specifications for a new two-seat fighter capable of night operations, bombardment, and reconnaissance. A special three-seat version was also desired as a "command fighter" to direct single-seat craft into action. In 1936 Louis Coroller unveiled the Potez 63 prototype to fulfill all these tasks. This was a large, all-metal airplane, one of the first "strategic" fighters then in vogue. Like its German counterpart, the Messerschmitt Bf 110, it possessed twin engines, twin rudders, and a large greenhouse canopy. After teething problems were resolved, the Potez 630 and slightly modified Potez 631s entered service in 1938. They proved to be underpowered and were retained only as trainers. But the company went on to develop the Potez 633 ground-attack version, along with the Potez 63.11 reconnaissance version. The latter model featured an extensively redesigned

nose with glazed windows and a shorter canopy moved aft along the fuselage. With 1,360 machines built in various versions, the Potez 63 series was the most numerous French design of World War II.

A Potez 63 has the distinction of being the first Allied aircraft lost in the West, when one was downed on September 8, 1939. Once the Battle of France commenced in May 1940, the Potez aircraft equipped several *groupes de chasse* (fighter groups) in northern France and were heavily engaged. Others saw front-line service with numerous reconnaissance outfits.

Lacking adequate fighter escort and committed to low-altitude attacks, both types suffered heavy losses. In fact, several Potez 631s were sometimes shot down by British aircraft who mistook them for Bf 110s. By the time of France's capitulation, more than 400 machines had been destroyed. Many surviving craft were exported to Romania in time to be used against the Soviet Union in 1941. Small handfuls of Potez 63.11s were also retained by Vichy forces in North Africa, where they flew briefly against Allied forces.

Type: Fighter

Dimensions: wingspan, 35 feet, 2 inches; length, 24 feet, 9 inches; height, 9 feet, 4 inches
Weights: empty, 2,529 pounds; gross, 3,968 pounds
Power plant: 1 × 645–horsepower Bristol Mercury VIS radial engine
Performance: maximum speed, 242 miles per hour; ceiling, 26,250 feet; range, 435 miles
Armament: 2 × 7.92mm machine guns
Service dates: 1935–1939

When it first appeared in 1935, the *Jedenastka* was arguably among the world's finest fighter planes. Four years later this distinctive craft was flown with great skill and courage in the defense of Poland.

For many years the fledgling *Lotnictowo Wojskowe* (Polish air force) groped with imported and usually mediocre aircraft. However, in 1929 Zygmunt Pulawski, a brilliant young designer working at the National Aircraft Factory (PZL), conceived a unique, parasol-winged fighter design, the P 1. This was followed two years later by the P 7, which was high-powered, constructed entirely of metal, and covered by stressed skin. Its introduction pushed Poland to the forefront of aviation technology at a time when most Western powers were still designing fabric-covered biplanes. In 1931 Pulawski, before his death in a plane crash, began designing an improved version of the P 7, which became known as the P 11. It enjoyed a more powerful engine and numerous aeronautical refinements that rendered it an even better airplane than the P 7. The P 11, affectionately known by pilots as the *Jedenastka* (Eleventh) was ruggedly built, fast for its day, and outstandingly maneuverable. It was so impressive that Romania purchased 50 machines outright and applied for a license to construct them. However, within a few years these world-famous gull-wing wonders were overtaken by low-wing monoplane aircraft—most notably Germany's Messerschmitt Bf 109—and rendered obsolete.

By the advent of World War II in September 1939, the PZL P 11s constituted the bulk of Poland's first line of defense. Polish pilots, seemingly helpless in the face of modern opposition, proved fanatically brave in defending their homeland. In fact, the first German aircraft shot down in World War II fell to the guns of a P 11 on September 1, 1939. Although ultimately overrun, these brave aviators managed to claw down 124 German aircraft with a loss of 114 P 11s. Of the 258 *Jedenastkas* constructed, one survives in Warsaw and is displayed as a cherished symbol of national resistance.

Type: Light Bomber; Reconnaissance

Dimensions: wingspan, 45 feet, 9 inches; length, 31 feet, 9 inches; height, 10 feet, 10 inches
Weights: empty, 4,251 pounds; gross, 7,771 pounds
Power plant: 1 × 680–horsepower Bristol Pegasus VIII radial engine
Performance: maximum speed, 199 miles per hour; ceiling, 23,950 feet; range, 783 miles
Armament: 3 × 7.7mm machine guns; up to 1,543 pounds of bombs
Service dates: 1937–1939

The *Karas* was another formerly advanced Polish machine that had fallen behind technologically by 1939. Flown with fanatical bravery, they inflicted heavy losses upon German armored formations.

In 1931 the Polish government sought to acquire a new light bomber based upon the unsuccessful PZL P 13 civilian transport. Several prototypes were then constructed until the cowling was lowered somewhat to improve the pilot's forward vision. This change gave the new P 23 *Karas* (Carp) its decidedly humped appearance. It was an all-metal machine with fixed, spatted landing gear and a spacious glazed canopy. The P 23 also mounted a bombardier/tailgunner's ventral gondola just aft of the main wing. At the time it debuted, the *Karas* possessed radically modern features such as stressed skin made from sandwiched alloy/balsa wood. This innovation conferred great strength and light weight to the machine. Initial production models were powered by a 590-horsepower Bristol Pegasus radial engine, but their performance proved limited and they served as trainers. Subsequent models featured more powerful engines and greater payload, entering frontline service in 1937. By 1939 P 23s equipped 12 bombing and reconnaissance squadrons in the Polish air force. Bulgaria also expressed interest in the P 23, purchasing 12 and ordering an additional 42 in 1937. Nonetheless, by the eve of World War II the *Karas* had become outdated as light bombers and helpless in the face of determined fighter opposition.

The initial German blitzkrieg of September 1, 1939, failed to destroy many P 23s on the ground, and they struck back furiously at oncoming armored columns. Several Panzer forces lost up to 30 percent of their equipment in these raids, although many P 23s were claimed by ground fire and enemy fighters. Toward the end of the month-long campaign, a handful of surviving *Karas* fought their way to neutral Romania. Within two years these machines were reconditioned and flown against the Soviet Union. A total of 253 were built.

Type: Medium Bomber

Dimensions: wingspan, 58 feet, 8 inches; length, 42 feet, 4 inches; height, 16 feet, 8 inches
Weights: empty, 9,293 pounds; gross, 19,577 pounds
Power plant: 2 × 925–horsepower Bristol Pegasus radial engines
Performance: maximum speed, 273 miles per hour; ceiling, 19,685 feet; range, 1,616 miles
Armament: 3 × 7.7mm machine guns; up to 5,688 pounds of bombs
Service dates: 1938–1939

The *Los* (Elk) was a world-class attack bomber and Poland's most formidable air weapon of World War II. It arrived in only limited quantities but nonetheless performed heroic work throughout a hopelessly lopsided campaign.

The amazing P 37 *Los* had its origins in the experimental P 30 civilian transport of 1930, which failed to attract a buyer. That year a design team under Jerzy Dabrowksi conceived a modern bomber version of the same craft and proffered it to the government in 1934. A prototype was then authorized, first flying in 1936. The P 37 marked a pinnacle in medium bomber development for, in terms of design and performance, it was years ahead of contemporary machines. This was a sleek, all-metal, low-wing monoplane employing stressed skin throughout. Although relatively low-powered, its broad-chord wings permitted amazing lifting abilities, and it could hoist more than 5,000 pounds of bombs aloft—the equivalent of half its own empty weight! No medium bomber in the world—and few heavy bombers for that matter—could approach such performance. The *Los* entered production in 1937, and the first units became operational the following year. The government originally ordered 150 machines, but resistance from the Polish High Command, which viewed medium bombers as expensive and unnecessary, managed to reduce procurement by a third. Meanwhile, other countries expressed great interest in the P 37, with Bulgaria, Turkey, Romania, and Yugoslavia placing sizable orders. A total of 103 machines were built.

By the advent of World War II in September 1939, the Polish air force could muster only 36 fully equipped P 37s. Several score sat available in waiting but lacked bombsights and other essential equipment. Nonetheless, the *Los* roared into action, inflicting considerable damage upon advancing German columns. When the outcome of the fight became helpless, around 40 surviving machines fled to neutral Romania and were absorbed into its air force. Within two years these fugitives were reconditioned and flown with good effect against the Soviet Union.

Type: Fighter

Dimensions: wingspan, 36 feet, 1 inch; length, 27 feet, 5 inches; height, 10 feet, 2 inches
Weights: empty, 5,265 pounds; gross, 6,989 pounds
Power plant: 1 × Daimler-Benz DB 601A liquid-cooled in-line engine
Performance: maximum speed, 339 miles per hour; ceiling, 39,205 feet; range, 646 miles
Armament: 2 × 7.7mm machine guns; 2 × 12.7mm machine guns
Service dates: 1939–1945

The *Falcos* were a capable series of Italian fighters, but available in only limited numbers. They enjoyed greater success as export machines, being operated by Sweden, Hungary, and Germany.

In 1938 the new Reggiane design office rolled out its first Re 2000 *Falco* (Falcon), which had been designed by Roberto Longhi. Superficially resembling the U.S. Seversky P 35 fighter of the same period, it was stubby and possessed large, elliptical wings. However, the Italian design offered clear improvements, being more streamlined and having retractable undercarriage that recessed into wing wells. Flight tests also revealed that the Re 2000 was an outstanding dogfighter and superior to the Bf 109 in a contest of slow turns. However, like all Italian fighters of the late 1930s, being driven by a low-power radial engine meant that it was relatively slow. This, and the fact that fuel was carried in unarmored tanks near the wing roots, caused the Regia Aeronautica (Italian air force) to reject the design. However, Sweden and Hungary expressed interest,

and the Re 2000 was acquired by both air forces in considerable numbers. The Regia Marina (Italian navy) also acquired 12 for possible catapult work aboard Italian battleships.

After Italy entered World War II in June 1940, Reggiane had greater access to advanced German engine technology. Longhi wasted no time refitting the Re 2000 with a powerful Daimler-Benz 601A in-line engine—quite a feat considering the rotund fuselage—and created the Re 2001 *Falco II*. As predicted, this version possessed superior performance to the original design. It was deployed with some success over Malta in 1941, but a shortage of German engines limited its production to only 237 machines. Final development of the series culminated in the Re 2005 *Sagittario* (Archer) when the DB 605A engine was fitted to a totally redesigned, slender fuselage. This was quite possibly the greatest Italian fighter of the war, and the Germans co-opted all 48 machines for their own use. These aircraft actively flew in the defense of Berlin until 1945.

Type: Reconnaissance

Dimensions: wingspan, 35 feet; length, 29 feet, 6 inches; height, 10 feet, 2 inches
Weights: empty, 1,274 pounds; gross, 1,600 pounds
Power plant: 1 × 70–horsepower Renault liquid-cooled in-line engine
Performance: maximum speed, 70 miles per hour; ceiling, 10,000 feet; range, 200 miles
Armament: up to 1 × .303–inch machine gun; 100 pounds of bombs
Service dates: 1912–1918

The slow, anachronistic BE 2s were among the first British aircraft dispatched to France in World War I. Despite staggering losses, bureaucratic inertia kept them in frontline service until the end of that conflict.

The BE 2a was designed and constructed in 1912 by Geoffrey de Havilland and was Britain's first purely military aircraft. It was a two-bay biplane constructed entirely of wood and fabric, powered by an 80-horsepower engine. Despite its obvious frailty, the BE 2a possessed good performance for its day, was inherently stable, and was pleasant to fly. It therefore entered into production and, by the advent of World War I in August 1914, equipped three reconnaissance squadrons. BE 2s were the first British airplanes dispatched to France during the war, and in August 1914 they conducted the first British reconnaissance missions.

The pace of war quickly transformed the stately BE 2s into relics, a fact painfully underscored when the machine gun–totting Fokker *Eindekker* debuted in 1915. The slow-flying BE 2s, unarmed and incapable of evasive maneuvers, were shot down in droves. The Royal Aircraft Factory was cognizant of these deficiencies and tried numerous modifications to improve performance, but to no avail. For many months in a service career that should have terminated speedily, the BE 2 remained the staple of "Fokker fodder."

In light of the BE 2's demonstrated obsolescence, it is difficult to account for why it was kept in frontline service for so long. The British government was certainly culpable on this point. In 1916 the most numerous version, the BE 2e, was introduced with a stronger engine and better armament, but the results were the same. The aging craft was finally transferred from the front in mid-1917 and relegated to training duties. It is regrettable that this docile aircraft was responsible for more Royal Air Corps casualties than any other type. A total of 3,535 of all models were built

Type: Fighter; Light Bomber

Dimensions: wingspan, 47 feet, 9 inches; length, 32 feet, 3 inches; height, 12 feet, 7 inches
Weights: empty, 1,993 pounds; gross, 2,970 pounds
Power plant: 1 × 120–horsepower Beardmore liquid-cooled in-line engine
Performance: maximum speed, 80 miles per hour; ceiling, 9,000 feet; range, 250 miles
Armament: 2 × .303–inch machine guns; up to 350 pounds of bombs
Service dates: 1916–1918

The venerable "Fee" was one of several capable pushers fielded by England during the World War I. It counted among many victims Max Immelmann, the noted German ace.

The FE 2 (Fighter Experimental) evolved from a series of pusher aircraft constructed at Farnborough in 1912. It was among the earliest warplanes designed in Great Britain, first flying there in 1913. The FE 2 consisted of a two-seat plywood and fabric-covered nacelle that also housed an engine. This unit sat suspended on struts between two wings of equal length, while four wooden booms extended rearward to a rudder and high-mounted tailplane. The forward nacelle seat contained a forward-firing machine gun and a second, telescopic-mounted weapon firing rearward over the top wing. To operate this weapon, the gunner stood up inside the cockpit while the aircraft was in flight. For all its relative crudeness, the FE 2 was a sound, good-handling machine, and a fine fighter for its day.

The first FE 2s did not reach the front until December 1915, but their impact was immediate. In concert with the de Havilland DH 2, the Fees outclassed the rampaging Fokker *Eindekkers* and helped eradicate them. On June 18, 1916, an FE 2 operated by No. 25 Squadron shot down and killed the famous ace Max Immelmann. Other German pilots like Karl Schaefer and Manfred von Richthofen were also injured while combating the deceptively doughty craft. The appearance of Albatros and Halberstadt D II fighters that fall spelled the end of the FE 2's career. However, being stable in flight and solidly built, they next took on responsibilities as night bombers. On April 5, 1917, the FE 2's initial raid was against von Richthofen's own aerodrome at Donai. The remaining craft were subsequently employed as trainers and in home defense units. FE 2s continued serving until the Armistice of 1918. An estimated 1,989 were constructed.

Type: Reconnaissance

Dimensions: wingspan, 42 feet, 7 inches; length, 32 feet, 7 inches; height, 11 feet, 4 inches
Weights: empty, 1,803 pounds; gross, 2,869 pounds
Power plant: 1 × 150–horsepower RAF 4a liquid-cooled in-line engine
Performance: maximum speed, 103 miles per hour; ceiling, 13,500 feet; range, 400 miles
Armament: 2 × .303–inch machine guns; up to 250 pounds of bombs
Service dates: 1917–1918

The lumbering "Harry Tate" was built in greater numbers than any other British reconnaissance craft of World War I. Intended as a replacement for the unpopular BE 2, it was equally inadequate yet remained in production through the end of hostilities.

By the spring of 1916, the heavy loss of BE 2 aircraft forced the Royal Air Corps to request better machines capable of defending themselves. The Royal Aircraft Factory at Farnborough responded with the RE 8, which in many respects was simply a scaled-up BE 2. It too was a hulking, two-bay biplane with staggered wings of unequal length. Construction was plywood and fabric throughout, save for the metal cowling, and the upward-sloping rear fuselage gave it a decidedly "broken-back" appearance. It also had a small tail that during service life had to be enlarged to prevent spinning. But the RE 8 was well-armed by contemporary standards, possessing a synchronized Vickers machine gun for the pilot and a ring-mounted Lewis for the gunner. Like

the BE 2, the RE 8 was predictable and easy to fly, but it was inherently too stable for defensive maneuvers. Nonetheless, more than 4,077 were constructed over the next two years, with the first units reaching the Western Front in 1917.

Predictably, the RE 8s fended no better in combat than their earlier stablemates. The slow, stately craft simply lacked the agility to defend themselves against the fast, maneuverable German scouts, and they sustained heavy losses. With no suitable successor on the horizon, the RE 8s soldiered on, providing useful work in reconnaissance, artillery-spotting, and some occasional ground-attack work. Flight crews eventually admired its reliable qualities and nicknamed it "Harry Tate" after a noted vaudeville comedian. Despite their glaring shortcomings, RE 8s continued to provide valuable service through the end of the war. But it is unconscionable that the British Air Ministry allowed such a derelict to serve as long as it did—and at such great cost.

Type: Fighter

Dimensions: wingspan, 26 feet, 7 inches; length, 20 feet, 11 inches; height, 9 feet, 6 inches
Weights: empty, 1,531 pounds; gross, 2,048 pounds
Power plant: 1 × 200–horsepower Hispano-Suiza liquid-cooled radial engine
Performance: maximum speed, 126 miles per hour; ceiling, 17,500 feet; range, 250 miles
Armament: 2 × .303–inch machine guns; up to 100 pounds of bombs
Service dates: 1917–1918

The SE 5a formed half of a famous British fighter duo from World War I. Although not as maneuverable as a Sopwith *Camel*, it was faster, more stable, and the preferred choice of several leading aces.

In 1916 the Royal Aircraft Factory began designing a new fighter around the 150-horsepower Hispano-Suiza engine. It was a standard two-bay biplane with rather angular features, for the wings, tail surfaces, and radiator were square. But the prototype SE 5 (Scout Experimental) successfully flew on November 16 with impressive results. It was fast, easily handled, and could dive with complete safety. Moreover, consistent with all Royal Aircraft Factory products, great emphasis had been placed on overall stability. Hence, it was an excellent gunnery platform, well-armed with a nose-mounted Vickers machine gun and a Lewis weapon firing over the top wing.

The SE 5 entered production in the spring of 1917, flew its first operational sorties that April, and demonstrated mastery over the German Albatros D Vs, Pfalz D IIIs, and Fokker Dr Is opposing them. It could also hold its own against the superb Fokker D VII of 1918. The SE 5 was decidedly faster and could outclimb and outdive all its adversaries with ease. These features, combined with stable flying, made it the favored mount of leading aces like Edward Mannock, Albert Ball, and William Bishop. Possessing an in-line engine, it was not as maneuverable as the famous Sopwith *Camel*, but for the same reason it afforded novice pilots an easier time. By the summer of 1917 a stronger version, the SE 5a, appeared with the geared 200-horsepower French-manufactured Hispano-Suiza engine. This power plant was egregiously defective at first, and a series of similar British engines were installed in its place. By the 1918 Armistice 5,205 SE 5as had been delivered while another 50 were manufactured in the United States by Eberhardt. Most were retired immediately after the war.

Type: Reconnaissance

Dimensions: wingspan, 41 feet, 6 inches; length, 27 feet, 7 inches; height, 10 feet, 8 inches
Weights: empty, 2,376 pounds; gross, 3,366 pounds
Power plant: 1 × 260–horsepower Mercedes D IVa liquid-cooled in-line engine
Performance: maximum speed, 106 miles per hour; ceiling, 21,000 feet; range, 330 miles
Armament: 2 × 7.92mm machine guns
Service dates: 1917–1918

The excellent Rumplers were a common sight in the skies of Europe throughout World War I. They were among the highest-flying reconnaissance machines to serve during that conflict.

Since 1915 the Rumpler Flugzeugwerke had provided the German army with numerous two-seat aircraft, both armed and unarmed. The firm's C I was a masterpiece of aeronautical engineering that debuted in 1915 and soldiered on at the front lines three years later. Toward the end of the war Dr. Edmund Rumpler decided to update his long-lived design with one better suited for long-range reconnaissance work. The new version, the C IV, was a departure from earlier conceptions. A two-bay biplane, it possessed slightly swept, highly efficient wings constructed of wood and fabric. The fuselage was also highly streamlined and mounted a pointed spinner on the propeller hub. The tail surfaces had also been revised and lost the triangular shape that was a Rumpler trademark. But more important, this craft was fitted with an excellent Mercedes D IVa engine, which gave it plenty of power at all altitudes.

The Rumpler C IV appeared at the front in February 1917 and was strikingly successful. It was one of the few aircraft that could routinely reach altitudes of 20,000 feet at speeds of 100 miles per hour. Consequently, Rumplers were considered among the most difficult German aircraft to shoot down. They were also ruggedly constructed and could absorb great damage. That fall work on an even better version was commenced, and the C VII emerged that winter. Externally, it was almost indistinguishable from the C IV but was powered by a high-compression Maybach Mb IV engine. This plane functioned as a high-altitude long-range reconnaissance platform. An even more highly specialized form, the *Rubild* (Rumpler photographic) also materialized. It was a stripped-down C VII fitted with heaters and oxygen equipment for the crew. Thus rendered, it easily reached unprecedented altitudes of 24,000 feet, where no Allied fighters could follow. The exemplary Rumpler machines continued serving with distinction until the war's end.

Type: Fighter; Light Bomber

Dimensions: wingspan, 36 feet, 1 inch; length, 33 feet, 2 inches; height, 12 feet, 3 inches
Weights: empty, 10,141 pounds; gross, 17,637 pounds
Power plant: 1 × 5,000–pound thrust de Havilland Ghost turbojet engine
Performance: maximum speed, 659 miles per hour; ceiling, 45,000 feet; range, 1,677 miles
Armament: 4 × 20mm cannons; up to 24 × 76mm rockets
Service dates: 1951–1976

The odd-looking J 29 set an important precedent by establishing Sweden at the forefront of military aviation. It was the first European jet with swept wings and enjoyed a lengthy service life.

Even before World War II had ended, the Swedish government resolved to enforce its long-standing policy of neutrality by acquiring modern warplanes. In 1945 Project 1001 was initiated by Saab to provide Sweden with its first jet fighter. The original design intended to mount straight wings and utilize the relatively weak de Havilland *Goblin* turbojet. However, awareness of German swept-wing technology, coupled with invention of the more powerful *Ghost* engine, caused fundamental revisions in the program. The design was modified, providing the wing with 25 degrees of sweep, and the fuselage was made more portly to accommodate the new engine. The resulting J 29 prototype first flew in September 1948 with excellent results. It was fast, ruggedly built in the tradition of Saab products, and highly maneuverable.

When wing-mounted air brakes were found to cause excessive flutter, they were subsequently relocated to the fuselage. The tricycle landing gear were also unique in that they inclined inward before retracting inside the fuselage. Three more years lapsed before the J 29 entered production and became operational as Europe's first swept-wing jet fighter. Pilots took an immediate liking to the tubby craft, giving it the appropriate nickname *Tunnan* (Barrel).

A total of 661 J 29s were built until 1958 in six versions, all with successively better performance and endurance. The definitive model was the J 29F, constructed for ground-attack purposes and employing the effective Bofors rocket clusters. It also sported an afterburner and a sawtooth leading edge for better performance in the transonic range. The beloved *Tunnans* were slowly phased out after 1958, but several examples remained on active duty until 1973. In 1961 Austria obtained 30 J 29Fs and retained them in frontline service until 1993.

Type: Fighter

Dimensions: wingspan, 30 feet, 10 inches; length, 50 feet, 4 inches; height, 12 feet, 9 inches
Weights: empty, 18,188 pounds; gross, 25,132 pounds
Power plant: 1 × 12,790–pound thrust Volvo RM6C turbojet engine
Performance: maximum speed, 1,321 miles per hour; ceiling, 49,200 feet; range, 350 miles
Armament: 1 × 30mm cannon; up to 6,393 pounds of air-to-air missiles
Service dates: 1960–1999

The *Draken*, distinct with its double-delta configuration, was one of the world's most advanced aircraft. It confirmed Sweden's reputation for constructing high-performance aircraft with originality and flair.

In 1949 the *Flygvapen* (Swedish air force) issued stringent specifications for a new supersonic aircraft to replace the J 29 *Tunnan*. This evolved at a time when the only craft capable of such speeds was Bell's famous experimental X-1. Nonetheless, the new machine had to be fast and display unprecedented rates of climb. It was also required to possess good STOL (short takeoff and landing) capabilities for operating off of highways and unprepared strips during dispersal. That year a Saab design teamed under Erik Bratt set about creating a minor aviation masterpiece when they opted to employ a unique double-delta. Such an arrangement promised great strength and internal volume with very little frontal area. The new machine could thus be crammed with fuel and avionics yet be difficult to ascertain head-on. It also promised excellent handling at fast as well as slow speeds. Several small-scale models and mock-ups followed before the first J 35 flew in October 1955. The aircraft was an outstanding success, although its engine failed to produce the Mach 2 speeds anticipated. It nonetheless entered production that year as the *Draken* (Dragon), reaching operational status in 1960. Production amounted to 660 machines.

Over time the *Draken* passed through successive variants that gradually improved its performance. Conceived as a bomber interceptor, the new J 35F mounted a pulse doppler radar, automatic fire-control systems, and advanced Hughes *Falcon* air-to-air missiles. This model could also fly at speeds in excess of Mach 2, exhibiting performance equal to the English Electric *Lightning* on only one engine. *Drakens* served Sweden well over four decades and were retired only in 1999. As they aged, they also became available for export, with Denmark and Finland obtaining several copies. However, the biggest user was Austria, which purchased 24 machines that are still in service.

Type: Fighter; Light Bomber; Reconnaissance; Trainer

Dimensions: wingspan, 34 feet, 9 inches; length, 53 feet, 9 inches; height, 19 feet, 4 inches
Weights: empty, 33,069 pounds; gross, 45,194 pounds
Power plant: 1 × 28,100–pound thrust Volvo RM8B turbofan engine
Performance: maximum speed, 1,321 miles per hour; ceiling, 60,040 feet; range, 621 miles
Armament: 1 × 30mm cannon; up to 13,000 pounds of missiles, rockets, or bombs
Service dates: 1971–

The racy _Viggen_ (Thunderbolt) was history's first canard fighter and a formidable interceptor. Until recently it formed the bulk of Swedish air strength, operating from hidden roadways deep in the woods.

In the 1960s Sweden began considering a replacement for its aging Saab J 32 _Lansens_. It was determined to develop a totally integrated approach to aerial defense called System 37, whereby a single airframe could be slightly modified to perform fighter, bomber, reconnaissance, and training functions economically. At length Saab took one of its usual departures from conventional wisdom by designing the J 37 _Viggen_ in 1967. It was a sophisticated design for the time by incorporating small delta canards, equipped with flaps, just behind the cockpit. This complemented the larger, conventional delta wing perfectly, affording greater lift and maneuverability at lower speeds than plain deltas enjoyed. More important, canards allowed the _Viggen_ to take off in relatively short distances. This was essential given the

wartime strategy of dispersing air assets into the woods and taxiing off roadways. To shorten landing distances even further, J 37s are equipped with built-in thrust reversers that automatically engage upon touchdown. This is an added safety feature for, given Sweden's nominally icy conditions, applying airplane brakes in winter can be a chancy proposition at best. These machines became operational in 1971.

The first _Viggens_ were optimized for ground attack, but subsequent variants successfully fulfilled interceptor, reconnaissance, and training missions. All look very similar at first glance, but the SK 37 trainer has a staggered second canopy behind the student cockpit. The final version, the JA 37, arrived in 1977 as a dedicated fighter intent on replacing the redoubtable J 35 _Drakens_. These are fitted with advanced multimode look down/shoot down radar and an uprated RM8B engine. The total production of all _Viggens_ is 330; they will remain in service until replaced by superlative JAS 39 _Gripens_ within a few years.

Type: Fighter; Light Bomber; Reconnaissance

Dimensions: wingspan, 26 feet, 3 inches; length, 46 feet, 3 inches; height, 15 feet, 5 inches
Weights: empty, 14,599 pounds; gross, 27,498 pounds
Power plant: 1 × 18,100–pound thrust Volvo RM12 turbofan engine
Performance: maximum speed, 1,321 miles per hour; ceiling, classified; range, 497 miles
Armament: 1 × 27mm cannon; up to 14,330 pounds of rockets, missiles, or bombs
Service dates: 1997–

The futuristic *Gripen* (Griffon) is the third generation of advanced Saab fighters. Its lightweight, high-performance profile, coupled with digital avionics, make it one of the world's most sophisticated warplanes.

By 1980 the JA 37 *Viggen* was showing its age, so the Swedish government initiated studies for a successor. At length stringent performance and fiscal conditions were established, which more or less ensured that the new machine would be lighter and smaller than the *Viggen* but even more capable. Furthermore, it was expected to simultaneously fulfill fighter, bomber, and reconnaissance missions currently performed by three versions of the former craft. This led to the new designation JAS (*Jakt*, *Attack*, and *Sparing*). Facing such requirements, Saab resurrected its previous canard-delta planform, although with some important changes. The new JAS 39 *Gripen* is a single-engine design with the wing moved from low- to midbody position. The small fixed canards were replaced with completely all-moving ones above the engine inlets. The new machine is constructed almost entirely of composite materials for lighter weight and greater strength. As before, the JAS 39 is designed with a fast sink rate for hard, abbreviated landings; in the absence of reverse thrusters, the canards point downward to act as air brakes. To ensure quick stops, the main wing is also fitted with a variety of flaps and elevons for additional drag. But the biggest changes are in the avionics. The JAS 39 is inherently unstable for greater maneuverability and utilizes fly-by-wire technology. Its onboard computers also allow the craft to perform any of three mission profiles by simply changing the software.

The first JAS 39 prototype flew in 1988 and demonstrated excellent, cost-effective qualities but was lost to a programming error. A second prototype also crashed in a stall, but most problems have since been rectified. The first *Gripens* became operational in 1997 and are slated to replace the *Viggen* within a decade. They are among the most advanced fighters ever built.

Type: Reconnaissance

Dimensions: wingspan, 38 feet, 8 inches; length, 27 feet, 10 inches; height, 9 feet, 6 inches
Weights: empty, 1,354 pounds; gross, 2,954 pounds
Power plant: 1 × 260–horsepower Salmson Canton-Unne liquid-cooled radial engine
Performance: maximum speed, 115 miles per hour; ceiling, 20,505 feet; range, 300 miles
Armament: 3 × 7.7mm machine guns
Service dates: 1918–1920

This sturdy machine was one of the best French reconnaissance aircraft of World War I. It was a fine, if unexpected, achievement, considering how its designer was previously known for manufacturing engines.

In 1909 French industrialist Emile Salmson established the Societe des Moteurs Salmson firm for the express purpose of manufacturing water-cooled radial engines for aircraft. In the period prior to World War I, his products gained a reputation for reliability, which was further enhanced during the war years. In 1916 Salmson tried designing aircraft to go along with his engines. The first attempt, the Salmson SM 1, was an awkward-looking craft with propellers driven by chains—and a total failure. The following year he had better luck by completing the prototype Type 2, which utilized a more conventional approach. The new machine was a standard biplane with two-bay, unstaggered wings of equal length. The fuselage was circular in cross-section, made of fabric-covered wood, and mounted a heavily louvered metal cowling. A crew of two sat in separate cockpits, although at such distance that communication was difficult. Nonetheless, French authorities were impressed, and the airplane went into production as the Salmson 2A2 in the fall of 1917.

In service the Salmson was not particularly fast but proved robust and mechanically reliable. It was well adapted for photo reconnaissance and ar-tillery-spotting, being sufficiently armed to defend itself. A total of 3,200 were constructed and outfitted 24 French squadrons during final phases of the war. Of this total, 705 2A2s were also purchased by the United States for the American Expeditionary Force. These machines were likewise extensively employed and won the admiration of their new owners. In one instance, a 2A2 flown by Lieutenant W. P. Irwin of the 1st Aero Squadron claimed eight attacking German fighters with his front gun! The Salmson was phased out shortly after the war, although it was subsequently exported to Japan. Others were refitted with enclosed rear cabins and flown as passenger ships by early European airlines.

Type: Medium Bomber; Torpedo-Bomber; Reconnaissance

Dimensions: wingspan, 69 feet, 6 inches; length, 51 feet, 10 inches; height, 14 feet, 1 inch
Weights: empty, 14,991 pounds; gross, 23,104 pounds
Power plant: 3 × 780–horsepower Alfa-Romeo 126 RC34 radial engines
Performance: maximum speed, 267 miles per hour; ceiling, 21,325 feet; range, 1,180 miles
Armament: 3 × 12.7mm machine guns; 2,755 pounds of bombs or torpedoes
Service dates: 1936–1952

The famous *Sparviero* (Sparrow) was the most capable Italian warplane of World War II. It gave excellent service as a bomber, torpedo plane, and reconnaissance craft.

The SM 79 was originally designed by Alessandro Marchetti as a high-speed, eight-passenger transport craft. It was a very streamlined, trimotor machine with retractable landing gear and constructed of steel tubing, wood, and fabric covering. It first flew in 1934 and established several international speed and distance records. Eventually the Regia Aeronautica (Italian air force) expressed interest in it as a potential bomber, and a prototype emerged in 1935. The military *Sparviero* was outwardly similar to the transport save for a bombardment gondola under the fuselage and a somewhat "humped" top profile to accommodate two gun turrets. Consequently, crew members nicknamed it *Il Gobbo* (The Hunchback) and several were deployed to fight in the Spanish Civil War. The SM 79 quickly established itself as a fast, rugged aircraft that handled extremely well under combat conditions. Its reputation induced Yugoslavia to import 45 machines in 1938. The following year a torpedo-bomber version, the SM 79-II, was deployed. Italy had helped pioneer the art of aerial torpedo bombardment, so when their efficient weapons were paired with the *Sparviero*, a formidable combination arose. By the time Italy entered World War II in 1940, SM 79s formed half of that nation's bomber strength.

Early on, the SM 79 established itself as the most effective aircraft in the Italian arsenal. It performed well under trying conditions in North Africa and gave a good account of itself as a bomber. *Sparvieros* were also responsible for torpedoing several British warships in the Mediterranean. After the 1943 Italian surrender, surviving machines served both sides, with Germany developing a final version, the SM 79-III, which was deployed in small numbers. After the war, many *Sparvieros* reverted back to transports with the new Italian air force. These served capably until being replaced by more modern designs in 1952.

Type: Medium Bomber; Transport

Dimensions: wingspan, 78 feet, 8 inches; length, 58 feet, 4 inches; height, 14 feet, 7 inches
Weights: empty, 13,890 pounds; gross, 23,040 pounds
Power plant: 3 × 700–horsepower Piaggio P.X radial engines
Performance: maximum speed, 211 miles per hour; ceiling, 26,240 feet; range, 1,336 miles
Armament: up to 6 × 7.7mm machine guns; 2,205 pounds of bombs
Service dates: 1935–1944

The handsome SM 81 was among the world's best bombers when it first appeared. Despite growing obsolescence, they appeared wherever Italian troops fought in World War II.

In 1934 the appearance of the successful SM 73 commercial transport led to its development for military purposes. The prototype SM 81 emerged the following year with very similar lines. It was a large, low-wing monoplane in trimotor configuration, and in the course of a very long career a variety of differing engines was mounted. The craft was made of metal framework throughout, covered in fabric, and possessed two large, spatted landing gear. Although intended as a dedicated bomber, its roomy fuselage could also accommodate up to 18 fully equipped troops. SM 81s were rushed into service during the invasion of Ethiopia, where they rendered good service in bomber, transport, and reconnaissance roles. It thereafter served as the standard Italian bomber type until the appearance of the much superior SM 79s in 1937. Mussolini so liked the easy-flying

craft that he adopted one as his personal transport, and flew it regularly.

The *Pipistrello* (Bat) enjoyed an active service career that ranged the entire Mediterranean. They were among the first Italian aircraft to assist Franco's Spanish Nationalist forces in 1936, performing well against light opposition. In 1940, after Italy's entrance into World War II, the aging craft flew missions wherever Italian forces deployed. They bombed British targets in East Africa up through 1941, but the lightly armed craft took heavy losses. Thereafter, it became necessary to employ SM 81s exclusively as night bombers throughout the North African campaign. They raided Alexandria on numerous occasions but were subsequently employed in transport and other second-line duties. In 1942 alone, the 18 *Stormo Traspori* (transport squadron) made 4,105 flights, conveying 28,613 troops and 4.5 million pounds of supplies. A handful of SM 81s survived up to the 1943 Italian surrender, and they found service with both sides until war's end. Production amounted to 534 machines.

Type: Fighter; Light Bomber; Trainer

Dimensions: wingspan, 28 feet, 6 inches; length, 57 feet, 6 inches; height, 16 feet
Weights: empty, 15,432 pounds; gross, 34,612 pounds
Power plant: 2 × 5,115–pound thrust Rolls-Royce Turbomeca Adour Mk 102 turbofan engines
Performance: maximums peed, 1,056 mile per hour; ceiling, 45,930 feet; range, 530 miles
Armament: 2 × 30mm cannons; up to 10,000 pounds of bombs and rockets
Service dates: 1972–

The highly capable *Jaguar* is one of the most successful multinational aircraft designs. Although originally designed as a trainer, it has since matured into a potent strike fighter.

By 1965 the great expense of modern military aircraft induced France and Great Britain to enter a joint program for developing an advanced jet trainer that could also double as a ground-attack craft. At length British Aircraft Corporation (now British Aerospace, or BAe) and Breguet (now Dassault) were tasked with designing such machines on a cost-effective basis. A basic prerequisite was the ability to deliver heavy ordnance at low level, high speed, and considerable range with great accuracy. The *Jaguar* prototype emerged in September 1968 as a high-wing jet with a sharply streamlined profile and highly swept wings. It featured tall landing gear to facilitate ease of loading large weapons on the numerous wing hardpoints. Being powered by two high-thrust Adour turbofan engines ensured that the craft possessed good STOL (short takeoff and landing) capabilities,

even when fully loaded. The first version, the *Jaguar A*, was a single-seat strike fighter deployed in France in 1972. This was followed by the *Jaguar E*, an advanced two-seat trainer. Britain, meanwhile, received deliveries of the single-seat *Jaguar GR* Mk 1 and the dual-seat Jaguar B trainer. Total production of European variants reached 400 machines. Both France and Britain have also operated them abroad, during the 1991 Gulf War, in Chad, and in Mauritania. The *Jaguars* are currently being phased out by the more advanced Panavia *Tornado*, but they maintain their reputation as excellent aircraft.

The good performance and easy maintenance of the *Jaguar* made them ideal for the overseas market, so an export version, the *Jaguar International*, was created. This variant was based upon the British *GR 1* and could be fitted with advanced Agave radar and *Sea Eagle* antiship missiles. Thus far, India has proven the biggest customer, although small orders have also been placed by Ecuador, Nigeria, and Oman.

Type: Fighter; Light Bomber

Dimensions: wingspan, 30 feet, 2 inches; length, 48 feet, 11 inches; height, 12 feet, 9 inches
Weights: empty, 12,700 pounds; gross, 22,045 pounds
Power plant: 2 × 5,730–pound thrust Liming Wopen R-9BF turbojets
Performance: maximum speed, 900 miles per hour; ceiling, 58,725 feet; range, 370 miles
Armament: 2 × 30mm cannons; up to 1,100 pounds of bomb or rockets
Service dates: 1958–

The J 6 remains the single-most important aircraft in China's arsenal. Continually improved since its inception, it remains a formidable dogfighter.

The Russian MiG 19 interceptor first flew in 1953 and subsequently became one of the world's earliest mass-produced supersonic fighters. It was acquired in great quantities by the Soviet Union and Warsaw Pact before being supplanted by more modern MiG 21s in 1960. Two years previously, China contemplated construction of the MiG 19 under license. The craft was rugged, endowed with high performance, and exhibited excellent powers of maneuverability and climb. In 1958 the Shenyang Factory at Mukden obtained blueprints to the craft and manufactured its first example as the J 6. A handful of the craft had been turned out by the advent of the Cultural Revolution in 1961, which virtually gutted the Chinese aviation industry. Mass production could not resume until 1973; close to 3,000 have since been built. Like its Russian counterpart, the J 6 is a rakish all-metal jet with midmounted, highly

swept wings and tail surfaces. For added stability, the wings display pronounced fences across the chord. J 6s have since been fitted with a succession of more powerful engines and maintain a high-performance profile. To date it still fulfills numerous fighter, ground-attack, and reconnaissance missions within the People's Liberation Air Force.

To improve its leverage with Third World nations, many of them desperately poor, China cultivated their friendship by offering the J 6 for export. Ready client states include Albania, Bangladesh, Egypt, and North Korea. But the most notable customer in this instance is Pakistan, which continues operating several squadrons of constantly refurbished J 6s. In combat with more advanced Indian aircraft, the redoubtable warhorse has unequivocally held its own, despite being based on obsolete technology. The J 6 and its export models will undoubtedly see continued use well into the twenty-first century. They have since received the NATO designation FARMER.

Type: Antisubmarine; Patrol-Bomber; Air/Sea Rescue

Dimensions: wingspan, 108 feet, 9 inches; length, 109 feet, 9 inches; height, 32 feet, 8 inches
Weights: empty, 51,367 pounds; gross, 99,200 pounds
Power plant: 5 × 3,493–horsepower General Electric T46 turboprop engines
Performance: maximum speed, 318 miles per hour; ceiling, 23,600 feet; range, 2,372 miles
Armament: none
Service dates: 1968–

The US 1 is the most advanced and capable flying boat ever built. Using sophisticated air boundary control technology, it can take off and land in amazingly short distances.

Japan is preponderantly a maritime nation, its destiny closely linked to control of the seas surrounding it. For this reason flying boats have always been something of a specialty in Japan's history, and during World War II it produced some of the finest machines of that conflict. By 1965 the Japan Maritime Defense Force sought modern replacements for its Korean War–vintage Grumman UF-2 *Albatroses*. This was being sought for improved search-and-rescue capability, as well as antisubmarine warfare (ASW). They approached ShinMaywa (previously Shin Meiwa and, before that, Kawanishi) to develop such a machine. A team headed by Dr. Shizuo Kikuhara, who was responsible for the superb H8K *Emily* of World War II, responded with a large and modern four-engine craft. The PS 1 was a high-wing, all-metal monoplane with a single-step hull and a high "T" tail. The aircraft also employed a fifth engine driving a unique air boundary control device. This vents engine gases and blows them directly against the lowered flaps, providing extra lift for takeoffs and landings. Such technology allowed the big craft to operate from relatively short distances. The hull also permits working in waves as high as 10 feet. ShinMaywa ultimately constructed 23 PS 1s, all of which were retired from ASW service in 1989.

In 1974 ShinMaywa tested the first prototype US 1, a dedicated search-and-rescue amphibian. It is outwardly identical to the earlier PS 1 save for the presence of retractable landing gear in the hull. The new craft has been stripped of all submarine detection equipment to make room for up to 36 stretchers. A maximum of 100 persons could be carried in emergency situations. A total of 13 have been acquired thus far, and a new version, the US 1*kai*, with improved Allison turboprop engines, is under evaluation.

Type: Torpedo-Bomber

Dimensions: wingspan, 63 feet, 6 inches; length, 40 feet, 7 inches; height, 13 feet, 6 inches
Weights: empty, 3,703 pounds; gross, 5,363 pounds
Power plant: 1 × 225–horsepower Sunbeam liquid-cooled in-line engine
Performance: maximum speed, 88 miles per hour; ceiling, 9,000 feet; range, 150 miles
Armament: 1 × .303–inch machine gun; 1 × 14-inch torpedo
Service dates: 1915–1918

The lumbering Short 184 was an illustrious veteran of World War I with an impressive combat record. It was actively engaged in the Battle of Jutland and also launched the first aerial torpedo attack against enemy vessels.

The Short 184 had its origins in the beliefs of Commodore Murray F. Sueter, who in 1914 convinced the British Admiralty to develop an airplane capable of dropping torpedoes. This was then a revolutionary new concept. Accordingly, the Short 184 prototype flew the following year, so designated by the Admiralty practice of naming aircraft types by numbers assigned to the first example. The Short 184 was a standard, three-bay biplane of wood-and-fabric construction. The wings were extremely long, with the top ones sporting ailerons and the lower ones tipfloats. The fuselage was also somewhat attenuated and mounted two pontoon-type floats. Despite its somewhat fragile appearance, the craft handled well and could hoist a heavy torpedo aloft. A total of 650 were acquired.

The Short 184 made aviation history while attached to the floatplane tender HMS *Ben-my-Chree* during the Dardanelles campaign. On August 12, 1915, a Short 184 torpedoed and severely damaged a Turkish steamer. This success was repeated five days later when a steam tug was sent to the bottom, again demonstrating the validity of Sueter's theories. During the next three years, these creaking floatplanes distinguished themselves in a variety of missions and climes. Throughout the spring of 1916, five Short 184s operated from the Tigris River at Ora, Iraq, dropping supplies to the beleaguered garrison at Kut-al-Imara. On May 31, 1916, a Short 184 conducted history's first naval reconnaissance flight when it espied part of the German battle fleet and successfully relayed coordinates. The ubiquitous Short 184 flew from every conceivable British naval base, be it in England, the Mediterranean, the Aegean, the Red Sea, Mesopotamia, or the French coast. They retired from British service after the war, but several examples were operated by Greece and Estonia as late as 1933.

Type: Heavy Bomber

Dimensions: wingspan, 99 feet, 1 inch; length, 87 feet, 3 inches; height, 22 feet, 9 inches
Weights: empty, 43,200 pounds; gross, 70,000 pounds
Power plant: 4 × 1,650–horsepower Bristol Hercules XVI radial engines
Performance: maximum speed, 270 miles per hour; ceiling, 17,000 feet; range, 2,010 miles
Armament: 8 × .303–inch machine guns; up to 14,000 pounds of bombs
Service dates: 1941–1945

The slab-sided _Stirling_ was Britain's first strategic bomber and the first to achieve operational status during World War II. Visually impressive, it suffered from poor altitude performance and was eventually eclipsed by the Avro _Lancaster_ and Handley Page _Halifax_.

In 1936 the British air staff sought acquisition of its first strategic bomber, so the Air Ministry issued Specification B.12/36 for a four-engine aircraft. Several prototypes were entered by different firms, but Short's model proved the most successful. It was a large, high-wing monoplane with smooth, stressed skin. The fuselage was rather long, was slab-sided, and housed three power turrets for defense. Because the wing was so far off the ground, enormous landing gear were required, causing the aircraft to appear larger than it actually was. A potential problem was the wingspan. Because ministry specifications mandated that the new craft should fit into existing hangars, its wings could not exceed 100 feet. Thus, the _Stirling_, which was rather large, always suffered from insufficient lift.

Nonetheless, the decision was made to acquire the bomber in 1939, and within two years the first squadrons were outfitted.

In service the _Stirling_ enjoyed a rather mixed record. The big craft was structurally sound and, at low altitude, quite maneuverable for its size. However, its short wing enabled it to reach barely 17,000 feet while fully loaded—an easy target for antiaircraft batteries and enemy fighters. Another unforeseen shortcoming was the bomb bay, which was constructed in sections and could not accommodate ordnance larger than 2,000 pounds—the largest weapon available in 1938. Thus, unlike the _Halifaxes_ and _Lancasters_ that followed, its utility as a strategic weapon was decidedly limited. _Stirlings_ nonetheless performed good service with RAF Bomber Command until 1944, when they were relegated to secondary tasks. Foremost among these was glider-towing, which they extensively performed at Normandy in June 1944. By 1945 _Stirlings_ had flown 18,446 sorties and dropped 27,281 tons of bombs. A total of 2,373 were constructed.

Type: Patrol-Bomber

Dimensions: wingspan, 112 feet, 9 inches; length, 85 feet, 3 inches; height, 32 feet, 10 inches
Weights: empty, 37,000 pounds; gross, 65,000 pounds
Power plant: 4 × 1,200–horsepower Pratt & Whitney R-1830 Twin Wasp radial engines
Performance: maximum speed, 213 miles per hour; ceiling, 17,900 feet; range, 2,980 miles
Armament: 10 × .303–inch machine guns; 2,000 pounds of bombs
Service dates: 1938–1959

The large, graceful *Sunderland* was among World War II's best flying boats. Because it bristled with armament, the Germans regarded it as the "Flying Porcupine."

The advent of successful Short *Empire C*-class flying boats in 1933 persuaded the British Air Ministry to consider its adoption for military purposes. That year it issued Specification R.2/33 to replace the aging biplane flying boats with a new monoplane craft. The prototype *Sunderland* was heavily based upon the civilian craft when it first flew in 1937. It was a high-wing, four-engine airplane with stressed-skin construction and a very deep, two-step hull. The spacious hull of the *Sunderland* allowed for creature comforts not associated with military craft. These included comfortable bunks, wardrooms, and a galley serving hot food, all of which mitigated the effects of 10-hour patrols. The craft was also the first flying boat fitted with powered gun turrets in the nose, dorsal, and tail positions, as well as the first to carry antishipping radar. Despite its bulk, the

Sunderland handled well in both air and water and became operational in 1938. World War II commenced the following year, and *Sunderlands* ultimately equipped 17 Royal Air Force squadrons.

This capable aircraft played a vital role in the ongoing battles in the Atlantic. They cruised thousands of miles over open ocean, providing convoy escorts and attacking U-boats whenever possible. The first submarine kill happened in January 1940 when a *Sunderland* forced the scuttling of U-55. The big craft, by flying low to the water, could also defend itself handily. On several occasions, *Sunderlands* beat off roving bands of Junkers Ju 88s with considerable loss to the attackers. The Germans held the big craft in such esteem that they nicknamed it the *Stachelschwein* (Porcupine). *Sunderlands* performed useful service in the Atlantic and Pacific theaters throughout the war. They were retained in frontline service until 1959, giving them—at 21 years—the longest service record of any British combat type. A total of 721 were built.

Type: Fighter

Dimensions: wingspan, 27 feet, 4 inches; length, 18 feet, 8 inches; height, 8 feet, 11 inches
Weights: empty, 1,190 pounds; gross, 1,620 pounds
Power plant: 1 × 160–horsepower Siemens-Halske rotary engine
Performance: maximum speed, 118 miles per hour; ceiling, 26,240 feet; range, 250 miles
Armament: 2 × 7.92mm machine guns
Service dates: 1918–1919

The barrel-chested Siemens-Schuckert D III and D IV were among the finest fighters developed during World War I. At high altitude they possessed superior performance to the legendary Fokker D VII.

Since 1916 the famous Siemens-Schuckert Werke firm had been experimenting with numerous rotary-engine fighter designs. Eventually the program came under the sway of designer Harald Wolf, who originated a unique aircraft suitable for the large Siemens-Halske Sh III rotary engine. Called the D III, it was a squat, barrel-chested machine possessing rather sleek lines. It had two-bay wings of conventional wooden construction, with the upper wing of considerably lower chord than the lower one. The massive engine was completely enclosed by a close-fitting cowling and drove a four-blade propeller. To counteract strong torque forces, the right wing was actually four inches longer than the left. In sum, this was a compact, powerful design of unusual military promise.

In the winter of 1917 small batches of D IIIs arrived at the front for evaluation under combat conditions. Pilots were awed by its aerial agility and phenomenal climb. In level flight, however, it was somewhat slower than other fighters, and the SH III engine was prone to overheating. Engine seizures were frequent, and by February 1918 all 20 D IIIs returned to the factory for modifications. They reappeared at the front by summer, along with 60 production models, having the lower part of their cowling cut off to facilitate cooling.

Concurrently, an improved version, the D IV, was also under development. Outwardly this model appeared identical to the D III, but it possessed a redesigned top wing and a large spinner with cooling louvers. These modifications endowed the D IV with greater speed and even faster climb. By the fall of 1918 a total of 118 had been constructed, which equipped four squadrons. In service the D IVs proved the only German fighter capable of tackling the formidable Sopwith *Camels* and *Snipes* on equal terms. In 1919 several examples were flown by German against Bolshevik forces in the Baltic.

Type: Heavy Bomber

Dimensions: wingspan, 97 feet, 9 inches; length, 56 feet, 1 inch; height, 15 feet, 6 inches
Weights: empty, 8,378 pounds; gross, 12,125 pounds
Power plant: 4 × 150–horsepower Sunbeam liquid-cooled in-line engines
Performance: maximum speed, 85 miles per hour; ceiling, 10,500 feet; range, 435 miles
Armament: 7 × 7.7mm machine guns; 2,200 pounds of bombs
Service dates: 1914–1924

The massive *Ilya Muromets* was the world's first four-engine bomber—and a good one at that. In three years it dropped 2,200 tons of bombs on German positions, losing only one plane in combat.

In 1913 the Russo-Baltic Wagon Works constructed the world's first four-engine aircraft under the direction of Igor Sikorsky. Dubbed the *Russki Vitiaz* (Russian Knight), it was also the first to mount a fully enclosed cabin. This giant craft safely completed 54 flights before being destroyed in a ground accident. In 1914 Sikorsky followed up his success by devising the first-ever four-engine bomber and christened it *Ilya Muromets* after a legendary medieval knight. The new machine possessed straight, unstaggered, four-bay wings with ailerons only on the upper. The fuselage was long and thin, with a completely enclosed cabin housing a crew of five. On February 12, 1914, with Sikorsky himself at the controls, the *Ilya Muromets* reached an altitude of 6,560 feet and loitered five hours while carrying 16 passengers and a dog! This performance, unmatched any-

where in the world, aroused the military's interest, and it bought 10 copies as the Model IM.

After World War I commenced in 1914, Sikorsky went on to construct roughly 80 more of the giant craft, which were pooled into an elite formation known as the *Vozdushnykh Korablei* (Flying Ships) Squadron. On February 15, 1915, they commenced a concerted, two-year bombardment campaign against targets along the eastern fringes of Germany and Austria. The *Ilya Muromets* carried particularly heavy loads for their day, with bombs weighing in excess of 920 pounds. This sounds even more impressive considering that ordnance dropped along the Western Front was usually hurled by hand! The mighty Russian giants were also well-built and heavily armed. In 422 sorties, only one was lost in combat, and only after downing three German fighters. Operations ceased after the Russian Revolution of 1917, with many bombers being destroyed on the ground. A handful of survivors served the Red Air Force as trainers until 1922.

Type: Fighter; Reconnaissance

Dimensions: wingspan, 27 feet, 6 inches; length, 20 feet, 4 inches; height, 9 feet, 1 inch
Weights: empty, 897 pounds; gross, 1,490 pounds
Power plant: 1 × 80–horsepower Gnome air-cooled rotary engine
Performance: maximum speed, 73 miles per hour; ceiling, 11,482 feet; range, 200 miles
Armament: up to 2 × 7.62mm machine guns
Service dates: 1916–1924

The diminutive S 16 was one of the earliest fighters to mount forward-firing interrupter gear. A mediocre craft, its robust construction permitted useful service under very harsh operating conditions.

The Russo-Baltic Wagon Factory had gained considerable renown through the efforts of its chief engineer, Igor I. Sikorsky. His four-engine *Ilya Muromets* bombers were among the most advanced in the world, and in the spring of 1914 he was instructed to design an escort fighter to assist the giant craft. The prototype emerged in February 1915 as the S 16. This was a small machine of conventional appearance and construction. It possessed a wire-braced wooden fuselage and a spacious cockpit for two crewmen. The single bay wings were affixed to the fuselage by dual struts, and the craft was built entirely of wood and canvas covering. The S 16 was originally designed to be powered by a 100-horsepower Gnome Monosoupape rotary engine, but shortages necessitated using a smaller, 80-horsepower version. Consequently, the S 16, which pos-

sessed excellent flying characteristics, remained slow and underpowered. However, it was unique in mounting robust, four-wheeled landing gear. These allowed operations from the plowed fields that Russian forces utilized as airstrips. In winter, the S 16 could also be fitted with skis.

The S 16 was only marginally successful, but it is notable in being among the first Allied aircraft to utilize Russian-designed interrupter gear for machine guns to fire through the propeller arc. This system, conceived by naval Lieutenant G. I. Lavrov, was somewhat faulty (as were most early systems) and was usually complemented by a second, wing-mounted gun firing over the propeller. Only 34 S 16s were built by 1917, but they saw widespread service as reconnaissance craft. They were also deemed unsatisfactory for escorting the giant *Ilya Muromets* bombers, which proved very capable at defending themselves. After the Russian Revolution, the surviving S 16s were impressed into the Red Air Force as trainers. They dutifully served until being retired in 1924.

Type: Fighter; Light Bomber; Reconnaissance

Dimensions: wingspan, 33 feet, 6 inches; length, 25 feet, 3 inches; height, 10 feet, 3 inches
Weights: empty, 1,259 pounds; gross, 2,150 pounds
Power plant: 1 × 130–horsepower Clerget rotary engine
Performance: maximum speed, 106 miles per hour; ceiling, 15,000 feet; range, 400 miles
Armament: 2 × .303–inch machine guns; up to 230 pounds of bombs
Service dates: 1916–1918

Sopwith 1 1/2 _Strutters_ sported several technical innovations for their time and were exceptionally fine-looking aircraft. They compiled an exemplary combat service record in World War I as fighters, bombers, and scouts.

In 1915 the British Admiralty issued new specifications for a two-seat fighter, the first British tractor-type equipped with a synchronized machine gun for firing through the propeller arc. Sopwith completed the prototype in December of that year as a handsome, two-bay biplane powered by a rotary engine. In fact, the new craft sported two interesting innovations. The first was a form of air brake, consisting of two square sections on the lower wing that were hinged and could be lowered upon landing. The second was a variable-incidence tailplane that allowed the craft to be trimmed in flight. Like all Sopwith machines, the new Type 9400 was delightful to fly, responsive, and maneuverable. It was also heavily armed for its day, mounting both a forward-firing machine gun for the pilot and a ring-mounted weapon for the observer. Production began the following

spring; the first units reached the front in April 1916. Crews immediately dubbed it the 1 1/2 _Strutter_ on account of the "W"-shaped inboard struts.

Strutters were operated by both Royal Flying Corps and Royal Naval Air Service units and acquired a jack-of-all-trades reputation. They initially functioned as escort fighters and enjoyed considerable success, for very few two-seat aircraft were armed with interrupter gear. By that fall the newly arrived Albatros D I and Halberstadt fighters terminated this role, for the craft was too stable for violent defensive maneuvers. Fortunately, their versatility made them excellent bombing platforms, and several hundred single-seat versions were deployed by both services. The British ultimately constructed 1,513 _Strutters_, but its biggest customer was France, which manufactured an additional 4,500 machines. They were also employed by the American Expeditionary Force, which purchased 514 machines to serve as trainers in 1918. _Strutters_ continued to function in various capacities until supplanted by more advanced types in 1918.

Type: Fighter

Dimensions: wingspan, 28 feet; length, 18 feet, 9 inches; height, 8 feet, 6 inches
Weights: empty, 929 pounds; gross, 1,453 pounds
Power plant: 1 × 140–horsepower Clerget rotary engine
Performance: maximum speed, 113 miles per hour; ceiling, 19,000 feet; range, 200 miles
Armament: 2 × .303–inch machine guns
Service dates: 1917–1919

The immortal *Camel* was the finest British fighter of World War I. A snubbed-nosed dervish, it helped wrest air superiority away from Germany and counted among its victims the legendary Manfred von Richthofen (the Red Baron).

Development of a new fighter to succeed the Sopwith *Pup* commenced in 1916 when Herbert Smith conceived a machine capable of greater maneuverability. He accomplished this by placing the heaviest parts—the engine, armament, and pilot—all within 8 feet of the nose section. This arrangement, coupled with the tremendous torque generated by a Clerget rotary engine, gave the ensuing Sopwith F1 fighter unparalleled turning ability. It was also the first British fighter designed to be equipped with twin Vickers machine guns firing through the propeller arc. These were closely enclosed in a distinctive hump that inspired the nickname *Camel*.

The *Camel* was unlike any British fighter to date and certainly differed from the Sopwith designs preceding it. Whereas the famous *Pup* and Triplane designs possessed gentle, almost sedate characteris-

tics, the new machine was both unstable and unforgiving. These attributes rendered it a first-class fighter in the hands of an experienced pilot, for the *Camel* could outturn any German aircraft except the vaunted Fokker Dr I triplane. However, novice pilots found it a vicious handful and dangerous to fly, for careless turning inevitably led to fatal spins. Attrition among beginning pilots was appreciable high, but those who mastered the craft managed to shoot down an estimated 1,300 German airplanes, more than any other Allied fighter. Among the many victims was Baron von Richthofen himself, purportedly bagged by Captain Roy Brown of Naval Squadron No. 209 on April 21, 1918. A total of 5,490 *Camels* were built, including the 2 F1, a navalized version featuring shorter wings and a detachable fuselage for shipboard storage. Like its Royal Flying Corps counterparts, the navy *Camels* fought tenaciously, scored well, and even claimed the last Zeppelin shot down during the war. The mighty Sopwiths were all retired within months of the November 1918 Armistice and were replaced by an even finer machine, the *Snipe*. It remains a classic British warplane.

Type: Fighter; Light Bomber

Dimensions: wingspan, 32 feet, 6 inches; length, 22 feet, 3 inches; height, 8 feet, 6 inches
Weights: empty, 1,391 pounds; gross, 2,008 pounds
Power plant: 1 × 200–horsepower Hispano-Suiza Vee liquid-cooled in-line engine
Performance: maximum speed, 112 miles per hour; ceiling, 20,000 feet; range, 250 miles
Armament: up to 4 × .303–inch machine guns; 100 pounds of bombs
Service dates: 1918–1919

The ungainly _Dolphin_ was the first multigun British fighter ever produced. It had fine high-altitude performance but, ironically, performed more useful work on the deck.

In 1917 Sopwith commenced work on a fighter that maximized vision and firepower at the expense of maneuverability. The new craft was an even bigger departure from traditional company norms in that it utilized an in-line, not rotary, engine. The prototype emerged in May 1917 and immediately raised eyebrows. The wings of equal length were set back in a negative stagger to afford the pilot greater frontal view. To that end, the top wing's center section was also cut out and mounted low to the fuselage, allowing the pilot's head to protrude. This afforded him a splendid field of vision but also guaranteed a broken neck—or worse—in the event of a noseover. The in-line motor gave the deep fuselage a rather pointed profile and mounted outboard radiators on either side. The armament was also worthy of note. In addition to two synchronized machine guns in front, it possessed a pair of drum-fed Lewis machine guns mounted at an angle over the pilot's enclosure. This craft, christened the 5F1 _Dolphin_, displayed excellent flying qualities, especially at high altitude, and the decision was made to enter production. Within a year 1,532 had been acquired.

Dolphins reached France in the spring of 1918 and were immediately viewed with suspicion. The geared Hispano-Suiza engine caused endless difficulties, and—owing to the wing arrangement—its stall characteristics caused many accidents. But pilots came to appreciate the fine high-altitude performance of the _Dolphin_ and its robust construction. Curiously, many squadrons found the twin Lewis guns burdensome and discarded them altogether. _Dolphins_ functioned as fighters for several months but found even greater success as ground-attack craft. Armed with four 25-pound bombs, they proved extremely effective at dispersing infantry formations. The novel Sopwiths served well until war's end and were phased out of service the following year.

Type: Fighter

Dimensions: wingspan, 26 feet, 6 inches; length, 19 feet, 3 inches; height, 9 feet, 5 inches
Weights: empty, 790 pounds; gross, 1,225 pounds
Power plant: 1 × 80–horsepower Gnome Monosoupape rotary engine
Performance: maximum speed, 111 miles per hour; ceiling, 17,500 feet; range, 310 miles
Armament: 1 × .303–inch machine gun
Service dates: 1916–1917

When first introduced, the elegant *Pups* were hailed as the most perfect flying machines of their day. They were also capable dogfighters and compiled an astonishing combat record.

In 1915 Sopwith's Herbert Smith decided to produce a new fighter based on a personal aircraft owned by test pilot Harry Hawker. The resulting prototype looked like a scaled-down, single-seat version of the already capable 1 1/2 *Strutter*. It was a small, handsome craft driven by a rotary engine and constructed of wood and fabric. This new Model 9901 possessed broad wings of equal length, a reduced center section to improve pilot vision, and the same distinctive inboard struts as the 1 1/2 *Strutter*. This close visual association gave rise to the craft's popular name—the "pup" of the previous airplane. Although distinctly underpowered, the *Pup* was in every respect a pilot's machine. It was docile yet sensitive, and by virtue of very low wing loading it was able to maintain altitude during violent acrobatic maneuvering. The tidy craft equipped several

naval squadrons and arrived in France during the spring of 1916.

In combat, the pugnacious *Pup* became the terror of the Western Front. It tackled the feared Albatros scouts with ease and outflew them at high altitude. The Royal Flying Corps was then hard-pressed owing to heavy casualties, and a number of *Pup*-equipped Royal Navy squadrons were dispatched to assist. The most famous of these, Naval Eight, flew for only three months and accounted for 20 enemy craft. Having themselves received the *Pup*, air corps units also asserted their superiority at great expense to the enemy. The diminutive plane gained further distinction by participating in landing experiments aboard the carrier HMS *Furious*. On August 2, 1917, a *Pup* flown by Commander F. J. Rutland became the first land plane to touch down on a moving ship at sea. By the fall of 1917, the splendid little Sopwiths were gradually withdrawn and replaced by the newer *Camels* and Royal Aircraft Factory SE 5s. A total of 1,770 had been manufactured.

Type: Fighter

Dimensions: wingspan, 30 feet, 1 inch; length, 19 feet, 9 inches; height, 9 feet, 6 inches
Weights: empty, 1,312 pounds; gross, 2,020 pounds
Power plant: 1 × 230–horsepower Bentley BR 2 rotary engine
Performance: maximum speed, 121 miles per hour; ceiling, 20,000 feet; range, 300 miles
Armament: 2 × .303–inch machine guns
Service dates: 1918–1926

Had World War I endured beyond the November 1918 Armistice, the *Snipe* might have gained renown as the best all-around fighter of the war. Accordingly, it served as the last rotary-engine airplane of the postwar period.

Throughout 1917 Herbert Smith worked on a more powerful successor to his already famous *Camel*. The new craft shared similar outlines with its predecessor but was built around the new 230-horsepower Bentley BR 2 rotary engine. Several prototypes were built, flown, and successively modified until rendered proficient. The 7F1 *Snipe*, as it was named, was a four-bay biplane design with a short fuselage and relatively long wings. Unlike the *Camel*, both wings were given several degrees of dihedral, and the top one had its center section reduced to improve pilot vision. The slab-sided fuselage of the former had also given way to a rounder, more streamlined form. And like its precursor, the *Snipe* possessed twin machine guns in a distinctive fairing over the engine, only now the hump was even more pronounced. Flight-testing concluded success-

fully, and production commenced in the spring of 1918.

Only 200 *Snipes* had been completed by the time of the Armistice, equipping three squadrons. Nonetheless, the new fighter quickly gained repute as being quite possibly the best aircraft of its class during the war. It climbed better than the *Camel*, retained all the legendary maneuverability, and possessed none of the latter's vicious spin characteristics. These traits were summarily displayed on October 27, 1918, when a *Snipe* flown by Canadian Major W. G. Barker single-handedly engaged 15 superb Fokker D VIIs, gaining him the Victoria Cross.

After the war, *Snipes* continued on as the first major Royal Air Force service fighter. Given their great aerial agility, they remained standard fare at aviation shows throughout the early 1920s, although their rotary-engine technology was approaching obsolescence. By 1926 the weary *Snipes* had been eclipsed by newer radial-engine fighters like the Gloster *Grebe* and the Armstrong-Whitworth *Siskin*. Production totaled 2,103 machines.

Type: Reconnaissance; Light Bomber

Dimensions: wingspan, 25 feet, 6 inches; length, 20 feet, 4 inches; height, 8 feet, 5 inches
Weights: empty, 720 pounds; gross, 1,120 pounds
Power plant: 1 × 80–horsepower Gnome rotary engine
Performance: maximum speed, 93 miles per hour; ceiling, 15,000 feet; range, 300 miles
Armament: none
Service dates: 1914–1915

The *Tabloid* was a fast, groundbreaking design of the early aviation era. In 1914 it became the first single-seat scout to enter military service and also made the first successful air raid on German soil.

In 1913 Tommy Sopwith established a small aircraft firm at Kingston-upon-Thames and commenced his lifelong ambition of designing airplanes. His first effort was a small racing biplane named the *Tabloid* that possessed amazing performance for its day. It was a standard two-bay biplane constructed when monoplanes seemed the future of aviation. Of standard wood-and-fabric construction, it sported a neatly fitting metal cowl and a broad fuselage seating two occupants side by side. The wings were rake-tipped and utilized warping for lateral control. When Harry Hawker flew the *Tabloid* at the Hendon Air Show on November 29, 1913, he reached a blazing 93 miles per hour and climbed 1,200 feet a minute while carrying a passenger and two and a half hours of fuel! Such outstanding performance quickly garnered military attention, and shortly before World War I the nifty biplane was acquired in

small numbers by both the Royal Flying Corps and the Royal Naval Air Service. Around 40 were built, modified to carry ailerons.

Military aircraft at this juncture were little more than civilian flying contraptions pressed into service. However, the speedy *Tabloids* were among the first aircraft dispatched to France and soon commenced reconnaissance operations. The craft was never formally armed, but on one occasion a *Tabloid* piloted by Lieutenant Norman Spratt forced a German machine down by constantly circling it! A more ominous action transpired on October 8, 1916, when two *Tabloids* flown by Commander Spenser Gray and Lieutenant Marix conducted the first allied bomb run over Germany. Spenser became lost in the mist and dropped his small bombs on the Cologne railway station, but Marix enjoyed spectacular success by destroying Zeppelin Z IX in its shed. Following some brief Mediterranean service, the famous *Tabloids* were finally retired. But Tommy Sopwith had made his mark and went on to become a renowned aircraft manufacturer.

Type: Fighter

Dimensions: wingspan, 26 feet, 6 inches; length, 18 feet, 10 inches; height, 10 feet, 6 inches
Weights: empty, 1,101 pounds; gross, 1,541 pounds
Power plant: 1 × 130–horsepower Clerget rotary engine
Performance: maximum speed, 117 miles per hour; ceiling, 20,500 feet; range, 250 miles
Armament: 1 × .303–inch machine gun
Service dates: 1917

Coming on the heels of the vaunted *Pup*, the Sopwith Triplane was an even bigger surprise to the Germans. The little *Tripehound* was faster and could outturn and outclimb the Albatros scouts with ease.

The Sopwith Triplane originated when Herbert Smith attempted to wring even more maneuverability out of his exiting *Pup* design. The prototype flew in May 1916 and shared some outward similarities with the earlier machine, but little else. Like the *Pup*, the Triplane was compact and good-looking. It employed three wings of equal length, but each was fitted with an aileron to enhance turning and roll rates. Being a triplane, the wings were also of less chord, which gave the pilot better fields of vision. The fuselage was conventionally built of wood and fabric with the engine, armament, fuel, and pilot concentrated toward the front. This arrangement, in concert with torque forces from the spinning rotary engine, contributed to its very sharp turning rate. Trial flights were successful, and the Triplane was

ordered in quantity for both the Royal Flying Corps and the Royal Naval Air Service. A majority of the 140 Triplanes constructed were flown by navy pilots, who dubbed it the *Tripehound*.

The little Sopwiths appeared on the Western Front in the spring of 1917 and completely mastered the formidable Albatros D III scouts. The leading triplane exponent was Lieutenant Raymond Collingshaw, a Canadian commanding B Flight of Naval Ten. This unit fancied itself the "Black Flight" because all five Triplanes were painted black and christened *Black Death*, *Black Maria*, *Black Roger*, *Black Prince*, and *Black Sheep*. In three months of combat, Collingshaw's flight accounted for no less than 87 German aircraft. Other units enjoyed similar success, and for seven months *Tripehounds* dominated the air. By the fall of 1917 they were replaced by newer Sopwith *Camels* and relegated to training duties. The reign of this little Sopwith was brief, but the Germans paid it a direct compliment by bringing out a triplane of their own—the famous Fokker Dr I.

Type: Light Bomber; Trainer

Dimensions: wingspan, 32 feet, 5 inches; length, 40 feet, 2 inches; height, 14 feet
Weights: empty, 6,993 pounds; gross, 13,890 pounds
Power plant: 1 × 4,000–pound thrust Rolls-Royce Viper turbojet engine
Performance: maximum speed, 565 miles per hour; ceiling, 49,200 feet; range, 807 miles
Armament: up to 2,646 pounds of gunpods, bombs, or rockets
Service dates: 1985–

The *Super Galeb* is a competent trainer/light attack craft that saw active duty during the Yugoslavian civil war. Several were consequently shot down by NATO air forces.

No sooner had the straight-wing G 2 *Galeb* (Seagull) trainer been deployed in 1970 than the Yugoslavian Federal Air Force began agitating for a more advanced design with greater ground-attack capability. The government, wishing to expand its ties to Third World governments through arms trading, was in complete agreement. By 1978 SOKO, the state-run airplane factory, had unveiled its first G 4 *Super Galeb* prototype, which shared little commonality with the previous craft beyond the name. It possessed a pointed profile, a swept wing, and tail surfaces that sloped slightly downward. This last feature was unique for a training craft, as the fins were an all-moving arrangement for greater maneuverability. The crew of two sat tandem under a spacious bubble canopy in staggered seats. Production commenced in 1980, and by 1985 the G 4 had largely

superceded the older *Galebs* as advanced trainers. In service the *Super Galeb* was reasonably fast and could carry a useful load of ordnance, making it ideal as a cheap strike fighter. Around 130 G 4s were built before production ceased in 1992.

Despite their status as trainers, G 4s acquired a controversial reputation as a ground-attack craft. In 1990 the military government of Myanmar (Burma), beset by guerilla movements, purchased 12 of the sleek craft for counterinsurgency operations. Yugoslavia willingly sold machines in the face of international sanctions against the oppressive local regime. Two years later *Super Galebs* were in action against Yugoslavians after the civil war commenced. Transferred to the largely Serbian Yugoslav state, G 4s pounded ethnic Muslim civilian centers for some time until ordered by the United Nations to observe a no-fly zone. On February 28, 1994, three *Super Galebs* disobeyed and were downed in NATO's first-ever hostile action. It is not known how many G 4s remain operational.

Type: Light Bomber

Dimensions: wingspan, 31 feet, 6 inches; length, 48 feet, 10 inches; height, 14 feet, 7 inches
Weights: empty, 13,007 pounds; gross, 22,267 pounds
Power plant: 2 × 5,000–pound thrust Roll-Royce Viper turbojet engines
Performance: maximum speed, 721 miles per hour; ceiling, 41,010 feet; range, 329 miles
Armament: 2 × 23mm cannons; up to 3,307 pounds of bomb and rockets
Service dates: 1979–

Politics and aviation make for strange bedfellows. This axiom is borne out in the case of the jointly produced *Orao*, an indifferent fighter-bomber with great national pride attached.

In 1970 two maverick communist states, Romania and Yugoslavia, announced a decision to jointly develop a new ground-attack aircraft. This move could hardly be viewed as unexpected, as Yugoslavia under Marshal Tito had thumbed its nose at the Soviet Union since 1946. Moreover, Romania's dictator Nicolae Ceausescu—his country a nominal member of the Warsaw Pact—was a pragmatist determined to forge links outside of the communist bloc. Given the prickly sensibilities of Balkan nationalism, however, each side went to inordinate lengths not to outstage the other. The new craft hoisted a lot of national pride on its back, so, despite common origins, it was also assigned different names! The Romanian version would be designated the IAR 93, whereas its Yugoslavian counterpart became the SOKO J 22 *Orao* (Eagle).

Early on the two national state aviation industries SOKO and CNIAR elected a relatively simple, if outwardly modern, design. The J 22/IAR 93 was a single-seat, shoulder-wing jet with swept wings and tail surfaces. It was powered by two Rolls-Royce Viper turbojet engines with afterburners, to be manufactured locally. The new craft was destined as a low-level ground-attack machine with possible interception functions. Plans were also entertained to produce a two-seat trainer version. Construction moved forward haltingly, and it was not until October 31, 1974, that two prototypes flew—on the *same day* in both countries. Production had finally geared up by 1979, and the first models arrived for service shortly thereafter. The initial machines lacked afterburners and were immediately consigned to reconnaissance duties. Subsequent models were fitted with the thrust-enhancing device, but even that addition did not translate into supersonic performance. Consequently, the *Orao* remains a poor man's attack plane. Romania has acquired about 200, but Yugoslavian production halted at about 50 after that country splintered in 1995.

SPAD XIII — France

Type: Fighter

Dimensions: wingspan, 26 feet, 6 inches; length, 20 feet, 4 inches; height, 7 feet, 8 inches
Weights: empty, 1,255 pounds; gross, 1,808 pounds
Power plant: 1 × 220–horsepower Hispano-Suiza liquid-cooled in-line engine
Performance: maximum speed, 138 miles per hour; ceiling, 21,800 feet; range, 220 miles
Armament: 2 × 7.7mm machine guns
Service dates: 1916–1923

The magnificent SPAD XIII was the best French fighter of World War I and a radical departure from earlier design philosophies. Although not as nimble as the lighter Nieuports, the sacrifice in maneuverability was offset by speed and ruggedness.

In 1916 the inability of the Societe Pour les Appareils Deperdussin (SPAD) to market the SPAD A 1 two-seat fighter induced designer Louis Bechereau to rethink his approach. In April 1916 his prototype SPAD VII emerged as a completely new aircraft sporting beautifully clean lines. It was a conventional biplane with unstaggered, four-bay wings and a round cross-section fuselage housing a 160-horsepower in-line V engine. Armament was restricted to one machine gun. Test flights proved the SPAD VII possessed great speed and strength, so the craft entered service within months. The new fighter was immediately successful, being faster than German fighters in both climb and level flight. Moreover, SPAD VIIs could absorb amazing amounts of damage and return safely. By 1917 more than 5,000 had been produced, and they equipped

virtually every French fighter squadron, along with many in Italy, Belgium, and Russia. Reputedly, Italian ace Francesco Baracca grew so attached to his SPAD VII that he refused to trade it when later models became available.

In 1917 Bechereau capitalized on his success by developing the mighty SPAD XIII. This was a further refinement of his earlier masterpiece, with two machine guns, longer wings, and a stronger engine. In combat the SPAD XIII repeated the success of the earlier design, and it became the chosen mount of numerous French aces such as Rene Fonck, Georges Guynemer, and Charles Nungesser. By 1918 more than 8,472 had been constructed, equipping no less than 71 French squadrons. It also replaced rickety Nieuport 28s of the American Expeditionary Force and was flown with great success by Captain Eddie Rickenbacker. More than any other airplane, the SPAD XIII helped turn the air war's tide in favor of the Allies. Afterward it was widely exported abroad and continued in frontline service for nearly a decade.

Type: Light Bomber

Dimensions: wingspan, 45 feet, 3 inches; length, 61 feet, 6 inches; height, 16 feet, 5 inches
Weights: empty, 36,155 pounds; gross, 42,989 pounds
Power plant: 1 × 24,802–pound thrust NPO Saturn AL-21F-3 turbojet engine
Performance: maximum speed, 870 miles per hour; ceiling, 49,870 feet; range, 715 miles
Armament: 2 × 30mm cannons; up to 2,205 pounds of bomb or rockets
Service dates: 1971–

Russian aircraft builders display great ingenuity in wringing every last ounce of performance from existing machines. The long-lived Su 17 is such an example, and it continues to be upgraded and employed long after the basic design became obsolete.

In 1956 the Sukhoi design bureau created its first tactical jet bomber, the Su 7, a modern-looking machine built in large numbers to offset its relative simplicity. It was a capable fighter-bomber and ruggedly built but also somewhat underpowered. Moreover, it suffered from long runway rolls and rather short range. In 1967 the Sukhoi bureau decided to upgrade this family of bombers by adding variable-geometry wings to enhance takeoff, landing, and load-carrying abilities. Early on it was judged impossible to fit wing-retracting equipment into the narrow fuselage, so engineers compromised by making the wings pivot midway along their length. The added lift increased the Su 7's takeoff performance, and operational radius and ordnance payload were improved as well. Commencing in 1971 the new Su 17 became operational in large numbers, and they were deployed by Warsaw Pact allies and Soviet client states. It has since received the NATO designation FITTER.

During the past three decades, the basic Su 17 design has undergone numerous modifications and upgrades that render this marginally obsolete machine still useful as an attack craft. The latest variant, the Su 17M, is distinguished by a close-fitting clamshell canopy with a high spine ridge running the length of the fuselage. The tail fin is also somewhat taller and employs a single airscoop at its base. This model has been exported abroad as the Su 22, with somewhat lowered-powered avionics, but otherwise it remains an effective bombing platform. After the breakup of the Soviet Union in the late 1980s, many former Warsaw Pact countries were eager to unload their aging Sukhois, but Russia alone seems content to maintain its stable of 800-plus Su 17s. Their rugged design, combined with good reliability and performance, ensures a long service life.

Sukhoi Su 24

Type: Medium Bomber; Reconnaissance

Dimensions: wingspan, (spread) 57 feet, 10 inches; length, 80 feet, 5 inches; height, 16 feet
Weights: empty, 41,887 pounds; gross, 87,522 pounds
Power plant: 2 × 24,802–pound thrust NPO Saturn AL-21F-3A turbofan engines
Performance: maximum speed, 1,441 miles per hour; ceiling, 57,415 feet; range, 1,300 miles
Armament: 1 × 23mm cannon; up to 17,637 pounds of nuclear or conventional bombs
Service dates: 1974–

The formidable Su 24 is among the most potent weapons of the Russian tactical air arm. It can attack at low level, high speed, and with pinpoint accuracy under any weather conditions.

Up through the late 1960s, Soviet tactical aviation, though possessing huge quantities of airplanes, still lacked genuine nighttime all-weather attack capability. Moreover, in view of the increasing sophistication of antiaircraft defenses, low-level operations were becoming a matter of survival. The existing Il 28 and Yak 28s then in service were simply too old or too incapable to meet such rigorous standards. To remedy this shortfall and place the Red Air Force on par with Western adversaries, the Sukhoi design bureau was entrusted with designing a new generation of ground-attack craft. Commencing in 1970 it experimented with a bizarre variety of delta and vertical-takeoff prototypes before settling on a machine very reminiscent of the General Dynamics F-111. Like that groundbreaking U.S. design, the new Su 24 employed variable-geometry wings

that sweep forward to assist takeoff and landings, then sweep back for high-speed operations. Around 900 were constructed since 1974, and they received the NATO code name FENCER.

In service the Su 24s were the first Russian aircraft to incorporate a totally integrated avionics system, one linking bombsight, weapons control, and navigation into one central computer. The new Su 24, in fact, was initially viewed as a "mini-F-111" owning to the obvious side-by-side placement of the two-member crew. This was proof that a Soviet warplane, for the first time, flew with a dedicated weapons-systems officer to operate an advanced avionics suite. Approaching a target at low altitude and high speed, Su 24s can deliver a host of conventional or nuclear weapons with great accuracy at night and in bad weather. An equally adept tactical reconnaissance version, the Su 24MR, has also been developed. With continual upgrades, these formidable warplanes will remain in service for years to come.

Type: Antitank; Light Bomber

Dimensions: wingspan, 47 feet, 1 inch; length, 50 feet, 11 inches; height, 15 feet, 9 inches
Weights: empty, 21,605 pounds; gross, 41,005 pounds
Power plant: 2 × 9,921–pound thrust NMPK R-195 turbojet engines
Performance: maximum speed, 590 miles per hour; ceiling, 22,965 feet; range, 308 miles
Armament: 1 × 30mm cannon; up to 9,700 pounds of bombs or rockets
Service dates: 1984–

The Su 25 is successor to the famous Il 2 *Shturmovik* of World War II. Fast and heavily armed, it is reputedly the most difficult plane in the world to shoot down.

The air war in Vietnam highlighted the need for simple close-support aircraft able to operate from unpaved strips close to the front. Such warplanes would also have to deliver heavy ordnance against targets with great accuracy and be able to survive intense ground fire. The United States parlayed its experience into the Fairchild A-10 *Thunderbolt II*, a heavily armored twin-engine bomber. The Soviets also watched these developments closely before deciding that they, too, needed similar aircraft and capabilities. During World War II Russia had deployed the redoubtable Il 2 *Shturmovik* aircraft for identical reasons, so in 1968 the Sukhoi design bureau became tasked with developing an equivalent machine for the jet age. The bureau settled upon a design reminiscent of the Northrop YA-9, which had lost out to the A-10 in competition. The new Su 25 was an all-metal,

shoulder-wing monoplane constructed around a heavily armored titanium "tub" that housed both pilot and avionics. Engines were placed in long, reinforced nacelles on either side of the fuselage, and the fuel tanks were filled with reticulated foam for protection against explosions. To assist slow-speed maneuvering, the wingtip pods split open at the ends to form air brakes. Its profile is rather pointed, but a blunt noseplate covers a laser range finder/target designator. The Su 25 is somewhat faster than the A-10, trusting more in speed to ensure survival than a dependency on agility and heavy armor. It is nonetheless an effective tank destroyer.

A series of preproduction aircraft was subsequently deployed to Afghanistan, where the planes performed useful service against guerilla forces. They flew some 60,000 sorties, losing 23 machines in the process, but the decision was made to enter production in 1980. Since then 330 Su 25s have been built; they have received the NATO designation FROGFOOT.

Type: Fighter

Dimensions: wingspan, 48 feet, 3 inches; length, 72 feet; height, 19 feet, 6 inches
Weights: empty, 38,580 pounds; gross, 72,750 pounds
Power plant: 2 × 27,557–pound thrust Saturn/Lyulka AL-31F turbofan engines
Performance: maximum speed, 1,553 miles per hour; ceiling, 59,055 feet; range, 2,285 miles
Armament: 1 × 30mm cannon; up to 10 air-to-air missiles
Service dates: 1985–

The fantastic Su 27 is probably the world's most impressive interceptor. Fast, capable, and heavily armed, it was the first aircraft to perform the famous "cobra" maneuver.

By 1969 the forthcoming generation of U.S. fighters—the Grumman F-14 *Tomcat* and the McDonnell-Douglas F-15 *Eagle*—caused great consternation within Soviet aviation circles. These new planes were projected to be faster, more maneuverable, and able to carry more missiles than their Russian counterparts. That year Pavel Sukhoi began development of a fighter-interceptor with the range, armament, and ultramodern avionics to counter them. It was imperative that the new craft be able to detect and intercept low-flying targets and meet agile U.S. fighters on equal terms. Several unsuccessful prototypes were developed before Sukhoi died; his successor, Mikhail Simonov, hit upon a functional solution. The new Su 27 was a big fighter by virtue of the 4-foot-wide radar dish utilized in the nose. It also employed widely separated twin turbofan engines in a beautifully blended forebody and

high-lift wing. The craft was deliberately made unstable for enhanced maneuverability and is flown with computer-assisted fly-by-wire technology. Moreover, the Su 27 does not require in-flight refueling, as it carries 10 tons of fuel aloft. The NATO code word for the big craft is FLANKER, a name adopted by Russian pilots themselves.

In 1986 pilot Viktor Pugachev impressively flew an Su 27 from Moscow to the Paris Air Show nonstop, then stunned observers by demonstrating the famous "cobra" maneuver. In this acrobatic stunt, the pilot raises the nose of the Su 27 at high speed until the aircraft virtually stands still on its tail in midair; the pilot then lowers it without loss of altitude—the effect is a cobralike appearance. In service the FLANKER is designed for long-range interception, being the first Russian fighter unshackled from ground-controlled intercept radar. It can launch up to 10 missiles before closing in for the kill with a heavy cannon. China, wishing to replace its aging fighter fleet, purchased several for its own air force. The Su 27 is a formidable fighting machine and will remain so for years.

Type: Fighter

Dimensions: wingspan, 36 feet, 10 inches; length, 32 feet, 8 inches; height, 12 feet, 8 inches
Weights: empty, 6,600 pounds; gross, 8,500 pounds
Power plant: 1 × 2,050–horsepower Rolls-Royce Griffon liquid-cooled in-line engine
Performance: maximum speed, 448 miles per hour; ceiling, 44,500 feet; range, 460 miles
Armament: 2 × 20mm cannons; 4 × .303–inch machine guns; up to 500 pounds of bombs
Service dates: 1938–1954

The immortal *Spitfire* remains *the* symbol of British aerial prowess during World War II. Beautiful, fast, and lethal, this thoroughbred warrior was the quintessential fighter pilot's dream—and more.

Reginald J. Mitchell was an accomplished designer of racing craft when, in 1934, he set about designing Britain's first all-metal eight-gun fighter. His initial attempt, to be named the *Spitfire*, was a crank-winged apparition that flew as bad as it looked. However, development continued as a company project. The revised machine was a rakish, highly streamlined aircraft with a pointed spinner, retractable undercarriage, and beautiful elliptical wings. It exuded the persona of a racehorse. The new *Spitfire* flew just less than 350 miles per hour, making it the fastest fighter in the world. Moreover, its handling and maneuverability were intrinsically superb, traits that carried over through a long and exemplary service life. The usually dubious British Air Ministry was so singularly impressed by the craft that a new specification was issued "around it" to facilitate production. *Spitfire Is* entered squadron service in 1938, and the following year, when Europe was plunged into war, they constituted 40 percent of Britain's frontline fighter strength.

Commencing with the 1940 Battle of Britain, *Spitfires* captured the imagination of the world. They fought the equally capable Messerschmitt Bf 109Es to a draw, leaving the more numerous Hawker *Hurricanes* to drub bomber formations. As the war developed, so did the *Spitfire*, into no less than 40 major versions. Prior to 1941 they were indelibly associated with the equally famous Rolls-Royce Merlin engine, but the appearance of the Focke-Wulf Fw 190 in 1942 caused better engines to be sought. Eventually the powerful Griffon in-line engine was married to the *Spitfire* fuselage, endowing it with greater speed and climb without infringing upon its legendary handling. The new *Spitfire XIV* was so fast that it successfully engaged the dreaded Me 262 jet fighters, downing several. The last marks were assembled in 1947 and remained in service until 1954. More than 20,000 of these peerless warriors were built.

Type: Patrol-Bomber

Dimensions: wingspan, 85 feet; length, 54 feet, 10 inches; height, 21 feet, 9 inches
Weights: empty, 11,250 pounds; gross, 19,000 pounds
Power plant: 2 × 875–horsepower Bristol Pegasus X radial engines
Performance: maximum speed, 165 miles per hour; ceiling, 18,500 feet; range, 1,000 miles
Armament: 3 × .303–inch machine guns; up to 1,000 pounds of bombs
Service dates: 1938–1942

The _Stranraer_ was the last in a dynasty of flying boats that spanned the interwar period. It was also the fastest flying boat ever employed by the Royal Air Force.

In 1924 the British Air Ministry released specifications for a new biplane flying boat to replace the World War I–vintage Felixstowe F5. The following year, Reginald J. Mitchell, future designer of the legendary _Spitfire_, conceived a new machine based upon his successful Supermarine _Swan_, a civilian machine. Christened the _Southampton_, 78 machines were manufactured for the Royal Air Force. The Mk II variant sported an all-metal hull, and in 1927–1928 _Southamptons_ of No. 205 Squadron successfully completed a 27,000-mile tour of the Far East. They served capably for nearly a decade before being supplanted by a more refined model, the _Scapa_, in 1933. This machine bore many similarities to its forebear but differed in having double rudders, a fully enclosed cockpit, and relocated engines at the bottom of the top wing. By 1935 15 ex-

amples had been delivered; they were withdrawn by 1938.

In 1931 the government drew up specifications for a new all-purpose flying boat. Mitchell created a scaled-up version of the _Scapa_ that was initially designated the _Southampton V._ It was longer than the _Scapa_, with an extra set of interplane struts and a tailgunner position. The prototype was powered by two Bristol Pegasus IIIM engines driving two-blade wooden propellers, but production models utilized three-blade metal ones. Consequently, the new craft, which was renamed the _Stranraer_, became the fastest flying boat ever acquired by the RAF. A total of 24 were delivered in 1935, but _Stranraers_ were rapidly overtaken by technology and soon rendered obsolete. They actively patrolled in 1939, but the following year gave way to greatly superior Short _Sunderlands_. However, _Stranraers_ received a second lease on life in 1941 when the Royal Canadian Air Force acquired an additional 47 examples. They performed coastal patrolling until being retired in 1944.

Type: Air/Sea Rescue; Reconnaissance

Dimensions: wingspan, 45 feet, 10 inches; length, 37 feet, 3 inches; height, 15 feet, 3 inches
Weights: empty, 4,900 pounds; gross, 7,200 pounds
Power plant: 1 × 775–horsepower Bristol Pegasus radial engine
Performance: maximum speed, 135 miles per hour; ceiling, 18,500 feet; range, 600 miles
Armament: 2 × .303–inch machine guns; up to 760 pounds of bombs
Service dates: 1936–1945

The homely "Shagbat" was one of the most welcome sights in the skies of World War II. It rescued thousands of downed airmen and performed useful service as a naval gunnery spotter.

As early as 1921 Reginald J. Mitchell had designed a small flying boat that he deemed the *Seagull*. It continued on as a private venture for many years until 1933, when the Australian government purchased 24 examples of the latest version, the *Seagull V.* This craft was ugly but functional. It was a single-bay biplane with a fuselage mounted below the lower wing; a pusher-configuration engine stood affixed on struts above it. The hull was made of metal and stressed for shipboard catapulting and, hence, very strong. Flying surfaces were all fabric-covered, and there was a fully enclosed cockpit and two gunner positions. At this time the Fleet Air Arm closely scrutinized Mitchell's creation and in March 1936 adopted it as the *Walrus I.* They were deployed on capital ships throughout the fleet and engaged in reconnaissance and gunnery spotting. Once fitted with fixed landing gear, the little amphibians could also operate from airstrips. As events proved, the *Walrus* was adept at convoy patrolling and antisubmarine warfare. A total of 287 *Walrus Is* were produced.

During World War II the ubiquitous *Walrus* served in virtually every theater of the war. Antiquated appearances notwithstanding, it was a tough little craft capable of absorbing great amounts of punishment. In addition to naval service, Shagbats also equipped numerous squadrons of the Royal Air Force Air/Sea Rescue Service. This force was responsible for saving thousands of downed airmen, and its stately gait and noisy drone were reassuring sights in the combat theaters. By 1940 a new version, the *Walrus II,* was introduced, with a completely wooden hull. Production of Mk IIs amounted to 453 machines, with many serving in the Australian, New Zealand, and other Commonwealth navies. Most were phased out shortly after 1945.

Type: Light Bomber

Dimensions: wingspan, 66 feet, 8 inches; length, 40 feet, 3 inches; height, 10 feet, 8 inches
Weights: empty, 10,511 pounds; gross, 17,372 pounds
Power plant: 2 × 960–horsepower M-103 liquid-cooled in-line engines
Performance: maximum speed, 280 miles per hour; ceiling, 25,590 feet; range, 1,429 miles
Armament: 6 × 7.62mm machine guns; 1,323 pounds of bombs
Service dates: 1936–1943

Fast-flying SB 2s were among the world's best bombers when they appeared in 1936. They enjoyed a distinguished career in Spain, Mongolia, and Finland before suffering heavy losses in World War II.

In 1933 the Soviet government announced specifications for an entirely new light bomber, one so fast that it could operate without escort fighters. The Tupolev design bureau finessed the problem with great skill, and in 1934 it built two prototypes with radial and in-line engines respectively. The new SB 1 was Russia's first stressed-skin aircraft, a mid-wing, all-metal monoplane bomber. It was modern in every respect to Western contemporaries and possessed such advanced features as retractable landing gear and flush-riveting. A crew of four was comfortably housed, and the plane flew faster than any fighter or bomber then in service, including the highly touted Bristol *Blenheim*. In 1936 the in-line-engine prototype entered production as the SB 2, and nearly 7,000 were produced. These modern, capable craft formed the bulk of Soviet tactical aviation over the next five years and played a major role in modernizing and revitalizing the Soviet bomber forces.

SB 2s were bloodied in the Spanish Civil War (1936–1939), where they proved impervious to slower Nationalist fighters. They also enjoyed similar success in Mongolia against the Japanese and were exported to China in quantity. Several new versions were also introduced with more powerful engines, but this robust design was growing obsolete in light of developments elsewhere. SB 2s again fought well against Finland during 1939–1940, but when Germany invaded Russia the following year they lost their speed advantage. Being somewhat flammable, scores were quickly dispatched by formidable Messerschmitt Bf 109 and Bf 110 fighters. But they were abundantly available, and so the Soviets had little recourse but to continually employ them. They did so in a wide variety of roles, including that of night intruder and torpedo-bomber. By the time SB 2s withdrew in 1943, they had sustained the heaviest losses of any Russian aircraft in World War II.

Type: Heavy Bomber

Dimensions: wingspan, 132 feet, 10 inches; length, 82 feet, 8 inches; height, 18 feet
Weights: empty, 22,000 pounds; gross, 54,020 pounds
Power plant: 4 × 730–horsepower M-34R liquid-cooled in-line engines
Performance: maximum speed, 179 miles per hour; ceiling, 25,365 feet; range, 1,550 miles
Armament: 4 × 7.62mm machine guns; up to 12,790 pounds of bombs
Service dates: 1931–1944

The mighty TB 3 was the world's most advanced heavy bomber throughout most of the early 1930s. Despite archaic looks, it was a solid, capable design and served admirably through most of World War II.

Russian proclivities for giant aircraft dated back to the Sikorsky *Ilya Muromets* of 1914, and in time they accumulated sufficient knowledge and expertise to build even bigger machines. In 1925 Andrei N. Tupolev fielded the TB 1, an advanced metal monoplane that was the best in its class. Three years later he received orders to build a four-engine bomber with prodigious range and lifting abilities. He complied, and the new TB 3 emerged as an all-metal, low-wing monoplane with fixed landing gear and a crew of ten. Initial models were covered in corrugated metal, stressed to great strength. Consequently, in 1931 the TB 3 could lift more than 12,000 pounds on short flights—a payload unmatched until the Avro *Lancaster* and Boeing B-29 *Superfortress* a decade later. Stalin appreciated the propaganda

value of such huge machines, and during the 1934 May Day parade no less than 250 TB 3s overflew Moscow. The production run concluded by 1938 with 808 machines built, with latter versions possessing smooth, stressed skin.

In service the TB 3s proved ruggedly adaptable and easily maintained. They made international headlines by transporting scientific teams during a number of expeditions to the Arctic Circle. TB 3s were also used during the mid-1930s to train embryonic Soviet parachute forces, who deployed by jumping off the aircraft's broad wing. An even more controversial use was the so-called parasite experiments, whereby the lumbering craft carried their own fighter escorts. One TB 3 could successfully carry, launch, and retrieve no less than three I 15 biplanes and two I 16 monoplanes. The giant craft was marginally obsolete at the start of the 1941 German invasion and, being vulnerable to enemy fighters, served as a night bomber and transport. All these versatile machines were retired from service by 1944.

Type: Medium Bomber

Dimensions: wingspan, 61 feet, 10 inches; length, 45 feet, 3 inches; height, 13 feet, 9 inches
Weights: empty, 18,524 pounds; gross, 28,219 pounds
Power plant: 2 × 1,850–horsepower Shvetsov radial engines
Performance: maximum speed, 342 mile per hour; ceiling, 31,170 feet; range, 1,553 miles
Armament: 1 × 12.7mm machine gun; 2 × 20mm cannons; up to 5,004 pounds of bombs
Service dates: 1944–1961

The Tu 2 was a Soviet medium bomber that compiled an impressive record in World War II. Its success is especially remarkable considering that it was designed in a prison.

In 1937 the Russian aircraft engineer Andrei Tupolev was accused of passing secrets to the Germans and was incarcerated in a Soviet gulag. He and his entire staff languished for two years until they obtained promises of early release in exchange for designing a new bomber for the Red Air Force. Work commenced from behind prison walls, and in January 1941 the prototype first flew. It was designated "Aircraft 102," for Tupolev's status as a nonperson precluded using his initials! The new machine was a strikingly clean, twin-engine design with smooth engine cowlings, a pointed profile, and twin rudders. During flight tests it demonstrated even better performance than the Petlyakov Pe 2s then in service. It was slow going at first, but the German invasion of the Soviet Union in June 1941 dramatically accelerated the pace of production.

The Tu 2 proved itself a fine machine, especially in terms of speed, payload, and handling. The big, rugged craft was especially popular with crews for its amazing ability to absorb damage and remain aloft. Initial deliveries did not commence until late 1944, and then in only limited numbers. This was because the Tu 2 was more complicated to build than the Pe 2 and took longer to assemble. Another reason is that the Pe 2 was already serving capably—and in large numbers—so Tupolev's new machine did not receive priority production. Nonetheless, by 1945 Tu 2s were a common sight in the skies over Eastern Europe, and they had a devastating effect upon German troops and armor. Consequently, Tupolev was rehabilitated and received the Stalin Prize for his achievement. Tu 2s remained in production until 1948, following a production run of 2,557 machines. Forces under the United Nations encountered them during the Korean War in 1950, and Tu 2s also flew with communist satellite air forces until 1961.

Type: Medium Bomber; Reconnaissance

Dimensions: wingspan, 108 feet, 3 inches; length, 14 feet, 2 inches; height, 34 feet
Weights: empty, 82,012 pounds; gross, 167,110 pounds
Power plant: 2 × 20,920–pound thrust Mikulin RD-3m–500 turbojets
Performance: maximum speed, 616 miles per hour; ceiling, 40,350 feet; range, 4,000 miles
Armament: 6 × 23mm cannons; up to 6,600 pounds of nuclear bombs or standoff missiles
Service dates: 1955–

One of the classic aviation designs of the 1950s, the Tu 16 was Russia's most successful jet bomber. It remains in active service today as a missile platform and maritime reconnaissance craft.

The origins of the famous Tu 16 trace back to 1944, when bad weather forced down three U.S. Boeing B-29s on a Russian airfield in Siberia. The Soviet Union, neutral toward Japan, promptly detained the crews and confiscated the aircraft. This technological windfall handed Soviet dictator Josef Stalin the world's most advanced bomber aircraft, and he immediately ordered reverse-engineered copies for the Red Air Force. They became known as the Tupolev Tu 4 and received the NATO designation BULL. By 1950 the Americans and British were developing and deploying advanced jet-powered bomber designs, so Stalin authorized production of Soviet models as well. The new Tu 16 thus became the first successful Soviet jet bomber, the first with swept-back wings, and the first with engines buried

in the wing roots. It was revealed to the West in 1954 as a midwing aircraft of extremely sleek lines. The landing gear were uniquely positioned in trailing-edge pods, as the wing was too thin to contain them. Tupolev's conservative approach gave the Tu 16 a robust construction that in turn led to a long and varied service life. Around 2,000 were manufactured and given the NATO code name BADGER.

Initial models of the Tu 16 were tactical nuclear bombers, but, lacking the necessary range to hit the United States, they were quickly phased out by more modern designs. Most were shunted over to the Soviet navy, which employed them in long-range reconnaissance and antishipping strike roles. Many BADGERS encountered at sea were usually configured with one or more cruise missiles in the bomb bay or under the wings. The type was also exported to China in the late 1950s and was produced there in some quantity. An estimated 70 Tu 16s fly with Russian naval aviation and will continue serving for years to come.

Type: Medium Bomber; Reconnaissance

Dimensions: wingspan, 77 feet; length, 139 feet, 9 inches; height, 35 feet
Weights: empty, 83,995 pounds; gross, 207,230 pounds
Power plant: 2 × 27,560–pound thrust Dobrynin RD-7M-2 turbojet engines
Performance: maximum speed, 920 miles per hour; ceiling, 43,365 feet; range, 2,600 miles
Armament: 2 × 23mm cannons; up to 22,046 pounds of nuclear weapons or missiles
Service dates: 1961–

The Tu 22 was the Soviet Union's first supersonic bomber. Hobbled by poor range, it spent most of a long life as a maritime reconnaissance platform or performing antishipping functions.

Throughout the late 1950s, Western air defenses acquired new levels of sophistication and effectiveness. The Soviet Union, saddled with lumbering subsonic bombers, had little hope of mounting effective attacks in the event of war. It therefore became imperative to develop new jet bombers with a minimum supersonic dash capacity for successful penetration of enemy air space. Around 1956 the Tupolev design bureau began creating Russia's first supersonic bomber, one that could compete with the General Dynamics B-58 *Hustler* and Dassault *Mirage IV*. The Tu 22 emerged four years later as a machine configured for high speed and high altitude without sacrificing subsonic handling. Its most unusual aspect was the twin engines mounted high on the rear fuselage. This obviated the need for long inlet ducts and the

drag penalties they imposed. The wings were also carefully rendered with a compound sweep that facilitated high speeds yet performed well in a subsonic regime. Moreover, the Tu 22 was the first Soviet bomber to dispense with traditional glazed noses and numerous gun turrets: The new craft employed internal bombing/navigation radar and a remote-controlled tail turret. In service the Tu 22 flew well and could reach supersonic speeds for brief periods, but it possessed abysmally short range. Around 250 were constructed, known to NATO as BLINDER A.

The Tu 22 did not survive long as a nuclear bomber, for in the early 1960s most were siphoned off into Soviet naval aviation. They were fitted with various antishipping strike missiles and redesignated BLINDER B. A maritime reconnaissance version, BLINDER C, with numerous electronic protuberances, was also developed. Only a few Tu 22s remain operational at present in Russia. Several others are currently employed by the Libyan air force.

Type: Medium Bomber; Reconnaissance

Dimensions: wingspan, (spread) 112 feet, 6 inches; length, 139 feet, 4 inches; height, 36 feet
Weights: empty, 119,059 pounds; gross, 278,660 pounds
Power plant: 2 × 55,115–pound thrust Kuznetsov KKBM MN25 turbofan engines
Performance: maximum speed, 1,320 miles per hour; ceiling, 59,055 feet; range, 7,457 miles
Armament: 2 × 23mm cannons; up to 52,910 pounds of bombs or missiles
Service dates: 1975–

Once the object of intense diplomatic debate, the celebrated Tu 22M was merely the latest failed attempt by the Soviet Union to acquire strategic bombing capability. It is nonetheless a formidable aircraft with extensive service in the Russian naval air arm.

In the early 1960s the Tu 22's shortcomings prompted the Tupolev design bureau to consider major revisions. Wind-tunnel studies indicated that a variable-geometry arrangement (known as the "swing wing") could nearly double its combat radius while halving takeoff distance. Because the Soviet Union still lacked a bona fide supersonic bomber capable of reaching the United States, Tupolev was authorized to develop an improved Tu 22. The first model emerged in 1969 as a highly modified BLINDER, replete with an area-ruled fuselage and podded landing gear on the wing's trailing edges. The wing itself was conservatively designed and pivoted only midway down the span. The new machine entered service soon thereafter, receiving the NATO designation BACKFIRE A. Because of the plane's high drag and other deficiencies, only small numbers were built.

In 1969 Tupolev fielded a new and radically altered prototype, soon internationally known as the BACKFIRE B. This craft employed the nose section of the old Tu 22, but the thin fuselage was joined to two lengthy engine nacelles with massive air intakes at the front. The landing gear were also repositioned from wingpods to the fuselage. In service the new craft displayed marked improvement over earlier models and entered production as the Tu 22M. This may have been a deliberate ruse on the part of the Soviets, who wished to regard it as simply a Tu 22 variant during the SALT arms-reduction negotiations. The United States, fearful that the new plane possessed sufficient range as a strategic bomber, insisted that it be included in negotiations. As it turns out, even with in-flight refueling the Tu 22M could barely reach Cuba. However, the BACKFIRE remains a formidable antishipping weapon and continues serving in that capacity with Russian naval aviation. Production peaked at around 250 machines.

Type: Strategic Bomber; Antisubmarine; Reconnaissance

Dimensions: wingspan, 167 feet, 7 inches; length, 155 feet, 10 inches; height, 39 feet, 9 inches
Weights: empty, 189,544 pounds; gross, 407,848 pounds
Power plant: 4 × 14,795–horsepower Kuznetsov NK-12M turboprop engines
Performance: maximum speed, 757 miles per hour; ceiling, 39,370 feet; range, 5,150 miles
Armament: 2 × 23mm cannons; up to 25,000 pounds of bombs; torpedoes, or missiles
Service dates: 1955–

The legendary BEAR is the world's fastest propeller-driven aircraft. It is also the world's largest combat aircraft, with a distinguished service record dating back nearly half a century.

In the early 1950s the Soviet quest to crash-build a viable intercontinental strategic bomber took two distinct paths. The more conventional, jet-powered approach culminated in the unsatisfactory Mya-sishchev M 4, a promising design that simply lacked sufficient range to be strategic. Recognizing the pitfalls of early jet-engine technology, the Tupolev design bureau opted to utilize newly developed turboprop engines as a practical compromise. The four massive Kuznetsov power plants chosen would drive eight contrarotating propellers that were huge—18 feet in diameter! The fuselage was also conservatively conceived, as were the enormous swept wings. When the Tu 95 premiered at Moscow in 1955, the aviation world gasped, as Russia had apparently constructed an aircraft that should not have worked at all. In fact, the Tu 95 functioned well as a strategic bomber, being

almost supersonic and, thanks to the economy of the engines, possessing great range. With in-flight refueling, the Soviets now fielded an aircraft that could hit the United States and return. This point was well taken by the Americans, who spent billions of dollars developing new missiles and interceptors to thwart it. Around 300 Tu 95s of various types were constructed; all were assigned the NATO code name BEAR.

The first Tu 95s were intended as nuclear bombers, but the increasing sophistication of surface-to-air missile technology rendered them obsolete by 1960. Thereafter, great numbers were outfitted with nuclear-tipped standoff missiles. They functioned as the pride of Soviet Naval Long Range Aviation, as does a new version, the Tu 142. This is a revamped BEAR with a longer fuselage, longer inboard nacelles, and totally redesigned wings. The Tu 142 functions today as a dedicated antisubmarine warfare weapon of tremendous range and punch. At least 100 BEARs are still thought to remain in service with Russia and India.

Tupolev Tu 160 ━━━━━━━━━━━━━━━━━━━━━━━━━━━━━━ **Russia**

Type: Strategic Bomber

Dimensions: wingspan, (spread) 182 feet, 9 inches; length, 177 feet, 6 inches; height, 43 feet
Weights: empty, 260,140 pounds; gross, 589,947 pounds
Power plant: 4 × 30,843–pound thrust Kuznetsov NK-321 turbofan engines
Performance: maximum speed, 1,243 miles per hour; ceiling, 49,200 feet; range, 7,640 miles
Armament: up to 36,000 pounds of nuclear bombs and missiles
Service dates: 1987–

The mighty Tu 160 (designated BLACKJACK by NATO) is the most powerful and heaviest warplane ever constructed. It is designed to penetrate enemy airspace in high- or low-altitude configurations with greater speed and heavier payload than the rival North American/Rockwell B-1B *Lancer*.

Up through the early 1970s, the United States developed an advanced strategic bomber capable of hitting targets in the Soviet Union with speed, altitude, and excellent prospects for survival. The Soviet government summarily ordered its aviation industry to design a similar machine, even after U.S. President Jimmy Carter canceled the B-1 program in 1977. Three years later President Ronald Reagan resurrected it as the B-1B, which to save money became slated for low-altitude operations. No such cost-cutting measures were enacted in the Soviet program, however, and when the new Tu 160 materialized in 1981, it was capable of operating at any altitude. The design team under Vladimir I. Bliznuk fulfilled its tasks well, for the Tu 160 was 30 percent bigger than the B-1B, faster, and more capable. The

Soviet craft employed a similar planform to its American counterpart, possessing a blended fuselage and variable-geometry wings. The four podded engines are similarly housed under the fixed portion of the wings. The underside also sports two cavernous rotary bomb bays carrying a variety of freefall and guided nuclear weapons. Finally, the Tu 160 is almost completely operated by 100 computerized systems, and the two pilots are equipped with fighterlike joysticks plugged into multiple fly-by-wire systems. The Soviet government authorized 100 to be built, and NATO granted it the designation BLACKJACK.

After 1991 the intended role of this massive bomber is largely irrelevant. With the collapse of the Soviet Union, former Russian President Boris Yeltsin ordered a halt to production of most strategic weapons, and the run of Tu 160s appears to have ended at 38 machines. Half of them were marooned in the newly independent Ukraine, pending return to Russia. The final disposition of these formidable aircraft remains unknown.

Type: Reconnaissance

Dimensions: wingspan, 31 feet, 2 inches; length, 24 feet, 4 inches; height, 8 feet 8 inches
Weights: empty, 1,654 pounds; gross, 2,536 pounds
Power plant: 1 × 230–horsepower Hiero liquid-cooled engine
Performance: maximum speed, 118 miles per hour; ceiling, 16,076 feet; range, 360 miles
Armament: 2 × 7.92mm machine guns
Service dates: 1918–1919

The little-known Ufag C I was among the best Austrian two-seaters of World War I and was often more popular with pilots than the celebrated Phonix C I. It became the preferred machine for low-level artillery-spotting and reconnaissance work.

In January 1917 the Ungarische Flugzeugfabrik firm entered competition against the Phonix firm to build a new reconnaissance aircraft for the Luftfahrtruppe (Austrian air service). Like its rival, it was based upon the Hansa-Brandenburg C I, one of the infamous "Star-strutter" designs. The new Ufag machine dispensed with complicated bracing in favor of a conventional, single-bay approach. In addition, the nominally swept wing was highly modified into a straightened form with rounded tips that curved slightly inward. A crew of two sat in separate cockpits that were placed in a rather deep fuselage. The gunner also stood in a built-up ring that afforded him an excellent field of fire. Test results were impressive, and during flight trials against the Phonix machine the Ufag design proved faster and more maneuverable at lower altitudes. The Austrian

government saw virtues in both aircraft, and the respective companies were allowed to begin production. The Ufag machine entered Austrian service as the C I in the spring of 1918.

Ufag C Is were deployed almost exclusively along the Italian front and gained a reputation as rugged, durable weapons. Given its superior low-level performance, it was the choice of many pilots for dangerous artillery-spotting service, whereas the Phonix C I was favored for high-level reconnaissance work. The relatively fast Ufag was also praised for its ability to evade and outrun most Italian fighters. Subsequent models introduced increased wingspan and a modified empennage with a smaller tailplane and a plain, unbalanced rudder to enhance maneuverability. As reconnaissance platforms they equaled anything fielded on the Western Front. By war's end, a total of 244 C Is had been delivered by Ufag with an additional 40 machines contributed by Phonix. In 1919 several machines participated in the Hungarian Revolution and were also procured in small quantities by the fledgling Romanian air force.

Type: Fighter

Dimensions: wing span, 36 feet, 6 inches; length, 27 feet, 2 inches; height, 11 feet, 6 inches
Weights: empty, 1,220 pounds; gross, 2,050 pounds
Power plant: 1 × 100–horsepower Gnome Monosoupape rotary engine
Performance: maximum speed, 70 miles per hour; ceiling, 9,000 feet; range, 240 miles
Armament: 1 × .303–inch machine guns
Service dates: 1915–1916

The slow, sturdy "Gunbus" was among the world's earliest warplanes and the first British fighter. It performed useful, if undistinguished, service in World War I before being withdrawn.

The giant Vickers firm had established an airplane division as early as 1911 and was the first English company to market that new technology for military purposes. At the Olympia Air Show in 1913 Vickers unveiled its Type 18 "Destroyer," a controversial pusher design sporting a belt-fed Maxim machine gun operated by the observer. With successive refinements a final form, the FB 5 (Fighting Biplane), emerged in 1914. This, too, was a biplane pusher with two-bay, equal-length, unstaggered wings. A large nacelle was fastened to the lower wing, housing a crew of two and the motor. The tailbooms, four in number, were made of steel and converged on a structure that formed the rudder. Despite its fragile appearance, the FB 5 was sturdy and possessed viceless flying characteristics. The Vick-

ers firm, convinced that war with Germany was imminent, began construction before it was ordered by the government. When war did erupt in August 1914, several machines were available for military use, and it became the first British fighter accepted into service.

The first FB 5s did not reach France until the spring of 1915, and by summer they were flying in squadron strength. In combat it flew slow and stately, but it performed well against the equally primitive German craft of the day. On one occasion, a "Gunbus" piloted by Lieutenant G.S.M. Insall downed an Aviatik but was forced to land from damage. He subsequently repaired his plane under fire and flew it home the following day, winning the Victoria Cross. That fall the notorious Fokker *Eindekker* appeared, firing a synchronized gun through the propeller, which ended the FB 5's military career. By 1916 surviving machines functioned only as trainers, a somewhat anticlimactic finale for Britain's first fighter craft.

Type: Strategic Bomber; Tanker

Dimensions: wingspan, 114 feet, 4 inches; length, 108 feet, 3 inches; height, 32 feet, 4 inches
Weights: empty, 75,881 pounds; gross, 175,000 pounds
Power plant: 4 × 10,050–pound thrust Rolls-Royce Avon turbojet engines
Performance: maximum speed, 567 miles per hour; ceiling, 54,000 feet; range, 4,500 miles
Armament: up to 21,000 pounds of nuclear or conventional bombs
Service dates: 1955–1964

The *Valiant* was the first of the famous V-bombers and became the first British aircraft to test-drop nuclear weapons. Ironically, metal fatigue terminated their short and rather useful service.

The aftermath of the U.S. bombings of Hiroshima and Nagasaki underscored the necessity of nuclear deterrence to maintain peace and security in the postwar period. This was especially true in a world dominated by East-versus-West confrontation. Such prerogatives were in mind when the British Air Ministry issued Specification B.35/46 in 1946 for a fleet of jet-propelled nuclear bombers. Both Avro and Handley Page submitted designs that were extremely advanced and complicated, culminating in the splendid *Vulcan* and *Victor* bombers. However, rather than go charging off into uncharted waters, Vickers forwarded a plan that was deliberately less complicated and promised lower performance. The Air Ministry, wishing it as insurance in case the more advanced machines failed to materialized, then drew up Specification B.9/48 around the craft. The prototype *Valiant* first flew in 1951 as an ultramodern, all-metal jet bomber. It was a high-wing configuration, with four jets buried in the wing roots, and a high tail. The *Valiant* flew well enough to warrant production, so in 1955 the first 30 examples of the B 1 model became operational. These were followed by 11 B(PR) 1 reconnaissance versions, 14 B(PR) K 1 reconnaissance/tankers, and 48 BK 1 bomber/tankers. Total production amounted to 104 machines.

Operationally, *Valiants* highlighted all the diplomatic and military perils of the age. In 1956 several flew from Malta and dropped bombs on Egypt during the Suez Crisis. On October 11 of that same year a *Valiant* test-dropped the first British atomic weapon over northern Australia. The feat was duplicated on May 15, 1957, when a *Valiant* dropped Britain's first thermonuclear device in the Pacific. But as the more capable and modern *Vulcans* and *Victors* became operational, *Valiants* gradually were transferred to refueling duties. They were thus employed until 1964, when widespread metal fatigue caused the active fleet to be scrapped.

Type: Torpedo-Bomber; Liaison

Dimensions: wingspan, 49 feet; length, 37 feet, 8 inches; height, 14 feet, 8 inches
Weights: empty, 4,724 pounds; gross, 8,500 pounds
Power plant: 1 × 825–horsepower Bristol Perseus radial engine
Performance: maximum speed, 156 miles per hour; ceiling, 17,000 feet; range, 630 miles
Armament: 2 × .303–inch machine guns; 1 × 18–inch torpedo, or 1,000 pounds of bombs
Service dates: 1933–1942

The hulking *Vildebeest* was a capable machine that flew for nearly a decade. Totally obsolete by World War II, it suffered heavy losses during the defense of Singapore.

In 1925 a British Air Ministry specification sought to replace the Hawker *Horsley* torpedo-bomber with a more modern design. Three years later Vickers fielded the prototype *Vildebeest* as a possible contender. It was a large, two-bay biplane with fixed landing gear and an uncowled radial engine. The two square-tipped wings were unstaggered and of equal span, being made of metal framework and fabric covering. The fuselage was circular in cross-section and seated a crew of two in widely spaced seats. The landing gear were also widely spaced to hold an 18-inch-wide torpedo slung between them. It took a succession of different engines before the *Vildebeest* was successfully flown, but in 1933 it became the RAF Coastal Command's standard torpedo-bomber. The *Vildebeest* served capably for many years, and in 1935 a new model, the Mk IV, introduced a third

cockpit. Total production orders amounted to 194 machines, with 15 of them being diverted to the Royal New Zealand Air Force. When developmental problems delayed the appearance of the new Bristol *Beaufort*, the *Vildebeest*'s anticipated successor, they remained in service long after their operational usefulness had ended. This fact was painfully underscored in December 1941 when the Japanese attacked Malaysia. *Vildebeests* of No. 36 and No. 100 Squadrons fought with great courage—and little results—while taking heavy losses. The aging craft simply could not withstand the onslaught of modern fighter craft. Only two surviving bombers managed to reach Sumatra before being destroyed.

In 1934 the RAF sought an army cooperation version of the *Vildebeest* to replace the aging Fairey IIIs and Westland *Wapitis*. This craft, known as the *Vincent*, differed only in having an additional fuel tank and specialized communications equipment. A total of 197 were built, and they served throughout the Middle East until 1941.

Type: Heavy Bomber

Dimensions: wingspan, 68 feet; length, 43 feet, 6 inches; height, 15 feet
Power plant: 2 × 207–horsepower Hispano-Suiza water-cooled in-line engines
Performance: maximum speed, 103 miles per hour; ceiling, 12,000 feet; range, 900 miles
Armament: 2 × .303–inch machine guns; 2,476 pounds of bombs
Service dates: 1919–1930

The Vickers *Vimy* was a standard Royal Air Force heavy bomber between 1919 and 1930. However, it is best remembered for two highly successful long-range flights to Ireland and Australia.

The *Vimy* originated from a 1917 design specification for heavy bombers capable of hitting Berlin from the British Isles, much like the Handley Page O/400 and de Havilland DH 10. The prototype first flew in November 1917 as a standard three-bay biplane of wood-and-canvas construction. The engines hung midway between equal-span wings on struts; the fuselage sported a large biplane tail unit, and the whole thing touched down on paired, fixed wheels. Three preproduction machines reached Europe before the 1918 Armistice but saw no combat. Thereafter *Vimys* formed the bulk of RAF heavy bombardment units until their gradual replacement by Vickers *Virginias* in 1924. Toward the end of their service life, around 80 *Vimys* were refitted with radial engines and assigned training duties. They were finally withdrawn in 1930 after a production run of 221 machines.

In the course of its long career, the *Vimy* became indelibly associated with two historic flights. The first staged out of Newfoundland, Canada, on June 15, 1919, when a modified *Vimy* flown by Captains John Adcock and Arthur Whitten-Brown successfully reached Ireland in the world's first transatlantic crossing. The second, more ambitious flight took off from London on November 12, 1919, and was flown by Captain Ross Smith and his brother, Lieutenant Keith Smith. They successfully reached Australia by air on December 10, 1918, after 136 hours of flying time. A third, less-celebrated venture transpired on February 4, 1920, when a *Vimy* piloted by Lieutenant-Colonel Pierre van Rynevld and squadron leader Christopher J. Q. Brand, both of the South African air force, pioneered a mail link between London and Cape Town. Having crash-landed in Egypt, they were loaned another *Vimy* and proceeded as far as Bulawayo, Rhodesia, before being stalled again by mechanical problems. They finally touched down in Cape Town on March 20, 1920, in a third aircraft—a de Havilland DH 9.

Type: Light Bomber

Dimensions: wingspan, 74 feet, 7 inches; length, 39 feet, 3 inches; height, 12 feet, 4 inches
Weights: empty, 6,690 pounds; gross, 11,100 pounds
Power plant: 1 × 950–horsepower Bristol Pegasus XX radial engine
Performance: maximum speed, 228 miles per hour; ceiling, 19,680 feet; range, 1,110 miles
Armament: 2 × .303–inch machine guns; up to 2,000 pounds of bombs
Service dates: 1937–1944

The *Wellesley* was one of the longest-spanned single-engine bombers ever built. It set a world range record in 1938 and helped pioneer the geodetic building techniques applied to the famous Vickers *Wellington*.

In 1931 a British Air Ministry specification called for a long-range bomber, and Vickers constructed two aircraft. The first was a biplane built in precise conformity to the specification; it proved singularly unimpressive. The second, undertaken as a private venture, was radically different and successful. The new craft was a low-wing monoplane of exceptionally long span and powered by a cowled radial engine. A crew of two sat in separate, fully enclosed canopies. But the most distinguishing feature was its construction. Designers Barnes Wallis and Rex Pierson had previously collaborated on building airship R100 for Vickers and decided to incorporate its geodetic structure into a large aircraft. This technique entailed building a crisscross lattice structure of metal, promoting great strength with very little weight. The fuselage and wings of the new

craft were accordingly built along these lines with impressive results. It proved so superior to the biplane entry that the Air Ministry canceled the old specifications and rewrote them with the new monoplane in mind. In 1937 it entered service as the Vickers *Wellesley;* 176 were constructed.

By the advent of World War II in 1939, the *Wellesley* was marginally obsolete, but at least 100 were maintained in and around the Middle East. Many of them dropped bombs on Italian targets during the East African campaign and conducted long-range reconnaissance throughout the western Mediterranean. After 1941 most *Wellesleys* were declared surplus and scrapped. However, this craft is best remembered for efforts by the RAF Long Range Development Flight. In 1938 three modified *Wellesleys* took off from Ismailia, Egypt, for Darwin, Australia. Two arrived safely exactly 48 hours later, having covered 7,162 miles in poor weather. This was the greatest distance ever flown in a straight line, and the record remained unbroken until 1945.

Type: Medium Bomber

Dimensions: wingspan, 86 feet, 2 inches; length, 64 feet, 7 inches; height, 17 feet, 5 inches
Weights: empty, 18,970 pounds; gross, 34,000 pounds
Power plant: 2 × 1,500–horsepower Bristol Hercules XI radial engines
Performance: maximum speed, 255 miles per hour; ceiling, 19,000 feet; range, 1,540 miles
Armament: 8 × .303–inch machine guns; 4,500 pounds of bombs
Service dates: 1938–1953

The "Wimpy" was built in greater numbers than any other British multiengine aircraft. Its geodetic structure allowed it to absorb extensive damage and keep flying.

In 1932 the British Air Ministry sought development of a new twin-engine heavy bomber and issued Specification B.9/32. A Vickers design team under Barnes Wallis decided to capitalize on prior success with the *Wellesley* by incorporating the same geodetic construction techniques. The prototype was unveiled in 1936 as a midwing monoplane employing the trademark basket-weave lattice structure in the wings and fuselage, all covered by fabric. The resulting craft was relatively light for its size but phenomenally strong. It was also heavily defended by powered gun turrets in the nose and tail and additional beam positions. The *Wellington* entered squadron service in 1938 as the most advanced medium bomber in the world. Known as "Wimpy" after a cartoon character, it helped form the backbone of RAF Bomber Command when World War II commenced in 1939.

Wellingtons, in concert with several Bristol *Blenheims*, made the first British raid of the war when they hit naval targets at Wilhelmshaven on September 4, 1939. However, the practice of daylight bombing, in the teeth of determined fighter opposition, usually resulted in heavy losses. Consequently, a return raid over Wilhelmshaven on December 18 resulted in 10 out of 24 *Wellingtons* being lost. Thereafter, they were restricted to nighttime operations, and by helping establish the RAF strategy of nighttime saturation bombing, the "Wimpy" made its greatest contribution. Almost impervious to flak, many sustained great damage yet survived. Until the advent of bigger, more capable four-engine aircraft from 1942 on, *Wellingtons* bore the brunt of strategic bombing with excellent results. Large numbers also served with the RAF Coastal Command throughout the Atlantic and Mediterranean theaters, sinking no less than 26 U-boats. Production totaled 11,462 machines. Many remained in service until 1953, almost three decades after the original specifications had been announced.

Type: Transport; Antisubmarine; Reconnaissance

Dimensions: rotorspan, 42 feet; length, 49 feet, 9 inches; height, 12 feet
Weights: empty, 6,772 pounds; gross, 10,750 pounds
Power plant: 2 × 1,135–horsepower Rolls-Royce Gem turboshaft engines
Performance: maximum speed, 159 miles per hour; ceiling, 10,600 feet; range, 392 miles
Armament: 6 × TOW antitank missiles or 6 × *Sea Skua* antiship missiles
Service dates: 1977–

The versatile *Lynx* is one of the world's foremost tactical helicopters. Jointly built by Britain and France, it serves in navies around the world and performs many military functions.

The *Lynx* can trace its origins to the Westland WG.13, a design submitted in fulfillment of the Anglo-French helicopter accord of 1968. Through this expedient, both countries would jointly build and deploy three basic helicopters. The first two, the *Puma* and *Gazelle*, were of entirely French design, but the WG.13 was an original Westland product. It was a sleek pod-and-boom configuration utilizing the new semirigid rotor technology. Thirteen prototypes were built, with the first flying in March 1971. Test results were excellent and revealed the machine to be fast, agile, and extremely acrobatic. Christened the *Lynx*, it is one of few helicopters in the world that can be routinely looped and rolled in complete safety. Production commenced in 1976, with Britain responsible for 70 percent of the parts and France the remainder.

The *Lynx* is currently available in two versions. The navy *Lynx* possesses tricycle landing gear and a rotorhead capable of a negative 6 degrees of pitch that, in effect, "pushes" the machine down on a rolling ship deck to keep it in place. These helicopters are outfitted with advanced avionics that permit all-weather operations while being flown by only one pilot. Furthermore, they are extremely versatile and can fulfill a variety of antisubmarine, antishipping, and surveillance missions. In 1982 *Lynxes* became the first helicopter to fire *Sea Skua* missiles in anger when they damaged the Argentine submarine *Santa Fe* near South Georgia Island. The Royal Navy has acquired 91 of these useful machines; 200 more fly with navies around the world.

The military *Lynx* version is immediately recognizable by its landing skids. It can carry up to 12 fully armed troops but is usually outfitted with eight TOW missiles and a roof-mounted sight for antitank work. The British army maintains and operates a large fleet of 100 *Lynxes*.

Type: Liaison; Reconnaissance

Dimensions: wingspan, 50 feet; length, 30 feet, 6 inches; height, 14 feet, 6 inches
Weights: empty, 4,365 pounds; gross, 6,318 pounds
Power plant: 1 × 870–horsepower Bristol Mercury XX radial engine
Performance: maximum speed, 212 miles per hour; ceiling, 21,500 feet; range, 600 miles
Armament: 3 × .303–inch machine guns
Service dates: 1938–1945

Possessing excellent STOL (short takeoff and landing) characteristics, "Lizzie" was a useful liaison and reconnaissance aircraft. It became renowned for its ability to drop off and retrieve secret agents throughout occupied Europe.

In 1934 the British Air Ministry, wishing to replace the aging Hawker *Hector* biplanes as army co-operation craft, issued Specification A.39/34. It called for a new monoplane aircraft with good STOL characteristics for operating from small fields. Westland entered a design called *Lysander*, one of the most unique-looking airplanes ever flown by the Royal Air Force. It was a braced monoplane with large, spatted wheels and braced, lozenge-shaped wings. The wings were metal-covered from the leading edge to the main spar, then covered by fabric. Slotted flaps were fitted to the trailing edges, which when deployed allowed the craft to land and take off at speeds as slow as 65 miles per hour. The rotund fuselage consisted of steel tubing and wooden formers, also fabric-covered. The *Lysander* was somewhat heavily armed for a liaison aircraft, sport-ing two forward-firing machine guns and one for the observer. It entered production in 1938 and equipped several squadrons by the advent of World War II.

In September 1939 *Lysanders* were deployed to France as part of the British Expeditionary Force. They performed useful reconnaissance and artillery-spotting services as long as the RAF maintained local air superiority. However, commencing with the Battle of France in May 1940, the slow-flying airplanes were easy prey for fast, heavily armed German fighters. They were called upon to perform ground-attack and air-supply missions, often in the teeth of enemy opposition. No less than 112 were lost in a single month, by which time the British had been driven from the continent. Thereafter, new work was found for the "Lizzie" in the form of training and glider-towing. Its ability to land and abruptly depart made it ideal for dropping and retrieving special agents throughout Europe. A total of 1,593 *Lysanders* were built; all were declared obsolete by 1946.

Westland *Scout/Wasp* ──────────── Great Britain

Type: Antitank; Reconnaissance; Antisubmarine

Dimensions: rotorspan, 32 feet, 3 inches; length, 30 feet, 4 inches; height, 8 feet, 11 inches
Weights: empty, 3,452 pounds; gross, 5,500 pounds
Power plant: 1 × 1,050–horsepower Rolls-Royce Nimbus turboshaft engine
Performance: maximum speed, 132 miles per hour; ceiling, 12,500 feet; range, 478 miles
Armament: 4 × SS.11 antitank missiles or 2 × Mk 44 torpedoes
Service dates: 1963–1998

The *Scout* was a useful light utility helicopter for the British army. A naval derivative, the *Wasp*, became the first helicopter deployed in large numbers aboard Royal Navy frigates.

Shortcomings of the Saunders Roe *Skeeter* helicopter induced that company to initiate design of a larger, more capable craft in 1956. Designated P 531, it was a standard pod-and-boom machine with a fully enclosed cabin, large glazed windows, and landing skids. The prototype first flew with good results in 1958, although a more powerful version, the P 531–2, flew the following year. In 1960 Saunders Roe was absorbed by Westland, but work continued apace on the production models, which entered service in 1963 as the *Scout*.

The British army ordered 150 examples of the AH 1 *Scout* for use as light utility/liaison aircraft. Despite their small size, *Scouts* were applauded for strength and reliability in the field. They performed sterling service throughout the 1982 Falkland Is-

lands War as reconnaissance and medevac vehicles. Toward the end of their long career, many were outfitted with SS.11 wire-guided missiles for antitank work. By 1994 all had been retired in favor of the more modern *Lynx*. A solitary example remains in flyable condition at Middle Wallop.

In the early 1960s the Royal Navy needed a standard light helicopter to perform antisubmarine warfare work aboard its frigates. The *Scout* seemed like a logical place to begin, so a navalized version, the *Wasp*, was developed in 1962. It differed from army versions mainly in possessing castor landing gear and a folding tail section for shipboard storage. It also employed locking brakes to keep the helicopter from pitching on deck during heavy seas. In service the *Wasp* flew without sensors, relying instead on sonar findings from its mothership for guidance. The Royal Navy acquired 98 *Wasps*, with an additional 35 being exported to Brazil, New Zealand, and South Africa. All have been retired since 1998.

Type: Light Bomber; Reconnaissance

Dimensions: wingspan, 46 feet, 5 inches; length, 32 feet, 6 inches; height, 11 feet, 10 inches
Weights: empty, 3,280 pounds; gross, 5,400 pounds
Power plant: 1 × 460–horsepower Bristol Jupiter VI radial engine
Performance: maximum speed, 140 miles per hour; ceiling, 20,600 feet; range, 360 miles
Armament: 2 × .303–inch machine guns; up to 580 pounds of bombs
Service dates: 1927–1939

The inelegant *Wapiti* was Westland's first airplane and a stalwart machine of the 1930s. They served conspicuously throughout the empire and final variants even overflew Mount Everest.

As the 1920s drew to a close, the British Air Ministry decided that new aircraft were needed to better maintain order throughout the British Empire. Specification 26/27 was therefore issued, calling for a new general-purpose aircraft. As a cost-cutting expedient, it also mandated that the winning candidate would utilize as many parts of the old de Havilland DH 9a as possible. Fortunately, Westland had constructed DH 9s during 1916–1918, and in 1927 a Westland prototype beat out six other competitors to win a government contract. The new craft, called the *Wapiti*, used the same wings, interplane struts, and tail unit as the DH 9a. However, they were wedded to a new, much deeper fuselage. Once fitted to a 420-horsepower Bristol Jupiter VI radial engine, the new craft flew exceedingly well, and in 1927 the first 25 aircraft were delivered.

In service the *Wapiti* proved to be a rugged, functional design that went through five marks in five years. The most significant of these was the Mk II, which introduced an all-metal framework. *Wapitis* flew the length and breadth of the British Empire, serving as army cooperation planes, light bombers, and reconnaissance craft. In fulfilling these duties there evolved a seaplane *Wapiti* on twin floats, an Arctic *Wapiti* with skis, a long-range *Wapiti* with additional fuel tanks for desert patrol, and the *Wapiti* trainer with dual controls. By the time production ceased in 1932, 521 machines had been constructed for the Royal Air Force, with another 500 exported to other countries. Commencing in 1932 around 80 *Wapitis* were upgraded to a successive model, the *Wallace*, with lengthened fuselages and bigger engines. On April 3, 1932, two of these aircraft climbed to 29,026 feet and ranged over Mount Everest in the Himalayas. The last *Wapitis* were finally retired in 1939.

Type: Fighter; Light Bomber

Dimensions: wingspan, 45 feet; length, 32 feet, 9 inches; height, 11 feet, 7 inches
Weights: empty, 8,310 pounds; gross, 11,388 pounds
Power plant: 2 × 885–horsepower Rolls-Royce Peregrine liquid-cooled in-line engines
Armament: 4 × 20mm cannons; up to 1,000 pounds of bombs
Service dates: 1940–1943

The futuristic, spectacular *Whirlwind* was one of Britain's most conspicuous aviation failures of World War II. Conceived as a fast and hard-hitting escort fighter, it flew well but suffered from insurmountable engine problems.

In 1935 the Air Ministry issued the highly secret Specification F.37/35 to obtain the world's first twin-engine, single-seat fighter. Moreover, the new design was also intended to be the world's first cannon-armed fighter. A Westland design team under W.E.W. "Teddy" Petter conceived a very advanced solution the following year, and the government quietly issued a contract for two prototypes. The first ones flew in September 1938, being among the most advanced warplanes of the time. The *Whirlwind* appeared radically different from contemporary fighters. It possessed a long fuselage, the cross-section being less than those of the engine nacelles. Moreover, the wing was set far forward on the fuselage, and the distinct, cruciform tail sat high in the rear. It was also one of the first fighters to possess a bubble canopy for unimpeded all-around vision. The aircraft was formidably armed with four 20mm concentrated cannons,

closely packed together in the nose, for unprecedented firepower. The *Whirlwind* displayed excellent range and maneuverability, and thus, in great secrecy, the government decided to produce them in quantity.

In view of its great potential, the *Whirlwind* proved a major disappointment. The problem source was the Roll Royce Peregrine engines, which were unreliable, low-powered, and required high maintenance time. The *Whirlwind* also exhibited high landing speeds, despite the presence of Fowler flaps, which rendered it unsuitable for a majority of British airfields. Ultimately, 112 were constructed and equipped only two squadrons. Commencing in 1941, *Whirlwinds* performed useful work as escort fighters and subsequently distinguished themselves as low-level fighter-bombers. Their specialty was a cross-channel foray dubbed the "Rhubarb." Roaring in low and fast, Westland fighters appeared suddenly and wreaked havoc on enemy transportation and railway systems. But in view of mechanical unreliability, their operational days were limited. By 1943 all were replaced by the initially temperamental, but ultimately more successful, Hawker *Typhoon*.

Type: Fighter

Dimensions: wingspan, 30 feet, 2 inches; length, 27 feet, 10 inches; height, 7 feet, 11 inches
Weights: empty, 4,641 pounds; gross, 5,864 pounds
Power plant: 1 × 1,300–horsepower VK 105PF liquid-cooled in-line engine
Performance: maximum speed, 407 miles per hour; ceiling, 35,105 feet; range, 559 miles
Armament: 2 × 12.7mm machine guns; 1 × 20mm cannon
Service dates: 1944–1946

The Yak 3 was a highly successful low-altitude interceptor during World War II. It sprung from a family of fighters renowned for their maneuverability, and German pilots were warned to avoid it.

In late 1942 attempts were made to wring even better performance out of existing Yak fighters. Russian aircraft performed better at low altitude than their German counterparts, but the latter were generally faster. Because the majority of air battles along the Eastern Front were waged at low altitude, the Red Air Force wanted a weapon that would ensure air superiority close overhead. Consequently, a Yak 1M fuselage was modified to accept an advanced VK 107 engine. To accomplish this, the already light frame was lightened even further, and special care was taken to reduce drag through streamlining. The most notable modification was moving the bulky chin oil cooler to the wing roots. The fuselage was also cut down toward the rear and a simple bubble canopy installed. Finally, a smaller wing was fitted, and armament was pared down to save weight. When teething problems delayed the availability of the VK 107 engine, the existing VK 105PF was substituted. In service the new fighter, designated the Yak 3, proved an even better dogfighter than its more numerous Yak 9 stablemates.

Yak 3s made their appearance in the summer of 1944 and were strikingly successful. Not only could they outturn Messerschmitt Bf 109s and Focke-Wulf Fw 190s at low altitude, the new Yaks climbed and accelerated faster. In the hands of skilled pilots it proved deadly. On July 14, 1944, eight Yak 3s encountered 60 enemy aircraft and claimed three Junkers Ju 88s and four Me 109s without loss. In another swirling engagement, 18 Yak 3s tangled with 30 Bf 109s, downing 15 with the loss of a single plane. The Germans quickly took stock of this streamlined dervish and advised pilots to avoid Yak 3 fighters below 16,000 feet. A total of 4,848 were built.

Type: Fighter

Dimensions: wingspan, 32 feet; length, 28 feet; height, 9 feet, 8 inches
Weights: empty, 5,988 pounds; gross, 6,830 pounds
Power plant: 1 1,650–horsepower Klimov VK 107A liquid-cooled in-line engine
Performance: maximum speed, 434 miles per hour; veiling, 39,040 feet; range, 541 miles
Armament: 2 × 12.7mm machine guns; 1 × 20mm cannon; up to 220 pounds of bombs
Service dates: 1942–1950

The Yak 9 was the Soviet Union's most numerous and important wartime fighter during 1942–1945. It helped to wrest away air supremacy from German invaders and facilitated the ultimate Russian victory.

Responding to a 1939 Soviet directive for new fighters, young Alexander Yakovlev originated a promising design, while attempting to build the smallest possible airframe around a powerful VK 105 engine. It was built of steel tubing and covered with wood. First flown in 1940, the craft handled extremely well and was rushed into production as the Yak 1. Latter models eventually acquired a lower fuselage and a bubble canopy for better vision. From there the new Yak 7 evolved, incorporating lighter construction and additional fuel. It retained the fully enclosed, old-style canopy and served mainly in ground-attack roles. Both fighters did valuable work blunting the German aerial onslaught, but by 1942 a newer version was needed to acquire air superiority. Thus was born the Yak 9, which, numerically speaking, was the largest and

most important member of this burgeoning family of aircraft.

The Yak 9 was essentially a lightened version of the earlier Yak 7, although fitted with the Yak 1's bubble canopy. A smaller wing with metal spars was also fitted, along with revised tail surfaces and a retractable tailwheel. Moreover, it featured metal skinning instead of wood, as well as additional streamlining. Yak 9s debuted during the 1942 Battle of Stalingrad and demonstrated marked superiority over Messerschmitt Bf 109s at low altitude. This ruggedly versatile craft was subsequently adopted for an entire range of activities, including long-range escort and tankbusting. By 1943 the second generation of Yak 9s appeared with stronger engines and a higher proportion of metal parts. These also sported a redesigned fuselage and bigger wings and proved to be the most maneuverable members of the series. Yak 9s remained in service until about 1950. Total production of this variant reached 16,769 out of a grand total of 30,000 Yak machines.

Type: Fighter

Dimensions: wingspan, 24 feet; length, 50 feet, 10 inches; height, 14 feet, 4 inches
Weights: empty, 16,501 pounds; gross, 25,794 pounds
Power plant: 1 × 14,991–pound thrust NMPK turbojet; 2 × 7,175–pound thrust RKBM turbojet
Performance: maximum speed, 627 miles per hour; ceiling, 39,370 feet; range, 230 miles
Armament: up to 2,200 pounds of air-to-air missiles
Service dates: 1976–

The complicated Yak 36 remains the Russian navy's lone operational shipborne attack craft. It operates on the same principle as the more famous British *Harrier*, although it is lacking in payload and sophistication.

Throughout the late 1950s and into the 1960s, Russia and Great Britain experimented heavily with VTOL (vertical takeoff and landing) aircraft for military applications. By 1969 the British arrived at a viable solution by deploying the British Aerospace *Harrier*, the world's first VTOL attack craft. Russian efforts, by comparison, were conducted with much less imagination. They did not field a working prototype until 1967 with the appearance of a Yakovlev bureau prototype designated FREEHAND by NATO. It was a crude, if functional, machine compared to the sophisticated *Harrier*, apparently constructed as a testbed for follow-on designs. The pace of Yakovlev's research increased by 1969, when construction of the Soviet Union's first VTOL-dedicated aircraft carrier, the *Kiev*, commenced. However, it was not until 1976 that the *Kiev* sailed with a com-

pliment of new Yak 36 fighters as standard equipment. Around 100 were apparently built, receiving the NATO designation FORGER.

Despite outward similarities to the *Harrier*, the Yak 36 is more primitive and less capable. It employs a main thrust engine for both vertical and horizontal flight, assisted by two smaller engines during liftoff. The engines are arrayed in vectoring nozzles, two forward and two aft. Thus configured, the Yak 36 cannot make conventional takeoffs from a carrier deck, lacking forward thrust. It is therefore constricted to fuel-consuming vertical-lift operations. Neither does the FORGER employ wingtip nozzles like the *Harrier*, making it incapable of such dazzling maneuvers as vectored thrust in combat ("viffing"). For all its limitations, the Yak 36 is still a viable shipborne strike aircraft, much better armed than the helicopters most Russian ships employ. It certainly represents a threat to unarmed maritime reconnaissance craft like the *Orion* and *Nimrod*. The Yak 36 apparently remains an interim type, pending arrival of a more advanced successor.

Type: Dive-Bomber; Reconnaissance

Dimensions: wingspan, 37 feet, 8 inches; length, 33 feet, 6 inches; height, 12 feet, 3 inches
Weights: empty, 5,514 pounds; gross, 10,267 pounds
Power plant: 1 × 1,400–horsepower Aichi AE1P Atsuka liquid-cooled in-line engine
Performance: maximum speed, 357 miles per hour; ceiling, 34,450 feet; range, 945 miles
Armament: 2 × 7.7mm machine guns; 1 × 12.7mm machine gun; 1,234 pounds of bombs
Service dates: 1943–1945

The D4Y was the fastest carrier-based dive-bomber of World War II. Although suffering from lack of armor and armament, it also fulfilled reconnaissance, night-fighter, and kamikaze functions.

In 1937 the Imperial Japanese Navy staff requested a replacement for its Aichi D3A dive-bombers. They approached the design staff at the Yokosuka Naval Air Arsenal with stringent requirements that included a 1,380-mile range, a 550-pound payload, and a top speed of 320 miles per hour. This was a departure from prevailing norms, for most dive-bombers were by necessity relatively slow, stable machines. To meet these new specifications, it was decided to employ a relatively small fuselage powered by an in-line engine. The power plant chosen was the Aichi Atsuka, a licensed copy of the Daimler-Benz DB 600. The prototype D4Y first flew in November 1940 as a sleek, all-metal, midwing monoplane. It had a pointed outline, a long canopy seating two crew members, and was stressed for catapult operations. The craft was fast and handled

well, but it suffered from chronic engine problems. Two more years of development followed before a handful of preproduction models served aboard the carrier *Soryu* in 1942. They functioned as high-speed reconnaissance craft and were lost when the *Soryu* sank at Midway in June 1942. It was not until 1943 that the persistent engine problems were resolved and mass production commenced. Eventually the D4Y *Suisei* (Comet) gained the Allied designation *Judy*.

Several hundred D4Ys were deployed on nine Japanese carriers by the fall of 1944 and experienced their baptism of fire off Truk. There, and in a host of successive encounters, *Judys* performed well but were inevitably intercepted by hordes of U.S. fighters without ever reaching their targets. Lacking self-sealing tanks and armor, they also proved extremely vulnerable to attack. Nonetheless, new CR models were introduced with a more reliable radial engine; kamikaze and night-fighter versions were also deployed. A total of 2,319 D4Ys were built.

Type: Suicide Craft

Dimensions: wingspan, 16 feet, 9 inches; length, 19 feet, 11 inches; height, 3 feet, 9 inches
Weights: empty, 970 pounds; gross, 4,718 pounds
Power plant: 3 × Type 4 MK1 rocket motors with 1,765 pounds of thrust
Performance: maximum speed, 535 miles per hour; range, 23 miles
Armament: 2,646 pounds of explosives
Service dates: 1945

Born out of Japan's desperation to stem the Allied march through the Pacific, the *Oka* was a hideously ingenious and potentially formidable weapon. It might have wreaked havoc on Allied forces had the bombers carrying them been able to penetrate American fighter screens.

By the summer of 1944 Japanese military planners were beginning to sense futility in defending the empire against the Allied onslaught. Navy Ensign Mitsuo Ohta then conceived of an idea that was at once simple and barbaric. He proposed creating a small manned aircraft, part glider and part rocket, that could be released near an objective and destroy itself in the finest tradition of kamikaze warriors. That fall the Yokosuka Naval Air Arsenal constructed a functioning prototype of what came to known as the MXY 7 *Oka*. The name, which means "Cherry Blossom," was chosen for the traditional reverence shown it by samurai warriors: Both were expected to enjoy lives that were brilliant—and brief. It was a small gliding platform made from wood and metal, fitted with stubby wings and twin rudders. However, once powered by three small rocket motors, it could streak toward targets at speeds in excess of 500 miles per hour. Moreover, the *Oka* packed nearly 3,000 pounds of high explosives in the nose, which detonated on contact. The most ghoulish feature was that pilots were sealed into their cockpit before launching without any thought of survival. It was envisioned that fleets of such destructive craft, in concert with more conventional propeller-driven kamikazes, would convince the United States not to invade Japan or sign a more favorable peace treaty. By the spring of 1945 more than 800 MXY 7 *Okas* had been assembled. The Allies came to know them as *Baka*, the Japanese term for "idiot."

The *Okas* were first deployed in March 1945, when 16 specially rigged G4M bombers approached the U.S. fleet. However, most were shot down by Navy fighters, and the *Okas* that did manage to be launched were too distant to be effective. Other attacks were more successful, and an MXY 7 sank the destroyer USS *Mannert L. Abele* in April 1945. Fortunately, the war ended before more lives, Japanese and American alike, could be claimed by such insidious technology.

Type: Medium Bomber; Torpedo-Bomber; Dive-Bomber

Dimensions: wingspan, 65 feet, 7 inches; length, 49 feet, 2 inches; height, 14 feet, 1 inch
Weights: empty, 16,017 pounds; gross, 29,762 pounds
Power plant: 2 × 1,820–horsepower Nakajima NK9B Homare radial engines
Performance: maximum speed, 340 miles per hour; ceiling, 30,840 feet; range, 3,337 miles
Armament: 2 × 20mm cannons; up to 2,205 pounds of bombs or torpedoes
Service dates: 1945

The P1Y1 was a fine multimission aircraft in the tradition of the Junkers Ju 88 and de Havilland *Mosquito*. However, it remained plagued by teething problems and mechanical unreliability.

In 1940 the Japanese naval staff established demanding specifications for a new high-speed medium bomber. The craft had to be capable for level-bombing, dive-bombing, and torpedo-bombing while possessing great speed, range, and armament. It fell upon a design team headed by Tadanao Mitsuzi and Masao Yamana to formulate the design into a functioning prototype. This took three years to accomplish, and it was not until 1943 that the first P1Y1 took flight. It was an extremely clean, appealing machine, with a streamlined fuselage, cowls, and tapering wings. More important, it was fitted with self-sealing fuel tanks and armor for the crew of three. Test pilots marveled at the big machine's speed and maneuverability, but ground crews grumbled over its complex hydraulics and unreliable

Homare radial engines. At this stage in the war, Japan very much needed a more capable bomber, so the navy elected to commence production before persistent design flaws had been corrected. Machines rolled off the assembly line up through 1944, but not a single P1Y1 *Ginga* (Milky Way) was accepted into service until properly debugged. By the time this transpired in January 1945, the Japanese Empire was in dire straits indeed. Around that time it received the Allied designation *Frances*.

In service the P1Y1 proved something of a mixed blessing. When running properly it was fast, extremely robust, and able to outrun Allied fighters at low altitude. However, operations were bedeviled by shoddy workmanship, a lack of trained mechanics, and spare-parts shortages. At length it became necessary to adapt the P1Y1 as a night fighter, but it lacked the necessary performance at high altitude. Many were thus expended as kamikazes. A total of 1,098 were built.

Type: Heavy Bomber

Dimensions: wingspan, 138 feet, 5 inches; length, 72 feet, 6 inches; height, 20 feet, 8 inches
Weights: empty, 17,426 pounds; gross, 26,066 pounds
Power plant: 4 × 245–horsepower Maybach Mb IV liquid-cooled in-line engines
Performance: maximum speed, 84 miles per hour; ceiling, 14,170 feet; range, 800 miles
Armament: 7 × 7.92mm machine guns; up to 4,409 pounds of bombs
Service dates: 1917–1918

The gigantic, lumbering Zeppelin Staaken R bombers were the most remarkable aircraft of World War I. They raided England with impunity and hoisted some of the largest bombs dropped in that conflict.

As early as 1915 the famous Count Ferdinand Zeppelin expressed interest in *Riesenflugzeug* (giant aircraft) as possible weapons; that year, in concert with engineers Gustav Klein and Helmut Hirth, a factory was founded at a field provided by the Gothaer Waggonfabrik firm. The following year the company reestablished itself as the Zeppelin Werke Staaken outside of Berlin. For two years the count and his cohorts developed numerous R-class prototypes with varying degrees of success. It was not until June 1917 that the first production model, the R VI, emerged. It was a huge, multibay biplane with a slab-sided fuselage and a large biplane tail assembly. The R VI was powered by no less than four Maybach engines positioned in tandem cowls, with two pushers and two

tractors per side. A crew of seven was carried, including two pilots who were seated in a fully enclosed cabin. The R VI was so large that its landing gear utilized no less than 16 wheels, grouped in fours, under the wing. A smaller set of nosewheels was also employed to prevent noseovers upon landing. All told, the R VIs were crude but perfectly functional strategic bombers. A total of 18 were acquired, bringing the entire number of R types constructed to 32.

The R VIs began operations against France and England in the summer of 1917. They raided London several times and, on one occasion, delivered a bomb weighing 2,205 pounds—the heaviest dropped during the entire war. Surprisingly, no R ship was ever shot down during 28 raids over England, although several were lost in accidents. Two were subsequently downed on the continent, but by war's end the R VIs enjoyed a higher percentage of successful raids than their more famous Gotha rivals. This was a formidable warplane in its day.

AIRCRAFT BIBLIOGRAPHY

ARGENTINA

FMA
IA 58 *Pucara*
Donald, David. "FMA IA-58 Pucara: Pampas Warrior," *World Air Power Journal* 6 (Summer, 1991): 136–145.
Ethell, Jeff. "Pucara," *War in the Falklands: Air Combat Special Report* (1983): 42–45, 80–85.
Huertas, Salvadore M. "Pucara's Wrong War," *Air International* 50 (April, 1996): 248–251.
"Latin American Flying 'Fortress,'" *Air International* 13 (October, 1977): 165–172.

AUSTRALIA

Commonwealth Aircraft Corporation
Hill, Brian. *Wirraway to Hornet: A History of the Commonwealth Aircraft Corporation, Pty. Ltd., 1936 to 1985*. Bulleen, Victoria: Southern Cross Publications, 1988.
Vella, Joe. "From Fisherman's Bend: The Aircraft of the Commonwealth Aircraft Corporation," *Air Enthusiast* No. 61 (January/February, 1996): 25–35.
CA 1 *Wirraway*
Justo, Craig P. "Facing a Challenge," *Fly Past* No. 169 (August, 1995): 71–73.
_____. "Together Again," *Aeroplane Monthly* 25 (March, 1997): 12–17.
Owers, Colin. "Australia's Warlike Trainer," *Air Enthusiast* 50 (May/July, 1993): 11–19.
Pentland, Geoffrey. *Wirraway and Boomerang Markings*. Dandinong, Victoria: Kookaburra Technical Publications, 1970.
Research Staff. *Commonwealth Wirraway*. Aircraft in Profile No. 154. Windsor, UK: Profile Publications, 1967.
Wilson, Stewart. *Wirraway, Boomerang, and CA-15 in Australian Service*. Weston Creek, ACT: Aerospace Publications, 1992.
CA 12 *Boomerang*
Francillon, Rene J. *Commonwealth Boomerang*. Aircraft in Profile No. 178. Windsor, UK: Profile Publications, 1967.
Grant, James R. "Boomerang!" *Fly Past* No. 130 (May, 1992): 62–63.
Green, William. "Boomerang, the Digger's Delight," *Air International* 2 (February, 1972): 91–98.
Harding, Stephen. "Return of the Boomerang," *Air Classics* 28 (September, 1992): 34–43, 46.

Pentland, Geoffrey. *Commonwealth Boomerang Described*. Melbourne: Kookaburra Technical Publications, 1966.

AUSTRIA-HUNGARY

Aviatik
C I
Grosz, P. M. *Aviatik C I*. Windsock Datafile No. 63. Berkhamsted, UK: Albatros Productions, 1997.
Krzyzan, Marian K. "Aviatik C. III," *World War I Aero* No. 76 (November, 1979): 27–35.
"Les Aviatiks," *Cross and Cockade Great Britain Journal* 13 (Spring, 1982): 1–17.
D I
"The Austrian Berg Single-Seater," *Cross and Cockade Journal* 1 (Autumn, 1960): 14–27.
Grosz, Peter M. *Aviatik D.I.* Windsock Datafile No. 45. Berkhamsted, UK: Albatros Productions, 1994.
Grosz, Peter M., and George Haddow. "Austria-Hungary's First Indigenous Fighter," *Air Enthusiast* 21 (April/July, 1983): 63–76.
Haddow, George W. O. *Aviatik (Berg) D. I.* Aircraft in Profile No. 151. Windsor, UK: Profile Publications, 1967.
Meindl, Karl, and Walter Schroeder. *Brandenburg D. I.* Stratford, CT: Flying Machine Press, 1997.

Etrich
Taube
DeVries, John A. *Taube, Dove of War*. Temple City, CA: Historical Aviation Album, 1978.

Hansa-Brandenburg
C I
Kopanski, Tomasz. "The Brandenburg C. I in Polish Air Force Service," *Windsock International* 11 (March/April, 1995): 25–28.
D I
Connors, John F. "The Star-Strutter," *Wings* 6 (October, 1976): 54–60.
Meindl, Karl, and Walter Schroeder. *Brandenburg D. I.* Stratford, CT: Flying Machine Press, 1997.

Lloyd
C V
Owers, Colin. "The Lloyd C. V.," *Windsock International* 6 (January/February, 1990): 4–13.

Lohner
B VIII
Evans, Bill, and George Haddow. "Lohner B VIII: A Photographic Study," *Cross and Cockade International* 12 (Winter, 1981): 166–174.

Phonix
C I
    Owers, Colin A. "Phonix Colours," *Windsock International* 15 (1999): 25–32.
D I
    Grosz, P. M. *Phonix D I -II*. Windsock Datafile No. 31. Berkhamsted, UK: Albatros Productions, 1992.
    Haddow, George W. *Phonix Scouts*. Aircraft in Profile No. 175. Windsor, UK: Profile Publications, 1967.

BRAZIL

Embraer
Tucano
    "Embraer: The Brazilian Phenomenon," *Air International* 28 (February, 1985): 65–73.
    Fricker, John. "Embraer's Tractable Tucano," *Air International* 24 (June, 1983): 7–14.
    _____. "More Power for the Pupil," *Air International* 35 (September, 1988): 113–121.
    "RAF Prepares for Tucano," *Air International* 32 (May, 1987): 237–239.

CANADA

Avro Canada
    Hotson, Fred W. *The de Havilland Story*. Toronto: CANAV Books, 1983.
CF 100 *Canuck*
    Baeglow, Bob. *Canucks Unlimited: Royal Canadian Air Force CF-100 Squadrons and Aircraft, 1952–1963*. Ottawa: Canuck Publications, 1985.
    Dean, Jack. "The Other 'Hundred,'" *Wings* 23 (February, 1993): 10–24, 43–51.
    Milberry, Larry. *The Avro CF-100*. Toronto: CANAV Books, 1981.
    Page, Ron D. *Avro Aircraft Canuck: CF-100 All-Weather Fighter*. Erin, ON: Boston Mills Press, 1981.
    Rankin-Lowe, Jeff. "CF-100 Variants," *Wings of Fame* 18 (2000): 102–131.

Canadair
    Dumigan, Eric. "Canadair's First Fifty," *Air Classics* 30 (September, 1994): 14–18, 54–59.
    Pickler, Ronald A., and Larry Milberry. *Canadair: The First 50 Years*. Toronto: CANAV Books, 1995.
CL 28 *Argus*
    Ashworth, R. C. B. "Canada's All-Seeing Monster: Almost a Quarter-Century of Argus Operations," *CAHS Journal* 30(3) (1990): 82–89.
    Fisher, Douglas J. "Classic Argus," *Air Classics* 20 (June, 1984): 34–36.
    Foster, Peter. "Canadair Argus," *Fly Past* No. 76 (November, 1987): 48–51.
    MacDougal, Larry J. "Canadair Argus," *Air Pictorial* 36 (March, 1974): 86–94.
    Wilson, Tom. "Argus—Canada's Watchful Guardian," *Air Combat* 4 (November, 1976): 20–29.

CL 41 *Tutor*
    Johnson, Bill. "Snowbird through the Lens," *Air Enthusiast* 21 (April/July, 1983): 51–62.
    Wilson, Tom. "Canadair's Tutor," *Air Combat* 9 (May, 1981): 64–74.

de Havilland Canada
    Bain, Gordon. *De Havilland: A Pictorial Tribute*. St. Catharines, ON: Vanwell Publications, 1992.
    Hotson, Fred W. *The DH Canada Story*. Downsview, ON: de Havilland Aircraft of Canada, 1978.
DHC 1 *Chipmunk*
    Birtles, Philip. "Timeless Trainer from Toronto," *Air International* 50 (May, 1996): 284–294.
    Davisson, Budd. "Chipmunk," *Flying Classic Warbird: Air Combat Special* (Summer, 1989): 56–57, 90–91.
    Fillingham, W. P. E. "Flying the First Chipmunk," *Aeroplane Monthly* 14 (June, 1986): 311–314.

CHINA

Nanchang
Q 5
    "Fantan: A Sino-Soviet Melange," *Air International* 19 (September, 1980): 135–138.
    "Fantan . . . the Chinese Gamble," *Air International* 35 (September, 1988): 7–14.
    Lake, Jon. "Fantan Fantasy," *World Air Power Journal* 1 (Spring, 1990): 126–131.

Shenyang
J 6/F 6
    Fricker, John. "Problems for Pakistan's Air Force," *Air International* 20 (April, 1980): 163–168, 205.
    Gordon, Yefim. "Mikoyan MiG-19 Variants," *Wings of Fame* 9 (1997): 116–149.
    Hali, Ultan M., and Eddy De Kruijff. "Sixshooter," *Aircraft Illustrated* 33 (October, 2000): 30–35.
    Stapfer, Hans-Herri. *MiG-19 Farmer in Action*. Carrollton, TX: Squadron/Signal Publications, 1994.

CONSORTIA

Dassault-Dornier
Alphajet
    "Alphajet: A Franco-German Solution," *Air Enthusiast* 7 (October, 1974): 167–173.
    Braybrook, Roy. "Alphajet," *Air Combat* 7 (March, 1979): 22–32, 78–81.
    _____. "Training Maturity," *Air International* 26 (June, 1984): 269–276, 312–313.
    Fraidel, Herman. "Alphajet: A Great Leap Forward," *Interavia* 33 (June, 1978): 539–543.

Panavia
Tornado
    Evans, Andy. *Panavia Tornado*. Marlborough, UK: Crowood, 1999.

Hawkins, Hugh. *Tornado ADV: Protecting Britain's Skies*. Edinburgh: Pentland Press, 1995.

Lake, Jon, and Mike Crutch. *Tornado: Multi-Role Combat Aircraft*. London: Aerospace, 2000.

Paxton, Tony. *Tornado*. Shepperton, Surrey: Ian Allan, 1992.

Peters, John, and John Nichol, with Neil Hanson. *Team Tornado: Life on a Front-Line Squadron*. London: Michael Joseph, 1994.

SEPECAT
Jaguar

Evans, Andy. *SEPECAT Jaguar*. Marlborough, UK: Crowood, 1998.

"Ferocious Feline," *Air Enthusiast* 3 (September, 1972): 120–128, 153.

Gething, Michael J. *Jaguar*. London: Arms and Armour Press, 1989.

Jackson, Paul. "SEPECAT Jaguar," *World Air Power Journal* 11 (Winter, 1992): 52–111.

Lake, Jon. "The Jaguar Sharpens Its Claws," *Air International* 59 (December, 2000): 356–375.

CZECHOSLOVAKIA

Aero
L 29 *Delfin*

Hudson, Chris. "Red 64," *Fly Past* No. 227 (June, 2000): 47–54.

L 39 *Albatros*

Braybrook, Roy. "Aero L-39 Albatross," *Air Combat* 7 (July, 1979): 20–26.

_____. "Aero L-139," *Air International* 49 (September, 1995): 157–164.

Jefferies, Mark. "Czech Mate: Aero Vodochody's Light Attack Aircraft Evaluated," *Air International* 58 (February, 2000): 93–98.

Lake, Jon. "Aero L-39 Variant Briefing," *World Air Power Journal* 43 (Winter, 2000): 116–131.

Avia
B 534

Craig, James F., and Zdenek Titz. "The Last Biplane Kill," *Air Classics* 9 (March, 1973): 12–17, 71–72.

Green, William. "The Last Belligerent Biplane," *Air International* 7 (July, 1974): 25–35.

Krybus, Josef. *Avia B. 534*. Aircraft in Profile No. 152. Windsor, UK: Profile Publications, 1967.

Westburg, Peter. "Fighting Czech: The Story of the Avia B-534," *Air Classics* 12 (June, 1976): 18–27, 80.

_____. "Avia Update," *Air Classics Quarterly Review* 4 (Spring, 1977): 99–111.

_____. "Dogfight over Ruthenia," *Air Power* 13 (November, 1983): 38–55.

Letov
S 328

"A Biplane's War," *Flying Review International* 21 (November, 1966): 214–216.

FRANCE

Aerospatiale

Geddes, Philip J. *Special Issue, Aerospatiale: A French Perspective*. Alexandria, VA: International Defense Images, 1989.

Dauphin

Francillon, Rene J., and Carol A. McKenzie. "To the Throne...on the Third Try," *Air International* 49 (July, 1995): 14–19.

CM 170 *Magister*

Francillon, Rene J. "Masterful Magister," *Air International* 50 (June, 1996): 362–368.

Henson, Robert. "Fouga Fanfare," *World Air Power Journal* 21 (Summer, 1995): 34–37.

Gazelle

"Franco-British Antelope," *Air International* 13 (December, 1977): 277–283, 300.

Rees, Elfan ap. "Aerospatiale/Westland Gazelle," *Air Pictorial* 40 (June/July/August, 1978): 208–213, 262–266, 306, 309.

Super Puma

Dalling, John. "Puma or Mountain Lion," *Air Classics* 13 (July, 1985): 58–62.

Jackson, Paul. "Super Puma," *Air International* 26 (January, 1984): 7–12, 33–35.

Norman, Tony. "Puma in Service," *Aircraft Illustrated* 9 (May, 1976): 210–213.

Amiot
143

"The Angular Amiot," *Flying Review International* 20 (June, 1965): 49–51.

Geiger, George J. "Amiot's Angular Airframes," *Air Classics* 19 (February, 1983): 18–23, 66–70.

"A Study in Angular Ugliness," *Air International* 35 (December, 1988): 306–313.

Bleriot
XI

"Bleriot XI," *World War I Aero* No. 51 (May, 1975): 6–16.

Crouch, Tom D. *Bleriot XI: The Story of a Classic Aircraft*. Washington, DC: Smithsonian Institution Press, 1982.

Elliot, Brian. *Bleriot: Herald of an Age*. Stroud, Gloucestershire, UK: Tempus Publishing, 2000.

Provensen, Alice. *The Glorious Flight: Across the Channel with Louis Bleriot, July 25, 1909*. New York: Viking Press, 1983.

Bleriot-SPAD
510

Riviere, Pierre, and Jerry Beauchamp. "France's Last Biplane Fighter," *Air Classics* 13 (March, 1977): 60–65.

Bloch
MB 152

Cristesco, Michel. *Marcel Bloch 151/152*. Aircraft in Profile No. 210. Windsor, UK: Profile Publications, 1971.

Leyvastre, Pierre. "The Contentious Combatants," *Air Enthusiast* 14 (April, 1978): 179–189, 205–205.

Breguet
Atlantique
"The New Atlantique Emerges," *Air International* 21 (November, 1981): 213–218, 252–253.
14
Bruce, J. M. *Breguet 14.* Windsock Datafile Special. Berkhamsted, UK: Albatros Productions, 2000.
Connors, John. "The Breguet Battlewagons," *Airpower* 7 (July, 1977): 42–47.
Davilla, Dr. James, and Arthur M. Soltan. "French Day Bombers," *Over the Front* 4 (Autumn, 1989): 196–234.
Hibbard, Tom. "The Breguet 14," *Cross and Cockade Journal* 7 (Autumn, 1966): 232–236.
Stroud, John. "Wings of Peace," *Aeroplane Monthly* 16 (August, 1988): 496–501.
19
Leyvastre, Pierre. "The Saga of the Ubiquitous Breguet," *Air Enthusiast* 7 (July/September, 1978): 161–181.

Caudron
G IV
Flanagan, Brian P. "Caudron G. IV," *Cross and Cockade Journal* 7 (Summer, 1966): 185–189.
Owers, Colin. "Caudron G. 4," *Windsock International* 7 (September/October, 1991): 207.

Dassault
Carlier, Claude, and Luc Berger. *Dassault—50 Years of Aeronautical Adventure, 1845–1995.* 2 Vols. Paris: Editions du Chere, 1996.
_____. "From the Eclair Propellor to the Mirage: Marcel Dassault," *Aerospace Historian* 35 (Summer/June, 1995): 80–93.
Dassault, Marcel. *The Talisman: The Autobiography of Marcel Dassault, Creator of the Mirage Jet.* New Rochelle, NY: Arlington House, 1971.
Haddaway, George E. "Marcel Dassault: The Last of the Titans," *Aviation Quarterly* 8 (Summer/Fall, 1988): 192–211, 292–317.
Ulsamer, Edgar E. "The Designers of Dassault: Men Who Take One Step at a Time," *Air Force and Space Digest* 53(8) (1970): 32–39.
Mirage III
Decock, Jean-Pierre. *Mirage.* Maidstone, UK: Arms and Armour Press, 1985.
Huertas, Salvador M. *Dassault-Breguet Mirage III/5.* London: Osprey, 1990.
_____. "Mirage and Dagger in the Falklands," *Wings of Fame* 6 (1997): 4–27.
_____. *Mirage: The Combat Log.* Atglen, PA: Schiffer Publishing, 1996.
Jackson, Paul. "Mirage III/5/50 Variant Briefing," *World Air Power Journal* 14 (Autumn/Fall, 1993): 112–137; 15 (Winter, 1993): 1001–119; 16 (Spring, 1994): 90–119.

_____. *Mirage.* Shepperton, Surrey: Ian Allan, 1985.
Mirage 2000
Braybrook, Roy. "Mirage 2000: Dassault's Export Fighter for the Eighties," *Air International* 19 (September, 1980): 111–116.
Jackson, Paul. "Dassault Mirage 2000," *World Air Power Journal* 10 (Autumn/Fall, 1992): 52–97.
Mirage F 1
"Dassault's Mid-life Mirage," *Air International* 34 (March, 1988): 121–133.
Francillon, Rene J. *Dassault Mirage F.1.* Arlington, TX: Aerofax, Inc., 1986.
_____. "Mirage at War," *World Air Power Journal* 4 (Winter, 1990/1991): 22–25.
Grassot, Philippe. "The Tangible Mirage," *Air Combat* 3 (November, 1975): 44–52, 80–82.
Jackson, Paul. "Dassault F.1 Mirage: Gallic Guardian," *World Air Power Journal* 17 (Summer, 1994): 46–95.
Super Etendard
Huertas, Salvador M. "Super Etendard in the Falklands," *Wings of Fame* 8 (1997): 22–29.
Jackson, Paul. "France's Super Standard," *Air International* 30 (February, 1986): 59–69.
Super Etendard. Yeovil: Foulis, 1983.

Dewoitine
D 510
Leyvastre, Pierre. "The Day of the Dewoitine," *Air Enthusiast Quarterly* No. 1: 17–19, 84–96.
D 520
Danel, Raymond. *Dewoitine D-520.* Aircraft in Profile No. 135. Windsor, UK: Profile Publications, 1967.
Botquin, Gaston. "Forty Years after the Battle of France: A Dewoitine D.520 Flies Again," *Aerospace Historian* 28(4) (1981): 259–261.

Farman
F 222
Brindley, John. "Farman F221/222 Family," *Air Pictorial* 42 (November, 1980): 92–98.

Hanriot
HD 1
Bruce, J. M., and R. L. Rimell. *Hanriot HD-1.* Windsock Datafile No. 12. Berkhamsted, UK: Albatros Productions, 1988.
_____. *Hanriot HD-1.* Aircraft in Profile No. 109. Windsor, UK: Profile Publications, 1967.
"Hanriot-Dupont HD-1," *World War I Aero* No. 106 (September, 1985): 12–30.

Liore et Olivier (LeO)
LeO 451
Danel, Raymond. *Liore et Olivier LeO 45 Series.* Aircraft in Profile No. 173. Windsor, UK: Profile Publications, 1967.
"France's Finest Bomber," *Flying Review International* 20 (July, August, 1965): 65–67; 35.

Morane-Saulnier

A 1

Bruce, J. M. "Type A.I," *Windsock International* 8 (May/June, 1992): 16–23.

Carlson, John R. "The Morane-Saulnier A.I," *Cross and Cockade Journal* 4 (Autumn, 1963): 264–271.

L

Bruce, J. M. *Morane-Saulnier Type L.* Windsock Datafile No. 16. Berkhamsted, UK: Albatros Productions, 1989.

Rimell, Ray. "Warneford VC: Giant Killer," *Fly Past* No. 26 (September, 1983): 38–43.

MS 406

Botquin, Gaston. *Morane Saulnier 406.* Aircraft in Profile No. 147. Windsor, UK: Profile Publications, 1967.

Leyvastre, Pierre. "Gallic Guardian," *Air Enthusiast* 5 (September, October, 1973): 130–136; 183–191.

Nieuport

Bruce, J. M. *Nieuport Aircraft of World War One.* London: Arms and Armour Press, 1989.

Connors, John F. "Nieuport Chronicles," *Air Power* 3 (September, 1973): 24–31, 62–65.

Cooksley, Peter G. *Nieuport Fighters in Action.* Carrollton, TX: Squadron/Signal Publications, 1997.

Franks, Norman L.R. *Nieuport Aces of World War I.* Oxford: Osprey Publishing, 2000.

Nieuport 11

Bruce, J. M. *Nieuport 11.* Windsock Datafile No. 68. Berkhamsted, UK: Albatros Productions, 1998.

Nieuport 17

Andrews, C. F. *Nieuport 17.* Aircraft in Profile No. 49. Windsor, UK: Profile Publications, 1966.

Bruce, J. M. *Nieuport 17.* Windsock Datafile No. 20. Berkhamsted, UK: Albatros Productions, 1990.

_____. "Those Classic Nieuports," *Air Enthusiast Quarterly* No. 2: 137–153.

Nieuport 28

Bowers, Peter M. *Nieuport N. 28C-1.* Aircraft in Profile No. 79. Windsor, UK: Profile Publications, 1966.

Cavanagh, Robert L. "94th and Its Nieuports, April 15–June 11, 1918," *Cross and Cockade Journal* 21 (Autumn, 1980): 193–222.

Crean, Michelle, and Joseph Ventulo. "Nieuport 28," *World War I Aero* 111 (September, 1986): 31–40.

Gutman, Jon. *Nieuport 28.* Windsock Datafile No. 36. Berkhamsted, UK: Albatros Productions, 1992.

"The Nieuport 28 Described," *Cross and Cockade Journal* 12 (Summer, 1971): 117–128.

Nieuport-Delage

Ni-D 29

Foxworth, Thomas G. "The Quest for Vitesse," *Aero Album* 2 (Summer, 1968): 43–50.

Potez

63

Danel, Raymond. *Potez 63* Series. Aircraft in Profile No. 195. Windsor, UK: Profile Publications, 1971.

"Last of the Sixty-Threes," *Air International* 25 (August, 1983): 72–78.

Salmson

2A2

Owers, Colin A., et al. *Salmson Aircraft of World War I.* Boulder, CO: Flying Machine Press, 2001.

SPAD

XIII

Bruce, J. M. *SPAD Scouts S VIII–S XIII.* New York: Arco Publishing, 1969.

_____. *SPAD XIII.* Windsock Datafile No. 32. Berkhamsted, UK: Albatros Productions, 1992.

Connors, John. *SPAD Fighters in Action.* Carrollton, TX: Squadron/Signal Publications, 1989.

Richardson, Roland W. "SPAD XIII," *Aerospace Historian* 27(4) (1980): 257–261.

Zorn, Peter A. *SPAD XIII and SPAD VII.* New York: Crown, 1982.

GERMANY

AEG

C IV

Grosz, P. M. *A.E.G. C IV.* Windsock Datafile, No. 67. Berkhamsted, UK: Albatros Productions, 1998.

G IV

"AEG G.IV Bomber," *Windsock International* 3 (Winter, 1987): 13–20; 4 (Spring, 1988): 16–18.

"The A.E.G. G.IV Bomber," *Cross and Cockade Journal* 15 (Summer, 1974): 97–117.

Grosz, P. M. *A.E.G. G.IV.* Windsock Datafile No. 51. Berkhamsted, UK: Albatros Productions, 1995.

Knauer, John H. "Flying the A.E.G. IV," *Cross and Cockade Journal* 15 (Summer, 1974): 118–126.

Leaman, Paul. "AEG G.IV: Technical Report," *Cross and Cockade International* 1 (Autumn, 1970): 39–47.

Albatros

Connors, John F. *Albatros Fighters in Action.* Carrollton, TX: Squadron/Signal Publications, 1981.

Franks, Norman. *Albatros Aces from World War I.* Oxford: Osprey Publishing, 2000.

Schaedel, Charles. *Albatros Scouts Described.* Victoria, Australia: Kookaburra Technical Publications, 1971.

D V

"Agile and Aggressive Albatros," *Air Enthusiast Quarterly* No. 1 (1975): 36–51.

Chionchio, John A. "Albatros—Defeat by Design," *Air Enthusiast* 38 (January/April, 1989): 67–78.

Gray, Peter L. *Albatros D-V.* Aircraft in Profile No. 127. Windsor, UK: Profile Publications, 1967.

Mikesh, Robert C. *Albatros D.Va: German Fighter of World War I.* Washington, DC: Smithsonian Institution Press, 1980.

Rimell, R. L. *Albatros D.V.* Windsock Datafile No. 3. Berkhamsted, UK: Albatros Productions, 1987.

Arado

Bowers, Peter M. "Arado and the Emergent Luftwaffe,"*Airpower* 20 (May/July, 1990): 10–19, 33–43; 10–17, 48–53.

Kranzhoff, Jorg A. *Arado: The History of an Aircraft Company.* Atglen, PA: Schiffer Publishing, 1997.

Ar 68

"The Arado 68: The Last of the Luftwaffe's Fighter Biplanes," *Flying Review International* 21 (February, 1966): 379–381.

Grosz, Peter M. "Arado's Biplane Fighters," *Air Classics* 13 (August, 1977): 68–77.

Ar 96

"The Arado Ar-96B: Germany's Standard Military Trainer," *Aero Digest* 37 (September, 1940): 111–112.

Ar 196

Dabrowski, Hans-Peter. *Arado Ar-196: Germany's Multi-Purpose Seaplane.* Atglen, PA: Schiffer Publishing, 1993.

Grosz, Peter M. "Arado Ar-196: Germany's Sea-going Scout," *Air Classic Quarterly Review* 3 (Summer, 1976): 60–64.

Rye, John. "Eyes of the Kriegsmarine," *Fly Past* No. 192 (July, 1997): 32–34.

Ar 234 *Blitz*

Brown, Eric. "Like Greased Lightning," *Air International* 4 (February, 1973): 78–81.

Kober, Franz. *The World's First Jet Bomber: Arado Ar-234.* Atglen, PA: Schiffer Publishing, 1993.

Myhra, David. *Arado AR 234C.* Atglen, PA: Schiffer Publishing, 2000.

Price, Alfred. "Arado's Blitz," *Air International* 51 (November, 1996): 304–308.

Smith, J. Richard, and Eddie J. Creek. *Arado 234 Blitz.* Sturbridge, MA: Monogram Aviation Publications, 1992.

Blohm und Voss

Amtmann, Hans. "Blohm und Voss Remembered," *Aeroplane Monthly* 26 (March, 1998): 12–15.

Bowers, Peter M. "The Flying Hamburgers," *Wings* 13 (August, 1983): 10–21, 48–53.

Wixey, Ken. "Flugboots from Hamburg," *Air Enthusiast* No. 82 (July/August, 1999): 42–50.

Bv 138

"Die Fligende Holzschuh: The Oddity from Hamburg," *Air International* 17 (November, 1979): 229–235, 253–255.

Nowarra, Heinz J. *BV-138: 'Der Fliegende Holzschuh.'* Atglen, PA: Schiffer Publishing, 1997.

Bv 222 *Wiking*

Amtmann, Hans H. "Vogt's Viking," *Aeroplane Monthly* 22 (July, 1994): 18–23.

Brown, Eric. "Das Grosflugboot Wiking," *Air International* 20 (April, 1981): 180–188.

Nowarra, Heinz J. *Blohm and Voss Bv 222 Wiking, Bv 238.* Atglen, PA: Schiffer Publishing, 1997.

Seely, Victor D. "Bv-222," *Aero Album* 6 (Summer, 1969): 22–27.

DFS

230

Nowarra, Heinz J. *German Gliders in World War II.* Atglen, PA: Schiffer Publishing, 1992.

DFW

C V

Abbott, Dan-San. "The Colors of the Halberstadt-Built DFW C V," *Cross and Cockade International* 30 (Summer, 1999): 80–89.

Grosz, Peter M. *DFW C.V.* Windsock Datafile No. 53. Berhamsted: Albatros Productions, 1995.

Stair, Ian. "DFW C.V," *Windsock International* 7 (May/June, 1991): 10–16.

Dornier

"A Dornier Anniversary," *Air Classics* 20 (October, 1984): 58–67, 81–82.

Bowers, Peter M. "The Dornier Design Works," *Airpower* 24 (March, 1994): 10–19, 46–55.

Griehl, Manfred. *Dornier Bombers and Reconnaissance Aircraft, 1925–1945.* London: Arms and Armour Press, 1990.

Ogden, Bob. *Dornier.* Stamford: Key, 1983.

Wixey, Kenneth E. "Dornier Flying Boats," *Aircraft Illustrated* 13 (August, September, 1980): 368–372; 400–403.

Do 18

Bowers, Peter M. "Dr. Dornier's Flying Whales," *Wings* 3 (June, 1973): 50–65.

"Do-18: Dornier's Whale Calf," *Air International* 18 (April, 1980): 181–188.

Wixey, Ken. "Dornier's Flying Boat Dynasty," *Air Enthusiast* No. 51 (August/October, 1993): 61–73.

Do 23

Dabrowski, Hans Peter. *The Dornier Do-23: First Bomber of the Wermacht.* Atglen, PA: Schiffer Publishing, 1996.

Do 24

"The Cosmopolitan Dornier," *Air Enthusiast* 21 (April/July, 1983): 9–20.

Chapman, Rich. "The Luftwaffe's Last Mission," *Aeroplane Monthly* 13 (April, 1985): 202–205.

Do 27

Gerhardt, P. M. *The Dornier Do-27.* Tonbridge: Air Britain, 1987.

Do 217

"Annals of the 'Pencil,'" *Air Enthusiast* 30 (March/June, 1986): 38–53.

Griehl, Manfred. *Dornier 217-317-417: An Operational History.* Atglen, PA: Schiffer Publishing, 1991.

Nowarra, Heinz J. *The Flying Pencil: Dornier Do-17-215.* Atglen, PA: Schiffer Publishing, 1990.

Smith, J. Richard. *Dornier Do-17 and 215.* Aircraft in Profile No. 164. Windsor, UK: Profile Publications, 1967.

Toll, Karl. "The Lufthansa Bomber," *Air Power* 3 (January, 1973): 35–51.

Fieseler

Fi 156 *Storch*

Bateson, Richard P. *Fieseler Fi-156 Storch.* Aircraft in Profile No. 228. Windsor, UK: Profile Publications, 1972.

Brown, Eric. "The Slow and Foolproof," *Air International* 11 (December, 1976): 282–288.

Davisson, Budd. "Flying the Storch," *Flight* 4 (April, 1999): 24–31.

Nowarra, Heinz J. *Fieseler 156 'Storch.'* Atglen, PA: Schiffer Publications, 1997.

Trimble, Robert. "Fieseler's Amazing Storch," *Air Classics* 11 (March, 1975): 28–37, 74, 80–81.

Flettner

Flettner, Anton. *The Story of the Rotor.* New York: F. O. Willhofft, 1926.

Nowarra, Heinz J. *German Helicopters, 1928–1945.* West Chester, PA: Schiffer Military History, 1990.

Fl 282 *Kolibri*

"A Page from Helicopter History: The Flettner Story," *Flying Review International* 20 (February, 1965): 49–51.

Flettner FL 282 'Kolibri.' Atglen, PA: Schiffer Publications, 1996.

Holcomb, Mal. "Vertical Lift," *Airpower* 20 (March, 1990): 10–21, 38–45.

Kay, Anton. "The Flettner Episode," *Aeroplane Monthly* 3 (November, December, 1975): 576–580; 488–493.

Focke-Wulf

Smith, J. Richard. *Focke-Wulf: An Aircraft Album.* London: Ian Allan, 1973.

Wagner, Wolfgang. *The History of German Aviation: Kurt Tank, Focke-Wulf's Designer and Test Pilot.* Atglen, PA: Schiffer Military/Aviation History, 1998.

Fw 189

Brown, Eric. "Flying the Eye," *Air Enthusiast* 7 (October, 1974): 183–189.

"Das Fliegende Auge: Focke-Wulf's Versatile Owl," *Air Enthusiast* No. 37 (September/December, 1988): 25–38.

Punka, George. *Focke-Wulf Fw-189 in Action.* Carrollton, TX: Squadron/Signal Publications, 1993.

Toll, Karl. "The Obsolete Observation Fleet," *Wings* 12 (April, 1982): 28–37.

_____. "Utmost Utility," *Air Power* 31 (January, 2001): 10–23, 50–55.

Fw 190

Jesson, Morton. *Focke-Wulf Fw 190: The Birth of the Butcher Bird.* London: Greenhill Books, 1998.

_____. *Focke Wulf FW 190: Defending the Reich, 1943–1945.* London: Greenhill Books, 2000.

Griehl, Manfred. *Focke-Wulf Fw 190.* Atglen, PA: Schiffer Publishing, 1995.

Price, Alfred. *Focke-Wulf Fw-190 in Combat.* Thrupp, Stroud, UK: Sutton, 1998.

Spenser, Jay. *Focke-Wulf Fw-190: Workhorse of the Luftwaffe.* Washington, DC: Smithsonian Institution Press, 1987.

Fw 200 *Condor*

Brown, Eric. "Condor: An Elegant Improvisation," *Air Enthusiast* 7 (September, 1974): 143–151.

Nowarra, Heinz J. *Fw 200 Condor: Battle Companion of the U-boats.* West Chester, PA: Schiffer Publications, 1990.

Poolman, Kenneth. *Focke-Wulf Condor: Scourge of the Atlantic.* London: Macdonald's and Jane's, 1978.

Toll, Karl. "Condor: Scourge of the Atlantic!" *Air Power* 10 (November, 1980): 42–51.

Wixey, Ken. "Incidental Combatant: Focke-Wulf Fw-200 Condor," *Air Enthusiast* No. 66 (November/December, 1996): 42–46; No. 67 (January/February, 1997): 68–75.

Fokker

Dierikx, M. C. J. *Fokker: A Transatlantic Biography.* Washington, DC: Smithsonian Institution Press, 1997.

Fokker, Anthony H. G. *Flying Dutchman: The Life of Anthony Fokker.* New York: Arno Press, 1972.

Hegener, Henri. *Fokker: The Man and His Aircraft.* Letchworth, Hertfordshire, UK: Harleyford Publications, 1961.

Imrie, Alex. *Fokker Fighters of World War One.* London: Arms and Armour Press, 1987.

Postma, Thiji. *Fokker: Aircraft Builders to the World.* London: Jane's, 1980.

Weyl, Alfred R. *Fokker: The Creative Years.* London: Putnam, 1965.

D VII

Brannan, Edgar. *The Fokker D. VII.* Carrollton, TX: Squadron/Signal Publications, 1997.

Grosz, P. M. *Fokker D. VII.* Windsock Datafile No. 9. Berkhamsted, UK: Albatros Productions, 1989.

Nowarra, Heinz J. *The Fokker Dr. I and D. VII in World War I.* Atglen, PA: Schiffer Publications, 1991.

Westburg, Peter. "Deadly D-VII," *Wings* 9 (April, 1979): 4–53.

D VIII

Connors, John F. "Fokkers Flying Razors," *Wings* 4 (August, 1974): 44–50.

Grosz, Peter M. "Fokker D. VIII: The Facts as They Stand Today," *World War I Aero* No. 86 (September, 1981): 28–38.

_____. "Fokker's D. VIII: The Reluctant Razors," *Air Enthusiast* No. 17 (December, 1981–March, 1982): 61–73.

_____. *Fokker D. VIII.* Windsock Datafile No. 25. Berkhamsted, UK: Albatros Productions, 1991.

Hucker, Robert. "D. VIII . . . Was It the Best Fokker?" *Air Classics* 14 (February, 1978): 70–79.

Dr I

Brannan, Edgar. *Fokker V5/Dr. I.* Carrollton, TX: Squadron/Signal Publications, 1997.

Imrie, Alex. *The Fokker Triplanes.* London: Arms and Armour Press, 1993.

Nowarra, Heinz J. *Fokker Dr. I in Action.* Carrollton, TX: Squadron/Signal Publications, 1990.

Rimell, R. L. *Fokker Triplane.* Windsock Datafile No. 5. Berkhamsted, UK: Albatros Productions, 1987.

Schuster Wolfgang. *Fokker V5/Dr. I.* Atglen, PA: Schiffer Publishing, 1998.

E III

Brannon D. Edgar. *Fokker Eindecker in Action.* Carrollton, TX: Squadron/Signal Publications, 1996.

Bruce, J. M. *Fokker Monoplanes.* Aircraft in Profile No. 38. Windsor, UK: Profile Publications, 1965.

Grosz, P. M. *Fokker E. III.* Windsock Datafile No. 15. Berkhamsted, UK: Albatros Productions, 1989.

Hucker, Robert. "Fokker Scourge: Fact or Fiction?" *Air Classics* 15 (June, 1979): 14–18, 96.

Jarrett, Philip. "Fokker Five-O-Nine," *Cross and Cockade Journal* 12 (Spring, 1981): 1–17.

Friedrichshafen

G III

Friedrichshafen G. "III/G.IIIA," *Windsock International* 7 (September/October, 1991): 14–21; 8 (January/February, March/April, 1992): 5–12, 20–23.

Grosz, P. N. *Friedrichshafen G. III.* Windsock Datafile No. 65. Berkhamsted, UK: Albatros Productions, 1997.

"Report on the Friedrichshafen Bomber," *Cross and Cockade Journal* 26 (Summer, 1985): 61–79.

Gotha

"The Gothas," *Air Progress* 19 (February/March, 1963): 18–23.

Grosz, Peter M. *Gotha I-V.* Aircraft in Profile No. 115. Windsor, UK: Profile Publications, 1967.

G V

Fredette, Raymond H. "First Gotha Over London," *Aerospace Historian* 8 (October, 1961): 194–206.

"Gotha G V: A 'Flight' Magazine Technical Evaluation," *Over the Front* 15 (September, 2000): 50–62.

Grosz, Peter M. *Gotha!* Windsock Datafile Special. Berkhamsted, UK: Albatros Productions, 1994.

White, C. M. *The Gotha Summer: The German Daytime Air Raids on England, May-August, 1917.* London: R. Hale, 1986.

Go 242

"Gotha's Twin-boom Troopers," *Air International* 37 (December, 1989): 286–292, 309.

Gunston, Bill. "Gotha's Glider," *Air Classics* 13 (November, 1977): 69–73, 98.

Halberstadt

Grosz, Peter M., and A. A. Ferko. "Biplanes for the Fliegertruppe," *Air Enthusiast* No. 17 (1981): 57–68.

C V

Grosz, P. M. *Halberstadt C. V.* Windsock Datafile No. 69. Berkhamsted, UK: Albatros Productions, 1998.

CL

Grosz, P. M. *Halbertstadt CL. IV.* Windsock Datafile No. 43. Berkhamsted, UK: Albatros Productions, 1993.

"The Halberstadt CL II," *Cross and Cockade Journal* 2 (Summer, 1961): 131–149.

Levy, Howard. "Handle with Care," *Aeroplane Monthly* 23 (May, 1995): 48–50.

"Report on the Halberstadt Two-Seater, Type Cl. IV: An Evaluation," *Cross and Cockade Journal* 18 (Winter, 1977): 370–379.

Van Wyngarden, Greg. "Colors: The Halberstadt CL. II," *Over the Front* 11 (June, 1996): 176–179.

D II

Grosz, Peter M. "The Halbersdtadt Fighters," *Cross and Cockade Journal* 11 (Autumn, 1970): 267–280.

_____. "Biplanes for the Fliegertruppe," *Air Enthusiast* No. 14 (December, 1980–March, 1981): 57–67.

_____. *Halberstadt Fighters.* Classics of World War I Aviation No. 1. Berkhamsted, UK: Albatros Productions, 1997.

"Halbersdtadt D. II," *Cross and Cockade Journal* 10 (Summer, 1969): 164–165.

Hannover

Grosz, Peter M. "Hannover Aircraft, 1915–1919," *Air Pictorial* 33 (July, August, 1971): 252–256; 290–293.

CL

Grosz, Peter M. *Hannover CL III.* Windsock Datafile No. 23. Berkhamsted: Albatros Productions, 1990.

"Report on the Hannoveraner Biplane," *Cross and Cockade Journal* 3 (Summer, 1962): 124–138.

Van Wyngarden, Greg. "Colors: The Hannover CL II, III, and IIIa," *Over the Front* 12 (Winter, 1997): 358–364.

Hansa-Brandenburg

W 29

Grosz, P. M. *Brandenburg W. 29.* Windsock Datafile No. 55. Berkhamsted, UK: Albatros Productions, 1996.

Owers, Colin A. "Brandenburg W. 29: 1918 German Defense Seaplane Fighter," *Windsock International* 5 (Summer, 1989): 10–15.

_____. "Zeebrugge's Hornets," *Air Enthusiast* No. 73 (January/February, 1998): 58–62.

Heinkel

Bowers, Peter M. "Ernest Heinkel: Aviation Pioneer," *Airpower* 14 (July, September, 1984): 34–47; 10–23, 34–47.

Geiger, George J. "Heinkel's Waterbirds," *Air Classics* 11 (August, September, October, 1975): 66–71; 68–73; 68–76.

Griehl, Manfred. *Heinkel Combat Aircraft.* London: Arms and Armour Press, 1992.

Heinkel, Ernst. *He 1000.* London: Hutchinson, 1956.

Turner, Paul St. John. *Heinkel: An Aircraft Album.* New York: Arco Publishing, 1970.

He 51

"The Cadre Creator: Heinkel's Last Fighting Biplane," *Air Enthusiast* No. 36 (May-August, 1988): 11–24.

Kortbein, Harro. "Tooth-Cutter of the Jadgflieger," *Air International* 10 (May, 1976): 232–236.

Orange, Vincent. "Fortunate Fascist Failures: The Case of the Heinkel Fighters," *Historical News* 47 (1983): 7–13.

He 70 *Blitz*

Amtmann, Hans. "Heinkel's Hot Ship," *Aeroplane Monthly* 25 (January, 1997): 30–36.

"The Beautiful Blitz," *Air International* 40 (January, 1991): 25–33.

"The Blitz: Heinkel's Elegant Trendsetter," *Air Enthusiast* 8 (February, 1975): 76–80, 89–92.

Green, William. "The Most Elegant Heinkel," *Flying Review International* 21 (October, 1965): 116–119.

Stroud, John. "Wings of Peace," *Aeroplane Monthly* 13 (June, 1985): 321–325.

He 111

Bowers, Peter M. "Blitz Bomber: Heinkel 111," *Airpower* 4 (March, 1974): 36–57.

Feist, Uwe, and Mike Dario. *Heinkel He-111 in Action.* Warren, MI: Squadron/Signal Publications, 1973.

Kober, Franz. *Heinkel He-111.* Atglen, PA: Schiffer Publications, 1991.

Michulec, Robert. *Heinkel He-111.* Farnborough, UK: Books International, 1994.

Nowarra, Heinz. *Heinkel He-111: A Documentary History.* London: Jane's, 1980.

He 115

Bowers, Peter M. "Torpedoes Los!" *Wings* 8 (June, 1978): 40–55.

Dabrowski, Hans-Peter. *Heinkel He-115: Torpedo/Reconnaissance/Mine Layer, Seaplane of the Luftwaffe.* Atglen, PA: Schiffer Publishing, 1994.

"Last of a Genus," *Air International* 32 (February, March, 1987): 96–101; 154–156.

He 177 *Greif*

Brown, Eric. "The Grievous Griffon," *Air Enthusiast* 8 (April, 1975): 177–184.

Griehl, Manfred, and Joachim Dressel. *Heinkel He 177, 277, 274.* Shrewsbury, UK: Airlife, 1998.

Hirsch, Robert S. *Heinkel He-177.* Fallbrook, CA: Aero Publishers, 1969.

Price, Alfred. *Heinkel HE-177 Greif (Griffon).* Aircraft in Profile No. 234. Windsor, UK: Profile Publications, 1972.

Toll, Karl. "Terror Bomber," *Wings* 2 (August, 1972): 28–39.

He 219 *Uhu*

Brown, Eric. "Heinkel's Nocturnal Predator Viewed from the Cockpit," *Air International* 9 (July, 1975): 23–29.

"Heinkel's Nocturnal Predator," *Air Enthusiast* No. 40 (September/December, 1989): 8–19.

Nowarra, Heinz J. *German 'Uhu': He-219 Aircraft.* Atglen, PA: Schiffer Publishing, 1989.

Remp, Ronald. *Heinkel He 219: An Illustrated History of German's Premier Nightfighter.* Atglen, PA: Schiffer, 2001.

Spencer, Jay. "Caged Owl," *Wings* 9 (August, 1979): 10–25.

Henschel

Hs 123

"Legacy of Udet: The Henschel Hs-123," *Air International* 15 (August, 1978): 75–79.

Woodman, Harry. "Angelito," *Air Power* 2 (September, 1972): 40–51.

Hs 129

Grinsell, Robert. "Winged Can Opener," *Airpower* 2 (May, 1972): 18–24.

"The Henschel Hs-129," *Air International* 19 (December, 1980): 277–283, 303–304.

Pegg, Martin. *Hs-129 Panzer Jaeger!* Burgess Hill, UK: Classic Publications, 1997.

Smith, Richard J. *Henschel Hs-129.* Aircraft in Profile No. 69. Windsor, UK: Profile Publications, 1966.

Vanags-Baginski, Alex. *Tank Buster v. Combat Vehicle.* Shrewsbury, UK: Airlife, 1990.

Junkers

Fischer von Potsurzya, Friedrich A. *Junkers and World Aviation: A Contribution to German Aeronautical History, 1909–1934.* Munich: R. P. Flaum, 1935.

Griehl, Manfred. *Junkers Bombers.* Poole, Dorset, UK: Arms and Armour Press, 1987.

Schmitt, Gunter. *Hugo Junkers and His Aircraft.* Leicester, UK: Midland Counties, 1988.

Turner, Paul St. John. *Junkers: An Aircraft Album.* New York: Arco Publishing, 1971.

Walters, Brian. *Junkers.* Stroud, UK: Chalford, 1997.

CL I

Cowin, Hugh W. *The Junkers Monoplanes.* Aircraft in Profile No. 187. Windsor, UK: Profile Publications, 1967.

Hucker, Robert. "Junkers' Tin Donkeys," *Air Classics* 15 (May, 1979): 24–37.

D I

Grosz, Peter M., and Gerard Terry. "The Way to the World's First All-Metal Fighter," *Air Enthusiast* 25 (August-November, 1984): 60–76.

_____. *Junkers D. I.* Windsock Datafile No. 33. Berkhamsted, UK: Albatros Productions, 1992.

J I

"The Flying Furniture Van," *Windsock International* 4 (Autumn, 1988): 4–9.

Grosz, P. M. *Junkers J. I.* Windsock Datafile No. 39. Berkhamsted, UK: Albatros Productions, 1993.

Ju 52

Bowers, Peter M. "Old Ironsides," *Wings* 10 (September, October, 1980): 21–35; 10–21, 40.

Brown, Eric. "Iron Annie from Dessau, Viewed from the Cockpit," *Air International* 9 (October, 1975): 180–184.

Cadin, Martin. *The Saga of Iron Annie.* Garden City, NY: Doubleday, 1979.

Feist, Uwe, and Mike Dario. *Junkers Ju-52 in Action.* Warren, MI: Squadron/Signal Publications, 1973.

Nowarra, Heinz J. *Junkers Ju 52: Aircraft and Legend.* Sparkford, Somerset, UK: Haynes, 1987.

Ju 86

Chapin, Seymour L. "Funky Junkers' Planes: Junkers Research and Development at High Altitude in the 1920s and 1930s," *Aerospace Historian* 28 (Summer/June, 1981): 94–101.

Dressel, Joachim, and Manfred Griehl. *Junkers Ju-86.* Atglen, PA: Schiffer Publishing, 1998.

"Junkers Ju-86: The Dimorphous Dessauer," *Air Enthusiast* No. 20 (December, 1982/March, 1983): 15–30.

Ju 87

Smith, Peter C. *Stuka Spearhead: The Lightning War from Poland to Dunkirk, 1939–1940.* London: Greenhill Books, 1998.

_____. *Stuka Squadron: Stukagruppe 77: The Luftwaffe's 'Fire Brigade.'* Wellingborough, UK: Patrick Stephens, 1990.

Toll, Karl. "Blitzkrieg: The Making of a Myth," *Wings* 9 (October, 1979): 10–23.

Vanags-Baginski, Alex. *Stuka: Ju-87.* London: Jane's, 1982.

Zobel, Fritz X. *The Junkers Ju-87 Stuka.* Atglen, PA: Schiffer Publications, 1996.

Ju 88

Bowers, Peter. "Junkers Ju 88: Demon in the Dark," *Wings* 12 (August, 1982): 10–23.

Filley, Brian. *Junkers Ju-88 in Action.* Carrollton, TX: Squadron/Signal, 1991.

Griehl, Manfred. *Junkers Ju 88: Star of the Luftwaffe.* London: Arms and Armour Press, 1990.

Ju 188

"The Fortuitous Avenger," *Air International* 22 (April, 1982): 179–182.

"The Junkers Ju-188," *Air Pictorial* 18 (March, 1956): 79–80, 86.

Ju 290

Cruz, Gonzalo Avila. "Singular Giant: Spain's One-off Ju-290," *Air Enthusiast* No. 82 (July/August, 1999): 50–54.

"Facts by Request," *Flying Review International* 21 (June, 1966): 640–641.

Hitchcock, Thomas H. *Junkers 290.* Boylston, MA: Monogram Aviation Publications, 1975.

Nowarra, Heinz J. *Junkers Ju 290, Ju 390, etc.* Atglen, PA: Schiffer Publications, 1997.

LFG Roland

C II

Grosz, P. M. *Roland C. II.* Windsock Datafile No. 49. Berkhamsted, UK: Albatros Productions, 1995.

_____. *Roland C-II.* Aircraft in Profile No. 163. Windsor, UK: Profile Publications, 1967.

Owers, Colin A. "Roland C. II," *Windsock International* 6 (March/April, 1990): 17–21.

D II

Bowers, Peter M. "The Song of Roland," *Airpower* 7 (March, 1977): 44–62.

Davis, George W. "LFG Roland Fighters: D. I to D. V," *Cross and Cockade Journal* 21 (Autumn, 1980): 249–260.

Grosz, Peter M. *Roland D. II.* Windsock Date File No. 47. Berkhamsted, UK: Albatros Productions, 1994.

Grosz, Peter M., and Dan S. Abbott. "The Beknighted Rolands," *Air Enthusiast Quarterly* No. 3: 38–49.

Van Wyngarden, Greg. "Colors: The Roland D. II and D. IIa," *Over the Front* 5 (Autumn, 1990): 266–272.

LVG

C V

Grosz, P. M. *L.V.G. C. VI.* Windsock Datafile No. 17. Berkhamsted, UK: Albatros Productions, 1989.

_____. *L.V.G. C. VI.* Windsock Datafile No. 71. Berkhamsted, UK: Albatros Productions, 1998.

"Les L.V.G.," *Cross and Cockade International* 14 (Spring, 1983): 1–21.

"The L.V.G. C. V," *Windsock International* 8 (November/December, 1992): 6–16.

"The L.V.G. Two-Seater Biplanes," *Cross and Cockade Journal* 21 (Summer, 1980): 133–145.

Messerschmitt

Baur, Isolde. *A Pilot's Life: Chief Test Pilot for Messerschmitt.* Winnepeg, Manitoba: J. J. Fedorowicz Publishing, 2000.

Ebert, Hans J. *Willy Messerschmitt, Pioneer of Aviation Design.* Atglen, PA: Schiffer Publications, 1999.

Ishoven, Armand van. *Messerschmitt, Aircraft Designer.* Garden City, NY: Doubleday, 1975.

Pritchard, Anthony. *Messerschmitt.* New York: Putnam, 1975.

Smith, J. Richard. *Messerschmitt: An Aircraft Album.* New York: Arco Publishing, 1971.

Vann, Frank. Willy *Messerschmitt: First Full Biography of an Aeronautical Genius.* Yeovil, UK: Patrick Stephens, 1993.

Bf 109

Feist, Uwe. *The Fighting Me-109.* London: Arms and Armour Press, 1993.

Lande, David. *Messerchmitt 109.* Osceola, WI: MBI, 2000.

Patterson, Dan. *Messerschmitt Bf-109: Luftwaffe Fighter.* Shrewsbury, UK: Airlife, 1997.

Radinger, Willy. *Messerschmitt BF-109: The World's Most Produced Fighter from Bf 109A to E.* Atglen, OPA: Schiffer Publications, 1999.

Shacklady, Edward. *The Messerschmitt Bf-109.* Stroud, UK: Tempus, 2000.

Bf 110

Brown, Eric. "BF-110: Hermann's Destroyer," *Air Enthusiast* 4 (October, 1973): 177–181.

Hirsch, R. S., and Uwe Feist. *Messerschmitt Bf-110.* Fallbrook, CA: Aero Publishers, 1967.

Ishoven, Armand van. *Messerschmitt Bf-110 at War.* London: Ian Allan, 1985.

MacKay, Ron. *Messerschmitt Bf-110.* Marlborough, UK: Crowood, 2000.

Vasco, John J. *Zerstorer: The Messerschmitt 110 and Its Units in 1940.* Norfolk, UK: JAC Publications, 1995.

Me 163 *Komet*
    Brown, Eric. "A Brush with Exoticism," *Air Enthusiast* 3 (September, 1972): 129–136.
    Ethell, Jeffrey L. "Rocket Fighter," *Wings* 7 (April, 1977): 10–19.
    _____. "Rocket Fighter," *Airpower* 7 (May, 1977): 38–49, 64–65.
    Hemingway, Albert. "The Man Who Rode the Komet," *Aviation Heritage* (January, 1991): 19–25.
    Ziegler, Herman E. *Rocket Fighter: The Story of the Messerschmitt Me-163.* London: Arms and Armour Press, 1976.

Me 262 *Schwalbe/Sturmvogel*
    Brown, Eric. "No Harbinger of Summer: Messerschmitt's Swallow," *Air Enthusiast* 3 (November, 1972): 241–248.
    Hecht, Heinrich. *The World's First Turbojet Fighter: Me-262.* Atglen, PA: Schiffer Publications, 1990.
    Morgan, Hugh. *Me-262: Stormbird Rising.* London: Osprey Publishing, 1994.
    Radinger, Willy. *Messerschmitt Me-262: Development, Testing, Production.* Atglen, PA: Schiffer Publishing, 1993.
    Smith, J. Richard, and Eddie J. Creek. *Me-262.* 4 vols. Crowborough, UK: Classic Publications, 1998.

Me 321/323 *Gigant*
    Dabrowski, H. P. *Messerschmitt Me-321/323: Giants of the Luftwaffe.* Atglen, PA: Schiffer Publications, 1994.
    "Die Giganten . . . Messerschmitt's Monsters," *Air International* 24 (May, 1983): 233–241, 256–257.
    Gunston, Bill. "Gigant," *Aeroplane Monthly* 5 (June, 1977): 284–289.
    Hammer, Arthur. "Giant Size: World War II's Largest Aircraft—the Messerschmitt Me-323," *Airpower* 11 (March, 1981): 38–47.
    Lattke, Horst, and John Manderville. "Gigant: The Story of Messerschmitt's Monsters," *Air Combat* 3 (November, 1975): 12–23.

Me 410 *Hornisse*
    "Hornisse: The Last Zerstorer," *Air International* 21 (October, November, 1981): 181–185; 229–235.
    Punka, George. *Messerschmitt Me-210/410 in Action.* Carrollton, TX: Squadron/Signal Publications, 1994.
    Smith, J. Richard. *Messerschmitt. Me-210/410 Series.* Aircraft in Profile No. 161. Windsor, UK: Profile Publications, 1967.
    Spenser, Jay. "Gray and Green Hornet," *Wings* 13 (February, 1983): 10–27.

MBB
BO 105
    Allward, Maurice. "MBB BO-105 Helicopter," *Air Pictorial* 43 (April, 1981): 128–133.
    "BO-105: A Versatile Success," *Air International* 16 (May, 1979): 215–221, 246–248.

Pfalz
    Grosz, Peter M. *Pfalz: World War I Aircraft.* Glendale, CA: Aviation, 1975.
    Herris, Jack. *Pfalz Aircraft of World War I.* Boulder, CO: Flying Machine Press, 2001.
D IIIa
    Gray, Peter L. *Pfalz D-III.* Aircraft in Profile No. 43. Windsor, UK: Profile Publications, 1965.
    Grosz, P. M. *Pfalz D. IIIa.* Windsock Datafile No. 21. Berkhamsted, UK: Albatros Productions, 1990.
    Rimell, R. L., and P. M. Grosz. *Pfalz D. III.* Windsock Datafile No. 7. Berkhamsted, UK: Albatros Productions, 1988.
    Stasinos, Nick. "The Old Eagle," *Airpower* 1 (November, 1971): 27–33.
D XII
    Bowers, Peter M. "Tracking the Pfalz," *Flight Journal* 5 (October, 2000): 60–68.
    Connors, John F. "Stand-in Fokker," *Airpower* 6 (November, 1976): 56–63.
    Grosz, P. M. *Pfalz D. XII.* Windsock Datafile No. 41. Berkhamsted, UK: Albatros Productions, 1993.
    Hucker, Robert. "Pfalz D XII: The Bogus Fokker," *Air Classics Quarterly Review* 8 (Fall, 1979): 30–37.
    Lawson, Stephen T. "Pfalz D XII: A Workhorse in Foreign Fields," *Cross and Cockade International* 30 (Winter, 1999): 222–229.

Rumpler
C IV
    Grosz, P. M. *Rumpler C. IV.* Windsock Datafile No. 35. Berkhamsted, UK: Albatros Productions, 1992.
    Kelly, Paul. "Les Avions Rumpler," *Cross and Cockade Great Britain Journal* 15 (Spring, 1984): 1–19.
    "Rumpler C. IV," *Windsock* 1 (Autumn, 1985): 15–23.

Siemens-Schuckert
    Kruger, Egon, and Peter M. Grosz. "A History of Siemens-Schuckert Aircraft and Missiles, 1907–1919," *Cross and Cockade Journal* 13 (Autumn, 1972): 193–229.
    Siemens, Georg. *History of the House of Siemens.* Freiberg: K. Alber, 1957.
D III/IV
    Bennet, Dick. "Siemens Schuckert D. III," *World War I Aero* No. 123 (February, 1989): 8–25.
    Grosz, P. M. *SSW D. III-IV.* Windsock Datafile No. 29. Berkhamsted, UK: Albatros Productions, 1991.
    Levy, Howard. "Purple Pursuit," *Aeroplane Monthly* 23 (February, 1995): 42–44.
    McCracken, Jack. "The Best World War I Fighter," *Over the Front* 14 (Spring, 1999): 50–59.

Zeppelin Staaken
    Eckener, Hugo. *Count Zeppelin—the Man and His Work.* London: Massie Publishing, 1938.
    Guttery, Thomas E. *Zeppelin: An Illustrated Life of Count Ferdinand von Zeppelin, 1838–1917.* Aylesbury, UK: Shire Publications, 1973.
    Vaeth, J. Gordon. *Graf Zeppelin: The Adventures of a Great Aerial Globe Trotter.* London: F. Miller, 1959.
    Vissering, Harry. *Zeppelin: The Story of a Great Achievement.* Chicago: Wells, 1922.

R

Avram, Valeriu. "A German Giant in Rumanian Hands," *World War I Aero* No. 157 (August, 1997): 28–34.

Haddow, G. W., and Peter M. Grosz. *The German Giants: German R Planes, 1914–1918.* Baltimore: Nautical and Aviation Press, 1989.

GREAT BRITAIN

Airspeed

Middleton, Don H. *Airspeed—the Company and Its Aeroplanes.* Leavenham, Suffolk: T. Dalton, 1982.

_____. "The Origins of Airspeed," *Fly Past* No. 71 (June, 1987): 36–40.

Taylor, H. A. *Airspeed Aircraft since 1931.* London: Putnam, 1970.

Horsa

Johnston, Alexander. "The Saxon's Return: Flying the Airspeed Horsa," *Air Enthusiast* 2 (April, 1972): 213–214.

Middleton, Don H. "Airspeed's Silent War Horse," *Aeroplane Monthly* 7 (October, November, December, 1979): 508–513; 564–569; 620–626.

Morrison, Alexander. *Silent Invader: A Glider Pilot's Story of the Invasion of Europe in 1944.* Shrewsbury, UK: Airlife, 1999.

Oxford

Middleton, Don H. "Airspeed Oxford," *Aeroplane Monthly* 8 (May, June, 1980): 243–249; 322–326.

Rawlings, John D. R. *Airspeed Oxford.* Aircraft in Profile No. 229. Windsor, UK: Profile Publications, 1972.

Armstrong-Whitworth

"'Pioneers of Progress': An Outline History of the Sir W.G. Armstrong-Whitworth Aircraft Company," *Aircraft Illustrated* 7 (November, 1974): 442–449.

Tapper, Oliver. *Armstrong-Whitworth Aircraft since 1913.* London: Putnam, 1973.

Williams, Ray. *Armstrong-Whitworth Aircraft.* Stroud, UK: Chalford Publishing, 1998.

FK 8

Bruce, J. M. "The Armstrong-Whitworth," *Air Pictorial* 22 (November, 1960): 387–389.

_____. *Armstrong-Whitworth FK. 8.* Windsock Datafile No. 64. Berkhamsted, UK: Albatros Productions, 1997.

Siskin

Gobeil, Fowler M. "Siskin Pilot," *CAHS Journal* 15 (Spring, 1977): 3–9.

Williams, Ray. "Siskin Supreme," *Air Enthusiast* No. 72 (November/December, 1997): 26–39.

_____. "The Siskin Saga," *Aeroplane Monthly* 6 (February, March, 1978): 66–72; 124–129.

Whitley

"Armstrong-Whitworth's Willing Whitley," *Air Enthusiast* No. 9 (February/March, 1979): 10–25.

Donnelly, G. L. *"The Whitley Boys: 4 Group Bomber Operations, 1939–1940.* Walton-on-Thames, Surrey: *Air Research*, 1998.

Philip, J. R. *Armstrong-Whitworth Whitley.* Aircraft in Profile No. 103. Windsor, UK: Profile Publications, 1967.

Williams, Ray. "Armstrong-Whitworth's Night Bomber," *Aeroplane Monthly* 10 (August, 1982): 402–407.

Avro

Hardy, M. J. *Avro.* Cambridge, UK: Patrick Stephens, 1982.

Harlin, E. A., and G. A. Jenks. *Avro: An Aircraft Album.* London: Ian Allan, 1973.

Holmes, Harry. *Avro: The History of an Aircraft Company.* Shrewsbury, UK: Airlife, 1994.

Jackson, A. J. *Avro Aircraft since 1908.* London: Putnam, 1965.

504

Bruce, C. M. *Avro 504K.* Windsock Datafile No. 28. Berkhamsted, UK: Albatros Productions, 1991.

Jackson, A. J. "Avro 504," *Aeroplane Monthly* 6 (May, July, 1978): 243–249; 370–376.

Anson

Hall, Alan W. *The Avro Anson.* London: Almark, 1972.

Holmes, Harry. *Avro Anson: Images of Aviation.* Stroud, UK: Tempus Publishing, 2000.

Middleton, Don. "Avro Anson," *Aeroplane Monthly* 8 (April, 1986): 187–192.

Sturtivant, Ray. "The Chronicles of 'Faithful Annie,'" *Air Enthusiast* No. 42 (1991): 37–51.

_____. *The Anson File.* Tonbridge, Kent, UK: Air Britain, 1988.

Lancaster

Holmes, Harry. *Avro Lancaster: The Definitive Record.* Shrewsbury, UK: Airlife, 1997.

Jacobs, Peter. *The Lancaster Story.* London: Arms and Armour Press, 1996.

Mason, Francis K. *The Avro Lancaster.* Bourne End, Buckshire, UK: Aston, 1989.

Randell, Nick, and Mike Vines. *Lancaster: A Bombing Legend.* London: Osprey Aerospace, 1997.

Shackleton

Ashworth, Charles. *Avro's Maritime Heavyweight: The Shackleton.* Bournes End, Buckshire, UK: Aston, 1990.

Bentley, John. "Airborne Watchkeeper," *Flight* 96 (November 27, 1969): 843–848.

Calvert, Denis J. "Ten Thousand Rivets Flying in Formation: The Shackletons of the Royal Air Force's No. 8 Squadron," *Air Combat* 11 (September, 1983): 38–47, 70–72.

Chartres, John. *Shackleton at War and Peace.* London: Ian Allan, 1989.

Holmes, Harry. *The Avro Shackleton: The First Forty Years.* Manchester, UK: BAe, 1989.

Vulcan

Brookes, Andrew J. *Avro Vulcan.* London: Ian Allan, 1985.

Cubitt, Duncan, and Ken Ellis. *Vulcan: Last of the V Bombers.* London: Osprey Aerospace, 1996.

Darling, Kev. *Royal Air Force Vulcan.* Leicester, UK: Midland Counties, 1999.

Jackson, Robert. *Avro Vulcan*. Cambridge, UK: Patrick Stephens, 1984.

Pace, Steve. *Avro Vulcan*. North Branch, MN: Specialty Press, 1999.

Blackburn

Jackson, A. J. *Blackburn Aircraft since 1909*. London: Putnam, 1989.

Sherry, Alan M. *The Blackburn: Dumbarton's Aircraft Factory*. Ochiltree: Richard Stenlake, 1996.

Beverly

Chinnery, Phil. "The Beverly," *Fly Past* No. 52 (November, 1985): 38–42.

Gilchrist, Peter. "Blackburn Beverly," *Air Classics* 16 (November, 1980): 52–61.

Overton, Bill. *Blackburn Beverly*. Leicester, UK: Midland Counties, 1990.

Swanborough, Gordon. "Beverly: The General Idea," *Air International* 41 (November, 1991): 251–258.

Wixey, Ken. "Big, Beautiful Beverly," *Fly Past* No. 227 (June, 2000): 87–90.

Shark

"Blackburn Shark," *Aircraft Illustrated* 6 (October, November, 1973): 414–415; 462–463.

Coles, Bob. "Blackburn's Shark Biplane," *Air Classics* 11 (December, 1975): 56–66.

Vincent, Carl. *The Blackburn Shark*. Stittsville, ON: Canada's Wings, 1974.

Woodman, Harry. "Blackburn's Battleships," *Wings* 3 (August, 1973): 38–49.

Skua/Roc

Brown, Eric. "Blackburn's Ill-fated Duo," *Air Enthusiast* 13 (November, 1977): 231–238.

London, Peter. "The Mismatched Skua," *Aeroplane Monthly* 23 (February, 1995): 48–52.

Lumsden, Alec, and Terry Heffernan. "Probe Probare," *Aeroplane Monthly* 18 (February, March, 1990): 105–109; 146–150.

Buccaneer

"Buccaneer: The 15-Year Stop-Gap," *Air International* 23 (August, 1982): 59–67, 93–97.

Calvert, Denis J. "Bucc-shots," *Aircraft Illustrated* 27 (June, August, 1994): 20–25; 34–37.

Gething, Mike. "The Buccaneer Bows Out," *Air International* 46 (March, 1994): 137–144.

Laming, Tim. *Buccaneer: The Story of the Last All-British Strike Aircraft*. Somerset, UK: Patrick Stephens, 1998.

Larsen, Jim. "The Buccaneers of Honington," *Air Combat* 6 (March, 1978): 32–47.

Boulton-Paul

Brew, Alec. *Boulton-Paul Aircraft since 1915*. London: Putnam, 1993.

Kinsey, Gordon. *Boulton and Paul Aircraft: The History of the Companies at Norwich and Wolverhampton*. Lavenham, UK: Terence Dalton, 1997.

Defiant

Bowyer, Chaz. "Boulton-Paul Defiant," *Air International* 41 (July, August, 1991): 33–41; 87–92.

Brew, Alec. *The Defiant File*. London: Air Britain, 1997.

Chambers, John. *Defiant: The True Story*. Swindon: BJ and M Productions, 1997.

Whitehouse, J es. "The Disappointing Defiant," *Air Enthusiast* No. 5 (November, 1977–February, 1978): 44–57.

Woodman, Harry. "The Magnificent Failure," *Air Classics* 7 (May, 1971): 36–49, 54, 64–65.

British Aerospace

Coulson, Phil, ed. *Proud Heritage: A Pictorial History of British Aerospace Aircraft*. Fairfield, UK: Royal Air Force Benevolent Fund Enterprises, 1995.

Tapper, Oliver. *Roots in the Sky: A History of British Aerospace Aircraft*. London: Published for Flight International by IPC Transport Press, Special Publications Department, 1980.

Harrier

Davies, Peter E. *The Harrier Story*. Annapolis, MD: Naval Institute Press, 1996.

Price, Alfred. *Harrier at War*. London: Ian Allan, 1984.

Ward, Sharkey. *Sea Harrier over the Falklands: A Maverick at War*. Annapolis, MD: Naval Institute Press, 1992.

Hawk

Fricker, John. "BAe Hawk," *World Air Power Journal* 22 (Autumn/Fall, 1995): 46–111.

_____. "Poised to Strike," *Air Enthusiast* 15 (September, 1978): 131–142.

Braybrook, Roy M. "Hawk Update No. 2," *Air Combat* 6 (January, 1978): 20–31, 72–82.

March, Peter R. *Hawk Comes of Age*. London: RAF Benevolent Fund, 1995.

Reed, Arthur. *BAe Hawk*. London: Ian Allan, 1985.

Bristol

Barnes, C. H. *Bristol Aircraft since 1910*. London: Putnam, 1988.

Dean, Jack. "The Phoenix Bombers," *Airpower* 27 (January, 1997): 8–23, 34–54.

James, Derek. *The Bristol Aeroplane Company*. Stroud, Gloucestershire, UK: Tempus Publishing, 2000.

Oughton, James D. *Bristol: An Aircraft Album*. London: Ian Allan, 1973.

Russell, D. A. *The Book of Bristol Aircraft*. Leicester, UK: Harborough, 1946.

Beaufort

Bowyer, Michael J. F. "The Bristol Beaufort," *Air Pictorial* 32 (November, December, 1976): 401–405; 440–445.

"Bristol's First Beau," *Air International* 15 (November 1978): 225–237.

Haywood, Robert. *Beaufort File*. Tonbridge, Kent, UK: Air Britain, 1990.

Nesbit, Roy C. *Torpedo Airmen. Missions with Bristol Beauforts, 1940–1942*. London: William Kimber, 1984.

Robertson, Bruce. *The Beaufort Special*. London: Ian Allan, 1976.

Beaufighter

Bingham, Victor F. *Bristol Beaufighter.* Shrewsbury, UK: Airlife, 1994.

Bowyer, Chaz. *Beaufighter at War.* London: Ian Allan, 1976.

_____. *Beaufighter.* London: Kimbler, 1987.

Scutts, Jerry. *Beaufighter in Action.* Carrollton, TX: Squadron/Signal Publications, 1995.

Swanborough, Gordon. "Beaufighter: Innovative Improvisation by Bristol," *Air International* 6 (January, 1974): 25–47.

Blenheim

Boiten, Theo. *Blenheim Strike: The History of the Bristol Blenheim in RAF Service between 1935 and 1942.* Surrey, UK: Air Research Publications, 1995.

Bowyer, Chaz. *Bristol Blenheim.* London: Ian Allan, 1984.

Franks, Norman. *Valiant Wings: The Battle and Blenheim Squadrons over France, 1940.* Somerton, UK: Crecy, 1994.

Mackay, Ron. *Bristol Blenheim in Action.* Carrollton, TX: Squadron/Signal Publications, 1988.

Warner, Graham. *The Forgotten Bomber: The Story of the Restoration of the World's Only Airworthy Bristol Blenheim.* Sparkford UK: Patrick Stephens, 1991.

Bulldog

Andrews, C. F. *Bristol Bulldog.* Aircraft in Profile No. 6. Windsor, UK: Profile Publications, 1964.

"The Bulldog Breed," *Air Enthusiast* 4 (January, February, 1973): 30–35; 91–95.

Lumsden, Alec, and Terry Heffernan. "Probe Probare," *Aeroplane Monthly* 14 (June, 1986): 284–288.

Luff, David. *Bulldog: The Bristol Bulldog Fighter.* Shrewsbury, UK: Airlife, 1987.

Owers, Colin A. "RAAF Bristol Bulldog," *Skyways* No. 26 (April, 1993): 30–41.

F 2B

Bowyer, Chaz. *Bristol F2B: King of the Two-Seaters.* London: Ian Allan, 1985.

Bruce, J. M. *The Bristol Fighter.* London: Arms and Armour Press, 1985.

Cooksley, Peter. *Bristol Fighter in Action.* Carrollton, TX: Squadron/Signal Publications, 1993.

Scout

Bruce, J. M. "Bristol's Fighter Marque," *Air Enthusiast* No. 32 (December, 1986/April, 1987): 1–21.

_____. *Bristol Scouts.* Windsock Datafile No. 44. Berkhamsted, UK: Albatros Productions, 1994.

_____. *Bristol Scouts C and D.* Aircraft in Profile No. 139. Windsor, UK: Profile Publications, 1967.

de Havilland

Birtles, Philip J. *de Havilland.* London: Jane's, 1984.

Davis, Mick. *Airco: The Aircraft Manufacturing Company.* Marlborough, Wilts.: Crowood Publishing, 2001.

Hannah, Donald. *de Havilland.* Stamford: Key, 1982.

Jackson, A. J. *de Havilland Aircraft since 1909.* London: Putnam, 1987.

Owers, Colin A. *De Havilland Aircraft of World War I.* 2 vols. Boulder, CO: Flying Machine Press, 2001.

Riding, Richard. *de Havilland: The Golden Years, 1919–1939.* Sutton, Surrey, UK: IPC Transport Press, 1981.

Sharp, C. Martin. *DH: A History of de Havilland.* Shrewsbury, UK: Airlife, 1982.

DH 2

Cooksley, Peter. *de Havilland DH 2 in Action.* Carrollton, TX: Squadron/Signal Publications, 1996.

Gray, Barry J. *Airco DH. 2.* Windsock Datafile No. 48. Berkhamsted, UK: Albatros Productions, 1994.

Hall, John S. "Thorpe Park's Pusher," *Aeroplane Monthly* 8 (February, 1980): 72–75.

Hucker, Robert. "de Havilland's DH 2 Pusher," *Air Classics* 5 (August, 1979): 82–85.

DH 4

Bowers, Peter M. "Damnable DH-4," *Wings* 10 (December, 1980): 37–45.

_____. "Diabolical DH-4 Myth and Reality," *Wings* 8 (April, 1978): 48–58.

Bruce, J. M. *The DH 4.* Windsock Datafile Special. Berkhamsted, UK: Albatros Productions, 2000.

Sturtivant, Ray, and Gordon Page. *DH4/9 File.* Tonbridge, Kent, UK: Air Britain, 2000.

DH 9

Bruce, J. B. *Airco DH. 9.* Windsock Datafile No. 72. Berkhamsted, UK: Albatros Productions, 1998.

Cooksley, Peter J. *de Havilland DH 9 in Action.* Carrollton, TX: Squadron/Signal Publications, 1996.

Jarrett, Philip. "By Day and by Night," *Aeroplane Monthly* 20 (June, July, 1992): 8–13; 43–47.

Owers, Colin A. "DH-9a," *World War I Aero* No. 141 (August, 1993): 22–32.

Thetford, Owen. "By Day and by Night," *Aeroplane Monthly* 20 (August, 1992): 17–22.

DH 10 *Amiens*

Bruce, J. M. "Airco D. H. 10: The Amiens," *Air Pictorial* 93 (March, 1961): 70–73.

_____. *Airco DH. 10.* Windsock Datafile No. 38. Berkhamsted, UK: Albatros Productions, 1993.

Jarrett, Philip. "By Day and by Night," *Aeroplane Monthly* 20 (September, 1992): 15–20.

Thetford, Owen. "By Day and by Night," *Aeroplane Monthly* 20 (October, 1992): 6–10.

Wixey, Ken. "Airco DH. 10 Amiens," *Fly Past* No. 36 (July, 1984): 34–38.

DH 82 *Tiger Moth*

Bramson, Alan E. *The Tiger Moth Story.* Shrewsbury, UK: Airlife, 1987.

Jackson, A. J. "DH 82 Tiger Moth," *Aeroplane Monthly* 7 (October, 1979): 523–530.

Jerram, Michael F. *Tiger Moth.* Sparkford, Yeovil, Somerset, UK: Haynes, 1984.

McKay, Stuart. *de Havilland Tiger Moth: Legendary Biplane Trainer.* Leicester, UK: Midland Counties, 1999.

_____. *The Tiger Moth: A Tribute.* Shrewsbury, UK: Airlife, 1987.

DH 98 *Mosquito*
  Bishop, Edward. *Mosquito: The Wooden Wonder.* Washington, DC: Smithsonian Institution Press, 1990.
  Bowman, Martin W. *de Havilland Mosquito.* Marlborough, UK: Crowood Press, 1997.
  Howe, Stuart. *de Havilland Mosquito.* Wilmslow, UK: Crecy, 1999.
  Simons, Graham. *Mosquito: The Original Multi-role Aircraft.* London: Arms and Armour Press, 1990.
DH 100 *Vampire*
  Birtles, Philip. *de Havilland Vampire, Venom, and Sea Vixen.* London, Ian Allan, 1986.
  Mason, Francis K. *de Havilland Vampire 5 and 9.* Aircraft in Profile No. 48. Windsor, UK: Profile Publications, 1965.
  Moyes, Philip. "Spider Crab," *Airpower* 9 (January, 1979): 34–49.
  Poe, Bryce II. "Flying King Haaken's Vampires," *Aerospace Historian* 3(2) (1984): 94–100.
  Watkins, David. *de Havilland Vampire: The Complete Story.* Stroud, UK: Sutton, 1996.
  _____. "RAF Training and the Vampire," *Air Enthusiast* No. 86 (November/December, 1999): 41–48.
DH 110 *Sea Vixen*
  Birtles, Philip "Sea Vixen: Britain's First Missile Specialist," *Air International* 40 (April, 1991): 194–201.
  Butler, Tony. "Secrets of the Sea Vixen," *Air Enthusiast* No. 87 (May/June, 2000): 49–61.
  Fiddeler, Brian. *Sea Vixen.* Yeovil, Somerset, UK: Society of Friends of the Fleet Air Arm Museum, 1985.
DH 112 *Venom/Sea Venom*
  Birtles, Philip. "de Havilland Venom," *Air Pictorial* 33 (July, August, 1971): 242–247; 281–283.
  Lindsay, Roger. "de Havilland Venom," *Aeroplane Monthly* No. 6 (July, 1978): 378–381.
  Morgan, Eric. "Vickers Venom Interceptor," *Aeroplane Monthly* 10 (September, 1982): 502–507.
  Sturtivant, Ray. "A Naval Twin Boomer," *Air International* 39 (August, 1990): 81–90.
  Wixey, Ken. "Vampire with Attitude," *Air Enthusiast* No. 85 (January/February, 2000): 35–41.

English Electric
  Ransom, Stephen, and Robert Fairclough. *English Electric Aircraft and Their Predecessors.* London: Putnam, 1987.
Canberra
  Delve, Ken. *English Electric Canberra.* Leicester, UK: Midland Counties, 1992.
  Jones, Barry. *English Electric Canberra and Martin B-57.* Marlborough, UK: Crowood, 1999.
  Lashmar, Paul. "Canberras over the U.S.S.R," *Aeroplane Monthly* 23 (February, 1985): 32–35.
Lightning
  Black, Ian. *Lightning.* Shrewsbury, UK: Airlife, 1988.
  _____. *Last of the Lightnings: A Nostalgic Farewell to the RAF's Favorite Supersonic Fighter.* Somerset, UK: Patrick Stephens, 1996.

  Bowman, Martin W. *English Electric Lightning.* Marlborough, UK: Crowood, 1997.
  Darling, Kev. *Lightning: The Operational History.* Shrewsbury, UK: Airlife, 1995.
  Lake, Jon. "English Electric Lightning," *Wings of Fame* 7 (1997): 36–101.

Fairey
  Desmond, Kevin. "Richard Fairey," *Aeroplane Monthly* 16 (January, February, 1988): 34–37; 110–113.
  Sturtivant, Ray. *Fairey Aircraft.* Stroud, UK: Alan Sutton Publishing, 1996.
  Taylor, H. A. *Fairey Aircraft since 1918.* London: Putnam, 1988.
IIIF
  Isaacs, Keith. "The Fairey IIIF in Australia," *Air Enthusiast* No. 24 (April/July, 1984): 40–49.
  Jarrett, Philip. "Fairey IIIF," *Aeroplane Monthly* 22 (March, April, June, 1994): 59–63; 51–54; 12–20.
  Lumsden, Alec, and Terry Heffernan. "Per Mare Probare," *Aeroplane Monthly* 15 (August, September, 1987): 438–441; 458–461.
  Mason, Francis K. *Fairey IIIF.* Aircraft in Profile No. 44. Windsor, UK: Profile Publications, 1965.
  Wixey, Ken. "Fairey IIIF," *Fly Past* No. 48 (July, 1985): 40–43.
Barracuda
  Brown, Eric. "Fairey's Mighty Monster—the Barracuda," *Air International* 12 (May, 1977): 236–242.
  Hadley, Dunstan. *Barracuda Pilot.* Shrewsbury, UK: Airlife, 1992.
  Smith, Peter. "Fairey Barracuda," *Fly Past* No. 28 (November, 1983): 12–16.
  Sturtivant, Ray. "Barracuda in Action," *Aeroplane Monthly* 9 (March, April, 1981): 116–121; 200–205.
  Trimble, Robert L. "Barracuda," *Air Classics* 18 (October, 1982): 14–23, 70.
Battle
  Dean, Jack. "Bred for Battle," *Airpower* 26 (November, 1996): 34–47.
  "Elegantly Obsolete," *Air International* 20 (March, 1981): 127–134.
  Franks, Norman. *Valiant Wings: The Battle and Blenheim Squadrons over France, 1940.* Somerton, UK: Crecy, 1994.
  Isby, David. "Too Little, Too Late," *Air Classics* 8 (December, 1972): 46–53, 62–63.
  Shail, Sidney. *Fairey Battle File.* Tonbridge, Kent, UK: Air Britain, 1998.
Firefly
  Brown, Eric. "A Ship Board Luminary," *Air International* 17 (July, 1979): 24–32.
  "Firefly: A Masterpiece for Malelots," *Air Enthusiast* 2 (March, May, 1972): 139–147; 309–315.
  Harrison, William A. *Fairey Firefly: The Operational Record.* Shrewsbury, UK: Airlife, 1992.
  Larson, George C. "The Fairey Firefly," *Flying* 154 (April, 1974): 47–51, 96–97.

Trimble, Robert L. "Firefly," *Air Classics* 19 (May, June, 1983): 48–62,82; 16–27, 64–74.

Flycatcher

Cross, David. "Return of the Flycatcher," *Air Classics* 16 (January, 1980): 53–56.

Sturtivant, Ray. "Fairey's First Fleet Fighter," *Air Enthusiast* No. 37 (September/December, 1988): 1–14.

Taylor, H. A. "Testing at Martlesham . . . and the Flycatcher Flaps," *Air International* 14 (May, 1978): 232–237.

Thetford, Owen. *Fairey Flycatcher*. Aircraft in Profile No. 56. Windsor, UK: Profile Publications, 1965.

Fulmar

Brown, David. *Fairey Fulmar Mks I and II*. Aircraft in Profile No. 254. Windsor, UK: Profile Publications, 1973.

Brown, Eric. "The Fortuitous Fulmar," *Air International* 13 (August, 1997): 74–79.

Trimble, Robert L. "Fairey Fulmar," *Air Classics* 19 (April, 1983): 42–44, 72–80.

Zichy, Count. "Fulmar Flight," *Aeroplane Monthly* No. 10 (July, 1982): 394–396.

Swordfish

Harrison, William A. *Swordfish Special*. London: Ian Allan, 1977.

_____. *Swordfish at War*. Shepperton, UK: Ian Allan, 1987.

Felixstowe

Bruce, J. M. "The Felixstowe Flying Boats," *Flight* 63 (December 2–23, 1955): 842–846; 895–898; 929–932.

Kinsey, Gordon. *Seaplanes—Felixstowe: The Story of the Air Station, 1913–1963*. Lavenham, UK: T. Dalton, 1978.

F2A

Bruce, J. M. *Felixstowe F.2A*. Windsock Datafile No. 82. Berkhamsted, UK: Albatros Productions, 2000.

_____. "The Felixstowe Flying Boats," *Aeroplane Monthly* 10 (October, November, 1982): 536–540; 622–625.

"The Fabulous Felixstowe," *Windsock International* 7 (March/April, May/June, 1991): 12–22; 18–21.

Livock, G. E. *To the Ends of the Air*. London: HMSO, 1973.

Folland

James, Derek N. *Spirit of Hamble: Folland Aircraft*. Stroud, Gloucsester: Tempus, 2000.

Gnat

Birtles, Philip J. "Folland's Midget Fighter," *Air Classics* 13 (November, 1977): 46–53, 88.

Braybrook, Roy. "Quarts in Pint Pots," *Air International* 15 (July, 1978): 21–24.

Burnet, Charles. "Folland's (G)Natty Fighter," *Air International* 24 (April/July, 1984): 1–10.

Choprin, Pushpindar. "Fly with a Sting," *Air Enthusiast* 7 (August, 1974): 68–75.

General Aircraft

Butler, P. H. *British Glider*. Liverpool, UK: Merseyside Society, 1980.

Hamilcar

Gunston, Bill. "Hamilcar: Tank-Carrying Glider," *Aeroplane Monthly* 5 (December, 1977): 636–640.

Jarrett, Philip. "Nothing Ventured...," *Aeroplane Monthly* 20 (February, 1992): 16–22.

Prower, Charles W. "Gliding Tanks," *Aeroplane Monthly* 22 (July, August, 1993): 26–31, 52–55.

Gloster

James, Derek M. *Gloster Aircraft since 1917*. London: Putnam, 1987.

Gauntlet

"Annals of the Gauntlet," *Air Enthusiast Quarterly* No. 2: 163–176.

Lumsden, Eric, and Terry Heffernan. "Probe Probare," *Aeroplane Monthly* 13 (August, 1985): 396–400.

Mason, Francis K. *Gloster Gauntlet*. Aircraft in Profile No. 10. Windsor, UK: Profile Publications, 1965.

Rawlings, J. D. R. "Gloster Gauntlet—Expansion Fighter," *Air Pictorial* 35 (May, 1973): 185–191.

Wixey, Kenneth. "Gloster Gauntlet Story," *Aircraft Illustrated* 14 (January, 1981): 13–17.

Gladiator

"Epitome of an Era...The R.A.F's Last Fighting Biplane," *Air Enthusiast* 4 (March, 1973): 125–137.

Guhnfeldt, Cato. "A Norse Saga," *Aeroplane Monthly* 8 (June, 1980): 311–313.

Lumsden, Alec. "Nothing Ventured...," *Aeroplane Monthly* 20 (April, May, 1992): 8–15, 8–15.

Mackay, David. "Flying the Gladiator," *Aeroplane Monthly* 29 (March, 2001): 44–52.

Mason, Francis K. *The Gloster Gladiator*. London: Macdonald, 1964.

Javelin

Allward, Maurice. *Gloster Javelin*. London: Ian Allan, 1983.

Lake, Jon. "Classics Compared: Javelin and Tornado G.3," *Air International* 54 (February, 2001): 97–105.

Lindsay, Roger. "Gloster Javelin," *Aeroplane Monthly* 6 (January, 1978): 19–24, 35.

Morgan, Eric, and Edward Shacklady. "Delta Developments," *Aeroplane Monthly* (February, March, April, 1996): 28–32; 28–33; 62.

Wixey, Ken. "Javelin—Gloster's Innovative Delta," *Air International* 49 (December, 1995): 348–356.

Meteor

Bowyer, Chaz. *Gloster Meteor*. London: Ian Allan, 1985.

Derek, James N. "Fighters of the Fifties—Gloster Meteor NF.11–14," *Aeroplane Monthly* 3 (November, 1975): 549–558.

Jones, Barry. *Gloster Meteor*. Wiltshire, UK: Crowood Press, 1998.

Philpott, Bryan. *Meteor*. Wellingborough, UK: Patrick Stephens, 1986.

Williams, Ray. "Meteor Night Fighters," *Aeroplane Monthly* 23 (April, 1995): 6–10.

Handley Page

Barnes, C. H. *Handley Page Aircraft since 1907.* London: Putnam, 1987.

Bowyer, Chaz. *Handley Page Bombers of the First World War.* Bourne End, Buckshire, UK: Aston Publications, 1992.

Clayton, Donald C. *Handley Page: An Aircraft Album.* London: Ian Allan, 1970.

Halifax

Bingham, Victor. *Halifax Second to None: The Handley Page Halifax.* Shrewsbury, UK: Airlife, 1986.

"Bomber Command's Second String . . . the Halifax," *Air Enthusiast* 15 (April/June, 1981): 11–30.

Merrick, Kenneth A. *Halifax: An Illustrated History of a Classic World War 2 Bomber.* London: Ian Allan, 1980.

Rapier, Brian J. *Halifax at War.* London: Ian Allan, 1987.

Scutts, Jerry. *Halifax in Action.* Carrollton, TX: Squadron/Signal Publications, 1984.

Hampden

Bowyer, Chaz. *Hampden Special.* London: Ian Allan, 1976.

Halliday, Hugh A. "Canada and the Hampden," *CAHS Journal* 36 (Spring, Summer, 1998): 22–32; 52–59.

"Hampden: Defender of Liberty," *Air International* 27 (November, 1984): 244–252.

Moyle, Harry. *The Hampden File.* Tonbridge, Kent, UK: Air Britain, 1989.

Woods, Eric. "Surely You Didn't Fly in That Thing?" *Fly Past* No. 195 (October, 1997): 72–76.

Heyford

Jarrett, Philip. "By Day and by Night: Handley Page Heyford," *Aeroplane Monthly* 23 (November, December, 1995): 13–18; 16–21.

Lumsden, Alec, and Terry Heffernan. "Probe Probare," *Aeroplane Monthly* 12 (September, 1984): 456–462.

Moyes, Philip. "Big Sticks," *Wings* 9 (April, 1979): 30–39, 54.

Thetford, Owen. "By Day and by Night: Handley Page Heyford," *Aeroplane Monthly* 24 (February, 1996): 63–66.

Wixey, Ken. "Handley Page Heyford," *Fly Past* No. 69 (November, 1986): 39–42.

O/400

Barnes, C. H. "Handley Page's 'Bloody Paralyzer,'" *Air Enthusiast* 5 (August, 1973): 74–83.

Halley, Jack. "The Kabul Raid," *Aeroplane Monthly* 7 (August, 1979): 437–441.

Hucker, Robert. "The Bloody Paralyzer," *Air Classics Quarterly Review* 6 (Summer, 1979): 69–72, 99.

Wixey, Ken. "Handley Page O/400, V/1500," *Fly Past* No. 32 (March, 1984): 39–44.

Victor

Brookes, Andrew. *Handley Page Victor.* London: Ian Allan, 1988.

Laming, Tim. *V Bombers—Vulcan, Victor, and Valiant: Britain's Airborne Deterrent.* Somerset, UK: Patrick Stephens, 1997.

Moyes, Philip P. "V for Victor," *Wings* 10 (August, 1980): 28–47.

Hawker

Blackmore, L. K. *Hawker: Aviator, Designer, Test Pilot.* New York: Orion Books, 1991.

_____. *Hawker—One of Aviation's Greatest Names: A Biography of Harry Hawker.* Shrewsbury, UK: Airlife, 1993.

Hawker, Muriel. *H. G. Hawker, Airman: His Life and Work.* London: Hutchinson, 1927.

James, Derek M. *Hawker: An Aircraft Album.* London: Ian Allan, 1972.

Mason, Francis K. *Hawker Aircraft since 1920.* London: Putnam, 1991.

Fury

"Barrier-Breaking Fury,"*Air Enthusiast Quarterly* No. 3 (1976): 1–17.

Butler, Tony. "The RAF Hath No Fury," *Air Enthusiast* No. 86 (March/April, 2000): 46–55.

"El Fury Espanol," *Air International* 18 (June, 1980): 285–289, 305.

Westburg, Peter. "Fury from Hawker," *Air Classics* 11 (July, 1975): 72–82; 12 (August, September, 1976): 2–32; 74–85; 13 (April, 1977): 20–31, 76.

Woodman, Harry. "Hawker's Flying Thoroughbred," *Air Classics* 6 (October, 1969): 38–54, 57, 59, 63, 65.

Hart

Holmes, J. Gordon. "The Hart Family," *Air Pictorial* 39 (April, May, June, July, 1977): 146–150; 185–189; 228–231; 274–276.

Jarrett, Philip. "Radial-Engined Harts," *Aeroplane Monthly* 25 (October, November, 1997): 62–67; 50–54.

Lumsden, Alec, and Terry Heffernan. "Probe Probare," *Aeroplane Monthly* 12 (July, 1984): 352–356, 375.

Thetford, Owen. "Hawker Hart and Hind," *Aeroplane Monthly* 23 (August, 1995): 35–43.

Wixey, Ken. "Hawker Hart," *Fly Past* No. 60 (July, 1980): 22–25.

Hunter

Braybrook, Roy. *Hunter: A Personal View of the Ultimate Hawker Fighter.* London: Osprey, 1987.

Duke, Neville. "Hunter's Quarter-Century," *Aeroplane Monthly* 4 (September, 1976): 458–465.

Jackson, Robert. *Hawker Hunter: The Operational Record.* Washington, DC: Smithsonian Institution Press, 1990.

Jones, Barry. *Hawker Hunter.* Marlborough, UK: Crowood Press, 1998.

Mason, Francis K. *Hawker Hunter: Biography of a Thoroughbred.* Wellingborough, UK: Patrick Stepens, 1985.

Hurricane

Barker, Ralph. *Hurricats: The Fighters That Could Not Return.* Stroud, Gloucestershire, UK: Tempus Publishing, 2000.

Bishop, Edward. *Hurricane.* Washington, DC: Smithsonian Institution Press, 1990.

Fozard, John W., ed. *Sydney Camm and the Hurricane: Perspectives on a Master Builder and His Finest Achievement.* Washington, DC: Smithsonian Institution Press, 1991.

Jacobs, Peter. *Hawker Hurricane.* Wilshire, UK: Focus Publishing, 1998.

Mason, Francis K. *Hawker Hurricane.* Winslow, UK: Crecy, 2000.

Sea Fury

Brown, Eric. "Finae Furioso . . . the Era-Ending Sea Fury," *Air International* 18 (February, 1980): 82–86, 94–97.

Mackay, Ron. *Hawker Sea Fury in Action.* Carrollton, TX: Squadron/Signal Publications, 1991.

Trimble, Robert A. "Last of the Breed," *Air Classics Quarterly Review* 5 (Spring, 1978): 20–31, 90–98.

Williams, Ray. "Sea Fury," *Aeroplane Monthly* 13 (December, 1985; January, 1986): 635–638; 31–35.

Wilson, Stewart. *Sea Fury, Firefly, and Sea Venom in Australian Service.* Western Creek, ACT: Aerospace Publications, 1993.

Tempest

Beaumont, Roland. *Tempest over Europe.* Shrewsbury, UK: Airlife, 1994.

Halliday, Hugh A. *Typhoon and Tempest: The Canadian Story.* Toronto: CANAV Books, 1997.

Mason, Francis K. *Hawker Tempest, Mks. I-V.* Aircraft in Profile No. 197. Windsor, UK: Profile Publications, 1971.

Reed, Arthur, and Roland Beaumont. *Typhoon and Tempest at War.* London: Ian Allan, 1974.

Thomas, Chris. *The Typhoon and Tempest Story.* London: Arms and Armour Press, 1988.

Typhoon

Bickers, R. T. *Hawker Typhoon: The Combat History.* Shrewsbury, UK: Airlife, 2000.

Demoulin, Charles. *Firebirds: Flying the Typhoon in Action.* Shrewsbury, UK: Airlife, 1987.

Mason, Francis K. *Hawker Typhoon.* Aircraft in Profile No. 81. Windsor, UK: Profile Publications, 1966.

"The More Violent Hurricane," *Air Enthusiast* 3 (August, 1992): 91–100.

"Typhoon," *Air Classics* 10 (March, 1979): 14–24.

Hawker-Siddeley

Nimrod

Chartres, John. *BAe Nimrod.* London: Ian Allan, 1986.

De Graef, Stefan. "Millennium Nimrods," *Air Combat* 26 (May/June, 1998): 57–62.

"Hawker Siddeley's Mighty Hunter," *Air Enthusiast* 5 (December, 1993): 259–267.

Laming, Tim. "Sea Scanner," *Airpower* 15 (November, 1985): 30–37.

Williams, Ray. *The Comet and Nimrod.* Stroud, Gloucestershire, UK: Tempus Publishing, 2000.

Martinsyde

Bruce, J. M. "The History of Martinsyde Aircraft," *Royal Aeronautical Society Journal* (1968): 755–770.

Sanger, Ray. *The Martinsyde History.* Tonbridge, Kent, UK: Air Britain, 1999.

G 100 *Elephant*

Bowyer, Chaz. *The Flying Elephants: A History of No. 27 Squadron, Royal Flying Corps, Royal Air Force, 1915–1969.* London: Macdonald, 1972.

Bruce, J. M. *Martinsyde Elephant.* Windsock Datafile No. 70. Berkhamsted, UK: Albatros Productions, 1998.

_____. *Martinsyde Elephant.* Aircraft in Profile No. 200. Windsor, UK: Profile Publications, 1971.

Leaman, Paul. "The 'Elephants' of Twenty Seven," *Cross and Cockade Journal* 30 (Spring, 1999): 16–47.

Miles

Brown, Don L. *Miles Aircraft since 1925.* London: Putnam, 1970.

Lukins, A. H. *The Book of Miles Aircraft.* Leicester, UK: Harborough Publishing, 1946.

Simpson, R. W. *Miles Aircraft.* Stroud, Gloucestershire, UK: Chalford, 1998.

Master

Amos, Peter. "Master I and II," *Aeroplane Monthly* 8 (August, September, 1980): 412–418; 460–469.

Lumsden, Alec, and Terry Heffernan. "Probe Probare," *Aeroplane Monthly* 17 (October, November, 1989): 586–590; 650–654.

Royal Aircraft Factory

Hare, Paul R. *The Royal Aircraft Factory.* London: Putnam Aeronautical, 1990.

_____. *Aeroplanes of the Royal Aircraft Factory.* Marlborough, UK: Crowood, 1999.

BE 2

Bruce, J. M. *RAF BE. 2e.* Windsock Datafile No. 14. Berkhamsted, UK: Albatros Productions, 1989.

Cooksley, Peter. *B. E. 2 in Action.* Carrollton, TX: Squadron/Signal Publications, 1992.

Hare, Paul. "Aerial Reconnaissance and the B. E. 2c," *World War I Aero* No. 148 (May, 1995): 45–50.

Leaman, Paul. "Evolution of the BE.2 Airplane," *Cross and Cockade International* 8 (Winter, 1977): 168–176.

FE 2

Bowyer, Chaz. "Fee Portfolio," *Cross and Cockade Great Britain* 3 (Summer, 1972): 58–67.

Bruce, J. M. *RAF FE. 2b.* Windsock Datafile No. 18. Berkhamsted, UK: Albatros productions, 1989.

Waugh, Colin, and Raymond Vann. "Story of the Fifty Fees," *Cross and Cockade Journal* 18 (Winter, 1977): 342–348.

RE 8

Bowyer, Chaz. "Harry Tate: The RE. 8," *Cross and Cockade Great Britain* 4 (Autumn, 1973): 118–124.

Bruce, J. M. *RE-8.* Windsock Datafile No. 24. Berkhamsted, UK: Albatros Productions, 1991.

"Royal Aircraft Factory RE. 8," *World War I Aero* No. 136 (April, 1992): 48–58.

SE 5a

    Bourget, Charles L. *Royal Aircraft Factory S.E. 5a.* West Roxbury, MA: World War I Aero Publishers, 1965.

    Bruce, J. M. *RAF Se. 5a.* Windsock Datafile No. 10. Berkhamsted, UK: Albatros Productions, 1989.

    Connors, John F. *S.E. 5a in Action.* Carrollton, TX: Squadron/Signal Publications, 1985.

    Sturtivant, Ray, and Gordon Page. *The S.E. 5a File.* Tonbridge Wells: Air Britain, 1996.

Short

    Barnes, C. H. *Shorts Aircraft since 1900.* London: Putnam, 1989.

    Donne, Michael. *Pioneers of the Skies: A History of Short Brothers PLC, the First Manufacturers of Aircraft in the World.* Nicholson and Bass, 1987.

    Hannah, Donald. *Shorts.* Stamford: Key, 1983.

    "The Short Story," *Air Pictorial* 19 (March, April, May, June, 1957): 74–76; 112–114; 148–151; 185–188, 214.

    Taylor, Michael J. H. *Shorts.* London: Jane's, 1984.

184

    Bruce, Jack. "The Question of Launching Torpedoes," *Aeroplane Monthly* 15 (March, April, May, 1987): 146–149; 215–217; 270–273.

    _____. *Short 184.* Aircraft in Profile No. 74. Windsor, UK: Profile Publications, 1966.

    Bruce, J. M. *Short 184.* Windsock Datafile No. 85. Berkhamsted, UK: Albatros Publications, 2001.

Stirling

    Bowyer, Michael J.F. *The Stirling Bomber.* London: Faber and Faber, 1980.

    Falconer, Jonathan. *Stirling Wings: The Short Stirling Goes to War.* Gloucestershire, UK: A. Sutton Publishing, 1995.

    MacKay, Ron. *Short Stirling in Action.* Carrollton, TX: Squadron/Signal Publications, 1998.

    Peden, D. Murray. "Avenger in the Shadows," *Wings* 6 (October, 1976): 40–53.

    _____. "Salute to the Stirling," *Aeroplane Monthly* 5 (November, 1977): 564–569.

Sunderland

    Bowyer, Chaz. *Sunderland at War.* London: Ian Allan, 1976.

    _____. *The Short Sunderland.* Bourne End, Buckshire, UK: Aston, 1989.

    Delve, Ken. *Short Sunderland.* Marlborough, UK: Crowood, 2000.

    Hendrie, Andrew. *Short Sunderland in World War II.* Shrewsbury, UK: Airlife, 1998.

    "Sunderland Story," *Air International* 21 (September, 1981): 125–134.

Sopwith

    Arango, Javier. "Revolutionary Aircraft Designer Tommy Sopwith," *Aviation History* 11 (March, 2001): 42–48, 74–76.

    Baxter, Raymond. "The Sopwith Interview," *Aeroplane Monthly* 12 (July, August, 1984): 348–351; 404–407.

    Bramson, Alan E. *Pure Luck: The Authorized Biography of Sir Thomas Sopwith, 1888–1989.* Wellingborough, UK: Patrick Stephens, 1990.

    Bruce, J. M. *The Sopwith Fighters.* London: Arms and Armour Press, 1986.

    Davis, Mick. *Sopwith Aircraft.* Marlborough, UK: Crowood, 1999.

    King, H. F. *Sopwith Aircraft, 1912–1920.* London: Putnam, 1980.

    Robertson, Bruce. *Sopwith: The Man and His Aircraft.* Letchsworth: Air Review, 1970.

1½ Strutter

    Bruce, J. M. "The Sopwith 1½ Strutter," *Flight* 78 (September 28; October 5, 1956): 542–546; 586–591.

    _____. *Sopwith 1½ Strutter.* Windsock Datafile No. 80. Berkhamsted, UK: Albatros Productions, 2000.

    _____. *Sopwith 1½ Strutter.* Aircraft in Profile No. 121. Windsor, UK: Profile Publications, 1967.

Camel

    Bowyer, Chaz. *Sopwith Camel: The King of Combat.* Falmouth, UK: Glasney Press, 1978.

    Bruce, J. M. *Sopwith Camel.* London: Arms and Armour Press, 1990.

    Macmillan, Norman. "A Fierce Little Beast," *Aeroplane Monthly* 12 (October, 1984): 528–531, 556.

    Pudney, John. *The Camel Fighter.* London: Hamish Hamilton, 1964.

    Sturtivant, Ray, and Gordon Page. *The Camel File.* Tonbridge: Air Britain, 1993.

Dolphin

    Bruce, J. M. "The Sopwith 5F.1 Dolphin," *Air Pictorial* 79 (May, 1961): 132–135, 150.

    _____. *Sopwith Dolphin.* Windsock Datafile No. 54. Berkhamsted, UK: Albatros Productions, 1994.

    _____. *Sopwith Dolphin.* Aircraft in Profile No. 169. Windsor, UK: Profile Publications, 1967.

    Carnes, John F. "11th Hour Sopwiths," *Wings* 6 (February, 1976): 8–19.

    Jarrett, Philip. "Sopwith 5F.1 Dolphin," *Aeroplane Monthly* 29 (February, 2001): 53–73.

Pup

    Bruce, J. M. "The Sopwith Pup," *Cross and Cockade International* 19 (Spring, 1988): 1–25.

    _____. *Sopwith Pup.* Windsock Datafile No. 2. Berkhamsted, UK: Albatros Productions, 1987.

    _____. *Sopwith Pup.* Bourne End, UK: Aston, 1991.

Snipe

    Bruce, J. M. "Sopwith Snipe: The RAF's First Fighter," *Air Enthusiast* 6 (April, June, 1974): 190–195, 206–207; 289–302.

    _____. *Sopwith Snipe.* Windsock Datafile No. 46. Berkhamsted, UK: Albatros Productions, 1994.

    _____. *Sopwith Snipe.* Aircraft in Profile No. 50. Windsor, UK: Profile Publications, 1966.

    Shennan, Anthony. *Sopwith Snipe Described.* Toronto, ON: Kookaburra Technical Publications, 1967.

Tabloid

    Bruce, J. M. *Sopwith Tabloid.* Mini-Datafile No. 9. Berkhamsted, UK: Albatros Productions, 1997.

Triplane

Bowers, Peter M., and Ernest R. McDowell. *Triplanes: A Pictorial History of the World's Triplanes and Multiplanes.* Osceola, WI: MBI, 1993.

Bruce, J. M. "The Sopwith Triplane," *Flight* 71 (April 19; April 26, 1957): 507–510; 553–557.

_____. *Sopwith Triplane.* Windsock Datafile No. 22. Berkhamsted, UK: Albatros Productions, 1990.

Connors, John F. "Sopwith's Flying Staircase," *Wings* 5 (June, 1975): 46–54.

Hadingham, Evan. *The Fighting Triplanes.* New York: Macmillan, 1969.

Supermarine

Andrews, C. F., and F. B. Morgan. *Supermarine Aircraft since 1919.* London: Putnam, 1981.

Holt, Peter. "Supermarine Super Designer R. J. Mitchell," *Aviation History* (September, 1995): 34–41.

Mitchell, Gordon. "R. J. Mitchell: My Father," *Aerospace Monthly* 14 (March, April, 1986): 123–126; 177–180.

Spitfire

Dibbs, John M. *Spitfire: Flying Legend—the Fighter and the Few.* London: Osprey Aviation, 1996.

Jackson, Robert. *Spitfire: The Combat History.* Osceola, WI: Motorbooks International, 1995.

Morgan, Eric B., and Edward Shacklady. *Spitfire: The History.* Hemel Hempstead, UK: Nexus Special Interests, 2000.

Price, Alfred. *The Spitfire Story.* London: Arms and Armour Press, 1999.

Wilson, Stewart. *Spitfire.* Shrewsbury, UK: Airlife, 2000.

Stranraer

Andrews, C. F. "The Southampton Saga," *Aeroplane Monthly* 4 (September, 1976): 452–457.

Tate, Harry. "The Stranraer in the RCAF," *CAHS Journal* 8 (Fall, 1976): 68–72.

Wixey, Ken. "Flying Boats of the Royal Air Force," *Fly Past* No. 133 (August, 1992): 65–67.

Walrus

Davies, Richard. "The Time Has Come, the Walrus Said," *Aeroplane Monthly* 23 (October, 1995): 50–54.

Franks, Norman. *Another Kind of Courage: Stories of the UK-based Walrus Air-Sea Rescue Squadrons.* Sparkford, UK: Patrick Stephens, 1994.

Gault, Owen. "Shagbat the Magnificent," *Air Classics* 28 (January, 1992): 58–63.

London, Peter. "From Seagull to 'Shagbat': The Life and Times of the Supermarine Walrus," *Air Enthusiast* No. 74 (March/April, 1998): 34–39; No. 76 (July/August, 1998): 68–71.

Wixey, Ken. "Flying Boats of the Royal Air Force," *Fly Past* No. 139 (February, 1993): 62–63; No. 142 (May, 1993): 55–56.

Vickers

Andrews, C. F., and E. B. Morgan. *Vickers Aircraft since 1908.* London: Putnam, 1988.

Barfield, Norman. *Vickers Aircraft.* Stroud, Gloucestershire, UK: Chalford, 1997.

Morpugo, J. F. *Barnes Wallis: A Biography.* New York: St. Martin's Press, 1992.

Scott, J. D. *Vickers: A History.* London: Weidenfeld and Nicolson, 1962.

FB 5

Franks, Norman. "The Gunbus in Combat," *Aeroplane Monthly* 4 (May, 1976): 255–261.

Bruce, J. M. "Vicker's First Fighter," *Air Enthusiast* No. 12 (April/July, 1980): 54–70.

_____. *Vickers FB. 5.* Windsock Datafile No. 56. Berkhamsted, UK: Albatros Productions, 1996.

_____. *FE-2, 2A, and 2B.* Aircraft in Profile No. 133. Windsor, UK: Profile Publications, 1967.

Valiant

Andrews, C. F. *Vickers Valiant.* Aircraft in Profile No. 66. Windsor, UK: Profile Publications, 1966.

Burnet, Charles, and Eric B. Morgan. "The V-Bombers: Vickers Valiant," *Aeroplane Monthly* 8 (August, September, 1980): 396–401; 452–456.

Jones, Barry. *V-Bombers: The Valiant, Vulcan, and Victor.* Marlborough, UK: Crowood, 2000.

Moyes, Philip. "Valiant: First of Britain's V-Bombers," *Wings* 10 (June, 1980): 29–41.

Vildebeest

Jarrett, Philip. "Vildebeest and Vincent," *Aeroplane Monthly* 23 (February, 1995): 17–22.

Thetford, Owen. "Vildebeest in Service," *Aeroplane Monthly* 23 (April, 1995): 37–42.

Trimble, Robert. "Vildebeest," *Air Classics* 21 (November, 1985): 20–21, 78–79, 82.

Wixey, Ken. "Vildebeest and Vincent," *Fly Past* No. 66 (January, 1987): 22–25.

Woodman, Harry. "The Weybridge Beast," *Air Classics* 5 (February, 1969): 22–25, 28–33, 36–37, 65.

Vimy

Bruce, J. M. *Vicker Vimy.* Windsock Special. Berkhamsted, UK: Albatros Productions, 1994.

McMillan, Peter. "Flying the Vimy," *Aeroplane Monthly* 23 (October, 1995): 10–15.

Turner, Paul St. John. *The Vickers Vimy.* London: Patrick Stephens, 1969.

Wixey, Ken. "Vickers Vimy," *Fly Past* No. 38 (September, 1984): 24–28.

Wellesley

Adkin, Fred. "Erk's Progress," *Aeroplane Monthly* 7 (April, 1979): 214–219.

Moyes, Philip. "The Basketweave Bomber," *Air Power* 11 (March, 1981): 11–19.

Pelly-Fry, James. "Wellesleys over the Sudan," *Aeroplane Monthly* 12 (March, April, May, 1984): 136–141; 177–179; 239–241.

"The Wellesley: Geodetics in Action," *Air International* 19 (July, 1980): 25–33, 49–50.

Wixley, Ken. "Vickers Wellesley," *Fly Past* No. 74 (September, 1987): 48–50.

Wellington

Bowman, Martin W. *Wellington: The Geodetic Giant.* Shrewsbury, UK: Airlife, 1989.

Bowyer, Chaz. *Wellington at War*. London: Ian Allan, 1982.
_____. *The Wellington Bomber*. London: Kimber, 1986.
Cooksley, Peter G. *Wellington: Mainstay of Bomber Command*. Wellingborough, UK: Patrick Stephens, 1987.
Delve, Ken. *Vickers-Armstrong Wellington*. Wiltshire, UK: Crowood Press, 1998.

Westland
Boyne, Walt. "Penrose of Westland: Fabulous Flightlog of Westland's Chief Test Pilot," *Wings* 9 (April, 1979): 8–22.
James, Derek N. *Westland Aircraft since 1915*. London: Putnam, 1991.
Lukins, A. H. *The Book of Westland Aircraft*. Leicester, UK: Harborough, 1945.
Mondey, David. *Planemakers 2: Westland*. London: James, 1982.
Taylor, John W. R., and Maurice F. Allward. *Westland 50*. London: Ian Allan, 1965.
Lynx
Braybrook, Roy M. "Westland Lynx," *Air Combat* 11 (September, 1983): 6–15, 56–57.
"Lynx in Battledress," *Air International* 38 (April, 1990): 105–111.
"The Lynx Leaps Ahead," *Air International* 10 (April, 1976): 163–170.
"Lynx—Yeovil's Revolutionary Yearling," *Air Enthusiast* 2 (June, 1972): 283–290.
Rawlings, John D. R. "With the Lynx at Sea," *Air Pictorial* 41 (October, 1979): 384–389.
Lysander
Mason, Francis K. *Westland Lysander*. Aircraft in Profile No. 159. Windsor, UK: Profile Publications, 1967.
Robertson, Bruce. *Lysander Special*. London: Ian Allan, 1977.
Sephton, Andy. "Getting to Know Lizzie," *Aeroplane Monthly* 78 (January, 2000): 74–80.
Taylor, H. A. "The Westland Lysander Viewed from the Cockpit," *Air Enthusiast* 3 (July, 1972): 33–35.
Verity, Hugh. *We Land by Moonlight: Secret RAF Landings in France, 1940–1944*. Wilmslow, UK: Air Data, 1995.
Scout/Wasp
Burford, Andrew. "Life Begins Again at 30," *Air International* 45 (September, 1993): 138–140.
Wapiti
Andrews, C. F. *Westland Wapiti*. Aircraft in Profile No. 32. Windsor, UK: Profile Publications, 1965.
Jarrett, Philip. "Wapiti and Wallace," *Aeroplane Monthly* 22 (May, July, 1994): 18–23; 58–63.
Thetford, Owen. "Westland Wapiti," *Aeroplane Monthly* 22 (October, 1994): 33–39.
Wixey, Ken. "Wallace and Wapiti," *Fly Past* No. 54 (January, 1986): 22–25.
Whirlwind
Bingham, Victor F. *Whirlwind: The Westland Whirlwind Fighter*. Shrewsbury, UK: Airlife, 1987.

Coyne, J. P. "Flying the Whirlwind," *CAHS Journal* 37 (March, 1999): 124–133, 154.
Heffernan, Terry. "Something Special from Somerset," *Aeroplane Monthly* 13 (January, February, 1985): 8–12; 60–64.
Lake, Jon. "Whirlwind at War," *Combat Aircraft* 1 (September, 1997): 186–190.
Price, Alfred. "The Vortex from Yeovil," *Air International* 48 (March, 1995): 157–164.

INDIA

Hindustan
Singh, Pushpindar. "Diamonds in the Sky: HAL 60 Years On," *Air International* 59 (December, 2000): 368–374.
HF 24 *Marut*
Chopra, Pushpindar Singh. "Harnessing the Storm Spirit," *Air Enthusiast* 4 (May, 1973): 215–222.
"HAL Fighters . . . Hope and Hazard," *Air International* 11 (September, 1976): 129–132.

ISRAEL

Israel Aircraft Industries
Allen-Frost, Peter R. "IAI: Israel's Dynamic Aviation Industry," *Air Classic Quarterly Review* 4 (Summer, 1977): 24–29.
Sherman, Arnold. *Lightning in the Skies: The Story of Israeli Aircraft Industries*. London: Stone, 1993.
Kfir
Allward, Maurice. "Israel's Kfir C-2," *Air Pictorial* 39 (September, 1977): 341–343.
Braybrook, Roy M. "Hebrew Lion," *Air Combat* 6 (January, 1976): 44–55, 84–85.
Eyal, Eli. *From Mirage to Kfir*. Hod Hasharon, Israel: Eshel Dramit, 1979.
"Israel's Pride of Lions—Shotgun Marriage . . . or Love Match?" *Air International* 11 (November, 1976): 220–225, 248.

ITALY

Aermacchi
Braybrook, Roy M. "Aermacchi," *Air Classics* 20 (December, 1984): 62–75; 21 (January, 1985): 20–25, 70–79.
MB 339
Braybrook, Roy M. "Aermacchi MB-339," *Air Combat* 8 (July, 1980): 46–49, 62–69.
_____. "Aermacchi MB-339," *Air International* 43 (September, 1992): 137–143.
Huertas, Salvadore M. "Targets of Opportunity," *Air Enthusiast* No. 76 (July/August, 1990): 45–50.
"Mentor with a Pedigree," *Air Enthusiast* 14 (June, 1978): 267–276, 310–311.

Wilson, Stewart. *Vampire, Macchi, and Iroquois in Australian Service.* Weston Creek, ACT: Aerospace Publications, 1994.

Agusta

Forror, Mark. "The Agusta Renaissance," *Rotor and Wing* 34 (July, 2000): 42–47.

A 109 *Hirundo*

"The Agusta A 109A—Agusta's Pacesetter," *Air Enthusiast* 13 (October, 1978): 159–166, 198.

A 129 *Mangusta*

Niccoli, Riccardo. "A 129—Italy's Mean Mongoose," *Air International* 41 (November, 1991): 233–240.

Ansaldo

SVA 5 *Primo*

Alegi, Gregory. *Ansaldo SVA 5.* Windsock Datafile No. 40. Berkhamsted, UK: Albatros Productions, 1993.

Cattaneo, Gianni. *SVA (Ansaldo) Scouts.* Aircraft in Profile No. 61. Windsor, UK: Profile Publications, 1966.

Grant, Jim. "A Slap in the Face: Italy's Leaflet Raid on Vienna, August, 1918," *Air Enthusiast* 91 (January/February, 2001): 70–73.

Hagen, H. W. "Ansaldo Restoration," *Aeroplane Monthly* 7 (April, 1979): 187–190.

Ludovico, Domenico. *Italian Aviators from Rome to Tokyo in 1920.* Milano: Edizioni Etas Kompass, 1970.

CANT

Z 501 *Gabbiano*

"A Record Holder: Cantieri CANT Z. 501," *Aeroplane* 34 (September, 1935): 178–179.

Z 506 *Airone*

Nesbit, Roy C. "Flight of the Heron," *Aeroplane Monthly* 11 (August, 1983): 452–454.

Z 1007 *Alcione*

Apostolo, Giorgio. "Viva Zappata!" *Airpower* 12 (May, 1982): 8–15.

Green, William. "Zapatta's Wooden Kingfisher," *Air International* 43 (August, 1992): 81–89.

Caproni

Abate, Rosario. *Aeroplani Caproni: Gianni Caproni and His Aircraft, 1910–1983.* Trento, Italy: Museo Caproni, 1992.

Caproni, Gianni. *Gli Aeroplani Caproni: The Caproni Airplanes.* New York: Arno Press, 1980.

Caproni's Warfare: August, 1915–February, 1918. Milano: La Panagrafica Bodoniana, 1919.

Donnini, Frank P. "Douhet, Caproni, and Early Air Power," *Air Power History* 37 (Summer, 1990): 45–51.

Ca 3

Alegi, Gregory. *Caproni Ca 3.* Windsock Datafile, No. 78. Berkhamsted, UK: Albatros Productions, 1999.

"Caproni Ca 3: Trimotor WW I Bomber," *Windsock International* 6 (November/December, 1990): 12–27.

Fitch, Willis S. *Wings in the Night.* Nashville, TN: Battery Press, 1938.

Lamberton, W. M. "The Caproni Bombers," *Cross and Cockade Journal* 6 (Autumn, 1965): 215–227.

Ca 310

"The Caproni That Nearly Joined the RAF," *Air Enthusiast* 1 (July, 1971): 95–103.

Gaal, Julius R. "A Coven of Dangerous Witches," *Air Combat* 7 (November, 1979): 72–82.

Micrander, Bengt. "Capricious Caproni," *Aeroplane Monthly* 24 (November, December, 1996): 672–675; 762–767.

Fiat

McKay, D. A. S. "The Fiat Story," *Air Pictorial* 21 (June, July, August, 1958): 188–190; 250–253; 282–285.

Vergame, Peter. *The Fiat Fighters, 1930–1945.* Genoa: Intyrama, 1969.

BR 20 *Cignona*

Apostolo, Giorgio. *Fiat BR. 20.* Aircraft in Profile No. 110. Windsor, UK: Profile Publications, 1967.

Carunana, Richard J. "Fiat BR. 20," *Air International* 13 (December, 1977): 302–305.

"Fiat BR.20: Stork à la mode," *Air International* 22 (June, 1982): 290–294, 307–312.

CR 32 *Chirri*

Cattaneo, Gianni. *Fiat CR. 32.* Aircraft in Profile No. 22. Windsor, UK: Profile Publications, 1965.

McCullough, Anson. "La Cucaracha," *Airpower* 28 (September, 1998): 44–53.

Punka, George. *Fiat CR. 32/CR. 42 in Action.* Carrollton, TX: Squadron/Signal Publications, 2000.

"Rosatelli's Italian Fighter," *Air Enthusiast* 22 (August/November, 1983): 52–63.

Westburg, Peter. "'That Italian Fighter': The Story of the Fiat CR-32," *Air Classics* 13 (July, 1977): 94–108.

CR 42 *Falco*

Cattaneo, Gianni. *Fiat CR. 42.* Aircraft in Profile No. 16. Windsor, UK: Profile Publications, 1965.

"Fighter Biplane Finale: The Falco," *Air Enthusiast* No. 20 (December, 1982/March, 1983): 1–14.

Gaal, Julius R. "Biplane against the Red Bear," *Air Combat* 2 (Spring, 1974): 10–17.

Maio, Enzo. "Falconry by Fiat," *Airpower* 16 (July, 1986): 44–55.

Malizia, Nicola. "The Fireflies of Rhodes: Italian Night Fighters over the Aegean," *Aeroplane Monthly* 28 (February, 2000): 38–44.

G 50 *Freccia*

Cattaneo, Gianni. *Fiat G. 50.* Aircraft in Profile No. 188. Windsor, UK: Profile Publications, 1967.

Ghergo, Giuseppe. "Blunted Arrow," *Airpower* 7 (November, 1977): 12–18, 56–57.

"A Second-String 'Arrow,'" *Air International* 34 (May, June, 1988): 251–258; 295–298, 308–311.

G 91Y

Braybrook, Roy. "Aeritalia G.91Y," *Aeroplane Monthly* 1 (October, 1973): 281–286.

Foster, Peter. "Arrivederci, Gina!" *Air Illustrated* 29 (February, 1996): 76–79.

Lopes, Mario C. "Portugal's Ginas," *Air Enthusiast* No. 36 (May/August, 1988): 61–77.

Niccoli, Riccardo. "Gina's Story," *Air Enthusiast* No. 65 (September/October, 1996): 48–57; No. 66 (November/December, 1996): 4–9.

Schakelaar, H. J. "Low-level Luftwaffe," *Air Combat* 6 (May, 1978): 51–59.

Macchi

Braybrook, Roy. "Italian Excellence: A History of the Macchi/Aermacchi Dynasty," *Air Enthusiast* No. 50 (May/July, 1993): 22–36.

M 5

Alegi, Greg. *Macchi M. 5.* Windsock Datafile No. 86. Berkhamsted, UK: Albatros Productions, 2001.

"Macchi M.5: Italy's Classic Flying Boat Fighter," *Windsock International* 6 (November/December, 1990): 2–7.

MC 200 *Saetta*

Cattaneo, Gianni. *Macchi MC 200.* Aircraft in Profile No. 64. Windsor, UK: Profile Publications, 1966.

"The Spritely Saetta," *Air International* 13 (December, 1977): 284–291, 311–312.

MC 202 *Folgore*

Cattaneo, Gianni. *Macchi MC 202.* Aircraft in Profile No. 28. Windsor, UK: Profile Publications, 1965.

Gentilli, Roberto, and Luigi Gorena. *Macchi C. 202 in Action.* Carrollton, TX: Squadron/Signal Publications, 1980.

"Lightning from Lombardy," *Air Enthusiast* 2 (January, 1972): 17–24, 46.

MC 205 *Veltro*

"The Interim Veltro: the Ultimate Castoldi," *Air Enthusiast* 24 (April/July, 1984): 11–21.

Geiger, George J. "Thunder and Lightning and Flashes of Brilliance," *Wings* 5 (April, 1975): 30–41, 50–51.

Piaggio

Stevens, James H. "The Piaggio Story," *Air Pictorial* 30 (August; September, 1968): 290–293; 334–339.

P 108

Apostolo, Giorgio. "Italy's Flying Fortress," *Wings* 9 (December, 1979): 10–21, 50–55.

Bignozzi, Giorgio. "The Italian Fortress," *Air International* 31 (December, 1986): 298–305; 32 (January, 1987): 29–31, 47–49.

Reggiane

Longhi, Roberto. "Reggiane and I . . . a Fighter Designer Recalls," *Air Enthusiast Quarterly* No. 2: 214–224.

Prato, Piero. *The Caproni-Reggiane Fighters, 1938–1945.* Genova: Intyrama, 1968.

Re 2000 *Falco*

Brindley, John F. *Caproni Reggiane RE-2000 Falco II, RE-2002 Ariete, and RE-2005 Sagittario.* Aircraft in Profile No. 244. Windsor, UK: Profile Publications, 1973.

Cattaneo, Gianni. *Reggiane RE-2000.* Aircraft in Profile No. 123. Windsor, UK: Profile Publications, 1967.

Green, William. "The Too Advanced Fighter: The Story of the Re-2000," *Flying Review International* 21 (July, 1966): 703–707; 22 (September, October, 1967): 870–873; 937–939.

"RE-2000: The 'State of the Art' Reggiane," *Air Enthusiast* No. 41 (Midsummer, 1990): 54–69.

Savoia-Marchetti

SM 79 *Sparviero*

Geiger, George J. "The Hunchback Hawks," *Airpower* 4 (May, 1974): 32–48.

Gentilli, Roberto. *Savoia Marchetti S. 79 in Action.* Carrollton, TX: Squadron/Signal Publications, 1986.

La Trenta, Aldo. "Fallen Eagles," *Wings* 24 (December, 1974): 42–53.

"S. 79: Hunchback Sparrowhawk," *Air International* 27 (July, August, 1984): 26–32; 76–84.

SM 81 *Pipistrello*

Apostolo, Giorgio. *Savoia Marchetti SM-81.* Aircraft in Profile No. 146. Windsor, UK: Profile Publications, 1967.

Passingham, Malcom B. "Savoia-Marchetti SM 81," *Aircraft Illustrated* 10 (May, 1977): 182–187.

JAPAN

Aichi

D3A

"Pacific Predator . . . the Aichi Type 99," *Air International* 33 (December, 1987): 285–301.

Smith, Donald, and M. C. Richards. *Aichi D3A ("Val") and Yokosuka D4Y ("Judy").* Aircraft in Profile No. 70. Windsor, UK: Profile Publications, 1966.

Smith, Peter C. *Aichi D3A1/2 Val.* Marlborough, UK: Crowood, 1999.

Kawanishi

H6K

"Kawanishi's Parasol Patroller," *Air International* 29 (December, 1985): 293–298, 304–305.

Richards, M. C. *Kawanishi Four Motor Flying Boats (H6K Mavis and H8K Emily).* Aircraft in Profile No. 223. Windsor, UK: Profile Publications, 1972.

H8K

Mikesh, Robert C. "Emily Was No Lady," *Air Classics Quarterly Review* 3 (Fall, 1976): 5–19.

"The Unrivaled Emily," *Air International* 24 (April, 1983): 179–187.

N1K2 *Shiden Kai*

Francillon, Rene J. *Kawanishi Kyofu, Shiden, and Shiden Kai Variants.* Aircraft in Profile No. 213. Windsor, UK: Profile Publications, 1971.

Huggins, Mark. "Japanese Lightning," *Fly Past* No. 183 (October, 1996): 76–78.

Mikesh, Robert S. "Japanese Fighter, By George!" *Wings* 25 (April, 1995): 20–25, 33–42.

"Nipponese Antiquity: The Story of the Kawanishi Violet Lightning," *Air Enthusiast* 4 (April, 1973): 178–187.

Werneth, Ron. "Memoir of a Japanese Fighter Pilot," *Flight Journal* 5 (April, 2000): 80–85.

Kawasaki

Ki 45 *Toryu*

Huggins, Mark. "Slayer of Dragons," *Fly Past* No. 202 (May, 1998): 28–30; No. 203 (June, 1998): 28–30.

"Slayer of Dragons," *Air Enthusiast* 5 (November, December, 1973): 225–230; 276–287.

Ki 48

Buechel, Richard M. *Kawasaki Ki-48 I/II Sokei in Japanese Army Air Force. CNAF and IPSF Service*. Reading, UK: Osprey Publishing, 1972.

"Made in Japan," *Airpower* 3 (March, 1973): 16–23, 62–64.

Ki 61 *Hien*

Daniels, C. M. "Sword of the Samurai," *Airpower* 5 (March, 1975): 32–41, 53.

House, Arnold. "Kawasaki Ki-61 Tony," *Wings* 29 (February, 1999): 44–55.

Hyashi, Kyoto. "Kawasaki's Swallow: The Fighter That Almost Failed," *Air Classics* 9 (December, 1973): 18–24.

"An Oriental Swallow," *Air International* 9 (August, 1975): 75–83.

Ki 100

Bueschel, Richard M. *Kawasaki Ki-61/Ki-100 Hien in Japanese Army Air Force Service*. Atglen, PA: Schiffer Publishing, 1996.

"The Last Swallow of Summer . . . the Extraordinary Story of the Ki. 100," *Air International* 11 (October, 1976): 185–191.

Mitsubishi

A5M

"The Zero Precursor," *Air Enthusiast* No. 19 (August/November, 1982): 26–43.

A6M *Zero*

Meyer, Corky. "Zero—Myth, Mystery, and Fact," *Flight* 3 (February, 1998): 30–41.

Mikesh, Robert C. *Zero Fighter*. New York: Crown Publishers, 1980.

Horikoshi, Jiro, and Shojiro Shindo. *Eagles of Mitsubishi: The Story of the Zero Fighter*. Seattle: University of Washington Press, 1981.

Nohara, Shigeru. *Mistubishi A6M Zero Fighter*. Toyko: Dai Nippon Kaiga, 1993.

Yoshimura, Akira. *Zero Fighter*. Westport, CT: Praeger, 1996.

G3M

Bueschel, Richard M. *Mitsubishi G3M1/2/3, Kusho L3Y1/2 in Japanese Naval Air Service*. Reading, UK: Osprey Publishing, 1992.

Francillon, Rene J. *The Mitsubishi G3M Nell*. Aircraft in Profile No. 160. Windsor, UK: Profile Publications, 1967.

Grinsell, Robert. "G3M Nell: Twin-Finned Belle or Demon from Hell," *Wings* 1 (October, 1971): 8–18, 56.

G4M

"A Bomber Called Betty," *Fly Past* No. 320 (October, 2000): 73–78.

Dean, Jack. "Bomber on Fire," *Airpower* 21 (January, 1991): 10–22.

"Flying Lighter: Mitsubishi's 1-Rikko," *Air International* 27 (December, 1984): 298–302, 314–318.

Jasmer, Leroy. "Betty's Final Mission," *Air Classics* 31 (September, 1995): 12–19.

Tagaya, Osamu. *Mitsubishi Type 1 Rikko "Betty" Units of World War 2*. London: Osprey, 2000.

J2M *Raiden*

Gallagher, James P. "Operation Save a Jack," *Air War, 1939–1945: Air Classics Special* (1986): 48–53.

Heumann, Gert W. "The Mitsubishi Raiden," *Air Pictorial* 21 (September, 1959): 331–332, 334.

McCullough, Anson. "Fortress Killer," *Wings* 3 (October, 1973): 40–48.

"Raiden: The Asiatic Thunderbolt," *Air Enthusiast* 1 (July, 1971): 67–73, 103.

Ki 21

Dean, Jack. "Ever Wonder What Became of Sally?" *Airpower* 29 (September, 1999): 8–19, 50–55.

Francillon, Rene J. *The Mitsubishi Ki-21*. Aircraft in Profile No. 173. Windsor, UK: Profile Publications, 1967.

"Mitsubishi Ki-21," *Air International* 31 (August, 1986): 74–80, 100–101.

Ki 46

Ashley, Glenn. *Mitsubishi Ki-46 "Dinah."* Shelford: Delta Aviation, 1997.

Cross, David W. J. "The Mitsubishi Ki-46 I/II Dinah," *Air Classics* 12 (February, 1976): 53–55.

Francillon, Rene J. *The Mitsubishi Ki-46*. Aircraft in Profile No. 82. Windsor, UK: Profile Publications, 1966.

Huggins, Mark. "A Fast Lady Called Dinah," *Fly Past* No. 223 (February, 2000): 80–86.

"Mitsubishi's Ki-46: The Aesthetic Asian," *Air International* 19 (November, 1980): 227–233.

Ki 67 *Hiryu*

Bueschel, Richard M. *Mitsubishi Ki-67/Ki-109 Hiryu in Japanese Army Air Force Service*. Atglen, PA: Schiffer Publications, 1997.

"Mitsubishi's Final Bomber," *Air International* 25 (July, 1983): 25–33, 47.

T 2/F 1

Lake, John. "Mitsubishi T-2: Supersonic Samurai," *World Air Power Journal* 18 (Autumn/Fall, 1994): 136–147.

_____. "Mitsubishi F-1," *World Air Power Journal* 23 (Winter, 1995): 50–71.

Sekigawa, Eiichiro. "Mitsubishi Mentor," *Air Enthusiast* 8 (April, 1975): 170–176.

Nakajima

B5N

Hawkins, M. F. *The Nakajima B5N Kate*. Aircraft in Profile No. 141. Windsor, UK: Profile Publications, 1967.

J1N1 *Gekko*

Mikesh, Robert C. *Moonlight Interceptor: Japan's "Irving" Night Fighter.* Washington, DC: Smithsonian Institution Press, 1985.

Ki 27

"The Agile Asian . . . Japan's Type 97 Fighter," *Air Enthusiast* No. 6 (March/June, 1978): 81–89, 107–110.

Bueschel, Richard M. *Nakajima Ki-27A/B, Manshu Ki-79 A/B in Japanese Army Air Force Service.* New York: Arco, 1970.

Izawa, Yasuho. "64th Flying Sentai," *Aero Album* 3 (Spring, 1970): 2–8.

Ki 43 *Hayabusa*

Bueschel, Richard M. *Nakajima Ki-43 Hayabusa I-III in Japanese Army Air Force—RTAF-CAF-IPSH Service.* Atglen, PA: Schiffer Publishing, 1995.

"Pacific Peregrine . . . the Nakajima K43 Hayabusa," *Air International* 18 (January, 1980): 26–31, 44–46.

Phillips, Ward. "The Last Samurai," *Air Classics* 13 (October, 1973): 32–43.

Stanaway, John. *Nakajima Ki-43 "Hayabusa": Allied Code Name Oscar.* Bennington, VT: Merriam Press, 2000.

Windrow, Martin C., and Rene Francillon. *Nakajima Ki-43 Hayabusa.* Aircraft in Profile No. 46. Windsor, UK: Profile Publications, 1965.

Ki 44 *Shoki*

Brindley, John F. *Nakajima Ki-44 Shoki (Tojo).* Aircraft in Profile No. 255. Windsor, UK: Profile Publications, 1973.

Bueschel, Richard M. *Nakajima Ki-44 Shoki Ia,b,c/IIa,b,c in Japanese Army Air Force Service.* Reading, UK: Osprey Publishing, 1971.

Green, William. "Nakajima Demonology: The Story of the Shoki," *Air International* 3 (July, 1972): 17–25.

Grinsell, Bob. "Demon Drivers," *Wings* 9 (February, 1979): 38–47.

Huggins, Mark. "Imperial Demon," *Air Enthusiast* No. 85 (January/February, 2000): 62–67.

Ki 49 *Donryu*

Bueschel, Richard M. *Nakajima Ki-49 Donryu in Japanese Army Air Force Service.* Atglen, PA: Schiffer Publications, 1997.

"Made in Japan," *Airpower* 3 (March, 1973): 16–23; 62–64.

Ki 84 *Hayate*

Busechel, Richard M. *Nakajima Ki-84 A/B Hayate in Japanese Army Air Force Service.* Atglen, PA: Schiffer Publishing, 1997.

"The High Wind from Ota," *Air International* 10 (January, 1976): 22–28, 43–46.

Nakajima Ki-84. Fallbrook, CA: Aero Publishers, 1965.

Trimble, Robert. "The Ki-84 Hayate," *Air Combat* 1 (Winter, 1973): 24–29, 74.

ShinMaywa

US 1

David, Donald. "Japan's Big Boat," *World Air Power Journal* 15 (Winter, 1993): 126–133.

Sekigawa, Eiichiro. "Shin Meiwa US-1 . . . Epitaph for the Big Boat," *Air International* 22 (February, 1982): 72–77, 90–92.

Wisneski, Daniel. "Japan's Sea-Going Hunter," *Air Combat* 4 (September, 1976): 56–65.

Yokosuka

D4Y *Suisei*

Smith, Donald, and M. C. Richards. *Aichi D3A ("Val") and Yokosuka D4Y ("Judy").* Aircraft in Profile No. 70. Windsor, UK: Profile publications, 1966.

Smith, Peter. "Yokosuka D4Y Suisei "Judy,'" *Fly Past* No. 43 (February, 1985): 10–13.

MXY 7 *Oka*

Drake, Hal. "The Bomb with a Human Brain," *Mankind* 3 (December, 1973): 52–58.

Maloney, Edward T. *Kamikaze.* Fallbrook, CA: Aero Publishers, 1966.

Mikesh, Robert C. "Mission of No Return," *Airpower* 27 (November, 1997): 40–54.

Wolf, William. "Suicide Samurai," *Wings* 7 (February, 1977): 18–23, 66.

NETHERLANDS

Fokker

C V

Kamphuis, G. H. *Fokker C.V.* Aircraft in Profile No. 87. Windsor, UK: Profile Publications, 1966.

Owens, Colin. "Fokker's Fifth: The C.V. Multirole Biplane," *Air Enthusiast* No. 53 (Spring, 1994): 60–68.

D XXI

Eberspacher, Warren. *Fokker D-XXI.* St. Paul, MN: Phalanx Publishing, 1994.

Kamphuis, G. H. *Fokker D. XXI.* Aircraft in Profile No. 63. Windsor, UK: Profile Publications, 1966.

Overest, Henk J. Van. "Last of the Fighting Fokkers," *Air International* 13 (October, 1977): 178–183.

Stenman, Kari. "First and Last: Finnish Fokker D XXIs," *Air Enthusiast* No. 88 (July/August, 2000): 50–57.

Toll, Karl. "Last of the Fighting Fokkers," *Airpower* 12 (January, 1982): 10–17.

G I *Faucheur*

"Fokker G. I in Focus," *Air Combat* 1(1) 1968: 4–6.

"Le Faucheur . . . Fokker's Formidable G. I," *Flying Review International* 22 (April, 1967): 507–511.

"The Mower-Fokker's Final Fighter," *Air Enthusiast* 7 (October, November, December, 1974): 178–183; 239–244; 286–289.

Van der Klaauw, B. *Fokker G. I.* Aircraft in Profile No. 134. Windsor, UK: Profile Publications, 1967.

POLAND

PZL

Eberspacher, Warren. *Poland's PZL Gull-Wing Fighters.* St. Paul, MN: Phalanx Publishing, 1995.

P 11

Cynk, Jerzy B. "First Kill," *Air Enthusiast* No. 48 (December, 1992–February, 1993): 68–73.

Liss, Witold. *PZL P-11*. Aircraft in Profile No. 75. Windsor, UK: Profile Publications, 1966.

Plulawski, Zygmunt. "The Era of the Gull," *Air Enthusiast* No. 28 (July-October, 1985): 35–53.

Wolf, Bill, and Jin Lansdale. "First Kill," *Air Classics* 29 (March, 1993): 12–22, 64–65.

P 23 *Karas*

Cynk, Jerzy B. "Poland's Karas," *Air Pictorial* 26 (September, 1964): 279–283.

_____. *The PZL P-23 Karas*. Aircraft in Profile No. 104. Windsor, UK: Profile Publications, 1967.

P 37 *Los*

Cynk, Jerzy B. "PZL P. 37 Los—a Notable Polish Bomber," *Air Pictorial* 30 (February, 1968) 53–58.

"The Elegant Elk," *Air International* 35 (October, 1988): 216–218.

RUSSIA

Antonov

An 2

Anderson, Robert M. *Antonovs over the Arctic: Flying to the North Pole in Russian Biplanes*. Auckland, NZ: David Bateman, 1990.

Fricker, John. "Annuska, Irina, and Me," *Air International* 24 (March, 1983): 128–134.

_____. "Flying Russia's Biggest Biplane," *Aeroplane* 91 (September, 1956): 385–358.

Stroud, John. "Antonov An-2," *Aeroplane Monthly* 23 (February, 1985): 65–68.

An 12

Lake, Jon. "Anontov An-12 'Cub' Variant Briefing," *World Air Power Journal* 27 (Winter, 1996): 102–121.

Staszak, Richard. *Military Transports in Detail*. Oceanside, CA: Air Transport, 1994.

An 124 *Ruslan*

Davies, Malory. "When Only the Ruslan Will Do," *Global Transport* No. 9 (Spring, 1999): 44–46.

"The Mighty Dream," *Air International* 36 (March, 1989): 146–147.

Veronico, Nicholas A., and Jim Dunn. *Giant Cargo Planes*. Osceola, WI: MBI, 1999.

Beriev

Nemecek, Vaclav. "Beriev's Seaplanes," *Flying Review International* 22 (May/June, 1967): 563–564; 681–683.

Be 12 *Tchaika*

Hayles, John. "Russia's Coastal Guardian," *Air International* 49 (August, 1995): 82–88.

Oliver, David. *Flying Boats and Amphibians since 1945*. Annapolis, MD: Naval Institute Press, 1987.

Ilyushin

Il 2 *Shturmovik*

Duffy, Paul. "Ilyushin Shturmovik," *Air International* 50 (May, 1996): 306–313.

"The Annals of Ilyusha: Ilyushin's Proliferous Shturmovik," *Air Enthusiast* 12 (April/July, 1980): 1–10; 13 (August/November, 1980): 26–34.

Geiger, George J. "Stormavik," *Wings* 12 (December, 1982): 28–51.

Liss, Witold. *Ilyushin Il-2*. Aircraft in Profile No. 88. Windsor, UK: Profile Publications, 1966.

Stapfer, Hans-Herri. *Il-2 Stormovik in Action*. Carrollton, TX: Squadron/Signal, 1995.

Il 4

"From DB-3 to Il-4," *Air International* 30 (February, March, 1986): 81–86; 133–138, 154–155.

Geiger, George J. "The Red Bomber Brigades," *Airpower* 13 (May, 1983): 44–55.

Il 28

Braybrook, Roy M. "The Ilyushin Il-28 Beagle," *Flying Review International* 19 (July, 1964): 42–45.

Geiger, George J. "Ilyushin's Illusion," *Wings* 13 (October, 1983): 44–55.

"Il-28: A Quadragenarian Ilyushin," *Air Enthusiast* No. 36 (May/August, 1988): 39–51.

"Il-28, A Soviet 'Canberra,'" *Air Enthusiast* 1 (December, 1971): 351–357.

Il 38

Gordon, Yefim. "Il-18 Family Variant Briefing," *World Air Power Journal* 41 (2000): 108–135.

Lake, Jon. "Ilyushin Il-38," *Combat Aircraft* 1 (July, 1998): 514–517.

Il 76

Gordon, Yefim, and Dimitriy Kommissarov. *Ilyushin Il-76: Russia's Versatile Freighter*. Leics.: Midland Counties, 2001.

"The Ilyushin 'Candid' Family," *Air International* 38 (April, 1990): 173–186.

Kamov

Butowski, Piotr. "Kamov Shipborne Helicopters," *Jane's Soviet Intelligence Review* 2 (May, 1990): 200–203.

_____. "Kamovs for the Navy," *Air International* 56 (May, 1999): 284–292.

Ka 25

Gunston, Bill. "Kamov 'Hormone' and 'Helix' Family," *World Air Power Journal* 5 (Spring, 1991): 117–125.

"Kamov Ka-27 Helix," *Air Pictorial* 62 (August, 2000): 539–542.

Taylor, John W. R. "The Contra-rotating Kamovs," *Air International* 39 (November, 1990): 257–267, 303–304.

Ka 50

Butkowski, Piotr. "Alligator Supports Black Shark," *Air International* 53 (July, 1997): 29–35.

Lake, Jon. "Kamov Ka-50 Hokum," *World Air Power Journal* 19 (Winter, 1994): 34–45.

Wheeler, Barry. "HOKUM: An Enigma Variously Described," *Air International* 42 (April, 1992): 194–197.

Lavochkin

La 5/7

Abashin, Michael E. *Fighting Lavochkin*. Lynwood, WA: Aviation International, 1993.

Geiger, George J. "Red Star Ascending," *Airpower* 14 (November, 1984): 10–21, 50–54.

Liss, Witold. *Lavochkin LA-5 and 7*. Aircraft in Profile No. 149. Windsor, UK: Profile Publications, 1967.

Stapfer, Hans-Herri. *La-5 in Action*. Carrollton, TX: Squadron/Signal Publications, 1998.

Valousek, Ladislav. "Flying the Wooden Wonder," *Air Enthusiast Quarterly* No. 2: 113–125.

LaGG 3

"LaGG-3: Lavochkin's Timber Termagant," *Air International* 20 (January, 1981): 23–30, 41–43.

Stapfer, Hans-Herri. *LaGG Fighters in Action*. Carrollton, TX: Squadron/Signal Publications, 1996.

Mikoyan-Gurevich

Beliakov, R. A., and J. Marmain. *MiG: Fifty Years of Secret Aircraft Design*. Annapolis, MD: Naval Institute Press, 1994.

Butowski, Piotr, and Jay Miller. *OKB MiG: A History of the Design Bureau and Its Aircraft*. Arlington, TX: Aerofax for Specialty Press, 1991.

Gunston, Bill, and Yefim Gordon. *MiG Aircraft since 1937*. London: Putnam, 1998.

Mikoyan, Stepan A. *Stepan Anastasovich Mikoyan: An Autobiography*. Shrewsbury, UK: Airlife, 1999.

Oliver, David. *MiG Dynasty*. Osceola, WI: Motorbooks International, 1990.

MiG 3

Geiger, George J. "The First MiGs," *Airpower* 12 (November, 1982): 40–48.

Green, William. "The First MiG," *Flying Review International* 22 (January, 1967): 327–329.

_____. "MiG-3: Undistinguished Forebear of a Distinguished Line," *Air Enthusiast* 1 (October, 1971): 252–260.

MiG 15

Gordon, Yefim. *MiG-15*. Osceola, WI: MBI, 1993.

Spick, Mike. "Sabre versus MiG-15," *Air International* 48 (April, 1995): 246–250.

Stapfer, Hans-Heri. *MiG-15 in Action*. Carrollton, TX: Squadron/Signal Publications, 1991.

Wilson, Stewart. *Sabre, MiG-15, and Hunter*. Weston Creek, ACT: Aerospace Publications, 1995.

MiG 21

Gunston, Bill. *Mikoyan MiG-21*. London: Osprey, 1986.

Gunston, Bill, and Yefim Gordon. *MiG-21 Fishbed: The World's Most Widely Used Supersonic Fighter*. Leicester, UK: Aerofax, 1991.

Linn, Don. *MiG-21 Fishbed in Action*. Carrollton, TX: Squadron/Signal Publications, 1993.

Stapfer, Hans-Heri. *MiG-21: Cold War Warrior*. London: Arms and Armour Press, 1991.

MiG 23/27

Gunston, Bil. *MiG-23/27*. London: Osprey, 1986.

Lake, Jon. "Mikoyan MiG-23/27 Flogger," *World Air Power Journal* 8 (Spring, 1992): 40–85.

"Mikoyan Flogger," Air International 32 (January, 1987): 16–23, 50–52.

Stapfer, Hans-Heri. *MiG-23/27 in Action*. Carrollton, TX: Squadron/Signal Publications, 1990.

Sweetman, Bill. "Mikoyan's Multifaceted Middleweight," *Aeroplane Monthly* 4 (September, 1976): 466–477.

MiG 25

Barron, John. *MiG Pilot: The Final Escape of Lieutenant Belenko*. New York: McGraw-Hill, 1980.

Gordon, Yefim. *MiG-25 Foxbat and MiG-31 Foxbat: Russia's Defensive Frontline*. Leicester, UK: Aerofax, 1990.

"Mikoyan Foxbat in Soviet Service," *Air International* 17 (November, 1979): 242–252.

Sweetman, Bill. "Foxbat—Something Completely Different," *Aeroplane Monthly* 4 (September, 1976): 466–477.

MiG 29

Gordon, Yefim. *Mikoyan MiG-29 Fulcrum: Multi-Role Fighter*. Osceola, WI: MBI, 1999.

Hildebrandt, Erik. "Hornet versus Fulcrum," *Flight Journal* 4 (June, 1999): 42–51.

Lambeth, Benjamin S. *From Farnborough to Kublinka: An American MiG-29 Experience*. Santa Monica, CA: Rand, 1991.

Stapfer, Hans-Heri. *MiG-29 Fulcrum in Action*. Carrollton, TX: Squadron/Signal Publications, 1991.

Zuyev, Alexander. *Fulcrum: A Top Gun Pilot's Escape from the Soviet Empire*. New York: Warner Books, 1992.

MiG 31

Butowski, Piotr. "Foxhound: Inside the MiG-31," *Combat Aircraft* 2 (October/November, 2000): 980–991.

Braybrook, Roy. "Foxhound: Son of Foxbat," *Air International* 41 (September, 1991): 121–126, 130.

Lake, Jon. "Russia's 'Manned Patriot,'" *World Air Power Journal* 13 (Summer, 1993): 30–45.

Zaloga, Steven J. "MiG-31 Foxhound," *Jane's Intelligence Review* 3 (October, 1991): 454–463.

Mil

"The Mighty Mils," *Flying Review International* 21 (October, 1965): 69–73.

Mi 17

Lake, Jon. "The 'Hip' and 'Haze' Family," *World Air Power Journal* 10 (Autumn/Fall, 1992): 110–129.

Mi 24

Butowski, Piotr. "M-24 Hind," *Combat Aircraft* 2 (September, 2000): 890–899; 3 (December 2000): 66–70.

Lake, Jon. "Mil Mi-24 Hind Variant Briefing," *World Air Power Journal* 18 (Autumn/Fall, 1994): 110–135.

Spick, Mike. *Mil Mi-24* Hind. London: Osprey, 1988.

Stapfer, Hans-Heri. *Mi-24 Hind in Action*. Carrollton, TX: Squadron/Signal Publications, 1988.

_____. *Mi-24 Hind*. London: Arms and Armour Press, 1990.

Mi 26

Lambert, Mark. "Mi-26: The First, True Heavy Lift Helicopter," *Interavia* 36 (August, 1981): 764–768.

"Siberian Halo," *Air International* 24 (June, 1983): 313–315, 318.

Myasishchev

M 4 *Molot*

Gordon, Yefim, and Bill Gunston. "The Extinct Bison," *Air International* 49 (October, November, December, 1995): 222–229; 275–279; 342–347.

Jacobs, G. "'Bison' Close Up," *Jane's Soviet Intelligence Review* 2 (November, 1990): 486–489.

Petlyakov

Pe 2

"From Sotka to Peshka," *Air International* 17 (August, 1979): 76–83, 93–94.

Passingham, Malcom, and Waclaw Klepacki. *Petlyakov Pe-2 Variants.* Aircraft in Profile No. 216. Windsor, UK: Profile Publications, 1971.

Smith, Peter. "Petlyakov," *Fly Past* No. 23 (June, 1983): 48–52.

Pe 8

Guttman, Jon. "Red Stars over Berlin," *Aviation History* 8 (March, 1998): 22–28, 60–61.

"The Petlyakov Pe-8," *Flying Review International* 20 (April, 1964): 57–58.

"Pe-8: Last of a Generation," *Air International* 19 (August, 1980): 76–83, 101.

Polikarpov

Nemecek, Vaclav. "Polikarpov: The Prolific Pioneer," *Flying Review International* 23 (July, August, 1968): 404–407; 455–456.

Stapfer, Hans-Herri. *Polikarpov Fighters in Action, Part 1 and Part 2.* Carrollton, TX: Squadron/Signal Publications, 1995–1996.

I 15/I 153

Brodie, Ian, and Tom Middleton. "Mad about the Gull," *Aeroplane Monthly* 28 (May, 2000): 44–53.

Green, William. "Chato and Chaika," *Flying Review International* 23 (January, 1968): 45–48.

———. "End of an Era: Polikarpov Chaika," *Air Enthusiast* 1 (June, 1971): 9–15.

"Of Chaika and Chato," *Air Enthusiast* No. 11 (November, 1979–February, 1980): 9–29.

I 16

Green, William. "Polikarpov's Little Hawk," *Flying Review International* 25 (November, December, 1969): 58–63; 60–64; 26 (January, 1970): 62–66.

Heumann, Gert W. "Polikarpov's Remarkable I-16," *Air Pictorial* 20 (December, 1958): 425–426.

Liss, Witold. *Polikarpov I-16.* Aircraft in Profile No. 122. Windsor, UK: Profile Publications, 1967.

"Soviet Flies in Spanish Skies," *Air Enthusiast Quarterly* No. 1: 1–16.

Po 2/U 2

Fricker, John "Dawn Flight to Zagreb," *Air International* 21 (December, 1981): 278–280.

Williams, William J. "Bedcheck Charlie and the AN-2," *Air Power History* 43(4) (1996): 4–13.

R 5

Alexandrov, Andrew. "Russian R-5," *Skyways* No. 20 (October, 1991): 2–15.

Sikorsky

Bartlett, Robert M. *Sky Pioneer: The Story of Igor I. Sikorsky.* New York: Charles Scribner's Sons, 1997.

Cochrane, Dorothy. *The Aviation Careers of Igor Sikorsky.* Seattle: University of Washington Press, 1989.

Delear, Frank J. *Igor Sikorsky: His Three Careers in Aviation.* New York: Dodd, Mead, 1969.

Finne, K. N., Carl J. Bobrow, and Von Hardesty. *Igor Sikorsky: The Russian Years.* Washington, DC: Smithsonian Institution Press, 1987.

Sikorsky, Igor. *The Story of the Winged S: An Autobiography.* New York: Dodd, Mead, 1958.

RBVZ *Ilya Muromets*

Bibrow, Carl. "A Technical Overview of the Evolution of the Grand and the Ilya Muromets," *World War I Aero* No. 127 (February, 1990): 40–55.

Meos, Edgar. "The Russian Giants," *Cross and Cockade Journal* 4 (Summer, 1963): 168–179.

Woodman, Harry. "The Big Il'ya," *Windsock International* 6 (May/June, July/August, September/October, 1990): 16–24; 4–11; 4–10.

Woodman, Harry. *Ilya Muromets: Type VEH.* Berkhamsted, UK: Albatros Productions, 2000.

S 16

Alexander, J. P. "Sikorsky Scouts," *Air Pictorial* 26 (April, 1964): 111–114.

Fleischman, John. "Igor Sikorsky's Little Bird," *Air and Space Smithsonian* 12 (February/March, 1998): 60–65.

Mikheyev, Vadim. *Sikorsky S-16.* Stratford, CT: Flying Machine Press, 1997.

Stamper, George L. "The Sikorsky S-16 and Russian Aviation during the Great War," *War in History* 7(1) (2000): 65–81.

Sukhoi

Alexander, Jean P. "Sukhoi—Pioneer Soviet Aircraft Designer," *Air Pictorial* 38 (April, 1976): 136–139.

Antonov, Vladimir, with Lenox Carruth and Jay Miller. *OKB Sukhoi: A History of the Design Bureau and Its Aircraft.* Earl Shilton, Leicester, UK: Aerofax, 1996.

Geiger, George J. "The Aircraft of Pavel Sukhoi," *Air Combat* 5 (September, November, 1977): 12–19, 94–98; 12–18, 92–97.

Su 17

Stapfer, Hans-Heri. *Sukhoi Fitter in Action.* Carrollton, TX: Squadron/Signal Publications, 1989.

"Survival of the Fitter," *Air International* 20 (April, 1981): 169–172, 205.

Su 24

Dawes, Alan. "Fencer Parries Critics," *Air Force Monthly* No. 151 (October, 2000): 62–67.

Fricker, John. "Fencer Unveiled," *Air International* 43 (September, 1992): 129–135.

Lake, Jon. "Sukhoi Su-24 Fencer: Soviet Striker," *World Air Power Journal* 5 (Spring, 1991): 42–49.

"Sukhoi Fencer," *Air International* 33 (September, 1987): 111–113, 151.

Zaloga, Steve J. "Sukhoi Su-24 'Fencer' Strike Aircraft," *Jane's Soviet Intelligence Review* 2 (July, 1990): 290–300.

Su 25

Braybrook, Ray. "Sukhoi Frogfoot," *Air International* 30 (May, 1986): 222–226.

Skrynnikov, Sergey. *Sukhoi Su-25 Frogfoot.* Hong Kong: Concord Publishing, 1994.

Stapfer, Hans-Herri. *Su-25 Frogfoot in Action.* Carrollton, TX: Squadron/Signal Publications, 1992.

Su 27

Fomin, Andrei. *Su-27 Flanker Story.* Moscow: R. A. Intervestnik, 2000.

Gordon, Yefim. *Sukhoi Su-27 Flanker: Air Superiority Fighter.* Shrewsbury, UK: Airlife, 1999.

Halbertstadt, Hans. *Sukhoi Su-27: Design and Development of Russia's Super Interceptor.* Osceola, WI: MBI, 1992.

Jenkins, Dennis R. *Sukhoi Su-27 Flanker.* Stillwater, MN: Specialty Press, 1991.

Lake, Jon. *Sukhoi Su-27 Flanker, Including Su-30 to Su-35.* London: Aerospace Publications, 1994.

Tupolev

"Dean of the Red Bombers," *Wings* 2 (February, 1972): 52–59, 62–67.

Duffy, Paul R. "Tupolev: Russia's Prolific Designer," *Air International* 45 (July, 1993): 16–22.

Duffy, Paul R., and Andrei Kandalov. *Tupolev: The Man and His Aircraft.* Shrewsbury, UK: Airlife, 1997.

Gunston, Bill. *Tupolev Aircraft since 1922.* Annapolis, MD: Naval Institute Press, 1995.

Kerber, Leonard L. *Stalin's Aviation Gulag: A Memoir of Andrei Tupolev and the Purge Era.* Edited by Von Hardesty. Washington, DC: Smithsonian Institution Press, 1996.

SB 2

Geiger, George J. "The Red Bomber Brigades," *Airpower* 13 (May, 1983): 44–55.

Martinez, Luis G. "Los Katiuskas," *Air Enthusiast* 32 (December, 1986/April, 1987): 45–55.

"SB: The Radical Tupolev," *Air International* 36 (January, February, March, 1989): 44–51; 77–81, 100–102; 148–155.

Stenman, Kari. "The Anti-Soviet Tupolevs," *Air Enthusiast* No. 27 (March/June, 1985): 9–20.

"The Tupolev SB-2 Medium Bomber," *Flying Review International* 23 (March, 1967): 446–451.

TB 3

Vanags-Baginskis, Alex. "Chronicle of the Remarkable ANT-6: Progenitor of Blackjack," *Air Enthusiast* No. 35 (January/April, 1988): 1–18.

Tu 2

"Tupolev's Tractable Twin," *Air International Quarterly* No. 4: 173–186.

"Tupolev Tu-2," *Flying Review International* 23 (March, 1968): 157–159.

Tu 16

Bock, Robert. *Tu 16 Badger in Action.* Carrollton, TX: Squadron/Signal Publications, 1990.

Lake, John. "Tupolev's 'Badger' Family," *World Air Power Journal* 11 (Winter, 1992): 118–141.

Tu 22

Braybrook, Roy M. "The Tupolev Tu-22 Blinder," *Flying Review International* 20 (August, 1964): 28–31.

Gordon, Yefim, and Vladimir Rigmant. *Tupolev Tu-22 Blinder/Tu-22M Backfire: Russia's Long-Range Supersonic Bombers.* Leicester, UK: Aerofax, 1998.

Marmain, Jacques. "Tu-22 Blinder—New Details on an Old Aircraft," *Jane's Intelligence Review* 5 (October, 1993): 446–450.

Tu 22M

Beckett, Neville. "Backfire Unveiled," *Air International* 45 (July, 1993): 23–30.

Sweetman, Bill. "Backfire: The Bogeyman Bomber," *Flight International* 112 (December 17, 1977): 1810–1815.

"Tupolev Backfire," *Air International* 34 (June, 1988): 267–275.

Tu 95/142

Beckitt, Neville. "Strategic Strike," *Air International* 45 (December, 1993): 333–337.

Bowman, Martin. "Friendly Bear?" *Air Combat* 23 (August/September, 1995): 4–15.

Gordon, Yefim. *Tupolev Tu-95/142 "Bear": Russia's Intercontinental-Range Heavy Bomber.* Leicester, UK: Midland Publishing, 1997.

Gunston, Bill. "Bear Briefing," *World Air Power Journal* 1 (Spring, 1990): 98–117.

"Tupolev Bear," *Air International* 32 (April, May, 1987): 223–226, 255–258; 172–179, 208.

Tu 160

Braybrook, Ray. "The Tupolev Tu-160 Blackjack," *Air International* 40 (January, 1991): 9–15.

Butowski, Piotr. "Close upon Tu-160 Blackjack," *Jane's Intelligence Review* 4 (March, 1992): 119–123.

_____. "Steps towards 'Blackjack': Soviet Supersonic Intercontinental Bombers before the Tu-160," *Air Enthusiast* 73 (January/February, 1998): 36–54.

_____. "Blackjack Profile," *Air International* 58 (May, 2000): 285–292.

Davis, Malcom. "Blackjack and Beyond," *Air International* 55 (November, 1998): 274–278.

Yakovlev

Gordon, Yefim, and Bill Gunston. *Yakovlev Aircraft since 1924.* London: Putnam, 1997.

Kosminkov. "Red Star Rising," *Wings* 26 (October, 1996): 42–55.

Stapfer, Hans-Herri. *Yak Fighters in Action.* Carrollton, TX: Squadron/Signal Publications, 1986.

Yakovlev, Alexandre. *Notes of an Aircraft Designer.* Moscow: Foreign Language Publishing House, 1961.

_____. *The Aim of a Lifetime: The Story of Alexander Yakovlev, Designer of the Yak Fighter Plane.* Moscow: Progress Aviation, 1972.

Yak 3

Kosminkov, Konstantin Y. "Red Star Rising," *Wings* 26 (October, 1996): 42–55.

"Second Generation Yaks," *Air International* 9 (November, 1975): 229–240, 247.

Tillman, Barrett. "Hatching Stalin's Falcons," *Flight Journal* 6 (April, 2001): 22–28.

Yak 9

"First of the Yaks," *Air International* 7 (June, 1975): 297–305.

Liss, Witold. *Yak 9 Series.* Aircraft in Profile No. 185. Windsor, UK: Profile Publications, 1967.

Stockton, Harold E. *Red Beauty: Yak 1 and Yak 7.* Round Rock, TX: Snow Leopard Productions, 1996.

Yak 36

Braybrook, Roy. "Yakovlev Forger," *Air International* 31 (August, 1986): 81–86.

Fricker, John. *Yakovlev's V/STOL Fighters: Yak-36, Yak-38, Yak-41, and Yak-141.* Leicester, UK: Aerofax, 1995.

Geiger, George J. "Soviet VTOL," *Air Combat* 20 (February, 1992): 22–27, 58–70.

Hirschberg, Michael J. *Soviet V/STOL Aircraft: The Struggle for Shipborne Combat Capability.* Reston, VA: American Institute of Aeronautical and Astronautics, 1997.

"In Soviet Service, I: Yakovlev 36 MP," *Air International* 16 (January, 1979): 18–20.

SPAIN

CASA

C 101 *Aviojet*

"The Iberian Instructor," *Air International* 15 (August, 1978): 65–69, 98–99.

SWEDEN

Saab

Andersson, Hans G. *Saab Aircraft since 1937.* London: Putnam, 1989.

"From Seventeen to Thirty-Nine," *Air Enthusiast* No. 33 (May/August, 1987): 9–25.

Geiger, George J. " Saab Story," *Wings* 4 (April, 1974): 8–25.

James, Derek N. *Saab Aircraft.* Stroud, Gloucestershire, UK: Chalford, 1997.

Widfelt, Bo. "Saab Story," *Air Pictorial* 25 (February, March, April, 1965): 34–39; 72–75; 114–117.

J 29 *Tunnan*

Gunston, Bill. "Saab J-29," *Aeroplane Monthly* 4 (March, 1976): 154–159.

Widfeldt, Bo. *Saab J-29.* Aircraft in Profile No. 36. Windsor, UK: Profile Publications, 1965.

J 35 *Draken*

Butler, Tony. "Draken: A Swedish Masterpiece," *Air International* 58 (March, April, 2000): 170–174; 240–244.

Delbro, Ulf. "Saab Draken," *Aeroplane Monthly* 1 (May, 1973): 19–23, 35.

Dorr, Robert F. *Saab J35 Draken.* Arlington, TX: Aerofax, 1987.

Jorgensen, Jan. *Saab 35 Draken: Scandinavian 'Cold War' Warrior.* Shrewsbury, UK: Airlife, 1997.

Peacock, Lindsay. "Saab Draken Briefing," *World Air Power Journal* 17 (Summer, 1994): 116–135.

JA 37 *Viggen*

Dahlin, John S. "Swedish Success Story: The Viggen Family in the Swedish Air Force," *Air Combat* 11 (January, 1983): 32–37.

Dorr, Robert F. *SAAB Viggen.* London: Ian Allan, 1985.

English, Malcom. "Saab's Classic Canard," *Air International* 56 (February, 1999): 92–102.

Jackson, Paul. "Saab 37 Viggen," *World Air Power Journal* 13 (Summer, 1992): 46–89.

Nicolaou. Stephan. "Thor's Thunderer," *Wings* 17 (December, 1987): 12–35, 45–55.

JAS 39 *Gripen*

"An Ambitious 'Jack of All Trades,'" *Air International* 33 (November, 1987): 224–230.

Braybrook, Roy. "Sweden's JAS-39 Gripen," *Air International* 44 (February, 1993): 71–75.

Handleman, Philip. "In the Lair of the Eagle/Lion," *Wings* 23 (October, 1993): 24–33.

Hewson, Robert. "Saab JAS-39 Gripen," *World Air Power Journal* 20 (Spring, 1995): 30–51.

_____. "Saab JAS 39 Gripen," *World Air Power Journal* 42 (Autumn/Fall, 2000): 60–103.

YUGOSLAVIA

SOKO

G 4 *Super Galeb*

Emil, Pozer. "Yugoslav Galeb G-4," *Air Combat* 17 (August, 1989): 25–27.

J 22 *Orao*

"Balkan Belligerent," *Air International* 25 (August, 1983): 68–71.

GENERAL BIBLIOGRAPHY

Argentina

"Fuerza Aerea Facelift," *Air Enthusiast* 3 (August, 1972): 72–77.

Huertes, Salvador Mafe. *Argentine Air Forces in the Falklands Conflict.* Poole, UK: Arms and Armour Press, 1987.

Steinemann, Peter. "Argentina's Air Force," *Air International* 39 (July, 1990): 16–24, 33.

Australia

"Australian Naval Aviation," *Aerospace Historian* 23 (December, 1976): 182–188.

Bennett, John. *The Imperial Gift: British Aeroplanes Which Formed the RAAF in 1921.* Maryborough, QLD: Banner Books, 1996.

Coulthand-Clark, C. D. *The Third Brother: The Royal Australian Air Force, 1921–39.* North Sydney, NSW: Allen and Unwin, 1991.

Gillet, Ross. *Australian Air Power.* Sydney, NSW: The Book Company International, 1996.

_____. *Wings across the Sea.* Sydney: Aerospace Publications, 1988.

Isaacs, Keith. *Military Aircraft of Australia, 1909–1918.* Canberra: Australian War Memorial, 1971.

Jones, Ray. *Seagulls, Cruisers, and Catapults: Australian Naval Aviation.* Hobart, Tasmania: Pelorus Publications, 1989.

McCarthy, John. *Australia and Imperial Defense, 1918–1939: A Study in Air and Sea Power.* St. Lucia: University of Queensland Press, 1976.

_____. *A Last Call of Empire: Australian Aircrews, Britain, and the Empire Training Scheme.* Canberra: Australian War Memorial, 1988.

Meggs, Grey. *Australian Air Power Today.* Melbourne: Kookaburra Technical Publications, 1988.

Odgers, George. *The Royal Australian Air Force: An Illustrated History.* Brookvale, NSW: Child and Henry, 1984.

Parnell, Neville M. *Australian Air Force since 1911.* Sydney, NSW: Reed, 1976.

Pearson, Ross A. *Australians at War in the Air, 1939–1945.* 2 Vols. Kenthurst, NSW: Kangaroo Press, 1995.

Pentland, Geoffrey G. *Aircraft and Markings of the R. A. A. F., 1939–1945.* Melbourne: Lansdowne Press, 1970.

Pentland, Geoffrey G., and Peter Malone. *Aircraft of the RAAF 1921–1971.* Melbourne: Kookaburra Technical Publications, 1971.

Stephens, Alan. *Going Solo: The Royal Australian Air Force, 1946–1971.* Canberra: Australian Government Publishing Service, 1995.

_____. *Power Plus Attitude: Ideas, Strategy, and Doctrine in the Royal Australia Air Force, 1921–1991.* Canberra: AGPS Press, 1992.

Wilson, Stewart. *Military Aircraft of Australia.* Western Creek, ACT: Aerospace Publications, 1994.

Austria-Hungary

Cowin, Hugh W. *German and Austrian Aviation of World War 1: A Pictorial Chronicle of the Airmen and Aircraft That Forged German Airpower.* Oxford: Osprey, 2000.

Gaal, Julius R. "Austro-Hungarian Air Corps, 1918–1920: History of a Little-Known Air War," *Air Classics* 14 (September, 1978): 75–81.

Grosz, Peter M. *Austro-Hungarian Army Aircraft of World War One.* Mountain View, CA: Flying Machine Press, 1993.

_____. "Some Reflections on Austro-Hungarian Aviation in World War I," *Over the Front* 2 (Summer, 1987): 99–107.

Kerr, James L. III. "Against All Comers: Operations of the K. u. K. Luftfahrtruppen," *Cross and Cockade Journal* 15 (Winter, 1974): 291–356.

Nelsen, Stephen. "Austrian Naval Aircraft," *Cross and Cockade Journal* 7 (Summer, 1966): 112–133.

O'Connor, Martin D. *Air Aces of the Austro-Hungarian Empire, 1914–1918.* Mesa, AZ: Champlin Fighter Museum Press, 1986.

_____. "Markings and Camouflage of Austro-Hungarian Aircraft," *Cross and Cockade International* 17 (Spring/Summer/Autumn, 1986): 1–23; 76–87; 131–131; 18 (Spring/Summer/Autumn/Winter, 1987): 31–36; 75–87; 97–118; 168–173.

Pfister, Rudolph. "Birdmen of Austria," *Cross and Cockade Journal* 5 (Spring, 1964): 39–47.

Rothenberg, Gunter. "Military Aviation in Austria-Hungary, 1893–1918," *Aerospace Historian* 19 (June, 1972): 77–82.

Thompson, Jesse D. "Notes on the Austro-Hungarian Flying Corps, 1910–1918," *Cross and Cockade Journal* 3 (Winter, 1972): 281–295.

Brazil

Andrade, John M. *Latin American Military Aviation.* Leicester: Midland Counties, 1982.

da Costa, Thomaz G. " The Formation of Defense Policy in Brazil: Grand Strategy and Air Power, Politics and Doctrine during the Cold War, 1945–1974." Ph.D. dissertation, Columbia University, 1997.

Canada

Berg, Glen. "Scrambling for Dollars: Resource Allocation and the Politics of Canadian Fighter Procurement, 1943–1983." Ph.D. dissertation, Royal Military College of Canada, 1994.

Carroll, Warren H. *Eagles Recalled: Air Force Wings of Canada, Great Britain, and the British*

Commonwealth, 1913–1945. Atglen, PA: Schiffer Publications, 1997.

Data, Shabham K., and Fred W. Crickard. *Canadian Military Aviation in the Year 2000: Proceedings of a Conference Held in Halifax, N.S., May, 1990.* Halifax, NS: Center for Foreign Policy Studies, Dalhousie University, 1991.

Dunmore, Spencer. *Wings for Victory: The Remarkable Story of the British Commonwealth Air Training Program in Canada.* Toronto: McClelland and Stewart, 1994.

English, Allan D. *The Cream of the Crop: Canadian Aircrew, 1939–1945.* Montreal: McGill-Queen's University Press, 1996.

Foster, Tony. *Sea Wings: A Pictorial History of Canada's Waterborne Defense Aircraft.* Toronto: Methuen, 1986.

Halliday Hugh A. *Chronology of Canadian Military Aviation.* Ottawa: National Museum of Canada, 1985.

Hatch, F. J. *The Aerodrome of Democracy: Canada and the British Commonwealth Air Training Plan, 1939–1945.* Ottawa: Directorate of History, Department of National Defense, 1983.

Hendrie, Andrew. *Canadian Squadrons in Coastal Command.* St. Catharines, ON: Vanwell, 1997.

Kostenuk, Samuel. *RCAF: Squadron Histories and Aircraft, 1924–1968.* Toronto: Hakkert, 1977.

McQuarrie, John. *Canadian Wings: The Passion and the Force.* Toronto: McGraw-Hill, Ryerson, 1990.

Milberry, Larry. *Canada's Air Force at War and Peace.* 3 Vols. Toronto: CANAV Books, 2000.

_____. *Sixty Years: The Royal Canadian Air Force and Canadian Force Air Command, 1924–1984.* Toronto: CANAV Books, 1984.

_____. *Canada's Air Force Today.* Toronto: CANAV Books, 1987.

_____. *AIRCOM: Canada's Air Force.* Toronto: CANAV Books, 1991.

Molson, Kenneth M., and H. A. Taylor. *Canadian Aircraft since 1909.* Stittsville, ON: Canada's Wings, 1982.

Rankin-Lowe, Jeff. "Royal Canadian Air Force, 1950–1959," *Wings of Fame* 2 (1996): 142–156; 3 (1996): 142–157.

Weicht, Christopher. *Jericho Beach and the West Coast Flying Boat Stations.* Chemainus, BC: MCW Enterprises, 1997.

China

Allen, Kenneth W., Glenn Krumel, and Jonathan D. Pollack. *China's Air Force Enters the 21st Century.* Santa Monica, CA: Rand, 1995.

Bueschel, Richard M. *Communist Chinese Air Power.* New York: Praeger, 1968.

Czechoslovakia

Fricken, John. "Czech Republic and Slovakia," *World Air Power Journal* 25 (Summer, 1996): 142–157.

Hall, David J. "The Czechoslovakian Air Force in Britain, 1940–1945." Ph.D. dissertation, University of Southampton, 1998.

Titz, Zdenek. *The Czechoslovakian Air Force, 1918–1970.* New York: Arco, 1971.

France

Beauchamp, Gerry. "Falcons of France: The Demise, Destruction, and Death of French Fighter Forces in World War II," *Wings* 26 (June, 1996): 8–37, 47–55.

_____. "A Short History of French Fighter Airplanes, 1918–1934," *Skyways* No. 42 (April, 1997): 22–31; No. 44 (October, 1997): 6–18; No. 47 (July, 1998): 26–39.

Brindley, John. *French Fighters of World War Two.* Windsor, UK: Hylton Lacy Publishers, 1971.

Bruner, Georges. "Fighters a la Francaise," *Air Enthusiast Quarterly* No. 3: 85–93; No. 4: 212–224.

Cain, Anthony C. "Neither Decadent, nor Traitorous, nor Stupid: The French Air Force and Air Doctrine in the 1930s." Ph.D. dissertation, Ohio State University, 2000.

Camelio, Paul, and Christopher Shores. *Armee de l'Air: A Pictorial History of the French Air Force, 1937–1945.* Warren, MI: Squadron/Signal Publications, 1976.

Chillon, J., J. P. Dubois, and J. Wegg. *French Post-War Transport Aircraft.* Tonbridge, Kent, UK: Air Britain, 1980.

Christienne, Charles. *A History of French Military Aviation.* Washington, DC: Smithsonian Institution Press, 1986.

Davilla, James J. *French Aircraft of the First World War.* Stratford, CT: Flying Machine Press, 1997.

Dean, Jack. "The Armistice Air Force," *Airpower* 2 (July, 1972): 52–57, 66.

Ehrengardt, Chris J. "The Aeronavale in the Battle for France," *Air Pictorial* 42 (April/May, 1980): 144–150, 192–193.

_____. *Camoflage and Markings: #1, French Air Force, 1938–1945.* Fleurance, France: Aero Editions, 2000.

"The Falcons of France," *Air Classics* 5 (April, 1969): 26–26.

Franks, Norman L. R. *The Storks: The Story of the Les Cigognes, France's Elite Fighter Group of World War I.* London: Grub Street, 1998.

Griffin, David E. "The Role of the French Air Force, the Battle of France, 1940," *Aerospace Historian* 21 (Fall, 1974): 144–153.

Jackson, Paul A. *French Military Aviation.* Leicester, UK: Midland Counties Publications, 1979.

Kane, Francis X. "French Air Power in the Thirties," *Aerospace Historian* 13 (Autumn, 1966): 105–113.

Kenneth, Lee. "Aeronavale, 1912–1962," *Aerospace Historian* 26 (December, 1979): 238–244.

Ketley, Barry. *French Aces of World War 2.* Oxford: Osprey Aviation, 1999.

Kirkland, Faris R. "French Air Strength in May, 1940," *Air Power History* 40 (Spring, 1940): 22–34.

Krauskopf, Robert W. "French Air Power Policy, 1919–1939." Ph.D. dissertation, Georgetown University, 1965.

Liron, Jean, and Raymond Liron. "The French Air Force in 1939–40," *Air Pictorial* 25 (May/June, 1963): 128–132, 169–172.

Mizrahi, Joseph V. "Farewell to the Falcons of France," *Wings* 1 (December, 1971): 39–55, 64.

Opdyke, Leonard E. *French Aeroplanes before the Great War.* Atglen, PA: Schiffer Publications, 1999.

Rivere, Pierre. " Five French Fighters, 1939–1940," Air Combat 3(4) (1970): 108–114.

Van Haute, Andre. *Pictorial History of the French Air Force.* 2 Vols. London: Ian Allan, 1974–1975.

Germany

Abbott, Dan-San. *The Unit and Personal Markings of the German Air Force, 1914–1918.* Ceres, CA: World War I Aviation Documentation Services, 1995.

Aders, Gebhard. *History of the German Night Fighter Force, 1917–1945.* London: Jane's, 1979.

Bender, Roger J. *Air Organizations of the Third Reich.* Mountain View, CA: R. J. Bender, 1972.

Blanco, Richard L. *The Luftwaffe in World War II: The Rise and Decline of an Air Force.* New York: J. Messner, 1987.

Boiten, Theo. *Nachtjagd: The Night Fighter versus Bomber War over the Third Reich, 1939–45.* Wiltshire, UK: Crowood Press, 1997.

Brown, Eric M. *Wings of the Luftwaffe: Flying German Aircraft of the Second World War.* Novato: Presidio Press, 1987.

Clark, Chad G. "Trampled Underfoot: The Story of Attack Aviation in the German Spring Offensives of 1918," *Air Power History* 45 (Summer, 1998): 16–25.

Cooksley, Peter. *German Bombers of World War I in Action.* Carrollton, TX: Squadron/Signal Publications, 2000.

Cooper, Peter J. "Thor's Flawed Hammer: Bureaucratic Influence on Offensive Aircraft in Hitler's Luftwaffe." Master's thesis, St. John's University, 1982.

Corum, James S. *The Luftwaffe: Creating the Operational Air War, 1918–1940.* Lawrence: University Press of Kansas, 1997.

_____. "Development of Strategic Air War Concepts in Interwar Germany, 1919–1939," *Air Power History* 44 (Winter, 1997): 18–35.

_____. *The Luftwaffe Way of War: German Air Force Doctrine, 1911–1945.* Baltimore: Nautical and Aviation Publications, 1998.

Delve, Ken. *Night Fighter: The Battle for the Night Skies.* London: Arms and Armour, 1995.

Donald, David, ed. *Warplanes of the Luftwaffe.* London: Aerospace Publications, 1994.

Drendel, Lou. *The New Luftwaffe in Action.* Warren, MI: Squadron/Signal Publications, 1974.

Dressel, Joachim. *Fighters of the Luftwaffe.* London: Arms and Armour Press, 1993.

_____. *Bombers of the Luftwaffe.* London: Arms and Armour Press, 1994.

"Early Days of German Aviation," *Cross and Cockade Journal* 17 (Spring, 1976): 57–68.

Emme, Eugene M. "German Air Power and International Politics, 1899–1946." Master's thesis, State University of Iowa, 1946.

Feist, Uwe. *Luftwaffe in Action.* Warren, MI: Squadron/Signal Publications, 1972.

Fleuret, Alain. *Luftwaffe Camouflage, 1935–40.* Melbourne: Kookaburra Technical Publications, 1981.

Galland, Adolph. *The Luftwaffe Fighter Force: The View from the Cockpit.* London: Greenhill Books, 1998.

Geiger, George J. "Nazi Germany's Strategic Bombers," *Air Classic* 23 (August, 1987): 22–31, 56–62.

Gray, Peter, and Owen Thetford. *German Aircraft of the First World War.* Garden City, NY: Doubleday, 1971.

Green, William. *Warplanes of the Third Reich.* New York: Galahad Books, 1986.

Griehl, Manfred. *Fighters over Russia.* London: Greenhill Books, 1997.

_____. *German Jets of World War Two.* New York: Arms and Armour Press, 1988.

_____. *Night Fighters over the Reich.* London: Stackpole Books, 1997.

_____. *German Heavy Bombers: Do-19—Fw-200—He-177—He-274—Ju 89—Ju-290—Me 264 and Others.* Atglen, PA: Schiffer Publishing, 1994.

_____. *German Short-Range Reconnaissance Planes, 1930–1945.* West Chester, PA: Schiffer Publishing, 1989.

_____. *German Twin Engine Bombers of World War II.* West Chester, PA: Schiffer Publishing, 1989.

_____. *Luftwaffe Combat Aircraft, 1939–1945: Development, Production, Operations.* Atglen, PA: Schiffer Publishing, 1994.

Grosz, Peter M. *German Aircraft of World War I.* Stratford, CT: Flying Machine Press, 1999.

Haddow, G. W. *The German Giants: The Story of the R Planes, 1914–1919.* New York: Funk and Wagnalls, 1969.

Herwig, Dieter. *Luftwaffe Secret Projects: Strategic Bombers, 1935–1945.* Leicester: Midland Counties, 2000.

Homze, Edward L. *Arming the Luftwaffe: The Reich Air Ministry and the German Aircraft Industry, 1919–1939.* Lincoln: University of Nebraska Press, 1976.

_____. *German Military Aviation: A Guide to the Literature.* New York: Garland, 1984.

Hooton, E. R. *Phoenix Triumphant: The Rise and Rise of the Luftwaffe.* London: Arms and Armour Press, 1994.

_____. *Eagle in Flames: The Fall of the Luftwaffe.* London: Arms and Armour Press, 1997.

Hyland, Gary, and Anton Gill. *Last Talons of the Eagle: Secret Nazi Technology Which Could Have Changed the Course of World War II.* London: Headline, 1998.

Imrie, Alex. *German Naval Air Service.* London: Arms and Armour Press, 1989.

_____. *German Bombers of World War One.* London: Arms and Armour, 1990.

Jackson, Paul A. *German Military Aviation, 1956–1976.* Hinckley, UK: Midland Counties Publications, 1978.

Kilduff, Peter. *Germany's First Air Force, 1914–1918.* London: Arms and Armour Press, 1996.

Kosin, Rudiger. *The German Fighter since 1915.* London: Putnam, 1988.

Luftwaffe Camouflage and Markings, 1935–1945. 3 vols. Melbourne: Kookaburra Technical Publications, 1973–1977.

Mason, Francis K. *German Warplanes of World War II.* New York: Crescent Books, 1983.

Mason, Herbert M. *The Rise of the Luftwaffe: Forging the Secret German Air Weapon, 1918–1940.* New York: Dial Press, 1973.

Merrick, Kenneth A. *German Aircraft Interiors, 1935–1945.* Sturbridge, MA: Monogram Aviation, 1996.

_____. *German Aircraft Markings, 1939–1945.* London: Ian Allan, 1977.

Meyer, Michael. *The Luftwaffe: From Training School to the Front: An Illustrated Study, 1933–1945.* Atglen, PA: Schiffer Publications, 1996.

Morrow, John H. *Building German Air Power, 1909–1914.* Knoxville: University of Tennessee Press, 1976.

_____. *German Air Power in World War I.* Lincoln: University of Nebraska Press, 1982.

Munson, Kenneth. *German Warbirds from World War I to NATO Ally.* Poole, UK: New Orchard Editions, 1986.

O'Connor, Neal W. *Aviation Awards of Imperial Germany in World War I.* Princeton: Foundation for Aviation, 1988.

Philpott, Bryan. *The Encyclopedia of German Military Aircraft.* New York: Crescent Books, 1981.

_____. *German Maritime Aircraft: A Selection of German Wartime Photographs from the Bundesarchiv, Koblenz.* Cambridge: Patrick Stephens, 1981.

_____. *The History of the German Air Force.* Twickenham, UK: Hamlyn, 1986.

_____. *Luftwaffe Camouflage of World War 2.* Cambridge: Patrick Stephens, 1975.

Price, Alfred. *The Luftwaffe, 1933 to 1945.* London: Arms and Armour Press, 1981.

_____. *The Last Year of the Luftwaffe: May 1944 to May 1945.* London: Arms and Armour Press, 1991.

Procter, Raymond L. *Hitler's Luftwaffe in the Spanish Civil War.* Westport, CT: Greenwood Press, 1983.

Reynolds, Mike. *Camouflage and Markings: Luftwaffe, 1939–1945.* Hemel Hempstead, UK: Argus Books, 1992.

Ries, Karl. *The Luftwaffe: A Photographic Record, 1919–1945.* Blue Ridge Summit, PA: Aero, 1987.

_____. *Markings and Camouflage Systems of Luftwaffe Aircraft in World War II.* Finthen Bei Mainz: Verlag Dieter Hoffman, 1963.

Rimmell, Raymond L. *The German Air Service in World War One.* London: Arms and Armour Press, 1988.

Roba, Jean-Louis. *Seaplanes on the Black Sea: German-Romanian Operations, 1941–1944.* Bucharest: Editura Modelism, 1995.

Rosch, Barry. *Luftwaffe Codes, Markings, and Units, 1939–1945.* Atglen, PA: Schiffer Publications, 1995.

Shepherd, Christopher. *German Aircraft of World War II.* New York: Stein and Day, 1976.

Smith, J. Richard. *German Aircraft of the Second World War.* London: Putnam, 1972.

_____. *Luftwaffe Colors.* Boylston, MA: Monogram Aviation Publications, 1976.

Sundin, Charles. *Luftwaffe Fighter Aircraft in Profile.* Atglen, PA: Schiffer Publications, 1997.

Tegler, John H. "One Man—One Taube: The German Imperial Air Force–Far East," *Cross and Cockade Journal* 3 (Summer, 1962): 153–159.

Vajda, Ferenc A. *German Aircraft Industry and Production, 1933–1945.* Warrendale, PA: SAE International, 1998.

Wadman, David. *Aufklarer: Luftwaffe Reconnaissance Aircraft and Units.* Aldershot, UK: Hikoki, 1997.

Wagner, Ray, and Heinz Nowarra. *German Combat Planes.* Garden City, NY: Doubleday, 1971.

West, Kenneth. *The Captive Luftwaffe.* London: Putnam, 1978.

Williams, Roger A. "The Development of Luftwaffe Aircraft in the Nazi Era." Ph.D. dissertation, University of Minnesota, 1971.

Windrow, Martin. *Luftwaffe Colour Schemes and Markings, 1935–45.* New York: Arco, 1971.

Wood, Tony. *Hitler's Luftwaffe: A Pictorial History and Technical Encyclopedia of Hitler's Air Power in World War II.* London: Salamander Books, 1977.

Great Britain

Ball, S. J. *The Bomber in British Strategy: Doctrine, Strategy, and Britain's World Role, 1945–1960.* Boulder: Westview, 1995.

Beaver, Paul. *British Naval Air Power, 1945 to the Present.* London: Arms and Armour Press, 1985.

_____. *Encyclopedia of the Fleet Air Arm since 1945.* Wellingborough, UK: Patrick Stephens, 1987.

Benbow, Tim. "The Impact of Air Power on Navies: The United Kingdom, 1945–1957." Ph.D. dissertation, Oxford University, 1999.

Bialer, Uri. *The Shadow of the Bomber: The Fear of Air Attack and British Politics, 1932–1939.* London: Royal Historical Society, 1980.

Boot, Roy. *From Spitfire to Eurofighter: 45 Years of Combat Aircraft Design.* Shrewsbury, UK: Airlife, 1990.

Bower, Chaz. *Coastal Command at War.* London: Ian Allan 1979.

_____. *The Encyclopedia of British Military Aircraft.* New York: Crescent Books, 1982.

_____. *RAF Operations, 1918–1938.* London: W. Kimber, 1988.

Bowyer, Michael J.F. *Fighting Colours: RAF Fighter Camouflage and Markings, 1937–1969.* London: Patrick Stephens, 1969.

_____. "RAF Expansion, 1934–1939," *Air Pictorial* 24 (October/November/December, 1962): 323–326, 338–342, 381–383.

_____. *Interceptor Fighters for the Royal Air Force, 1935–45.* Wellingborough, UK: Patrick Stephens, 1984.

British Aviation Colours of World War Two: The Official Camouflage, Colours, and Markings of RAF Aircraft. London: Arms and Armour Press, 1976.

Brown, Eric M. *Wings of the Navy: Flying Allied Carrier Aircraft of World War Two.* Annapolis: Naval Institute Press, 1987.

Bruce, J. M. *The Aeroplanes of the Royal Flying Corps.* London: Putnam, 1982.

Cole, Christopher, and E. F. Cheeseman. *The Air Defense of Britain, 1914–1918*. London: Putnam, 1914.

Coombs, L. F. E. "The Expanding Years, 1936–1939," *Aeroplane Monthly* 12 (November/December, 1984): 568–573, 626–630; 13 (January/February/March/April, 1985): 20–23, 66–71, 143–146, 187–189.

_____. *The Lion Has Wings: The Race to Prepare the RAF for World War II, 1935–1940*. Shrewsbury, UK: Airlife, 1997.

Cooper, Malcom. *The Birth of Independent Air Power: British Air Policy in the First World War*. London: Allen and Unwin, 1986.

Cronin, Dick. *Royal Navy Shipboard Aircraft Developments, 1912–1931*. Tonbridge, Kent, UK: Air Britain, 1990.

Dibbs, John M. *RAF Frontline: The Royal Air Force—Defending the Realm*. Shrewsbury, UK: Airlife, 1998.

Donne, Michael. *Per Ardua ad Astra: Seventy Years of the Royal Flying Corps and the Royal Air Force*. London: F. Mullen, 1982.

Dowling, John. *RAF Helicopters: The First Twenty Years*. London: HMSO, 1992.

Driver, Hugh. *The Birth of Military Aviation: Britain, 1903–1914*. Rochester, NY: Boydell Press, 1997.

Duval, G. R. *British Flying Boats and Amphibians, 1909–1952*. London: Putnam, 1966.

Dymott, Roderick. *Fleet Air Arm*. London: Ian Allan, 1981.

Edmonds, Martin, ed. *British Naval Aviation in the 21st Century*. Lancaster, UK: Center for Defense and International Security Studies, Lancaster University, 1997.

Ellis, Paul. *Aircraft of the Royal Navy*. London: Jane's, 1982.

_____. *Aircraft of the Royal Air Force*. London: Macdonald and Jane's, 1978.

English, Malcom. *RAF Colour Album*. London: Jane's, 1986.

Evans, Andy. *Elite Fliers: The Men, the Machines, the Missions*. London: Arms and Armour Press, 1995.

Everett-Heath, John. *British Military Helicopters*. London: Arms and Armour Press, 1986.

Farrar-Hockley, Anthony. *The Army in the Air: The History of the Army Air Corps*. Phoenix Mill, UK: A. Sutton, 1994.

Flintham, Victor. *Aircraft in British Military Service: British Service Aircraft since 1946*. Shrewsbury, UK: Airlife, 1998.

Foster, Peter R. *Strike Command at NATO's Frontline*. London: Arms and Armour Press, 1991.

Friedman, Norman. *British Carrier Aviation: The Evolution of the Ships and Their Aircraft*. Annapolis: Naval Institute Press, 1988.

Gander, Terry. *Modern Royal Air Force Aircraft*. Wellingborough, UK: Patrick Stephens, 1987.

Gardner, Richard E. *British Service Helicopters: A Pictorial History*. London: R. Hale, 1985.

Gollin, A. M. *The Impact of Air Power on the British People and Their Government, 1909–1914*. Stanford: Stanford University Press, 1989.

Goulding, James. *Camouflage and Markings: RAF Fighter Command, Northern Europe, 1936 to 1945*. London: Ducimus Books, 1971.

Great Britain. Central Office of Information. *The Aircraft Builders: An Account of British Aircraft Production, 1935–1945*. London: HMSO, 1947.

Hall, David J. "The Birth of the Tactical Air Force: British Theory and Practice of Air Support in the West, 1939–1943." Ph.D. dissertation, Oxford University, 1998.

Halley, James J. *The K File: The Royal Air Force of the 1930s*. Tonbridge, Kent, UK: Air Britain, 1995.

Hamilton, Pierson M. "Bombing and the British Public, 1938–1939." Master's thesis, Arizona State University, 1989.

Hoare, John. *Tumult in the Clouds: A Story of the Fleet Air Arm*. London: Joseph, 1976.

Hobbs, David. *The Fleet Air Arm in Focus*. Liskeard, UK: Maritime, 1990.

_____. *Aircraft of the Royal Navy since 1945*. London: Maritime Books, 1997.

Hyde, H. Montgomery. *British Air Policy between the Wars, 1918–1939*. London: Heinemann, 1996.

Jackson, Robert. *Strike from the Sea: A Survey of British Naval Air Operations, 1900–1969*. London: Barker, 1970.

_____. *The RAF in Action: From Flanders to the Falklands*. Poole, Dorset, UK: Blandford Press, 1985.

John, Douglas B. "The Debate on British Military Air Policy, 1937–1939." Ph.D. dissertation, University of Kentucky, 1969.

Jones, Neville. *The Beginnings of Strategic Air Power: A History of the British Bomber Force, 1923–1939*. London: Frank Cass, 1987.

Keaney, Thomas A. "Aircraft and Air Doctrinal Development in Great Britain, 1912 to 1914." Ph.D dissertation, University of Michigan, 1975.

King, Bradley. *Royal Naval Air Service, 1912–1990*. Aldershot, UK: Hikoki, 1997.

Lansdown, John R. P. *With the Carriers in Korea: The Fleet Air Arm Story, 1950–1953*. Wilonslow, UK: Crecy Publishing, 1997.

Layman, R. D. *Before the Aircraft Carrier: The Development of Aviation Vessels, 1849–1922*. Annapolis: Naval Institute Press, 1989.

Lewis, Peter H. M. *The British Fighter since 1912: Fifty Years of Design and Development*. London: Putnam, 1965.

_____. *The British Bomber since 1914: Fifty Years of Design and Development*. London: Putnam, 1967.

Mason, Francis K. *The British Fighter since 1912*. Annapolis: Naval Institute Press, 1992.

_____. *The British Bomber since 1914*. Annapolis: Naval Institute Press, 1994.

Mondey, David. *The Hamlyn Concise Guide to British Aircraft of World War II*. London: Hamlyn/Aerospace, 1982.

Morcen, Neil. *Fleet Air Arm*. Shrewsbury, UK: Airlife, 1994.

Omissi, David E. *Air Power and Colonial Control: The Royal Air Force, 1919–1939*. Manchester, UK; Manchester University Press, 1990.

Paris, Michael. *Winged Warfare: The Literature and Theory of Aerial Warfare in Britain, 1854–1917.* Manchester, UK: Manchester University Press, 1992.

Penrose, Harald. *British Aviation: The Great War and Armistice, 1915–1919.* New York: Funk and Wagnalls, 1969.

_____. *British Aviation: The Ominous Skies, 1935–1939.* London: HMSO, 1980.

Popham, Hugh. *Into Wind: A History of British Naval Flying.* London: Hamilton, 1969.

Powers, Barry D. *Strategy with Slide Rule: British Air Strategy, 1914–1939.* New York: Holmes, Meier, 1976.

_____. "The Development of British Air Defense Concepts in Theory and Practice, 1919–1931." Ph.D. dissertation, University of Delaware, 1973.

Rawlings, John D.R. *The History of the Royal Air Force.* London: Aerospace, 1984.

_____. *Coastal, Support, and Special Squadrons of the RAF and Their Aircraft.* London: Jane's, 1987.

Reynolds, Mike. *Camouflage and Markings, Royal Air Force, 1939–1945.* Hemel Hempstead: Argus Books, 1992.

Rimell, Ray. *R.A.F. between the Wars.* London: Arms and Armour Press, 1985.

Ritchie, Sebastian. *Industry and Air Power: The Expansion of British Aircraft Production, 1935–1941.* London: Frank Cass, 1997.

Robertson, Bruce. *Bombing Colours: British Bomber Camouflage and Markings, 1914–1937.* London: Patrick Stephens, 1972.

Robertson, Scott. *The Development of RAF Strategic Bombing Doctrine, 1919–1939.* Westport, CT: Praeger, 1995.

Rogers, Les. *British Aviation Squadron Markings of World War I.* Atglen, PA: Schiffer Publishing, 2001.

Smith, Malcom. *British Air Strategy between the Wars.* New York: Claredon Press, 1984.

Spencer, H. J. C. *Ordinary Naval Airmen.* Tonbridge Wells, UK: Spellmount, 1992.

Sturtivant, Ray. *British Naval Aviation: The Fleet Air Arm, 1967–1990.* Annapolis: Naval Institute Press, 1990.

_____. *British Research and Development Aircraft: Seventy Years at the Leading Edge.* Newbury Park, CA: Haynes, 1990.

_____. *Fleet Air Arm, 1920–1939.* London: Arms and Armour Press, 1990.

_____. *Fleet Air Arm Aircraft, 1939 to 1945.* Tonbridge Wells, UK: Air Britain, 1995.

_____. *Fleet Air Arm at War.* London: Allan, 1982.

_____. *The History of Britain's Training Aircraft.* North Yeovil, Somerset, UK: Haynes Publishing Group, 1987.

Swanborough, Gordon. *British Aircraft at War, 1939–45.* St. Leonards-on-Sea, UK: HPC Publishing, 1997.

Thetford, Owen G. *Aircraft of the Royal Air Force.* London: Putnam, 1976.

_____. *British Naval Aircraft since 1912.* Annapolis: Naval Institute Press, 1991.

_____. *On Silver Wings: RAF Biplane Fighters between the Wars.* London: Osprey, 1993.

Till, Geoffrey. *Air Power and the Royal Navy, 1914–1945: A Historical Survey.* London: Macdonald and James, 1979.

Treadwell, Terry L., and Alan C. Wood. *The Royal Naval Air Service.* Stroud, Glouchestershire, UK: Tempus Publishing, 1999.

Tress, Harvey B. *British Air Strategic Bombing Policy through 1940: Politics, Attitudes, and the Formation of a Lasting Pattern.* Lewiston, NY: Edwin Mellen Press, 1988.

Turner, John F. *British Aircraft of World War 2.* New York: Stein and Day, 1976.

Turner, Michael. *Royal Air Force: The Aircraft in Service since 1918.* Feltham, Middlesex, UK: Temple Press, 1981.

Vicary, Adrian. *Naval Wings: Royal Navy Carrier-Bourne Aircraft since 1916.* Cambridge: Patrick Stephens, 1984.

Williams, George K. *Biplanes and Bombsights: British Bombers in World War I.* Maxwell AFB, AL: Air University Press, 1999.

Williams, Ray. *Royal Navy Aircraft since 1945.* Annapolis: Naval Institute Press, 1989.

_____. *Fly Navy.* Shrewsbury, UK: Airlife, 1989.

Winter, John. *Find, Fix, and Strike! The Fleet Air Arm at War, 1939–45.* London: Batsford, 1980.

Wixey, Kenneth F. *Forgotten Bombers of the Royal Air Force.* London: Arms and Armour Press, 1997.

Wynn, Humphrey. *Forged in War: A History of the RAF Transport Command, 1943–1967.* London: HMSO, 1996.

India

Chatterji, A. K. *Naval Aviation: A World History.* New Dehli: Allied, 1985.

Chaturvedi, Air Marshal M. S. *History of the Indian Air Force.* New Dehli: Vikas Publishing House, 1978.

Chopra, Pushpindar S. "Indian Ocean Air Power," *Air Enthusiast* 3 (December, 1992): 275–281.

_____. "Spinal Cord of Indian Air Defense," *Air Enthusiast* 8 (January/February, 1975): 7–12, 69–75.

"Defending India's Frontiers," *Air International* 33 (December, 1987): 267–276.

Fricker, John. *Battle for Pakistan: The Air War of 1965.* London: Ian Allan, 1979.

Green, William, Pushpindar Singh Chopra, and Gordon Swanborough, eds. *The Indian Air Force and Its Aircraft.* London: Ducimus Books, 1982.

Lake, Jon. "Indian Air Power," *World Air Power Journal* 12 (Spring, 1993): 138–157.

Lal, Pratap Chandra. *My Years with the IAF.* New Dehli: Lancer International, 1986.

"Quality or Quantity: The Indian Dilemma," *Air Enthusiast* 9 (October, 1975): 170–180.

Seth, Vijay. *The Flying Machines–Indian Air Force, 1933–1999.* New Dehli: Seth Communications, 2000.

Singh, Pushpindar. *Aircraft of the Indian Air Force, 1933–73.* New Dehli: English Books Store, 1974.

Tanham, George K., and Marcy Agmon. *The Indian Air Force: Trends and Prospects.* Santa Monica, CA: RAND, 1995.

Touching the Sky: The Indian Air Force Today. New Delhi: Narosa Publishing House, 1991.

Verma, Vivendra. *Hunting Hunters: Battle of Longewala, December, 1971*. Dehradun: Youth Education Publications, 1997.

Israel

Aloni, Shlomo. "Israel, 1950–1959," *Wings of Fame* 7 (1997): 142–157.

Borovik, Yehuda. *Israeli Air Force, 1948 to the Present*. London: Arms and Armour Press, 1984.

Braybrook, Roy M. "The Israeli Aerospace Industry," *Air Combat* 12 (May, 1984): 26–28, 70–76.

Cohen, Eliezer. *Israel's Best Line of Defense: The First Full Story of the Israeli Air Force*. New York: Orion Books, 1993.

Eshel, David. *Israel Air Force*. Hod Hashron, Israel: Eshel-Dramit, 1981.

Gunston, Bill. *An Illustrated Guide to the Israeli Air Force*. New York: Arco, 1982.

Handleman, Philip. *Mid-East Aces: The Israeli Air Force Today*. London: Osprey, 1991.

Huertas, Salvador M. *Israeli Air Force, 1947–1960: An Illustrated History*. Atglen, PA: Schiffer Publications, 1998.

"Israel's Pride of Lions," *Air International* 11 (November, 1976): 220–225, 248–249.

Jackson, Robert. *The Israeli Air Force Story*. London: Tom Stacey, 1970.

Mersley, Peter B. *Israeli Fighter Aces: The Definitive History*. North Branch, MN: Speciality Press, 1997.

Mizrahi, Joe. "A Time for Testing," *Wings* 28 (February, 1998): 44–55.

Nordeen, Lon. *Fighters over Israel: The Story of the Israeli Air Force from the War of Independence to the Bekkar Valley*. New York: Orion Books, 1990.

Norton, William. *Fifty Years on the Edge: The Aircraft of the Israeli Air Force since 1948*. Leicester: Midland Counties, 1999.

Rubsenstein, Murray. *Shield of David: An Illustrated History of the Israeli Air Force*. Englewood Cliffs, NJ: Prentice-Hall, 1978.

Stevenson, William. *Zanek! A Chronicle of the Israeli Air Force*. New York: Viking Press, 1971.

Yonay, Ehud. *No Margin for Error: The Making of the Israeli Air Force*. New York: Pantheon Books, 1993.

Italy

Apostolo, Giorgio. "The Birth of Italian Aviation," *Air Power History* 9 (July, 1962): 184–188.

_____. *Italian Aces of World War 2*. London: Osprey, 2000.

Arena, Nino. *Italian Air Force Camouflage in World War II*. Modena, Italy: Mucchi, 1983.

Beale, Nick. *Air War Italy, 1944–1945: The Axis Forces from the Liberation of Rome to the Surrender*. Shrewsbury, UK: Airlife, 1996.

Caruana, Richard J. *Camouflage and Markings: Italian Air Forces, 1935–1945*. Valleton, Malta: Modelaid International, 1988.

_____. *Italian Air Forces, 1943–1945: The Aviazone Nazionale Republicana*. Malta: Modelaid International Publications, 1989.

Catalanotto, Baldassare. *Once upon a Sky: 70 Years of the Italian Air Force*. Rome: Lizard, 1994.

D'Amico, Ferinando, and Gabriele Valentini. *Regia Aeronautica, Volume 2: 1943–1945*. Carrollton, TX: Squadron/Signal Publications, 1986.

Dean, Jack. "The White Eagles: More on Mussolini's WW II Air Force," *Air Classics* 3 (May, 1967): 30–43.

_____. "Mussolini's Paper Tigers," *Air Classics* 3 (November, 1967): 17–24, 51–67.

_____. "Doomsday for the Regia Aeronautica," *Wings* 15 (April, 1985): 40–55.

Dunning, Chris. *Combat Units of the Regia Aeronautica: Italian Air Force, 1940–1942*. Surrey, UK: Air Research Publications, 1988.

_____. *Courage Alone: The Italian Air Force, 1940–1943*. Aldershot, UK: Hikoki Publications, 1998.

Elliott, Christopher R. "Italian Raids on Britain," *Air Pictorial* 31 (September, 1969): 332–335.

Gaal, Julius. "Winged Shadows: Italy's Aerial Transports During World War II," *Air Combat* 6 (May, 1978): 12–21, 96.

Gentilli, Roberto. "The Italian Air Force in Russia," *Air Classics* 8 (October, 1972): 20–25.

Ghergo, Giuseppe F. "The Italian Air Force in World War II," *Air Pictorial* 45 (January/February/March, 1983): 10–18, 52–58, 100–107.

"The Italian Air Force: An Official History," *Aerospace Historian* 20 (December, 1973): 178–185.

McMeiken, Frank. *Italian Military Aviation*. Leicester, UK: Midland Counties, 1984.

Mattioli, Guido. *The Italian Air Force in Spain*. London: United Editorial, 1938.

Mizrahi, Joe V. "Desert Ace: An Exclusive Interview with One of Italy's Leading Combat Fliers," *Air Classics* 4 (June, 1968): 8–15.

Niccoli, Riccardo, and Renzo Sacchetti. *Italian Military Aviation Today*. Milano: Editrice Militare, 1992.

Potts, Thomas. "L'Operazione Cizzano," *Air Power History* 28 (March, 1981): 23–37.

Segne, Claudio G. *Italo Balbo: A Fascist Life*. Berkeley: University of California Press, 1987.

Sglarato, Nico. *Italian Aircraft of World War II*. Warren, MI: Squadron/Signal Publications, 1979.

Shores, Christopher. *Regia Aeronautica: A Pictorial History of the Italian Air Force*. 2 Vols. Warren, MI: Squadron/Signal Publications, 1976–1986.

Thompson, Nathan. *Italian Civil and Military Aircraft, 1930–1945*. Fallbrook, CA: Aero Publishers, 1963.

Vergnano, Piero. *Origin of Aviation in Italy, 1783–1918*. Genoa: Edizioni Intyprint, 1969.

Walker, Wayne T. "Italian Warplanes," *World War II Magazine* 3 (April, 1974): 44–52.

Japan

Baker, Ian K. *Japanese Army Aircraft Colours and Markings in the Pacific War and Before*. Camberwell, Victoria: I. K. Baker, 1992.

_____. *Nippon's Naval Air Force: Japanese Navy Aircraft Colours and Markings in the Pacific War and Before.* Camberwell, Victoria: I. K. Baker, 1989.

Bueschel, Richard M. *Japanese Aircraft Insignia, Camouflage, and Markings.* West Roxbury, MA: World War I Aero Publishers, 1966.

Collier, Basil. *Japanese Aircraft of World War II.* New York: Mayflower Books 1979.

Coox, Alvin D. "The Rise and Fall of the Imperial Japanese Air Forces," *Air Power History* 27 (June, 1980): 74–94.

Dews, Jule Neville. *Wing-Smiths of Japan: A Story of Japan's WW II Aircraft.* Frederick, MD: Politico-Socio-Economics Press, 1993.

Francillon, Rene J. *Japanese Aircraft of the Pacific War.* London: Putnam, 1979.

_____. *Japanese Bombers of World War Two.* Garden City, NY: Doubleday, 1969.

General View of Japanese Military Aircraft in the Pacific War. Tokyo: Published for Airview by Kantosha, 1956.

Green, William, and Gordon Swanborough. *Japanese Army Fighters.* New York: Arco, 1977.

Guttman, Jon. "Shigeno: The First Flying Samurai," *Windsock International* 7 (March/April, 1991): 24–27.

Harvey, A. D. "Army Air Force and Navy Air Force: Japanese Aviation and the Opening Phase of the War in the Far East," *War in History* 6 (April, 1999): 147–173.

Hata, Ikuhiko. *Japanese Naval Aces and Fighter Units of World War II.* Annapolis: Naval Institute Press, 1989.

Izawa, Yasuho. "Ace's Aircraft: Lt. Moritsugu Kanai," *Aero Album* 4 (Summer, 1971): 19–23.

_____. "Fighting Floatplanes of the Imperial Japanese Navy," *Air Enthusiast* 31 (July-November, 1986): 7–22.

_____. "Japan's Red Eagles: The 64th Flying Sentai," *Air Classics* 8 (July-August, 1972): 11–17, 38–47; 9 (May, 1973): 24–29, 74–75, 82.

Japanese Military Aircraft Illustrated. 3 Vols. Tokyo: Burin-do, 1982–1983.

Mikesh, Robert C. *Broken Wings of the Samurai: The Destruction of the Japanese Air Force.* Shrewsbury, UK: Airlife, 1993.

_____. *Japanese Cockpit Interiors.* Boylston, MA: Monogram Aviation Publishers, 1976.

_____. *Japanese Aircraft: Code Names and Designations.* Atglen, PA: Schiffer Publications, 1993.

_____. "Wings of the Samurai," *Aviation Heritage* (November, 1992): 38–35.

Mikesh, Robert C., and Shorzoe Abe. *Japanese Aircraft, 1910–1941.* Annapolis: Naval Institute Press, 1990.

Pelvin, Richard. *Japanese Air Power, 1919–1945: A Case Study in Military Dysfunction.* Fairburn, ACT: Air Power Studies Center, 1995.

"Reluctant Samurai," *Air International* 29 (August/September, 1985): 65–74, 123–128, 143–146.

Sakaida, Henry. *Japanese Army Air Force Aces, 1937–1945.* London: Osprey, 1997.

_____. *Imperial Japanese Navy Aces, 1937–1945.* London: Osprey, 1998.

Scott, Peter. *Emblems of the Rising Sun: Imperial Japanese Army Air Force Unit Markings.*

Ottringham, East Yorkshire, UK,: Hikoki Publishing, 1999.

Sekigawa, Eiichiro. "The Paradox of Japan's Maritime Wings," *Air Enthusiast* 8 (May, 1971): 222–227.

_____. *Pictorial History of Japanese Military Aviation.* London: Ian Allan, 1974.

_____. "The Undeclared Air War," *Air Enthusiast* 4 (May/June, 1973): 245–250, 294–302.

_____. "Development of Japanese Army Aviation," *Air International* 10 (February, 1976): 64–69, 97.

Thorpe, Donald W. *Japanese Army Air Force Camouflage and Markings, World War II.* Fallbrook, CA: Aero Publications, 1968.

_____. *Japanese Naval Air Force Camouflage and Markings, World War II.* Fallbrook, CA: Aero Publishers, 1977.

Tindal, James A. "A Brief History of Early Japanese Aviation," *World War I Aero* No. 120 (July, 1988): 6–7, 14.

Netherlands

Casius, Gerard, and Peter Boer. "NEIAF: The Story of an Unusual Air Force," *Air Combat* 4 (March/May, 1975): 62–71, 28–29.

Jackson, Paul A. *Dutch Military Aviation, 1945–1978.* Leicester, UK: Midland Counties Publications, 1978.

Kamphuis, G. H. "The Royal Netherlands Air Force," *Air Pictorial* 25 (July, 1963): 198–201.

Poland

Arct, Bohdan. *Polish Wings in the West.* Warsaw: Interpress, 1971.

Cynk, Jerzy. "Blitzkrieg," *Airpower* 13 (July, 1983): 30–53.

_____. *History of the Polish Air Force, 1918–1968.* Reading, UK: Osprey Publishing, 1972.

_____. "Poland's Part in the Air War, 1940–45," *Air Pictorial* 27 (June, 1965): 194–198.

_____. *Polish Aircraft, 1893–1939.* London: Putnam, 1971.

_____. *The Polish Air Force at War: The Official History.* 2 Vols. Atglen, PA: Schiffer Publications, 1998.

Gretzyngier, Robert. *Polish Aces of World War 2.* London: Osprey, 1998.

Kolinski, Izydor. *Polish Aviation Past and Present.* Warszawa: Publications of the Ministry of National Defense, 1967.

Koniarek, Jan. *Polish Air Force, 1918–1945.* Carrollton, TX: Squadron/Signal Publications, 1994.

Lisiewicz, M., ed. *Destiny Can Wait: The Polish Air Force in the Second World War.* London: Heinnemann, 1949.

Meissner, Janusz. *Polish Wings over Europe.* Harrow, Middlesex, UK: Atlantis, 1943.

Orwovski, J. S. "Polish Air Force versus the Luftwaffe," *Air Pictorial* 21 (October/November, 1959): 378–383, 388, 395–400, 418.

Peczkowski, Robert, and Bartolomieji Belcaiz. *White Eagles: The Aircraft, Men, and Operations of the Polish Air Force, 1918–1939.* Ottringham, East Yorkshire, UK: Hikoki Publications, 1999.

Peszke, Michael A. "Pre-War Polish Air Force: Budget, Personnel, Politics, and Doctrine," *Aerospace Historian* 27 (September, 1981): 186–204.

_____. "The Operational Doctrine of the Polish Air Force in World War II: A Thirty-Year Perspective," *Aerospace Historian* 23 (September, 1976): 140–147.

"Polish Wings: An Official History," *Aerospace Historian* 20 (March, 1973): 10–16.

Rivere, Pierre. "Air Force on the Run," *Air Combat Yearbook* (1978): 22–29.

Zamoyski, Adam. *The Forgotten Few: The Polish Air Force in the Second World War.* New York: Hippocrene Books, 1995.

Russia

Aleksandrov, A. O. *Naval Planes of Russian Origin.* St. Petersburg, Russia: n.p., 1996.

Alexander, Jean. *Russian Aircraft since 1940.* London: Putnam, 1975.

Andersson, Lennart. *Soviet Aircraft and Aviation, 1917–1941.* London: Putnam, 1994.

Arold, Louis. *U.S.S.R. Helicopters and Utility Aircraft.* La Puente, CA: Airlandco, 1977.

_____. *U.S.S.R. Aircraft: Fighter and Bomber.* La Puente, CA: Airlandco, 1976.

Baidukov, Georgi. *Russian Lindberg: The Life of Valery Chkalov.* Washington, DC: Smithsonian Institution Press, 1991.

Bailes, K. E. "Technology and Legitimacy: Soviet Aviation and Stalinism in the 1930s," *Technology and Culture* 17 (November, 1976): 55–81.

Baker, David. *The Soviet Air Force.* Vero Beach, FL: Rourke Publications, 1988.

Ballatine, Colin. *Vintage Russian: Props and Jets of the Iron Curtain.* Osceola, WI: MBI Publishing, 1998.

Bayless, Stuart W. "Soviet Inter-war Aviation, 1917–1941: The Heroic Years." Master's thesis, University of Washington, 1991.

Berman, Robert P. *Soviet Air Power in Transition.* Washington: Brookings Institute, 1978.

Bobrow, Carl. "Early Aviation in Russia," *World War I Aero* No. 114 (April, 1987): 18–29.

Braybrook, Roy. *Soviet Combat Aircraft: The Four Post War Generations.* London: Osprey, 1991.

Cain, Charles W. *Military Aircraft of the U.S.S.R.* London: Jenkins, 1952.

Dean, Barry. *Kiev and Kuznetsov: Russian Aircraft Carriers.* New Territories, Hong Kong: Concord Publications, 1993.

Dick, Charles J. "Military Reform and the Russian Air Force," *Journal of Slavic Military Studies* 13 (March, 2000): 1–12.

Dimitroff, James S. "Give Russia Wings: The Confluence of Aviation and Russian Futurism, 1909–1914." Ph.D. dissertation, University of Southern California, 1998.

Durkota, Alan, Thomas Darcey, and Victor Kulikov. *The Imperial Russian Air Service: Famous Pilots and Aircraft of World War One.* Mountain View, CA: Flying Machine Press, 1995.

Dzhus, Alexander M. *Soviet Wings: Modern Soviet Aircraft.* London: Greenhill Books, 1991.

Epstein, Joshua M. *Measuring Military Power: The Soviet Air Threat to Europe.* Princeton: Princeton University Press, 1984.

Everett-Heath, John. *Soviet Helicopters: Design, Development, and Tactics.* London: Jane's, 1983.

Geiger, George J. "The Mystery Fighters: An Exclusive Look at World War II's Soviet Air Force," *Air Classics* 7 (March, 1971): 6–17.

———. "Russia's Two-Seat Fighters," *Combat Aircraft* 24 (April, 1988): 52–67, 73.

George, Mark, and Vic Sheppard. "Russia's Air Force in War and Revolution, 1914–1920," *Cross and Cockade International* 17 (Winter, 1986): 145–153; 18 (Summer, 1987): 49–54.

Gething, Michael J. *Soviet Air Power Today.* London: Arms and Armour Press, 1988.

Geust, Carl-Fredrik. *Red Stars: Soviet Air Force in World War Two.* Tampere, Finland: Apali, 1995.

Gordon, Yefim. *Soviet Combat Aircraft of the Second World War.* 2 Vols. Leicester, UK: Midland Publishing, 1998.

Green, William, and Gordon Swanborough. *Soviet Air Force Fighters.* New York: Arco, 1977.

Gunston, Bill. *The Encyclopedia of Russian Aircraft, 1875–1995.* Osceola: MBI International, 1995.

Halberstadt, Hans. "The Best from Russia," *Air Combat* 21 (February, 1993): 34–45.

_____. *Red Star Fighters and Ground Attack.* London: Windrow and Greene, 1994.

Hardesty, Von. *Red Phoenix: The Rise of Soviet Air Power, 1941–1945.* Washington, DC: Smithsonian Institution Press, 1982.

Higham, Robin, and Jacob W. Kipp, eds. *Soviet Aviation and Air Power: A Historical View.* Boulder: Westview Press, 1978.

Higham, Robin, John T. Greenwood, and Von Hardesty, eds. *Russian Aviation and Air Power in the Twentieth Century.* Portland, OR: Frank Cass, 1998.

Jones, David R. "The Birth of the Russian Air Weapon, 1909–1914," *Aerospace Historian* 21 (Fall, 1974): 169–181.

Kilmarx, Robert A. *A History of Soviet Air Power.* New York: Praeger, 1962.

_____. "The Russian Imperial Air Force of World War I," *Airpower Historian* 10 (July, 1963): 90–95.

Korolkov, B. *A Guide to the Russian Federation Air Force Museum at Monino.* Atglen, PA: Schiffer Publications, 1996.

Lake, John. "The Toothless Bear?" *Combat Aircraft* 1 (September, 1998): 624–633.

Lambeth, Benjamin S. *Russia's Air Power in Crisis: A Rand Research Study.* Washington, DC: Smithsonian Institution Press, 1999.

_____. *Russia's Air Power at the Crossroads.* Santa Monica, CA: Rand, 1996.

Layman, R. D. "Euxine Wings: Russian Shipboard Aviation in the Black Sea, 1913–1917," *Cross and Cockade Journal* 15 (Summer, 1974): 143–178.

Lesnitchenko, Vladimir. "Combat Composites: Soviet Use of Motherships to Carry Fighters, 1931–1941," *Air Enthusiast* No. 84 (November/December, 1999): 4–21.

Mason, R. A. *Aircraft, Strategy, and Operations of the Soviet Air Force*. London: Jane's, 1986.

Miller, Russell. *The Soviet Air Force at War*. Alexandria, VA: Time-Life Books, 1983.

Morgan, Hugh. *Soviet Aces, 1939–45*. London: Osprey, 1997.

Munro, Colin. *Soviet Air Forces: Fighters and Bombers*. New York: Sports Car Press, 1972.

Myles, Bruce. *Night Witches: The Untold Story of Soviet Women in Combat*. Novato, CA: Presidio Press, 1981.

Nemecek, Vaclav. *The History of Soviet Aircraft from 1918*. London: Willow Books, 1986.

_____. "Parasites," *Fly Past* No. 61 (August, 1986): 36–38.

_____. "Trapeze Artists—with a Red Star," *Air Pictorial* 27 (January, 1965): 8–11.

Noggle, Anne. *A Dance with Death: Soviet Airwomen in World War II*. College Station, TX: Texas A&M University Press, 1994.

Nowarra, Heinz J. *Russian Civil and Military Aircraft, 1884–1969*. London: Fountain Press, 1971.

_____. *Russian Fighter Aircraft, 1920–1941*. Atglen, PA: Schiffer Publications, 1997.

Oliver, David. *Soviet Battlefield Helicopters*. London: Osprey Aerospace, 1991.

Polak, Tomas, and Christopher Shores. *Stalin's Falcons: The Aces of the Red Star: A Tribute to the Notable Fighter Pilots of the Soviet Air Forces, 1918–1953*. London: Grub Street, 1998.

"The Predacious Parasite," *Air Enthusiast* 19 (August-November, 1982): 1–7.

Red Stars in the Sky: Soviet Air Force in World War II. Espoo, Finland: Tietotcos, 1979–1983.

Russia's Top Guns. New York: Gallery Books, 1990.

Rustam-Bek-Tageev, B. *Aerial Russia: The Romance of the Giant Aeroplane*. London: John Lane, 1918.

Seidl, Hans D. *Stalin's Eagles: An Illustrated Study of the Soviet Aces of World War II and Korea*. Atglen, PA: Schiffer Publications, 1998.

Sglarlato, Nico. *Soviet Aircraft of Today*. London: Arms and Armour Press, 1978.

Spick, Mike. *Modern Soviet Aircraft*. London: Osprey Publishing, 1987.

Stapfer, Hans-Heri. *Soviet Military Helicopters*. London: Arms and Armour, 1991.

_____. *Red Ladies in Waiting*. Carrollton, TX: Squadron/Signal Publications, 1994.

Stroud, John. *Soviet Transport Aircraft since 1945*. New York: Funk and Wagnalls, 1968.

Sweetman, Bill. *The Hamlyn Concise Guide to Soviet Military Aircraft*. London: Hamlyn/Aerospace, 1981.

Ward, Richard. *Soviet Military Aircraft Design and Procurement: A Historical Perspective*. Fort Worth, TX: General Dynamics, 1983.

Weeks, Albert. "Muromets to Black Jack: The VVS at 66," *Air University Review* 35 (November, 1983): 39–49.

Whiting, Kenneth R. *Soviet Air Power*. Boulder: Westview Press, 1986.

Zaolga, Steve J. *Modern Soviet Warplanes: Fighters and Interceptors*. Hong Kong: Concord Publications, 1991.

_____. *Russian Falcons: The New Russian Aircraft*. Hong Kong: Concord Publications, 1992.

_____. *Modern Soviet Warplanes: Strike Aircraft and Attack Helicopters*. Hong Kong: Concord Publications, 1991.

Spain

Andrade, John M. *Spanish and Portuguese Military Aviation*. Leicester, UK: Midland Counties Publications, 1977.

Ghergo, Emiliani. *Wings over Spain: History and Images of the Civil War, 1936–1939*. Milano: Giorgio Apostolo, 1997.

Howson, Gerald. *Aircraft of the Spanish Civil War, 1936–1939*. London: Putnam Aeronautical, 1990.

Huertas, Salvadore M. "Spanish Army Aviation," *Air Combat* 10 (January, 1982): 26–29, 73–74.

_____. "Winged Anchors: The Spanish Navy's Fleet Air Arm," *Air Combat* 10 (July, 1982): 48–55, 74.

Miranda, Justo. *World Aviation in Spain (The Civil War), 1936–1939: American and Soviet Warplanes*. Madrid: Silex, 1988.

Salas Larrazabal, Jesus. *From Fabric to Titanium: Aeronautical Creativeness in Spain, Past and Present*. Madrid: Espasa-Calpe, 1983.

Shores, Christopher. *Spanish Civil War Air Forces*. London: Osprey Publishing, 1977.

Sweden

Bohme, Klaus-Richard. *The Growth of the Swedish Aircraft Industry, 1918–1945: The Swedish Air Force and Aircraft Industry*. Manhattan, KS: Sunflower University Press, 1987.

_____. Swedish Air Force Defense Doctrine, 1918–1936," *Aerospace Historian* 24 (June, 1977): 94–99.

Farmer, James H. "At Russia's Front Door," *Air Combat* 16 (March/April, 1988): 34–41, 67–71, 74.

Jorgensen, Hans. *Nordic Air Power*. Shrewsbury, UK: Airlife, 1993.

Larsson, Gunnar. "Flygvapnet: Lion of the North," *Air Combat* 7 (March, 1979): 34–45, 64–76.

"The Swedish Air Force: An Official History," *Aerospace Historian* 27 (December, 1975): 218–230.

Yugoslavia

Ellison, Alan. "Phoenix or Dodo," *Air Force Monthly* No. 86 (May, 1995): 39–42.

"Of Gulls and Eagles: The Yugoslav Aircraft Industry," *Air International* 28 (January, 1985): 7–13, 46–48.

APPENDIX 1: AIRCRAFT BY MISSION

Air Supremacy
Mikoyan-Gurevich MiG 29
Sukhoi Su 27

Air-Sea Rescue
Aerospatiale *Dauphin*
Aerospatiale *Super Puma*
Beriev Be 12 *Tchaika*
Heinkel He 59
ShinMaywa US 1
Supermarine *Walrus*
Westland *Lynx*
Westland *Scout/Wasp*

Antisubmarine
Aerospatiale *Dauphin*
Aerospatiale *Super Puma*
Avro *Shackleton*
Beriev Be 12 *Tchaika*
Beriev MBR 2
Breguet *Atlantique*
Canadair CL 28 *Argus*
Hawker-Siddeley *Nimrod*
Ilyushin Il 38
Kamov Ka 27
ShinMaywa US 1
Tupolev Tu 95
Westland *Lynx*
Westland *Scout/Wasp*

Antitank
Aerospatiale *Gazelle*
Agusta A 109 *Hirundo*
Agusta A 129 *Mangusta*
Henschel Hs 129
Ilyushin Il 2 *Shturmovik*
Kamov Ka 50
MBB BO 105
Mil Mi 24
Sukhoi Su 25
Westland *Scout/Wasp*

Assault Glider
Airspeed *Horsa*
DFS 230
General Aircraft *Hamilcar*
Gotha Go 242
Messerschmitt Me 321/323

Attack Helicopter
Agusta A 129 *Mangusta*
Kamov Ka 50
Mil Mi 24

Dive-Bomber
Aichi D3A
Blackburn *Skua*
Fairey *Barracuda*
Henschel Hs 123
Junkers Ju 87 *Stuka*
Petlyakov Pe 2
Yokosuka D4Y *Suisei*
Yokosuka P1Y1 *Ginga*

Early Warning
Avro *Shackleton*
Ilyushin Il 76

Escort Fighter
Caudron R 11
Halberstadt CL IV
Hannover CL III
Sikorsky S 16

Fighter
Albatros D V
Arado Ar 68
Armstrong-Whitworth *Siskin*
Avia B 534
Aviatik D I
Avro 504
Avro Canada CF 100 *Canuck*
Blackburn *Buccaneer*
Blackburn *Roc*
Bleriot-SPAD S510
Bloch MB 152
Boulton-Paul *Defiant*
Bristol *Beaufighter*
Bristol *Bulldog*
Bristol F2B
Commonwealth CA 12 *Boomerang*
Dassault *Mirage 2000*
Dassault *Mirage F 1*
Dassault *Mirage III*
Dassault-Breguet *Super Etendard*
de Havilland DH 2
de Havilland DH 98 *Mosquito*
de Havilland DH 100 *Vampire*
de Havilland DH 110 *Sea Vixen*
de Havilland DH 112 *Venom/Sea Venom*
Dewoitine D 510
Dewoitine D 520
English Electric *Lightning*
Fairey *Firefly*
Fairey *Flycatcher*
Fairey *Fulmar*

Fiat CR 32 *Chirri*
Fiat CR 42 *Falco*
Fiat G 50 *Freccia*
Fiat G 91Y
Focke-Wulf Fw 190
Fokker C V
Fokker D VII
Fokker D VIII
Fokker D XXI
Fokker Dr I
Fokker E III
Fokker G I
Folland *Gnat*
Gloster *Gauntlet*
Gloster *Gladiator*
Gloster *Javelin*
Gloster *Meteor*
Halberstadt D II
Hanriot HD 1
Hansa-Brandenburg D I
Hansa-Brandenburg W 29
Hawker *Fury*
Hawker *Hunter*
Hawker *Hurricane*
Hawker *Sea Fury*
Hawker *Tempest*
Hawker *Typhoon*
Heinkel He 51
Hindustan HF 24 *Marut*
IAI *Kfir*
Junkers D I
Junkers Ju 88
Kawanishi N1K2 *Shiden Kai*
Kawasaki Ki 45 *Toryu*
Lavochkin La 5/7
Lavochkin LaGG 3
LFG Roland D II
Macchi M 5
Macchi MC 200 *Saetta*
Macchi MC 202 *Folgore*
Messerschmitt Bf 109G
Messerschmitt Bf 110
Messerschmitt Me 163 *Komet*
Messerschmitt Me 262 *Schwalbe*
Messerschmitt Me 410 *Hornisse*
Mikoyan-Gurevich MiG 3
Mikoyan-Gurevich MiG 15
Mikoyan-Gurevich MiG 21
Mikoyan-Gurevich MiG 23/27
Mikoyan-Gurevich MiG 25
Mikoyan-Gurevich MiG 29
Mikoyan-Gurevich MiG 31
Mitsubishi A5M

Mitsubishi A6M
Mitsubishi J2M
Mitsubishi Ki 46
Morane-Saulnier A 1
Morane-Saulnier L
Morane-Saulnier MS 406
Nakajima Ki 27
Nakajima Ki 43
Nakajima Ki 44
Nakajima Ki 84 *Hayate*
Nieuport 11
Nieuport 17
Nieuport 28
Nieuport-Delage Ni-D 29
Panavia *Tornado*
Pfalz D IIIa
Pfalz D XII
Phonix D I
Polikarpov I 15
Polikarpov I 16
Potez 63
PZL P 11
Reggiane Re 2000 *Falco*
Royal Aircraft Factory FE 2
Royal Aircraft Factory SE 5a
Saab J 29 *Tunnan*
Saab J 35 *Draken*
Saab JA 37 *Viggen*
Saab JAS 39 *Gripen*
SEPECAT *Jaguar*
Shenyang J 5/F 6
Siemens-Schuckert D IV
Sikorsky S 16
Sopwith 1½ *Strutter*
Sopwith *Camel*
Sopwith *Dolphin*
Sopwith *Pup*
Sopwith *Snipe*
Sopwith Triplane
SPAD XIII
Sukhoi Su 27
Supermarine *Spitfire*
Vickers FB 5
Westland *Whirlwind*
Yakovlev Yak 3
Yakovlev Yak 9
Yakovlev Yak 36

Floatplane
Arado Ar 196
CANT Z 506B *Airone*
Hansa-Brandenburg W 29
Heinkel He 59
Heinkel He 115
Macchi M 5
Short 184

Flying Boat
Beriev Be 12 *Tchaika*
Beriev MBR 2
Blohm und Voss Bv 138

Blohm und Voss Bv 222 *Wiking*
CANT Z 501 *Gabbiano*
Dornier Do 18
Dornier Do 24
Felixstowe F2A
Kawanishi H6K
Kawanishi H8K
Macchi M 5
ShinMaywa US 1
Short *Sunderland*
Supermarine *Stranraer*
Supermarine *Walrus*

Heavy Bomber
AEG G IV
Avro *Lancaster*
Caproni Ca 5
de Havilland DH 10
Farman F 222
Friedrichshafen G III
Gotha G V
Handley Page *Halifax*
Handley Page *Heyford*
Handley Page O/400
Heinkel He 177 *Greif*
Petlyakov Pe 8
Piaggio Pe 108B
Short *Stirling*
Sikorsky RBVZ *Ilya Muromets*
Tupolev TB 3
Vickers *Vimy*
Zeppelin *Staaken* R VI

Helicopter
Aerospatiale *Dauphin*
Aerospatiale *Gazelle*
Aerospatiale *Super Frelon*
Aerospatiale *Super Puma*
Flettner Fl 282 *Kolibri*
Kamov Ka 27
MBB BO 105
Mil Mi 17
Mil Mi 24
Mil Mi 26
Westland *Lynx*
Westland *Scout/Wasp*

Liaison
Antonov An 2
Dornier Do 27
Fairey IIIF
Fieseler Fi 156 *Storch*
Heinkel He 70 *Blitz*
Polikarpov Po 2
Vickers *Vildebeest*
Westland *Lysander*

Light Bomber
AEG C IV
Aermacchi MB 339
Aero L 29 *Delfin*

Aero L 39 *Albatros*
Aerospatiale CM 170 *Magister*
Arado Ar 234 *Blitz*
Avro 504
Blackburn *Buccaneer*
Bloch MB 174
Breguet 14
Breguet 19
Bristol *Blenheim*
British Aerospace *Harrier*
Canadair CL 41 *Tutor*
Caproni Ca 310
CASA C 101 *Aviojet*
Caudron G IV
Commonwealth CA 1 *Wirraway*
Dassault *Mirage 2000*
Dassault *Mirage F 1*
Dassault *Mirage III*
Dassault-Dornier *Alphajet*
de Havilland DH 4
de Havilland DH 9a
de Havilland DH 98 *Mosquito*
de Havilland DH 100 *Vampire*
de Havilland DH 112 *Venom/Sea Venom*
English Electric *Canberra*
Fairey *Battle*
Fiat G 91Y
FMA IA 58 *Pucara*
Focke-Wulf Fw 190
Fokker C V
Fokker G I
Folland *Gnat*
Halberstadt CL IV
Hannover CL III
Hansa-Brandenburg C I
Hawker *Hart*
Hawker *Hunter*
Hawker *Hurricane*
Hawker *Sea Fury*
Hawker *Tempest*
Hawker *Typhoon*
Hawker-Siddeley *Hawk*
Heinkel He 51
Heinkel He 70 *Blitz*
Henschel Hs 123
Hindustan HF 24 *Marut*
IAI *Kfir*
Ilyushin Il 2 *Shturmovik*
Ilyushin Il 28
Junkers CL I
Junkers J I
Kawasaki Ki 45 *Toryu*
Kawasaki Ki 61 *Hien*
Lohner B VII
Martinsyde G 100
Messerschmitt Me 262 *Schwalbe*
Messerschmitt Me 410 *Hornisse*
Mikoyan-Gurevich MiG 21
Mikoyan-Gurevich MiG 23/27
Mikoyan-Gurevich MiG 29

Mitsubishi T 2/F 1
Nakajima B5N
Nanchang Q 5
Panavia *Tornado*
Petlyakov Pe 2
Polikarpov R 5
Potez 63
PZL P 23 *Karas*
Saab J 29 *Tunnan*
Saab JA 37 *Viggen*
Saab JAS 39 *Gripen*
SEPECAT *Jaguar*
Shenyang J 6/F 6
SOKO G 4 *Super Galeb*
SOKO J 22 *Orao*
Sopwith 1½ *Strutter*
Sopwith *Dolphin*
Sopwith *Tabloid*
Sukhoi Su 17
Sukhoi Su 25
Tupolev SB 2
Vickers *Wellesley*
Westland *Wapiti*
Westland *Whirlwind*

Medium Bomber
Amiot 143
Armstrong-Whitworth *Whitley*
CANT Z 1007 *Alcione*
Dornier Do 23
Dornier Do 217
Fiat Br 20 *Cignona*
Handley Page *Hampden*
Heinkel He 111
Ilyushin Il 4
Junkers Ju 86
Junkers Ju 88
Junkers Ju 188
LeO 20
LeO 451
Mitsubishi G3M
Mitsubishi G4M
Mitsubishi Ki 21
Mitsubishi Ki 67 *Hiryu*
Nakajima Ki 49 *Donryu*
PZL P 37 *Los*
Savoia-Marchetti SM 79 *Sparviero*
Savoia-Marchetti SM 81 *Pipistrello*
Sukhoi Su 24
Tupolev Tu 2
Tupolev Tu 16
Tupolev Tu 22
Tupolev Tu 22M
Vickers *Wellington*
Yokosuka P1Y1 *Ginga*

Night-Fighter
Boulton-Paul *Defiant*
Bristol *Beaufighter*
Bristol *Blenheim*
de Havilland DH 98 *Mosquito*

de Havilland DH 112 *Venom/Sea Venom*
Dornier Do 217
Gloster *Javelin*
Gloster *Meteor*
Heinkel He 219 *Uhu*
Junkers Ju 88
Kawasaki Ki 45 *Toryu*
Nakajima J1N1 *Gekko*

Patrol-Bomber
Avro *Shackleton*
Beriev Be 12 *Tchaika*
Beriev MBR 2
Blohm und Voss Bv 138
Canadair CL 28 *Argus*
CANT Z 501 *Gabbiano*
CANT Z 506B *Airone*
Felixstowe F2A
Focke-Wulf 200 *Condor*
Hawker-Siddeley *Nimrod*
Heinkel He 59
Junkers Ju 290
Kawanishi H6K
Kawanishi H8K
ShinMaywa US 1
Short *Sunderland*
Supermarine *Stranraer*
Vickers *Wellington*

Reconnaissance
AEG C IV
Aerospatiale *Gazelle*
Aerospatiale *Super Puma*
Agusta A 109 *Hirundo*
Albatros C XII
Anatra D
Ansaldo SVA 5
Antonov An 12
Arado Ar 196
Arado Ar 234 *Blitz*
Armstrong-Whitworth FK 8
Aviatik C I
Avro 504
Avro *Anson*
Beriev MBR 2
Blackburn *Shark*
Bleriot XI
Bloch MB 174
Blohm und Voss Bv 138
Blohm und Voss Bv 222 *Wiking*
Breguet 14
Breguet 19
Breguet 691
Bristol *Beaufort*
Bristol F 2B
Bristol Scout D
CANT Z 506B *Airone*
Caproni Ca 310
Caudron G III
DFW C V

de Havilland DH 98 *Mosquito*
Dornier Do 18
Dornier Do 24
English Electric *Canberra*
Etrich *Taube*
Fairey IIIF
Fairey *Firefly*
Fairey *Swordfish*
Fieseler Fi 156 *Storch*
Flettner Fl 282 *Kolibri*
Focke-Wulf Fw 189
Halberstadt C V
Handley Page *Halifax*
Handley Page *Victor*
Hansa-Brandenburg C I
Hawker-Siddeley *Nimrod*
Heinkel He 70 *Blitz*
Heinkel He 115
Ilyushin Il 38
Junkers Ju 86
Junkers Ju 188
Junkers Ju 290
Letov S 328
LFG Roland C II
Lloyd C III
Lohner B VII
LVG C V
MBB BO 105
Mitsubishi Ki 46
Myasishchev M 4 *Molot*
Nakajima J1N1 *Gekko*
Phonix C I
Polikarpov Po 2
Potez 63
PZL P 37 *Los*
Royal Aircraft Factory BE 2e
Royal Aircraft Factory RE 8
Rumpler C IV
Saab JA 37 *Viggen*
Saab JAS 39 *Gripen*
Salmson 2A2
Savoia-Marchetti SM 79 *Sparviero*
Sikorsky S 16
Sopwith 1½ *Strutter*
Sopwith *Tabloid*
Sukhoi Su 24
Supermarine *Walrus*
Tupolev Tu 16
Tupolev Tu 22
Tupolev Tu 22M
Tupolev Tu 95
Ufag C I
Westland *Lysander*
Westland *Wapiti*
Westland *Wasp/Scout*
Yokosuka D4Y *Suisei*

Strategic Bomber
Avro *Vulcan*
Handley Page *Victor*
Myasishchev M 4 *Molot*

Tupolev Tu 95
Tupolev Tu 160
Vickers *Valiant*

Suicide Aircraft
Yokosuka MXY 7 *Oka*

Tanker
Handley Page *Victor*
Myasishchev M 4 *Molot*
Vickers *Valiant*

Torpedo-Bomber
Blackburn *Shark*
Bristol *Beaufighter*
Bristol *Beaufort*
CANT Z 1007 *Alcione*
Caproni Ca 310
Fairey *Barracuda*
Fairey *Swordfish*
Handley Page *Hampden*
Heinkel He 111
Heinkel He 115
Junkers Ju 188
Mitsubishi G3M
Mitsubishi G4M
Mitsubishi Ki 67 *Hiryu*
Nakajima B5N
Nakajima B6N

Savoia-Marchetti SM 79 *Sparviero*
Short 184
Vickers *Vildebeest*
Yokosuka P1Y1 *Ginga*

Trainer
Aermacchi MB 339
Aero L 29 *Delfin*
Aero L 39 *Albatros*
Aerospatiale CM 170 *Magister*
Airspeed *Oxford*
Arado Ar 96
Avro 504
Avro *Anson*
Canadair CL 41 *Tutor*
CASA C 101 *Aviojet*
Caudron G III
Caudron G IV
Dassault-Dornier *Alphajet*
de Havilland DH 82 *Tiger Moth*
de Havilland Canada DHC 1
    Chipmunk
Embraer EBB 312 *Tucano*
Folland *Gnat*
Hawker-Siddeley *Hawk*
Miles *Master*
Mitsubishi T 2/F 1
Polikarpov Po 2
Saab JA 37 *Viggen*

SEPECAT *Jaguar*
SOKO G 4 *Super Galeb*

Transport
Aerospatiale *Dauphin*
Aerospatiale *Super Puma*
Agusta A 109 *Hirundo*
Airspeed *Horsa*
Antonov An 2
Antonov An 12
Antonov An 22
Antonov An 124 *Ruslan*
Blackburn *Beverly*
Blohm und Voss Bv 222 *Wiking*
DFS 230
Dornier Do 27
Focke-Wulf Fw 200 *Condor*
General Aircraft *Hamilcar*
Gotha Go 242
Ilyushin Il 76
Junkers Ju 52
Junkers Ju 290
Kamov Ka 27
Kawanishi H6K
Kawanishi H8K
Messerschmitt Me 321/323 *Gigant*
Mil Mi 17
Mil Mi 26
Savoia-Marchetti SM 81 *Pipistrello*

APPENDIX 2: MUSEUMS

ARGENTINA
Museo Nacional de Aeronautica
Avenida Rafael Obligado 4550
Buenos Aires

Museo Naval de la Nacion
Paseo Victoria 602
Tigre, Buenos Aires

AUSTRALIA
Australia's Museum of Flight
RAN Air Station Albatross
Nowra, New South Wales

Darwin Aviation Museum
557 Stuart Highway
Winnelle, Northern Territory

Moorabin Air Museum
PO Box 242
Mentone, Victoria 3194

Queensland Air Museum
GPO Box 2315
Brisbane, Queensland 4001

AUSTRIA
Technisches Museum fur Indistrie
    und Gewerbe
Mariahilfer Str. 212
A-1140 Vienna

BELGIUM
Musee Royal de l'Armee
Parc du Cinquantenaire
Jubel Park 3
B-1040 Brussels

BRAZIL
Museu Aerospacial
Avenue Mal Fontenelle
Campo dos Afonsos
Rio de Janeiro

CANADA
Canadian Museum of Flight
5333 216th St.
Langley Airport
Langley, BC V3A 4R1

Canadian Warplane Heritage
Hamilton Civic Airport Hangar 84
Mississauga, ON LOR 1W0

National Aviation Museum
Rockliffe Airport
Ottawa, ON K1A 0M8

CZECH REPUBLIC
Vojenske Museum
Kbely
Praha 9
19796 Prague

FINLAND
Suomen Ilmailumusen
PL42
01531 Vantaa Lento
Helsinki

Keksi Suomen Ilmailumusen
PL 1
41161 Tikkakoski

FRANCE
Jean Salis Collection
Aerodrome de la Ferte Alais
91590 la Ferte Alais

Musee de l' Air et de l' Espace
93350 Le Bourget
Paris

GERMANY
Deutsches Museum
Museumsinsel 1
8000 Munich

Hubschrauber Museum
Postfach 1310
Sableplatz, 2062 Buckeburg

Luftwaffen Museum
Marseille-Kaserne Airfield
2081 Appen

GREAT BRITAIN
Aerospace Museum
RAF Cosford
Shifnal, Shropshire
TF11 8UP

Fleet Air Arm Museum
RNAS Yeovilton
Ilchester, Somerset

Imperial War Museum
Lambeth Road
London SE 1 6HZ

Imperial War Museum
Duxford Airfield
Cambridgeshire CB2 4QR

Newark Air Museum
Winthrope Airfield
Newark, Nottinghamshire

North East Aircraft Museum
Sunderland Airport, Sunderland
Tyne and Wear SR5 3HZ

RAF St. Athan Historic Aircraft
    Collection
RAF St. Athan, Barry, Glamorgan
CF6 9WA WALES

Battle of Britain Museum
Aerodrome Road, Hendon
NW9 5LL London

Shuttleworth Collection
Old Warden Aerodrome
nr. Biggleswade SG18 9ER
Bedfordshire

Warbirds of Great Britain
Blackbushe Airport, Camberly
Surrey

Royal Air Force Museum
Grahame Park way
Hendon, London NW9 5LL

Royal Scottish Museum
Chambers Street
EH1 1JF Edinburgh

Glasgow Museum of Transportation
25 Albert Dr.
G41 2PE Glasgow
SCOTLAND

Wales Aircraft Museum
Cardiff Airport
South Glamorgan
WALES

INDIA
Indian Air Force Museum
Palam Air Force Station
New Dehli 110010

ISRAEL
Israel Air Force Museum
Hatzerim AFB
Beersheba

ITALY
Museo Storico dell Aeronautica
    Militaire
Aeroporto di Vigna di Valle
00062 Vigna di Valle

Museo Nazionale della Scienza e della
    Tecnica
Via San Vittore 21
20123 Milano

NETHERLANDS
Aviodome
Schiphol Centrum
1118A, Amsterdam

Militaire Luchtvaart Museum
Kamp von Zeist
3769 ZK Soesterberg

POLAND
Muzeum Wojska Polskiego
Palac Kultuty i Nauki
Warsaw

Muzeum Lotnictwa Astronautyki
Radkowice Airport 30-969
Krakow 28

PORTUGAL
Museo do Ar
Alverca do Ribatejo 2615
Alverca

RUSSIA
Gagarin Academy/Red Banner
    Academy
141170 Monino
Moscow

SPAIN
Museo de Aeronautica y Astronautica
Carretera de Extremadura
km 10.500 Cuatra Vientos

SWEDEN
Luftfartmuseet
Stiftelsen Luft-och Rymdartmuseet
Museivagen 7
S115 27 Stockholm

Flygvapenmuseum
Box 13300
S580 13 Linkopping

Svedinos Bil Ochs Flygmuseum
S31050 Sloinge
Ugglarp

SWITZERLAND
Verkehrhaus de Schweiz
Lidostrasse 5
CH-6006 Lucerne

Museum der Schweizerischen
    Fliegertuppe
Abteilung der Militarflugplatz
CH-8600 Dubendorf

YUGOSLAVIA
Muzej Jugoslovenskog
    Vazduhplovsta
Aerodrom Surcin
Beograd 1100d Belgrade
SERBIA

APPENDIX 3: AIRCRAFT JOURNALS AND MAGAZINES

ARGENTINA

Aerospacio/Aerospace
Fuerza Aerea Argentina
Paraguay 748, Piso 3
1057 Buenos Aires

AUSTRALIA

Australian Aviation
Aerospace Publications
PO Box 1777
Fyshwick, ACT 2609

Aviation Heritage
PO Box 2007
South Melbourne, Victoria 3205

CANADA

CAHS Journal
Canadian Aviation Historical Society
Box 224, Sta. A
Willowdale, Ontario M2N 5S8

CHINA

Aerospace China
Institute for Aeronautics Information
PO Box 1408
1 Binhe Lu, Hepingi
Beijing 100013

FRANCE

Aero Journal
50 blvd Paul Valery
32500 Fleurance

Air Fan
48 bd. des Batignolles
75017 Paris

Avions
39 rue Aristide Briand
62200 Boulonge sur Mer

Fana de l'Aviation
Editions Lariviere
12 rue Mozart
92587 Clichy Cedex

Icare
Syndica and National des Pilotes de
    Ligue Francais
Tour Essor 93
14–16 rue de Scandicci
93508 Pantin Cedex

Jets
39 rue Aristide Briand
62200 Boulogne sur Mer

Pegase
Association des Amis du Musee de
    l'Air
BP 173, Aeropart du Bourget
93350 Le Bourget

Le Trait D'Union
107 Alee D. Casanova
93320 les Pavillions Sous Bois

GERMANY

Flieger Review
Flug Verlag Berolina GmbH
Schonhauser Allee 6/7
10119 Berlin

Flug Revue
Vereinigte Motor-Verlag GmbH
Leusohner Str 1
70174 Stuttgart

Flugzeug
Thomas-Mann Str. 3
89257 Ilertissen

Jet & Prop
Verlag Heinz Nickel
Kasernenstr. 6-10
66482 Zweibrucken

GREAT BRITAIN

Aeromilitaria
Air Britain
1 East St.
Tonbridge, Kent TN9 1 HP

Aeroplane Monthly
IPC Magazines
King's Reach Tower
Stamford St.
London SE1 9LS

Air Action
Key Publishing
PO Box 100
Stamford, Lincs.
PE9 1XQ

Air Enthusiast
Key Publishing, Ltd.
PO Box 100
Stamford, Lincs.
PE9 1XQ

Air Forces Monthly
Key Publishing, Ltd.
PO Box 100
Stamford, Lincs.
PE9 1XQ

Air International
Key Publishing, Ltd.
PO Box 100
Stanford, Lincs.
PE9 1XQ

Air Pictorial
HPL Publishing
Drury Lane
St. Leonards-on-Sea
E. Sussex TN38 9BJ

Aircraft Illustrated
Ian Allan, Ltd.
Riverdene Business Park
Molesey Rd.
Hersham, Surrey KT12 4RG

Cross and Cockade International
First World War Aviation Society
Cragg Cottage
Braham, Wetherby
W. Yorks LS23 6QB

Defense Helicopter
111 High St.
Barnham, Bucks. SL1 7 JZ

Fly Past
Key Publishing, Ltd.
PO Box 100
Stamford, Lincs. PE9 1XQ

Helicopter International Magazine
Avia Press Associates
75 Elm Tree Rd.
Locking, Weston-super-Mare
Somerset BS24 8EL

Insignia
Blue Rider Publishing
43a Glasford St.
London SW17 9HL

Warbirds Worldwide
PO Box 99
Mansfield, Notts. NG19 9GU

Warplane
Orbis Publishing, Ltd.
179 Dalling Dr.
London W6

Windsock International
Albatross Productions
10 Long View
Berkhamsted, Herts. HP4 1BY

Wingspan International
AOB Publishing, Ltd.
Aldbury House, Dower Mews
Berkhamsted, Herts. HP4 2BL

ISRAEL
Israel Society of Aeronautics
PO Box 3144
Rishon-le Zion 75131

Knafaim
Aero Club of Israel
PO Box 26261
Tel Aviv 63432

ITALY
Aerofan
via Ampere, 49
20131 Milano

JP 4 Aeronautica
via Guinicelli, 4
50133 Florence

JAPAN
Aireview
Kantosha Co., Ltd.
601 Kojua Blvd.
8-7, 6-chome
Ginza, Chuo-ku, Tokyo 104

Air World
12-8, Roppongi, 4-chome
Minato-ku, Tokyo 106

NETHERLANDS
Aero-Journal
Postbus 3/2
7400 Deventer

Luchtvaartkennis
Afdeling Luchtvaartkennis
Jozef Israelsplein 8
2596 AS The Hague

NEW ZEALAND
Aviation Historical Society of New Zealand
PO Box 12-009
Wellington 6038

RUSSIA
Aerospace Journal
35 Mosfilmovskaya, Bldg. 1
Moscow 117330

Air Fleet Review
PO Box 77
Moscow 125057

ILLUSTRATION CREDITS

The photographs, cited by page number, are courtesy of the following:

National Archives, 7, 49, 58, 96, 101, 116, 120, 207, 245, 256, 312, 333

San Diego Aerospace Museum, 2, 13, 14, 21, 25, 27, 28, 32, 34, 35, 42, 47, 50, 51, 52, 55, 56, 61, 62, 67, 74, 77, 80, 82, 84, 85, 88, 109, 111, 112, 115, 118, 122, 125, 127, 128, 130, 131, 133, 142, 143, 144, 147, 148, 153, 158, 159, 160, 167, 172, 186, 195, 200, 208, 213, 214, 215, 216, 219, 226, 229, 233, 234, 239, 241, 248, 254, 257, 258, 259, 261, 265, 276, 279, 289, 290, 291, 293, 294, 295, 296, 297, 299, 300, 302, 314, 322, 326, 329, 330, 332, 334, 336

Smithsonian Institution, 1, 6, 8, 10, 15, 16, 17, 18, 20, 26, 29, 30, 31, 33, 36, 37, 38, 40, 45, 46, 48, 53, 54, 57, 59, 60, 66, 68, 69, 70, 72, 73, 79, 81, 83, 86, 87, 89, 90, 91, 92, 93, 94, 95, 97, 98, 99, 100, 102, 105, 106, 107, 108, 110, 113, 114, 117, 119, 121, 123, 124, 126, 129, 132, 134, 135, 136, 137, 138, 139, 140, 141, 145, 146, 150, 151, 154, 155, 156, 161, 164, 165, 166, 169, 170, 171, 175, 176, 180, 181, 182, 183, 184, 185, 187, 188, 191, 192, 193, 194, 196, 197, 198, 199, 201, 202, 203, 206, 210, 211, 212, 217, 218, 225, 228, 230, 231, 235, 236, 238, 240, 242, 243, 244, 246, 247, 249, 251, 252, 253, 262, 263, 264, 266, 267, 268, 269, 270, 271, 272, 273, 274, 275, 277, 278, 281, 282, 283, 286, 287, 288, 298, 303, 307, 308, 309, 310, 311, 319, 321, 323, 324, 327, 328, 331, 335

Courtesy of Arvo Haav, 19, 152, 202, 204, 260, 318

Courtesy of Gerald Frawley, 3, 9, 11, 12, 75, 76, 301

Courtesy of Leo Opdyke, 205

Courtesy of Igor S. Sikorsky Historical Archives, 292

Paul Laurence Dunbar Library, Wright State University, 209

PRO, Indian Air Force via Bharat Rakshak, 173

British Aerospace, 39, 43, 44, 63, 71, 103, 104, 149, 157, 162, 163, 174, 190, 250, 255, 284, 320, 325

National Museum of Naval Aviation, 65

Naval Institute, 41, 64, 168, 177, 178, 220, 224, 232, 280, 313, 315

Defense Visual Information Center, 22, 23, 24, 78, 179, 221, 222, 223, 227, 237, 304, 305, 306, 316

Aero Vodochody, 4, 5

Avia World, 189, 317

Stephen Innes, 285

ABOUT THE AUTHOR

John C. Fredriksen is a recognized authority on the War of 1812 manuscripts and other resources. He holds degrees from UCLA, the University of Michigan, the University of Rhode Island, and Providence College. He has received numerous research grants and departmental awards.